'Gary Murphy's eye for the telling detail is rivalled only by the breadth of his overall analysis and the depth of his superbly balanced exploration of the life and politics of one of the most fascinating figures in twentieth-century Irish politics, which eschews the rough trade of gossip for the integrity of case-hardened research and assessment.'

Professor John Horgan

'In the absence of an autobiography, Gary Murphy's fine book is probably the closest we'll ever get to what Charles Haughey actually thought about the various controversies in which he was embroiled. It is an indispensable read for anyone with an interest in modern Irish history.'

David McCullagh

'Charles Haughey has been the most controversial figure in Irish public life since the civil war, but his own perspective on the events of his time has not been chronicled up to now. Professor Murphy's sweeping biography, informed by unique access to Haughey's personal papers, makes good this deficiency. Haughey offers much new detail – and not a few surprises – about the personality and career of a political titan who is still, in equal measure, revered and reviled in twenty-first-century Ireland.'

Conor Brady

HAUGHEY

GARY MURPHY

Gill Books

Gill Books
Hume Avenue
Park West
Dublin 12
www.gillbooks.ie

Gill Books is an imprint of M.H. Gill and Co.

978 07171 9364 6

Designed by Bartek Janczak
Edited by Jane Rogers
Proofread by Sally Vince
Indexed by Adam Pozner

Printed by Clays Ltd, Suffolk
This book is typeset in 11 on 16pt, Minion Pro

A CIP catalogue record for this book is available from the British
Library.

5 4 3 2 1

For my mother, Margaret.

So we'll live,
And pray, and sing, and tell old tales, and laugh
At gilded butterflies, and hear poor rogues
Talk of court news; and we'll talk with them too,
Who loses and who wins; who's in, who's out

WILLIAM SHAKESPEARE, *KING LEAR*, ACT V, SCENE III

A man of genius makes no mistakes. His errors
are volitional and are the portals to discovery.

JAMES JOYCE, *ULYSSES*

CONTENTS

INTRODUCTION

In 2010 the family of the late Taoiseach and Fianna Fáil leader Charles J. Haughey donated his private papers to Dublin City University. Once they had been catalogued by the university, the Haughey family gave me access to these papers, which has given me a unique advantage in writing this book. They cover Haughey's life from his birth in September 1925 in a small house in Castlebar, County Mayo to his death at his home in Kinsaley[1] in June 2006. The house in Castlebar, called Mountain View, was Free State army property for the use of the commanding officer of the 4th Battalion, Western Command, 2nd Brigade of the Irish Free State army. Commandant Seán Haughey (who was known as Johnnie) lived there with his wife, Sarah (née McWilliams) and their growing family. Cathal Haughey, as Charles Haughey was known throughout his childhood and teenage years, was their third child and second son.

The James Gandon-designed house in Kinsaley, which was part of an estate named Abbeville, was Charles Haughey's family home, where he and his wife Maureen (née Lemass) had moved in 1969 with their four children. It would become the subject of much controversy relating to both its purchase and its upkeep over the course of the nearly forty years Haughey lived in it. It was both a family home and a workplace for Haughey. It bustled on Saturdays, when it functioned as a sort of community hub for the residents of Kinsaley, and when local people mingled with visitors of all sorts over copious amounts of food and drink. As Maureen Haughey described it: 'We had a kind of open house on Saturday morning. You'd have barristers and judges and the local farmer. Kinsaley was a farming community and we had friends there all our life who kept coming Saturday after Saturday right to the end.'[2]

On Sundays it would often be full of civil servants and Haughey's political aides discussing state and party business. Scouts used its grounds for camping. Army showjumpers used it for training. It was rarely quiet during Haughey's public life. When he retired in 1992 the hectic pace eased, but it was still open house on Saturdays. As Haughey aged and his health deteriorated, Abbeville became a place of refuge from a hostile world as first the McCracken and later the Moriarty tribunals of inquiry exposed the intricacies of his finances and his reliance on a number of wealthy donors. The visitors still came, but there were fewer of them.

Abbeville is central to the second half of the Haughey story. The first half was more peripatetic; the young Haughey moved with his family from Castlebar to Mullingar, to Limerick, to Dunshaughlin, and finally to Dublin, where Johnnie and Sarah Haughey settled into the working-class area of Donnycarney at 12 Belton Park Road in 1933. Belton Park was a small estate of some forty-eight private houses in an enclave of corporation houses, but there was no public/private demarcation amongst those who lived there. Cathal Haughey was seven when his family moved there, and his experience as a child of Donnycarney was to shape his whole life. His father was sick throughout his childhood. Johnnie suffered from multiple sclerosis, and the young Cathal Haughey's entire existence in Donnycarney revolved around that illness. He witnessed his mother physically lift his father up and down the stairs until he and his brothers became old enough and strong enough to do it. They also fed their father while his wife did the housework in the morning. Raising seven children on an army pension in a two-up two-down terraced house was difficult for his mother. Haughey was inspired by her struggle to make ends meet, and was keen to enter the workforce as soon as possible to help with the family finances. His more far-sighted mother made sure that he continued with his education. In 1986, introducing his mother in the Channel 4 documentary *Charles Haughey's Ireland*, he said, 'Things were difficult when we were young but like most Irish mothers she was determined that whatever else we would all get a good education.'[3] It was that determination to see her son succeed that in turn drove Haughey to go as far as he could in his chosen career. That career would become his life and that life was politics.

The Haughey papers provide a rich tapestry of the story of a life of a politician and a state. Haughey was born as the fledgling state began to make its way in the world and when the party with which he was later synonymous, Fianna Fáil, had not even been founded. He faced the poverty that enveloped much of the northside of Dublin city in the 1930s and 1940s. His escape route from that poverty was education. Dublin Corporation scholarships to St Joseph's secondary school in Fairview, commonly known as Joey's, and then to University College Dublin in Earlsfort Terrace gave Haughey the opportunity to look beyond the narrow confines of Donnycarney that eluded many of his contemporaries and schoolfriends. His expanding horizons included training as a barrister in the King's Inns.

From the 1950s they also included Fianna Fáil. For Haughey, Fianna Fáil was the vehicle that allowed children like him the opportunity to advance in society. But it was also a great national movement that enabled the Irish nation itself to advance. Haughey was attracted to its grand gestures of inspiration in social, economic and national progress. For the whole of his political career, spanning more than four decades, Haughey was convinced that only Fianna Fáil could show the Irish people the way forward. But he also believed that Fianna Fáil could only succeed if it had a strong leader to show the faithful the path to righteous truth. That truth was based on national unification and on using the state to engineer wealth. For Haughey, this had been partly on show in the leadership of Éamon de Valera and even more so under Seán Lemass. He was of the view that it mostly disappeared under Jack Lynch but returned in full in December 1979 when Haughey himself became Fianna Fáil's fourth leader.

Less than ten years earlier his political career had seemed ruined when he was charged with assisting in the illegal importation of arms. The ruination of his career, however, was very much secondary to the real danger that, if convicted, he would lose his liberty for perhaps a decade. Jail was not something the forty-five-year-old Haughey looked forward to when he went on trial in September 1970. Haughey's acquittal led to a bout of introspection about both his personal and his political future. He bet on himself by staying in Fianna Fáil when many were urging him to leave and form a new party. But, perhaps for the first time, he was riven with doubt as to his future within Fianna Fáil, given his spectacular fall from grace and his ostracism from its decision-making structures. It was then that he turned to Fianna Fáil's ordinary members, who forced his return to the frontbench, which in turn led to ministerial office and ultimately the leadership of the party.

Haughey's years as Taoiseach and leader of the opposition between December 1979 and February 1992 were tumultuous ones for the Irish state. Ireland was engulfed in turmoil over a stagnating economy, and how to fix it, riven with factionalism over questions of sexual morality, and tormented over the continuing and seemingly never-ending violence in Northern Ireland. These same issues also engulfed Fianna Fáil, split the party and forced Haughey to fend off several attempts to replace him as party leader. Still, many in Ireland, both North and South, looked to him for answers, some of which he had, some he had not. Power forced him to compromise with enemies and discard friends.

Haughey was forced out of office in February 1992, a victim of a power play within Fianna Fáil of which one suspects he would have approved had he not been the target. His ousting from power brought more introspection as he was faced with a retirement he had hoped not to contemplate for some years. That retirement, initially brooding, soon became sedate and calm as he enjoyed the quiet life and the company of family and friends. Within a few years, however, it became wearying and at times unbearable as two tribunals of inquiry investigated his private finances, and his family life came under considerable strain with the revelation of a long-standing extramarital relationship with the socialite Terry Keane. But Haughey's family, led by his stoical, indefatigable and, most important, loving wife Maureen, stood by him. They remained his rock over the course of the long and remorseless final act in Abbeville until it finally came to an end in the early summer of 2006.

The Haughey who stalks the pages of twentieth-century Irish history is more often than not a venal, shallow, one-dimensional character who pursued ambition to the exclusion of everything else. His purchases of Abbeville and Inishvickillane, his island off the coast of County Kerry, are viewed as evidence of a gauche, empty character obsessed with material things. Such is his reputation that he can be accused of almost any misdeed, from subverting the state from within to behaving like some sort of South American dictator while Taoiseach. To some of his critics he was a kept man who undermined and debased Irish democracy through a series of supposedly corrupt acts, committed in return for huge sums of money to support his lavish lifestyle. The reality is far more complex and nuanced. There is the Haughey who rose from Donnycarney to the office of Taoiseach. There is the Haughey of the arms trial and the Haughey at the beginning of the peace process. There is Haughey at the birth of social partnership. There is Haughey on the international stage engulfed in controversy over the Argentinian invasion of the Falkland Islands and the British military response. There is Haughey on the international stage as President of the EU's Council of Ministers at the heart of the debate about the reunification of Germany. There is the defiant Haughey of the tribunal era. Ultimately there is the Haughey at the centre of Irish politics for over three decades and the Haughey whose legacy still casts a large shadow on the Irish state.

It is time for a reassessment of Haughey. His papers allow us to do just that. In them we get a unique view of what he thought about many of the crises and controversies he was involved in. We also get to see Haughey the man as he negotiates his way in the world and comes across all manner of people from the poorest of his north Dublin constituency to the great and good of international politics. We are with Haughey as he navigates from the north Dublin working-class suburbs to the gentrified halls of UCD, where he meets Maureen Lemass, graduates with a first-class honours commerce degree and experiences private life as an accountant and public life within the sometimes fiercely cliquish nature of Dublin Fianna Fáil. We accompany him as he finally achieves political success after years of failure, enters the Dáil, and climbs the Fianna Fáil hierarchy through a series of ministries, culminating in his appointment as Minister for Finance in 1966. We see him at the centre of Fianna Fáil as the party's links with business burgeon in the 1960s. We are at his side as he is sacked from office while just out of his hospital bed, arrested and tried for the illegal importation of arms. We hear what he really thinks of his trial. After his acquittal we journey with him on his lonely, soul-destroying but ultimately fruitful route across the country to political redemption in the 1970s. We ascend with him as he achieves his lifelong ambition to become Taoiseach, only to find himself thwarted by a series of attempts within his own party to challenge his leadership, missteps, ill luck and poor judgement. We look on at his frustration out of office, epitomised by his opposition to the Anglo-Irish Agreement of 1985. We see his maturity in office and share the controversies of coalition, the self-doubts over breaking one of Fianna Fáil's core values, the shattering trauma of the 1990 presidential election, and the painstaking attempts to bring peace to Northern Ireland. We are there as his lonely political end comes quickly and painfully, and as public life recedes only to re-emerge unwelcomingly as the tribunals delve into his financial affairs. We get Haughey's first-hand view of Seán Doherty's allegations that he knew of the tapping of the telephones of Bruce Arnold and Geraldine Kennedy when he was Taoiseach in 1982. Finally, we are with him as his life comes to an end, slowly and in agony as he fights cardiac attacks and cancer while living as a virtual recluse in Abbeville, his days filled with loving family care but with a hostile public baying for his imprisonment as his reputation is shredded.

But there was more to Haughey than his multiple public personas. There was the Haughey who enjoyed horses, holidays, international travel, bees, deer, the GAA, the sea, wine, children, grandchildren, sailing and fast cars. There were car crashes, an aeroplane crash, a near-fatal sailing accident and numerous and often lengthy hospital stays. We see his correspondence, some of it just one-way, with such luminaries as Gerry Adams, Bruce Arnold, Robert Ballagh, Vincent Browne, Bono, Gay Byrne, Bishop Edward Daly, Len Deighton, Theo Dorgan, Frank Dunlop, Hilton Edwards, Garret FitzGerald, Seamus Heaney, John Hume, Ted Kennedy, Helmut Kohl, Louis le Brocquy, Hugh Leonard, Micheál Mac Liammóir, Mary McAleese, Archbishop John Charles McQuaid, John Major, Seamus Mallon, Vincent O'Brien, Fr Alec Reid, Mary Robinson, Peter Sutherland, Margaret Thatcher, Gore Vidal, T.K. Whitaker, and many others. We also see correspondence with the forgotten people of Ireland, those who could not find the means to get by in the changing Ireland which Haughey represented during his forty years as a public representative.

In our quest to understand Haughey we must, however, move beyond his papers. This biography is also substantially informed by dozens of interviews with contemporaries of Haughey including members of his family, civil servants, political advisers, supporters and opponents, journalists and friends. A number of these have since died and a few others have asked to remain anonymous. Those who have gone on the record are mentioned in the sources section at the end of this book. Their recollections provide crucial insights into Haughey's life beyond what official state papers, party archives and personal correspondence can offer the biographer.

Haughey was fond of saying that he was from all four corners of Ireland. He was born in Mayo; his parents were from Derry and he went there often as a child. He holidayed in Kerry and considered himself a sort of son of Dingle; and he was a quintessential northside Dubliner. His impact on all parts of Ireland was profound. It is the aim of this biography to explain how and why.

CHAPTER 1

CATHAL

INTRODUCTION

On 21 January 1980 the Department of the Taoiseach received a letter for the newly installed incumbent of the office, Charles J. Haughey. Haughey had been in office just over a month, and his incoming mail was filled with congratulatory letters, telegrams and cards. This particular letter came from one of Haughey's regular correspondents, the founder, publisher and editor of *Magill* magazine, Vincent Browne, who was at that stage working on his own biography of the Fianna Fáil leader. Browne and Haughey had known each other for over a decade and just six months later, Browne would publish his explosive arms trial material based on the diaries of the former secretary of the Department of Justice, Peter Berry. The day after Haughey had unexpectedly won the Fianna Fáil leadership contest against George Colley, Browne had told Haughey that *Magill* was running a special 'Making of the Taoiseach' feature and urged Haughey to contribute to it.[1] Haughey refused. Browne had known Haughey for over a decade. He was constantly offering Haughey advice in his letters and kept demanding an official interview, which the Taoiseach's private secretary, Seán Aylward, on his boss's behalf, kept refusing. Haughey's post into the department was triaged by his private secretary and a number of secretaries, who decided what he would see; but he did want to know who was writing to him, and there were a number of people whose correspondence he would demand to see. Browne was one of them.[2] In this particular letter Browne told Haughey that for his book he had 'interviewed your mother, sister Maureen and brother Fr Owen in the recent past and they have revealed terrible things about your childhood'.[3] What these terrible things were was left unsaid.

We know something of Haughey's childhood, but there is no real evidence of anything awfully terrible in it beyond the usual deprivations experienced by the northside working classes. Much of the poverty the family endured was due to Johnnie Haughey's illness. Johnnie was born in Knockaneill, just outside Swatragh, Derry, on 26 December 1897 (some put the date as 18 January 1898) into a staunch republican household and played an extremely active role in the Irish revolutionary period. After the War of Independence and the Civil War he stayed in the new national army, but ill health forced him to resign his commission in April 1928, when he was only thirty years of age. In 1928 the army was being reduced in strength and senior officers were offered two years' pay as inducement to retire. Haughey, knowing his health was rapidly declining, took the offer and retired. It was a bitter pill for his professional pride and a savage economic blow to his wife and young family. They temporarily moved to Burrow Road in Sutton before Johnnie Haughey attempted a career in farming at the Riggins in Dunshaughlin, County Meath in 1929. The Haughey children were sent to the local school in Cushinstown.

DERRY

Johnnie Haughey's military pension file was released in 2018. It tells a grim story from when he first applied for a military pension as early as 1925 to the death of his wife Sarah Haughey in 1989. The file, in which Haughey is called John, relates to his receipt of a military service pension in respect of his service with the Irish Volunteers, IRA and National Forces in the service periods between 1 April 1919 and 30 September 1923 during the War of Independence, the truce period and the Civil War. He claimed unsuccessfully for service in the periods between 1 April 1917 and 31 March 1919. The file refers to his receipt of a disability pension under the Army Pensions Acts and further refers to Sarah Haughey's (née McWilliams) receipt of a widow's allowance in respect of John Haughey under the Army Pensions Acts between 1962 and her death in September 1989. Sarah McWilliams, who was born in Stranagone on 18 October 1901, received a military pension for her service in Cumann na mBan from 1 April 1920 to 31 March 1923 during the War of Independence, truce period and Civil War.

The curator of the military archives provides a very useful summation of Haughey's army activities as described in his file.[4] During the War of Independence and truce period John Haughey served with the IRA as a company officer commanding, a vice-battalion officer commanding, a battalion officer commanding and a vice-brigade officer commanding. According to Haughey and the references he supplied when applying for his pension, in 1919 and 1920 he took part in a number of Irish Volunteer and IRA arms raids on homes of members of the Ulster Volunteer Force and retired British Army officers. He was also involved in organisational and training work. He stated that he was on the run and his family home was constantly raided, including on ten different occasions in one year alone. He further claimed that as a result his father and sister were forced to emigrate to the USA.

During 1920 and 1921 Haughey was involved in the disruption and destruction of communications links in his area. He took part in an IRA ambush at Swatragh in June 1921 in which, he stated, two members of the Royal Irish Constabulary (RIC) were killed and one wounded; and in another ambush at an unnamed location, the outcome of which does not appear on file. He claimed to have been in receipt of information from named members of the RIC. He also took part in what were described as 'Divisional reprisals' at Doon, County Tyrone in which 'a creamery, dwelling houses, shops [and] … mills were destroyed.' Haughey stated that during the truce period he took part in an IRA officers' training camp at Glenasmole, County Dublin in August 1921, and established training camps and munition manufacturing in his own battalion area.

According to Haughey and a reference from Patrick J. Diamond, he also took part in the IRA capture of Maghera RIC barracks in March 1922 and attacks on Draperstown Barracks in May 1922 and on Pomeroy Barracks at a date not on file. John Haughey joined the National Army in August 1922 and served throughout the remainder of the Civil War. Despite the fact that the truce with the British was signed in July 1921 the situation in Northern Ireland was violent and volatile well into 1922 and there was no hope that John Haughey and Sarah McWilliams could marry in their native Derry. They decided that they would cross the Foyle and wed in Donegal and were duly married on 1 August 1922 in St Patrick's Church, Murlog, by an uncle of Sarah McWilliams, Fr Robert Fullerton, who had helped to found the Gaelic League in Belfast. The witnesses were James Mallon and Ellie McEldowney, and the newly wed couple had their wedding breakfast in Argue's Hotel in Lifford. They travelled by boat from Magilligan to Greencastle, where they stayed the night and afterwards started their brief honeymoon. When Charles Haughey was Taoiseach, John Hume, with whom he had a friendly but at times difficult relationship, tracked down the boatman, John McCormack, and brought him to a pub in Greencastle from where Haughey spoke to him by phone from Dublin with what he described as a hilarious, but alas unrecorded, result.[5] In October 1989 Haughey, while he was Taoiseach, travelled to Derry and met informally with Bishop Edward Daly of the Roman Catholic Church, Bishop James Mehaffy of the Church of Ireland and representatives of the other churches in Derry. Daly presented him with a copy of his parents' wedding certificate, prompting Haughey to remark that it was 'another of the many links in the chain which will always bind me to Derry.'[6]

According to Major Daniel McKenna, the senior IRA commander in the North, John Haughey had 'done his utmost to make British law impossible in his area' and his 'enemies were of the opinion, and indeed not without reason, that he was the cause of all their woes in his area'.[7] McKenna and Haughey were involved in a number of operations transferring guns from Donegal to Tyrone. Tim Pat Coogan's biography of Michael Collins recounts an affidavit of another IRA volunteer, Thomas

Kelly, who told of a dangerous mission in which 'rifles and ammo were brought by army transport to Donegal and later moved into County Tyrone in the compartment of an oil tanker. Only one member of the IRA escorted the consignment through the Special Constabulary Barricade at Strabane/Lifford Bridge. He was Seán Haughey, father of Charles Haughey.'[8]

One of Charles Haughey's later correspondents, Louis Walsh, told him in the early 1980s of a conversation he had with James McCloskey of Derry, who had served with Commandant Haughey and who was then eighty-seven years of age. McCloskey reminisced that 'he often slept in a dugout with your father around his home. Apparently, your father could not sleep in his own house after a certain incident in Swatragh and after a time McCloskey acted as your father's bodyguard when he got across the Lifford. I asked him about Dan McKenna and he said your father was a brave man.'[9]

According to John Haughey and references he supplied, he served in counties Donegal, Mayo and Sligo as well as at Athlone, Limerick, Dublin and the Curragh during that conflict. He retired to the Defence Forces reserve with the rank of commandant on 21 April 1928. The large file includes original handwritten material submitted and signed by John Haughey in support of his service pension application; material relating to the subject's National Army and Defence Forces service record; undated unsigned handwritten notes of evidence given by John Haughey before the Board of Assessors, Military Service Pensions Act 1924 and signed handwritten statements and letters regarding John Haughey's service from Lieutenant Michael Quinn, N. Collins, Eoin Ua Dubhaigh (Eoin O'Duffy), Major Domhnaill Mac Cionnaith (Daniel McKenna), Garda Síochána Sergeant Patrick J. Diamond, and Garda Síochána Inspector Thomas Kelly.

Johnnie Haughey's service in the War of Independence and Civil War hit him hard. He was now an officer in an army that faced much resentment from those on the losing side in the Civil War. In his pension file, Commandant A. Fitzpatrick said that in 1923, when Haughey was stationed in Mayo, he operated in an environment where the civilian population were 'almost entirely hostile to the army'.[10] A former soldier under Haughey's command, Seán Clancy, later recalled that while the army was not by any means popular with the civilian population in those days, the personnel of the 4th Battalion integrated reasonably well and several officers and men of other rank married girls from Mayo.[11] Nevertheless, it is clear that conditions both within the barracks and in the wider community were tough.

Haughey and his men often had to sleep out and their clothes were ruined. They were billeted in accommodation in Ballina which had no heating, lighting or windows. Fitzpatrick bluntly stated that all 'these hardships endured by NCOs and men had a very detrimental effect on the health of ex-commandant Haughey as he continually endeavoured to improve the conditions of the men under his command, without result.'[12] And indeed the health of Johnnie Haughey dramatically worsened during the 1920s. In his application for a military pension, Haughey said that his disseminated sclerosis, or MS, was 'caused by nervous and physical strain during my service in the IRA' and claimed that he was suffering from what he termed nervousness, which led to bouts of insomnia and him traipsing around the house in the middle of the night. Haughey's claim that his MS was a direct result of his service was not accepted by the Army Pensions Board in 1925, but reconsidered and granted on appeal on 6 October 1927, when it was decided on re-examination that the disease was 'excited by service'.[13] In a profile of the then Minister for Finance Charles Haughey in June 1969, the *Irish Times* claimed that Sarah Haughey believed it was a fall from a horse which was responsible for the gradual onset of Johnnie Haughey's MS.[14]

While this profile mistakenly calls Haughey the second son in the family and misspells Eoghan Haughey, the story about Johnnie Haughey's fall from a horse would appear to be true. Charles Haughey was always intrigued about his heritage and where his family came from. Once he became a minister he was inundated with letters from Haugheys all across the globe wondering if they were related to him. In the mid-1970s he asked a local history teacher in St Aidan's CBS in Whitehall, Tommy Broughan, to undertake research into the Haughey family name.

Broughan completed his mammoth 400-page work on the Haughey name and sent it to Haughey in January 1980, just after he had become Taoiseach. Haughey replied to him on 6 February declaring that he could see 'even at first glance that it is a marvellous piece of work on your part'.[15] In his account of Johnnie Haughey, Broughan stated that during his time in Mullingar, where he had been stationed after Castlebar, Haughey was becoming worried about a physical disability which he could not shake off. Although an enthusiastic and skilful horseman, something his second son inherited from him, he fell badly on one occasion. Broughan notes that it is impossible to tell if this aggravated a condition that was already present. It certainly could not have helped, and Johnnie's illness was made worse by the fact that he refused over a number of years to go to hospital to have treatment or to be X-rayed for his progressive disability.[16]

Johnnie was officially diagnosed with multiple sclerosis in 1933 but was manifestly showing signs of the disease five years earlier when he left the army. He had difficulty walking after 1934. His youngest son, Eoghan, who was born in 1934, never saw him walking.[17] By 1941 Haughey was so incapacitated that he was completely bedridden. He was so affected by the disease that his pension statement had to be marked with an X as he was unable to write his own name. In 1942 a doctor who had examined him over the previous decade and a half noted his fits of 'marked moroseness and depression' and that his gait was 'definitely spastic in character'.[18] He died five years later on 3 January 1947, just over two weeks short of his forty-ninth birthday, leaving a devastated wife and seven children. His condition had been such for over a decade that it was considered to be 100 per cent debilitating.

The family home that Charles Haughey grew up in was one in which the father figure was an invalid who was forced to lie in bed all day and could only get out of it to be fed. In that context there were indeed terrible things about Haughey's childhood. He and his siblings went to school while their father was in bed and when they came home he was in bed. But Haughey was immensely proud of his father and, as Taoiseach, instructed his private secretaries that any letter about his father was to be given directly to him. One of Haughey's earliest congratulatory letters came from Henry MacErlean from Belfast who told him it was a 'source of considerable pleasure to me personally that the son of a county Derryman, with whom I was once associated in the fight for the freedom of the country, has been elected to membership of Dáil Éireann'.[19] Moreover, Haughey asked the officer in charge of the Military Archives, Commandant Peter Young, to notify him directly of any records he might come across pertaining to his father. In May 1983 Young contacted Haughey to pass on a variety of documents about Johnnie Haughey's service, including one describing the difficult conditions under which Haughey and his fellow soldiers operated.[20] A number of years later Lieutenant Colonel Bill Egar sent Haughey a copy of *An Cosantóir* (the Defence Forces' journal) of November 1983, which recounted much of the history of the 4th Infantry Battalion, noting: 'your father contributed to the foundation of this proud unit, being commanding officer from April 1924 to April 1928.'[21] That edition of *An Cosantóir* featured the reminiscences of retired Lieutenant Colonel Seán Clancy, who noted that Commandant Haughey commended him on the speed with which he finished his first mission, when Clancy was expecting a reprimand.[22]

In retirement Charles Haughey occasionally pondered writing his memoirs. He was not short of offers from publishers. Fergal Tobin of Gill and Macmillan had been trying to persuade him to write his life story even when he was still in the heat of the political action. In 1984 Tobin suggested to Haughey that it was 'hardly an exaggeration to say that you have not had the sympathetic ear of the media in recent years; perhaps you should now consider the possibility of telling your own story in your own words.'[23] Haughey replied that he would very much like to do so but simply did not have the time. Just under a decade later, after the publication of Bruce Arnold's biography of Haughey with its pejorative subtitle *His Life and Unlucky Deeds* in 1993, Tobin tried again. He told Haughey that while he understood that Haughey did not want to do an autobiography it meant 'leaving the field clear for hostile witnesses like Bruce Arnold to continue their never-ending campaign of vilification … you owe it to yourself to do something.'[24] Haughey's reply this time noted while there was a great deal in what Tobin said, he was still not persuaded that he should commit himself to all that would be involved in producing something that would be worthwhile. In 1997 Haughey was offered an advance of £60,000 sterling by British publisher Hodder and Stoughton to write his memoirs. Roland Phillips of the publishing house told him that he had edited the memoirs of Roy Jenkins, Barbara Castle and Edward Heath and was also involved in publishing Garret FitzGerald in both Ireland and the UK. He also offered research and writing help, but once again Haughey was unmoved.[25]

But while Haughey spurned all professional offers to write his memoirs he did draft some paragraphs about his parents, noting that they were born and reared practically next door to each other on two small farms in adjacent townlands, Knockaneill and Stranagone near Swatragh in County Derry. His mother's family were from Stranagone and a number of the McWilliams family still live there to this day. It was a typical south Derry small farm where the family followed the traditional patterns of small farming. They were self-sufficient, with produce from the farm feeding them and a nearby bog supplying turf for heating and cooking. Haughey recalled that he spent a good part of his school summer holidays there and gained at first hand an insight into how at that time rural communities were firmly divided along sectarian lines.[26]

Haughey's mother, Sarah McWilliams, was also extremely active during the revolutionary period, if in a slightly different manner to Johnnie Haughey. On 7 November 1940 she travelled to Collins Barracks to give evidence on her own behalf to an army interview board in relation to her pension. She joined Cumann na mBan in Swatragh in 1919. She learned first aid, did some drilling and fundraised for the Volunteers through ceilidh and dances and collections among friends. She was not involved in either firing or storing arms, saw no action, and her main duty was looking after the needs of the men who were in a dugout three miles from her home, which was occupied for over twelve months. She went three times a week to this dugout bringing food, clothing and tobacco to the men – usually there were up to three in the trench at any one time – and acting as a messenger between them and their commanding officer, the company captain James McAleary, who lived a mile away in the other direction.

Sarah's activities in Cumann na mBan continued until her marriage in August 1922. At the end of her brief testimony there is a rather begrudging and unsympathetic note from one of the interviewing officers: 'As will be seen from the evidence, this lady's principal service consisted in attending to the wants of men in a dugout. One of them has since become her husband.'[27] A week later Sarah Haughey politely wrote to the secretary of the Military Pensions Service Board saying that she would accept the verdict of the referee in regards to her claim of a pension.[28] Ultimately the referee found in her favour and on 30 January 1941 awarded her one and seven-ninth years' service for pension purposes, for which she was granted the princely sum of £8 17s 9d per year with effect from 1 October 1934 under the Military Service Pensions Act of that year.[29]

Throughout his teenage years and all his adult life, Haughey was extremely protective of his mother. His keenness to enter the workforce at as early an age as possible to contribute to the family's dire financial situation stemmed from his love of his mother. There is a snippet in his archive that reveals his devotion to her. When pondering writing his memoirs after his retirement, Haughey engaged Eoin Neeson to help with this project. Neeson, a contemporary of Haughey's, being just two years younger, was a journalist, historian and had been the director of the Government Information Bureau in the late 1960s. In 2005, Neeson drafted a section about Haughey's birth and early years. While that draft is not in Haughey's papers, his reaction to it was underwhelming. He noted that the 'description of my arrival into the world is totally lopsided. The focus is almost entirely on the poker game. My mother is barely mentioned.'[30] Haughey was generally unhappy with what Neeson sent him and cancelled the whole project.[31]

Regarding his birth, Haughey went on to say he was delivered by a well-known midwife in the area, a certain Mrs Minch, who had also delivered Enda Kenny's father, Henry (Haughey calls him Harry). The reference to the poker game comes from an article in the *Sunday World* newspaper on 20 September 2000 when Johnnie Haughey's fellow soldier

Seán Clancy recounts the night Charles Haughey was born.[32] To Clancy, Johnnie Haughey was a good friend and comrade, if a little hot tempered. A poker game took place once a week in Johnnie Haughey's house outside the barracks and was attended by some soldiers, a couple of local priests and some local gardaí. On the night of Charles Haughey's birth, Johnnie Haughey was called away from the poker game just after 11 p.m. The others continued, but at some time after midnight were told by a maid working in the house that the doctor had come to attend to Mrs Haughey and they should take their leave, which they duly did. The following morning word reached the barracks that a son, to be named Cathal (although he would be christened Charles), had been born to Johnnie and Sarah Haughey. The young Cathal was baptised two days later by the local parish priest, Chancellor Corcoran, and the witnesses were Captain Eamon Young and his wife Jane Young. Haughey's original birth certificate correctly states the date of his birth as 16 September but registers his Christian name as James. His baptismal certificate gives his full name, Charles James, but incorrectly records his date of birth as 15 September. This might be due to the fact that he was born in the early hours of 16 September.[33] Some fifty-three years later, in 1978, the priest who had christened Charles Haughey sent him well wishes and declared that he had 'made a good job' as Minister for Health and Social Welfare.[34] According to family lore, as told by Haughey's mother, he was born with a caul.[35] This is an extremely rare occurrence in birth; the baby is delivered with an intact amniotic sac which covers its face and head. It is then lifted off the baby's head by the midwife in a fairly simple procedure.[36] Since medieval times this has been interpreted as good luck and a sign that the child is destined for greatness. It was something that Sarah Haughey certainly believed in when it came to her second son.

Charles Haughey's northern heritage had a significant impact on his upbringing and later political life. In his 1986 collection of Haughey's speeches and statements, Martin Mansergh, his long-time adviser, stated that Haughey had no input into the choice of material: the only item he saw in advance was the section of a biographical note about his early life.[37] That biographical sketch noted that while holidaying with his grandmother in Swatragh, Haughey attended the local school in Corlecky. The details of Haughey's childhood visits to Swatragh are sketchy, but the principal reason for them was to give his mother a break from her children in her constant battle to cope with her husband's ever-increasing disability. Every summer, once school was over, Charles Haughey and his brothers were sent north on the train to Belfast, where they caught another train to Maghera. At that small station, which ran until 1950, they were picked up by Sarah Haughey's brother, Owen McWilliams, who was a local cattle dealer, one of many in the area. McWilliams put up the money to buy a lorry for a number of dealers, including his own brother, Patsy McWilliams, and Patrick Heaney, father of the poet Seamus Heaney.[38]

McWilliams took the Haugheys with him when visiting local marts all across south Derry and trained them in the art of cattle dealing. He lived in Stranagone before moving to Kilrea just before the outbreak of the Second World War, and treated the Haughey boys as if they were his own sons. They helped with his business, played GAA with the local teams, took part in athletics competitions and went to dances, particularly in the local parish hall in Kilrea, with the grocer's daughters from across the street where McWilliams lived. Beyond that the only other entertainment at night was a small cinema in Maghera. The four Haughey boys were outstanding athletes in their youth and were of great benefit to the local GAA teams, but their victories in various races at the Maghera festival in the summer led to much resentment from locals who initially took against these 'blow-ins' coming in and taking the glory. After a few years, however, the rage of the locals subsided and the Haughey boys began to be accepted.[39]

But Derry was not all idyllic summers for the Haugheys. Cathal Haughey witnessed sectarian riots in Maghera in 1935 when he was just ten years old.[40] Owen McWilliams was a great fan of the cinema and often took his nephews Seán and Cathal with him.[41] The author David Burke claimed that after one such trip in 1938 they emerged from the building to witness a riot in which loyalists were firing rifles at unarmed Catholics. The event made a lasting impression on the young Cathal Haughey.[42] In 1939, as war broke out across Europe, Owen McWilliams bought new winter coats for Seán and Cathal Haughey, the eldest two of the Haughey boys, who would have been fifteen and fourteen years of age. These were a farewell present from Derry and would do the boys throughout the winter to come. On the way home the train was boarded by members of the Ulster Special Constabulary (B Specials) in Armagh, who took the two Haughey boys off the train and questioned them as to their new coats. They were removed from the train, had their coats taken, were held for the day and then put back on the last train to Dublin.[43] The psychological impact on the teenage Haugheys can only be guessed at but it was part of a reality that they put up with on their visits to Derry. They were often stopped at night by local B Specials who were known to them when they were returning to Stranagone from Swatragh, Kilrea or Maghera. Haughey was reported as finding these intrusions sinister and threatening, feeling that there was an element of 'croppies lie down' in the behaviour of their B Specials tormentors.[44]

DONNYCARNEY

While Haughey's summers were spent in Derry, the rest of his childhood was very much based around Dublin's northside. When Johnnie Haughey realised he would have to leave the army he began approaching his senior officers to help him adjust to civilian life. Like so many of his generation who had spent his late teens and early adulthood in the IRA and later in the Free State army he had nothing to fall back on, since he had had no time to learn a trade or engage in business. His lack of security in relation to his future career prospects was intensified by his problematic living arrangements; during his service he had been supplied with basic army quarters, which he would now lose. The future looked grim. Haughey was ill, had a growing family and very little in the way of job or housing prospects. Moreover, while he had a pension, it was, as one old soldier described it, 'barely enough to feed a canary'.[45] On his retirement on 21 April 1928 to the Reserve of Officers he was granted a pension under the Military Service Pension Act of £90 per year.[46]

The Haugheys decided that farming was the solution to their problems. Both had grown up in the Swatragh farming community and reckoned they could eke out a decent living. They also felt that the fresh air of County Meath would help with Johnnie's declining health.

In April 1928 the secretary of the Land Commission, Kevin O'Shiel, wrote to General Sean McKeon, then quartermaster general of the National Army, who had asked whether anything could be done to help Seán Haughey, as he was soon to retire, and in ailing health. O'Shiel stated: 'I think you know our difficulties about providing land for ex-army officers ... However, I shall do what I can in the case of Haughey. In the meantime would it not be well to have Haughey sent a list of prospective auctions of defaulting annuitants? You will remember I spoke to you about this aspect of the situation and I think you agreed that many of the National Army Officers would be able to acquire holdings at these auctions.[47] O'Shiel told McKeon that he was having a list of such auctions prepared to be sent to Haughey. A note attached to this file states that Commandant John Haughey was the son of a farmer, could farm tillage and was looking for a farm in north Dublin or Kildare. It added that he had some money and was the nephew of Fr Fullerton of Belfast. In fact, Fr Fullerton was the uncle of Sarah McWilliams. But rather than Dublin or Kildare, the Haugheys ended up in Dunshaughlin, County Meath. They bought a small farm called the Riggins in 1928. Here they set up their business farming dairy and vegetables, and educated their children, while every year Johnnie Haughey returned to the army to give six-week training courses to new recruits.

The Riggins, while having an address in Dunshaughlin, is technically in the parish of Skryne, and the farm was located on the road from Rathfeigh to Halltown Cross on the Skryne–Ratoath road. But Cathal Haughey went to school in Cushinstown in the corner of Duleek parish because his parents had to get milk to the creamery, which involved bringing their cans to the main road near Kilmoon where the Premier Dairies cart from Finglas would collect them. Their means of transport was a donkey with a saddle. When the milk cans were being collected in the evening the Haughey children would be collected and brought home. Cushinstown was a small two-teacher primary school, and Cathal Haughey's teacher was Rita Dardis.[48] Peter McDermott, who captained

Meath to win the All-Ireland Gaelic Football Championship in 1954, went to school in Cushinstown and knew the Haughey family well during their time in the Riggins. In 2003 he reminisced to the *Meath Chronicle* that a few times a week he would cycle to his uncle's house, near the Haugheys, to collect eggs, and often carried young Cathal home on the handlebars: 'I think a stop was put to it, as we would go flying down Painstown Hill and it was dangerous'[49] – particularly since McDermott was seven years older than Cathal Haughey. It was, however, typical of the young Haughey's daredevil attitude.

But while the Haughey children lived a relatively carefree existence, life was much more difficult for their parents. Johnnie Haughey became progressively sicker and the farm eventually failed, forcing the family to move to Dublin, where they settled in Belton Park Road in the growing suburb of Donnycarney. A decade into the new state Dublin was short of money, but the new Fianna Fáil government led by Éamon de Valera engaged in a large-scale housing expansion. Sarah Haughey persuaded her husband that it would be better if they moved to the northside of Dublin, where there were many serving army officers living in the areas around Griffith Avenue, Collins Avenue, and the neighbouring boroughs. There they would at least have some support structure for their young family.

They would also be going to an area with new churches, new schools, sound well-built houses and space for her outgoing children to play. And so the seven-year-old Cathal Haughey packed the few clothes and books he owned and off he went again with his family to the house where his mother would live for the remaining fifty-six years of her life. One of the things Haughey brought with him was a workbook from school. It is the earliest surviving possession of his. He writes the word 'dad' beautifully for a six-year-old child and is rewarded with a flourish of his teacher's red pen on a page dated 24 February 1932.[50]

Those early years of Sarah Haughey's life in Belton Park were taken up tending to her new baby, Eoghan, the only Haughey child to be born in Dublin, and raising her young family. At this stage she had seven children, all born in a ten-year period: four boys, Seán, Cathal, Pádraig and Eoghan; and three girls, Eithne, Bridget and Maureen. She attempted to get her husband treated for his multiple sclerosis in St Bricin's Military Hospital in Stonybatter,[51] but the hospital only treated serving members of the defence forces. For Sarah Haughey there was virtually no help from the state that she and her invalided husband had played their own part in establishing. There was no nursing help to assist with Johnnie, no children's allowances for her seven children, and no free secondary education.

Sarah Haughey had her indomitable Catholic faith, her love for her husband and children and little else. One of her neighbours remembers seeing her, 'coat tightly buttoned against the wind, pedalling along on her high bicycle with a spade tied to the handlebars on her way to one of the war-time allotments near us where she grew most of her own vegetables. I'd see her later cycling home with her carrier-basket full. She always reminded me of the women of the Bible and I thought she was aptly named, Sara. She had the mettle, the back for the burden without a doubt.'[52] Another neighbour recalls her as always being very well turned out when going to mass and wearing one of her array of hats. She was a daily mass-goer and instilled a deep religious faith in all her children. The young Cathal Haughey was reported to be a child of strong Catholic faith. On one occasion, when the family thought their father was dying, Haughey ran to the nearby Ormonde family on Hazel Road begging Mrs Ormonde to come and help as 'my daddy is dying'. He particularly wanted some religious relics so that everyone would be holding something as the family prayed around his bed. On rooting out some relics, Mrs Ormonde recalled Haughey bolting off like a racehorse back to his own house as she followed in his wake.[53] Johnnie Haughey recovered on that occasion but his sickness dominated the lives of his wife and children.

In an Ireland where the investigation of social class has often been avoided, the subject of Charles Haughey's background and its influence on his later political life has been the topic of much debate. While many take the view that his straitened upbringing is the key to understanding his later love of the lavish lifestyle, Haughey himself never saw it in those terms. In a contribution to a seminar given by this author in Trinity College in 2017 the journalist Deaglán de Bréadún stated that in a number of interviews he had done with Haughey during his career, he always thought of himself as middle class: 'Sure, wasn't my father an officer in the Irish army.'[54] Haughey's long-time cultural adviser and friend Anthony Cronin also pointed out that Haughey considered himself middle class. In a searing critique of the 2015 RTÉ drama series *Charlie*, Cronin said that one of its greatest errors arose from the question of Haughey's origins. The actor playing P.J. Mara 'asserts loudly that Charlie was a working-class boy from Donnycarney. The real P.J. would certainly have known better. In cold hard fact, Charlie was not working-class. He was the son of an army officer and he went, like Garret FitzGerald – and it sometimes seemed in those days every frontbench politician of any party – to UCD, where he distinguished himself socially and academically, as well as in many respects, humanly.'[55]

Well into retirement from public life, Haughey told a research student that he was the product of his 'working-class background'.[56] The only reason he was able to go to UCD in the first place was because he was able to go to secondary school. The only reason he was able to go to St Joseph's secondary school in Fairview was because he got a Dublin Corporation scholarship. And the precise nature of these scholarships was to provide the bright children of the Dublin working classes with access to secondary education. The Christian Brothers provided a ladder between different elements of Ireland's indistinct and little-studied social class divisions in a way that contributed powerfully to the growth of Ireland's middle classes in the post-war generation. And Charles Haughey was certainly one of those who benefited from that Christian Brothers education.

CHAPTER 2

EDUCATION

SCHOOL

On moving to Donnycarney, Sarah Haughey's first job was to enrol her children in primary school. Because they had only recently arrived in the parish, she had to bring her children with her to the interview by the principal in Scoil Mhuire, Marino. The oldest two boys, Seán and Cathal, were immediately accepted and proved two of the cleverest students ever to attend the school. On Charles Haughey's election as Taoiseach in 1979 a former teacher at Scoil Mhuire, John Campion, wrote to congratulate him, saying it was the day he had waited nearly half a century for. He told Haughey that he always regarded him as 'one of the cleverest in the school and a stylish hurler and footballer in the middle thirties'.[1]

And indeed the two Haugheys were among the ablest in the school. In 1937 Seán Haughey was placed second out of five hundred students who sat the Dublin Corporation examination for scholarships to secondary school. About eighty scholarships were awarded each year. The following year his younger brother Cathal was placed first. The *Irish Press* of 17 August 1938 put a photo of the then nearly thirteen-year-old Haughey on its front page. In a colour piece the *Irish Independent* of the same day stated that the twelve-and-a-half-year-old Cathal Haughey had atoned for the disappointment of his 'younger' brother Seán after a twelve-month preparation. It noted, without irony, that Seán got only second place in five hundred entrants for the Corporation scholarships for secondary schools in 1937 and was worried as to why he had lost the few odd marks he would have needed to be placed first. It informed its readers that because of that 'Cathal has taken a hand. He got to the top this year and is the youngest pupil who ever made the grade.' The reporter who visited the house stated that both were celebrating and, though they were keenly interested in games, 'they both stated that they were going to keep on studying until they are able to bring wages in home as well as prizes.'[2] The young Cathal Haughey's prowess as a primary school student was recalled by one of his correspondents, Sarah Corr, after he became Taoiseach for the first time in December 1979. She reminded him that she was visiting his home 'when you got the result of your Primary Cert and as you went out with your hurley to play a game with your brother Seán, your father said to us, Cathal will go far. How true.'[3] His results were greeted with great jubilation and a chant of 'None of your, none of your, We're from Donnyer.'[4]

Scoil Mhuire's prowess in the academic world was matched by its achievements on the sporting field. In 1936 Cathal Haughey was part of the Scoil Mhuire Marino junior primary Dublin hurling champions. The following year they were Gaelic football champions, with Haughey again on the team. The names of the boys on the football team and a picture of the team was sent to Haughey by Eddie Ó Mórdha in 2003. Ó Mórdha was passing them on at the request of Val Marshell, who had played on the same team and still lived in Marino.[5] The passing on of memorabilia from his childhood, teenage years and early adulthood was a feature of Haughey's whole life. Long into his retirement old schoolmates from Scoil Mhuire, St Joseph's CBS, UCD and King's Inns would send him on little mementoes or personal reminiscences of his time with them.

Beyond the thrill of seeing Cathal's photograph on the front page of the *Irish Press*, the preferred newspaper of the Haughey household, there was a very practical reason for the joy in Belton Park that warm summer afternoon in August 1938 when the results of the Dublin Corporation scholarship examinations were released. The scholarship would allow Cathal Haughey to follow his brother Seán to St Joseph's CBS, or 'Joey's', in Marino. Most of his friends at that time were not as fortunate and their families had not the means to allow them to attend secondary school. For Haughey, it was to be a formative experience.

JOEY'S

Founded in 1888, St Joseph's in Marino was popular with local families and those from outside its immediate catchment area because of its reputation for excellence and the absence of other secondary schools in the vicinity. It was the natural secondary school for the Haughey boys. At this stage it was still a one-cycle school and students finished their secondary schooling after the Intermediate Certificate. That changed with the arrival as principal of Brother Tomás Ó Catháin to take charge of the school in 1938, the year Cathal Haughey entered its doors. Ó Catháin, known to the boys in the school as 'The Goof', was to have a dramatic impact on the school's academic and sporting prowess.[6] Ó Catháin taught religious education, mathematics and Latin. He also took over the training of the school teams and set about both dramatically increasing the school's numbers and refurbishing its rather dilapidated building. In 1946 new classrooms were added for the first time since 1906 to meet the growing demand for places in the school. There were 181 students in the school when Ó Catháin became principal and at the end of his first year in 1939, twenty-five students passed the Intermediate Certificate. But Ó Catháin was determined to give at least some of the boys the opportunity to sit the Leaving Certificate examination and began making preparations to persuade the Provincial of the Christian Brothers Order, Brother B.L. Ryan at Booterstown, that he had the pupils who could successfully take the exam. He eventually received the necessary permission and the Leaving Certificate was taken for the first time by twelve pupils of St Joseph's in 1942. All passed with honours, and four also took the Matriculation Examination of the National University of Ireland to study at University College, Dublin. The following year twenty-eight students, including Cathal Haughey, took the Leaving Certificate examination.[7] The decision by Brother Ó Catháin to offer the Leaving Certificate curriculum opened a new horizon to the young Haughey, ultimately enabling him to go to UCD.

What was the young Cathal like in secondary school? For his research Tommy Broughan was sent a description of both Seán and Cathal Haughey by Brother Ó Catháin, who noted in 1978 that some thirty-five years after he had left the school he still remembered them as being much more than ordinary pupils and with quite different characters. He recalled Seán as 'a very talented, receptive, gentle, honourable and manly boy'.[8] He was an outstanding athlete but as he tended towards soccer rather than Gaelic games he did not feature in many of the school teams. He went on to become a very good League of Ireland soccer player for Shelbourne, having begun his career at Home Farm. Seán Haughey did not finish secondary school as he won a place as a clerk in Dublin Corporation before he was due to complete his Leaving Certificate. After much discussion in the family home he felt it his duty to become its main breadwinner and thus took the position, rising eventually to assistant manager in 1978.

Cathal Haughey – it was as Cathal that he was registered on the school roll and known to his schoolmates and teachers alike – was different from his brother. According to Ó Catháin, while both Haughey brothers were co-operative, honourable and manly, Cathal was more determined and 'somewhat aggressive', but also was never reprimanded in his five years at the school. To Ó Catháin he was 'at least as brainy as any pupil I met during a long teaching career'. To his entrance scholarship, Haughey quickly added an Intermediate scholarship for his results in the 1941 Intermediate Certificate, one of just forty in the whole country. One of Haughey's traits that quickly became apparent in his school years was his clear-mindedness and quick decision-making. He was a standout performer in school debates and mock trials, all of which were held through Irish. Ó Catháin recalled one such trial where Haughey was counsel for the state and took apart the alibi of the accused by placing several simple questions to the defendant regarding time, place and companions during the time at which the alleged crime was committed. On a second questioning, due to the sheer number of questions, the accused got mixed up and forgot his original answers. The result was that he lost all coherence and was found guilty by the jury, leading Ó Catháin to express intrigue at the 'cleverness of the questioning' by the young Cathal Haughey.[9]

While being extremely clever brought Haughey to the attention of the school authorities, his athletic prowess also marked him out, and he played both hurling and football for various school teams. He was reported to be a clean, skilful and determined player but prone to retaliation when fouled, which led to the occasional sending-off. He is also remembered as being unusually determined and being in every game to win it.[10] While his quick temper occasionally got him into trouble, his skill and determination made him a core player for St Joseph's as it became a serious force in schools Gaelic games under Ó Catháin's watch. Haughey never won a Leinster Colleges title, but came agonisingly close in February 1943 in the football championship final played at Mullingar when St Joseph's lost by two points to St Mel's of Longford. Haughey's late shot, which would have won the game, was cleared off the line by a defender. The referee played nine minutes of injury time, on a very wet day, in which St Mel's went ahead only in the closing stages, which made the defeat more difficult to take. Two weeks later, sixteen of the football panel were also involved with the hurlers when they lost the Leinster Colleges hurling final to the famed Kilkenny hurling nursery St Kieran's College in a game played at Dr Cullen Park in Carlow. They were at a disadvantage at not having played a game in Dublin and were discommoded by the length of the grass on the pitch, which hampered their normal ground hurling game.[11] Ironically enough, St Kieran's were also noted for their ability in ground hurling and they inflicted a heavy defeat on St Joseph's, winning by 8-9 to 4-2.[12] Haughey was left disappointed again.

Haughey's ability and forcefulness on the pitch brought him to the attention of both the Leinster Colleges and Dublin minor selectors. He was picked in both hurling and football for the Leinster Colleges and in 1942 he was named on the Dublin minor hurling panel for the Leinster

Championship, which in the event was postponed until the following year. At a meeting of the Central Council of the GAA in May 1942, the All-Ireland minor championships were suspended until a new set of circumstances arose. This was an indirect reference to the Emergency, as the Second World War was known in Ireland. The GAA established an Emergency Committee to run its games in 1942 as a direct response to the challenges around the availability of transport and the stressed financial position of the association in the war years. Central Council further agreed in May 1943 not to proceed with the minor inter-county championships.[13] As war waged across Europe, the 1943 All-Ireland Senior Hurling Championship final, featuring a novel pairing of Cork and Antrim, took place on 5 September. The future Taoiseach, Jack Lynch, was selected in his normal centre field position for a Cork team going for its third All-Ireland win in a row. It was decided that the game would be preceded by the Leinster minor hurling final postponed from the previous year; Haughey, who would succeed Lynch as Taoiseach, was named at right corner forward. Dublin suffered an extremely heavy defeat, going down by 3-10 to 0-4. Haughey's underage club career at St Vincent's was much more successful and he was a central part of the club's minor hurling and football championship teams of 1942. He was known for wearing black boots with white laces, which would have been a very uncommon combination at the time.[14]

But once Haughey came out of the underage grades he transferred his allegiance from the St Vincent's club in Marino to Parnells, which was closer to where he lived in Donnycarney. Since he was a very promising young player, St Vincent's did not want to lose him and was reported as being very sore that he left the club to go to Parnells.[15] Parnells and St Vincent's were fierce rivals, both on the pitch and in attracting players. The famous parish rule by which GAA players play with their local club and find it almost impossible to transfer to other clubs within their own county never applied in Dublin and transfers between Dublin clubs were relatively commonplace.[16] Haughey's GAA career with Parnells was relatively short-lived. He transferred to Parnells to play as an adult and won a Dublin County Football Championship medal in May 1945 when he came on as a substitute for Parnells against the reigning county champions, Civil Service. Although this game was labelled the 'final of the Taoisigh' because Jack Lynch played with Civil Service in this period, he did not play in this particular game as he was injured.[17] Fifty years later the journalist Una Claffey wrote to Haughey, who had by then retired, to remind him of the event and sent him a photograph of the team, which showed her father, Brendan Claffey, who had been on the same team, holding his daughter on his knee. A wistful Haughey replied thanking her, noting 'weren't they really lovely innocent days, with Brendan holding your sister on his knee. I doubt if the hard-featured team managers of today would allow such a homely photograph to be taken!'[18] Haughey's GAA playing career eventually came to a rather abrupt end when he was sent off in a game for Parnells the following year after striking a linesman. He was suspended for a year and never went back.[19]

Haughey's main focus in 1943, however, was the conclusion of his Leaving Certificate. The scholarship he won for his Intermediate Certificate results allowed him to proceed for the final two years but he was troubled by the fact that he was in school, and thus not contributing to the family income, while his father was lying sick in bed. Haughey was anxious to alleviate the family's dire financial straits. He often spoke at home of leaving school and following his father into the army. His mother, however, was having none of it; recognising his obvious talent, she insisted he stay in school. On one occasion, when the teenage Haughey was again mooting the idea of joining the army, his mother asked him what she could give him to persuade him to go to college. Haughey immediately replied in monetary terms – 'Ten bob'. To his great surprise she pulled it out of her purse, to which he replied, 'I didn't believe you had ten bob.'

'What will I do with the ten bob?' he thought. 'I gave her my word and I took her money.' Then off he went with some friends and bought ten Woodbines and some sweets to celebrate his good fortune.[20]

The counterpoint for him, though, was that he had to enrol in the Leaving Certificate cycle, sitting the exam along with twenty-seven others in the fabled St Joseph's Leaving Certificate class of 1942. His classmates included his lifelong friend Harry Boland, and his later rival for the Fianna Fáil leadership, George Colley, both of whom came from hardcore Fianna Fáil families. Haughey, by contrast, was a political outsider. The cultural critic Declan Kiberd recalls his aunt telling him of seeing Haughey running up and down from Donnycarney to Marino in bedraggled trousers during his schooling while George Colley was always impeccably turned out and wonders whether Haughey perhaps felt like an outsider in the Christian Brothers ambience of St Joseph's.[21]

That 'outsider' tag would follow Haughey in his early Fianna Fáil days when, because of his father's association with Michael Collins, his membership of the party was treated with scepticism by some of its ruling cadres. Yet while Haughey's father was devoted to Collins, it would appear that this devotion was to Collins the army man, as distinct from Collins the Fine Gael hero. Haughey's brother Eoghan was adamant that the Haughey home was strongly Fianna Fáil and that the Haughey and McWilliams cousins who came to visit Donnycarney in the 1930s and 1940s were very much de Valera and Fianna Fáil supporters.[22] Cathal Haughey was influenced by his northern cousins and his nationalism was shaped by their visits and viewpoints. But as he was about to sit his Leaving Certificate in June 1943 and his time at St Joseph's was coming to an end, his thoughts about where he should go were focused very firmly on UCD, which he saw as a gateway to make the money so badly lacking in Belton Park. Cathal Haughey performed excellently in his Leaving Certificate and was awarded a Dublin Corporation university scholarship, one of five the school received that year.[23] Brother Ó Catháin asked him what course he intended to pursue at UCD. As they went through the various faculties they eventually came to medicine. Ó Catháin recalled that Haughey looked interested and asked, 'What would be my financial position when I am qualified? I do not want to be a penniless doctor.'[24] He eventually settled on commerce after being assured by Harry Boland's brother, Enda, that he could join the family firm, Boland Bourke accountants, once he graduated.[25] It was hardly a cast-iron guarantee but it settled Haughey on a route to the financial security that he wanted for his mother, and indeed for himself.

During the last two years of his secondary schooling the young Cathal Haughey had explored the option of making the army his full-time career. On his sixteenth birthday, 16 September 1941, as he entered his fifth year of school, he joined the Local Defence Forces as part of the North County Battalion based in Collinstown. Military service was to be an important part of his life for the following fifteen years. He raised his own platoon of part-time soldiers from the streets of Donnycarney. In his early CVs as a politician Haughey stated that he was a platoon leader in the Local Defence Forces from 16 September 1941 to December 1945. After the war was over he was commissioned into An Fórsa Cosanta Áitiúil (FCÁ) on 3 June 1947 as a second lieutenant and would stay there until his election as a TD in 1957, working his way up to the rank of lieutenant and officer commanding 'A' Company, North Dublin Battalion.[26]

Haughey took his FCÁ duties quite seriously right up to his election to Dáil Éireann. As late as October 1956 he was telling his company about the importance of an area inspection, the first since a new area commander had taken over: 'I am very anxious that we have the greatest possible attendance on that night. Please make a special effort to be present. It is essential that every rifle on issue be on parade.'[27] Four months later, in the middle of a general election campaign in which he was desperately trying to be elected to Dáil Éireann for the first time at his fourth attempt, he was still dealing with mundane matters, such as discharges from the FCÁ, for members of his company.[28] It is quite clear that Haughey was a popular and conscientious company commander. In August 1956 he wrote with concern to the secretary of Clontarf Golf Club about one of his men, Private H. Timmons, who had been ordered to attend a training course with the other members of the battalion from 4 to 18 August in Kilkenny and was thus away from his employment at the club. Haughey understood that Timmons had the appropriate leave to attend the training camp which he successfully completed. On his return to work, Timmons was informed that he was late coming back and was dismissed, leaving an anguished Haughey to write: 'I feel sure that there must have been some misunderstanding and, I need hardly say, that I am very perturbed indeed to say that any action on my part might have had such a serious result for this excellent young man ... I am very worried that I may inadvertently have brought about the present situation.'[29] Haughey was reassured when the secretary of the golf club replied that Timmons had resumed work on 20 August and that the club did not consider that Haughey had in any way interfered in its affairs, something he had stressed in his original letter that he was not trying to do.[30] Haughey eventually left the FCÁ when he was finally successful in the March 1957 election, being elected a Fianna Fáil TD for Dublin North East on the fourth count with 4,168 first preference votes: 10.3 per cent of the vote.

UCD

Charles Haughey's UCD days have received little attention in accounts of his life, but it was there he met his future wife, developed his early thinking about economics and the power of the state, and was involved in the famous burning of the British flag incident in Dublin city centre on VE Day in May 1945. What is in many ways remarkable about Haughey's time in UCD is that he went there at all. Notwithstanding his obvious intellectual abilities, he was far more interested in the outdoor life than in studying for his Leaving Certificate. Then there was the fact that so very few of his contemporaries went on to college. But discussions with his mother and Brother Ó Catháin persuaded him of the merits of furthering his education. Again the thorny matter of money had to be overcome. Dublin Corporation's scholarship scheme, which had enabled Haughey to go to secondary school, was to provide the answer; he was one of just seventeen students to be awarded a scholarship to UCD by the Corporation in 1943. Once he entered the doors of Earlsfort Terrace, having enrolled in the Bachelor of Commerce degree course, he was spectacularly successful in his academic career, winning a number of internal scholarships, while continuing his extra-curricular pursuits, including participation in the Local Defence Forces.

Haughey faced some gentle ribbing from his brothers, Seán, Jock and Eoghan, when he went to UCD in October 1943. Seventy years later Eoghan would recall that Haughey had no inferiority complex about attending UCD: 'I wouldn't say he was unduly impressed by the fact that he was going to UCD.'[31] The Haughey who entered UCD now went by the name of Charles – Cathal had been left behind in St Joseph's. The announcement of the Dublin Corporation university scholarships names him as Charles James Haughey. In his first UCD identity card he is known, rather oddly, as James Charles Haughey and signs his name in that order. He was student number 2411 in the UCD 1943–1944 session. By his final year in 1946 he was still recorded as James C. Haughey, but he was now signing his name Charles J. Haughey.[32]

But Haughey was indeed very much an outsider in UCD and was conscious of that status. He was often lampooned in college for being there courtesy of Dublin Corporation, when the vast majority of his fellow classmates came from private schools and their families were paying for them to go to university. His wife, Maureen, recalled that it was certainly different in college being a scholarship boy, but that never fazed Haughey, and he became an active member of the Commerce Society.[33] Haughey's great political rival of the 1980s, Garret FitzGerald, a contemporary of his at UCD, alluded to the contrast between the private and state schoolboys who attended UCD. In 2000 FitzGerald told the ground-breaking RTÉ history documentary *Seven Ages*, 'We were always contrasted in university. He was in different societies than the ones I was in. He was always, in the early part of the period, with men, I was always with girls. He was for the Germans, I was for the allies, so you know the division was there at the very beginning.'[34] But the reality was somewhat different. FitzGerald simply moved in different circles because he came from privilege, having been educated at Belvedere College. His father was one of the founding fathers of the state. As eighteen-year-olds entering UCD, Haughey and FitzGerald were about as far apart as two people who grew up in the same city could be. FitzGerald's contemporaries at UCD were from the same social class as he was. Haughey was their polar opposite when it came to class. FitzGerald, who studied history and modern languages, does recall in his autobiography being in some of the same classes as Haughey and meeting him in the company of Harry Boland, Colm Traynor and Peadar Ward, all sons of Fianna

Fáil ministers.[35] Moreover, Haughey, according to Maureen, had plenty of female friends, including herself, at UCD.[36] Finally, there is no evidence whatsoever that Haughey was pro-German. Haughey was clearly anti-British, as were pretty much all his friends in UCD, but the casual slur that he was 'for' the Germans has no basis in fact.

This allegation is probably based on the legendary story of Haughey's involvement in the burning of the British flag on VE Day, 7 May 1945. Early that afternoon Germany surrendered to the Allies in the town of Rheims in France, triggering scenes of jubilation all across Europe, including Dublin, where students at Trinity climbed on to the roof of the university building and raised the flags of the victors – the hammer and sickle of the Soviet Union, the French tricolour and, at the top, and largest of all, the British Union flag. Underneath them, the Irish tricolour was at the bottom of the mast, and trailing on the roof. Eventually all four flags were taken down and replaced by the Stars and Stripes of the United States of America. The students on the roof then attempted to burn the Irish tricolour; when they failed, they threw it onto the lawn, where there was a rush of people to rescue it.[37] News of the burning of the flag spread to nearby UCD and a number of students, led by Haughey, marched over to TCD to do something about it.[38] In truth they did not have much idea what they would do, but on they marched.

The counter-demonstration began in Middle Abbey Street at 8 p.m., and on their way to Trinity the UCD students were alleged to have torn down a Union flag hanging on a lamppost at the bottom of Grafton Street and set it alight. Bruce Arnold alleged that it was Haughey and his friend, the future barrister Seamus Sorohan, who did this.[39] The *Irish Times* reported that the crowd that descended on Trinity was led by a 'young man waving a large tricolour hoisted on the shoulders of his comrades'.[40] This man was later identified by some of his friends as Haughey. But as the gates of Trinity were closed the group tried to scale the railings of the university, at which point they were set upon by gardaí, who baton-charged them. Haughey's UCD friend Kevin Burke remembers seldom seeing some of his colleagues running as fast as they did that evening.[41] Contemporary newspaper reports suggest that attempts by other students to storm Trinity were also rebuffed successfully by gardaí. A dozen protesters were taken to hospital. Contrary to legend, Haughey never did get to the top of Trinity to run the tricolour up the flagpole and never did burn the Trinity Union flag. That he burned the Union flag on Grafton Street is speculative at best, with no eyewitness account to definitively place Haughey as the culprit. Maureen Lemass, who did not hear about the incident until the following day, remembers Haughey telling her then that the whole event was no big deal.[42] Eventually the UCD protesters left College Green with one of their number telling the *Irish Times*: 'Trinity has insulted the country by burning the Tricolour. We don't mind Trinity flying the Union Jack because we all know the outlook of these people, but what we do object is to the flying of a number of Irish flags insultingly on the bottom'.[43]

One of the eyewitnesses to the events at Trinity College was Garret FitzGerald, who was in town celebrating VE Day when he heard about what was going on in College Green. He recalled hearing that Haughey had taken down the flag that was flying over Trinity and that a riot had ensued. FitzGerald and his friends escaped by 'jumping over bicycles and going up Trinity Street. My views and his views would have been different. I was strongly pro-Allied as my friends would have been. I don't think he shared that view at all.'[44] In his account of the incident the academic Stephen Kelly states that Haughey's actions reflected a prevailing anti-British mood among many Irish people at the time, but adds that, unlike the 'unscrupulous young Haughey', very few people would have been involved in burning a Union flag.[45] He provides no adjective to describe those Trinity students who attempted to burn the Irish tricolour. The later labelling of Haughey as one of the Union flag burners is unsupported by contemporary descriptions of the incident or indeed by any description of any others supposedly involved. Moreover, ever since Armistice Day in 1919 there had been annual confrontations between Trinity students loyal to the idea of the Empire and UCD students who supported Irish nationalism.[46] The 1945 incident was the latest manifestation of that rivalry.

Haughey never spoke publicly of the flag-burning incident and there is no mention of it in his archive except for one cryptic line in a letter written some twenty-five years later to his friend, the Gate Theatre co-founder Micheál Mac Liammóir. Haughey was about to go on trial for his alleged role in arms importation, and in a letter to him Mac Liammóir asks him for forgiveness over an unstated gaffe: 'I mean the one at Trinity College. You were so wonderful about it that I will never cease to be grateful and really I suppose it is quite funny and makes a good story with suitable additions and subtractions.'[47] It is not clear what this incident was, but in turning down the invitation to dinner with Mac Liammóir and his partner, Hilton Edwards – because of the 'tiresome business of the trial' – Haughey noted, 'I have been dining out on the Trinity incident myself – suitably embellished of course!'[48] It is possible, but perhaps unlikely, that this is a reference to the incident in 1945. What is certain is that the nineteen-year-old Haughey was centrally involved in the demonstration at Trinity College on 7 May 1945. It was clearly a manifestation of his youthful nationalism and perhaps even his anti-Britishness. But he was far from unique in that in both the Ireland, and the UCD, of May 1945. It had nothing to do with any pro-German feelings and was also most likely fuelled by alcohol. Ultimately the incident itself did no harm to Haughey's nationalist credentials when he was ascending through the ranks of Fianna Fáil and was indeed embellished, by rumour, over the years. He never did anything to quell those rumours.

MAUREEN

Far more important in Haughey's life at UCD was meeting Maureen Lemass. Born two weeks before her husband, Maureen Lemass met Charles Haughey in the bike shed of UCD in the first few weeks of beginning college in 1943. They were in the same BComm class and it was another classmate, Haughey's close friend Harry Boland, who introduced them. She was the eldest child of Seán and Kathleen Lemass and knew Harry Boland through their Fianna Fáil connections. His father, Gerald Boland, had served in the same cabinet as Seán Lemass. Her father had fought in the War of Independence, and on the anti-Treaty side in the Civil War, and was Fianna Fáil's Minister for Supplies when she entered UCD. Even though her father was one of the most famous people in

Ireland, she enjoyed a normal if rather peripatetic middle-class lifestyle in the south Dublin of the 1930s and early 1940s. Her parents moved house on numerous occasions and the family lived in Rathgar, Churchtown and finally on Palmerston Road in Rathmines. She attended Muckross Park College, the all-girls' Dominican secondary school in Donnybrook. She had an active childhood, playing camogie and tennis, cycling in the Dublin mountains with a large circle of friends and going to local dances.[49]

But Maureen Lemass's happy existence was dramatically interrupted when she contracted tuberculosis. This disrupted her UCD studies and necessitated a prolonged stay in hospital. In fact, all three Lemass daughters were struck down with the illness, as their mother recalled some years later: 'My three daughters all got TB at the same time. My eldest, who was eighteen or nineteen, was very bad and she had to spend two years in hospital. It was before they had discovered the drugs to cure TB easily and people were dying from it in their thousands in this country. It was a real killer and I was worried to death.'[50] But Maureen recovered and resumed her studies in UCD. In May 1945 she took up the position of social secretary of the Commerce Society and Charles Haughey became auditor. They were both very forceful debaters. In 1945 Haughey won the society's Gold Medal for oratory and Lemass won the Dr Beddy Prize for Lady Speakers.[51] Some months after his retirement in 1992 a former contemporary of Haughey's in UCD, Wally Treanor, wrote to him enclosing a piece he had written about life in UCD in the 1940s. Treanor recalled that in the Literary and Historical Society (L&H) 'there was a higher level of rhetoric and the society provided early practice in reasoned if at times heated argument for two future prime ministers, Charles J. Haughey and Garret FitzGerald.'[52]

Haughey's UCD days were much like those of his contemporaries and indeed college students of all generations. He cycled to Earlsfort Terrace from Donnycarney, attended most, but not all, of his lectures, got involved in the Commerce Society and was an active member of the Student Representative Council. He drank with his classmates, sometimes during the day, more often at night. One of his former classmates remembered Haughey in his new camelhair coat in an argumentative mood on the steps at Earlsfort Terrace, debating at the L&H and at 'the final debate in the Singing Kettle around the corner'.[53] On Haughey's appointment as Minister for Justice, another of his old UCD classmates, Noel Mulvin, wrote to congratulate him, noting that it was 'a far cry back to those days in 1944 in UCD when we were both aspiring to achieve the then fantastical pinnacle of B. Comm!' Haughey's reply hinted at the good times he enjoyed as a student: 'it seems a long time now since we travelled home by various unorthodox methods from Earlsfort Terrace.'[54]

Haughey also had his Local Defence Forces duty and his GAA commitments with Parnells to keep him busy. But he was also acutely aware that he was in UCD to get a degree that was to be the pathway out of the poverty he had grown up in. The combination of his prodigious intellect and serious work ethic meant that the coursework and exams came relatively easily to him and he received first-class honours in each year, gaining results-based scholarships throughout his degree course. He graduated second in the November 1946 Bachelor of Commerce class in the college.[55]

The Haughey–Lemass romance flourished in the grim post-war years. They started dating as they were approaching their twentieth birthdays and had a steady romance until they married when they were both twenty-six, in September 1951. Maureen had been a major support to him when his father finally succumbed to his illness and died at his home in the early morning of 3 January 1947. Haughey was then just twenty-one years of age, and his father's death hit the household hard. His widowed mother was only forty-five. Many of Johnnie Haughey's old IRA and Irish National Army comrades, including his former commanding officer, Dan McKenna, came to the wake and funeral. Once the formalities of the funeral were over Sarah Haughey told her children that life had to go on for the whole family and that both she and her late husband expected their children to go out and live full and productive lives.[56] Her strong religious faith strengthened her in this difficult time and she devoted herself to working in the local church in Donnycarney. She spent so much time there that her grandchildren came to know it as 'Granny Haughey's church'.[57]

On graduating a few months earlier, Sarah's second son Charles Haughey did something rather unusual and decided to train for both the accountancy and legal professions at the same time. On 14 November 1946 he was articled to Michael J. Bourke of Boland, Bourke and Company of Dawson Street for a period of three years. This was the family firm of his great friend Harry Boland but, given his glittering academic career at UCD, the young Haughey would have clearly been an attractive apprentice for any of the large accountancy firms of Dublin. Just the previous month he had also enrolled in King's Inns, the institution that trains barristers, and studied part-time at night for the next three years before being called to the Bar in 1949. The rules of King's Inns mandated that any new student had to be nominated for study by a practising barrister of at least ten years' standing, who had to declare that they knew the applicant. Haughey was sponsored by Francis Vaughan Buckley, who himself had been called to the Bar in 1931. On successfully completing his exams, Haughey was proposed as a member of the Inns by Oliver D. Gogarty, and declared to be a fit and proper person for admission to the Bar by the former Attorney General, Cearbhall Ó Dálaigh in October 1949.[58] There were very few applicants from the northside of Dublin to King's Inns at this time or for some considerable time after.

Half a century later Haughey explained that while accountancy gave him a lot of scope he had decided to train as a barrister at the same time 'because in a political career I felt that a knowledge of the law and naturally of legislation and all that whole area would be important and also that doing the Bar would be a natural adjunct to the accountancy profession'.[59] Haughey's time at King's Inns saw him mix with fellow students who went on to become significant jurists. He learned a respect and an awareness of the instruments of law and law-making that he would not have captured otherwise in his undergraduate education and it stood him in good stead in his ministerial career.

Haughey retained a lifelong interest in King's Inns. When he was Taoiseach in the 1980s, he donated busts of the Supreme Court justices Brian Walsh and Cearbhall Ó Dálaigh, which stand at the entrance to the dining hall, and secured state funding to restore the building's facade in the 1980s.

POLITICAL BEGINNINGS

On 10 July 1947 Charles Haughey was awarded the National University of Ireland's Bursary in Commerce.[60] Part of his submission for that bursary was a long essay of over eighty handwritten pages entitled 'The Financing of Industry in Ireland'. Perhaps as a nod to his northern heritage and nationalist leanings he added in parentheses '(Excluding the Six Counties of Northern Ireland)'.[61] A close reading of Haughey's bursary essay shows the early manifestation of two things that dominated his economic thinking all his life: the power and necessity of state intervention in economic life; and that theory should not over-influence economic decision-making. Early in the essay he argues, 'there can be no doubt that Irish agriculture suffers from low productivity as a result of, among other things, underinvestment ... if a prosperous national economy is to happen based on a highly productive agriculture, that agriculture must have more capital investment.' At the end of the essay, he stresses that one of the main difficulties in financing industry is 'to prevent the discussion from wandering on the one hand into an unreal realm of theoretical generalisation or degenerating into a mere succession of statistical tables on the other'.[62] The draft in Haughey's papers is full of amendments and shows clear evidence of both much work and much editing. Over fifty years later, during his travails with the McCracken and Moriarty tribunals, his solicitor, Deirdre Courtney, noted what a skilful editor Haughey was when it came to deciding final drafts of correspondence to be sent to the tribunals.[63]

At the time of Haughey's success in the Bursary in Commerce he was a regular visitor to the Lemass house in Palmerston Road. He first met his future father-in-law at Maureen's twenty-first birthday party in September 1946 at the Country Shop restaurant on St Stephen's Green.[64] Haughey was interested in Seán Lemass's work and his plans for the future of Ireland. The two men talked about politics, business, books and sport, particularly horseracing. Haughey had expressed admiration for Lemass's work as Minister for Supplies during the Emergency and as he got to know Lemass that admiration grew. For her part, Maureen's first visit to Donnycarney left a lifelong impression: the downstairs living room was dominated by a huge picture of Michael Collins. She recalled telling her father this when she returned home, to which the dedicated Fianna Fáiler gruffly replied that it was fair enough given that Johnnie Haughey had fought for Collins.[65]

Any familial, political or class differences between their houses had, however, no impact on the Haughey–Lemass romance. In many ways it was a typical relationship of its time. They spent time cycling together in Malahide to the north of Dublin and in the Dublin mountains to the south. They went to the cinema and socialised with a group of friends they had known from their UCD Commerce Society days. On the political front Haughey was keen on Fianna Fáil's statist attitude to the economy as epitomised by Seán Lemass, and had little time for the conservative approach associated with Lemass's internal rival Seán MacEntee. It was Haughey's discussions with Lemass and, more important, his friendship with Harry Boland that led him to eventually join Fianna Fáil in late 1947, when he enrolled in the Tomás Ó Cléirigh cumann in Dublin North East. The constituency was home to two celebrated and long-serving TDs, Harry Colley and Oscar Traynor, who had both served in the 2nd Battalion of the Dublin Brigade of the old IRA. Haughey's first practical engagement in the art of politics was helping out at the February 1948 general election. Boland had asked him to get involved and one night he told Maureen that he would not be able to meet her as he was going out to canvass with Harry Boland and would later be having a drink with him and George Colley, who he had known from his schooldays at St Joseph's and was friendly with at UCD.

Haughey made an immediate impact on the Fianna Fáil organisation. When he was elected Taoiseach in 1979 he received a letter from Edward Haughey of New Zealand, one of his many namesakes who regularly wrote to him. Edward Haughey recalled going into Fianna Fáil head-quarters in 1948 to obtain a ticket for an address against partition that Éamon de Valera, now out of office for the first time in sixteen years, was to deliver in Glasgow: 'I happened to meet Mr. Boland there. He told me that his brother had a young colleague named Haughey who had a great future ahead of him. How right he was!'[66]

While Fianna Fáil's 1948 election defeat cast a cloud over the party's immediate future, given how comfortable it had become in government, Haughey was more concerned with his own future. In November 1948 he sat the intermediate examinations of the Institute of Chartered Accountants and just before Christmas received a letter informing him that he had 'obtained first place thus winning the "John Mackie" memorial prize', for which he received a cheque for £3 3s 0d.[67] It was a small but welcome boost to his coffers. The following year he took his King's Inns and Chartered Accountants of Ireland final exams. On 1 November 1949 he was one of only thirty-one students called to the Bar at a time when there were only 240 practising barristers in the whole of the country. Seven weeks later, on 20 December, Haughey received notice that he had passed his final accountancy examinations and was admitted as an associate member of the Institute of Chartered Accountants.

As the 1950s dawned, the boy from Donnycarney was now, at the age of 24, both a qualified barrister and an accountant. This was no small achievement. In 1989, Justice Gerard Buchanan of the Circuit Court wrote to then Taoiseach Charles Haughey inviting him to a fiftieth anniversary dinner of the class of 1949, of which they were both distinguished members, and enclosing the names of the students called to the Bar that year.[68] Neither man was to know it when that dinner was held, but Buchanan was to play a major role in the latter years of Haughey's life, leading the first investigation into the controversial Dunnes Stores payments to Haughey in 1996. That same year Justice Kevin Lynch of the Supreme Court, who had been in Haughey's King's Inn class, wrote to him enclosing a copy of the *Evening Herald* from the day they were called to the Bar. He also enclosed some statistics from that class of 1949, noting that of the thirty-one members of the class only ten were still practising twenty-five years later.[69] Haughey, of course, was one of those not at the Bar. He had decided not to practise, seeing accountancy and politics as the keys to his future. While he was diligent regarding the establishment and workings of his newly formed accountancy practice with Harry Boland, it was politics that would soon consume his life.

Fianna Fáil's defeat in the February 1948 general election came as a surprise to the party and a disappointment to its latest recruit in Dublin North East, Charles Haughey. But the election had given Haughey a taste for politics and he soon began to devote much of his energy to Fianna Fáil, becoming secretary of the Tomás Ó Cléirigh cumann within a year of joining after the retirement of Richard Moylan. For Haughey, one of Fianna Fáil's big problems was a lack of proper communication about what the party stood for and what its policies were. To him the 1948 election had shown that Fianna Fáil could not simply fight future contests on the sort of 'Up Dev' mantra that had long been its main rallying cry. But the party itself viewed the result differently. It felt hard done by following its removal from government and believed that its policies had played no part in its defeat. Increasingly it was becoming a party of old men who believed that all they needed to do was reorganise themselves for government to naturally fall back into the party's lap.[70] Haughey was not so sure. As it turned out there was very little reorganisation and Fianna Fáil remained imperviously unreceptive to new ideas and, indeed, new blood. But a number of young members were determined to at least offer some new ideas. Foremost among them were Charles Haughey and George Colley.

Haughey and Colley were the driving forces behind a small and short-lived local party publication called *Firinne Fáil*. The context was the 1948 election defeat. Both young men felt that the party could not just await its inevitable return to its natural seat of power. Their aim was to spread the word of Fianna Fáil's policies and its general outlook, originally in the Dublin North East constituency, and then to a wider audience beyond. The goal of getting the Fianna Fáil message across to as large a public as possible was to be a staple of Haughey's political life. Its organising committee, which called itself An Coisde Craoladh, was set up at a meeting of delegates from all cumainn in the area. Among its terms of reference was to explore the possibilities of engaging in propaganda activities. The committee's members were Haughey, George Colley, Micheál O'Murcada, Dermot Ring, Dermot O'Brien and F. Brady.[71]

In the summer of 1948 Haughey sought permission for the *Firinne Fáil* project from Dublin North East's comhairle ceantair (constituency council). On 13 July he was told that his committee could proceed with collecting and filing newspaper clippings, preparing and privately distributing pamphlets, reposting cumann meetings and lectures and collecting statistics.[72] He had originally also sought permission to acquire a printing machine, to host public meetings and to write letters to the newspapers, but was told that permission would have to be given by the party's National Executive. Haughey wanted to rejuvenate public meetings by training speakers and giving members the opportunity to practise public speaking so that they would be more polished at election time. Holding meetings between elections was also seen as advantageous; 'having the field more or less clear there will be a greater opportunity for successfully influencing the public mind.'[73] The committee also believed that writing judicious and well-framed letters to the newspapers could build considerable propaganda for the party. These specific plans were rejected by the Dublin North East comhairle ceantair. In general, Fianna Fáil at a national level was hostile to pretty much all local initiatives, although within a year Haughey was arranging public speeches outside churches in the constituency, with the approval of the comhairle ceantair. Nevertheless, there was enough goodwill in the constituency for the project to go ahead and the first edition of *Firinne Fáil* appeared in September 1948. It was edited and compiled in George Colley's house in Clontarf, which was, according to Vincent Browne, the social centre of the Fianna Fáil party in the constituency.[74]

Later that month, on 21 September 1948, Haughey drafted a letter outlining the aims of An Coisde Craoladh and *Firinne Fáil*, noting that the committee in charge of it was tasked to 'conduct by all possible means intensive propaganda on behalf of the organisation in the constituency. We feel sure that you and the members of your cumann will be glad to hear that an effort is being made to meet the long-felt want in this direction as a desire for something of this nature has often been voiced in all cumainn.'[75] In February 1949 he wrote to the secretaries of cumainn in the constituency that in order for *Firinne Fáil* to 'represent to as great an extent as possible the views of our organisation and to ensure continual freshness and variety in its contents it is our intention to compile a panel of regular contributors from amongst the members in the area. We hope that this panel of contributors will supply us with a regular flow of material (articles, poems, etc) and that they will write on anything that may come to their notice from time to time which they think merits attention.'[76] But *Firinne Fáil* soon ran into difficulty in the constituency: the Dick McKee cumann complained about being libelled as useless in the February 1949 edition. Nevertheless, it still had support from the party's two TDs, with Oscar Traynor submitting a short piece 'germane to, but not on, Defence plans' in March 1949. Traynor had been Minister for Defence between 1939 and 1948. In a gesture of support for the burgeoning publication he told Haughey that he would 'have no objection if the Editorial blue pencil comes actively into operation'.[77]

Another issue that the An Coisde Craoladh committee was anxious to make progress on was the question of what exactly it meant to be a member of Fianna Fáil. This was an important point for Haughey throughout his long career; in his later years, some internal Fianna Fáil critics suggested his family background meant he was an opportunist who had no understanding of the party's heritage and traditions. The phrase 'that wee Blueshirt' was often used against him.[78] In that context there is a fascinating two-page document in Haughey's papers entitled 'A Member of Fianna Fáil' which, although undated, clearly dates from his time in An Coisde Craoladh. Written on the top of the document in Haughey's handwriting is the name George Colley. Whether Haughey or Colley wrote it is unclear, but given that they were friendly at the time and the central forces behind An Coisde Craoladh it speaks to both their mindsets. The beginning of the document shows no subtlety and is an all-out defence of the party:

> You are a member of Fianna Fáil! Are you proud of it? You should be! You are a member of the greatest organisation ever founded for the betterment of this country – great in its achievements, great in its leaders, but above all great in its members. This is no idle boast made for political purposes but a fact which history will endorse … The object of Fianna Fáil was and is the setting

up of a 32-county Irish-speaking republic in which the natural resources of the country and the physical and mental abilities of its citizens should be utilised to the greatest possible advantage for the benefit of all its people.

The remainder of the document sets out Fianna Fáil's achievements: the establishment of the Constitution; the ability of public representatives to take the seats in the Dáil without swearing allegiance to the Crown; the ending of the occupation of Irish ports; the ending of the £5 million annuity payments to Britain; and the building of 130,000 local authority houses, 'relatively the greatest housing drive in history in any country in the world ... Are you not proud to be a member of an organisation which has done such sterling practical works for Ireland?' It went on to hail the membership of the party as people of 'every class and creed welded together for the furtherance of their country's good'. It decried attacks from detractors who alleged that Fianna Fáil members were in it for what they could get out of it but:

> [A]ll investigations of concrete charges have refuted this. If, however, there be any in our ranks let them take care. There is no room for them in [the] organisation and the ordinary decent members will soon discover them and will know how to deal with them. Is it not a privilege to be one of the great band who have carried Ireland through die-hard opposition, foul slander and the perils of global war ... Treasure that privilege which you have and be worthy of it.[79]

Beyond the hyperbole lay something that Haughey would return to again and again in the political crises he faced, particularly when he was leader of the party – the support of the ordinary members of Fianna Fáil, who he would call on to stand by him when he faced revolts from within the parliamentary party. This awareness of the ordinary membership was something George Colley neglected, and this rebounded on him when he ran against Haughey for the leadership of the party in December 1979.

It did become apparent, however, that *Firinne Fáil* did not have a future. The lack of a printing machine meant that it was not economically sustainable to print it in any large numbers and there was no enthusiasm for it outside the Dublin North East constituency. Still, its aims of promulgating the Fianna Fáil message professionally and to a wider audience stayed with Haughey.

In 1950 Haughey's professional and political lives began to intertwine when he decided to open up his own accountancy practice with his closest friend, and fellow Fianna Fáil cumann activist, Harry Boland. They rented offices at 13 Dame Street above O'Callaghan's gentlemen's outfitters, which catered to a well-to-do middle-class clientele. Haughey called their address 'Callaghan Chambers' and held an account with the shop to provide him with his work suits. But there was a big question for the budding entrepreneurs – was there enough business for them to make their way? The accountancy profession was dominated by long-standing practices, either Protestant or so-called 'Castle Catholics', and, given the dire nature of the economy it was a forbidding time to try to establish a new practice. But Haughey and Boland decided it was worth branching off on their own. Boland was comfortable mixing with big business and specialised in the detailed spadework while Haughey took it upon himself to expand the business. Boland's initial political contacts and Haughey's acumen were central to the expansion of the firm as the 1950s progressed. They also attracted some business as public works auditors. In June 1951 Haughey successfully applied to the Department of Industry and Commerce to be appointed as a public auditor and stated that he had a wide and varied practice in auditing, general accountancy and income tax work. He finished his letter of application by stating that he believed he had 'the requisite professional, academic and practical qualifications to justify my appointment'.[80] Haughey Boland as a practice was at the nexus of the worlds of business and politics.[81] And it was to the latter that Charles Haughey looked for his future.

His immediate future included his blossoming romance with Maureen Lemass. They had been dating for some four years when one afternoon, at a family gathering in the Lemass house in the spring of 1951, Maureen's maternal grandmother asked Haughey when he was going to ask Maureen to marry him. Haughey replied, 'As soon as she'll have me.' Later, when they were alone together, he proposed and she accepted.[82] They were married four months later on Tuesday 18 September 1951 in the same church where her parents had been married, the Church of the Holy Name on Beechwood Avenue, Ranelagh. The ceremony was conducted by no fewer than four priests, including the Haughey family's local priest from Donnycarney. Maureen Lemass was walked down the aisle by her father, who, following the general election of May of that year, had become Tánaiste and Minister for Industry and Commerce. Her bridesmaids were her sisters Peggy and Sheila Lemass, and Haughey's sister Maureen. His older brother, Seán, was the best man, while Harry Boland acted as his groomsman. Maureen Lemass wore a gown of white ottoman with an all-over trellis design in gold. Her tulle veil was held in place by a coronet of fresh rosebuds and she carried a bouquet of white roses and lilies of the valley. The bridesmaids wore bouffant gowns of turquoise slipper satin with shoulder-length veils held in place by chap-lets of fresh flowers and carried shower bouquets of bronze roses. The wedding breakfast was held at the Royal Marine Hotel in Dún Laoghaire, but it was in no way a lavish affair. It was, however, a very political wed-ding, given that the Tánaiste's daughter was marrying a defeated Fianna Fáil candidate from the general election just three and a half months earlier. Some commentators have argued that the wedding cemented Haughey's links with Fianna Fáil – as if Maureen Lemass had nothing much to do with it.[83] The more prosaic reality was that it was the coming together of two young people who had met in college, were attracted to each other, shared many of the same interests, including politics, and who had fallen in love. As one of Haughey and Lemass's UCD friends, Kevin Burke, noted, Maureen Lemass was a very strong-willed woman.[84] The idea that she would marry any man she did not love denies her the agency she so clearly possessed.

The wedding guests included Taoiseach Éamon de Valera, Minister for External Affairs Frank Aiken, Minister for Finance Seán MacEntee, Minister for Justice Gerry Boland and Minister for Defence Oscar

Traynor.[85] In the afternoon the newly wed Mr and Mrs Haughey left for their honeymoon in the south of France, where they would return often during their married lives. When they returned from their honeymoon, they lived for a few months with the Lemasses at Palmerston Road before moving to their first home at 332 Howth Road in Raheny.[86] Maureen's grandmother had helped them with the deposit for the house. Maureen's mother, Kathleen, was afraid that after moving to the northside her daughter might never be seen or heard of again, so far away was it from Palmerston Road.[87] But that area of Raheny on the Howth Road was becoming home to many of the young working and professional classes of Dublin and the Haugheys quickly settled into married life in an area that would very quickly become the centre of Charles Haughey's political power base. Yet the political power that Haughey craved would take some time to come, and he would first have to endure some serious and demoralising electoral defeats as the dismal decade of the 1950s continued.

CHAPTER 3

CHARLIE

DEFEAT

On 5 September 1951, just under a fortnight before his wedding, Charles Haughey wrote to the Taoiseach, Éamon de Valera, on behalf of the Dublin North East comhairle dáil ceantair, to express its deep gratitude for de Valera's nomination of the Tomás Ó Cléirigh cumann's chairperson, Sean O'Donovan, to the Seanad as one of his eleven nominees.[1] This was some consolation to the cumann after the defeat of its secretary, Haughey, in the 1951 general election. The Ó Cléirigh cumann was one of the most influential in the Dublin North East constituency and it was home to the party's two TDs, Oscar Traynor and Harry Colley. Harry Boland, George Colley and Charles Haughey had brought an infusion of new blood as Fianna Fáil went into opposition after the 1948 election. Haughey was not content to be simply one of its members and, as secretary from 1949, he was keen to boost the profile of both the cumann and the party. By March of 1951 he was the secretary of the Dublin North East comhairle dáil ceantair, and was known all across the constituency. The collapse of the first inter-party government in late April 1951 left Fianna Fáil scrambling to put together a list of candidates for the election to be held on 30 May 1951. Haughey, as the secretary of the comhairle dáil ceantair, was seen across the constituency as being one of a new breed who, while standing no chance of election, would gain political experience. He was thus selected to run in a type of political sweeper role alongside Eugene Timmons, who had also been a candidate for the first time in 1948.

The expectation across Fianna Fáil in Dublin North East was that the majority of the party votes would go to the sitting TDs, Oscar Traynor, who was then sixty-five, and the sixty-year-old Harry Colley. Haughey was just twenty-five and his time would come. But Haughey was determined to put up a good show and he engaged in a wide and enthusiastic canvass of the constituency. His canvassers were primarily drawn from his FCÁ colleagues and his friends from UCD.[2] They cycled across the constituency chanting his name, knocked on doors, urging people to vote for the local boy who had made good. Haughey polled a respectable 1,629 votes in the five-seat constituency. Colley and Traynor were returned for Fianna Fáil; Jack Belton took a seat for Fine Gael; the former Labour and Clann na Poblachta candidate Peadar Cowan won a seat as an independent; and the hugely popular former Lord Mayor of Dublin, Alfie Byrne, took a seat for the thirteenth election in a row. Haughey was far from discouraged by his performance. Over fifty years later one of his old friends, Stephen Fleming, sent him a sample ballot paper that Fianna Fáil had had printed for their canvassers in that election. That ballot paper stressed the importance of Fianna Fáil voters voting for Traynor with a 'Y', who was last on the ballot paper, as distinct from the Fine Gael candidate, James Trainor, who spelled his name with an 'I'. At this stage the party affiliation of candidates did not appear on the ballot papers and mistakes were common. Haughey's wistful reply thanked Fleming and noted that the 'ballot paper certainly revived old memories and battles [of] long ago!'[3]

Haughey was enthused by his experiences of his battles on the canvass and felt that, given his age, electoral success was just a matter of time. Fianna Fáil was back in power, his accountancy practice had survived its first year in business – no mean feat in the Ireland of 1951 – and he was getting married and due to move into a new home in the heart of the constituency. His future looked bright. In December 1951 he had an income of £720 from secretaryships and directorships in three companies. One of these was titled in Irish and called Comhlucht na Nua-Bhaile, Teoranta; another was called New Homes, Co-operative Society Limited. These businesses were essentially the same and had the same address – 13 Dame Street – the address of Haughey Boland. The final company was called Eva Della Limited, with an address at 70 Middle Abbey Street, Dublin.[4]

Haughey's return from honeymoon was marred by the first of what would be a recurring theme in his life: his rather unlucky habit of being involved in car accidents. According to P.J. Mara, who drove around the country with him in the 1970s, Haughey sometimes drove fearfully fast.[5] He was seriously injured in two car crashes and was involved in a number of more minor accidents, on top of a life-threatening boat accident and an equally serious small aeroplane crash.

In October 1951 his Austin A40 saloon car was struck from behind by another car. Haughey was totally blameless and uninjured. His attitude in these matters was, if at all possible, not to involve his own insurance company. In this particular instance he wrote to the insurance company of the other party that it was not his 'intention that my insurance company should in any way enter into this matter; your insured ran into the back of my car, and is entirely responsible for the damage resulting, and I am looking to him only for the amount involved.'[6] That amount was £9. Haughey's annoyance was made worse by the fact that just the previous month he had fully paid off the car hire purchase loan obtained from the Dublin branch of Friends Provident Building Society on College Green in May 1950. On paying the final instalment the building society told him that should he require any future hire purchase facilities he could expect that any new application would 'be passed through with the minimum of fuss to yourself'.[7]

As Haughey and Harry Boland worked to keep their accountancy business afloat, in 1952 the new Fianna Fáil government implemented the harshest budget in the history of the state, removing subsidies on bread, butter, tea, sugar, alcohol and petrol. In an attempt to cure the country's dire balance of payments situation it also raised income tax by a shilling in the pound. The Minister for Finance, Seán MacEntee, forecast a deficit of £50 million if corrective measures were not taken. Even the official, and conservatively inclined, historian of the Central Bank, Maurice Moynihan, called it a budget of unusual severity.[8] This policy of austerity had its critics within Fianna Fáil, of whom Lemass – now back at Industry and Commerce – was one. Outside the Dáil, Haughey was another.[9] The Fianna Fáil parliamentary party was riven over differing approaches to combating the economic stagnation that had gripped the country. Taoiseach Éamon de Valera was curiously removed from the realities of the situation for ordinary people, as 60,000 people emigrated from the state in the first year after Fianna Fáil's return to power. His only contribution to the debate about the usefulness or otherwise of economic orthodoxy was to insist that the government's policy was to pay its way and that any additional services called for by the people could only be paid for by taxation. He fell back on his old familiar rallying cry that 'increased production – principally from the land – was the remedy for most of our problems.'[10] But a growing number of Fianna Fáil's elected representatives were becoming critical of financial austerity. At a parliamentary party meeting in July 1953 twenty TDs put forward a motion stating that such austerity was no longer justified and instead a new progressive policy should be framed which would end undue restriction of credit by the banks and make available low-interest loans for farmers and house purchasers.[11] At the same time as this motion was being discussed, and summarily dismissed by the dominant conservative wing of the Fianna Fáil government, the party's newest public representative, Charles Haughey, was co-opted onto Dublin Corporation following the death of Senator Michael Colgan. Dublin Corporation's educational scholarships schemes had, of course, enabled Haughey to go to secondary school at St Joseph's, and then on to UCD. He was a firm believer that the corporation had enormous potential to benefit Dublin's citizens and he applied himself diligently to his work. He would serve for two years before unexpectedly, at least to himself, losing his seat in the local elections held in June 1955.[12]

But before that unwelcome surprise Haughey had once more suffered defeat at the hands of the electorate in Dublin North East in the May 1954 general election campaign. Fianna Fáil's failure to tackle the twin scourges of emigration and unemployment saw its vote drop from 46.3 per cent to 43.4 per cent nationally and it lost seven seats, falling to sixty-five. More worrying for Lemass and Fianna Fáil's other urban deputies was the party's slippage in Dublin to 39.3 per cent, down from 46.4 per cent in 1951. In Dublin North East the fall in the party's support was even more dramatic. The same four Fianna Fáil candidates polled 32 per cent of the vote in 1954, down from 42.8 per cent just three years previously. Labour's Denis Larkin took the seat of the independent Peadar Cowan, and Haughey barely increased his own vote to 1,812 (from 1,629 in 1951). It was an uninspired performance, although Haughey received only 1,500 fewer first preference votes than Harry Colley, who retained his seat. Both Colley and Haughey were outpolled on the first count by Eugene Timmons, but Colley proved the most transfer-friendly of the three and he took the second Fianna Fáil seat behind Oscar Traynor.[13]

Haughey's place on the Fianna Fáil ticket was by no means assured in 1954. In March, just two months before the election, the East Wall cumann wrote to Haughey in his capacity as honorary secretary of the Dublin North East comhairle dáil ceantair, nominating Oscar Traynor, Harry Colley and its own chairperson, J.J. Phelan, as candidates.[14] But Haughey had one big advantage over any other potential constituency rivals, and indeed many other Fianna Fáil candidates, and that was his ability to speak on behalf of the party on national questions. As he told the party's legendary secretary, Tommy Mullins, in early 1954: 'I can speak with authority and accuracy on any conceivable subject. I am particularly expert on subjects appertaining to economics, finance, currency.'[15] And he had the qualifications to back this up. In the electorally fluid mid-1950s, when it was becoming clear that Fianna Fáil's mantra of 'Up Dev' could not be relied upon to sway any undecided voters, this was a skill that his father-in-law and many of the party's influential members in Dublin were keen to make use of. Haughey was duly selected to stand in Dublin North East but was disappointed at the ballot box. He had seen no palpable movement in his vote in his second attempt to gain a seat in the Dáil. He was far more downhearted about the result than he had been in 1951, but two initiatives in the months after the election tied him ever closer to Fianna Fáil than just being a candidate. One led him to travel the country investigating the state of the party's organisation. The other saw him attempt to broaden the party's intellectual heft. Both would be crucial to Haughey's long-term vision for Fianna Fáil.

THE ORGANISER

On 5 August 1954 Seán Lemass wrote to Haughey telling him that he had proposed his name for co-option to membership of the party's Organisation Committee of the National Executive and that his recommendation had been agreed to.[16] The two men had previously discussed the issue. Impressed with Haughey's drive and, disquieted by Fianna Fáil's defeat in the general election, Lemass was determined to use Haughey's energy for the benefit of the party nationally. Haughey, after his own election disappointment, was also keen to play a larger role in the party. While his accountancy practice had flourished, he was still keen to make politics his full-time career. He took the view that immersing himself further in the party would be the key to eventually winning a Dáil seat. He had time on his side and the party's two TDs in his constituency were getting older, but he knew nevertheless that he would only get one, or maybe two, more chances to win the Dáil seat that he so cherished. The following week Haughey attended his first meeting of the organisation committee. A month later he began touring the country to assess the organisational strength of various cumainn and constituencies. He was one of a number of younger members of Fianna Fáil charged with this task. All were handpicked by Lemass. Others included Brian Lenihan, Eoin Ryan and Kevin Boland.[17]

Haughey began his countrywide travels in September 1954. Over the following two months he visited Fianna Fáil cumainn and met with members all across the country. He attended meetings in Longford, Roscommon, Cavan, Limerick, Cork and Meath in this period. This pattern of travel continued for the next four years in all weathers and seasons as he visited practically every constituency in the country. His mission was to investigate the state of the organisation and he took his instructions seriously. He wrote detailed reports for Lemass, including, for instance, the number of polling stations in an area, the numbers of councillors of all parties, numbers of cumainn, numbers of active members, the number of churches for the possibility of after-mass speeches, and the general issues that affected Fianna Fáil members.

He would often return to constituencies shortly after his first visit to see if any improvements had been made; for example, he was in Kerry three times between March and May 1955. He reported back to Lemass in April of that year that in the last local elections Fianna Fáil had received 34 per cent of the votes cast and 'our impression of the state of the organisation in the area is that it is very poor'. He was more impressed by the party's standing in Killorglin, which, he stated, was, by comparison to Killarney, quite good.[18] He was quite critical of cumainn that consisted of groups of individuals who just came together at election time. But he was also happy to praise those units of the organisation which he considered excellent. Some of these were urban, such as O'Donovan Rossa cumann in Dublin South West; others were rural, for example Cappamore in County Tipperary. On Sunday 12 February 1956 he attended the Cappamore comhairle ceantair, where he was minuted as being from 'Headquarters'. Two weeks later he sent his report to Lemass. It was a typically detailed portrait in which he noted that one of the things that struck him more than anywhere else he had visited in the country was the amount of Irish spoken by the members: 'it really is amazing. All the members, old and young, use as much Irish as they do English, if not more.' While this was put down to the influence of the chairman, Haughey was also impressed by the strong nationalist tradition in the area and noted that the three aspects of 'hurling, the language and the volunteers went hand in hand'.[19]

Haughey's links with the grassroots were essential throughout his long career in Fianna Fáil. Again, and again, he would turn to them for succour and support. While much has been made of his traversing the country to rehabilitate himself in the eyes of the grassroots in the 1970s, it was these trips in the 1950s that laid the groundwork for his later popularity among the ordinary members of Fianna Fáil. In fact, even when he was a minister in the 1960s he was always happy to go to constituencies to advise on organisation and strategy. Key to his success was his habit of staying around to mingle with the members after the business was done. For instance, in May 1962, when he was Minister for Justice, he travelled to Tipperary to attend the Borris comhairle ceantair. His account neatly sums up the problems Fianna Fáil, and indeed all parties, faced in the Ireland of this time. Beyond the minutiae of the organisation and criticisms of various state bodies such as Irish Sugar and CIÉ there was a report of a dispute in one cumann over a grievance held by one of the key local members and the whole organisation was agitated over a court case involving two sons of another prominent member. All Fianna Fáil politics was indeed local. Haughey finished by noting that as the meeting was held in a local public house he 'deemed it expedient to close the proceedings by buying a drink for everyone present – including myself. This was very much appreciated by all.'[20]

While the party's organisation took up much of Haughey's time in this period, his other preoccupation was with its intellectual development. Lemass wrote to him in October 1954 stating that a resolution of the Clár of the Fianna Fáil Ard Fheis maintained that while the party had achieved many of its core objectives, as set out at its foundation, it was now time for the National Executive to publish a statement of the party's future programme with a particular emphasis on the social ideals enshrined in the Democratic Programme of the First Dáil. For Lemass, this was the most important resolution on the Clár. He said that Fianna Fáil's programme needed to be re-examined and re-stated, and it was politically important that the general public know this. He warned that 'any idea that we are standing for the view that everything that the Fianna Fáil government did was perfect and remains perfect in all circumstances and that anything it did not do is not worth doing would be very damaging.'[21]

He suggested that Haughey speak on the matter – he wanted speakers who were certain to take the constructive line. This was a nod both to the importance of Haughey to Lemass's plans for Fianna Fáil and to the ongoing civil war in the party relating to economic policy. In March 1955 Haughey had been appointed honorary secretary of the Dublin Chomh Chomhairle, an organisation established by Lemass, both to widen Fianna Fáil's electoral appeal and to attract people into the party who might not wish to become full formal members but who could be encouraged to support it beyond election time. Conor Lenihan claims that its remit was to recruit fee-paying associate members. Portraying it as a precursor to the 1960s affiliate Taca, he notes that it led to an increase in the party's coffers.[22] But judging by what the Dublin Chomh Chomhairle actually did this seems overblown. In fact, its principal aim was to ensure that Fianna Fáil would be able to adapt politically to changing economic and social circumstances. Haughey described it as 'primarily a forum where our members can inform themselves on important topics by having experts in their fields talk to them on these topics. While we are associated with the Fianna Fáil organisation, the above is our only objective.'[23]

At the end of its first year of activities in March 1956 An Chomh Chomhairle Atha Cliath had ninety-seven members: five representatives of each of the eight Dublin constituencies and fifty-seven associate members. Subscriptions cost £5 for associate members, which brought in a total of £285. Expenses totalled just over £126. This was a tidy profit for Fianna Fáil, but not much more than that. In its first year the organisation met on six occasions. The first meeting was addressed by both de Valera and Lemass, who outlined the purpose and function of the Chomh Chomhairle, which was to provide a forum in Dublin where matters of national importance could be discussed and debated in public. The format of the meetings was to have a guest speaker present a paper on a topic of social and economic importance, with a discussant responding before the topic was opened up to the audience.[24] Haughey succeeded in persuading leading figures in business, the trade unions and the farmers' organisations to attend and outline their positions on the economic and social questions of the day. M.J. Costello, the managing director of the Irish Sugar Company, and a former lieutenant general in the Irish army, spoke on the topic of what the organised farmers could do for Ireland. His discussants were the president of the newly founded National Farmers' Association (NFA), Dr Juan Greene, and the editor of the *Irish Farmers Journal*, Paddy O'Keeffe. Many in Fianna Fáil were suspect of the NFA, seeing it as no more than a branch of Fine Gael, and its members, rather pejoratively, as simply Blueshirts on tractors.

But it was Haughey's aim to bring wide and varied views to a Fianna Fáil still smarting from defeat in the 1954 general election. One of the more exotic topics for discussion in the first year was at the pre-Christmas meeting, which heard a paper from the Cambridge-based academic sociologist Fr James Kavanagh on the topic of 'Sociology: A Luxury or a Necessity?' Kavanagh agreed to give the paper 'so long as some "crackpot" with a bee in his bonnet does not hold the floor for too long'.[25] For the discussant Haughey was keen to get a response to the paper on how society was developing in rural Ireland. He felt that this was important because, since the entire organisation was made up of city people, it was vital they should have first-hand information on the problems and difficulties faced by people in rural Ireland. He contacted the Irish Countrywomen's Association saying he was 'anxious to have a lady speaker'. But his charms proved unsuccessful on this occasion as the eventual respondent to the paper was a male speaker from Muintir Na Tire.[26]

The highlight of the Chomhairle's first year of activities was Lemass's famous Clery's ballroom speech on Tuesday 14 October 1955. The previous month, Lemass had written to Haughey stating that the party committee had considered a memorandum he had submitted entitled 'Proposals for a Full Employment Policy' and had authorised him to deliver an address to An Chomh Comhairle based on this memorandum.[27] The original memorandum was modified following doubts as to what appeared to be an attack on the banking system, and an even more audacious implication that native resources might not, in fact, be sufficient to grow the economy and finance the industrial expansion that was necessary for the country to flourish. The party would allow Lemass to give his speech as long as he omitted his references to the Central Bank and if he pointed out that 'our resources are ample to finance agricultural and industrial development.'[28] What the 60,000 people who were emigrating each year at the lack of such economic development might have made of this was not touched upon.

Given the changes required by the party, Lemass said that he would be ready to deliver the address in the first half of October. The original plan was that the address would be made on 1 October, but it was pushed back by a fortnight. Fianna Fáil's National Executive, the Ard Chomhairle, met on 12 September. Haughey's copy of the agenda is littered with various little doodles, including some noughts and crosses games, sketches of what certainly look like Lemass, and a handwritten note stating 'Lemass is going to make a big speech to Co – Comhairle [sic].'[29] The following day he wrote to the members of the Chomh Chomhairle inviting them to a meeting to prepare for Lemass's speech and urging them to make a special effort to attend as he understood 'that the paper will be a very important one'.[30] And indeed it was. It set out Lemass's philosophy on government intervention in the economy, and his proposals to create full employment in a country fast losing people to emigration. Full employment as a concept was criticised by Seán MacEntee, who was not happy with what he saw as Lemass's woolly definition. For Lemass it meant the creation of 100,000 new jobs over five years. This was to become a millstone around his neck and a stick for his political opponents to beat him with. It also, however, crucially provided the progressive wing in Fianna Fáil, long associated with Lemass, and including Haughey, with a certain psychological boost to morale.

After the excitement and importance of the Lemass speech the next meeting of the Chomh Chomhairle was a more mundane affair on prices and the importance of the price structure in the national economy. The year finished with Fr Kavanagh's sociology talk. Haughey was relatively pleased with the attendance at the meetings, but he voiced displeasure at the question-and-answer sessions, noting that the 'discussion which followed the reading of the papers was not of a very high standard'.[31] Nevertheless, this was an important forum for Fianna Fáil and would provide it with a useful avenue for the exchange of ideas. Haughey was always on the lookout for innovative and interesting speakers and new topics for discussion. These ranged from the role of banks in the community, to the importance of the fishing community in sustaining rural Ireland, to a national television service. It was the latter subject that provided the Chomh Chomhairle with its greatest triumph when Haughey, by now a TD, persuaded the television personality and host of *This is Your Life* Eamonn Andrews to come to Dublin and speak on the importance of television on 20 November 1958. Andrews was happy to accept the invitation, saying it was a subject that interested him deeply, but he wasn't sure he could speak for the forty to sixty minutes Haughey suggested. He offered to give a shorter talk, which would allow more time for questions. He spoke about television from his viewpoint as a performer in Britain, his experience in presenting other talent for television, and in packaging radio shows, which his firm had been doing in Ireland for a number of years. In accepting the invitation Andrews ended on a prescient note, telling Haughey that he was 'certain that television is going to have a big part to play one of these days at home'.[32] This would come true within a very short period of time and Haughey was soon to become one of the most frequent faces on RTÉ television. He was confident, both in defending Fianna Fáil policies and in attacking the opposition. He also remained friendly with Andrews, who would become chairman of the Radio Éireann Authority between 1960 and 1964. That authority oversaw the introduction of state television to Ireland and established the broadcaster as an independent semi-state body. Andrews's resignation from that position in 1964 caused a huge fissure in relations between RTÉ and Fianna Fáil over the content of the then fledgling *Late Late Show*.

RESILIENCE

Haughey's pre-Dáil Éireann political career faced a severe crisis when in the course of ten months he lost his seat on Dublin Corporation in the June 1955 local elections and came second in the two-man by-election in Dublin North East on 30 April 1956. The loss in the local elections in the electoral ward of Artane was a particular blow given that this was his local area, and it was where he had drawn his votes from in the 1951 and 1954 general elections. In the five-seater constituency of the Dublin No. 1

Area, he received 1,686 first preference votes, some way off the quota of 2,908. His running mate, Eugene Timmons, received just ten votes more. Haughey was placed fourth on the first count and seemed in a reasonable position to take a seat. However, he failed to pick up as many transfers as Timmons and was overhauled by candidates from the Dublin Ratepayers' Association, which did well across the city, and a Combined Residents candidate.[33] Timmons won Fianna Fáil's only seat. The other two seats were taken by the sitting Fine Gael TD, Jack Belton, and the left-wing former TD Peadar Cowan. This led Haughey to an initial bout of introspection regarding his political future, but he was quickly disabused of any notions of feeling sorry for himself. His first child, Eimear, had been born in February 1955 and in her early months he was away from home for long periods on his organisational tour for Lemass. His business was still in its early stages, and a string of political defeats, when he was still shy of thirty of years of age was, his wife pointed out to him, nothing to be ashamed of or worried about. Haughey was a traditional 1950s father. His job was to be the household's breadwinner and it was Maureen's job to mind the house and raise the children. He did not have time to mope around pondering his Dublin Corporation election defeat.[34] But his next entrance into the political arena brought another disappointment. The following year he was Fianna Fáil's candidate in the Dublin North East by-election triggered by the death of the long-standing, and legendary, TD and former Lord Mayor of Dublin, Alfie Byrne.

In December 1954 the areas of East Wall, North Strand and Fairview were severely flooded when the River Tolka burst its banks. Known as the Great North Strand Flood, it was reckoned by contemporary newspaper reports to be the worst flooding in a century and a state of emergency was declared in the city.[35] Lord Mayor Alfie Byrne started a relief fund for those affected, raising thousands of pounds. One of the earliest contributors was Councillor Charles Haughey, who donated £10 to the relief effort. Byrne thanked him for his 'very generous gesture and handsome subscription', noting that it was indeed very heartening for him as Lord Mayor 'to be again reminded, if indeed a reminder is necessary, of the goodness and benevolence of the Citizens of this City, our commercial concerns and of our friends and sympathisers throughout the country and across the water'.[36]

Byrne died in March 1956, just short of his seventy-fourth birthday, and, as one of the most famous men in Dublin, his funeral was one of the largest seen in the city for decades.[37] The immediate consequence of his death was the need for a by-election, and it quickly became clear that his son Patrick would be a candidate to succeed him. In attempting to make sure that Byrne would have a clear path to the seat, all other parties except Fianna Fáil gave him their support. Given Alfie Byrne's popularity, his well-known concern for the poor, and the expected large sympathy vote for his son, the Fianna Fáil candidate in the by-election faced a gargantuan task. The question remained as to who Fianna Fáil would put up as their standard-bearer. The obvious candidates were Haughey and Eugene Timmons, both of whom had run in the 1951 and 1954 general elections. Timmons had outpolled Haughey in both general elections and in the 1955 Corporation elections, but he had also run in 1948 without success. Timmons was a former St Joseph's CBS boy, was based in the Marino–Clontarf part of the constituency, and had been a member of Dublin Corporation since 1945. He served on the boards of Grangegorman Mental Hospital, and Dublin Port and Docks, and was president of the Marino and District Tenants' Association.[38]

While Timmons was well regarded in the constituency, Haughey was far more crucial to the wider Fianna Fáil organisation, given his work for Lemass in reorganising the party across the country and his stewardship of the Dublin Chomh Chomhairle. In that context he was chosen to be Fianna Fáil's representative in what all in the party acknowledged would be an uphill battle to win the seat. But the key thing for Haughey in this by-election was that he would be receiving Fianna Fáil votes that had gone to Oscar Traynor, Harry Colley and Timmons in previous general elections; and there was every chance that he could keep some of them when it came to the next general election. He ran a typically energetic campaign and was described by Éamon de Valera as 'a young man of proved ability ... If elected he will serve you well.'[39] It was a generally quiet campaign. Beyond the tried and traditional route of door-to-door canvassing and after-mass speeches, Haughey used the final week of the campaign to address a number of public meetings, including one on Drumcondra Bridge and a final rally outside Fairview Park on Sunday 29 April.[40] His speeches followed a particular pattern of attacks on the government, and an outline of what Fianna Fáil would do when it was back in power. One of his main charges was that, given the alliance of people of diverse views and interests who made up the inter-party government, it was inevitable that it would be weak, vacillating and incompetent. He complained about the failure of the national loan, high unemployment, and the collapse of the housing industry. He ended his final rally with a rousing call to young people in particular to get behind Fianna Fáil in its ideas, its enthusiasm and its nationalism.

The following day just under half of the electorate of Dublin North East cast their ballots. Counting began after the polls closed and the boxes had been moved to the Technical Schools in Bolton Street. Haughey increased the share of the Fianna Fáil vote from 32 per cent in 1954 to 43.5 per cent. He polled 13,950 votes, some 4,179 votes behind Patrick Byrne. Byrne began his acceptance speech by stating that he was aware that the result 'was not only a vote of confidence in the inter-party government', but at this stage he was drowned out by jeers from Haughey's supporters. In his own speech congratulating Byrne, Haughey stated that Fianna Fáil 'did not seek to defeat Paddy Byrne as such. We made it quite clear that we were asking people for a vote against the coalition government.'[41] On the same day, Fianna Fáil won the Laois–Offaly by-election, taking the seat from the Labour Party, and the party claimed a job well done in both con-stituencies. But if Haughey was disillusioned by losing his Corporation seat, he was far more upbeat about his chances of eventually taking a Dáil seat after this by-election loss. He figured that the rise in the Fianna Fáil vote would be mirrored in the next general election. Moreover, Harry Colley, who had never been a prolific vote-getter, was then sixty-seven years of age. Haughey was just thirty-one and felt that he was close to taking a seat.

A couple of days after his defeat he received a letter from Vivion de Valera, the managing director of the *Irish Press* newspaper group, in which de Valera told him that he had done very well in the 'hopeless task set him … Don't feel disappointed: you put up a great fight under very difficult conditions. You may feel happy that everybody appreciates the way you carried the party's banner through the battle and the next time can be faced confidently.[42] This prompted Haughey to write, not only to de Valera, but also to the editors of the *Evening Press*, Douglas Gageby, and the *Sunday Press*, Matt Feehan. He told de Valera that he was grateful for the support of the *Irish Press* group and its three newspapers, stating that he had probably got more publicity than any candidate for a very long time and adding that the party was generally pleased with the result.[43] He echoed these sentiments in his thank you letters to Gageby and Feehan.[44] In his reply Feehan told Haughey that the only people who wrote to editors were those who were seeing red over something or other and he had the 'unique distinction of being the only individual to send me a letter of thanks after an election'.[45]

And in fact Haughey did have his own issues with the *Irish Press*. Not long after his defeat in the Corporation elections, he wrote to Oscar Traynor about dissatisfaction in the Fianna Fáil organisation when it came to the attitude of the *Irish Press*, and what he saw as the inordinately friendly coverage the paper gave to the Ratepayers' Association. Haughey claimed it was generally accepted that it was the Ratepayers' Association which had led to the loss of Fianna Fáil seats in the Dublin Corporation elections. He said that as a councillor he was always aware of the *Irish Press*'s tendency to cover the speeches of members of the Ratepayers' Association in its reports of corporation business and ignore those coming from Fianna Fáil: 'I was always reluctant to say very much about them as I felt that it would be interpreted as being merely a personal complaint about lack of publicity for myself.[46] Traynor replied that he had raised the issue with the managing director of the *Irish Press*, who was looking into the matter, and there it must be left for the time being.[47] It is, however, an early example of Haughey's awareness of the power of the press. After his by-election defeat he was determined that future coverage from the *Irish Press* would be favourable. He clearly had his eyes on the next general election, and friendly *Irish Press* group coverage would certainly be advantageous in his efforts to finally take a Dáil seat.

One other letter of note from this by-election was one Haughey received in the middle of the campaign from Richie Healy, the honorary secretary of the Uaimh cumann, in Navan, County Meath. While appreciating that Haughey was up against it, Healy said the cumann members would be 'quite happy if you give the Byrne cum inter-party group a good shaking. You hold a special place in our hearts since your visit to us over 12 months ago.'[48] Haughey perhaps oversold his reply to Healy, telling him that his letter came as a 'wonderful tonic' in the middle of the campaign.[49] Yet there can be no doubt that Haughey's organisational tour for Lemass in the mid-1950s took him into the heart of the Fianna Fáil membership. And that membership was grateful to him. Over thirty years later Richie Healy, by then a member of the Fianna Fáil National Executive, and a staunch ally of Haughey in the party heaves of the 1980s, played a crucial role in the early stages of the peace process. He was one of the three-man team, along with Dermot Ahern and Martin Mansergh, handpicked by Haughey, who travelled to Dundalk for secret meetings with representatives of Sinn Féin, including Gerry Adams. Healy was, according to a later Fianna Fáil leader, Brian Cowen, a man of loyalty and discretion who had been picked for those secret talks because Haughey knew he would treat them with 'the privacy and discretion that was necessary at the time, within the constitutional and democratic principles of the party'.[50]

THE PARTITION QUESTION

Haughey's view of Northern Ireland in the 1950s, and indeed Fianna Fáil's constitutional and democratic principles in this period, are a matter of some historical controversy. The Ó Cléirigh cumann, of which Haughey was an increasingly important member, has been characterised by Donnacha Ó Beacháin as being symptomatic of a rising militancy in the grassroots organisation, on the evidence of a memorandum on the question of partition it sent to Fianna Fáil headquarters in January 1955.[51] While Haughey plays no role in Ó Beacháin's analysis, he is front and centre in Stephen Kelly's treatment of this memorandum. In his detailed study of Haughey's attitude to the Northern Ireland question,

Kelly places much store in the memorandum, which was sent from the Ó Cléirigh cumann in response to an invitation from Lemass seeking submissions from all cumainn on local and national issues. In this six-page memorandum, the Ó Cléirigh cumann argued that the Irish state should sponsor a guerrilla campaign in Northern Ireland on the model of the covertly sponsored Egyptian campaign in the Suez Canal zone, and supply arms to volunteers in an attempt to provoke a border incident to internationalise the problem. This would be followed by a period of guerrilla-style warfare and a campaign of civil disobedience. The memorandum argued that anti-partition sentiment was increasing and that Fianna Fáil, as the republican party, should be at the centre of it. Kelly argues that this memorandum is the key to understanding what he describes as Haughey's 'visceral anti-partitionism' and that previous authors have not understood it or have downplayed its significance.[52]

The Ó Cléirigh memorandum did indeed offer an aggressive case as to why Fianna Fáil should support the use of physical force in pursuit of Irish unity. It did so in the context of a speech by de Valera at the 1954 Fianna Fáil Ard Fheis, in which he said that he was unable to offer any credible solution to ending partition. At that Ard Fheis George Colley's idea of creating an incident on the border was dismissed out of hand by de Valera in a private meeting between the two. De Valera wondered whether Colley would be prepared to be a G (Green) Special along the border who, like the B Specials, would have to enforce the rule of law on the Protestant population of Northern Ireland.[53]

There is no evidence that Haughey was the author or co-author of this memorandum and it is not in his papers, although a summary of it is, having been sent to him in his capacity as a member of Fianna Fáil's Anti-Partition Committee for discussion at the first meeting of that committee.[54] The fact that it is not in his papers is significant because he tended to keep all Fianna Fáil reports, including copies of reports he drafted himself, as a member of the party's national organisation committee.

Over fifty years later when he was in the process of collating his papers, he told his nephew, Niall Haughey, who was helping him with the project, that he doubted he was involved in the authorship of the document.[55] Nevertheless, it is likely that Haughey contributed in some shape, most likely with Colley, to the drafting of the submission to Fianna Fáil headquarters. After all, he had a central leadership place in the Ó Cléirigh cumann, and had already stood twice for the party in general elections. The more important question is: to what extent does it lay bare Haughey's thinking on Northern Ireland at the time, and what impact did it have on him in the tumultuous events of the arms crisis fifteen years later and, indeed, as Taoiseach a decade after that? For Kelly it is strong, indeed damning, evidence of Haughey's disillusionment with the policies of de Valera, and even of Fianna Fáil itself, which had become complacent about partition, leading to the abandonment of the party's number one issue – a united Ireland. He portrays Haughey as a man of action who believed that because peaceful solutions to partition failed, the alternative route of physical force was justified. That analysis, however, seems overstated.

Just before Christmas 1954 Haughey was appointed to membership of a Fianna Fáil committee on the issue of partition. The committee members were made up of members of the party's National Executive and parliamentary party. The language informing Haughey of his appointment is strangely foreboding. The letter, written by Lemass and Joe Groome as joint honorary secretaries of the party, begins: 'We have to inform you that you have been appointed by the National Executive of Fianna Fáil, on the nomination of the President, Éamon de Valera, to be a member of a joint committee … which has been set up to maintain contact with all aspects of the problem of partition, to consider what action might usefully be taken by Fianna Fáil regarding it from time to time, and to act as advisers to the national executive in this respect.'[56] The first meeting was set for January 1955 and Haughey's views were requested in a form that might be put on the agenda or, in writing, to the other members of the committee. Kelly is of the view that the circumstantial evidence suggests Lemass, on reading the Ó Cléirigh memorandum, decided to bring Haughey on to the standing committee on partition matters in order to educate his son-in-law on the futility of violence in the attainment of a united Ireland.[57]

But a more plausible suggestion would be that the Ó Cléirigh memorandum produced a document for discussion, given that it was written after the invitation to Haughey to join the group. It was sent to Fianna Fáil headquarters on 15 January 1955, a full three weeks after that invitation to Haughey to join the group, and to advance some thoughts on partition in advance of the first meeting. In that context it is far more likely that the memorandum is a forceful statement of one option for discussion by the committee from an enthusiastic local cumann. It should not be seen as some master plan by Haughey, who at this stage had twice failed to get in to the Dáil, to be put into use when he was at the heart of power. Ultimately, Haughey supported a detailed unanimous report by the committee which categorically ruled out physical force as a solution to partition, and instead suggested that it was only through a process of co-operation and mutual respect between Belfast and Dublin that Irish unity could be achieved.[58] The report was eventually shelved after de Valera rejected some of its proposals as of doubtful value and that would give rise to serious controversy. He was particularly perplexed by the lack of any reference to the problems faced by the Northern nationalist minority, or Britain's role in Northern Ireland. Indeed, all Haughey's actions, or indeed inactions, in relation to Northern Ireland over the course of the next decade would suggest he paid no heed to the Ó Cléirigh memorandum as a way forward on the question of partition. He might well have co-authored it, but the reality is it had little or no lasting impact on him as a politician. Far more important to him in this period was getting elected to the Dáil.

VICTORY

Haughey finally won a seat at the 1957 general election held on 5 March. As it was his fourth attempt he was apprehensive in advance of the vote, and more relieved than jubilant at its outcome.[59] The 1957 election was the fourth in nine years and the latest in the line of 'put them out' elections where the opposition campaigned on the simple grounds that it was not the sitting government and would do a better job in office.[60] The second inter-party government had stumbled into the election having lost the support of the three Clann na Poblachta deputies who were keeping it in power, over its crackdown on the IRA's border campaign, which had begun in November 1956. Notwithstanding some internal tensions in Fianna Fáil, it supported the government's position on this issue but not to such an extent that it was going to forego an election. As it became clear that Clann na Poblachta was going to put down a motion of no confidence in the government when the Dáil resumed in the first week of February 1957, Fianna Fáil decided it was ready for an election and agreed to place its own motion.[61] Just a few weeks earlier, Lemass had again used the offices of the Dublin Chomh Chomhairle to test out his economic ideas with a speech entitled 'Proposals for Recovery'.[62] This was essentially an updated version of his Clery's speech of some fifteen months earlier. There was more sophistication in this speech. It called for foreign investment, which could be induced to come to the country by innovations such as tax breaks on exports. This was some way removed from the idea that native resources would be sufficient to grow the economy and finance the industrial expansion needed for social development that had been Fianna Fáil policy since the foundation of the state.

Although the campaign itself was relatively dull, the results for Fianna Fáil were nothing short of spectacular. It won seventy-eight seats with 48.3 per cent of the vote, up a full five points on its 1954 performance, giving it a majority of nine in the Dáil. In Dublin North East the party held its two seats on 41.5 per cent of the vote, down from Haughey's 43.5 per cent in the previous year's by-election, but well up on the dismal 32 per cent it received in 1954. Haughey polled 4,168 first preference votes, just over 10 per cent of all ballots cast, and was placed fourth after the first count. This was a marked improvement on his previous general election performances. Most important, it put him significantly ahead of his incumbent party colleague, Harry Colley, who received 2,549 votes. Oscar Traynor topped the poll and was elected on the first count with 10,059 votes, nearly a quota and a half. Traynor's surplus was 3,327 and the key thing for Haughey as the count continued was that he stay ahead of Colley.

There was a crowded field in the constituency. Fine Gael ran three candidates, including Paddy Byrne, who had joined the party shortly after his by-election victory. Labour was represented by the sitting TD Denis Larkin, and there were strong candidates from the Ratepayers' Association, the Residents' Committee and Sinn Féin. The decisive change in the Fianna Fáil strategy in Dublin North East was that, for the first time since the constituency became a five-seater in 1948, the party only ran three candidates. Given its relatively poor performance in the constituency and the fact that it had no chance of winning a third seat, the North East convention decided to run just three candidates, with Eugene Timmons losing out from those selected in 1954. Traynor and Colley were automatic choices as sitting TDs and Haughey's credible performance in the previous year's by-election saw him get the nod as the third candidate. Traynor was guaranteed to be re-elected. Colley's seat was far more precarious. He had never been a strong vote-getter and now, with only three Fianna Fáil candidates in the field, he was susceptible to a challenge from Haughey. Colley was sixty-four years of age; Haughey was thirty-one and an important organiser for the party. He was also on the party's national executive and a number of other committees. Haughey could not really afford a fourth election defeat as it would have lumbered him with an unwanted reputation as a political loser. In fact, it might well have ended his career as there was no guarantee he would get another chance to run, no matter who his father-in-law was. The stakes were enormously high.

There was much interest in where Traynor's surplus would go. Of the 3,327 transfers available, Colley received 2,011 and Haughey 977, giving him a lead of 585. The age-old adage that in the Irish electoral system (proportional representation by single transferable vote (PR-STV)) it is better to start with a lead proved true in this election. Over the course of the two-day count Haughey kept steadily ahead of Colley as the eliminations continued. On the seventh count Byrne was the second candidate elected. When Larkin reached the quota two counts later just three candidates were left, Haughey, Colley and Jack Belton of Fine Gael. The distribution of Larkin's surplus saw Colley eliminated and Haughey and Belton elected without having reached the quota. Haughey's final total of 6,562 put him 808 votes ahead of Colley.[63] It was a narrow but decisive victory. Haughey would fight ten more general elections. In every one he topped the poll and took his seat on the first count.

Just under two weeks after his first win, on 20 March 1957 Haughey entered Leinster House as part of the sixteenth Dáil. Over the next thirty-five years he would come to dominate its proceedings and become its most controversial figure.

CHAPTER 4

IN THE DÁIL

THE DÁIL AND CONSTITUENCY DEPUTY

Harry Colley's election defeat hit him hard. He had been a conscientious TD since 1944 and, while he had been around the political scene long enough to know that defeat in the 1957 election was a possibility, he was still sorely disappointed at the outcome. The fact that he lost his seat to Haughey made it harder still. His son George was still relatively friendly with Haughey, and his wife was reported to have long taken a maternal interest in Haughey and his career.[1] Colley resolved to stay in politics and took the established route of those who had lost their Dáil seats by running for the Seanad on the Labour panel. The trading of votes was common among Seanad candidates and Colley engaged in a number of deals where he promised support to candidates running on different panels in return for the pledge of a vote for himself. He had discussed this with Haughey after the general election, and they had arranged that Haughey would give his number one vote to those candidates to whom Colley had promised support in the other panels. After arranging deals with Patrick Fitzsimons on the Administrative panel, and Patrick Browne on the Industrial and Commercial panel, Colley wrote to Haughey telling him he would be grateful 'if you would give them your No. 1 vote as arranged recently'.[2] But while Colley was ultimately elected to the Seanad his heart was not really in it. He spoke only ten times over the course of the four-year duration of the ninth Seanad and, once it ended in September 1961, he retired from public life. He was joined in retirement by Oscar Traynor who, when the 1961 general election was called, also announced that he was leaving politics. The way was now open for Haughey to dominate the politics of Dublin North East.

After the retirement of both Colley and Traynor, Haughey, by then Minister for Justice, organised a farewell dinner and presentation to them both on 22 February 1962. The event, held in Clery's, was a who's who of Fianna Fáil royalty, with Taoiseach Seán Lemass, Tánaiste Seán MacEntee, Minister for Local Government Neil Blaney, Minister for Social Welfare Kevin Boland, Minister for Lands Micheál Ó Móráin and Minister for Defence Gerald Bartley all in attendance. The Lord Mayor of Dublin, Robert Briscoe, also attended. While it was very much a Fianna Fáil event, Haughey was anxious to widen the circle of attendees and, in his speech, adverted to the fact that many of the guests were not members of the organisation or associated with Fianna Fáil in any way. Rather, they had come to demonstrate the high regard and affection in which they held Traynor and Colley. They included old comrades from the 2nd Battalion of the Dublin Brigade of the old IRA, and members of Cumann na mBan. Haughey concluded his speech by telling the guests, 'We will miss Oscar and Harry. We will miss their wise counsel at our comhairle and cumann meetings, their calm strength in the hurly burly of elections, their inspiring courage in times of difficulty … If we can but learn the lessons that they have taught and practise the example they have shown us in patriotism, integrity, loyalty and courage, we need never doubt our ability to do so.'[3] Over the next thirty years, Harry's son, George Colley, would of course spend much time questioning Haughey's personal integrity and loyalty to the party.

Lemass's speech praised Traynor's part in the struggle for Irish independence and painted him as a man without personal ambition. Then, rather oddly for someone who never wrote his own autobiography, he urged Traynor to pen his life story as it was intimately bound up with the story of Dublin's contribution to the national struggle for freedom. Lemass's praise for Colley was no less effusive, if shorter in length. He described him as one of the few men who had the opportunity 'of looking to the future in the certain knowledge that he has helped to shape it'.[4] But that future now belonged to Haughey and George Colley. Haughey was delighted at the success of the evening and wrote to the owner of Clery's, Denis Guiney, noting that the 'excellence of the meal and the wonderful service were commented upon by everybody. I did not realise that it was possible to serve such a good meal so quickly to so many people. Mr. Reffo and his staff did a magnificent job and I would like you to know about it.'[5] The manager, Louis Reffo, wrote in turn to thank Haughey for his kind words to Guiney, assured him that he could look forward to future excellent service and wished him every success in his responsible position.[6]

That responsible position as Minister for Justice saw Haughey at the heart of government just four years after he had first entered the Dáil. Those years saw him move house and have three more children with Maureen. They also saw his accountancy business expand. Haughey was certainly a new type of politician. Not long after he was elected he engaged the *Irish Times* journalist Tony Gray to advise him on how best to publicise his political work. This was uncharted territory for an Irish politician and Gray advised Haughey on when best to speak in the Dáil for coverage in the daily and evening papers. He also suggested that Haughey take up a sport which would ensure that the young politician appeared on both the news and sports pages. Haughey's team sports days were long behind him at this stage and while Gray suggested something along the lines of yachting, Haughey initially took up horseracing.[7] Yachting and Haughey's love of the sea would come later.

Haughey's efforts to gain widespread public recognition did not succeed immediately. One of the stories he was fond of telling against himself, when Minister for Justice, was of arranging to meet some friends in the Gresham Hotel not long after he was first elected. On his arrival he could not find them, so he went to the doorman and asked whether anyone had been looking for him. The doorman looked at him and said,

'Name, sir?' Haughey was somewhat disappointed at this, given all the time and effort he had put into his public persona. However, he was somewhat consoled when he noticed a flicker of recognition in the doorman's eyes on hearing the name 'Haughey', only to become crestfallen when the doorman went on to ask if he was related to the famous Dublin footballer, Jock. This self-deprecating aspect of Haughey's character was often seen in Department of Justice functions. He told one of his civil servants, Paddy Terry, with mock indignation, how at one function a young woman inquired whether he worked in the department after he had asked her the same thing.[8]

As a new TD, Haughey was determined to make his mark. The Dáil, however, could be a very dispiriting place for new arrivals, and the role of a backbench TD in Leinster House could be extremely frustrating. On days when the Dáil sat, TDs spent much of their time waiting for votes through many tediously long afternoons and evenings. Dáil sitting hours were generally organised so that all lawyer TDs could spend mornings profitably in the High Court and then devote themselves to their auxiliary profession as legislators and representatives in the afternoons. Many backbenchers, Haughey included, spent large parts of those days and nights in the Dáil bar, which never closed while the House was sitting, and where all drinks were on the deputy's tab, to be settled at long intervals. The spacious Dáil restaurant looked well, but the food was basic and stodgy. Salaries and staff support were very poor. Seats hard won could be easily lost in a snap election. Life was certainly far easier for Dublin TDs, especially those who had alternative professional lives, such as barristers and accountants. From the time he first entered the Dáil Haughey ran pretty much all his constituency work from his large Dublin house or his accountancy office. This was a luxury not afforded to non-Dublin TDs, many of whom stayed in digs or small hotel bedrooms during the week, and shared a secretary. They headed home on the train on Thursday evenings, replete with dirty washing, and facing weekends full of constituency clinics, party dinners and Monday county council meetings to attend before heading back to Dublin early on Tuesday morning.[9] It certainly could not be described as a glamorous lifestyle.

Haughey was well aware of the difficulties backbench TDs faced and never lost sight of their importance to Fianna Fáil when he himself was promoted through the ministerial ranks. Salaries and conditions were considerably improved when Haughey became Minister for Finance in 1966. Fianna Fáil backbenchers would prove crucial to Haughey's election as Taoiseach in December 1979 after which he again took considerable steps to improve their conditions.[10]

Within two months of taking his seat, on 14 May 1957 Haughey gave his maiden speech in the Dáil. He was one of the government TDs who spoke in favour of the budget produced by the Minister for Finance, Dr James Ryan, the previous week. In his speech Haughey introduced a theme he was to return to again and again over the next three decades: the importance of private industry flourishing in order to help weaker sections of society. His view was that if industrialists were helped by the state to succeed in business, it would expand the economy to the benefit of all. He had no time for the dogma of the left that private industry, in and of itself, was bad; neither had he time for the dogma of the right that private industry only had an obligation to itself. At its heart his early economic policies were nationalist in orientation. He wanted private industry to succeed so that the state would flourish. His maiden speech was infused with the idea that economic progress needed industrialists to succeed and that it was the duty of all Irish citizens to play their part in the great goal of national recovery. Given that the budget increased taxes on tobacco, beer, petrol and diesel, Haughey was forced to conclude that it was not as easy on all sections of the community as Fianna Fáil would want: 'it will bring some hardship, I suppose, to practically every section. The Minister has not introduced it for fun; he has not introduced it because he is sadistic or because he prefers to see people having a lower standard of living. He has introduced it because he was forced to do so by the inescapable logic of facts and figures.'[11] The opposition was not impressed, accusing Haughey, and Fianna Fáil, of breaking promises it had made during the election campaign.

His maiden speech marked the beginning of Haughey's thirty-five-year love affair with the Dáil. As he had in his debating days in UCD, he revelled in the cut and thrust of debates with political opponents. He was an enthusiastic heckler. One such interjection came at the end of a long rambling speech by the left-wing independent TD for Roscommon, Jack McQuillan, which covered a myriad of topics and ended by stating that in the light of the ongoing IRA border campaign, the question of partition could be solved by constitutional means. These means remained unstated. This was too much for Haughey, who shouted across the chamber: 'What steps?'[12] McQuillan replied that Haughey was as bereft as his leaders about the possibilities of a constitutional approach but was prepared, like other members of the Dáil, to condemn the young men who were only emulating the performance of the members in the house who forty years ago took similar steps. Haughey retorted that this was the equivalent of trying to go in both directions at the same time, and repeated his 'What steps?' jibe. Happy he had made his point, he said no more. It was the only comment Haughey ever made on Northern Ireland before he was appointed Minister for Justice.

THE DEBATER

Haughey's style in Dáil debates was not to the liking of everyone in Fianna Fáil. In a long letter to the government chief whip, Donnchadh Ó Briain, in June 1958 he got straight to the point in the very first line: 'I have been somewhat distressed by a number of comments and suggestions which have been made about my part in the debate on the Finance Bill and I feel that I should put my point of view before you.'[13] He went on to state that since he had been elected he had endeavoured to follow two rules when speaking: he would contribute on specific matters when he felt he had something useful to say; and he would speak when called upon by the chief whip to do so. He claimed that he was not an over-frequent contributor, or particularly verbose, and confined himself to actively supporting government policy, or offering constructive suggestions. Given that he was an accountant, Haughey said, he thought if there was a piece of parliamentary business that he could contribute to, it was the Finance Bill, and he had devoted a great deal of time and energy to mastering the bill, which had been making its way through the Dáil, since the first week of May. He considered that he would be failing in his elementary duty as a TD if he had not done this and contributed to the debate. Haughey had, with the agreement of the Minister for Finance, Dr James Ryan, put down a number of amendments at committee stage, all of which were eventually withdrawn, after brief discussion. Haughey stated that he was unfairly criticised outside the Dáil for not putting up a reasonable fight for his amendments, but that the difficulty with the protracted nature of the bill was its complexity and the long-winded speeches made by the opposition deputies James Dillon and Gerard Sweetman. He ended his letter by stating that he now found himself in some difficulty regarding his position vis-à-vis Dr Ryan:

> There are occasions when because of my training I might be able to assist the Minister on some point of fact or explanation but I have taken the view that it would be presumptuous and impertinent for me to do so. On the other hand, I have disagreed with him on a few points. But surely I am not to be blamed for disagreement on matters which are purely related to technical interpretations of a complex bill. If there is any question of loyalty in these points I cannot see it … I cannot accept that the part which I have taken in this debate is anything more or less than that required of me as a deputy who is anxious to do his duty to the best of his ability.[14]

This disagreement was symptomatic of the debate in Fianna Fáil between the old guard, as represented by Ó Briain and Ryan, and the new generation, epitomised by Haughey. It is also early evidence of Haughey's eagerness to make his mark in the chamber, whatever the consequences, and of a certain resolve in the face of opposition from more senior members of the party. It also perhaps contributed to the misgivings many of the elderly revolutionary generation of Fianna Fáil had about him in this early part of his parliamentary career.

Unlike many of his political opponents and, indeed, his colleagues in Fianna Fáil, Haughey spent quite some time in the Dáil. An early draft of a script for his 1986 Channel 4 documentary *Charles Haughey's Ireland*, which he worked on with his long-term friend and adviser, Anthony Cronin, notes that 'you'll find me in the chamber oftener than most deputies.'[15] This was certainly true, and Haughey did have a great respect for the Dáil and its traditions, which developed over the more than three decades he was a TD. While Haughey spent much of his first months as a deputy in the chamber, Fianna Fáil's stable majority also allowed him to continue his work in relation to the party's organisation. He still journeyed to cumainn all across the country, and remained the driving force behind An Chomh Chomhairle, organising speakers to come and talk to its members, and guests, on an eclectic range of topics.

Haughey had a hectic end to 1957. He was called for jury service on 5 November, but was recused on the grounds that he was a member of the Oireachtas.[16] His first son, Conor, was born a few weeks later on 23 November. The following week he was engaged in protracted legal correspondence with a firm in Donegal after being involved in a crash with a car owned by the County Donegal Railway and driven by a Mr Raymond Curran, for which Haughey admitted culpability and paid damages and expenses of £6 2s 0d. The Donegal West Fianna Fáil TD Joseph Brennan interceded with the County Donegal Railway's solicitors on Haughey's behalf. Those solicitors, Dunlevy and Barry, suggested that the matter would be ended once Haughey paid the monies due. They also suggested he write a letter of apology to Curran, who was not going to press the issue but, 'was rather annoyed as the occurrence took place in the presence of some ladies'.[17] While Haughey was willing to pay the cost of the accident 'in accordance to my promise to Deputy Joe Brennan', that was as far as he would go.[18] Some years later, Brennan and Haughey would serve as cabinet colleagues in the Lemass government elected in 1965, and then the Lynch government, before Haughey was sacked in the wake of the arms crisis of 1970.

Two days before his final correspondence in the Donegal crash case, Haughey chaired a meeting of An Chomh Chomhairle at which Professor Louden Ryan of Trinity College Dublin spoke on the subject of the banks and the community.[19] Haughey was convinced that banks needed to be more active players in the communities in which they operated, and was keen to hear the views of the renowned economist. In 1957 Haughey began his legendary constituency operation of providing turkeys, chickens and hams to the poorer parts of his constituency at Christmas. Now that he was a Dáil deputy, he decided it was important to cultivate his vote through helping those he, and his constituency team, felt needed help to have a proper Christmas dinner. It started off as a relatively small operation in the Cromcastle area of Coolock, generally considered to be the poorest part of the constituency, but grew significantly over the years. Many of his constituents originally asked for chickens as they were unsure of the cooking time for turkeys, and whether their cookers could handle a larger bird. In later years the operation also included recipes for how to cook turkey.[20]

At this early stage of his Dáil career Haughey was an enthusiastic participant in various debates to which he was invited. He was always conscious of the importance of promulgating the Fianna Fáil message. As the organiser of the Chomh Chomhairle series of talks, he also knew how difficult it was to book speakers, so he tended to accept invitations to speak at debates. On 18 January 1958 he addressed the Dublin Institute of Catholic Sociology Debating Society in Eccles Street, on the motion that 'Ireland's foreign policy is losing her friends abroad'. He tended to take these debates quite seriously, and for this particular one he spoke to the Minister for Foreign Affairs, Frank Aiken, in advance. He later wrote to tell Aiken that the motion had been defeated 42 votes to 14 and that 'the whole discussion was very favourable from our point of view'.[21] The following month he accepted an invitation from a nineteen-year-old Owen Dudley Edwards to appear at the inaugural meeting of a group of university students called The 1913 Club, which was established to discuss Irish social, political and economic problems and would take the format of a brains trust. He replied that it was 'a very great honour to be asked and I have much pleasure in accepting.' Hyperbolic certainly, but also evidence of Haughey's willingness to speak to any audience.[22]

He was also keen to keep up to date with economic trends and statistics. He wrote to the private secretary in the Department of the Taoiseach in March 1958 seeking future copies of a number of economic publications: the *Monthly Trade Statistics of Ireland*; *Irish Trade Journal and Statistical Bulletin*; *Irish Statistical Survey*; *Trade and Shipping Statistics*; Statistical Abstract; Statement of Accounts of the Central Bank of Ireland; and Reports of the Central Bank of Ireland.[23] On the international front he was interested in the outcome of the Canadian general election held on 31 March 1958, which saw the then Prime Minister John Diefenbaker's Progressive Conservative party, which had been in a minority government for only eight months, win the largest majority in Canadian history. Haughey had called this election spectacularly wrongly, telling a Canadian correspondent, 'because of the recession and the personality of Diefenbaker that the Conservatives must undoubtly [*sic*] lose ground'.[24] His correspondent, Terry O'Leary, an infants' and children's wear manufacturer from Montreal, judged by his letter that Haughey had a low opinion of Diefenbaker. He told Haughey that Diefenbaker, by bringing Quebec into the Conservative camp, had accomplished something that no Canadian Prime Minister in history had ever achieved, by building the largest majority in history: 'The man has an evangelical fervour that seems to have taken hold of the Canadian imagination and thereby lies the story. Apart from the tremendously strong character of its leader, it would appear that the general public decided that the Conservatives deserve a chance to show their merit.' He drew a comparison between Fianna Fáil and the Canadian Liberals, who had been in power for twenty-two years and quoted the old Lord Acton adage, 'Power tends to corrupt, and absolute power corrupts absolutely.' O'Leary signed off wittily, saying that he had recently met a namesake of Haughey's from the Irish Export Board: 'We discussed you to some extent, but inasmuch as he seems like a very nice sort of fellow, and certainly not familiar with the more lurid facets of your character, I decided not to disillusion him and agreed that you are a bonny boy.'[25]

While that humorous phrase might not have stuck with Haughey, there is every chance that O'Leary's comparison of Fianna Fáil to the Liberals, and his tale of the attraction of Diefenbaker's strong personality to the Canadian public, resonated with the ambitious young TD from Dublin North East. A couple of months earlier a German correspondent who was disappointed with the performance of the Christian Democratic government called Haughey a 'conservative politician'.[26] Haughey replied that Germany was the envy of the world and he would happily swap 'some of our peace and quiet for some of your prosperity. I am very distressed that you should regard me as a conservative politician. I regard myself as very advanced, progressive, etc., etc.'[27] Politically, Haughey did think of himself, and indeed the Fianna Fáil of Lemass, as progressive. But the Fianna Fáil of de Valera was still a conservative organisation, and was seen as such by many international observers of Irish politics.

THE CHANGING OF THE FIANNA FÁIL GUARD

The decisive change in Ireland's woeful post-war economic performance is widely ascribed to the publication of the document *Economic Development* in November 1958 by the state's premier civil servant, the secretary of the Department of Finance, T.K. Whitaker. *Economic Development* was completed and presented to the government on 29 May 1958. It became the basis for the White Paper entitled *Programme for Economic Expansion* published six months later on 12 November 1958. The fact that *Economic Development* was published a further ten days later, on 22 November, is itself significant. By publishing it after the *Programme for Economic Expansion*, the government made it clear that it was not, and was not claimed to be, a policy prepared by Fianna Fáil. Rather it was a national policy programme prepared by the head of the civil service. This had the desired effect, and *Economic Development* was accepted as a type of national plan. Its most critical feature was its proposal to shift from protection towards free trade, and from discouragement to encouragement of foreign investment in Ireland. This involved a dramatic reversal of the rhetoric, and to a large extent the practice, of all industrial policy, but especially Fianna Fáil industrial policy, since 1932.[28]

Economic Development remains one of the most seminal documents in the independent Irish state. A popular history of Irish documents notes that for a rather dry policy document it has now taken on an iconic status.[29] Bryan Fanning has argued that as 'a post-independence cultural event the nativity of *Economic Development* was rivalled in the telling only by the story of the conflict surrounding the "Mother and Child scheme" in 1951.[30] Yet *Economic Development* did not impinge on the consciousness of the body politic immediately. The major newspapers gave it only cursory treatment, and the political parties showed a similar lack of interest. The Fianna Fáil parliamentary party minutes of the period all but ignore *Economic Development*. In its first discussion of the document it was recorded that 'the party be given a directive on the implications of the recent White Paper on economic expansion'. The Minister for Finance, James Ryan, gave this meeting, at which Lemass was not present, a general résumé of the contents of the paper, which was followed by a rather bizarre discussion 'in which arterial drainage and … certain very necessary drainage schemes was stressed by several members'.[31]

A planned session devoted to the White Paper on 6 January 1959 was deferred to 28 January, when Lemass 'explained that the proposals in the White Paper were to be regarded as an outline of minimum requirements for the future and do not exclude further proposals.'[32] The effects on agriculture of *Economic Development* were not discussed until March. While this seems to have occupied the party somewhat more as the debate ran into April, the minutes of these discussions are even more sparse than usual, although they state that the debate continued with contributions from various deputies.[33] It would appear that few politicians, whether in Fianna Fáil or elsewhere, were greatly struck by the attempt to revolutionise national economic policy-making. Such an attitude was memorably captured by John Healy of the *Irish Times*, who would later consider himself a close confidant of Haughey. He wrote that it was 'a myth to even think of a huddle of Fianna Fáil deputies solemnly considering the implications of the Whitaker Grey Paper … The poor whores, most of them still don't know what GNP means and "indices" looks like a dirty word.'[34]

There was at least one Fianna Fáil TD who had some idea of the importance of the *Programme for Economic Expansion*. The week before it was published Haughey wrote to his brother-in-law, Lieutenant

Jack O'Brien, who was serving with Irish troops as part of a United Nations (UN) mission in the Lebanon: 'Sean F announced a new five-year economic plan at FF Ard Fheis. It will be published in detail in a few days' time and looks like being what we were all waiting for.'[35] The 1958 Ard Fheis, held in October, was de Valera's last as party leader, and was notable for Lemass's announcement that the government would shortly publish a £220 million five-year plan to 'redefine the objectives of national economic policy'.[36] O'Brien was the husband of Maureen Haughey's sister Peggy, and was appointed Seán Lemass's aide-de-camp when he became Taoiseach in 1959.

The main theme of both the *Programme for Economic Expansion* and *Economic Development* was that an increase in investment, and an expansion in demand – coming from agriculture – would set in motion a general expansion in the national product. In conjunction with this was the aim of attracting foreign investment. Whitaker outlined two ways to attract foreign corporations: removing restrictions; and giving foreign firms incentives to establish bases in Ireland. The Control of Manufactures Acts were amended and a series of proposals intended to attract outside investors to Ireland were recommended. Whitaker proposed that the Industrial Development Authority (IDA) should expand its staff, particularly in North America, in an intensification of its efforts to attract foreign capital. He further proposed increasing the capital available for outright industrial grants. While there were some differences between *Economic Development* and the *Programme for Economic Expansion*, which arose out of their different parentage, such differences were for the most past cosmetic – the main thrust of both documents was the same. Where Whitaker had argued for intensive cattle production as the foundation of agricultural prosperity, the *Programme for Economic Expansion* did not want to abandon completely Fianna Fáil's traditional preference for tillage. Whitaker's proposal to locate new factories in large urban centres was omitted from the White Paper owing to Fianna Fáil's policy of decentralisation of industry, despite Lemass's own doubts about his party's line.[37] His son-in-law undoubtedly felt the same.

THE MERGING OF THE PUBLIC AND PRIVATE

While Haughey was communicating with some of his family members about politics and policy-making, the equally important matter of Gaelic football consumed the minds of a large number of Haugheys and McWilliamses in the summer and autumn of 1958. On 28 September Dublin beat Derry by the comfortable scoreline of 2-12 to 1-9 to win the All-Ireland football final for the first time since 1942. Playing at right half forward for Dublin was Pádraig Haughey, commonly known as Jock, but also called Paddy in the Haughey home. His brother, the TD for Dublin North East, was desperate for a pair of tickets for the big game but was having difficulty getting any. This was due to the fact that playing for Derry the same day was a relation through marriage of the Haughey brothers, Seán O'Connell. He also played at right half forward, and would later marry a cousin of the Haugheys, Margaret McWilliams.[38] Derry's first ever appearance in the final had spawned a frantic search for tickets across all nationalist areas of Northern Ireland, but particularly in the Gaelic football stronghold of south Derry. The Haughey and McWilliams families, and many others, came calling to Donnycarney looking for tickets for the big game. Jock Haughey used the connections he had in Dublin GAA circles to find a number of tickets for his Derry relatives, with the result that Charles Haughey was forced to look to GAA headquarters at Croke Park for tickets for himself. He wrote to the secretary of the GAA, Pádraig Ó Caoimh, that he was 'very conscious of the liberty I am taking in looking for these tickets and the pressure you are under in regard to same ... but, unfortunately, because of the fact that we have a relation playing for Derry, he (Paddy) has on this occasion had to give any tickets he could get to our friends in Derry. I have no option therefore but to appeal to you.'[39] He optimistically enclosed a postal order for fifteen shillings for two Cusack Stand tickets. While there is no response to this request in Haughey's papers, he ended up going to the game, which attracted a crowd of 73,371. He would later regale his northern cousins about how his brother played a key role in sending the McWilliams back to Derry empty-handed and he was there to cheer him on.[40] The *Irish Press* report of the game described Pádraig

Haughey as being part of a superb sextet of Dublin's key forwards who were responsible for winning the game, and Seán O'Connell, who scored five points, as Derry's cute forward who was only subdued in the second half once Dublin made a switch in their back line.[41]

As the debate about protectionism, free trade and industrial policy continued with some vehemence in the civil service between the departments of finance, and industry and commerce throughout 1959, Haughey's public and private life was beginning to merge. Politically, there was a presidential election and a referendum on proportional representation to be fought. Personally, he and his wife Maureen began to think of moving house and he had concerns about his health. In February and March, he began to travel around the country again, speaking at debates on proportional representation. At this stage he was rather impractically driving a Jaguar and continued to spend much of his weekends on Fianna Fáil matters. He spoke in Sligo on Sunday 15 February, where he linked the question of changing from proportional representation to first past the post with the issue of economic prosperity, telling his audience that 'economic survival is the issue. We may survive without the straight vote but I am certain that our task would be longer and harder and far more difficult than it need be … our very survival as a separate cultural, political and economic unit demands that we make this change now.[42] A month later, on Saturday 14 March, he gave a similar speech at the Cork School of Music in which he linked the first past the post system to stable government, articulating the view that only a strong Fianna Fáil government could bring about the prosperity the country needed.[43]

This was a theme also favoured by Lemass, who felt that proportional representation inhibited the potential involvement in political life by business and industrial leaders. (Coincidentally, these economic leaders shared his views.) It also reduced the talent pool available to any Taoiseach in choosing his ministers. Of course, he could not say this during the campaign as it would have been an implied criticism of the government he served in, and of his parliamentary colleagues. While he was confident that de Valera would win the presidential election, he was less sure about the proportional representation referendum because of the innate conservatism of the Irish people and so coined the slogan 'Vote Yes and de Valera' in an attempt to link the two campaigns in the minds of the voters.[44] In Haughey's case, the irony was that he had benefited electorally from proportional representation. On the one occasion he had fought a first-past-the-post election, the by-election of 1956, he had been decisively, if narrowly, beaten.

Haughey was director of finance for the campaign in Dublin and in this context he wrote to Fianna Fáil supporters prior to the vote saying it was vital that in order to elect de Valera and pass the referendum it was absolutely necessary that every possible supporter be brought to the polls on Wednesday 17 June: 'For this purpose we will need every car that we can get on that day and I would be grateful if you could place your car at our disposal. Your car will be fully insured by us for the day and you have our guarantee that the paintwork will not be harmed by the use of posters or otherwise.' He went on to say that petrol would be provided by the party and that if the owner could not do the driving themselves, 'we will supply a competent and reliable person to drive your car.'[45] The campaign yielded mixed results. Fianna Fáil's main problem in the referendum campaign was that it could not overcome the attacks from the opposition that abolishing proportional representation would result in perpetual Fianna Fáil government. The proposal was eventually defeated by just over 33,000 votes as 52.8 per cent of the people voted to keep the existing voting system. The most decisive rejection came in Dublin where, notwithstanding Haughey's call to ferry voters to the polling station, the capital voted heavily to retain proportional representation. The lessons of the defeat stuck with Haughey when Fianna Fáil would have another go at changing the system less than a decade later, although the result would be no different.

The presidential election brought better news for the party: Éamon de Valera was elected President having received over 538,000 votes, 56.3 per cent of the poll. Yet again Dublin was sceptical, and de Valera just edged out his opponent, Seán Mac Eoin, by 2,207 votes, with de Valera losing four constituencies.[46] One of these was Haughey's Dublin North East where Mac Eoin received 17,446 votes to de Valera's 16,417, a majority of 1,029.[47] Six days later, on 23 June, Seán Lemass was elected Taoiseach. On the same day, in one of his last acts as Taoiseach, de Valera wrote to Haughey in Irish, commenting rather unexpectedly about the potential medicinal value of Lucozade, and mineral water from Vichy, and its possible advertising in Ireland.[48] Whatever about the quixotic nature of the subject matter, Haughey was very cognisant of the date of de Valera's letter and told him, again in Irish, that he would cherish it for ever as a memento of Fianna Fáil's first leader.[49]

Haughey's own health was something that he was very conscious of in this early stage of his parliamentary career. In November 1958 he told one correspondent, Seán McDonnell of the University of British Columbia, 'like Hamlet I have gone fat and scant of breath.'[50] In February 1959 he began a diet, having corresponded with a physician in Chicago called Maurice B. Berger.[51] Haughey was a relatively small man, about 5 foot 8 inches and, at this time, he weighed, according to his own notes, 12 stone 11 pounds. This would have given him a body mass index of about 27, which would have put him in the medical category of over-weight. He resolved to lose one pound a week for twenty-three weeks to reach his target weight of 11 stone 2 pounds, which would have brought him to the ideal BMI of 22–23. Berger told him that he could have a total of 1,300 calories a day, was not to eat between meals, and had to avoid foods rich in fats and carbohydrates. The recommended calorie intake for a man of his age would be 2,500 per day.[52] Given that Haughey's target intake was 1,300 calories this was a serious effort, which would allow him reach his target weight in the six-month period he had set himself. His food intake seems normal enough. A poached egg for breakfast was common during the week, while he would have sausage and bacon at the weekends. His main course might be beef, lamb, pork or veal, and he seems to have been partial to dessert, with ice cream and pudding a particular favourite.

On Thursday 19 February 1959, one week after he began his diet, he recorded his calorie intake as 1,300, which might well have been due to an exuberant start. On Sunday 12 April, he noted, it was 2,317. Just over a fortnight later, on Monday 27 April, it was 1,790, while the following week, on Tuesday 5 May, it was 1,760. By the middle of April, he had reached his target weight – 11 stone 2 pounds, or 157 pounds. In mid-July, he recorded a calorie intake of, on average, 1,700 during the week, rising to over 2,800 on Saturday and 2,450 on Sunday.[53] Haughey's diet in the first half of 1959 shows rather remarkable self-discipline in achieving his weight loss. In later life he became far more fastidious about his food, with fish, particularly Dover sole, being a favourite both at home and when dining out.[54] His calorie counting was aided by a relatively active lifestyle. He tried to swim most days but complained that the Irish climate did not always come up to scratch.[55] He also began riding horses and joined the Ward Union Hunt in this period.

Haughey also smoked heavily in this period, which limited his appetite, and he could go through 100 cigarettes a day at the weekend. There is no mention of alcohol in Haughey's dietary plan, but he was partial to white wine and over the course of the following decade he led a rather high-octane lifestyle. It was the shock of the arms trial in 1970 that not only revived and deepened his political ambitions but also led to him considerably disciplining himself and moderating the excessive drinking and smoking of earlier years. He gave up smoking and limited his alcohol intake dramatically.

GRANGEMORE

The summer of 1959 saw Haughey, Maureen and their two young children move from their modest semi-detached house on the Howth Road to Grangemore in Raheny, a large Georgian house on forty-five acres of land, which cost the family in the region of £10,000 and where they would stay for a decade. It had been previously owned by the Walker family, one of whom wrote to Haughey two decades later congratulating him on becoming Taoiseach. Haughey replied that he and his family had greatly enjoyed their time at the 'lovely old house'.[56] When they moved in, Charles and Maureen had intended it to be the family home for the rest of their lives.[57]

A decade later Grangemore became the source of much controversy during the 1969 general election campaign when Gerard Sweetman of Fine Gael claimed that Haughey had avoided paying tax on its sale as a result of changes in the Finance Act of 1968, which he had introduced as Minister for Finance. This was seized on by Haughey's constituency rival, Conor Cruise O'Brien of the Labour Party, who denounced Haughey, saying that the deal epitomised 'the Fianna Fáil speculator-oriented oligarchy'.[58] An angry Haughey issued a denunciation of his political enemies and what he described as an attempt to lower the campaign to a level of personal denigration in an effort to gain political advantage. He claimed that he was putting a number of facts about its purchase and sale into the public sphere, not in an attempt to clarify his own position, but rather to avoid any damage to Fianna Fáil. He stated that Grangemore was then 'in the green belt and there did not seem to be any possibility that it would ever be involved in development. I bought it as a permanent home for my family.' He went on to point out that the Raheny area had expanded at a rapid rate, that many of the holdings around him had been sold for housing, and that it was becoming steadily clearer to him that his land, too, would have to be made available for housing sooner or later. Moreover, he argued, if he had held on to it, he would have had a different type of campaign waged against him. He thus claimed that it was with great reluctance that he had decided 'to break up my home and move elsewhere. I sold to the Gallagher Group because they were already building on adjoining lands and providing excellent houses, comfortable and well-finished and which I saw at first-hand were within the reach of most young married couples.'[59]

Haughey finished his personal statement by insisting that there was nothing secret about the transaction and that his decision meant that a number of people who badly needed houses would get them sooner than they otherwise would have. Fianna Fáil, however, was so exercised by the attack on Haughey's sale of Grangemore that it referred the matter to the Attorney General, Colm Condon, who would the following year play a key role in the arms trial. He issued a statement on 9 June 1969 exonerating Haughey and explaining that the sale of Grangemore did not come within the provisions of Part VII of the Finance Act of 1965, or any other Act, and there was thus no possibility of Haughey benefiting from the Finance (Miscellaneous Provisions) Act of 1968. In that context

Haughey had no personal interest in the enactment of the 1968 Act and therefore 'the question of disclosing a personal interest to parliament did not arise, and the charge is without foundation.'[60]

In 1998, Patrick Gallagher, the son of the Gallagher Group's founder, Matt Gallagher, claimed that his father had told Haughey to buy Grangemore. Patrick Gallagher stated that Matt Gallagher told Haughey that the Gallagher Group would buy Grangemore back from him for a much larger sum. Indeed this is what happened when the Gallagher Group paid some £204,000 for the house and lands.[61] Patrick Gallagher repeated this story in the RTÉ *Haughey* documentary in 2005, adding that it was 'the same type of advice one would give to a friend in a pub. Go and buy that. If my thinking comes true correctly, you can't sell it to anyone else, you must sell it to me.'[62] This story has come to be accepted as fact, but beyond Gallagher's recollection of what his father supposedly told him, there is no other evidence that Haughey bought Grangemore on insider information, as part of a long-term property deal. Certainly Haughey knew Gallagher in 1959, and Gallagher knew that Haughey and Maureen were looking for a larger home. The idea of a large Georgian house most likely appealed to Haughey, being about as far removed from his humble upbringing as it was possible to be while still situated only a few miles away from where he grew up. As a shrewd businessman who had built a successful accountancy practice from nothing, he was undoubtedly aware that Grangemore would appreciate in value. Notwithstanding his statement about it being in the green belt, the potential for the rezoning of Grangemore, in an ever-expanding Dublin, was also clearly a long-term possibility. Yet primarily, Haughey was looking for a larger family home in his constituency, a home where he could base his rising political career while he and his wife reared their family.

Two further children, Ciarán and Seán, were born in the first two years after the move to Grangemore, and the enlarged Haughey family would enjoy a decade of living there. It was the period in which Charles Haughey would move centre stage in Irish politics.

Before the Grangemore controversy arose, Haughey's property interests had for some years been the subject of various rumours. During the

1969 general election campaign, the former Fianna Fáil TD for Cork North, Batt Donegan, told him of a rumour 'promoted presumably by Fine Gael that you are now about to purchase two farms somewhere near Cork City'. Haughey wearily replied, 'It is of course untrue.'[63] Two years earlier, in July 1967, Justice Donagh MacDonagh of the District Court wrote to Haughey about a visit he had taken to the Mount Brandon Hotel in Tralee, which he judged the best hotel in Ireland. He had heard Haughey had an interest in it. Haughey replied that the only interest he had in the hotel was that he knew the owners and that he wished he had a stake in it. He noted that these 'persistent rumours that I own all sorts of things from public houses to office blocks are one of the peculiarities of Irish public life today. They keep cropping up. If you want to make some money I suggest that the next time you hear anybody mentioning this sort of thing that you bet him £100 it is not true.'[64] MacDonagh's reply was short and to the point: 'Fuck the begrudgers.'[65]

These various assertions that Haughey owned large amounts of property, that he had benefited from insider dealing, and that he had profited from illicit dealings worried many of the old guard in Fianna Fáil. He told one correspondent: 'I seem more than ever before to be the victim of a widespread campaign of rumours of every conceivable sort.'[66] In July 1966, Paddy Smith, who Haughey had replaced as Minister for Agriculture two years earlier, wrote to him about an allegation he had become aware of, that Haughey, or his wife, had bought land that had previously been rented by the state, and subsequently sold it to the state at a 'fabulous profit'.[67] Smith stated that he was sorry to trouble Haughey, knowing what it was like to deal with false charges, but he was anxious to nail this particular allegation. Haughey replied that it was of course 'entirely without foundation. Neither myself nor my wife nor any member of my family has ever had any dealings in property with any government or anybody even remotely connected with the state in any way. No such accusation has ever been made in the Dáil or elsewhere.'[68]

At the end of the decade Haughey would sell Grangemore and buy Abbeville, leading to even greater rumours, which haunted him for the rest of his life.

CHAPTER 5

JUSTICE

THE PARLIAMENTARY SECRETARY

Seán Lemass's choice of ministers in his first government was extremely cautious. He made only minimal changes to the cabinet, and at the rank of parliamentary secretary. There was no place for Charles Haughey. It was not until May of 1960, eleven months into Lemass's tenure as Taoiseach, that Haughey was promoted to parliamentary secretary – to his constituency colleague, Oscar Traynor, the Minister for Justice. Traynor was now seventy-four and suffering from hypertension. He had a busy agenda in Justice, which included steering through the Dáil the Intoxicating Liquor Bill, which was passed in June 1960, and the Criminal Justice Bill, dealing with sentencing and release, which was passed the following month. In that context Lemass offered him a parliamentary secretary.[1] Lemass was inclined towards Seán Flanagan from Mayo but, under pressure from the parliamentary party, opted for Haughey instead. The initial support for Haughey's appointment actually came from Traynor.[2] He was aware of Haughey's ability, had known him for over a decade in the constituency, and was intending to retire at the next election. Haughey was no threat to him politically.

Some commentators have maintained that Traynor was dismayed by Lemass's choice of Haughey; Bruce Arnold, for one, maintained that Traynor was strongly opposed to Haughey's appointment because he disapproved of his lifestyle. Arnold cites the diaries of the secretary of the Department of Justice, Peter Berry, as evidence for this.[3] Berry records Traynor as having serious misgivings about Haughey: 'if he had the remotest idea that he would be saddled with Deputy Haughey he would have turned down the offer in the first instance.'[4]

Yet there is no real evidence of any significant animosity between Haughey and Traynor. Given Lemass's inherently cautious approach to his government members at this time, it seems unlikely that if Traynor was hostile to Haughey's appointment the Taoiseach would have gone ahead with it. It is even more unlikely that Lemass would have told Traynor, as Berry alleges, that Haughey would turn down the proposal because of his accountancy practice, and the loss of earnings Haughey would suffer if he took the position.[5] Lemass had by now known Haughey for over fifteen years and was clearly aware of his son-in-law's determination to devote himself fully to political life.[6] There was no question of Haughey ever turning down this promotion. In that context, Lemass's famous quote when offering Haughey the position – 'As Taoiseach it is my duty to offer you the post of parliamentary secretary and as your father-in-law I am advising you not to take it' – has all the hallmarks of being said in jest.[7]

When Haughey was appointed parliamentary secretary, an election was at most two years away, but one was likely to come sooner than that. There was serious work to be done in Justice in a short period of time and, for Traynor, that work was more likely to get done if he was assisted by Haughey. One of the civil servants in Justice at the time, Paddy Terry, recalled that Traynor was not comfortable with many of the technicalities of the legislation that was on his desk as minister, and it was becoming obvious in the department that a large backlog of partially prepared legislation would never be cleared without some sort of assistance from a parliamentary secretary and additional staff.[8] Nevertheless, it is likely that Traynor came quickly to resent being so heavily and rapidly outshone in the public eye by his parliamentary secretary. The traditionally subordinate role of parliamentary secretary to minister had been turned on its head. Berry had a strong rapport with Traynor given that they met daily, and most probably correctly described Traynor's resentful attitude to his rapidly rising colleague. It remains a universal truth in Irish politics that politicians of the same party who share a constituency are ultimately rivals, never friends, and this was the case with Oscar Traynor and Charles Haughey, even if Traynor fully intended to retire at the next general election.[9] For Haughey, the appointment as parliamentary secretary was the opportunity to make his mark on a larger scale. It would clearly do him no harm in the constituency and had the potential to quickly offer him a route to a place at the cabinet table.

When Haughey arrived in the Department of Justice it occupied the top floor of the north block of Government Buildings and housed the minister and some forty officials. It was memorably described by the political journalist James Downey as a 'very dusty, backward, obscure place, the kind of place you'd almost be afraid to venture in for fear you'd never find your way out'.[10] On the day Haughey arrived to start work he was met by Paddy Terry, who told him that the only available business ready for him was the Rent Restrictions Bill of 1960, which was the final result of the 1952 Conroy Report on Rent Restrictions and aimed to restrict the increase of rents and the recovery of possession of premises in certain cases. Terry brought the papers with him to what he described as Haughey's pokey little room in a corridor of Leinster House. When Terry finished introducing himself Haughey immediately told him about a constituent who wanted to join the Gardaí but had been turned down because he was adopted, even though he had lived with his adoptive family since he was a baby. Haughey told Terry that he had made representations to the Garda Commissioner on the matter but to no avail. He added that this seemed terribly wrong and asked what the civil servant thought about it. For Terry, this was the worst possible start to his working relationship with Haughey. Terry's boss, Peter Berry, had a reputation for not tolerating any officials going to ministers behind his back. He felt that it was bad enough for civil servants to express opinions to ministers on matters for which they were responsible, but infinitely worse to do so on matters on which they had none. Terry was flummoxed. Sixty years later he remembered the episode:

> I think I blacked out after Charlie stopped speaking, but I heard myself saying, 'I thought they were all bastards.' He looked at me steadily for a few seconds, he had not yet developed the hooded eyes, as if weighing up a new species of animal. He then said, 'Tell me, what is the position in the civil service?' but went on quickly, 'Don't tell me!' A narrow escape for me, but also an example of his quick wit.[11]

The two men then got down to business on the bill. Haughey's working style was an eye-opener for Terry and indeed pretty much everyone else in the Department of Justice. Haughey, at thirty-five, was five years younger than Terry, and sixteen years younger than Berry. It was the first time in Terry's career that he worked with a politician who did not have to have everything written out for him when in the Dáil and Seanad. When the Rent Restrictions Bill finally passed through the Dáil in December 1960, Haughey recounted to his civil servant that the Fine Gael leader, James Dillon, had told him that he rarely complimented any member of the Fianna Fáil party for anything, but made an exception in this case, describing Haughey's handling of the bill as masterly. Haughey then told Terry, 'I suppose some of the credit for that should go to you.'[12] Haughey was not given to lavishing praise on either his political colleagues or his civil servants but he was also not averse to it when he considered a job well done.[13] This was one of these times. The Rent Restrictions Acts 1960–1981 were ultimately struck down in 1981 by the Supreme Court in the case of *Blake v Attorney General* and replaced by the Rent Tribunal, which was set up to fix the terms of tenancy, including the rent of the dwellings formerly controlled under these Acts. In 1983, Haughey bemoaned the Supreme Court's decision, telling a correspondent that it was he who had put the legislation through the Dáil and that it was 'satisfactory legislation and catered for the situation reasonably well'.[14]

Haughey had a benevolent attitude to many civil servants at the lower grades, as the case of Charlie Harkin shows. Harkin was an old Tyrone IRA/Republican Congress man, one of many such former republicans who was made a temporary civil servant through political patronage after the Second World War. These temporary appointees became a chronic problem because they were not eligible for pensions, and therefore departments were very reluctant to retire them. Harkin was based in the Department of Justice and worked out of an office on the top floor, but was not allowed to use the building's lift for unstated security reasons. His wife, Nora Harkin, believed that the virulently anti-communist Peter Berry was responsible for this state of affairs and that he hoped to force Charlie Harkin out of the department because of his IRA/communist background. In 1962, worried about her husband's heart, Nora Harkin, contacted Haughey, then Minister for Justice, through the Fianna Fáil activist Padraic O'Halpin, for whom she worked, to ask whether anything could be done. A short time later Haughey informed O'Halpin that the situation had been resolved and that he hoped Mr Harkin would be satisfied. Harkin was moved to a ground floor office and spent the rest of his time serenely in the department.[15]

The remainder of Haughey's time as parliamentary secretary in Justice was spent on a range of bills, most notably the Civil Liability Bill, the Defamation Bill, and two Courts bills, all of which he steered through the Oireachtas.

The 1961 Civil Liability Act abolished the last opportunity rule in determining liability for wrongdoing and codified the law in regard to the liability of concurrent wrongdoers, the contribution between concurrent wrongdoers and contributory negligence. The rule that the person who had the last opportunity to avoid the damage was liable for the full damage was amended, and replaced with a system of providing for apportionment of responsibility in assessing liability in proportion to each party's share of the blame. It also included a provision establishing the principle that the law relating to wrongs applies to an unborn child for his protection in the same way as if the child were born, provided the child was subsequently born alive. This provision brought Irish law into conformity with Roman and civil law. Haughey was particularly proud of this bill, telling the *Irish Times* in December 1960 that it was a 'great advance on the existing law even in Britain'.[16] A number of years later, as Minister for Justice, he told an international audience in Luxembourg that it was the 'first attempt at codification in the sphere of tort in any of the common law jurisdictions'.[17]

The Defamation Act provided for fair comment, had sections on unintentional defamation, the lawfulness of indemnifying a person against civil liability for defamation, and prescribed penalties for blasphemous libel. Its passage through the Dáil was completed in four months from mid-April to early August 1961. It would later be severely criticised by media organisations for being a draconian piece of legislation which curtailed legitimate media and public scrutiny of matters of public interest.[18] On the defence of innocent, or unintentional, defamation, Haughey declared that it was 'not in the interest of any section of the community that frivolous or unduly enterprising actions for defamation should be encouraged'.[19] He continued that it was a good defence in civil proceedings for defamation to prove justification in that the words complained of are true in substance, and in fact. In relation to fair comment, he argued that fair comment on a matter of public interest was to be regarded as an important safeguard in the maintenance of that freedom of expression of opinion which Article 40 of the Constitution was designed to protect.[20] Haughey's ultimate aim was to take all the old statute law and put it into one modern statute so that anyone who wanted to know the law of defamation would find it in this bill.[21]

Of the two Courts Bills, the first formally established in law the existing courts in order to comply with the requirement in Article 34 of the 1937 Constitution. The second was a very large supplemental provisions bill. While Haughey led all the bills with decisiveness, he was also prone to overconfidence in the Dáil, which was sometimes problematic. During the debate on the Courts Bill the former Fine Gael minister, Patrick McGilligan, was ridiculing the draftsman's formula for translating the bill from Irish to English. Paddy Terry was the civil servant aiding Haughey in the Dáil and spent the debate sending over speaking notes to him to counter McGilligan's arguments, but every time Haughey tried to do so, McGilligan retorted with a ready and effective answer. Terry recalled:

> I felt as if we were in a bunker in World War III and running out of ammunition fast. The speaking notes being handed over were getting progressively less and less effective. Finally, when he received the last one, C.J. read it, stared at me and kept staring while slowly crumpling the note into a small ball and then letting it drop onto the floor.[22]

While Terry suggested to Haughey that he could avoid the difficulties by stating that it was essentially a drafting matter and he would ask a parliamentary draftsman to look at it, Haughey insisted instead that the section in question was quite clear, which was a particular parliamentary tactic of his. Haughey also had a distinct antagonism towards McGilligan. This was based on what he perceived as McGilligan's dislike of the new, relatively well-off younger generation of Fianna Fáil politicians, as much as the ordinary political differences between their parties.[23] Beyond the intricacies of debating various pieces of legislation, McGilligan was fond of taunting Haughey that he had at one time been an admirer of Cumann na nGaedheal and perhaps even a member of Fine Gael. When this allegation, made in the Dáil in May 1962, was reported in the newspapers, Haughey, as Minister for Justice, was forced to deny any such suggestion. The *Sunday Review* noted his uncanny sense for handling publicity.[24] He initially wrote to the *Irish Times* to point out 'in the interest of historical accuracy' that he was 'never at any time a member, supporter or admirer of, or in any way associated with Cumann na nGaedheal or Fine Gael. The very fact that the article was written on the assumption that I might have been shows how difficult it is to catch up with a lie once it has been uttered.'[25] He reiterated this point to the *Irish Press*, stating that he would not permit something said about him that was untrue to go unchallenged even if many people felt it to be relatively unimportant: 'I feel perfectly entitled to seek to ensure that anything published about me is accurate.'[26]

Haughey's insistence on accuracy even went as far as correcting the Dáil record when it came to his own statements. Given Haughey's propensity for engaging in combative debate in the Dáil, he quickly developed a routine of demanding that his civil servants vet his contributions, not only for errors and accuracy, which would have been normal practice, but also for grammatical precision. Prior to this, if a minister said something that was factually inaccurate, the civil servants would go to the editor of the debates and correct the error in the proofs as they came from the stenographer. However, Haughey required his civil servants not only to correct any errors in the reporting of his contributions to debates, but also to polish up the text. He felt it was important that a permanent record should read properly, as well as correctly. The result of this practice was that civil servants often worked late into the night to ensure the parliamentary secretary was satisfied.[27] The practice was discontinued when Haughey left Justice in 1964.

Haughey's relationship with the Attorney General, Aindrias Ó Caoimh, was known to be difficult. On the Courts (Supplemental Bill), Paddy Terry had gone to Vincent Grogan in the draftsman's office to get a number of amendments drafted for the committee stage. In view of the legal and constitutional importance of the amendments, they were routed through the Attorney General's office. Haughey had given instructions to Terry to get them published immediately, so Terry had to take them to Ó Caoimh. As Terry described it, the Attorney General was not happy:

> [He] lectured me about the amendments, emphasising that it was he, and not anyone else, who was the final authority on drafting and also that it was his function to ensure that every bill or amendment to it was in accordance with the Constitution. I knew that while he was talking to me, it was all directed at Charlie. Just the same, it was a seriously uncomfortable experience![28]

While Ó Caoimh eventually approved the amendments it was an example of the power game at play between the ambitious parliamentary secretary and the Attorney General. Further clashes between the political and administrative branches would follow as Haughey and Peter Berry, who was formally appointed secretary of the Department of Justice in 1961, took the measure of each other. Close to four decades later Haughey would describe himself as having a very good working relationship with Berry in Justice. In 1998 he told Eleanor Walsh, a research student at University College Cork, who was working on a thesis related to his time in the Department of Justice:

> I always listened fully and carefully to his views, though of course, I would not always accept them. As secretary of the department he was a tower of strength for his minister, providing invaluable support in difficult situations, because of his long experience and comprehensive knowledge of every aspect of the work of the department and the administration of justice. His relationship with politicians was very proper; firmly based on the traditional separate roles of politician and civil servant.[29]

That relationship between Haughey and Berry would become severely strained over the next few years.

STIMULATION

Haughey's routine was extremely disciplined. He woke at six o'clock, ate his poached egg breakfast, dealt with some constituency matters, and drove into the city centre.[30] He attended Iris Kellett's riding school in Mespil Road, Ballsbridge, at half past seven in the morning, as often as he could, telling Terry that when he was at school his 'one passion was football. Now it's horse riding.'[31] He was part of a group known as the Early Risers' Club. After his riding lesson he would be in his office for nine o'clock and followed his father-in-law's routine of finishing his working day at five o'clock in the evening. His evenings would be taken up with Fianna Fáil business or some sort of speaking engagement, either in Dublin or, when the Dáil was not sitting, around the country. He rarely refused any invitation to speak at constituency events. He was no longer a backbencher but realised that the Fianna Fáil message had to be promulgated, and the next election won, if a full ministerial career was to be realised.

Due to his increased responsibilities as parliamentary secretary, Haughey decided to resign his position as secretary of An Chomh Chomhairle in July 1960. He told Lemass that he had been neglecting its affairs for some time and suggested George Colley as his replacement. Lemass readily agreed to this proposition.[32] Haughey had been secretary for five years and had built up a large array of contacts through inviting speakers and guests to its talks. One of these was the leading industrialist Colm Barnes, of the textile company Glen Abbey. Barnes was friendly with Lemass and supported his free trade initiatives of the early 1960s. He also saw Haughey as one of the upcoming generation of dynamic Fianna Fáil politicians who could lead Ireland to a more promising economic future.[33] In July 1960, Barnes wrote to Haughey deploring what he considered the unscrupulous tactics used by Fianna Fáil canvassers in the local elections held the previous month.[34] A particular canvasser had been claiming that a candidate could use his influence to get driving licences issued in two weeks, rather than the usual twelve months. Haughey replied that the practice was regrettable but admitted that it did happen with canvassers and that 'it is impossible to control or even know what they may say or do in support of their favourite candidate. I can assure you that there is no truth whatever in the suggestion made by the canvasser, as I think you suspected yourself.'[35] It was a small but telling indication of the difference between candidates and canvassers and the distance Haughey put between them. It was something he would return to as his political career developed.

In December 1960, the *Irish Times* conducted a major interview with Haughey. Despite his role as parliamentary secretary in the Department of Justice, he confirmed the view that his particular aim in politics was developing the economy so that everyone who wanted a job would be able to get one. He confirmed his position from his university days that while private enterprise was the bedrock of the Irish economy, it was necessary at times for the state to intervene to drive projects that the private sector could not do. It was also necessary, he believed, that all economic endeavour to increase national wealth should be accompanied by a social system that would ensure that such wealth was passed on to the entire community in a fair measure. For him, politics was about being able to do good, and political action, he argued, should be directed to building up the economic and social structure of the state rather than merely regulating a fully developed society. He criticised young Irish people for being too quick to emigrate and insisted that they had immense possibilities in the Ireland of the 1960s. While he acknowledged that the root cause of emigration was economic, and he resolved to do something about it, he concluded that it was also a matter of education and outlook, both of which needed to be expanded. Perhaps most important, he stated that for him politics was 'the most stimulating and fascinating form of activity there is'.[36] His accountancy practice was beginning to thrive, and he had started to farm chickens and hens on his land in Grangemore, but it was politics where all his ambition lay.

In this interview Haughey told the *Irish Times* that law reform was a key part of how he viewed his role as parliamentary secretary in Justice. He had no interest in legislation for the sake of it. He wanted the law to keep in touch with modern social and commercial developments, or else there would be frustration and injustice within the general population. He returned to this theme in greater detail when on 15 April 1961 he spoke at a meeting of An Chomh Chomhairle held, as usual, in Clery's Hotel. Having spent five years cajoling various speakers to address it, Haughey took the opportunity to use the Chomh Chomhairle as a vehicle to present a major speech of his own, one he had been planning for some time: 'The Reform of the Law'. He told George Colley, who organised the meeting, that he did not mind who proposed or seconded the vote of thanks as long as they 'would not be particularly long-winded'.[37] Colley arranged for senior counsel Colm Condon to deliver the vote of thanks and respond to the paper and for the solicitor Liam McGonagle to second it.[38]

Haughey got straight to the point in his address. He said that if the law was out of touch with social and economic development, or was not in conformity with the circumstances and needs of the people, it was bound to lead to serious injustices. He pointed to two specific areas: the law of inheritance; and the guardianship of children. He stated that he had for some time been considering the law that allowed a man to disinherit his wife and family, and maintained that:

> [The] law of inheritance is heavily weighted against the wife and in favour of the husband, and generally we are maintaining the whole law as to the distribution of property on death almost exactly as it was two hundred years ago. The law was originally devised for a feudal system when the wife was considered some kind of chattel and the eldest son as the pride and joy of the household.[39]

He then bemoaned the fact that because of a law enacted in 1886 the mother was in an inferior position to the father in relation to the guardianship of children. If Ireland was to consider itself a modern, progressive nation, Haughey suggested, it had to change this situation. For him, the law had to advance in step with the social, commercial and economic developments of the community, and should reflect the outlook and needs of the public. He left the audience in Clery's Hotel in no doubt that such progressive change was coming.

THE AGE OF TELEVISION

One other progressive change that was coming to Ireland in the early 1960s was television. Fianna Fáil was unsure how it would impact on Irish politics, and the party itself, so its national executive established a committee to report on the issue. Haughey was intensely interested in television as a medium through which to communicate politics. He was influenced by Eamonn Andrews's speech in November 1958 to the Chomh Chomhairle, in which Andrews stressed television's potential societal and political impact in the decade ahead. Haughey had also told the *Irish Times* in his December 1960 interview that the advent of television would compel Fianna Fáil to modernise itself.[40] Haughey was appointed to the committee, which reported in March 1961. It was divided in its view of the importance television would have for politics in the short to medium term. One perspective was that television had a very limited impact on political life, its influence was slight, and this was likely to remain the case. The other view was that television would revolutionise the whole approach to politics, and that political parties must adapt themselves to it, or go under. As part of its evidence for this position, the committee pointed to the importance of television in the election of John F. Kennedy in the American presidential election of November 1960, and the success of what it described as a number of celebrities in the British general election of October 1959.

The committee did agree that Fianna Fáil needed to prepare itself to make the fullest possible use of the opportunities for publicity and propaganda that television provided. It proposed that the party establish a permanent television and radio committee which would be charged with dealing with all matters concerning both media. It also suggested that Fianna Fáil and the other political parties work out, between them, the manner in which political matters would be handled by Radio Éireann. It advocated that the system adopted by the BBC should apply in Ireland; that Radio Éireann should set up a television training school that would be available to politicians and unspecified others for training in the medium; that proceedings in the Dáil and Seanad would not be televised; that at general elections an adequate amount of time would be placed at the disposal of the parties for free party political broad-casts in accordance with the numerical strength of the parties; and that between elections Radio Éireann should be free to decide for itself what political programmes it would show, but these should be impartial and give due regard to a proper balance in subject matter and personalities.[41] While Lemass was initially willing to let Telefís Éireann, as it became known from 31 December 1961, forge ahead on a politically independent path, he quickly came to resent what he considered biased attacks on the government.[42] Lemass was attuned to the importance of television as a medium, as was Haughey, who would himself become a vociferous critic of Telefís Éireann in his early ministerial career.[43] It was ironic that despite Lemass's well-founded suspicion of television, he was himself a most effective performer on it. His avuncular, no-nonsense style was ideally suited to the medium in that period. The same went for Haughey, who quickly gained a reputation within RTÉ for being extremely well prepared and the most able of the government's ministers on both radio and television.[44]

Fianna Fáil's television committee had concerns that the party would not be ready to adapt to the new medium if Radio Éireann's television service was up and running before the next general election. It need not have worried. Lemass called the election for 4 October 1961, a few months before Ireland's first television broadcast on New Year's Eve of that year. Haughey was, however, very aware that the arrival of television was imminent and that Fianna Fáil needed to be ready for it. In August 1962 he sent a detailed note to the Minister for Local Government, Neil Blaney, which began, 'I have given a lot of thought to our conversation regarding Fianna Fáil and the use of television.'[45] He wrote that anything that helped to improve performance on Telefís Éireann was very much in the interests of the service. He went on to advocate that when representatives of the party appeared on television they should have an experienced public relations officer with them to supervise and advise on their performance, even down to such details as clothes, posture and the use of notes. He suggested that preparation was key, that the subject should know whether what he was going to say would be used in full or edited; and even brief, hurried interviews should be prepared for before facing the cameras, even if it necessitated a slight delay. The advent of television would present Fianna Fáil and, indeed, all other parties with a problem in relation to who would represent them in front of the cameras. Haughey warned Blaney that although in the nature of things many political figures would be strong personalities on the screen, the party could not know who was or was not that kind of personality except by looking at the result through a camera or a screen, and many party representatives would get better with experience. He warned against the dangers of coaching, noting that unconventional mannerisms were as likely to be endearing as they were irritating and that a natural performance was better than an over-polished one. He did, however, advocate filming sessions for those the party were thinking of putting on television, which could be professionally criticised and shown back to the subjects. It was advice that Haughey himself would take over the course of his career when it came to representing Fianna Fáil on television, and he used a variety of public relations firms over the course of the next thirty years to improve and polish his own performances.[46]

In October 1961, however, Fianna Fáil's big concern was how it would fare in its first election without de Valera at its helm. It was right to be worried. Its vote fell from 48.3 per cent to 43.8 per cent and the majority of six Lemass had when he was appointed Taoiseach became a minority of two. The urbanite Lemass had failed to lift the party's vote in the cities. Fianna Fáil lost one of its three seats in Cork, and Dublin was particularly bad. Despite the fact that there were thirty-four seats in the capital (four more than in 1957), Fianna Fáil failed to win any of the extra seats.

The one bright spot for the party was Dublin North East. Here, for the first time since the establishment of the constituency in 1948, it took three of the five seats. Given that Oscar Traynor was not running again, there were fears that the party would struggle. It decided to run four candidates to maximise its vote. Haughey had been an effective parliamentary secretary for just under a year and a half but he was still a first-time TD. Of the other candidates, Eugene Timmons had been dropped from the ticket in 1957, and had not come near to winning a seat in three other elections, while George Colley and Stan O'Brien were first-time candidates. Colley had the advantage of his father's name and reputation in the constituency, but Harry Colley was never a prolific vote-getter and it remained to be seen whether his son would do any better. So there was much trepidation in Dublin North East as to how Fianna Fáil would fare. When the votes were counted, however, Fianna Fáil had won 46.5 per cent of the first preference vote, up a full five points from its 1957 performance. It benefited from the Labour Party's decision to run two candidates, which diluted Denis Larkin's vote. As Labour had declared it would not enter coalition with Fine Gael after the election, the contest was essentially framed as one between Fianna Fáil and Fine Gael and this was the way it turned out in Dublin North East. Haughey topped the poll with 8,566 votes and was elected on the first count with 1.2 quotas. Colley was third after the first count, having taken over 12 per cent of the first preference vote. He polled a very respectable 5,086 votes, coming in just behind Fine Gael's sitting TD, Jack Belton. Timmons was placed fifth, having polled just under 4,000 votes (9.5 per cent), with Fine Gael's Patrick Byrne just ahead of him. These five candidates were well ahead of the field after the first count and were all duly elected as the transfers and eliminations played out.

Haughey, as the senior politician in the constituency, had run a sophisticated canvassing operation with target lists of names and addresses and instructions that letters to voters should be personalised. The organisation levels in Dublin North East led one of his correspondents to reflect ruefully that if things had been organised better elsewhere the result might have been much more positive for the party.[47] In fact, much of the Fianna Fáil election campaign continued with the personalised theme that the party had adopted since its foundation. The only difference was that de Valera had been replaced, not altogether successfully, by Lemass. To a correspondent who was looking for a copy of Fianna Fáil's election programme which he understood 'will be available from Monday, you know a printer's Monday always means Tuesday; "absolute shower" those printers', Haughey replied that the party did not propose to issue any formal document containing an election programme and that its policies were contained in various speeches and advertisements.[48] It would take a full decade and a half before Fianna Fáil would start to issue manifestos.

Haughey did, however, apparently pick up twenty votes when one of his canvassers, John O'Sullivan, told him that the good nuns of Manor House Convent in Watermill Lane had agreed to vote after he had reminded them of their obligations to exercise their franchise. They had not voted in the previous election, and were not of a mind to do so in this election either, until called upon by the Haughey canvassing machine. It helped that Haughey's six-year-old daughter, Eimear, was a pupil at Manor House and the mother superior 'spoke in glowing terms of her acting ability. Did you know you had such talent in the house?

I'm quite sure that was the most decisive single factor in influencing the Superioress, as she assured me on leaving that all the nuns would go along to vote next Wednesday.[49] O'Sullivan urged Haughey to send a note of thanks to the nuns for receiving him as his emissary, which would, no doubt, clinch the twenty votes.

Haughey's huge vote, and his election on the first count, copperfastened his reputation as one of the rising stars of Fianna Fáil. The fact that he had brought in two running mates in what was regarded as a very tough constituency added to his lustre. This was even more impressive considering Fianna Fáil's difficulties in Dublin. Haughey was duly rewarded with a place at the cabinet table, as Minister for Justice, when Lemass formed his minority government. The sleepy hollow of Justice was about to be woken up.

THE WARDEN OF THE SEALS

In the 1950s and 1960s the civil servants in Leinster House christened the ministerial corridor in which they and their political masters worked the 'Burma Road' because working conditions were so primitive and crowded.[50] Offices were shared, working hours were long and there were few benefits. Many political careers also ended somewhat abruptly there. (Eventually the Office of Public Works replaced that ghastly ministerial corridor with a three-storey office block at the back of the Dáil chamber.) On his appointment to cabinet, Haughey resolved not to be one of those ministerial casualties.

Given the perceived success he had made of his role as parliamentary secretary, it was widely expected both within Fianna Fáil, and outside it, that Haughey would be promoted. He told one correspondent that he was 'very surprised to discover that my appointment was not criticised at all but in fact was widely welcomed. The accusation of nepotism has not been raised once.'[51] The congratulatory letters came from near and far. One was from a rising official in the Department of Finance, Maurice Doyle, who told Haughey that he trusted it would 'prove a stepping-stone to greater things. Not that I want to belittle the Department of Justice, but there are others!'[52] It was certainly clear to many, within the bureaucracy of the civil service, and across the political spectrum, that Justice was unlikely to be the limit of Haughey's ministerial ambitions. Nevertheless, he was keen to make his mark in his new role, replying to Doyle that there was 'plenty to do here'.[53] And indeed there was. Yet, at the same time, he was determined not to lose the 'common touch' he had with his constituents and wider circle of friends. When the *Irish Press* journalist Sheila Walsh addressed him as 'Mr Haughey' in a congratulatory letter, not having 'the nerve to call you Charlie now that you are a minister', he demanded she never do so again, plaintively asking, 'How the hell can a politician hope to stay in business if people start going around calling him "Mister".'[54]

Haughey faced his ministerial career in Justice with optimism and hope for the future. In reply to one of his younger correspondents who suggested that Ireland was drifting nowhere he stated that there was no more apathy, indifference or cynicism in Ireland than in any other country and that none of these nouns applied to Fianna Fáil. He asserted, 'I have not the slightest doubt about my capacity to face up to the future. I am equally confident about the capacity of Fianna Fáil, and, indeed, of the Irish people as a whole.'[55] That confidence would first be tested in Justice. A French friend, Henry Castelnau, one of the Early Risers' Club, who frequented Iris Kellett's riding school, told Haughey, on his appointment, that he now held the post which had 'in France a name which indicates the high responsibilities it implies: Le Garde des Sceaux (The Warden of the Seals)'.[56]

Haughey's first major act as minister was to intervene in a bitter row about Garda pay. Since the foundation of the state there had been complaints from gardaí about low pay, poor promotional prospects and, as rank and file members saw it, indifference to their plight from Garda management. Garda Commissioner Daniel Costigan, a career civil servant, was known to be sympathetic to the difficulties of gardaí, and keen to introduce what he considered necessary reforms, but was frustrated by the lack of any government efforts to resolve gardaí grievances. At the time rank and file gardaí were paid much the same as clerical officers in the civil service, although they had several allowances for uniforms, boots and rent. When a pay award was granted to clerical officers in 1960, it was applied in due course to the Gardaí. The difficulty was that the new salary scale gave little or no increase to those on the early points of the pay scale, a position a significant number of gardaí were in as a result of the large intake of recruits to replace those gardaí who had enlisted in 1922 and had just retired.[57] This left about 3,000 members of the force with less than five years of service exempt from a wage increase, while newer recruits were already becoming disillusioned by their poor working conditions and living arrangements.

Approaches to Garda pay in this period were very haphazard. There were a number of Garda representative bodies, representing each rank below assistant commissioner, and they would convene at infrequent intervals over a few days, in the course of which a delegation would see the minister to outline their grievances and demands. The aim of the civil servants in Justice was to find something in the various requests that could be conceded with little or no cost and the promise that a conciliation and arbitration scheme for gardaí, which would allow complaints about pay to be dealt with properly and satisfactorily, was imminent.[58] The Fianna Fáil government had agreed with the Minister for Justice, Oscar Traynor, in November 1958 to establish such a scheme, telling the Dáil that a draft scheme for the establishment of conciliation and arbitration machinery for the Garda Síochána up to and including the rank of inspector had been sent to the representative bodies concerned.[59] By the time Haughey became Minister for Justice the scheme still had not been legislated for.

Individual meetings of gardaí in separate Garda stations to discuss pay and conditions were banned, under the force's disciplinary code, once Costigan became aware that they were happening. This led to much dissent in the ranks and a mass meeting of gardaí was called at the Macushla Ballroom on Amiens Street on 4 November 1961. Despite attempts by more senior members of the force to dissuade the revolutionaries, hundreds of disgruntled gardaí turned up, to be met by a superintendent and a number of inspectors who had been sent to take the names of anyone at the meeting they recognised. This resulted in 160 gardaí receiving charge notifications for discreditable conduct. This incensed the rank and file, who responded with a go-slow policy in Dublin city centre, which involved ignoring minor infractions of the law such as illegal parking and street trading. Five days later, on 9 November, Haughey issued a statement stating that once he was satisfied that discipline had been restored, he would undertake an examination of the existing negotiating machinery available to the gardaí and if it proved wanting, improvements would be made. This placatory statement, however, seemed pointless, when on the very same day Costigan, as Garda Commissioner, dismissed eleven members of the force by declaring them unfit for retention in the Garda Síochána in exercise of the power conferred on him by article 24 of the Garda Síochána discipline regulations.

This unexpected development turned public opinion against the Commissioner and provided Haughey, always attuned to the public's perspective, with a difficulty very early in his tenure as minister. Would he back the Commissioner or side with the individual gardaí? Taking the latter course was never really an option as it would have spawned an unparalleled crisis in the relationship between the leadership of the department and the leadership of the Gardaí. At this stage the Archbishop of Dublin, Dr John Charles McQuaid, let it be known that he was willing to act as an intermediary between the gardaí and their leadership and Haughey accepted his intervention. McQuaid met on a number of occasions with Frank Mullen, one of the Garda representatives, and eventually persuaded him to postpone any further action in return for the reinstatement of the eleven sacked members.[60] McQuaid's intervention proved crucial and both Costigan and Haughey agreed to his solution. The eleven members were reinstated to the force and one of them, Jack Marrinan, was appointed general secretary of the Representative Body for Guards. The Macushla affair was a watershed for the Gardaí. Until then its representative bodies had been largely ineffective, but they would become much more confident and assertive in their demands for improved pay and conditions. It was also a watershed for Haughey. He had been tested in his first weeks in office with a difficult internal Garda problem and had resolved it quickly. It gained him much respect within the Garda representative bodies. He followed this up in 1962 by supporting the demand of the representative bodies that deduction of mortgage interest payments could be made from salaries, a facility that had been available to civil servants and staff in semi-state bodies. This allowed gardaí to benefit from 90 per cent loan advances from the banks.[61]

A decade later, in June 1971, during Haughey's post-arms trial political purgatory, the Garda Representative Body for Inspectors, Station-Sergeants and Sergeants wanted to employ him in an advisory capacity to represent them.[62] The request was rejected by Garda Commissioner Michael Wymes, but Haughey did agree to act for the body on an honorary basis. Twenty years after that, in November 1991, just after he had survived yet another challenge to his leadership of Fianna Fáil, Frank Mullen, one of the Garda representatives in the original dispute, wrote to congratulate him and recalled the dispute of 1961 when after 'lengthy discussions I agreed on a settlement with you through the Archbishop. I found you an honourable man then and through the years nothing has happened to change my mind.'[63] Haughey's sympathies may well have resided with the various representative bodies, but he resolved not to interfere with individual disciplinary or promotion matters while minister. As he told one correspondent in early 1963 who queried the lack of promotion of one member of the Gardaí: 'I am afraid, however, there is nothing I can do to help him as I never interfere in matters of this sort. I think it would be very undesirable and bad for the force generally if I were to do so.'[64]

The resolution of the Garda pay revolt was a good start to Haughey's tenure as Minister for Justice, but it was essentially a reactive matter. Far more important to him was his law reform agenda. He was ably assisted by Paddy Terry and Roger Hayes. Hayes was appointed assistant secretary in the Law Reform Division in September 1962. Both men were as committed to law reform as Haughey was. Peter Berry, as secretary of the department, had no interest in the area. Hayes, by contrast, was fervently dedicated to law reform and the introduction of a whole new

structure of what he, and Haughey, considered to be enlightened legislation. Hayes was by nature a passionate reformer. He was delighted to
get the opportunity that Haughey gave him to provide a comprehensive
programme of reform, and he dedicated himself to the work literally
night and day. Haughey described his civil servants in Justice as being
extremely talented and, like civil servants throughout the bureaucracy,
as only requiring 'clear political direction to enable them to produce
excellent results. I found that your average civil servant was happiest
when he or she worked with a political head of department who knew
what he or she wanted and indicated clearly what the policy was.'[65]

Haughey, from his first days as minister, asked his civil servants
for ideas on how to progress his reform agenda. One of Paddy Terry's
ideas was to expand legal aid, which until 1962 was restricted to murder
cases and allowed no provision for appeal. Peter Berry was lukewarm
about the idea, quoting the escalation of the legal aid bill in Britain over
the years. Haughey, by contrast, was firmly supportive of the proposal,
although Terry suspected this was partly because he had by then become
bitten by the legislation bug, or at least realised that legislation would be
a permanent record of his achievements in the department.[66] The Legal
Aid Bill, which became law in April 1962, allowed for aid in a wider
variety of offences a suspect was charged with, and was also allowable
in appeal cases. The initial criterion for granting free legal aid was that
the aid was essential, rather than desirable, as was the case in Britain,
but it was substantially widened over time.

Just a few months later, in July 1962, the second Intoxicating Liquor
Act in two years became law. It regulated opening hours, issuing licences
and serving alcohol in clubs and restaurants. While Haughey was not
responsible for the first Intoxicating Liquor Act, which had passed
through the Oireachtas just after he had been appointed parliamentary
secretary, he nevertheless became associated with it. In August 1964, the
assistant editor of the *Irish Times*, Donal O'Donovan, wrote to Haughey
'as the minister responsible for two excellent licensing acts', asking him
to write an introductory article, and preferably one which contained
some humour, for a special supplement the paper was producing on the

liquor trade.[67] Haughey declined: 'I can't write, and as regards humour, I find it very difficult to understand even the most obvious of cartoons!'[68]

DEATH AND SUCCESSION

Whatever about Haughey's insights into his writing style, sense of humour, and how civil servants worked best, he and his team of officials drove through a quite remarkable series of legislative initiatives during his three-year period as Minister for Justice. These included the renewal of legislation that predated the laws of the Oireachtas, and legislation relating to the courts system, legal aid, intoxicating liquor, the Garda Síochána, coroners, extradition, adoption and the guardianship of infants, the death penalty, child offenders and, perhaps most famously, succession.

In October 1998 the documentary film-maker Seán Ó Mórdha met with Haughey to discuss the former Taoiseach's participation in a television series telling the story of the Irish state. Haughey agreed to be filmed and Ó Mórdha sent him some handwritten and printed notes on broad areas and specific questions he wanted to discuss. They covered the full gamut of Haughey's career. One area Ó Mórdha did not mention specifically was Haughey's period as Minister for Justice, but in his own handwritten preparatory notes for the television interview, Haughey mentions the Succession Act twice in relation to his reform initiatives and his own personal political philosophy.[69] While no discussion of the Act made it into the final cut there can be little doubt that long into his retirement, Haughey viewed this piece of legislation as a particularly important part of his legacy, despite the fact that it was his successor as Minister for Justice, Brian Lenihan, who steered the legislation through the Dáil.

At its heart the aim of the Succession Act was to safeguard the rights of widows and children on the death of a father.[70] Until Haughey's initiative, property, particularly in rural Ireland, was passed down from eldest son to eldest son through the generations. It was possible for a surviving wife and children to be left destitute on the death of their husband and father, as family property could be sold against their interests. Haughey's aim was essentially to ensure that a man would have to provide for his wife and children after his death by, for the first time, giving women legal rights to their husbands' estates. For Haughey it was a simple matter of social justice and of the government trying to achieve a fair and equitable system for the distribution of property. In that context it was very much a progressive measure that removed one of the last vestiges of feudalism left in modern Ireland. He recalled being incensed that an elderly parent could capriciously bequeath his entire estate to anybody he wished and leave his widow and children with nothing.[71]

Haughey told a Fianna Fáil meeting in October 1964 that passing the Act meant that the law governing matters of succession would now be 'a law which the Irish people will have given to themselves, not something which has been handed to us by an alien jurisdiction. We must therefore make it the best possible measure. It must be fair and just and suited to our needs and conditions.'[72] While the reference to an alien jurisdiction was probably tailored for his internal audience, Haughey was keen to showcase the Succession Bill to as wide an international audience as possible, including the British. In July 1964 Haughey sent a copy of the Succession Bill to the British Attorney General, Sir John Hobson, telling him that he would be delighted 'to receive entirely personally and confidentially any comments which you might like to make'.[73]

A few months earlier, in March 1964, he delivered a wide-ranging speech on the Irish government's law reform legislative agenda to the International University of Comparative Sciences in Luxembourg. He noted that in framing the Succession Bill his department had made an exhaustive comparative study of the laws of succession in England, Scotland, France, Germany, Switzerland and certain states of the USA. He pointed out that the relevant provisions of the French, German and Swiss civil codes had also been examined and some of the world's leading experts in this field of law had been personally consulted: 'We have done everything possible to ensure that our proposed new law of succession will be as enlightened as that of any other country.'[74]

One of the experts consulted was Professor Ernst Joseph Cohn, who had been forced to leave Germany after the Nazis came to power, and eventually settled in England in 1937, where he worked as a barrister and lecturer. In 1957, the University of Frankfurt made him an honorary professor of German and English private and civil law, although he spent much of his time in England. Cohn wrote to Haughey in November 1964 lamenting that Haughey had been moved from Justice to Agriculture, noting: 'I only hope that your splendid law reform program will not suffer too much from this change ... I hope also the Succession Bill will remain a monument of your energetic work in the cause of law reform.'[75] This indeed proved to be the case. Three years later, in 1967, Justice Conor P. Maguire of the Circuit Court wrote to Haughey: 'Last week I heard what I was told by counsel was the first case to come to a hearing under the Succession Act. In view of your association with it I want to tell you that the act enabled the court to rectify what would have been an injustice to a widow. The provisions of the act are imaginative, and will, I feel sure, be a great benefit to the community.'[76] As late as 1990, Brian Lenihan, when stressing his achievements at the beginning of his speech accepting the Fianna Fáil nomination for President of Ireland, noted that he 'steered the Succession Act introduced by Charles Haughey through the Dáil which greatly improved the status of women'.[77] Lenihan's nod to Haughey was important, signalling, as it did, the ownership of this particular piece of progressive legislation, one Haughey always considered his.[78]

Haughey certainly believed that while his array of progressive legislation in Justice was beneficial to the entire community, it was of particular help to women. His outrage about the succession laws was, in part, motivated by the thought that his mother could in theory have been thrown out of her home after the death of her husband. In April 1964 he approved the nomination of Eileen Kennedy as the first woman appointed to the District Court. He told one of his correspondents, the Anglo-Irish novelist Pamela Hinkson: 'I hope it has not escaped your notice that last week for the first time ever in this country we appointed a woman to the District Court Bench.'[79] He saw the Guardianship of Infants Act of 1964 through a similar lens. The two primary considerations of the Act were that in any proceedings affecting a child, the interests of the child must be the first and paramount consideration and that the mother and father of a child should have equal rights of guardianship and custody. At the end of the 1960s he gave a speech entitled 'Women in Irish Society' to the Comhdhail Atha Cliath of Fianna Fáil in the Shelbourne Hotel, in which he said that the aim of the guardianship legislation was to give statutory effect to the principle that in all matters affecting guardianship and custody of their children, the father and mother should have equal rights and duties. He went on to stress the rights of mothers as the key influence in relation to the Succession Act. He began that particular meeting by saying that a progressive political party with an enlightened social conscience, like Fianna Fáil, must have a special place for women in its policies, arguing that a society which does not give full and complete recognition to the position of women, and does not accord them equality in every sense, must be regarded as being still in a formative stage. He ended with a quote from the Roman Emperor Justinian: 'he begins his famous Institutes with the following words: "Justice is the constant and perpetual will to give every man his due", if he were alive today he would undoubtedly have added and every woman as well.'[80]

Over two decades later, in early 1992, Haughey insisted on keeping a speaking engagement to the conference of the Council for the Status of Women entitled 'Women – Partners in Policy Making', the day after he had dramatically announced that he was stepping down as Taoiseach and leader of Fianna Fáil. In that speech he stated that by 1970 he had recognised that a comprehensive reassessment was needed to ensure that women could play a full role in Irish society and to identify the barriers they faced so that these obstacles could be progressively dismantled. This was the context for the introduction of the first Commission of the Status of Women established by Jack Lynch on 31 March 1970. Haughey again referenced the Succession Act in this speech, stating that he looked upon its enactment as 'the commencement of a new era of advance which is still continuing'.[81]

When Haughey began his tenure in Justice he was convinced of the need for a progressive legislative programme, but he was also acutely aware that the Irish state still faced a serious security threat from the IRA. The ongoing, if intermittent, IRA border campaign did not feature at all in the 1961 general election campaign but it still had the means to cause shock among the population, as it did with the killing of an RUC man, William Hunter, in Jonesboro in November of that year.[82] This prompted the government to reconstitute the Special Criminal Court, staffed by army officers, and authorise it to try offences under the Offences Against the State Act. The target was IRA men. Berry would later credit Haughey as being determined to break the IRA, emphasising that it was on the Minister for Justice's initiative that the government had reactivated the Special Criminal Court. In June 1970, Berry told the Taoiseach, Jack Lynch, after Haughey had been arrested on charges of conspiracy to illegally import arms, that it was a course which the Department of Justice had advocated and unsuccessfully urged on Haughey's predecessor for a considerable time: 'It was a tough measure.'[83]

The IRA's border campaign had little popular support. Sinn Féin polled poorly at the 1961 election, receiving just 35,000 first preference votes and losing all four seats it had won in 1957. The party had practically no resources and neither did the IRA. Yet the border campaign somehow lasted for five years.[84] This required the Irish state to invest significant monetary and legislative resources in defeating it, of which internment, which eventually ended in April 1961, and the Special Criminal Court were the most effective. Ultimately the government's crackdown and the lack of any popular support forced the IRA to abandon its campaign in February 1962. Haughey was an enthusiastic supporter of crushing the IRA and was at the forefront of a government publicity campaign to portray it as an illegal organisation that offered Irish people nothing in its futile attempts to secure a united Ireland by force.

When the IRA ended its campaign, Haughey issued a statement stating that it had contributed to the perpetuation rather than the abolition of partition, and declared that the government was not prepared to tolerate the existence of unofficial organisations. He reiterated that all resources necessary to put an end to illegal activities would be utilised against any IRA resurgence, and repeated an amnesty promise he had previously made that anyone with illegal arms could hand them into the guards without fear of prosecution. While bemoaning the ills of partition, Haughey urged supporters of the IRA, and even those who had played an active role in its campaign, to put their energies to a more constructive use in service of the Irish nation.[85] This rather unrealistic appeal was part of a pattern of Haughey's – he would routinely call on Irish people to play their role in the march of the nation. The same was true of some of his comments on emigration; somewhat like Éamon de Valera, he would often encourage people not to emigrate, or for emigrants to come home to support the state, without taking any cognisance of their economic circumstances. In 1965 he told a convent nun that he felt 'quite justified in asking any Irish people who can to return here. I think it is far better that their children be brought up here in an Irish atmosphere and given an Irish education.'[86]

In any event the end of the IRA campaign allowed Haughey to devote his full energy to his progressive legislative agenda. One significant component of this agenda was to remove the death penalty from the statute book. Although no one had been executed by the state since Michael Manning in 1954, Haughey was disgusted by the practice, and felt it had no place in a civilised society. Haughey visited Mountjoy Prison many times in his tenure as Minister for Justice; in 1984, he recalled that shortly after becoming minister he saw the condemned cell there and was so revolted by the whole atmosphere that he resolved to do away with the death penalty.[87] There was, however, significant opposition in the department to abolishing capital punishment. The secretary, T.J. Coyne, was a noted proponent of the ultimate sanction. Coyne was described by Paddy Terry as being unequivocal in his insistence on keeping it on the statute book for all murders, including those committed by subversives, such as the IRA. For such murders he quoted a remark sometimes attributed to Oliver Cromwell, and long used by proponents of the death penalty: 'Stone dead hath no fellow.'[88]

Coyne's successor, Peter Berry, although equally antagonistic towards the IRA, did not have the same strong feeling about the death penalty and supported the Criminal Justice Act of March 1964 which ultimately abolished it except for the murder of gardaí on duty, prison officers, foreign ambassadors and visiting heads of state or heads of government. As Haughey told the Dáil in November 1963, 'persons who murder from political motives will not be deterred by the prospect of imprisonment. Accordingly, the government decided that treason and any form of "political" murder must continue to be punishable by death.'[89] Other murders committed by subversives would be punished with a mandatory forty-year sentence with no possibility of parole. Haughey's original announcement in January 1963 that the government was in the process of preparing legislation to end capital punishment was widely welcomed by organisations as diverse as the Irish Association for Civil Liberties and the Gardaí.[90]

Over twenty years later, in June 1985, Haughey received a letter from the left-wing militant British Labour MP Bill Michie, asking him to support a bill being introduced in the Seanad by the independent senator Shane Ross, to abolish the death penalty in all circumstances and to explain himself if he would not. Haughey replied that it was he, as minister, who had abolished the death penalty for almost all offences, and that, even in the case of the murder of gardaí, the death sentence was invariably commuted. He argued that many people, while opposed to the concept of capital punishment, would 'nevertheless, have reservations about removing this symbolic mark of society's abhorrence for the murder of a garda officer, especially as there is no popular demand for it'.[91] Haughey was not one for taking lessons on any of his legislative achievements, particular from Britain, as his curt reply to Michie made clear. The following week Garda Patrick Morrissey was killed by subversives from the Irish National Liberation Army (INLA) after an armed robbery at the Ardee Labour Exchange in County Louth, bringing the question of the death penalty back to the fore of public opinion. His murderers were sentenced to death, which was later commuted.

The death penalty legislation was another building block in what Haughey considered his ongoing attempt to restructure Ireland's justice system. Another was the Extradition Act of 1965, which Haughey ordered his department to begin preparing in late 1963. As it stood, there was a gentlemen's agreement between Ireland and Northern Ireland on extradition, but Haughey was keen to put the relationship on a firmer footing.[92] This was a significant step in North–South co-operation on the island of

Ireland. It was based on the simple premise that an offender should not be permitted to escape justice by fleeing from the state where the offence had been committed to another jurisdiction. The legislation included a clause that explicitly stated that no suspect could be handed over to the British until they had had an opportunity to challenge the warrant in the Irish High Court.[93] In January 1964, during the Dáil debate on the second stage of the bill, Haughey placed it in an all-Ireland context, thanking the Northern and British authorities in connection with the examination of the extradition legislation. He was confident that 'the enforcement of the criminal law in these islands has been brought to a commendable degree of efficiency while preserving fully the rights of the individual.'[94] While Haughey saw the bill as uncontroversial, and an important updating of the state's criminal law procedures, as indeed it was in the mid-1960s, extradition would, some two decades later, present him with enormous political difficulties when the Irish courts began to narrow the definition of what constituted a political offence. This led to serious discontent among many in Fianna Fáil when various IRA and INLA suspects were extradited to Britain from the Republic of Ireland in the mid-1980s.

By the time Lemass moved him from Justice to Agriculture in October 1964, Haughey had led an ambitious and successful process of legislative reform, which would not have happened at the speed it did if he had not been minister. As Haughey was on his feet one day in the Dáil discussing one of his Bills, the Minister for Finance, Dr James Ryan, came along, prised open the folding doors enough to see inside, saw Haughey in action and said to a number of Justice officials waiting for their minister, 'That fellow will have us legislated out of existence.'[95] In his retirement Haughey described his motivation as one of simply securing justice for ordinary people:

> ... in particular to righting wrongs and establishing a fair, humane legal and penal system. In this I think I was a product of my work-ing-class background, my upbringing and experiences of what I saw happening in the lives of ordinary people around me. My

approach to legislation and reform was always understanding and sympathetic to the human condition, seeking the humanitarian, enlightened, and if possible, common-sense answers to difficult problems and human situations and trying to strike an equitable balance when a conflict of rights arose.[96]

The reference to a fair, humane legal and penal system is instructive as to Haughey's mindset in Justice. His abhorrence of the condemned cell in Mountjoy was matched by a deep unease at the overall conditions for prisoners there and indeed in prisons all across the country. On his move from Justice, the visiting committee of Mountjoy Prison wrote to him to express their thanks for his most commendable efforts in the field of penal reform and assuring him of their 'very deep appreciation of the very considerable improvements you initiated in regard to reform and rehabilitation of prisoners and of your most forward outlook in introducing the new training unit and the new prison hostel'.[97] If prisoner visiting committees were one end of the administration of justice, the Supreme Court lay at the other. At the end of his tenure in Justice, Haughey received handwritten letters from both the Chief Justice, Cearbhall Ó Dálaigh, and Brian Walsh, an associate justice, with whom he was friendly from their days in the Local Defence Forces.[98] Ó Dálaigh told Haughey: 'my office prevents me saying anything about recent changes but allows me to say that the law will gratefully remember your dynamic presence in Justice and will regret your leaving us.'[99] Walsh declared, 'the lawyers will be very sorry at your departure but their loss is the warble flies' gain.'[100] The letters from the highest court in the land, and from the Mountjoy visiting committee were, in their different ways, eloquent testimony to the difference Haughey had made in Justice. His ministerial career had by any definition been a political and administrative success. Agriculture would, however, provide him with a much greater test.

CHAPTER 6

AGRICULTURE

THE QUALITIES THAT MAKE A GOOD DÁIL DEPUTY

Charles Haughey's increasingly high profile in the Dublin North East constituency was not enough to help Fianna Fáil stave off defeat in the May 1963 by-election caused by the death of his old Fine Gael adversary Jack Belton. Belton's brother, Paddy, was the Fine Gael candidate in the by-election and won a comfortable victory over Fianna Fáil's Stan O'Brien, Labour's Denis Larkin, and the independent Seán Loftus. O'Brien polled 13,132 votes, some 3,200 behind Belton, but it was his share of the first preference vote – just 33.4 per cent – that worried Haughey. The figure was some thirteen points below what Fianna Fáil had received in the 1961 general election. Anti-government sentiment, sympathy for Belton, and Fianna Fáil's general historic difficulties in this constituency combined to produce a disappointing result for the party. During the campaign Haughey issued a note to voters: 'If I were asked briefly to list the qualities that make a good Dáil deputy I would say that he should be approachable at all times, with a wide variety of tastes and interests, and a great deal of energy and enthusiasm.'[1] This essentially summed up Haughey himself. Haughey got over the disappointment that summer by taking his normal holiday in the sun with Maureen. The Haugheys generally took two summer holidays during this period. Charles and Maureen usually went to the south of France on their own in late July or early August. Favourite locations were Cannes and Biarritz. They also holidayed with their children in a variety of locations across Ireland in late August. Their 1963 holiday was to Monaco and memorable for the fact that they were received by Prince Rainier and his wife, the former Hollywood actress Grace Kelly, at the royal palace.[2]

At the same time Haughey still had worries about his health. In November 1963 he sought the help of a former boxing instructor to the Gardaí, Tommy Maloney, after his friend Paddy Finnegan 'took one look at my waist-line recently and gave me your card; he decided I needed your help. I am inclined to agree.'[3] Maloney advertised himself as a boxing and physical culture masseur. As far back as 1928, he had written a pamphlet for the Gardaí entitled *The Value of Boxing for Police*. His regime involved skipping, shadow-boxing, ball-punching and exercising, followed by a warm bath, shower, massage and Turkish bath.[4] Haughey's health worries were for the most part based on an issue with kidney stones that plagued him throughout his adult life. He began seeing a consultant urologist, Dermot O'Flynn, in the early 1960s who told him in January 1964 that his last check-up was quite satisfactory and that he did not need anything further done until that November, when he would need an X-ray to check that all was in order.[5] For all Haughey's command of his brief, he was prone to bouts of stress, particularly when it came to big events, which contributed to his ongoing kidney problems.[6] As the decade moved on, Haughey's kidney issues would periodically re-emerge with increased levels of pain and discomfort.

November 1963 also saw Haughey receive a report from Desmond McCreevy on the public image of Fianna Fáil which had as its aim the objective to promote it as a 'centre party with no sectional ties, able to pursue a course across the board which will benefit all the community'.[7] As the revolutionary generation entered its fifth decade of leading the party, McCreevy pointed out that the principal advantage of the present image of the party was that it appeared to be the best of what was available; but he had never been able to formulate a clear concept of what Fianna Fáil actually stood for. He complained to Haughey that no progress had been made on the original aims of the party to unify the country and restore the national language. He painted a picture of a party that was engaging in a 'wheeler dealer' form of government, making agreements here and consolidating trade deals there, without any clear overall image of its ultimate goals. The result was a party and government that was only concerned with the immediate well-being of individual departments and had no idea of what lay ahead in the long term. The lack of planning worried Haughey. He knew from his own electoral problems that there was no guarantee that Fianna Fáil would continue to win elections from an increasingly fickle electorate unless it could present a long-term programme for the country's economic and social advancement.

A lecture entitled 'The Practice of Politics' given by Dr David Thornley of TCD's Department of Political Science at Haughey's old stomping ground of the Fianna Fáil Chomh Chomhairle Atha Cliath in August 1964 painted a grim picture of those who practised politics. In his lecture Thornley had pertinently asked whether Fianna Fáil, Fine Gael and the Labour Party were content to go on electing to the Dáil men who were on average less well educated, less professionally trained, and given less opportunity to acquire specialist knowledge than their continental counterparts with whom they were being brought into closer and more competitive contact. He decried the political system whereby cabinet ministers who were required to adjudicate on the most complex social and economic issues of the state had first of all to negotiate cut-throat constituency jockeying for position. Thornley was also extremely critical of Fianna Fáil's rigid pyramidical democratic organisational structure, which he claimed, quite validly, made it impossible for the top echelons of the party to introduce Dáil candidates from outside the local machine. Adding to Fianna Fáil's woes was a lack of professionalism in the party. It had only just increased its number of full-time staff from two to three and its affiliation fee was a ludicrously low ten shillings. For Thornley, there were immense difficulties in attracting the right calibre of people who might become ministers into politics because of the localism of constituency politics and the tendency to brand as 'carpetbaggers' those who joined local cumainn in order to become TDs. He wanted to know whether 'the constituencies of Ireland want to be represented by the potential legislators of the seventies? Or will they continue to demand of their unfortunate representatives that they should be part-time social workers first, whose ancillary legislative skills are encouraged neither by leisure nor by opportunity?'[8] He finished by stating that there would be a place in the political sun for any party that trained its candidates in the arduous profession of political legislator.

Thornley's lecture caused quite a stir in Fianna Fáil. The Taoiseach, Seán Lemass, ordered a copy of it to be sent to each member of the party's organisation committee. His message was typically blunt. He wanted the members to consider the points raised by Thornley and to decide whether, arising from them, they had any suggestions for changes within the party.[9] Organisational change, however, came slowly in Fianna Fáil, and the party continued to be distrustful of opinion from outsiders. Thornley was certainly one of those. The cumann structure was extremely valuable for Fianna Fáil and the party's tradition in selecting Dáil candidates would remain with the constituency cumainn for decades ahead. Fianna Fáil's organisational structure had served the party well in its first thirty-seven years and those charged with leading it saw no reason to change. Thornley's heretical voice was ultimately ignored. Some six years later, the week after Haughey had been arrested and charged by the Gardaí with conspiracy to import arms, Thornley wrote to him stating that 'no matter how our politics differ I wish you all the best personally. I hope you are making sure to preserve your health in these strenuous times for the years ahead.'[10] It was one of many such letters that sustained Haughey in his darkest hours.

Yet when Haughey was appointed Minister for Agriculture in October 1964, his hours were filled with light and promise. He had made a telling mark in Justice and his family life was fulfilling. Horseracing and hunting had quickly become his favourite pastimes when he moved to Grangemore. He had joined the Ward Union Hunt in 1960 and bought his first horse, Miss Cossie, a five-year-old bay mare, in 1962. She was a daughter of Le Lavandou and a half-sister to the dam of leading American horses Charger's Kin, Fleet Allied and Royal Eiffel. Miss Cossie won six times, first for Major Laurie Gardner (a brother-in-law of Lord Louis Mountbatten), then in the Haughey silks (of black, blue sash and cap), and was eventually listed as a Black Type horse. Miss Cossie bred five winners and became foundation mare at Haughey's stud farm, along with another horse called The Chaser, a mare by Fighting Don, who was a noted sire of sprinters. The Chaser, born a year after Miss Cossie, won eight times in all.[11] By the summer of 1965 Haughey owned three thoroughbred mares, Miss Cossie, The Chaser and Boots II, and had them included in the mailing list of General Stud Book Return Forms in London.

After his initial training in Iris Kellett's equestrian school, Haughey enjoyed both riding to hounds and riding for pleasure with his friend Standish Collen, and continued to do so long into his retirement. Collen ran a successful construction engineering firm for over four decades, with his brother Lyle, and built Haughey's home in Inishvickillane in the mid-1970s. He had a long involvement in the equestrian world and was one of the founders of Ballsbridge Sales (now Tattersalls Ireland). He also chaired Fairyhouse Racecourse and was a member of the Turf Club and the Irish National Hunt Steeplechase Committee. Other Ward Union hunting friends of Haughey's were Eric Craigie, Charlie McCann, Raymond Keogh and Frank Roe. Maureen Haughey was as captivated by horses as her husband and also began to hunt, with the Naas Harriers, in 1964.[12] She later hunted with the Fingal Harriers. Haughey's entry into 'big house' society came through his Ward Union Hunt connections and unquestionably helped the Haughey Boland accountancy practice in the early 1960s, although Haughey himself did not take part in the affairs of the company after first being appointed a minister in 1961.

THE MINISTER AND THE FARMERS

On the morning of 8 October 1964, Paddy Smith resigned as Minister for Agriculture over what he saw as Fianna Fáil's neglect of rural Ireland

and Lemass's prioritisation of industrial needs over those of agriculture. Smith specifically referenced his disagreement with his government colleagues on how to resolve the then seven-week-long building strike in Dublin.[13] Two hours after Lemass accepted Smith's resignation, Charles Haughey was appointed to take his place and that evening went to Áras an Uachtaráin to be presented with his seal of office by President de Valera. Smith saw Lemass's courting of the trade unions, in his efforts to present a united front to the European Economic Community (EEC), as sacrificing rural to urban interests and became the first Fianna Fáil minister to resign over a policy issue.[14] Smith's resignation was the source of much controversy. The United States embassy reported back to Washington that his resignation had caught his colleagues, and the public, by surprise and was principled and courageous.[15] The following week, however, it was telling a different story, maintaining that 'there are indications that Smith's action … may not have been as principled as was initially indicated. Various reports from generally reliable sources echo the theme that a cabinet reshuffle was contemplated and that Smith, along with one or two of his older colleagues, was to make way for the appointment of younger ministers.'[16] This was something that was being widely reported by the newspapers of the time. John Healy, the anonymous 'Backbencher' in the *Irish Times*, noted, 'the young men were preparing to take over with the blessing of Mr. Lemass. The berths were all but allocated.'[17] A later editorial in the same paper maintained that 'it is widely believed that he [Smith] anticipated only by a short time the end of his ministerial existence.'[18] Lemass was reported to have had up to seventeen resignation statements from Smith in his drawer and it was only when he learned that Smith was attempting to get the press to announce his resignation that Lemass himself acted in accepting it.[19] The appointment of Haughey was generally seen as a surprise given his urban Dublin base and the fact that the National Farmers' Association (NFA) was growing increasingly disenchanted with government policy on rural Ireland.

Smith had an acrimonious relationship with the NFA, which had, since its foundation in 1955, aggressively pushed farmers' interests in its dealings with government. For all Smith's disputes with the NFA, his views were those of the farming community in general, and the NFA expressed regret at his resignation – he had given up a position of influence that could have benefited the farming community.[20] Once the trade union movement began to move to centre stage in the new debates on Irish economic and social development in the early 1960s, it began to seem to many farmers that they were in danger of being relegated, if not exactly to the margins of Irish politics, then to at least a more subordinate role than they had traditionally enjoyed. Predictably, they felt threatened and resolved to remind the Lemass government that they were still a formidable power in the land. Moreover, the NFA, and the farming community in general, were extremely wary of the urban Lemass. As Todd Andrews, one of the founders of Fianna Fáil, said of Lemass: 'he had little real rapport with rural Ireland and, considering the amount of travelling he did when building up the Fianna Fáil organisation, he had surprisingly little intimate knowledge of the countryside and its people. He was essentially the Dublin Jackeen with the ready wit and derisive humour so common in the city.'[21] The worry for the farming community was that his son-in-law would be the same.

While the NFA supported the government's planned entry to the EEC, it was deeply worried by Lemass's courtship of the unions, which it saw as a threat to agricultural interests, and it feared that the rural community would be left behind in a rising tide of prosperity. An incident in late 1963 over the withholding of rates in Kilkenny by a proportion of farmers, who had the support of the NFA, epitomised the fraught relationship between the state and the farmer. For Lemass, if the NFA were involved in illegal activities, the government would be compelled to take whatever measures the situation required. He told the leader of the NFA, Rickard Deasy, that the NFA could not expect 'to ride two horses at once and that a wish for closer co-operation with the Department of Agriculture could not be reconciled with a course of action which would make conflict with the government inevitable'.[22]

The withholding of rates in Kilkenny mirrored events of less than three decades earlier that still resonated with many in Fianna Fáil. Kilkenny was a strong farming county and had been one of the Blueshirts' strongholds in the 1930s. Indeed, the very first appearance of the 'Blueshirt' was in Kilkenny in April 1933. Moreover, Kilkenny was at the heart of an anti-rates campaign in the summer and autumn of 1934; the county council, which had a strong anti-Fianna Fáil majority, refused to co-operate fully in the collection of rates. This resulted in the county council being dissolved by order of the Minister for Local Government.[23] Lemass and Smith would not have forgotten such incidents. Lemass declared that a campaign of this kind struck at the very roots of representative government, saying in the Dáil that if 'agitation of this kind could succeed in any degree whatever, or even seem to succeed, or even so develop as being capable of being misrepresented as having succeeded, it could bring the whole administration of local and central government into disorder. This is the road to anarchy and I want to make the Government's position in this regard clear beyond any possibility of misunderstanding. We will not allow it to happen.'[24]

Entering 1964, the Kilkenny rates controversy had still to be resolved but was close to being settled. Linked to it was the fact that the government was in the process of redefining its relations with the agricultural lobby. On 28 January Lemass sent a memorandum to the NFA stating that while his government was concerned at the lack of unity and cohesion among farmers' organisations it did recognise that the NFA was interested in all branches of agriculture, and welcomed 'the prospect of regular and comprehensive discussions with the NFA in connection with the formulation of agricultural policy in the broadest sense, as well as their practical co-operation in respect of specific areas of agriculture … It will be the ordinary practice of the Minister for Agriculture to inform the NFA about pending changes in his department, proposed new schemes … and to consider any representations they may wish to make to him in this regard.'[25]

The road to the negotiating table had been a rocky one, but once there the NFA remained steadfast in its goal of improving the position of its members. Alert to the emerging realities of European integration, the farming community did not view entry to the EEC purely in terms of prices and markets, but took a view of the wider economic and social picture. Farm leaders were only too well aware of the social consequences of underemployment, poverty and mass emigration. Despite a continually fractious relationship with government, and a view of themselves as poor relations when considered alongside the trade unions and the employers, the farming community rightly surmised that it was better to be inside the tent than outside it. Formal recognition by government of the role of farmer organisations in the formulation of policy did not, however, ease the tensions between the two. It was perhaps naive of Lemass to expect that, having been invited to sit at the policy table, the farmers would abandon the confrontational approach that had, in their eyes, won them that position. For all their Blueshirt antecedents, by the early 1960s the NFA had come to be seen by Fianna Fáil ministers as a troublesome but essentially apolitical grouping: ten years earlier they would have regarded them simply as Fine Gaelers on tractors. Once inside the charmed circle of power the NFA would continue its aggressive championing of the cause of farmers and Haughey would be its target.

There had been some significant discontent within Fianna Fáil as to Paddy Smith's performance as Minister for Agriculture. Erskine Childers, then Minister for Transport and Power, told Haughey that the public knew nothing of the progress being made by the party on agricultural matters. He urged Haughey to bring leadership to the department as there was a tremendous leeway to make up to enable agriculture to thrive, and to ensure that people realised that the government was responsible for a 'colossal farm aid programme'.[26] In welcoming Haughey's appointment, another correspondent, the managing director of Waterford Glass, Noel Griffin, remarked, 'No doubt Smith is a great patriot and loyal party member but … as everybody knows he has been disastrous as far as agricultural development and improvement has been concerned.'[27]

Haughey's appointment was welcomed in places as diverse as a yacht in Cannes, a chicken factory in Halifax, and the bureaucracy of the Department of Finance. The English playboy millionaire, Frederic Tinsley, wrote to Haughey from the yacht *Mavala III* stating that the ministry of agriculture was the key to the financial progress of nations and this was particularly the case in Ireland. He advanced the view that when the Common Market was extended, 'you will have still further opportunity to show your varied qualifications, courage and good leadership.'[28] Writing from Yorkshire, John Harrower of the poultry producers Thornberry Brothers told Haughey, 'It is an excellent thing in these days of fast-changing agriculture that an accountant and businessman should be at the helm.'[29] Closer to home, Maurice Doyle of the Department of Finance wrote to Haughey privately congratulating him on his 'elevation to the purple' and, somewhat tongue in cheek, said 'let catharsis commence' in the Department of Agriculture.[30]

Perhaps the most important, and strangest, letter Haughey received on his appointment was written just four days after he had taken office. It came from Rickard Deasy, the president of the NFA. Deasy painted Haughey as a new doctor who had four issues to face: the list of his new patients; prescription; the course of new treatment; and follow-up measures. For Deasy, the patients were either Irish agriculture in general, or the parts that made up Irish agriculture. These patients were ill, he claimed, but with suitable treatment their prognosis was excellent. While the medical jargon was sure to try Haughey's patience, Deasy did make a number of important points. One of these was to get to know J.C. (Jack) Nagle, who had been appointed secretary of the department in 1958, and had long experience of dealing with the NFA. Nagle had been described by the British Ministry of Agriculture as 'at first sight a lugubrious-looking individual – responsibility for maintaining Irish agricultural aspects in the face of European economic grouping from which the Republic is excluded is a daunting one – his gloomy appearance conceals a sharp intellect and a considerable flair for patient and astute negotiation.'[31] From Deasy's perspective, Nagle was extremely shy and highly suspicious but also gifted, able and sincere: 'Loyalty to his minister is his dominating precept ... Don't override his judgement unnecessarily but establish as soon as possible that the Minister decides.'[32] Given the hostility between the NFA and the Department of Agriculture since Fianna Fáil had returned to power in 1957, Haughey must have felt it extraordinary that he was being told how to run his new department by the very organisation that had spent years trying to undermine it.

If that bemused him, however, the next part of Deasy's missive must have raised a smile, and a widening of those famous hooded eyes, when the president of the NFA told him that all the outpatients who would want to visit him were overcharged with emotion and underequipped with basic factual information. In that context the advice from Deasy was to keep these deputations to facts and figures and to find out which ones were worth listening to. Deasy suggested that Haughey let it be known that he was in favour of farmer unity but recognised that this was a matter for the farmer organisations themselves. From its foundation the NFA had been dominated by large farmers, who traditionally supported Fine Gael, although Deasy would later run unsuccessfully for the Labour Party in Tipperary North in the 1969 general election. The smaller Irish Creamery Milk Suppliers Association (ICMSA) was based primarily in Munster and consisted mostly of small dairy farmers who were adamantly against aligning with the larger organisation in any fashion.

Haughey was conscious that Deasy's letter was basically an opening gambit by the NFA to influence his thinking on the thorny relationship between the Fianna Fáil government and the farmers' representatives. In that context he visited the offices of the NFA in his first month in office. He was also acutely aware that he was viewed with suspicion by much of rural Ireland. Haughey was of Dublin, as much as Lemass was, and his hunting pursuits cut little ice with small farmers. However, his many forays to Fianna Fáil cumainn across the length and breadth of the country had given him an awareness of the difficulties of rural Ireland. On his first day at work Haughey met with Nagle, and his new private secretary, Donal Creedon. Over two decades later, on being appointed secretary of the Department of Agriculture in 1988, Creedon recalled that his career only took off on the day he walked into Haughey's office when he became minister. He told the then Taoiseach: 'I still look back on the short spell I spent in that office with a great deal of satisfaction.'[33] Nagle recalled that on that same day Haughey told him that his goal was to raise farm incomes, serve the farmer by having harmonious relations with the farmer organisations, and disabuse people of the notion that he was somehow antithetical to rural Ireland: 'Sure, am I not a farmer myself?'[34]

THE PRACTICE OF POLITICS

Haughey was conscious that most farmers had relatively poor standards of living and low incomes, telling one Dublin city correspondent that very large numbers of farmers 'are living in remote areas with few facilities of any kind, inadequate houses often without water or sanitation and a whole lot of other things the city people take for granted. Very often too the total income is £5 or £6 a week or even less, and in a bad year would sometimes amount to nothing at all. This is not hearsay or exaggeration, it is the actual position as I have seen it time and time again.'[35] The urban–rural divide was something Haughey tackled in one of his first major speeches after becoming minister when he addressed the inaugural meeting of the Dublin Institute of Catholic Sociology debating society in late November. He made the point that the great majority of people who lived in the towns and cities came originally from the land or were only one generation removed from it. He pointed out that the problem of equating rural and urban conditions had been a pressing global issue since Pope John XXIII dealt with it in *Mater et Magistra*, his papal encyclical on Christianity and social progress. For Haughey, if Ireland was to have social justice it could not contemplate a permanent state of affairs where one substantial sector of the people lagged behind in living standards. In that context, he stated, it was the government's aim to bring to farmers the facilities that were available to the urban community. These included good housing and amenities, opportunities for cultural development and, above all, comprehensive educational opportunities for their children.[36]

Haughey complimented the new generation of farmers coming through in Ireland, who were trained in Macra na Feirme, and of whom any country would be proud. That year's Macra na Tuaithe young farmer of the year competition was held as normal in Dublin, but also spawned allegations of the government condoning the urban–rural bias. One of Haughey's correspondents, Elizabeth O'Brien, a Fianna Fáil member from Athlone, suggested that the competition be held in the west of Ireland as it was her experience that these functions are 'in the nature of a Roman holiday for the citizens of Dublin whose comment on the bogmen assembled in the luxurious settings of the Gresham Hotel are not very complimentary.[37] In disagreeing with O'Brien, Haughey replied that he had attended the competition for many years, and was always impressed with the self-confidence of the finalists, who were never overawed by the occasion which, as a national function, was better held in the capital city.[38] While the contestants might well have enjoyed their day out in the big city, there was no doubt that the friction between agricultural and industrial interests was a growing one in the Ireland of the mid-1960s.

In November 1964, across the river from the Gresham Hotel, in the equally salubrious surroundings of the Shelbourne Hotel, Haughey brought a party of friends to celebrate the fortieth anniversary of Seán Lemass's first election to the Dáil. Lemass had famously won a by-election for Sinn Féin in Dublin South in November of 1924. He had married Kathleen Hughes three months earlier, and the dinner in the Shelbourne commemorated both events.[39] For a cold Monday night in November, it was a gala affair with dancing to Earl Gill and his orchestra, and a dinner of roast Norfolk turkey and Limerick ham. As the night was organised by Lemass's Dublin South Central constituency organisation, Haughey was happy to enjoy it, as Lemass's son-in-law, in the company of his wife and friends, without, for once, having to make a speech. He was at this stage reading the report of the Warren Commission into the assassination of President John Fitzgerald Kennedy, having received a copy from the chargé d'affaires of the US embassy in Dublin to whom he described it as 'a truly remarkable work and of great personal as well as historic interest.[40] Haughey had met Kennedy when the US president visited Ireland just fifteen months earlier in late June 1963. As Minister for Justice, Haughey was on hand to meet Kennedy on the tarmac when his plane landed in Dublin and he had overall political charge of security for the visit.[41]

One of the issues that characterised this period of Haughey's political life was his staunch defence of the practice of politics. This was privately on show in early December 1964 when he wrote in stern terms to Fr Pearse O'Higgins SJ, rector of St Ignatius College in Galway, to chide him for comments in the newspapers which claimed that some politicians were inarticulate and some downright ignorant. If the reported comments were true, then O'Higgins should be ashamed of himself, suggested an indignant Haughey, demanding to know why there was this continual attempt to denigrate politicians: 'Recollections of inept, mumbling, sermons sat through Sunday after Sunday tempts me to retort that one could say the same with a great deal more justification about the clergy.'[42] In wondering whether such attacks on politicians served any useful purpose, Haughey made the point that politicians had to train themselves for their profession while carrying on their ordinary business in life at the same time.

Haughey had relinquished his position in Haughey Boland when he became Minister for Justice three years earlier, but was actively farming hens on his forty-five-acre farm at Grangemore. In July 1965, the *Tatler* magazine journalist Muriel Bowen sent Haughey a copy of a *Financial Times* report in which he had recounted to the Dáil that his two thousand hens had made a profit of £840 the previous year after one TD, Labour's Michael Pat Murphy, lamented that there were hens dying all over Ireland and they were dying in debt. Bowen's gentle comment, 'I expect it has made some of your colleagues hopping mad', was met with a pithy 'There were some comments.'[43] Haughey began farming hens in 1962 and by 1965 he had about two thousand hens and 180 cocks. The eggs his hens produced were sent to the hatcheries of Knocknagarm-Sykes Ltd in Sallynoggin, a branch of F. & G. Sykes Ltd, a leading poultry breeders' company in Britain. At Sallynoggin, the eggs were hatched and 90 per cent of the one-day-old chicks were exported to Northern Ireland. Haughey told the rather niche agricultural magazine *Pigs and Poultry* that eggs could be a very good business but that the right type of housing and equipment were needed. His flock was housed in a modern, prefabricated building with a temperature-controlled unit and various other amenities required for successful poultry-keeping. Haughey's flock was tended to by Tom Keilty, whose father, Christy Keilty, was the groom for his horses. Haughey's hens, which produced 202 eggs each in the laying year, were Hybrid 3 hens, described by *Pigs and Poultry* as 'world record holders for profit'. The magazine summed up Haughey's farm as a well-conducted business venture, nothing out of the ordinary but an efficiently run, intensively kept flock of breeding birds which anyone with the necessary capital and initiative could undertake successfully: 'We regard it as a practical demonstration of good husbandry.'[44]

Haughey began 1965 preparing for a week-long tour to London, Brussels, Bonn and Berlin from 25 January to 2 February. Among those he met on this trip were Fred Peart, the British Minister for Agriculture, Fisheries and Food; Leslie Kirkham, the General Secretary of Oxfam; Sicco Mansholt, the European Commissioner for Agriculture; and Willy Brandt, the leader of the Social Democratic Party, and later Chancellor, of West Germany. On his return he told Mansholt that he looked 'forward to the time when circumstances will make it possible for Ireland to play its full part in the development of a united Europe by becoming a member of the Community'.[45] In Berlin Haughey visited the famous Internationale Grüne Woche, the agricultural and food trade fair, and later thanked Brandt for his hospitality, noting, 'My visit to this bastion of freedom and symbol of the future reunification of Germany was for me a truly great occasion.[46] Membership of the EEC, Ireland's place in the process of European integration, and the reunification of Germany were all issues in which Haughey strove to play a key role over the following two and a half decades.

The day after writing to Mansholt, Haughey went to Belfast to take part in a debate at Queen's University Belfast on 'The Future of Irish Politics'. He again rolled out his defence of those practising politics, noting that 'politics is a science and like any other science it exists to serve the people'.[47] He alluded to his recent trip to Europe; he could not help feeling a little envious of what was being achieved there through the wisdom and skill of politicians who were overcoming the animosities of centuries, abolishing past dissensions and achieving new levels of harmony and co-operation. He pointed out that in Europe the ingenuity of economists and technocrats, spurred on by political ideals, was providing acceptable and workable solutions to what at one time would have been regarded as insoluble fiscal and economic problems. There was no reason why this could not happen in Ireland as well. He again committed the government to exploring every possible opportunity for useful co-operation between both parts of the island of Ireland. Haughey ended his speech on an optimistic note, maintaining that as long as all politicians used their combined experience, wisdom and intelligence to counteract prejudice, ignorance and low living standards, the future of Irish politics was brighter and more hopeful than it had been for a long time. These hopes would soon be dashed in the maelstrom of the eruption of the troubles in Northern Ireland just four short years later.

Three days after that debate in Queen's, the Northern Ireland Minister for Agriculture, Harry West, came south to dine with Haughey at his home in Grangemore. West was a progressive farmer from Fermanagh who was the first in the county to acquire a Ferguson International tractor, with pneumatic tyres, and a Ransome mechanical threshing mill. The West household was also among the first in the county to have its own electrical lighting plant.[48] His farming background and general knowledge of the sector made him extremely popular with northern farmers. Haughey was keen to learn about both West's farming techniques and his relationship with the farming organisations. Haughey's European trip just a few weeks earlier strongly influenced his growing belief that Irish, and indeed British, entry to the EEC could well negate the border and that it would become irrelevant in the new European structures that both countries were keen to be part of.[49] West and his wife, Maureen, stayed in Haughey's home at Grangemore, and West attended the Ireland vs England rugby international the following day in which Ireland won a dour struggle 5–0.[50] Haughey did not attend. While both de Valera and Lemass were avid rugby fans, Haughey never warmed to the sport. Like most northside Dubliners, rugby simply was not his sport and he could never summon himself to go to Lansdowne Road. After the visit to Haughey's home, West wrote to thank him, stating that the 'company was delightful, the hospitality overwhelming' and the two arranged to meet later in the year, which they did the following month, and again in May after Fianna Fáil had been returned to office in the April general election.[51]

West was not the only Unionist politician with whom Haughey enjoyed good relations in this period. On 24 January 1966 the Northern

Ireland Minister for Commerce, Brian Faulkner, gave an address at an American Chamber of Commerce lunch in Dublin, at which Haughey was present, and where, departing from his original script, he commented that the long distance politically from Dublin to Belfast would appear to have shortened.[52] In the course of his remarks Faulkner also talked of politicians' interests outside politics. Feeling that he had not been specific as to what he meant he sent a handwritten note to Haughey stating that people who had no interest in hunting may have wondered what he was talking about and that he hoped he had not embarrassed Haughey. More interesting perhaps was the fact that Faulkner thanked Haughey for his thoughtfulness in showing up: 'it was reassuring for me to have a friend at my right hand.'[53] Faulkner was an avid hunter and a regular attendee at the Dublin Horse Show. He had also hunted with Haughey at the Ward Union Hunt in Dublin. In his reply, Haughey told him not to worry about the reference to hunting and that he was glad to hear Faulkner's excellent account of the efforts 'which you are making up there in the industrial development field'.[54]

Just before the April 1965 election, on St Patrick's Day, Haughey gave a major address on Anglo-Irish relations at the Irish Club in London. The audience included the British Prime Minister, Harold Wilson. Haughey once again addressed two of his major themes: Irish men and women living in Britain should come home to build a modern, new, energetic Ireland; and politics was a noble profession. He began his usual defence of politics by saying that while it would be inappropriate for him to comment on Wilson's difficulties brought about by his narrow parliamentary majority of three, 'We politicians, on whatever side of the fence we may be, are entitled to have fellow-feeling for each other and as professionals to appreciate each other's problems and difficulties.'[55] Haughey's general message was that Ireland wished to go forward into the future with Britain in a spirit of mutual co-operation; both countries could collaborate to their mutual advantage, and in that they would be reflecting their people. It was an important speech for Haughey, speaking as he was on fundamental relations between Britain and Ireland, but it was relatively vague and bland, not committing itself to anything concrete. Things heated up considerably after he had finished, however, during Wilson's toast. He began by claiming, to much laughter, that he suspected he represented more Irishmen through his constituency of Huyton, near Liverpool, in the House of Commons than Haughey did in the Dáil, and that moreover they all voted for him.[56] Then, in a toast to the 'two islands', Wilson suggested tripartite talks between himself, Lemass and the Northern Ireland Prime Minister, Terence O'Neill. Wilson's off-the-cuff remarks caused much surprise as Britain had stayed out of any North–South dialogue and O'Neill had made clear his opposition to any tripartite meetings. Lemass, pragmatic as ever, interpreted the comments as a matter of goodwill between Britain and the Republic. There was some debate in British diplomatic circles as to whether Wilson, notably cautious in all political matters, would be making such statements, post-prandial or otherwise, without full and deliberate consideration.[57] Coming just two months after Lemass's famous visit to Stormont to meet Terence O'Neill on 14 January, it was, nevertheless, odd for Wilson to suggest tripartite meetings. Haughey was a strong supporter of the Lemass–O'Neill meeting, but he had not known about it in advance. He was, however, clearly committed to greater co-operation between the two parts of the island.

REJUVENATING FIANNA FÁIL

Haughey's St Patrick's Day speech came a week after the Dáil had been dissolved. Labour's Eileen Desmond had kept her late husband's seat in the Mid Cork by-election held on 10 March. Fianna Fáil's failure to win the seat led Lemass to go to the country before Desmond had even taken her seat. He had, in fact, been thinking of an election for quite some time and had declared in advance that if Desmond beat the Fianna Fáil candidate, Flor Crowley, it would precipitate a dissolution of the Dáil. This, as Lemass's biographer John Horgan points out, was something of a short-odds political bet. In three of the previous five by-elections, the deceased TD's widow had taken the seat, and in a fourth, it had been won by the deceased's son.[58] Desmond duly took the seat, with Crowley polling credibly, having topped the poll at the first count. Both would be elected in the following month's general election, as would a third candidate in that by-election, Fine Gael's Donal Creed. Crowley would go on to become one of Haughey's most vociferous supporters in the 1970s and 1980s. Haughey had canvassed for him in that by-election and they became firm friends.[59]

When Lemass called the election he appointed Haughey Fianna Fáil's director of elections and the party faced the April election with relative confidence. Worrying economic indicators in relation to balance of payments difficulties, and demands from the unions on income policies, had not yet become public. Relations between the government and the unions, the farmers and business interests were stable. That state of affairs would not last long but it held firm until after the election. The opposition was also mired in difficulty. Labour had once again declared it would not enter coalition, making it more or less irrelevant in the contest. Fine Gael was deeply divided over Declan Costello's 'Just Society' document which, with its rallying call for much larger involvement by the state in society, many saw as a signpost for the party's future. Many others, particularly in the senior echelons of the party, were very much less enthusiastic about the 'Just Society'. As a policy document, much less a manifesto, it had not even been finished when Lemass called the election. It did, however, become party policy for that election as Fine Gael had not really developed any other policies while in opposition. The 'Just Society' was officially launched on 18 March, but Fine Gael's leadership was lacklustre in the extreme in endorsing it as a policy on which to campaign. The party leader, James Dillon, told the audience at the shambolic launch, at which not enough copies of the document were available for the journalists attending, that Fine Gael would 'rely on private enterprise. We are a private enterprise party.' As Collins and Meehan pithily point out in their history of Fine Gael: 'In two short sentences he contradicted the content of a manifesto that advocated greater state involvement.'[60]

This was something Fianna Fáil quickly picked up on. Haughey, channelling his inner Abraham Lincoln, maintained that a 'house divided itself cannot stand and the Fine Gael party is now clearly and dramatically divided within itself.[61] He was particularly scathing about the 'Just Society', complaining that it had all the hallmarks of a document put together by a group of students who had flicked through their textbooks picking the bits that appealed to them and strung them together without any attempt to relate them to present circumstances. Notwithstanding his own urban background, he charged that Fine Gael had handed over control of the party to a city centre clique of back-room theorists who were out of touch with the vast majority of people in the country. In that context, it was no wonder, he claimed, that 'an unrealistic, irrelevant, textbook type of policy statement should have been foisted on the Fine Gael party, the great majority of whom haven't the faintest idea of what it is all about and certainly wouldn't approve of it if they did.'[62]

Fianna Fáil, meanwhile, was far more united in its overarching objective of staying in power and ran on the straightforward slogan 'Let Lemass Lead On'. Candidate selection was becoming an increasing problem for the party. Lemass, no more than the younger members of his party, was anxious to freshen up the ranks of candidates. This was easier said than done, and many of those targeted by Lemass and Haughey for deselection adamantly refused to go. In the cabinet, Aiken and MacEntee would not even contemplate stepping aside.[63] On the backbenches, Martin Corry in Cork, a TD since June 1927, and then aged seventy-four, was another who refused to go. After he was re-elected for the thirteenth time Corry wrote to Haughey complaining that Fianna Fáil headquarters had done everything to undermine him by adding a fourth candidate to the ticket in his constituency of Cork North East, which had cost the party a third seat. He luridly described the party as using 'contemptible gangster methods' including sending 'thugs and women of easy virtue' to support other candidates outside the polling booth. He bemoaned seeing men 'with short service, one-third of my brains and ability and one tenth of my common sense put in charge of departments to mess them around'. Corry's view that after thirty-eight years' service he was entitled to better might have received a more sympathetic hearing had he not ended his letter by telling Haughey, 'we here in Cork have a way of dealing with this kind of stuff.[64] Haughey was not easily intimidated, but even he must have been slightly bemused by this reference, given that Corry had a fearsome reputation within Fianna Fáil from over forty years earlier, when he was reputed to be the chief executioner of the IRA's Cork No. 1 Brigade, responsible for at least twenty-seven killings between 1920 and 1922.[65] In Haughey's reply he pleaded ignorance of the more colourful of Corry's charges and said that he was willing to meet the veteran TD at any time.

Haughey and Lemass had more success in the neighbouring constituency of Mid Cork where both Seán MacCarthy and Con Meaney stood down to be replaced by Meaney's son, Thomas, and the by-election candidate, Flor Crowley. Further north, another veteran of the revolutionary period, Dan Breen, was also persuaded to step aside in Tipperary. For Haughey it was simply a fact that the time had 'now come to get younger men going forward in all the constituencies'.[66] The manner of persuasion, however, left many underwhelmed at its indirectness, and indeed anxious as to their futures. MacCarthy, for instance, wrote to Haughey that it had been conveyed to him, through Senator Ted O'Sullivan, that Fianna Fáil headquarters wanted him to retire from the Dáil. While open to what he described as the 'very strong hint', MacCarthy pointed out that it would cost him dearly as he had no alternative source of income, and many cumainn members were asking him to stay on. He ended by saying he would do what was best for the party.[67]

Breen, given his celebrity-like status in the party, was a more difficult case. He had told Lemass prior to the election that he was retiring from public life but later complained that at the Tipperary South selection convention in Cahir he had been railroaded by Haughey, who was acting as chairman. He told Lemass that this was not the first, or even second, mean and low thing he had had done to him, but he had overlooked them for the good of the country, and the party. He ended on a rather ominous note: 'This is farewell. May your supposed friends never railroad you and double-cross you. Look out. Don't put your full trust in them.'[68] Lemass sent Breen's letter to Haughey, because he had been mentioned in it, saying that he had tried and failed to translate it. He suggested

Haughey write a placatory letter to Breen, as he himself had done.[69] Haughey took Lemass's advice. He told Breen that he had acted impartially throughout the convention and had in no way tried to influence the delegates. He was very sorry that 'you should be angry about anything I did as I have had nothing but regard and admiration for you since I first read your book at a very early age … In fact I opened the proceedings by paying tribute to yourself. I asked the delegates to give you a standing ovation and they responded eagerly to my invitation to do so.'[70] Breen, however, was not easily placated, telling Haughey that he credited him with more brain matter than to try any tricks on the day of the convention.[71] Whatever about the merits of Breen's complaints, Haughey and Lemass were relatively successful in their attempts to inject youth onto the ticket. First-time Fianna Fáil TDs elected included Flor Crowley in Mid Cork, David Andrews in Dún Laoghaire–Rathdown, Ben Briscoe in Dublin South West, Bobby Molloy in Galway West, and Pearse Wyse in Cork Borough. All would, to some extent, become players in the leadership battles Haughey faced within Fianna Fáil in the early 1980s.

Beyond these contretemps with prospective candidates, Haughey also had to endure the embarrassment of British envelopes being used by Fianna Fáil in the middle of a government Buy Irish campaign. This was brought to his attention by a sympathetic political supporter who was a manager in a Dublin envelope factory and who bemoaned having received a personal appeal from Haughey posted in an envelope produced in Hemel Hempstead, England. He then rather plaintively said that his company could have supplied similar quality envelopes at a cheaper price.[72] A chastened Haughey replied that, while he did not even see the envelopes and it was too bad that it happened, it 'was certainly a very serious mistake'.[73]

Fianna Fáil won an extra two seats at the general election, taking half of all the 144 seats in the Dáil, thus ensuring that it stayed in power. Haughey once again topped the poll in Dublin North East, polling 8,566 first preferences, and was elected on the first count. He was, however, humbled by the fact that Fianna Fáil only took two of the five seats on offer, with Eugene Timmons losing out to Labour's Denis Larkin. The

1965 Oireachtas elections saw Haughey's great adversary of the 1980s, Garret FitzGerald, enter public life when he ran for the Seanad on the Industrial and Commercial panel. Having voted for Fianna Fáil in 1961, FitzGerald reverted to his Fine Gael heritage, writing to Haughey that while he could not reasonably look for a high preference he hoped that 'you will at least consider me less undesirable than some of the other Fine Gael candidates!'[74] Haughey replied that he was 'very sad to see you going over to the enemy, particularly in view of the fact that I tried at one time to involve you in our affairs' but realised that one's family background and personal friendships had a strong influence in such matters and in that context he had no hesitation in treating FitzGerald as the 'least undesirable'.[75] FitzGerald was duly elected, thus beginning a rivalry that would last over two and a half tumultuous decades.

CONFLICT

Lemass reappointed Haughey Minister for Agriculture, and Haughey was welcomed back by his department secretary, Jack Nagle, who, writing from the abominable rain, wind and lightning of Rome, hoped 'things won't be too bad and that we don't try you too much'.[76] His friends Brian Lenihan and Donogh O'Malley were also appointed to cabinet. Lenihan continued as Minister for Justice, having taken that position when Haughey moved to Agriculture. O'Malley was appointed Minister for Health. As far back as 1966, Tim Pat Coogan described Lemass's last cabinet as the coming of the men in mohair suits and painted Haughey as the epitome of such men. He was a 'strange blend of confidence and uncertainty, concerned for his image and sensitive to newspaper commentary. He hunts, is a bon viveur and a generous host.'[77] Coogan, at this stage deputy editor of the *Evening Press*, and a commentator on Ireland for various international outlets, had written to Haughey in November 1964 seeking an interview for a book on contemporary Ireland, the tone of which was intended to be 'serious-popular'.[78] Haughey replied that he would be delighted to see Coogan and do anything he could to help. Coogan duly thanked him as one of his interviewees in the acknowledgements in the book *Ireland Since the Rising*. What Haughey thought of the book is unclear, but he later claimed that he never wore a mohair suit himself, having more taste than that.[79]

Whatever about their attire, Haughey, Lenihan and O'Malley socialised together in Dublin's more fashionable nightspots in this period, such as Groome's Hotel, the Shelbourne, the Russell, and the Hibernian Hotel.[80] Jammet's French haute cuisine restaurant was a particular favourite of Haughey's until it closed in 1967. He dined there, not only with the so-called three musketeers – himself, Lenihan and O'Malley – but also with his friends the architects Arthur Gibney and Sam Stephenson, and literary luminaries such as Micheál Mac Liammóir and Hilton Edwards.[81]

Nagle's quiet optimism in welcoming Haughey back to Agriculture was unfounded. Haughey endured a trying eighteen months, leading the department in a constant struggle with the farming organisations against a worsening economic background. He was immediately enmeshed in controversy when he attended a dinner in Dublin of the Irish Jersey Cattle Society in early May. At the dinner, the guest speaker, Eric Boston, an Oxfordshire cattle breeder and president of the Jersey Cattle Society of the UK, made a joke about an unmarried mother who sought to register her twins in the names of Harold Wilson Smith and George Brown Smith. This led to Haughey walking out of the dinner on the grounds that he could not remain in view of an attack on ministers of a country with such close relations with Ireland. He was complimented for his action by numerous people, including his British ministerial counterpart, Fred Peart, who told him that it was 'good to know that we have firm friends on your side of the water' and enclosed a clipping of the incident from the *Daily Telegraph*.[82] Peart had visited Ireland the previous week and enjoyed a friendly relationship with Haughey, who had sent him a bottle of Paddy Irish whiskey through the Irish embassy when Peart returned to Britain. They had been appointed ministers for agriculture within two days of each other the previous October. Haughey replied that while the incident was unfortunate, he had no hesitation in acting as he did and would have done so even if he had never met 'the Prime Minister and liked him so much as a person'.[83] Apologies came from Boston himself, who reported that he was deeply shocked and lamented that he had been told it was a social occasion, a funny story would be appropriate, and politicians were there to be shot at. Boston's host, the president of the Jersey Cattle Society, Garrett Tyrell, regretted a 'story which, though kindly meant, turned out to be in doubtful taste'.[84] Haughey told Tyrell that he had hoped to leave quietly and without any fuss and that his respect for the society and its members was undiminished.[85] He was somewhat more blunt with Boston, stating that his speech had placed him in a very awkward situation: the prime minister of Great Britain, and all his ministers, were, by virtue of their high office, entitled to and must receive the utmost respect at any public function in Ireland: 'I could not appear to condone anything in the nature of a slight upon them. For this I felt I should leave the dinner … My sole concern was to act with propriety as a member of the Irish government.'[86] Haughey's action was complimented by the *Irish Times* journalist Liam MacGabhainn, who told him that he often shuddered at English wit, to which Haughey acidly replied, 'I don't think these people will ever learn.'[87] Another correspondent, the auctioneer Henry Wilson, saluted Haughey's 'moral courage to defend the leaders of another country with whom you have worked for the betterment of both communities.'[88] The incident was a small but telling example of the seriousness with which Haughey took his office, and his understanding of the need for good relations with the British government, particularly when the Fianna Fáil government was striving to forge an Anglo-Irish trade agreement. It also stands in stark contrast to the view that Haughey was intrinsically anti-British.

Of far more importance to Haughey at this stage was an internal Fianna Fáil row about Jack Lynch's first budget as Minister for Finance. On Lynch's second day as Minister on 22 April 1965, he received an ominous memo from his redoubtable secretary, T.K. Whitaker. It painted a grim picture of balance of payments problems and decreasing external reserves. The solution was to cut; and these cuts had to be real. Facing into his first budget, Lynch, as his biographer Dermot Keogh notes, was 'given the clear message to cut and make more cuts'.[89] The main target for the Department of Finance was to cut the capital budget from £111 million to £100 million. The government accepted this figure in principle, but Lemass fatefully decided that the specifics would be decided between the Department of Finance and the other departments. There had long been a difficult relationship between the departments of Finance and Agriculture with the latter, as Mary Daly points out, adopting a rather semi-detached approach to economic planning.[90] Their own attempts at planning, the so-called 'Brown Book', vastly overstated what agricultural output might achieve in the mid-1960s and they then decided to ignore their own targets. All this was anathema to Whitaker.

On 27 April a revision in the Department of Agriculture's budget for capital services involving a cut of £350,000 was agreed and the Department of Finance directed that Haughey announce the revision in his estimates speech to the Dáil two days later. He refused, saying that the announcement was a matter for the Department of Finance, although traditionally such announcements, even of bad news, were made by ministers of the relevant department. Haughey's uncooperative attitude has been described by Keogh as an act of gross insubordination.[91] Perhaps it was, but it can also be viewed as an example of a strong minister standing up to bureaucrats in the Department of Finance who had long been used to getting their way. Politically, Haughey was in a difficult position given the rumblings across rural Ireland about how agricultural interests had been left behind in the growing prosperity of the 1960s. The NFA, notwithstanding its privileged access to the department, was becoming increasingly agitated. A budget that cut agricultural spending, and one that a Dublin minister had agreed to, was viewed by Haughey as potentially ruinous to his relationship with the farming community. Lynch's budget speech claimed that the estimated current expenditure on agriculture would be close to £33.7 million – £3.6 million more than actual expenditure the previous year – and that the improvement in farmers' incomes in 1964 should continue for the rest of 1965 and beyond.[92] Much of this was based on the idea coming from the Department of Agriculture that the volume of agricultural production was expected to be higher than in previous years. This was more wishful thinking than prophecy. The contents of Lynch's speech, when it came to agriculture, were relatively bland, and based on a very optimistic reading of Irish agricultural potential.

An earlier draft of his speech, however, spawned Haughey's gravest crisis since entering cabinet. On Friday 7 May, four days before Lynch's budget speech, Haughey and Lemass met to discuss what Lynch proposed to say. Haughey was very unhappy about the tone of the speech, and a specific reference in it, which he wanted removed, and told Lemass so. On the following Monday he sent Lemass 'a final appeal with regard to the reference in Jack Lynch's budget speech which we talked about on Friday. I thought a great deal about it over the weekend and am more unhappy than ever about it. As you know, I have no time for people who resign or, worse still, threaten to do so without meaning it. There is in fact, therefore, nothing effective that I can do. If the announcement is made, I shall be placed in a very difficult position. I cannot for the life of me see the necessity for it.'[93]

It is unclear what this reference in an earlier draft was, and the speech itself had nothing in it that could have embarrassed Haughey. The language Haughey used in his letter was ambiguous enough to be read as if he would resign. It could also, however, be interpreted as meaning that he would be desperately unhappy if the speech went ahead as was proposed. In any event it would seem that he got his way and the political bombshell that would have erupted at his potential resignation was avoided. His relationship with Lynch, however, was damaged irreparably. From Lynch's perspective it was bad enough that Haughey would not follow protocol in announcing cuts in his own department, thus implicitly undermining Lynch's political position; it was much worse for a minister to threaten to resign over the contents of the budget speech of the Minister for Finance, whether or not that minister thought it merited. It was, however, symptomatic of the increasingly evident lack of unity in Lemass's cabinet as his tenure as party leader and Taoiseach was coming to an end. Many of his ministers knew it and were becoming more assertive in their own briefs. Haughey was clearly one of these. His willingness to exert influence on Lemass by threatening to resign, no matter how subtle that threat, was indicative of how he saw himself within Fianna Fáil as a leadership contest moved ever closer.

CHAPTER 7

OF FARMERS AND ELECTIONS

THE REPRESENTATIVE OF RURAL IRELAND

When he became Minister for Agriculture, Charles Haughey had a reputation in the civil service for being dynamic, hardworking and difficult. Brendan O'Donnell, who had replaced Michael Creedon as Haughey's private secretary in 1965, recalled that on first meeting Haughey the new minister told him, 'The first priority is my re-election; second is make sure that you look after sympathetically representations from Fianna Fáil TDs and Senators and be courteous to the Fine Gael people; and after that if you've any time left look after the department.'[1] O'Donnell struck up a reasonable rapport with his minister, who he described as not being the easiest person to work with: 'He'd fuck you out of it quickly enough.' He also had a quick temper and an expectation that people would do their work without being congratulated for it. O'Donnell would later follow Haughey to the Department of Finance until Haughey was sacked in 1970, then to Health and Social Welfare when Haughey returned to cabinet in 1977, and finally to the office of Taoiseach in 1979.

Rural Ireland went through a process of significant change during Haughey's tenure as Minister for Agriculture. He spent much time cultivating the small farmer class, especially in the west of Ireland. In June 1965, a month after Lynch's difficult first budget, a government social welfare bill introduced by the Minister for Social Welfare, Kevin Boland, brought in a new method of assessing income from land by reference to its rateable valuation rather than actual income. It was designed to be of benefit to the thousands of smallholders in the congested areas and became popularly known as the 'farmers' dole'. Fianna Fáil was competing with the Labour Party for the vote of the rural/cottier-class throughout the country and this was part of its appeal to that particular cohort of voters.

Another significant aspect of the changing social and economic undercurrents running through Ireland in the mid-1960s was the growth of various meat factories run by groups such as Purcell Brothers, headed by Seamus Purcell, who would later introduce Haughey to the Libyan dictator, Colonel Gaddafi, and the Anglo-Irish meat group run by Larry Goodman that was originally called L. Goodman and Sons.[2] Haughey was first introduced to Goodman by the veteran Louth politician, and Minister for External Affairs, Frank Aiken. Aiken, although he abhorred Haughey, wrote a confidential note to him in January 1965 saying that he understood that Goodman, a fellow Louth man, had been appointed Chairman of the National Executive of the Livestock Association and that Haughey could be assured of Goodman's 'goodwill and support'.[3] In his brief reply, also marked confidential, Haughey stated that he was glad to have Aiken's assurance about Goodman and looked forward to dealing with him.[4] Some two and a half decades later, allegations about Goodman's relationship with Haughey would play no small part in Haughey's downfall as Taoiseach and leader of Fianna Fáil.

This was also the era of the beginning of the modern shopping centre. Ben Dunne Senior bought a huge site in Cornelscourt in south Dublin in 1965 and opened the Cornelscourt Centre, Ireland's first shopping centre, the following year. It was a manifestation of a changing Ireland; people drove there from all over the country to do their shopping.[5]

Parallel with these trends was the inexorable decline of market towns like Charlestown in Mayo, as chronicled by John Healy in his famous book *The Death of an Irish Town*.[6] Healy and Haughey had a thirty-year friendship which lasted from the early 1960s to Healy's death in January 1991. The three musketeers, Haughey, Lenihan and O'Malley, were Healy's private source for much of the gossip about Fianna Fáil that filled his 'Backbencher' column.[7] Healy was enamoured from an early stage and often referred to Haughey in his column as 'The Golden Boy'.[8] 'Backbencher' was started in the *Sunday Review* by the duo of John Healy and Ted Nealon. When the column moved to the *Irish Times* Healy became its sole author. Nealon later joined RTÉ before eventually going into politics, becoming a Fine Gael TD and junior minister. Healy assiduously cultivated the three musketeers as his inside track to political gossip, and even took Haughey fishing with him in Mayo on one occasion. He was also a guest of Haughey in both Grangemore and Abbeville. As much of the gossip in the 'Backbencher' column was accurate, it suited both gossiper and gossippee very well, although other cabinet members were less enamoured of the practice.[9] This was particularly the case over the issue of the leadership of Fianna Fáil, which began to circulate well in advance of Lemass's decision to step down in November 1966.

While Haughey was not averse to using Healy as a vehicle to advance his own cause, he was also careful not to overuse him. Their friendship was genuine, although in his column Healy exaggerated his relationship with Haughey by implication; he was in fact closer to Donogh O'Malley. Healy fancied himself as a confidant of Haughey's and was in the habit of sending him long and detailed letters of advice, much of which it seems Haughey took with a grain of salt. During Haughey's tenure in Agriculture, Healy advocated that he hire the CIÉ's head of publicity and public relations, Tim Dennehy; the department needed 'a bloody good professional', and this would have the twofold advantage that 'you get a good PR and you get a good long-stop and adviser in the matter of your own campaign.'[10] As it turned out, Dennehy did not leave CIÉ until 1970, when he set up his own public relations firm. The previous year he had played an important co-ordinating role when public relations officers from state and semi-state bodies were sent to embassies around the world to disseminate the Irish government's viewpoint after the outbreak of the

Troubles in Northern Ireland.[11] The reference in the letter to Haughey's own campaign was yet another pointer to the fact that Haughey very much had his eye on the leadership of Fianna Fáil.

Among Healy's other advice was that Haughey should ignore the rumour factory, keep his temper, or at least lose it in a calculated way at a calculated time, and that since he had been moved out of the political jet set he should stay out of it and tour the country. In this way he could see the Labour Party's Michael Pat Murphy's Sherkin Island dairy farm and visit the Aran Islands – islands had a romance about them, and newspapers were suckers for island stories. Healy's knowledge of Cork geography was somewhat awry as Murphy's stomping ground was further north and west, around Schull in particular, whereas Sherkin Island and Baltimore were more Fine Gael territory.[12] Rather more crudely, Healy also suggested that Haughey chase the women's vote, rehashing an old line commonly used by cynical urban journalists: 'Fish is food. Food is one of the prime ingredients of a news story. The three C's: Crime, Cunt and Cookery. Housewives are interested in food. CJH should be interested in the housewife.'[13] There was certainly a kernel of truth in the increasing importance of the women's vote in Irish politics and Haughey, as he had shown in much of his progressive legislation in Justice, was in prime position to take advantage of it.

For Haughey, however, a greater worry than the women's vote was the increasing militancy of the farmers' organisations. The signing of the Anglo-Irish Free Trade Agreement in December 1965, which came into effect the following July, did nothing to quell farmer resentment at what they continued to see as the sacrificing of rural interests to urban ones. The agreement was another step in the opening of the economy to trade and investment that had begun with the First Programme for Economic Expansion and the Fianna Fáil government's decision to seek entry to the EEC in 1961. Since 1964, Irish goods exported to Britain had been subject to a 15 per cent levy. This had been imposed by Britain's Labour government, led by Harold Wilson, in response to Britain's own weakening economy. The Irish government was anxious to negotiate an agreement to alleviate the difficulties this had caused Irish farmers.

The agricultural aspects of the free trade agreement were among its most important provisions. Haughey was careful to later tell the Dáil that Ireland did not want a free trade area in agriculture as the country could not possibly sustain that type of arrangement for even a matter of months. He categorised the Irish position in the negotiations, slightly audaciously, as saying to the British government, 'We want access to your markets in the most unrestricted fashion we can get and, at the same time, we want complete protection in our home market.' The upshot of the free trade agreement, as far as agriculture was concerned, was that that position had practically been achieved.[14] Haughey asserted that Irish farmers would now have unrestricted access for all agricultural produce, with the exception of two or three products in respect of which Ireland already had satisfactory arrangements. At the same time, the government had been required to concede only very minimum quantities of British produce into the Irish home market. There was to be unrestricted access to the British market, for the first time ever, for Irish store cattle, store sheep and store lambs; a doubling of the butter import quota in 1967; and improved benefits under the British fatstock subsidy scheme. Given Healy's reference to the importance of fisheries in Haughey's portfolio, the agreement must have been pleasing to Haughey as it established unrestricted access to the British market. Up to then Irish supplies of fish and agricultural produce could be restricted by the British in the interests of orderly marketing. The agreement involved the gradual reduction of Irish industrial tariffs and the immediate removal of all British duties on Irish goods. It was seen by Haughey as a tuning-up of the Irish economy for the stricter measures it would have to contend with on accession to the EEC's Common Market. He described the agreement in a Dáil debate at the beginning of January 1966 as 'the best deal we have ever been able to get for Irish agriculture'. If the government and all agricultural stakeholders worked together and were united and agreed on the objectives to be achieved, it would 'surely mark the beginning of a period of development and progress in Irish agriculture unparalleled in our history'.[15]

Eleven months later, as Haughey was getting ready to take up the position of Minister for Finance, and Jack Lynch had been elected

Taoiseach and leader of Fianna Fáil, Haughey wrote to his friend, and British ministerial counterpart, Fred Peart. He looked back 'with, I think, justifiable satisfaction on the fruitful outcome of last year's negotiation for the establishment of a free trade area between Ireland and the UK. Despite recent criticisms of the Free Trade Area Agreement, here as well as in Britain, and notwithstanding the present difficulties in the cattle sector I am firmly convinced that the agreement will prove to be of very significant benefit to the economies of our two countries.'[16] The reference to the difficulties of the cattle sector was instructive – these were the primary cause of the government's bitter dispute with the NFA that nearly derailed Haughey's ministerial career just before he left the department.

On 27 April 1966, the ICMSA, under the leadership of John Feely of Limerick, picketed Leinster House in protest against falling milk prices. Milk had been a perennial problem in post-war Irish politics. It was, after all, a row about the price of milk, and not the Mother and Child Scheme, that had been the final nail in the coffin of the first inter-party government in 1951. Fifteen years later twenty-seven ICMSA picketers were arrested under the Offences Against the State Act for breaking the law that forbade picketing the Dáil while it was in session. Over the following two days another 150 ICMSA men were arrested and public opinion began to turn against the government. Two weeks later the number of those arrested had risen to over 450. The dispute was widely seen as one between the ICMSA and Haughey, in his capacity as Minister for Agriculture, as distinct from the state. With Fianna Fáil facing an unexpected presidential election on 1 June, Haughey, as director of elections, was desperate to resolve the conflict. He was also determined, however, not to talk to the ICMSA while they were acting illegally. The ICMSA removed its picket to make way for talks, but no progress was initially made. Haughey was of the view that the state could not afford the farmers' demands for a rise in the price of milk; this could lead to a form of socialised agriculture that would ultimately make agriculture subservient to the state. Yet the following month he rather opportunistically announced in the Dáil a £5.5 million farm package with the bulk of the money to come from taxation. An increase in the basic price of milk of twopence a gallon, and a penny increase in the price of quality milk from April 1967, under the Creamery Milk Quality grading scheme, was enough to placate the ICMSA and the protest ceased. The cases of over 450 farmers were heard at Dublin District Court as the presidential election votes were being counted. Most were fined £5 each, which was later reduced to £1.[17]

WELCOME, CHIEF: THE 1966 PRESIDENTIAL ELECTION

All levels of the Fianna Fáil party were outraged when Fine Gael decided that it would put forward a candidate to contest the 1966 presidential election. That outrage gave way to downright worry that Fine Gael would mount a serious challenge when it nominated the forty-nine-year-old Tom O'Higgins, whose youth contrasted with the ageing de Valera, who was a frail eighty-three. O'Higgins, a TD for Laois–Offaly, was a successful barrister, and the youngest candidate to stand for the presidency. He was also an experienced politician who had been Minister for Health. He was a rather reluctant candidate; he had no real desire to be president, but he also did not want to be humiliated at the ballot box, so he ran a very energetic campaign with the aid of his national director of elections, Gerry Sweetman.[18] Fine Gael's concentration on O'Higgins's youth as being more reflective of a modern Ireland certainly contrasted with the staid vision offered by de Valera.

The 1966 campaign was the first to involve an incumbent president and Fianna Fáil decided to present de Valera as a type of 'father figure to the nation'. In a broadcast on Radio Éireann on 26 May 1966, just four days from polling, Lemass argued that rejecting de Valera would mean that the Irish people had undergone a very fundamental change in their national sentiment. While incumbency did not harm de Valera, O'Higgins benefited by campaigning on the idea that it was time for a modern Ireland to have a modern president. The election was also noteworthy because the jubilee celebrations for the 1916 Easter Rising took place just two months before polling day, a piece of timing which, as any student of Irish politics will readily agree, was hardly coincidental.

Although there were some grumblings from Fine Gael in advance of the election about the enhanced public profile of de Valera, given that he presided over many of the functions celebrating the Rising, the contest was fundamentally a partisan Fianna Fáil versus Fine Gael affair, notwithstanding Fianna Fáil's attempts to portray de Valera as being somehow above politics.[19] Fine Gael also attempted to use the Rising to their advantage. Their handbook for canvassers pointed out that the men of 1916 were progressive and forward-looking, as was O'Higgins, and that in the year of the fiftieth anniversary, it would be appropriate to elect someone who encapsulated those virtues.[20]

De Valera's official biographers noted that some people thought that it should be unanimously agreed that he remain as president, but he was 'still too controversial a figure to be allowed this honour'.[21] Yet the reality was that Lemass had announced de Valera's intention to stand for a second term at the Fianna Fáil Ard Fheis, and this endorsement basically politicised his candidacy. De Valera could have nominated himself, but Haughey, in a post-election report, explained that the decision had been taken to have him nominated by twenty members of the Oireachtas in order to demonstrate that, as president, he had the support of the majority of members of the Oireachtas and so that he could gather as much fringe support as possible. In that context the committee decided to have as many people as they could get to sign nomination papers and submit them to the returning office. This seemed a rather pointless exercise and backfired when many of the subsidiary supporting papers were ruled out as having no legal standing and were deemed invalid, leading to adverse publicity for the party.[22] If anything, this approach copperfastened the view that de Valera was very much the Fianna Fáil candidate, rather than being any kind of father figure to the nation. It could never have been any other way given de Valera's own political partisanship dating back some forty-five years.

Fine Gael's campaign theme – that the youth and vigour of O'Higgins better encapsulated the Ireland of 1966 – left Haughey in somewhat of a quandary. He had been appointed Fianna Fáil's Director of Elections on 28 March 1966 and led an election committee consisting of Neil Blaney,

Kevin Boland, Joe Groome and Tony Hederman.[23] Haughey told the secretary of each comhairle dáil ceantair, 'It is essential that our candidate
be returned with a sweeping majority. It is an historical necessity in the
interest of Irish nationhood that in this jubilee year Éamon de Valera be
re-elected President of Ireland.'[24] This was easier said than done given
that Fianna Fáil did not think it would have to fight an election in the
first place, farmers were protesting in Dublin over prices, and there was
deep industrial unrest across the country.

There was then the thorny problem of what to do with the incumbent
candidate now that he had to face an unexpected contest. Fianna Fáil's
national executive decided that the campaign proper should not commence until the 1916 commemoration ceremonies had ended on 26 April.
Lemass had already advised de Valera that it would not be good constitutional practice for him, as acting president, to participate actively in
an election campaign. Haughey decided that de Valera should continue
to attend various public events as part of his official presidential duties
but refrain from making any public comments that might somehow be
construed as political. This was an attempt to keep O'Higgins out of the
limelight. If de Valera could not make political speeches, neither should
the Fine Gael candidate. Fine Gael, however, was determined to run a
vibrant campaign and maintained that there was nothing to prevent de
Valera doing the same. Thus they promptly ignored Haughey.

Yet many of de Valera's engagements had the air of political rallies.
One such event took place in Mallow on 15 May, two weeks before the
election. De Valera attended an Easter Rising commemorative pageant
at the local racecourse and was greeted by the War of Independence
veteran and local TD Martin Corry, with the salutation 'Welcome,
chief.'[25] Such events were populated by old IRA veterans, wearing War
of Independence service medals, and providing guards of honour. The
Irish Press also loyally came to de Valera's aid by publishing fourteen days
of extracts, up to the eve of polling day, from what was expected to be
his upcoming official biography by the Earl of Longford and T.P. O'Neill,
although it would not be published for another four years. Fianna Fáil
even toyed with the idea of producing a poster with a picture of de Valera

with his 1916 court martial escort between the words 'Lest We Forget' at the top and 'He paved the way; his character, his life, have been the bridge that led to our time' at the bottom. Haughey rejected the proposal on the grounds that it was difficult to get this kind of picture across well in a poster.[26] Posters were a major problem for Fianna Fáil because the party was forced to move away from its traditional colour scheme of green and orange, primarily because Fine Gael started using it first. Instead, Fianna Fáil adopted dark green, 'the idea being to subtly suggest the volunteer uniforms of 1916 with all their historical implications. It was a complete failure, particularly on our posters,' admitted Haughey.[27]

It was a campaign marked by political vandalism, with each camp accusing the other of defacing their posters, especially in Dublin. Fine Gael's Dublin director of elections, Richie Ryan, wrote to Haughey to complain that thousands of O'Higgins's posters had been deliberately mutilated and destroyed by his candidate's supporters. He went on to say that the many voluntary workers who had put up these posters had been tempted to retaliate by destroying Fianna Fáil's posters but would refrain from doing so if Haughey took steps to stop the destructive tactics of de Valera's supporters: 'If there is any further mutilation or removal of the advertising matter of Mr. O'Higgins, however, the safety of your candidate's material cannot be assured.'[28] Fianna Fáil's response was that several thousand of their own posters had been mutilated, from which it could only conclude that Ryan was unable to control the actions of his own workers.[29] Fianna Fáil also accused Fine Gael of having no scruples in campaigning before the Easter Rising celebrations had finished and for forcing the president, in the first place, to undergo an election for what it seemed to think was virtually his constitutional right to an automatic second term.

Haughey's favourite stump speech tactic was to lambast O'Higgins for seeking the complete destruction of Fianna Fáil as a political party, which he claimed O'Higgins had advocated when he was Minister for Health. Haughey demanded that O'Higgins retract his statement, asking how anyone holding these views could legitimately aspire to the office of President, given that half the country voted Fianna Fáil. He also asserted that under the Constitution the president was entitled to serve two terms and that the election was thus about whether de Valera should be removed from office or not. He challenged Fine Gael to 'give their reasons for removing Éamon de Valera from his post as President ... Can it be suggested that he has not in his first term done his job well and carried out his duties with dignity and in a way that brought honour to his country?'[30]

Notwithstanding this rallying call, and the so-called historical necessity to re-elect de Valera, the Fianna Fáil campaign struggled. De Valera scraped over the line by a margin of just 10,717 votes, having won 558,861 votes against 548,144 for O'Higgins on a 65.3 per cent turnout. It was far from the sweeping majority that Haughey had sought. Fianna Fáil identified a number of deficiencies in its post-mortem report after the election. Among the disadvantages outlined were the external environment of economic difficulties and labour troubles, which had led to a loss of popularity for the government and *ipso facto* the candidate it was supporting. Adding to this were a number of internal factors, including the seeming contradiction that the president could not openly campaign for himself; his age; and his long period in public life. This disadvantage was somehow undermined by the fact that the report claimed that two of the advantages Fianna Fáil had were that their candidate had enormous prestige and national standing and that he performed magnificently throughout the campaign. Further problems were the delay in opening the campaign; organisational weaknesses in certain areas; the absence from party headquarters of the party's general secretary, Tommy Mullins, who was ill; and a general complacency throughout the organisation that de Valera could not be beaten in any circumstances.[31] A specific criticism was made of CIÉ for bottlenecks in distributing the party's communications to voters, with Haughey complaining that the party had been completely let down.

The narrow victory certainly worried Haughey, who suffered the added ignominy of seeing de Valera heavily defeated in his own constituency of Dublin North East by over 8,000 votes. The 28,676 votes cast for O'Higgins in Dublin North East were the largest he received in any constituency in the country and he won it with over 58 per cent of the vote. Haughey pointed out that the extent of Fianna Fáil's defeat in Dublin and Cork had very serious implications for the party and had to be the subject of anxious consideration throughout the whole organisation. He felt that a vital factor in the result was whether the Labour vote went for or against de Valera, but bemoaned the fact that having analysed various constituencies and having had many discussions with Dáil deputies, local directors of elections and other experienced observers, 'the results are completely inexplicable and show extraordinary variations and fluctuations from normal patterns.'[32] In other words, the results were not his fault.

After the election Haughey commissioned a report from Frank Ryan, who ran a public relations firm, and had worked at Fianna Fáil headquarters for the duration of the campaign, on what the result meant for the future of the party. Ryan had worked on the previous year's general election but complained in early 1966 that as the party's PR consultant he was being sidelined from the party's headquarters, which had removed him from its organising committee.[33] Haughey, however, was impressed by Ryan's abilities. He had discussed with him the possibility of modernising Fianna Fáil's headquarters and organisational structures in the aftermath of the 1965 general election, but this had met with resistance from others in the party's headquarters.

Ryan's post-mortem into the presidential campaign and result mirrored Haughey's own criticisms, but it was more upfront about the negative effect of de Valera's age on younger voters. Ryan made an ominous prediction that in every constituency in the country Fianna Fáil was faced with the grim prospect of losing up to ten percentage points in its vote in a general election. He further stated that no amount of special pleading from any constituency could ignore the national trends over the course of the thirty-four years since Fianna Fáil first won power in 1932:

> If we ignore these figures we do so at our peril ... The size of the challenge facing us is that we have to change the pattern which history has been weaving for over a third of a century ... The cards

are stacked against us – so we must take over the game in order to win. Let us accept that we have a very, very difficult task ahead – and then set all our energies and determination to reverse the pattern which history and tradition seem to have in store for us.[34]

Beyond the hyperbole of Fianna Fáil – on the one hand filling de Valera's destiny, on the other changing the negative patterns of history in the aftermath of a close victory – there can be little doubt but that the party, and Haughey, as its director of elections, was spooked by the result and what it meant for its future.

THE ODD LITTLE BIT OF PROGRESS: THE NFA PROTEST

Haughey's milk price concession to dairy farmers might have shored up Fianna Fáil's support in rural Ireland and done enough to get de Valera over the line, but it was the party's weakness in the cities that was the main cause of his political angst. He also realised that the farmers would not be placated for long. But he put his worries aside for a holiday in Spiddal, County Galway, in July with his north Dublin friends, the O'Connors, Murnanes and Dennises. In the same month the American embassy in Dublin reported to the State Department that Haughey was somewhat fed up with public life and was considering leaving it, noting rather excitedly: 'once considered heir apparent to Lemass, he has lost some popularity. He may have reached his peak in the government and might be considering going back into private life. He has an accountancy firm and other business interests which give him ample means.'[35] This was a spectacular misreading of both Haughey's future intentions and the past nine years of his public life. He did need some relaxation that summer, however, and also spent a day with his family visiting Rupert Baring, the fourth Baron Revelstoke, on Lambay Island. Revelstoke lived on the island for some six decades and turned it into a sanctuary for sea birds, in which Haughey had a lifelong interest.[36]

Haughey's return to his desk in August saw him faced with renewed demands from the NFA and other groups to establish a meat marketing board to enable farmers to market and sell their produce, along the lines of Bord Bainne, which had been established in May 1961. Bord Bainne's job description was to promote, facilitate, encourage, assist, co-ordinate and develop the exportation of milk and milk products. It was led by Tony O'Reilly, who was appointed its general manager at the age of twenty-five in 1962 and became friendly with Haughey.[37] Cattle prices had fallen significantly throughout 1966 and farmers' anger was palpable throughout the country. The problem for Haughey was that in its short existence Bord Bainne was costing the exchequer a staggering £14 million per year. No one who was advocating for a similar marketing board for meat could reconcile for him the initiative of the private entrepreneur with the requirements of such a board. He was also convinced that Rickard Deasy, the NFA president, was attempting to use the issue as a shuttlecock in his farming politics struggle. This had opened many people's eyes, as he told Tom Moran of Marks and Spencer in a letter in which he was rather sanguine about what he could do in his department: 'You seem to be worried about wasting your time. Don't be. I waste a great deal of mine, but occasionally achieve the odd little bit of progress.'[38]

Any progress Haughey had made in the Department of Agriculture over his two years in office was put at substantial risk a number of weeks later when the NFA upped the ante in relation to government–farmer relations. On 7 October 1966, Rickard Deasy set out on a 210-mile protest march from Bantry in west Cork to the Department of Agriculture in Dublin city. Along the route, he was joined by some 30,000 farmers from all parts of the country. They converged on the capital twelve days later to protest about what they saw as falling farm incomes and the government's unwillingness to do anything about them. The prime target for their ire was Haughey. The friendliness of Deasy's welcome letter to Haughey on his appointment as Minister for Agriculture two years earlier was long gone.

The march posed a major public relations problem for Haughey. A new RTÉ current affairs programme called *Division*, presented by David Thornley of Trinity College Dublin, had started earlier in the autumn and proposed to devote one of its shows to the NFA's dispute with the government. The march was scheduled to arrive in Dublin on a Friday, the day *Division* aired, and the programme's producer, Muiris Mac Conghail, wanted to interview both Deasy and Haughey on the day the march reached its destination. Mac Conghail had made arrangements with Haughey's department about being interviewed on the programme and that week's press was dominated by the proposed, and much anticipated, encounter between the two chief protagonists. Haughey then contacted RTÉ claiming that he had never agreed to appear on the programme, much less take part in a debate with Deasy, and he refused to do so. Mac Conghail, backed by Gunnar Rugheimer, the controller of programmes, decided to proceed. The journalist Ted Nealon would present the government's case and provide an overview of the entire dispute.[39] Haughey was enraged, making public a letter he sent to Rugheimer denouncing RTÉ for having the temerity to use someone not authorised by him to outline the position of the government and the Department of Agriculture.

When the march arrived in Dublin, nine farmers, led by Deasy, staged a twenty-one-day sit-out on the steps of Government Buildings in Merrion Street after Haughey, continuing the strategy he had adopted with the ICMSA in April, refused to meet them.[40] There was no doubt but that this was a tense time for Haughey. He was further outraged by an RTÉ news report on the six o'clock news that juxtaposed an interview he had given with one by Deasy and called the newsroom directly to complain. This resulted in the interview with Deasy being dropped from later bulletins. That decision by RTÉ's head of news, Pearse Kelly, and later supported by the broadcaster's director general, Kevin McCourt, brought howls of protest from the NFA, the newspapers and the National Union of Journalists (NUJ) over what they, and others, perceived as inappropriate ministerial interference in the work of RTÉ. The NUJ made the simple but brutally effective point that the report would not have been changed between the bulletins at six o'clock and nine o'clock but for Haughey's intervention.[41] Haughey, who had since he became a minister been a persistent critic of RTÉ's political reporting, was unrepentant. Moreover, he had the full backing of both Lemass (who made his famous statement about RTÉ being an instrument of public policy in relation to this event) and the entire Fianna Fáil parliamentary party.[42] Fianna Fáil was also united when it came to the dispute with the NFA, who were contemptuously known by some in the parliamentary party as the 'Nine Frozen Arses' due to the inclement weather when the protest began.[43] A placard on display at Dublin Airport welcoming Haughey home from a day trip to London on 31 October stated 'Blue Shirts Wear Black Berets'.[44] This was a dig at the black beret that Deasy wore everywhere he went and which was also sported by many protest marchers. There was a certain irony in this as Deasy would run for Labour in the 1969 general election. In general, however, Fianna Fáil politicians viewed the NFA membership as being rock-solid Fine Gaelers and its leaders as hypocrites who sought to personally ingratiate themselves with individual decision-makers while simultaneously pursuing an aggressive public line against the Department of Agriculture and the government as a whole. Haughey clearly saw the NFA in these terms and believed that the dispute had its origins in inter-farming politics between the NFA and the ICMSA.

Haughey also had the support, at least in private, of the Archbishop of Dublin, John Charles McQuaid, who wrote to offer his support: 'I am deeply sorry that it is you who should be called on to endure the present treatment meted out by the NFA. But be patient: so far you have not been betrayed under provocation into speech or action that is undignified.[45] That provocation, however, was never far from the surface. On the evening of Friday 21 October Haughey attended a Fianna Fáil cumann meeting in the Prince of Wales Hotel in Athlone. On his way out of the hotel after the meeting had finished he was clapped in the foyer by a group of supporters, but once outside was met by a hostile crowd of about five hundred angry farmers. Shouts of 'Traitor' and 'You're afraid to face us' were reportedly shouted at Haughey by farmers who had broken through a Garda cordon, and he was bundled into his car by gardaí. The crowd then prevented the car from moving, surging around it, kicking and pounding its doors and windows, until the gardaí eventually forced the farmers back, allowing Haughey's car to head back to Dublin.[46] At the same time the nine handpicked NFA volunteers were getting ready to hunker down for the night, with their leader Rickard Deasy announcing, 'We are going to give the people their money's worth tonight. We are going to bed down early.'[47]

Earlier in the day Deasy had warned against any interference by members or supporters of the NFA with Haughey's home or family, telling reporters that he had heard reports of unusual Garda activity in Raheny that day. Before the incident with Haughey's car in Athlone, the NFA had announced that all government ministers and members of their families had been banned from riding with all the hunts in the country. This was explicitly aimed at Haughey, who hunted with the Fingal and Ward Union hunts in Dublin, Meath and Louth. The Garda inspector in charge of the policing in Athlone that night, Thomas Keon, wrote the following week to congratulate Haughey on his composure 'when the rabble was endeavouring to intimidate you. I was certainly proud of you and of your attitude. It was a great pleasure to me to see you seated unconcernedly in your car.' Keon's letter blamed 'Hobos' from Offaly for the confrontation and complained that the people of Athlone had not much backbone or 'they would have driven these so-called farmers in to the Shannon to wash their dirty carcasses and dirtier souls'.[48] While Keon, judging from his letter, was most certainly a Fianna Fáil supporter, his comment about Haughey's composure was apt. Not only did Haughey's refusal to negotiate with its leadership infuriate the NFA, but his sangfroid in the face of their increasingly aggressive protests antagonised them even further and made the possibility of any breakthrough very remote indeed. When Haughey's tenure as Minister for Agriculture ended a couple of weeks later, Justice Conor Maguire of the Circuit Court, whose Fianna Fáil sympathies were well known, wrote to him noting, 'your personal courage during the last few weeks apart from everything else was of the highest order.'[49]

Haughey's courage was based on the fact that he viewed the NFA's demands as both unrealistic and unrealisable. He made it clear within the department, to the NFA, and to the general public at large, that he was not going to be intimidated into meeting the NFA or acceding to their demands.[50] This was a point Lemass made a few days later when complaining that even if Haughey did agree to meet the NFA, Deasy had made it clear that they would not call off their protests unless their demands were met. The government was not going to agree to any meetings under those conditions.[51] The ban on government ministers attending hunts sat uneasily with some of Fianna Fáil's political opponents. One was Haughey's friend, and a regular correspondent, Frank Roe, who had stood twice in general elections for Fine Gael, and whom he knew through the hunting scene. Five days after Deasy had begun his march, Roe wrote to Haughey to suggest he make a magnanimous gesture and meet Deasy as it would show he was not a man to keep up a quarrel or allow personalities to influence him.[52] Haughey was having none of it, however, telling Roe, that while it would undoubtedly be a popular thing to do he could not accept his advice on the NFA, as the right thing for him to do was to try to handle the situation with responsibility and restraint, going neither too far in one direction nor the other.[53] He was insistent, however, that the NFA could not be allowed to usurp the functions of government.

Some ten days later, when the protest had become angrier and relations between Haughey and the NFA had deteriorated significantly, Roe, who was a member of the NFA's Clogherhead branch in Louth, wrote to NFA headquarters that he strongly disapproved of the decision to prevent hunts travelling over members' lands if a government minister or family member was a follower of the hunt in question. He called this 'a very mean and low form of retaliation which could never be justified … It is quite unworthy of the great farmers, big and small, of Ireland.'[54] In Roe's view this was an attack on Haughey's private life and that was entirely his own business. He argued that it was a very good thing to have a Minister for Agriculture who was willing and able to hunt and that by bringing the minister's private life into the dispute the NFA was definitely hitting below the belt.

Roe wrote to Haughey again, urging him to reconsider his refusal to meet the NFA and arguing that 'the vast majority of farmers read very little and are highly emotional when it comes to farmers' rights. They cannot see your point of view at all and they think you are being pig-headed in refusing to meet them. We Irish are also a very sentimental people, and you know we all like the man who reveals an unexpected touch of humanity.'[55] He advocated that Haughey do the emotional rather than the logical thing and agree to meet the NFA, as he certainly was not too big to say he would not climb down. In fact, it was Roe's view that Haughey would climb up much higher in most people's estimation if he agreed to meet the NFA, if only to say to them that he would be happy to receive any memorandum, which would be treated in good faith by him and the government. Haughey, however, was not for turning. While he was grateful for Roe's efforts in relation to the hunt, 'I hope I don't sound too pompous when I say the issue is bigger than me or my personal standing.'[56]

Haughey received numerous letters of support and protest about his position. These tended to break down on political lines. At the beginning of the dispute one of his correspondents told him that Deasy 'is miffed because you, as Minister for Agriculture, are not willing to take a narrow, short-term sectional view of the present difficult situation.'[57] A correspondent from Leitrim, a member of both Fianna Fáil and the NFA, told him that there was 'an element in the NFA that is maliciously opposed to the present government and the Fianna Fáil party … I am sure that all the rank and file of the NFA are not in sympathy with the men on the steps.'[58] A similar view came from Westport: 'You displayed courage of the highest order by your responsible action on behalf of the farming community … 99 per cent of farmers irrespective of politics back your stand against NFA intimidation.'[59] Jim McGuire, the editor of the *Western People* newspaper, based in Ballina, told him that public opinion in the west was very much with him, except for a few hotheads who did not appreciate the real issues involved, and that the NFA realised that it must sink or swim with Deasy. He argued that the 'rank and filers hate him for what he has done in creating such an impossible situation in their name but deeper loyalty to the pledged Association keeps them on the go.'[60] McGuire, as editor of the most widely read of all of Ireland's provincial newspapers, was in a better position than most to know the mood of the farmers, particularly in the west, but the strength of public support for the NFA showed little sign of abating. Most of the supportive letters Haughey received sounded like wishful thinking of the highest order and Haughey knew it. His stock response to any correspondence about the dispute with the NFA was that he had no doubt but that it could be quickly resolved if the NFA really wanted a solution.

The question as to the extent of NFA support among the wider public was somewhat more opaque. The businessman Dermot Ryan, a founder of the Ryan Group of hotels, and a major player in Irish tourism, told Haughey he would undoubtedly have the support of many in this dispute, particularly as it dragged into early November and the protests showed no signs of abating.[61] The business community, which Haughey had been cultivating since his election to the Dáil, was keen to see an end to the dispute, but most continued to support him. The property developer Clayton Love, who had made his money in frozen foods, wrote to Haughey on Tuesday 1 November to let him know that 'with all the hounds yapping at your heels I am one of those that are with you and particularly now when you are about to enter a more strenuous and more worthwhile contest.'[62]

EVERYTHING WILL WORK OUT SATISFACTORILY: THE FIANNA FÁIL LEADERSHIP CONTEST OF 1966

Love's reference was to the upcoming Fianna Fáil leadership contest. On the same day Love wrote to Haughey, the *Irish Press* splashed the headline 'Mr. Lemass Expected To Retire This Week' on its front page.[63] The following day it declared that there had been leadership talks within the cabinet and following that Lemass had met with the main leadership candidates, Haughey and George Colley.[64] Until now the newspapers had been very quiet about any potential Lemass retirement. Michael Mills had first run the story in the *Evening Press* two days earlier, on Saturday 30 October, although it was removed from later editions when the Government Information Bureau refused to confirm the story. There had, however, been significant jockeying for position in the race to succeed Lemass in the higher echelons of Fianna Fáil over the previous number of weeks and months. Before the NFA's protest Haughey believed himself to be in a reasonably strong position to succeed Lemass. He was popular with many members of the parliamentary party and he had wide support among the grassroots, having cultivated them over the previous decade. Such popularity was articulated in a letter sent to him during the height of the struggle with the NFA by a correspondent from Dublin, who told him that 'of all in high office in the country you are from my experience easily the most accessible and the least pretentious'.[65] This was a view held by many Fianna Fáil members, both urban and rural.

Another view strongly held across the organisation was that the leadership contest could prove ruinous for the party. It had never experienced such a contest before. While there had been vigorous intellectual debate within the party in the mid-1950s over the course of economic policy, with Lemass and MacEntee heading up different factions, there had been little doubt that when de Valera eventually retired as leader of Fianna Fáil, Lemass would replace him. Seven years later, the situation was completely different. Although Lemass had been mulling over the issue for months and had started confiding in a variety of people since September, his decision to step down caused much surprise across the country, particularly among Fianna Fáil members. The main problem was that there was no obvious successor. Once the newspapers started openly speculating about when Lemass would step down and who would replace him, the disquiet among many in the organisation as to the consequences of a divisive campaign came to the fore. One of Haughey's correspondents from rural Cork, Michael O'Connor, wrote to him on 2 November to say that he was shocked and dismayed at the way the leadership struggle within the party had come into the open, particularly when the real strength of Fianna Fáil since its foundation had been the loyalty of its members to each other. He went on to state that he had expected that the leadership transition would have taken place in a calm atmosphere and that 'a man would have been found who would find favour with the party and rank and file alike. I sincerely hope that no cliques will be formed within the party, as if there will, jealously and intrigue will prove the death knell of the greatest political movement Ireland has ever known.'[66] Haughey replied thanking him for his concern for the future well-being of the party, but he was 'quite confident, however, that everything will work out satisfactorily.'[67] O'Connor's fears were well founded as the 1966 leadership contest opened up fissures in Fianna Fáil that essentially split the party in two for well over two decades. The divisions would not be resolved until Haughey left public life over a quarter of a century later. Haughey was not wholly responsible for this split but he was both an essential part of it and central to its very being.

By mid-September Lemass had decided to retire and had summoned Jack Lynch to his office to ask if he was interested in succeeding him. Lynch, according to an account he gave over thirteen years later in *Magill* magazine on his retirement as leader of Fianna Fáil, immediately rebuffed the advance.[68] Two of his biographers, Bruce Arnold and Dermot Keogh, paint a slightly different picture. According to them, Lynch was in no way a reluctant candidate; but he might need to talk his wife, Máirín, round.[69] Yet, certainly it was Lemass's view after his meeting with Lynch that he had been rebuffed. He received the same answer when he approached the Minister for Labour, Patrick Hillery.[70] By contrast both Haughey and George Colley were very interested. Lemass's initial approaches to Lynch and Hillery showed where his own thoughts lay on his succession.

Colley had the backing of the Minister for External Affairs, Frank Aiken, and some of the other old guard like Paddy Smith, but had little else going for him. Brian Lenihan, for instance, viewed him as being completely out of his depth.[71] He had only been a TD since 1961 and a minister since just after the 1965 election just eighteen months earlier. Like his father before him, he was not a prodigious vote-getter and had trailed well behind Haughey in the 1961 and 1965 elections in Dublin North East. His main advantage, it seems, was that he was not Haughey. Aiken and other old guard types considered Haughey brash and arrogant, and somehow, given Haughey's father's service in the Free State army, as not really Fianna Fáil. This said far more about Aiken than it did about Haughey. Aiken appealed to Lemass to stay on as Taoiseach for another two years. He believed that Colley would be the most acceptable successor to Lemass within the party, but could do with more experience. Many of the old guard seemed to like Colley's own cultivated image as being one of the true heirs of the Fianna Fáil revolutionary generation, unlike Haughey, and one who truly represented the party's Irish Ireland heritage. Aiken's misguided belief that most of the new deputies who were elected in the 1965 election would support Colley shows how far removed he really was from the machinations of Fianna Fáil's internal politics. Although he had been a senior figure in Fianna Fáil for decades, Aiken's influence over the parliamentary party had been eroded over many years by his frequent absences at the UN in New York.

Colley's belief in his own prospects of victory was enhanced by his conviction that Lynch, given that he was not running, would support him and bring many undecided TDs along with him.[72] The reality was that most of those deputies elected in 1965 favoured Haughey over Colley, but many were not over-enamoured with either of the two, and this view was reflected in the wider parliamentary party. Colley might also have been convinced of his chances by the fact that the *Irish Times* had continually expressed the view that Lemass favoured him. On 2 November, a day after Lemass had met both Colley and Haughey, making it clear that he would not publicly support either, but apparently favouring a contest, the front page of that newspaper noted that the Taoiseach had supported Colley but if an overwhelming number of party members supported Haughey he would come down on his side.[73] This was a spectacular hedging of bets given the paper's insistence that Lemass had long favoured Colley. There was no real evidence for such a belief. Despite the fact that Lemass had promoted Colley to the cabinet, he was entirely aware of his weaknesses, not least the fact that he was junior to Haughey in the constituency in terms of both experience and vote-getting ability. There was also the family angle to consider. According to Maureen Haughey, speaking some fifty years later, Lemass had told Haughey, when informing him of his intention to resign, that it was too early for him to become Taoiseach, but that his time would eventually come. Yet when Lemass could not initially convince Lynch to succeed him, Haughey felt that he himself had no choice but to run. He certainly was not going to leave the field open for Colley. When he told Lemass this, the Taoiseach responded by declaring that he would remain neutral in the contest.[74]

It seems clear that Haughey would certainly have beaten Colley in a two-man race. That prospect disappeared, however, when Kevin Boland, after numerous discussions with Neil Blaney, put forward the name of the Donegal man on the morning of Thursday 3 November. This certainly muddied the waters, and Boland was convinced that Blaney would win a three-way contest. This seems unlikely, however, as Blaney did not have much support outside the northwest and none at all in the cabinet apart from Boland, although Conor Lenihan maintains that his father, Minister for Justice Brian Lenihan, also believed that Blaney would have won such a race.[75] Blaney's biographer, Kevin Rafter, is more persuasive in his analysis, noting that, beyond his organisational abilities, Blaney was perceived within the party as a single-issue or at best two-issue candidate.[76]

What was certain was that a three-way contest would be extremely unpredictable. The prospect set off a frantic number of hours in the Fianna Fáil parliamentary party. Lemass again summoned Lynch and pressed on him the fact that he owed the party a duty to serve, even if that meant as leader and Taoiseach. The previous day Lynch had met a number of backbenchers who had asked him to run, assuring him that not only would he win but his election would be unanimous. After meeting Lemass, Lynch said he would like to talk the issue over once more with his wife, which he did so twice, once at lunch and again in the late afternoon. At this stage Lemass must have been suffering from at least some sort of ennui at Lynch's indecision. After Lynch's second meeting with his wife he returned to Government Buildings, met Lemass again, and told him he would stand.[77]

Then Lemass contacted Blaney, Haughey and Colley to ask them to withdraw in favour of Lynch. Blaney and Haughey agreed immediately, while Colley said he wanted to talk to Lynch. This was certainly understandable in light of the fact that Colley believed he had an assurance of support from Lynch.[78] It was, however, a poor misreading of the whole situation. Colley and Lynch agreed to meet the next morning, but things took a turn for the worse when Colley heard on RTÉ radio that Lynch had agreed to stand and all the other candidates had withdrawn. Instead of seeing that his candidacy was doomed, and retreating gracefully, Colley, in a fit of pique, rang RTÉ to say that he had not withdrawn. On the following morning, Friday 4 November, when all of the country's broadsheet newspapers, the *Cork Examiner, Irish Independent, Irish Press,* and *Irish Times* led with variations of the same headline that Lynch would be the next Taoiseach, Colley told Lynch that he was not withdrawing and that a contest would be good for the party. Probably the only person who thought this would be best for the party was Colley. His supporters, among them his original sponsor Frank Aiken, and others such as Paddy Smith from the old brigade, and Paddy Lalor and Bobby Molloy from the newer generation, valiantly supported him when the vote was taken on 9 November, but none of them could be described as being hostile to Lynch. Why Colley felt he had to bring the matter to a vote has never been properly explained. He may have felt he was putting down a marker for the future or maybe he actually thought he was in with a chance. The decisive nature of his defeat, fifty-two votes to nineteen, demonstrated that he had made a spectacular miscalculation. It would not be the last time he would severely overestimate his level of support within Fianna Fáil. The manner of his defeat also left him in no way positioned as the heir apparent to Lynch.

The day after Lynch was elected Taoiseach, Pearse Kelly, RTÉ's head of news, resigned. He wrote to Haughey a month later telling him that his resignation was not entirely voluntary. The director general, Kevin McCourt, had told him that the RTÉ Authority had decided they wanted a change and he felt there was little point in attempting to do anything about it.[79] A number of months later Kelly again wrote to Haughey in much more specific terms to say that his resignation was not unconnected with the final stages of the Fianna Fáil leadership contest and that he felt bitter and victimised at having been made a pawn in a malicious political game. He alleged that RTÉ's director general had accused him of bias by implicitly supporting first Haughey and then Lynch for Taoiseach in the crucial week before the election and that he was prepared to use RTÉ's bulletins to support that line. Part of the evidence presented by the director general was that Kelly had not sent a TV crew to interview Frank Aiken when he flew back from New York that week and that Kelly had on occasion met Haughey for lunch. McCourt felt that only the director general was entitled to meet ministers for lunch.

On the evening that Lynch agreed to be nominated, RTÉ reported that he was receiving unanimous support from within the party. Kelly was later quizzed by the director general on the inclusion of an unofficial statement in RTÉ's bulletins that evening. Kelly later told Haughey that the 'statement was given to me on the telephone by Paddy O'Hanrahan, as a statement for non-attribution, and O'Hanrahan told me that Mr. Lemass was responsible for the statement. The director general implied that I was responsible for having the statement written in the way it was and deliberately slanted to indicate that Mr. Lynch's nomination was unanimous, and that his election would also be unanimous.'[80] Kelly denied this was the case and went on to state that his ambition was to win the confidence of the public for the news service provided by RTÉ and to be seen as impartial and someone who could keep the news bulletins straight by the political parties. In that context he believed that Haughey was convinced of his integrity. The implication of Kelly's letters is that at least some people in the RTÉ Authority were in favour of Colley succeeding Lemass. Kelly's news bulletins on the evening Lynch agreed to stand appeared to have ruled Colley out of contention altogether. Colley was a Dubliner, and a Gaelgeoir, both characteristics widely shared in the RTÉ Authority at the time. Haughey also shared them, although neither characteristic could be attributed to Lynch. McCourt also shared a long and friendly correspondence with Haughey over many years and would seem to have had no animus against Haughey in this period.[81]

Kelly's second letter would seem in itself to be strong evidence of Lemass's desire that he be succeeded by Lynch. Kelly's self-admitted bitterness, however, means that his testimony must be treated with extreme caution. Haughey simply thanked him for letting him know about the situation, saying that he had a 'fair idea of what went on but it is very helpful for me to have confirmation of these aspects from yourself.'[82] Lemass certainly leaked when he viewed it in his interests to do so. Ó hAnnracháin was a de Valera and Lemass loyalist and if he told Kelly that he was speaking on Lemass's authority it is most likely he would have been telling the truth, notwithstanding that he never liked, and increasingly disliked, Lynch.

All the evidence would certainly tend to the view that Lemass wanted Lynch to succeed him. He finally got his man, but he came in for much criticism within the party over the nature of the succession and the fact that it was not the smooth transition he himself had benefited from when replacing de Valera. This is unfair to Lemass in that the context was completely different. Fianna Fáil had survived de Valera moving on from his long tenure as leader. A fear that the party would go into permanent decline after he left the leadership, which was profoundly felt throughout the organisation, was allayed by its results in the 1961 and 1965 general elections. By 1966 a new post-revolutionary generation was positioning itself to lead the party in an Ireland that was changing rapidly in all sorts of economic, social and political ways and the contest to succeed Lemass was symptomatic of that change. Lemass must have had his doubts, however, about Lynch's hesitancy to take the top position. A number of years later his aide-de-camp, and son-in-law, Jack O'Brien penned a note to Charles Haughey stating that on the night Lemass handed over to Lynch, Lemass and O'Brien had a conversation in which Lemass expressed the view that Lynch's succession was a mistake. O'Brien recounted the conversation as follows:

SL – What do you think, Jack?

JOB – A mistake, sir.

SL – I am afraid so. Lynch, through his lack of nationalism, patriotism and republicanism will smash the Fianna Fáil party and the Irish economy. I hope and I pray that I am wrong.

JOB – You did nothing about it?

SL – What could I do [gruffly]. Boland and Blaney let me down. Charlie is young, and anyway the finger of nepotism will never be pointed at me. Some will say that I went soft on republicanism. That is not true. I could have preached republicanism every day but I would have achieved nothing. The time was not opportune. I might as well have bashed my head against a stone wall.[83]

According to O'Brien, Lemass continued in the conversation to predict that the 'North will rise for the first time in 1969', and that the border should be ended in the same year, as Ireland could not afford this 'bleeding sore' that would help destroy the economy. Lemass also foresaw a day when 'so-called Irish politicians, newspapers, and RTÉ will be used for British propaganda' and that the Irish people 'should remember that it was more humane to be murdered in a gas chamber than to be dragged to death behind a black and tan tender, or murdered by famine in a land of plenty, or indiscriminately butchered by Cromwell'. O'Brien further claims that Lemass predicted that if the border remained savage deeds would be performed and that there would be 'no peace in Ireland while the British remain'. Finally, O'Brien asserts that Lemass predicted that the 'Arabs are not fools. They will seek an economic price for oil. This price rise will shake most western economies.'[84]

All of this seems extraordinarily prescient and extremely precise. Why did Lemass think that the North would erupt in violence in 1969 rather than 1970, for instance? Why did he not stay on if he was so worried about Lynch? Why did he approach Lynch in the first place, and try again, as he so clearly did, once Blaney entered the race? And, if Pearse Kelly is to be believed, why did Lemass have Paddy O'Hanrahan phone RTÉ to say that Lynch had unanimous support within the Fianna Fáil parliamentary party? The reference to Boland and Blaney (although O'Brien spells it as Blayney) must surely be a nod to the worry as to how the leadership might go if there were a three-way contest between Haughey, Colley and Blaney as distinct from an either/or choice of the two Dublin North East men. There must be some significant doubt as to the accuracy of O'Brien's recollection, given its extraordinary specificity and incendiary content, even though Peggy Lemass revealed in the 1970s, after her father had died, that he had predicted the bloodbath that Northern Ireland would become.[85] Lemass probably had some doubts about Lynch. It would, in itself, be strange if he did not, but to say that he thought Lynch would smash the Fianna Fáil party seems far-fetched in the extreme.

Lemass was extraordinarily taciturn and had almost no confidants. Moreover, according to Patrick Hillery, he never explained himself. He let others explain on his behalf.[86] It is very unlikely that O'Brien, although married to his daughter Peggy, was in any way a political confidant of his. Lemass had also ceased to be a militant nationalist long before he became Taoiseach in 1959. He was essentially an intellectually agile, highly skilled, progressive pragmatist and realist. There is indirect, but telling, evidence of this characteristic from an occasion when, in opposition, he was exploring some narrow boreen in the west of Ireland with his family in his own private car, to the increasing alarm of his passengers. He reassured them by telling them that he would never drive down anywhere he could not back out of.[87] He did not linger around the Dáil chatting to his sons-in-law, ministers, aides de camp, Dáil staff or TDs. Lemass always headed off home after his business was concluded with the gruffest of good nights to anyone he bumped into. On many working days, he even went home for lunch. It is even more likely that on the night he handed over to Lynch, he would want to get away early and keep his counsel. Lemass may not have ever warmed to Jack Lynch, who, while pleasant in manner, was distinctly lacking in the drive that was ingrained in both Lemass and Haughey. But if Lemass disliked Lynch as much as O'Brien later claimed he did (but without offering any evidence that could be checked), he surely would not have pushed him forward at all, not even as the compromise candidate. The more persuasive analysis is that Lemass backed Lynch as a compromise candidate, *faute de mieux*, and even if he had misgivings, which is of course not impossible, it is very unlikely that he would have forsworn his normally taciturn mode of communication to express them in such extraordinary detail, and in such terms, on the very day he left the Taoiseach's office. Ultimately O'Brien's letter bears the hallmarks of either wishful thinking, or a misinterpretation of something Lemass said, rather than being an accurate reflection of his thoughts on Lynch succeeding him as Taoiseach.

In any event, Colley's decision to force an election left Haughey with mixed feelings. He almost certainly would not have withdrawn from the race if he realised that there would be a contest. He had the support of Brian Lenihan and Donogh O'Malley in the cabinet, although there were rumours, albeit very unlikely to have been true, that O'Malley might support Blaney. While Haughey's brashness was not to everyone's liking, he had built up significant contacts at all levels in the party over the previous fifteen years and could well have prevailed in a three- or even four-man race. He might also, of course, have seen his support disappear in the light of the wider choice available to the parliamentary party.

The farmers' protest certainly did him no favours. While he had the support of the parliamentary party for his stance, the fact that it had not been resolved nearly a month after it began was leading to serious anxiety in the wider community. The crucial breakthrough in the dispute came on 8 November, the day before the leadership vote, when Haughey invited the NFA to talks with the Taoiseach and himself, provided the demonstrators left the front of his office. Lemass was anxious not to have the dispute drag on without some semblance of a resolution before he left the Taoiseach's office. Once he had decided to resign, the decision to offer to meet with the NFA became much easier. Haughey was destined to be moved from the Department of Agriculture in a matter of days and was equally keen that there would be some movement in the dispute before he left. After discussing the issue on numerous occasions in the previous few days, Lemass and Haughey decided to make the first move. With Haughey out of the leadership equation, the decision to invite the NFA for talks was Lemass's final push to avoid this issue becoming tangled up in the election the following day. A decision by a new Taoiseach to invite the NFA for talks would also have reflected poorly on Lemass and Haughey and neither man wanted that as they prepared to leave their respective positions.

The day before that decision was made, Haughey replied to a letter he had received a few weeks earlier from Cyril Clemens, the founding editor and publisher of the *Mark Twain Journal*, which had been in existence for some thirty years and was one of the oldest journals in the world dedicated to a single author. Clemens, who was a relation of Twain, wrote to Haughey to announce that in recognition of his outstanding contribution to agriculture he had been unanimously elected a 'Knight of Mark Twain'.[88] Haughey replied thanking Clemens for the honour, particularly as he had been a 'great admirer of his writings since my boyhood days'.[89] It was a rare moment of light relief in a difficult and tense period for Haughey.

That tension continued as Haughey and Lemass waited for word from the NFA. On receiving the offer of a meeting with the Taoiseach and the Minister for Agriculture, the NFA's national executive held a four-hour meeting at which they decided to accept the invitation, although some members were reported as wanting to escalate the protest. And so the squatters' chairs which had become emblematic of the protest were moved to the other side of Merrion Street, in what Deasy described as a gesture of goodwill to provide a better atmosphere for an exploratory talk. That evening at 7 p.m. Haughey and Lemass met no fewer than ten members of the NFA's national executive, led by Deasy. The others were the original eight squatters, a ninth representing Bob Stack, who had been taken to hospital, and the association's general secretary, Seán Healy. The meeting lasted until 9.40 p.m. with the outcome that Lemass had agreed that his successor as Taoiseach, and whoever was to be the new Minister for Agriculture, would meet with the NFA the following week for a full and comprehensive review of agricultural matters. He stated that there was no question of any progress being made at the meeting towards the ultimate settlement of the dispute. For his part, Haughey described the meeting as frank and fairly cordial and refused to say anything else about the dispute.

The NFA, conscious that there was still significant division in its ranks about how the dispute might be settled, called the meeting a free and frank discussion which covered all matters pertaining to the existing issues. Deasy was keen to stress the meeting did not mean that the NFA had 'bowed down' to the government and that it was the result of simultaneous action by the association and the minister.[90] This was a nod to those elements within the association who had wanted to escalate the dispute by bringing 100,000 farmers to Dublin on the day of the Fianna Fáil Ard Fheis later in the month in an unprecedented demonstration of their strength and their ability to bring the city to a halt. In that context the election of Lynch and the appointment of Neil Blaney as Minister for Agriculture presented the opportunity for a new start in state–farmer relations.

The NFA and ICMSA were no doubt happy to see the back of Haughey but some in the business community were sorry to see him go. One correspondent said that his progressive outlook would be missed, particularly in relation to the pressing issues of marketing and the presentation of Irish products for the all-important foreign markets.[91] And for all Haughey's disputes with the farmers' organisations he certainly had a vision for what he wanted to achieve in Agriculture. His preoccupations were not only local. Before he left the department he was due to travel to East Africa to visit a number of countries, including Kenya, but he had to cancel the visit. Informing the Kenyan Minister for Agriculture, Bruce McKenzie, he lamented that his departure from Agriculture was a source of real regret because being minister gave him the opportunity to discuss with his ministerial counterparts across the world 'the paramount problems confronting the world today – the production of more food' and that in situations like this one's personal preferences were of 'little account'.[92]

The core difficulties in Irish agriculture remained and were unlikely to be resolved without more state investment in agriculture and a loosening of the government's purse strings. That responsibility now lay with Charles Haughey. Lynch announced that he was appointing the man who wanted to be Taoiseach as his new Minister for Finance. The farmers' dispute, however, had left a significant scar on Haughey's psyche. In May 1968, he was invited to lunch by Tom Moran, who was also going to ask the editor of the *Irish Times*, Douglas Gageby, and, with Haughey's permission, Rickard Deasy. Haughey politely but curtly declined, saying nothing more than: 'I don't think so. I'm afraid the iron has eaten too deeply into my soul.'[93]

Haughey's appointment as Minister for Finance was overshadowed by a rather harrowing weekend in his home. On Saturday night, 12 November 1966, the day after Lynch announced the appointment, gardaí were called to the Haughey home in Grangemore when it was thought a burglar had broken in. Nobody was found on the premises after an intensive search of the house and surrounding grounds. Far more serious, however, were the events of the following night, when fire broke out in the Haughey home as Charles and Maureen Haughey were watching television downstairs and their four children were in bed upstairs. Five-year-old Seán Haughey was rescued from his smoke-filled bedroom shortly before midnight when his eleven-year-old sister Eimear, who had heard him crying, burst into his upstairs room, brought him downstairs and raised the alarm. Charles Haughey immediately dashed upstairs, grabbed his other children, Conor and Ciarán, and with his wife, and a housekeeper, Mary Sadler from Kildangan in Kildare, brought all the children outside to safety. He then phoned the fire brigade.

Two units of the fire brigade arrived and soon had the fire under control. Haughey's own bedroom and a downstairs study were damaged. The fire had started in a storeroom immediately beneath Seán Haughey's bedroom and destroyed two storage rooms in the house. Dublin fire brigade men ripped up part of the flooring to hack away the burning ceiling of the storerooms in which large bundles of papers were stored. Haughey believed that the heat from the boiler room on a cold night might have set the papers on fire. He was quoted in the following day's newspapers as praising the fire brigade members for quickly getting to his house and doing a marvellous job in rapidly extinguishing the fire. He also praised Mary Sadler, who, he said, had remained calm throughout the incident and looked after the children during the anxious moments of the fire's discovery and the evacuation of the house.[94] It was a salutary reminder that for all the drama of politics, there was a frailty to human life and Haughey was well aware of it.

CHAPTER 8

THE MINISTER FOR FINANCE

THE INEVITABLE ADVANCE

Haughey's elevation to the position of Minister for Finance, at the age of forty-one, gave him control of the state's purse strings at a time of increasing demands from both ministers and back-benchers, and the farmers and trade unions. He was enough of a realist to know that being in charge of the finances of the state would inevitably lead to more disputes with sectional interests. It also had the strong probability of bringing with it more conflict within the Dáil as other ministers and backbenchers looked for ever more resources for their own initiatives and to placate the demands of their constituents. He was, however, even more central to government decision-making and that is where he wanted to be.

Haughey's appointment was welcomed in various quarters. His counterpart in London, the Chancellor of the Exchequer Jim Callaghan, wished him 'favourable winds in the years ahead', noting that he had told Jack Lynch that 'the job of a Minister of Finance is quite as difficult as that of Prime Minister and I shall expect him to admit it in view of his past experience!'[1] That experience, of course, included serious difficulties with Haughey over budgetary cuts; and the relationship between Haughey and

Lynch, never close, would nevertheless be crucial to the government's success. Haughey's business acumen and experience was commented upon by a number of his correspondents. The veteran public servant J.P. Beddy, the chairman and managing director of the Industrial Credit Corporation, told him that although difficult tasks lay ahead, 'with your specially appropriate qualifications you welcome the opportunity of being responsible for this vitally important ministry'.[2] And indeed he did. On the day of his appointment, Noel Griffin of Waterford Glass welcomed the fact that Haughey, more than anyone else, had 'the capacity for the post and this is the first time that anyone has been appointed with a professional finance training'.[3] Always comfortable with the world of private industry, Haughey replied on the same day, stating that he had 'been away from the world of business and finance for some time and I know I will have to rely heavily on people like yourself'.[4] It was an early signal that Haughey, once more, would not simply be taking his advice from his civil servants.

Haughey's relationship with his new department's civil servants, led by the formidable and, in his own way, radically innovative T.K. Whitaker, had clear potential for danger. While the state's premier civil servant had gained a well-deserved reputation for dynamism in the decade he had been in charge of Finance, and possessed enormous intellectual capacity, he remained cautious about the state's money and had little interest in the spectacular spendthrift ideas of which Haughey, among others in Fianna Fáil, was enamoured. The most famous of these was the announcement in September 1966 by Minister for Education Donogh O'Malley, at a Saturday night dinner of the NUJ in the Royal Marine Hotel in Dún Laoghaire, that he planned to introduce free second-level education. The announcement was made without the knowledge or approval of the Department of Finance, or its minister, Jack Lynch, who was away in Turkey at a meeting of the World Bank. It was designed to ensure maximum publicity, as Noel Whelan pointed out, in front of a room full of journalists in plenty of time for the mass-circulation newspapers of the following morning and the Sunday lunchtime radio news, which had a large listenership.[5] Indeed, all three Sunday broadsheets led with the announcement and it dominated media coverage the following week.

O'Malley had only been in office for two months and he had seen Lemass privately to run his idea of a free education scheme past him just three days before the announcement. He believed, perhaps disingenuously, that he had Lemass's agreement for a policy that had not even been discussed at government level, never mind endorsed. The Department of Finance reacted furiously. Whitaker argued that announcing the policy without prior government approval or a cost analysis by his department would make the development of national planning programmes futile. Lemass issued a formal written warning to O'Malley about the inappropriate nature of his unilateral actions. This drew a response from O'Malley that he had understood he had Lemass's support for his announcement.[6] At the next cabinet meeting, an extremely fractious affair, an irate Lynch raised O'Malley's solo run on free education. O'Malley looked at Lemass, seeking moral or spoken support, and received only a non-verbal indication that he was on his own. But O'Malley succeeded, as he had probably hoped, and as Lemass probably knew he would, because it was so popular, and Lemass was certainly in favour of it anyway. It would have been inconceivable for Fianna Fáil, as a party, to have made such an announcement, no matter how unorthodox, and then resiled from it. Lemass knew this and in fact, it was he, as Taoiseach, who had created the conditions necessary for the announcement and the ultimate provision of free secondary education.[7] If Lemass had said an unequivocal no to O'Malley's overtures at their meeting of 7 September there would have been no announcement three days later. Nevertheless, Lemass was perturbed that O'Malley had turned his general support for the idea into approval of something very specific.

This was something Haughey alluded to in his memory of the entire episode. A scheme for a type of free education with a means test had been commissioned by the previous Minister for Education, Patrick Hillery, but had not been advanced when Lemass moved Hillery to head the Department of Labour in July 1966. According to Haughey, Lemass agreed that O'Malley should make a speech on the idea of free secondary education, not that it was going to happen almost immediately, as O'Malley subsequently implied in his famous speech, in which he stated that 61,500 pupils would benefit from it in the following year. Haughey's view was that the scheme opened up a whole new era in education and gave a tremendous new meaning to equal opportunity to people like himself who had received a scholarship education. Without scholarships, many people who Haughey grew up with never had the opportunity to go to secondary school.

O'Malley's initiative and the decision by Jack Lynch's first government to finance the scheme ultimately opened up a whole new dimension for the children of the working class and those on low incomes.[8] The results were dramatic, with the number of students attending secondary school rising from 104,000 to 140,000 between 1966 and 1969.[9] It was not all, however, an educational land of milk and honey. There were still discrepancies between vocational schools, which were not allowed by the state to offer a curriculum to Leaving Certificate, and privately run secondary schools; the result being that vocational schools were soon viewed as second class by parents and students alike. Moreover, there was no subsidisation for the poorest students and, even without fees, many parents took the decision that getting their children into the workforce as soon as possible was better for their families. In that context the long-cherished goal of Lemass, Hillery, O'Malley and Haughey of a single system of secondary education was still far from realised.[10] The decision to provide free second-level education did, however, begin to erase the 'dark stain on the national conscience' that O'Malley referenced in his original speech and would ultimately transform Irish education in the decades ahead.[11] In the short term, Haughey, the new Minister for Finance, had to find the money to fund it.

Donogh O'Malley died tragically young at the age of 47 in March 1968 when he suffered a heart attack while addressing after-mass meetings during a by-election at Sixmilebridge in Clare. His death led to 'nationwide shock and grief', as his local newspaper, the *Limerick Leader*, reported in an editorial entitled 'Limerick's great loss'.[12] It certainly shocked Haughey. He received many letters of condolence on the loss of his friend. A full thirty-one years later he told one of his regular correspondents, Mother Bernard of the Loreto nuns, with whom he carried on a three-decade correspondence, of O'Malley's 'sense of humour, brilliant conversation, outrageous behaviour and how wonderful it was just to be in his company'.[13] Twenty-eight years earlier he told her, 'I miss Donogh enormously ... and I would like to assure you that I intend to carry on.'[14] The last line was a reference to his period in the political wilderness after the drama of the arms trial when, on his acquittal, Fianna Fáil rallied round Jack Lynch and rumours abounded that Haughey would leave the organisation and establish his own rival party.

Not long after Haughey's appointment to Finance, one of his correspondents told him that he was 'delighted to see you continuing your inevitable advance by being appointed to Finance'.[15] That inexorable rise came to a shuddering halt when Haughey was sacked in May 1970 in the aftermath of the revelations of the attempted importation of arms. His three and a half years in Finance were marked by occasional flourishes of inspiration while keeping a steady hand on the economic tiller. It was also characterised by a sometimes difficult working relationship with Whitaker. The brilliant civil servant had been secretary for a decade when Haughey became minister and was used to his political masters accepting his advice. Haughey was the first minister who was younger than him, the first who had had professional training in accountancy and finance, and certainly the first to have felt he was Whitaker's intellectual equal. Whitaker saw it as his job to say no to any extravagant spending schemes proposed by his own or any government minister. Equally, Haughey, since he first became a minister, was used to getting his own way and felt that civil servants were there to offer advice and support but that he would take the decisions. That continued to be his attitude when he went to Finance, no matter who the secretary was, and what reputation he had.[16]

The relationship between Haughey and Whitaker was hampered in its first few months by an illness that forced Whitaker to undergo an operation in early January 1967 and kept him out of the office for a number of weeks. He told Haughey that it would take him some time to achieve a perfect balance – 'a desideratum that seems to elude me in all directions' – but was available at all times to his minister either on the phone or if Haughey wanted to call out to his home for a 'chat'.[17] In mid-January Haughey went to Las Palmas in the Canary Islands for two weeks, where he holidayed with Tony O'Reilly. The two men worked on the closing stages of the deal whereby Erin Foods established a joint company with H.J. Heinz of Britain to develop and market the products of Erin Foods Ltd in the United Kingdom.[18] O'Reilly had become managing director of the Irish Sugar Company, of which Erin Foods was a subsidiary, the previous year, having moved on from Bord Bainne. The joint company was incorporated in Ireland and became Heinz-Erin, as Haughey announced to the Dáil on 5 April 1967.[19] Thus Haughey and Whitaker actually saw very little of each other in the first months of Haughey's tenure. When Haughey returned to his office in early February, his thoughts turned to the forthcoming budget, just over two months away.

THE TACA CONUNDRUM

On Friday 13 January 1967, Liam McHale, a Fianna Fáil-supporting solicitor from Mayo, received a letter from Harry Boland informing him that he had been proposed and accepted for membership of Taca, the subscription for which was £100 per annum. McHale wrote to Haughey the same day lamenting that while he appreciated the honour of being accepted for membership, and would very much have liked to have been able to measure up to the Taca standard of subscriptions, he just could not afford it.[20] Haughey replied that he was 'very upset that you have been put in this position. It is completely against the procedure laid down. No name should be put forward unless the person has been approached personally and has agreed to become a member ... It is of course fully understood by all concerned that the work people like yourself do for the organisation is far more important than membership of Taca.'[21]

Taca, the Irish word for aid or support, had been established the previous year with the explicit aim of raising funds to defray Fianna Fáil's election expenses and giving businessmen, many of whom were in the construction and property industry, access to party figures. One of Taca's largest contributors was the building magnate Matt Gallagher, who was centrally involved in its administration, to which he devoted one day a month. Gallagher was one of fourteen children born to Matthew Gallagher, a small farmer from Cashel in County Sligo, and his wife, Margaret. He emigrated to England at the age of seventeen in 1932. Over the next three decades he developed and quickly grew a transport and building firm with some of his brothers before returning to Ireland to continue his entrepreneurial building exploits in 1950.[22]

Gallagher and Haughey had become acquainted in the late 1950s and regularly socialised together in both the Gresham Hotel and Groome's Hotel. Haughey Boland became the accountants to the Gallagher Group, and Gallagher employed Des Traynor as his financial adviser and Christopher Gore-Grimes as his solicitor. In 1951 the twenty-year-old Traynor had been hired as Haughey Boland's first articled clerk. A decade later, he had become a partner in Haughey Boland and joined the Gallagher Group as a director and small shareholder of some one hundred of the group's 10,420 issued shares.[23] Gore-Grimes, who was friendly with Haughey, also became a director of the Gallagher Group in 1961.

In the aftermath of the 1967 budget Fine Gael launched a vitriolic attack on Taca. Its presidential candidate from the previous year, Tom O'Higgins, was particularly vociferous in his condemnation. In the midst of a particularly bad-tempered Dáil debate in which he said that the responsibility for the direction of the country lay in the hands of a group of ministers who had no policy and no political philosophy except to stay in office, O'Higgins attacked Taca as being 'reprehensible in our circumstances. If the minister thinks that represents a charge of corruption, it is the hat he has made and he can wear it. Any political party that is driven to the extreme of getting people interested in business to join a silent and secret organisation ... and to pay money down for the doing of it, to parade themselves as fellows of influence, is reprehensible, in my opinion.' Earlier in the debate Haughey angrily rejected what he deemed to be a charge of corruption, noting that he did not mind criticism of Fianna Fáil's policy or its competence, but 'I will not take these charges of corruption. These I resent. Criticise my competence and policy as much as you like but I do not think you can expect me to sit and listen to these other charges.' Haughey was particularly embittered by what he saw as Fine Gael's Janus-faced approach to fundraising. During the increasingly bitter debate he accused O'Higgins of having champagne parties for £100 a head during his failed presidential election bid and of trying to wrap himself in a white sheet: 'I always distrust a man who parades his virtue.'[24]

Haughey defended Taca by insisting that any political organisation that hoped to achieve anything had to move with the times and find new ways of raising money when faced with the enormous task of looking after the finances of a voluntary organisation. He compared Taca's aims with those of many Catholic parishes in Dublin which, when faced with spiralling costs, adopted a system known as planned giving. Fianna Fáil's annual national collection had for many years been barely adequate to meet its annual running costs, allowing no margin at all to provide funds for fighting elections. In that context he claimed that it would be a negation of democracy if any political party, whether Fianna Fáil, Fine Gael or Labour, could not put its policies and programmes before the electorate, so the voters could make their minds up, and that is all Fianna Fáil was trying to do with Taca. Haughey's attitude to accepting money from private donors was summed up in a note he sent to long-time Fianna Fáil activist Padraic O'Halpin a number of years earlier in relation to a proposal to establish a library in honour of the deceased American president John F. Kennedy: 'Within certain limits we are prepared to take money from anybody.'[25]

After delivering his first budget on 11 April 1967, Haughey claimed that the surest sign of its success was the amount of time opposition deputies spent on the irrelevant matter of Fianna Fáil's fundraising activities. He insisted that this was a dereliction of the opposition's duty: instead of debating the merits of his budget they had thrown up a political smoke-screen with all their talk about Taca. He condemned those people who pretended to see something sinister in Taca as attacking the state's political institutions and argued that the people who came together in its establishment had no other end in view beyond supporting Fianna Fáil at election time: 'The vast majority of them are members of our party and so were their fathers before them. They have been subscribing to us for years. They want nothing from Fianna Fáil but good government and that is all they will get. It is quite absurd to suggest that they can gain in any material way. The administration of this country due to the high standards of two or three generations of administrators and politicians is completely watertight.'[26] From his own perspective, Haughey claimed that he had never seen a tender or contract document during his time in government and did not want to.

Fianna Fáil, like all other parties, found raising money in the traditional way somewhat difficult. Its annual collection was the party's only substantial source of revenue. Out of this it had to maintain headquarters and meet printing, publicity and organisational expenses, while at the same time building reserves to meet unexpected contingencies such as by-elections. In September 1966 the party's head office wrote to all officers and members in Dublin, 'The failure of the Organisation in Dublin to pull its full weight in the current national collection is evidence that members do not appreciate their obligations in this vital matter.'[27] Its concerns were well founded. In 1964 Dublin had contributed £5,421; by the autumn of 1966, the sum of its collections was £2,045, a drop of well over a half. This was the context in which Taca, operating from Room 547 of the Burlington Hotel, was born.[28]

Complaints about Taca were not just the prerogative of the opposition. In May 1967 George Colley urged those attending a Fianna Fáil youth conference in Galway not to be 'dispirited if some people in high places appear to have low standards'. It was widely assumed that Colley was alluding to Haughey, but Jack Lynch was none too amused by this attack on one of his own senior ministers from within, and Colley later suggested that he was referring to Fine Gael members of the previous inter-party government.[29] The timing of Colley's implicit attack on Haughey was curious considering it took place just weeks after what was widely considered to be a triumphant budget for Fianna Fáil. This was best summed up by the veteran Seán MacEntee, a former Minister for Finance himself, who wrote to Haughey the day after the budget to congratulate him on his 'magnificent achievement', not only in the Dáil, but later on television as well, telling him that there was 'an atmosphere of approval and confidence wherever I went today that I have not experienced for many years' and that he had left Fine Gael 'gasping'.[30] Haughey replied that to be 'commended by a person one has always admired is particularly gratifying.'[31] A common narrative about Haughey is that pretty much all the Fianna Fáil old guard routinely abhorred him and thought him likely to strike the party's death knell with his ostentatious lifestyle, brash friends and willingness to embrace new thinking, even if it meant overturning some of the party's established shibboleths, as Taca, for instance, inevitably did. Yet Haughey was often congratulated by many of these old guard soldiers for various initiatives during his period as a minister in the 1960s. And anything that inflicted pain on Fine Gael was particularly welcomed.

THE FIRST BUDGET

Haughey's first budget was delivered on Tuesday 11 April 1967. He spent the previous night at home going over the details of his speech, displaying in private his usual nerves before a large-scale event.[32] This event was particularly noteworthy. Not only was it Haughey's first budget as Minister for Finance, but a crucial part of it was opposed by the most powerful civil servant in his department, and indeed the state, T.K. Whitaker. Haughey woke early on budget morning, had his usual frugal breakfast, and was in his office for 9 a.m., ready to resume a battle he had been fighting for weeks with Whitaker. That battle continued right up to the moment Haughey finally descended the steps into the Dáil chamber. Whitaker did not give up trying to dissuade Haughey from taking the dramatic step of announcing both free electricity and free public transport for pensioners until the very moment Haughey entered the chamber. He announced that he was giving relief from the fixed charge on the ESB's domestic consumer tariff, providing an allowance of a hundred units of electricity free of charge in each period; and allowing for free public travel.

In its planning the scheme had already caused deep division within Finance. Whitaker was opposed to it from the outset, telling Haughey that 'once you started that sort of thing there was no knowing where you could stop because there are so many other free gifts you can make available and people will begin to expect them.'[33] Haughey had a different outlook. To him, social services were there to make people's lives better, not just to give them stuff.[34] The idea of free travel came from his mother. She had often complained to him about buses from Donnycarney being empty going into and out of the city centre during the mid-morning to mid-afternoon period and told him that her contemporaries in Belton Park and the surrounding areas would not go into the city for shopping as it was simply too expensive on the bus. Given that the buses were running anyway she wondered whether anything could be done to help pensioners.[35] The germ of free transport was planted in Haughey's mind.

In his budget speech he began by noting that he had a budget surplus of £800,000, which, although small, had an important economic significance in that it marked the success of the government's policy of curbing, largely through budgetary action, the excessive pressure which total national spending had been exerting on the balance of payments. The 1965–66 deficit of almost £8 million had been eliminated. Coupled with the stabilisation of public capital expenditure, this played a large part in bringing national spending within the resources likely to be continuously available to his and other governments to follow.

He then asserted that there was a growing consciousness in the community of the problems of the old and a good deal of voluntary personal service was being devoted to their welfare. While social welfare services were being continuously improved, there was considerable scope for voluntary effort in providing old people not just with the bare necessities of life but also with some comfort and companionship. In that context, the government had been particularly considering the difficult circumstances of elderly people who lived alone and had decided to give this group additional help by way of free electricity and transport. That pledge electrified the Dáil. He continued with words that were lauded by pensioners then and ever since: 'The electricity bill can be a worry when resources are limited. A scheme is being prepared which will remove this expense, or reduce it substantially, for all households consisting only of old age pensioners … A scheme is also being worked out in consultation with CIÉ whereby old age and blind pensioners will be able to travel free of charge on CIÉ buses and trains during periods when traffic is not heavy.[36] He gave no account of how much these schemes would cost the exchequer, except to say that they would be introduced during the course of the following number of months and that the net cost would be reimbursed to the ESB and CIÉ from public funds after some experience of their operation.

This was what worried Whitaker. As with Donagh O'Malley's free education scheme, it was the unseen cost and the possibility that they would lead to further unforeseen expenditures, rather than the principle of such schemes, that perturbed him. Nevertheless, the budget initiatives of free electricity and free public transport brought an enormous amount of correspondence Haughey's way, both in the immediate aftermath of the announcement and over the following decades. At their heart he considered both schemes instruments of social justice. To one of his correspondents who complained about surtax increases in the budget being shameful in a country that had not been involved in any devastating wars, he offered the withering reply that he and his correspondent had different concepts of what social justice meant.[37]

After the acrimony of the farmers' protest, Haughey used this budget to attempt to repair his relationship with them. His view of the farming community had always been that governments should help farmers who worked their land fully and efficiently to share equitably in rising national prosperity. He never saw the point of simply giving farmers grants for no return.[38] He was insistent, however, that state aid in the form of production incentives, price supports, credit facilities and helping farmers find new markets would be effective only if farmers used them to increase their production and incomes. Haughey was conscious of the support Fianna Fáil received from the west of Ireland and devoted a significant section of his speech to western development. In maintaining that the greatest physical, human and social problem facing Ireland was the preservation of the west of Ireland, he announced that the twelve western counties would be treated as a special development region and would benefit from a number of state initiatives, one of which was the introduction of tax allowances for machinery and plant. His aim was to grow the west as a location for industrial development. He ended his speech by claiming that it was his aim to improve the lot of the old and the needy and to develop a new urgency in the solution of western problems by bringing about a better economic climate through a substantial increase in the incomes of the farming community.[39] It was a clever nod to two constituencies essential to Fianna Fáil's political success.

The reaction from the west was encouraging. Jim McGuire, the editor of the *Western People,* and a friend of John Healy, told Haughey, 'that was a budget that made you as far as the west is concerned.'[40] McGuire, like Healy, was concerned about the potential long-term demise of the west and suggested that a programme of civil service decentralisation would make living there a privilege rather a privation. He further advocated an end to the negativity of official terminology which suggested that the west was constantly underdeveloped. Instead he urged the government to adopt an approach that there were opportunities for and in the west and that it could be developed. This, he argued, would do much to remove the stigma of second-class citizenship that many westerners were labelled with from birth. Haughey was very much open to the idea of decentralisation, and people like Healy and McGuire were strong supporters of it as a policy. Yet Haughey also knew that in an age where telecommunications were still primitive along most of the western seaboard, the Irish state was not ready for such an initiative, no matter how politically popular it might be in the west.

I WILL MAKE ENQUIRIES TO SEE WHETHER ANYTHING CAN BE DONE

A constant theme of Fianna Fáil policy in the nine years in which Haughey went from a first-time TD to Minister for Finance was the need to bring foreign direct investment into the country. It took the intervention of Whitaker in 1957 to bring Fianna Fáil to the realisation that protectionism and indigenous Irish industry could not provide full employment. Almost a decade later Haughey was still preaching the necessity for full employment. In his budget speech he referenced a report by the National Industrial Economic Council, just a month before, which stressed the need for Irish people to recognise the profit motive for individuals and companies wishing to invest in Ireland. In the context of providing jobs at adequate wages for everyone who wished to make their livelihood within the state, Haughey argued that as a country Ireland could not attract the capital needed for development unless those providing it could expect to receive a satisfactory return.

Haughey was constantly receiving advice about how best to attract investment into the state. Some of it was useful, much of it less so. He was a believer in agencies doing their jobs properly and was willing to use whatever political capital he had by virtue of his position to help them to do so. This was also to be a feature of his later period as Taoiseach. A month after the budget, the former Director General of RTÉ, the American Edward Roth, told Haughey that he had heard that the Industrial Development Authority (IDA) was thinking of revitalising its efforts in the USA. He was interested in the job, and would appreciate Haughey's support. Notwithstanding Haughey's well-known difficulties with RTÉ throughout the 1960s he replied that the IDA could very well do with a man like Roth in the USA and he would be happy to do anything he could to help.[41] When Roth left RTÉ at the end of 1962 he told the playwright Seán O'Casey that although he and his family had enjoyed Ireland, he would not want to repeat the experience and confessed that after close to three years in Ireland he still could not understand the Irish. Although nothing came of his IDA query to Haughey he still kept a keen eye on events in Ireland and eventually gave evidence at a United States Senate Committee hearing in 1971 on the outbreak of the Troubles in Northern Ireland and how the United States government might respond.[42]

Another correspondent of Haughey's who was eager to offer assistance in relation to tapping into the possible US investment market was an American author called Jack Cohane, who had relocated to Ireland, and with whom Haughey had become friendly in the mid-1960s. Cohane, with his wife, Heather, had established a small knitwear business in Pallaskenry, County Limerick, where he lived in a large mansion. He used Haughey Boland as his accountants and tax advisers in applying for a number of government grants. In the course of a long rambling letter to Haughey in June 1967 he suggested that there were thousands of Americans who had very intense feelings about Ireland, much as Jewish people had about Israel, and that many of them were used to backing up their feelings with hard cash. Cohane reckoned that these people could be persuaded to invest in some way in Ireland as long as there was some decent return. He offered to discuss this with some prominent American fundraisers in the course of a visit he was soon to undertake.[43] Haughey replied that the idea of Irish-Americans investing in Irish development had often been put forward but never adopted and was not a particularly live issue at the moment. The government's capital programme had been agreed and Haughey did not anticipate any difficulty in funding it. He had no objections to Cohane finding out for his own personal information what the situation was, but he 'would not wish, under any circumstances, word to get out that I or the government were even considering anything of this nature'.[44]

On 9 May 1967, the American folk singer and actor Burl Ives was involved in a car crash in Milltown, County Kerry and was initially charged with careless driving and driving while drunk. Three months later, on 11 August, he was convicted of careless driving at Killorglin Circuit Court and fined £10. The state had withdrawn the charge of driving while drunk.[45] A month after Ives's accident, Cohane wrote to Haughey informing him of the charges and of how they had put Ives in a state of 'black despair', which was quite likely to interfere with a feature that *Look* magazine in the USA was doing on him to be titled 'Burl Ives in Ireland'. Ives, according to Cohane, was willing to plead guilty to the careless driving charge but was adamant that he was not drunk and was going to fight it 'tooth and nail'. Cohane ended his letter by telling Haughey that no one knew he was writing to him but he thought he should know in any event.[46] Two weeks later Cohane began his letter about American investors by telling Haughey, 'Burl Ives couldn't appreciate more what you did for him and hope[s] he will have a chance of thanking you in person sometime soon … I have cautioned him not to tell anyone there was any intervention at the top.[47] Haughey made no mention of the Ives case in his reply. A few years earlier, in 1963, Cohane had been involved in one of Britain's most notorious divorce cases involving Margaret Campbell, the Duchess of Argyll. Cohane, who was alleged to have been one of her lovers, was described by the magistrate in the case as having 'the morals of a tomcat and the agility of a mountain goat'.[48]

The whole episode can be viewed in two different ways. In one way it is difficult to see what influence Haughey could have had on the case considering Cohane was writing to him in June and it was not settled until August. In another way it would certainly have been very easy for Haughey to have made known his views on the matter. There had been a number of adjournments in the case and in his second letter to Haughey Cohane mentioned that the local Garda sergeant and a priest at the seminary in the village believed that they had 'double-handed[ly] negotiated the reduction in the charge', adding the rider, 'so be it'.[49] When Ives's case came before the court in August he was not present at the hearing and the prosecuting guard, Superintendent Brendan Lynch, said his instructions were to withdraw the drunk driving charge and agree to the charge of careless driving. It is certainly possible that political pressure was brought to bear on the gardaí in this case. It is also possible that given that nobody was injured in the accident a charge of drunk driving might not have been provable and a decision to move ahead with the lesser charge was more prudent. The Ives case is an important one when it comes to Haughey, however, as it goes to the heart of the charges that have long been levelled at him that he used his political office to further his own personal interests and those of his acquaintances.

A few months earlier Haughey had received a letter from a Fianna Fáil supporter who worked in the Irish Life insurance company and wanted him to intervene on his behalf about being promoted to a supervisory position: 'I sincerely hope that you will see your way to assist me as I do not know even one supervisor who is a member of the party.'[50] In bringing this letter to Haughey's attention his private secretary, Brendan O'Donnell, in a handwritten note, wrote, 'Presumably you do not wish to pursue the matter.' The word 'No' is underlined in response on the same note.[51] Haughey sent his correspondent a reply stating that 'matters of this sort are usually very delicate but I will make enquiries to see whether anything can be done.'[52] Over half a century later, Brendan O'Donnell maintained that Haughey was plagued with requests of this sort while he was a minister, and always refused to have anything to do with them. He did think it prudent to reply to most of those entreaties from Fianna Fáil supporters along the lines that he did not think anything could be done but he would make enquiries. He then proceeded to do nothing about them.[53]

Haughey did make all sorts of representations to various government agencies and departments in this period. Sometimes these were in his own name. In many other cases they were in the name of one of his officials. For example, in April 1967 he was asked by one of his Garda drivers to intervene in the case of a vehicle imported from Northern Ireland by another individual and impounded by customs officials over non-payment of duty. One of Haughey's officials wrote to the Revenue Commissioners stating that the minister would be glad if favourable consideration could be given to releasing the vehicle without payment of duty.[54] As it turned out the individual involved was willing to pay the duty on the vehicle and that was the end of the matter.

Such representations were common across the political system and were often used by Fianna Fáil and Fine Gael to attack each other. In August 1967, Donogh O'Malley's private secretary sent Haughey a note with an attached letter from the Department of Education over the appointment of the headmaster of Portlaoise Vocational School. The letter outlined concerns the department had raised over filling the post. It had been reported back to the minister by his representatives on the selection board that the Vocational Education Commission in Laois, which was deciding on the shortlist of candidates, had agreed that the position would be filled by a candidate who would only be interviewed after his selection. O'Malley's contacts also reported to him the rather extraordinary view that 'the representatives of the committee stated that it was not necessary to select the best candidate.' Haughey was told that the chairman of the committee was the long-standing Fine Gael TD Oliver J. Flanagan.[55] Political influence in filling public posts had been an issue since the very foundation of the state and was not just associated with Fianna Fáil.

Decades later the McCracken and Moriarty tribunals would trawl through years of Haughey's decisions as a public figure in an attempt to link decisions made with monies given to him. In the particular case of Burl Ives it might well have been that Jack Cohane overestimated what Haughey in fact did for him and that Haughey was indeed happy to have it that way. Alternatively, Haughey could also, of course, have made informal contact with someone involved in the case. He was certainly able to use political influence in this way. Yet when Haughey helped people, he usually told them. A year and a half after the Cohane incident, in December 1968, the legendary racehorse trainer Vincent O'Brien wrote to Haughey asking could he help out with a problem Charles W. Engelhard had with customs officials when he came to Ireland. Engelhard had made his fortune in mining and metals and was a major figure in the US Democratic Party. He was apparently the inspiration for the character Goldfinger in Ian Fleming's James Bond novel and the film of the same name.[56] He had a long interest in horses and horseracing and owned a string of thoroughbreds, including the famous Nijinsky, trained by O'Brien. Engelhard was due to visit O'Brien and was arriving into Ireland in his private plane. O'Brien told Haughey that the last time Engelhard had visited Ireland he mentioned that Shannon Airport was the only place where customs questioned him and opened his cases: 'I feel sure you will agree he is above smuggling of any kind big or small.'[57] Haughey replied that he fully agreed that 'people like Charlie Engelhard should be given the appropriate treatment on their arrival and you can rest assured that I will see to it that this will be done on this occasion'.[58]

A MATTER OF GENUINE NATIONAL PRIDE

In early November 1967 Fianna Fáil fought and won two by-elections in Cork Borough and Limerick West. In the course of the campaigns Haughey, speaking in Cork, told a party rally for its candidate, Seán French, that it was a matter of genuine national pride that September 1967 would long be remembered in the economic history of the country as the month in which exports practically equalled imports.[59] The expansion of exports in the face of a more difficult global trading outlook confirmed for Haughey that the Irish economy could be geared up to meet the challenge of EEC membership. He was confident that the second application currently before the Community after being lodged the previous May could be pursued with assurance and confidence. He was also, however, aware that the success of the application was still doubtful at best, given the widely held expectation that the French President, Charles de Gaulle, would once again veto the British application as he had in 1963. Lynch, Haughey and a team of civil servants had visited the capitals of West Germany, Italy and the Benelux countries in June and July of 1967 to present the Irish position. A separate visit to Paris to see President de Gaulle and his team of ministers and officials took place on 3 November. Positive reports emanated from the meeting and Lynch even went as far as stating afterwards that the French had no objection in principle to British membership of the EEC. This seemed wildly over-optimistic, but was also probably part of Lynch's understanding of the realpolitik of the situation. He knew Ireland could not become a member in Britain's absence, and told reporters that it was difficult to see Ireland as part of an economic bloc of which Britain was not a member.[60]

It was well known throughout the Community that Ireland could not continue its application to the EEC independently of the British, although de Gaulle remained open, if somewhat lukewarm, to the idea of associate membership. The British, for their part, wanted nothing to do with any sort of interim agreement, seeing it as a pointless exercise. It took the view that it was either in or it was not. De Gaulle duly called time on the British application on 27 November 1967, leaving the Irish application in abeyance. The following month, the Council of Ministers decided against formally opening entry negotiations with any of the applicants. Lynch's hopes for Irish entrance and his optimism about de Gaulle's view of Britain was shown to be entirely wrong. Yet all was not lost. As Ireland's primary objective for joining the EEC was not political but economic, it did not have the same reluctance as Britain about an interim arrangement leading to membership. The Lynch government continued to explore all sorts of avenues, from thinking about at least trying to encourage Britain to look at some interim arrangement, to exploring whether Ireland could negotiate its own arrangement for some sort of associate membership with the Community independently of Britain, as de Gaulle had mooted.[61] At a wider level the EEC itself was very hesitant about any discussions on interim arrangements, notwithstanding making the odd noise that it was open to such a position. Instead it opted to leave the British application on the table, to be reactivated whenever it, as a community, saw fit – a euphemism for when de Gaulle was either retired or dead. The Irish application continued to remain firmly tied to Britain's.

Haughey was from an early stage a strong believer in Ireland's membership of the EEC for both economic and political reasons. On the economic front he saw the value of the Common Agricultural Policy when he was Minister for Agriculture and the benefits that guaranteed markets and prices would bring to Irish farmers. He was, however, enough of a realist to know that membership would bring obligations and difficulties to manufacturing industry. The need for industry to prepare itself for membership was a constant theme of his speeches in his tenure as Minister for Finance. On the political front he was convinced that the economic benefits of membership would lead to the enhancement of Irish sovereignty and that partition could be resolved. He was to be proved partially right in the former and very badly wrong in the latter.

Before their departure for Paris, Lynch and Haughey were involved in an internal wrangle about canvassing in the by-elections. Lynch complained of a disappointing attendance at an event in Cork the previous week and asked Haughey to attend the next event as early as possible and to stay for as long as possible.[62] In a handwritten addendum Lynch stated that this was a general issue and he was glad that Haughey would be in Cork on Wednesday, which was just before the two men left for Paris. Haughey, normally an enthusiastic canvasser, was weary from a very hectic travel schedule. He had only recently returned from a trip to the USA and South America, where he visited Argentina, Brazil, Chile and Peru, as part of a trade mission. He took time during the Peruvian part of the trip to call on the Missionary Sisters of St Columban in Lima to see the work they were doing.[63] On his return he went straight back to canvassing in the Cork and Limerick West by-elections. Gerry Collins, whose father, James, had held the seat from 1948 until his death in 1967, was the Fianna Fáil candidate in Limerick. Collins had met Haughey for the first time earlier in the decade when he was a student in UCD and would often visit his father in Leinster House. He was appointed Fianna Fáil's assistant general secretary in 1965, bringing him into further contact with Haughey in relation to the running of the party.[64] Collins's appointment was part of an ongoing attempt at professionalising the Fianna Fáil organisation, which Haughey was intimately involved in. Collins immediately became part of a sub-committee on organisation, which also included Haughey. In October 1966 that committee received a report from a party member, Liam McHale, about a visit he had made to see how the Democratic Party organised its election strategy and campaign in Long Island, New York, prior to state and gubernatorial elections that November. A full decade before its then general secretary, Seamus Brennan, famously went to study the Democratic Party's campaign to elect Jimmy Carter as president, Fianna Fáil was casting its net wide in order to improve its own electoral performance. McHale's report suggested to Fianna Fáil that it could certainly be doing more in relation to fundraising, canvassing, election literature and involving more women in its election efforts.[65] At the Limerick West by-election Collins was elected on the first count, with a surplus of over a thousand votes, while in Cork Seán French had a substantial lead of over 8,000 votes on the first count, and he was duly elected on transfers on the third count. It was Fianna Fáil's fourth by-election victory in a row after wins for John O'Leary in Kerry South and Patrick 'Fad' Browne in Waterford in December 1966 had got Jack Lynch's tenure as Taoiseach off to a very successful electoral start.

It was during another by-election in Clare, eventually won by Fianna Fáil's Sylvester Barrett, that Donogh O'Malley had his heart attack and died in March 1968. He was replaced two months later by his nephew, Des O'Malley, who took the vacant seat in Limerick East. He had been selected to run for Fianna Fáil over the minister's widow, Hilda, who remained bitter about it for evermore. Des O'Malley recalled that before confirming his interest in standing for the vacant seat he went to see Hilda, but, he claimed, she was not interested in contesting the election, and had a poor view of political life in general. He also maintained that she was very critical of Haughey and Blaney for their negative influence on her late husband.[66] Yet if Hilda O'Malley was initially happy to step aside for Des O'Malley, she quickly had second thoughts. She told Lynch after her husband's funeral that she was grateful to him for the warmth of his graveside tribute and for 'giving Donogh the great happiness of seeing some of his dreams realised; we have your word that the rest will be brought to fruition.'[67] She quickly soured on Lynch ever enacting her husband's vision, however, and just over a year later ran as an independent in the 1969 general election, against Des O'Malley, in which she polled reasonably well but did not take a seat.[68] Des O'Malley recalled being shocked by her decision to stand and blamed some disaffected local party members and other elements in Dáil Éireann for encouraging her to run in the hope that she would dislodge him.[69] This, of course, denied her any agency in the decision at all. It would appear that Des O'Malley under-estimated Hilda O'Malley's interest in becoming a TD and overestimated her antipathy towards Haughey. The following year, in the aftermath of Haughey's sacking as Minister for Finance, she wrote to support him, expressing deep sorrow for what had happened. She alluded to the 'hypoc-risy of the state funeral' for her husband and told Haughey that Neil Blaney, Kevin Boland and himself had many friends and supporters in Limerick.[70]

For his part, Des O'Malley would have a meteoric rise within Fianna Fáil, becoming a full minister within two years of his election to Dáil Éireann in the midst of the turmoil in the party when the alleged plot to import arms illegally into the state was revealed and Haughey and Neil Blaney were sacked by Lynch. Blaney had been instrumental in O'Malley's by-election win. He had the methods of canvassing for by-elec-tions down to a fine art and would arrive with his infamous 'Donegal Mafia' stormtroopers of canvassers in whatever constituency he was named director of elections. He ran the same operation for O'Malley in Limerick East, having taken over from the official director of elections, the much more mild-mannered Paudge Brennan.

That victory, while a personal triumph for Lynch and O'Malley, turned into a pyrrhic one for Blaney. He harboured suspicions over what he perceived as O'Malley's lack of proper Fianna Fáil pedigree and quickly grew to distrust and dislike him. The feeling was very much mutual. O'Malley, in turn, disliked the tactics Blaney had used in the by-election campaign and even thought that Blaney would cost him the seat over his antagonism towards non-Fianna Fáil partisans. He was also unimpressed with what he described as the new generation, who viewed politics through the prism of money and business. He quickly associated himself with both Lynch and George Colley. O'Malley's rise within the party was linked both to his closeness with Lynch and his implacable hostility to Haughey. He recalled that the group of ministers with which Donogh O'Malley had been associated had assumed that he would in turn be part of their coterie and he was an obvious disappointment to them. His suspicion of Haughey was evident from the off. After finishing his maiden speech in June 1968 on the Finance Bill, O'Malley received a note of congratulations, passed to him by one of the Dáil ushers, from Haughey. He immediately interpreted it not as a gesture of congratulations, nor even of a job well done. Rather, it was a signal that a minister with the leadership already in his sights was cultivating the backbencher.[71] The hostility O'Malley and Haughey held for each other significantly shaped the nature of Fianna Fáil for a generation and it never faded while both men were alive.

CHAPTER 9

HORSEMAN, PASS BY

FUNDING THE ARTS

On 28 March 1968, just over two weeks after Donogh O'Malley died, Haughey bought 127 acres at Ashbourne, County Meath, for some £30,000. He did not take out a mortgage when buying the lands. His Dáil and ministerial salary was £5,000.[1] He used this land as a stud farm, which he called Rath Stud. Rath Stud was a small operation managed for Haughey by Ingrid Lauterbach.[2] He sold it in December 1976 to Maurice Taylor from Northern Ireland for £350,000, which he used to pay a debt he had accumulated to the Northern Bank Financial Corporation. Close to a quarter of a century later, when giving evidence at the Moriarty Tribunal, Haughey described it as 'smallish, it would be considered a small stud farm, but nevertheless, stud farms are very labour intensive, there would have been two or three people there'.[3] From 1961 pretty much all of Haughey's financial transactions, including the purchase of Rath Stud, were run by Des Traynor. Within a decade and a half of becoming Haughey Boland's first articled clerk in 1951, Traynor, by the time Haughey was appointed Minister for Finance in 1966, had the authority to negotiate loans on Haughey's behalf, and how they would be paid back. He was authorised to do all this by Haughey without having to consult him. All this was done to allow Haughey to concentrate fully on his public role as TD and minister. It was an arrangement that would haunt the last decade of Haughey's life. While he insisted to the Moriarty Tribunal that he knew nothing of the intricacies of his finances, all of which, he maintained, were handled by Traynor without his knowledge, a sceptical tribunal and equally sceptical public were unconvinced.

March of 1968 was a busy month for Haughey. He flew to the United States to open the new Bord Fáilte headquarters in New York and an Irish trade fair for the export board Córas Tráchtála in the presence of Senator Robert Kennedy, the favourite for the Democratic nomination for president, and Cardinal Richard Cushing, the former Archbishop of Boston. It was at this fair where Haughey famously complained about Ben Dunne Senior displaying drip-dry Bri-nylon shirts, supposedly uttering the immortal line: 'What do you think this is, the fucking Iveagh market?'[4] This outburst sparked simmering resentment from some members of the Dunne family which would come back to haunt Haughey when the revelations that Ben Dunne Junior had given him extremely large sums of money led to the establishment of the McCracken Tribunal and exposed internecine warfare within the Dunne family. Ben Dunne Senior died in April 1983. The following February his daughter, Margaret Heffernan, received a letter from one of Haughey's personal assistants thanking her for her donation of sheets for deprived children in Haughey's constituency at Christmas. The letter went on to say that Haughey had indeed attended her father's funeral, as she had inquired, but could not remain to sign the book of condolences as he had to go to a meeting.[5] Margaret Heffernan's inquiry was perhaps a further sign that the Dunne family felt slighted by Haughey, over Ben Dunne Senior, and she surely could not have been impressed by the delay in replying to her inquiry.

In his first budget, Haughey promised to increase the Arts Council's grant-in-aid for 1967/68 from £40,000 to £60,000. Nearly a year later, in March 1968, he visited the Arts Council, where he outlined a series of plans for future state assistance to the arts. While he was not legally responsible for the Arts Council – that responsibility rested with the

Taoiseach, Haughey had assumed the role of Fianna Fáil's patron of the arts.[6] He told the shocked members of the Council that he intended to abolish it and replace it with three new separate councils responsible for the visual arts; drama and literature; and music. These new councils would be independent of each other and have separate staffs, premises and budgets. Haughey further declared that he intended to grant £100,000 to the Visual Arts Council and £50,000 each to the other two councils. Yet in his second budget, just five weeks after he had visited the Arts Council, he announced that he was giving a grant-in-aid allocation to the Arts Council for 1968/69 of £60,000, rather than £100,000. The Arts Council would not in fact be restructured until 1973.[7] According to Tim Pat Coogan, Haughey was given to telling people that he was the first 'real' Minister for Finance.[8] Whatever about the reality of that, he was certainly the first Minister for Finance in the state's short history who was genuinely interested in the arts and would make his presence felt in the area before his tenure abruptly ended.

Haughey had been an enthusiastic supporter of an international art exhibition called Rosc, which opened in the Royal Dublin Society in Ballsbridge in mid-November 1967 and ran until the second week of January 1968. While there were complaints about the exclusion of Irish artists and the choice of various international exhibitors, Rosc was an undoubted success. Over 50,000 people, many of them tourists, attended the exhibition and it marked Ireland as a place where, at least to some extent, international art was appreciated for its intrinsic value and where a senior government minister was interested in its development. In his speech opening the exhibition, Haughey described Rosc as a 'magnificent, breathtaking conception. The timid may suggest that in its greatness and daring it is too much for the Irish mind to encompass at this point of our development. I do not believe it.'[9] A touch of hyperbole, no doubt, but it was also part of a theme from Haughey, as Minister for Finance, that Ireland was no closed, insular society, but rather a vibrant, open country that appreciated and welcomed outside influences. The driving force behind Rosc was the Irish modernist architect Michael Scott, who became a lifelong friend of Haughey and hosted dinners for him in his Sandycove home over a number of decades, where guests included, among others, the Gate Theatre duo of Hilton Edwards and Micheál Mac Liammóir. Scott, Edwards, Mac Liammóir and Haughey were all sincere supporters of the arts. When Haughey was Taoiseach in the early 1980s, Scott had a direct line to Haughey's private secretary, Seán Aylward, which he would use to convey the dinner invitation to Haughey, reveal the guest list and ensure that Haughey knew they were politics-free evenings.[10]

By the time of his visit to the Arts Council, Haughey had begun to think seriously about his famous proposal to support creative talent in musical composition, literature, painting and sculpture by exempting artists from income tax. In November 1967, just after he had opened the Rosc exhibition, Haughey received a letter from his friend, the peripatetic author Constantine FitzGibbon. Born in America, but raised in England, FitzGibbon had toured Europe as a young man. He moved to Ireland in 1965 and the following year rang Haughey with a proposal about a scheme for exempting artists from income tax. He fleshed out the details in a later letter to Haughey, noting that his proposals were fairly radical but might appeal to the minister, given what he had said at Rosc. FitzGibbon added that the only two people he had mentioned the scheme to were the then senator Garret FitzGerald, and the secretary to the Arts Council, Mervyn Wall. Both, according to FitzGibbon, were very keen on the idea. FitzGerald was going to speak to T.K. Whitaker about it, and he suspected the secretary of the Department of Finance might well be favourable. He ended his letter by saying as a writer, who was married to a painter, how gratifying it was to see the ministry of finance headed by 'a man with so great an interest in the arts, and Ireland's position in contemporary culture'.[11] By February 1968 Haughey had told the editor of the *Irish Press*, Tim Pat Coogan, about his burgeoning plan. After a dinner Coogan wrote to ask Haughey whether he wanted him 'to keep your Arts proposal secret for the time being ... about these very exciting developments'.[12] Haughey replied that he was making no comment about them for the time being but would be happy to talk to Michael Mills, the paper's political correspondent, on the proposals, as Coogan had

suggested.[13] Mills was impressed by Haughey in this period but grew disillusioned with him in the post-arms crisis period and became a strong
admirer of Jack Lynch.[14]

It would take another full year for Haughey to finalise his tax exemption for artists scheme before publicly announcing it in the May 1969
budget when he simply said that as 'further encouragement to the creative artists in our midst and to help create a sympathetic environment
here in which the arts can flourish I will provide in the Finance Bill
that painters, sculptors, writers and composers living and working in
Ireland will be free of tax on all earnings derived from work of cultural
merit'.[15] Haughey's imaginative gesture was broadly welcomed by the
arts community. The renowned sculptor Edward Delaney commented
that he had underestimated the government and had not anticipated
anything like the budget announcement, even though the Minister for
Finance was known for his support and interest in the arts.[16] Delaney
was but one of a number of artists who had been thinking of emigrating
due to the difficulty of earning a living in Ireland. Many artists remained
grateful to Haughey for the rest of their careers and into retirement for
what they saw as an imaginative and progressive gesture.[17] Haughey's
various ministerial initiatives had to be paid for and he continued to
seek foreign investment into the state. In April 1968, for example, he held
preliminary talks with a Middle Eastern tycoon, Sheikh Ali Ahmed, who
expressed an interest in investing £10–20 million in possible ventures
in oil refineries, steel mills and hotels.[18] Nothing came of any of these
initiatives, but they were symptomatic of Haughey's general attitude of
considering any and all propositions about investment into the state.

THE PROPORTIONAL REPRESENTATION REFERENDUM DEBACLE

For Haughey to implement any of his ideas he had to remain in power. It
was this hunger for office that prompted Fianna Fáil to attempt to change
the electoral system for the second time in less than a decade when they
again sought to persuade the people to replace Ireland's unique form of
proportional representation with a first-past-the-post system. The latter

system, in which voters voted for just one candidate, as distinct from multiple candidates, had been a goal of Fianna Fáil's since long before the first referendum in 1959.

The referendum was held in mid-October 1968 and, spurred on by six wins in seven by-elections since Lynch took over the leadership, Fianna Fáil was confident that it would prevail. Lynch's huge popularity throughout the country was seen by the party as its trump card. It also thought that it could persuade non-Fianna Fáil partisans to its side because Fine Gael's leader, Liam Cosgrave, was widely known to have been in favour of it and was trying (unsuccessfully, as it turned out) to persuade senior party members to support the proposal.[19] Notwithstanding Cosgrave's penchant for the straight vote, every other member of Fine Gael's frontbench was against the proposal. In February 1968 Cosgrave gave an impassioned speech in favour of changing the electoral system at a Fine Gael parliamentary party meeting which went on long into the night and at which he fully expected to bring his party around to his view. He was badly mistaken. As Collins and Meehan perceptively note, he was devastated by the rejection of his colleagues who, to a man, opposed change.[20] It was a crushing blow to Cosgrave, but also a damaging one for his political opponents in Fianna Fáil, who could not now call upon any significant opposition figure to speak in favour of changing the electoral system. In some of its referendum literature Fianna Fáil stated that some of the best and most constructive minds in Fine Gael were in favour of the proposal and it would be a 'tragic, historical mistake' if those who out of genuine conviction normally voted Fine Gael decided to view the changes in the electoral system as simply a Fianna Fáil proposal that should be voted down for that reason.[21]

The main problem for Fianna Fáil was that it basically employed the same sterile arguments it had used back in 1959: that proportional representation essentially produced unstable and internally divided coalition governments, which could in time lead to a negation of democracy; and that the first-past-the-post system produced strong, effective, single-party governments. It also proffered its long-held view that the straight vote allowed the wishes of the voters to be more clearly known, in contrast to proportional representation, whose cross-voting led to all sorts of inefficiencies and injustices.[22] It reiterated its previous arguments that people could not understand how proportional representation worked, that it led to long, tedious, boring counts, and was basically a game of voting chance.

Fianna Fáil could not, however, refute the idea that had taken hold among pretty much all non-Fianna Fáil voters that it was a cunning plan to keep it in perpetual power. This was memorably summed up by the Labour Party's pithy slogan: 'The Straight Vote is Crooked – Vote No!'[23] Fianna Fáil tried in vain to counteract this view by maintaining that its proposal would be as challenging electorally for it as a party as for the opposition. Fianna Fáil claimed that it had the confidence to face that challenge in the spirit of all those who wanted to see reform and regeneration of the exciting times of the late 1960s.[24] Haughey's response to the Labour slogan was to argue that it was a political smokescreen. All politicians of the left, whether they were in Labour, Sinn Féin or the Connolly Clubs, had a vested interest in chaos and disorder, which was what proportional representation gave them.[25] Fianna Fáil considered all types of slogans to counteract the Labour charge but could come up with nothing more inspiring than 'The Straight Vote is Simple, Fair, Democratic – Vote Yes'. Among others, Haughey rejected 'A New Style for the Seventies – Change to the single seat and straight vote'; 'A New Style in Politics – The single seat, the straight vote'; and 'Change to the Single Seat – Vote for the Straight Vote'. He told the Fianna Fáil activist Neville Keery, who had sent him a list of suggested slogans, that one was more uninspired than the next and that he admired the effectiveness of the Labour slogan which, he thought was straight and to the point, if wrong.[26]

In a nod to the idea that all politics is local, Fianna Fáil introduced one novel approach to the debate. It argued that individual suburbs in Dublin could have their own TD if the straight vote was adopted and another referendum on the same day to change the number of TDs per constituency was also accepted by the electorate. To the voters of Raheny and Edenmore, Fianna Fáil advanced the view that in the new system constituencies would be small, compact and accessible, and the local TD would have a far more intimate knowledge of the particular area and its problems. The appeal to voter localism was stressed by insisting that the TD would be far closer to the people he represented and thus capable of giving them much better service, while at the same time having more time to devote to his parliamentary duties.[27] Haughey's friend P.J. Mara told him that the appeal to the voters of Raheny and Edenmore and the handout they received could easily be replicated for use in other areas of Dublin's northside, such as Drumcondra, Glasnevin, Donnycarney, Fairview and so on.[28] At a meeting in Carlow in September 1968 Haughey insisted that with the straight vote local areas would become more conscious of themselves as a community rather than as simply an area giving public support to one political party or the other.[29] For Haughey, one of the benefits of single-seat constituencies was that it would transform political life by eliminating those he described as 'mediocrities'.[30] This was hardly likely to endear him to his political contemporaries, regardless of party, as very many of them had been elected on later counts on transfers from sometimes unlikely quarters. As he told one of his correspondents who had argued that Ireland did not need a change in the electoral system but rather a fixed-term parliament, 'I am after ... a really first class legislature.'[31] This was in the context of increasing pay and conditions for politicians, which most certainly did endear him to his parliamentary peers.

In an attempt to counter the opposition's argument that the referendum was a waste of time and money and nothing more than a cynical ploy to keep Fianna Fáil in power for ever, the party brought the noted German political scientist Ferdinand Hermens of the University of Cologne to Dublin to speak at a public event in Dublin. In 1941 Hermens had written an important book on voting systems called *Democracy or Anarchy? A Study of Proportional Representation* and had analysed the impact that electoral systems had in structuring party competition. He was a member of an advisory council on electoral reform set up by the German Ministry of the Interior after the war, which recommended the plurality or first-past-the-post system. Fianna Fáil was anxious to dispel the belief that the proposed new system would lead to continuous government by one party – namely itself – and wanted international approval for its proposal. Haughey had contacted Hermens in August 1968 and asked him to come to Ireland to speak at a public debate on the merits of the first-past-the-post system. Hermens agreed, writing to Haughey that he had been following Ireland's debate on the issue in the press and would be glad to take part in the debate.[32] Fianna Fáil invested significantly in Hermens's visit. He spoke at a press conference at the Gresham Hotel, gave a lecture under the auspices of the financial magazine *Business and Finance* at the Royal Hibernian Hotel and met President Éamon de Valera.[33] In his lecture Hermens maintained that proportional representation led to paralysis. Then, rather darkly and dramatically, he argued that proportional representation was the method within which dictatorships lurked to take over those countries that used it as an electoral system. He argued that Ireland now had the opportunity to join the great nations where democracy had been safe, stable and efficient for over a century by switching to the plurality system.[34]

It was all in vain, however, as the people once more rejected the straight vote with just over 60 per cent voting no. This was a much more decisive no vote than nine years earlier, and only four of the state's thirty-eight constituencies (Clare, Donegal North East, Donegal South West and Galway West) had voted for change. The results in Dublin were particularly bad for Fianna Fáil with a No vote in the region of 70 per cent. Haughey's constituency of Dublin North East ignored his arguments and returned a majority of almost 20,000 against the proposal, the highest in the state.[35] It was a crushing blow to his argument that the straight vote would benefit the ordinary people of Dublin's northside.

A SLOW RECOVERY

Any disappointment Haughey felt at the defeat was overshadowed by the events of a month earlier when he was involved in serious crash in the early hours of Friday morning, 20 September 1968. Returning from a Fianna Fáil convention in Enniscorthy, Co. Wexford, Haughey's ministerial car crashed at 4.30 a.m. in torrential rain, gale force winds and poor visibility on the Cooladangan Bridge on the Wexford side of Arklow. He sustained a fractured kneecap, suspected fractures of the ribs and various minor abrasions. His driver, Garda Gerry Connolly from west Cork, also suffered a number of injuries. Another passenger, Captain John O'Carroll, the assistant general secretary of Fianna Fáil, was slightly injured. A passing local motorist contacted the Gardaí, who brought the three men to the home of Dr Declan Connolly in Arklow. From there Haughey was taken by ambulance to the Mater Private nursing home in one ambulance while Garda Connolly and Captain O'Carroll were taken to the Mater Hospital in another ambulance.[36]

Later that morning, Peter Berry, the secretary of the Department of Justice, rang Haughey's private secretary Brendan O'Donnell. He said, 'I wish to tell you the minister was involved in an accident last night and won't be in today' and then slammed down the phone.[37] O'Donnell immediately went to the Mater Private, where he found Haughey in considerable pain and discomfort, insisting that his ministerial bag be brought to him. His doctors refused and ordered O'Donnell to leave. Initial reports that Haughey would still be able to play a central role in the referendum campaign, on which he was one of Fianna Fáil's main and most effective spokesmen, proved very wide of the mark and he did not leave hospital until 1 November, nearly six weeks later. There has long been speculation and rumour that Haughey had been driving the car. Two years earlier the Minister for Justice, Brian Lenihan, had written to all ministers stating his concern about the very high incidence of crashes in ministerial cars, which he blamed on excessive speed. He had instructed the Garda Commissioner to bring to the notice of ministerial drivers the desirability of keeping speeds within reasonable limits in these high-powered vehicles, as Garda drivers were not required to keep to the speed limit.[38] Haughey was certainly driving the car that night. He told his wife Maureen in its aftermath that his Garda driver was tired so he did the driving himself.[39] Haughey had a full day of engagements the following day as Minister for Finance and Fianna Fáil's director of elections, and was anxious to get home. He had stayed long enough after the convention mixing with the party's grassroots. There was always drink involved after these Fianna Fáil conventions and it was most likely that Haughey would have imbibed somewhat. He had a reputation for driving fearfully fast and it seems he simply lost control of the powerful vehicle after a long night in the foul weather, leading to the accident.

Haughey had already had difficulties with at least one of his Garda drivers. A few days before Brian Lenihan wrote to ministers warning about excessive speed, Haughey asked him to remove one of his Garda drivers, Michael O'Sullivan, also from Cork, from his transport duties. He complained that he had been embarrassed by his driver when in the company of the Dutch ambassador. Earlier the same day, after Haughey had left his office he had spoken to Garda O'Sullivan about reading a newspaper in the car; it did not look very well, he said, for a ministerial driver to have a newspaper so prominently displayed at the windscreen while waiting in public. Later that evening, after a reception at the Dutch embassy, Haughey was accompanied to his car by the ambassador. He found Garda O'Sullivan engrossed in a newspaper again and making no attempt, contrary to protocol, to open the door for the minister. Haughey complained to Lenihan that O'Sullivan did not move at all and the general impression given to the ambassador and his wife was appalling. He reported that he spoke to O'Sullivan again about reading newspapers while on duty and the guard replied: 'Mr Haughey, I will read a newspaper whenever I like. It is a free country.'[40] Haughey said that he was completely astounded, as nothing in his driver's previous demeanour had suggested such a reaction. He also criticised O'Sullivan's driving as hesitant and cumbersome and said that he was clearly not cut out to be a ministerial driver. The following week there was a report of the incident in the *Cork Examiner*, in which the Garda was named as John O'Sullivan. The report stated that O'Sullivan had apologised for the first incident and believed that the rule about not reading newspapers applied only when the car was in the precincts of Leinster House, which explained the second incident. The article concluded by pondering whether there would be a relaxation to the rule, if indeed there even was a rule, which compelled a driver to sit outside a house for hours without permission to while the time away reading a newspaper or a book.[41]

Haughey's issue was not that the rule, either in spirit or letter, had been broken, but the fact that his driver, as he saw it, was not doing his job. He routinely praised his drivers, and other members of the Gardaí who had helped him. One early morning in February 1965 he was on the verge of running out of petrol near Kildare, while coming home from Limerick on his own, and was helped by two gardaí who, he later told the commissioner, were a credit to the force.[42] A quarter of a century later he praised another garda as a credit to the force to a different commissioner after the garda assisted him through heavy traffic on his way to a function when he was Taoiseach.[43] There were other similar notes in the intervening years. He had long and friendly relationships with Max Webster and Bobby O'Brien, who between them drove him when he was in office from the mid-1960s until he retired as Taoiseach in 1992. Both men were invariably invited to join the Haughey family at the breakfast table when they called for him in the morning.[44] Haughey was certainly a demanding minister and Taoiseach to work for. He worked his civil servants hard, did not engage in small talk with them, beyond the odd quip, and expected them to do their job and work the hours he did. If he did not think civil servants were up to the job he would have them reassigned.

Haughey's recuperation in the Mater Private nursing home was accompanied by a large volume of post and then visitors from the worlds of politics, the civil service, industry, literature, the arts and journalism. O'Donnell went to see him regularly and found him reflective and frustrated in equal measure.[45] The length of time Haughey spent in hospital surprised and in time worried his friends and acquaintances. The problem was that a few days after he was admitted to hospital he suffered an embolism, a partial blockage of a blood vessel caused by his injuries, and nearly died. His general fitness from regular hunting and swimming most likely saved him. Des O'Malley might have distrusted the Minister for Finance from the time he first entered the Dáil, but this did not stop him writing to Haughey a month after the accident to say how sorry he was to find him still in hospital.[46] One of Haughey's friends, the public relations consultant Frank Ryan, told him that his very many friends were becoming increasingly alarmed at reports about what he had been going through. Haughey's sense of humour was still intact; he replied to Ryan that, just like Mark Twain, reports of his demise had been greatly exaggerated.[47] The manager of the Gresham Hotel, Toddy O'Sullivan, and his wife, Niamh, visited him in late October and decided he needed building up. Niamh O'Sullivan, reputed to be one of the finest cooks in Ireland, promptly baked Haughey a cake and some bread after her visit and asked how he would rate that for devotion. He replied that it was a mystery 'how the great T.O.S. kept that immaculate figure with such temptation at hand'.[48] The Fianna Fáil organiser Padraic O'Halpin, a supporter of George Colley, told Haughey that he should get a good rest as he had a lot more to give to Ireland than a kneecap and a few ribs.[49]

In a reference to the crash happening in the middle of the referendum, one of his correspondents, Rosaleen Moore, told him that whatever about Fianna Fáil, the country would survive with or without PR and he should just concentrate on getting better, adding that it was 'hard to kill a bad thing – so you should survive'.[50] A common theme of much of the correspondence Haughey received after his accident was that he was much missed from the social and political scene around Dublin. The reaction of Denis Corboy, the director of the Irish Council of the European Movement, that Haughey's absence had been 'most unfortunate – even tragic', although hyperbolic, summed up the attitude of many of his wide circle of friends.[51] The journalist Michael Mills, at this stage still an admirer of Haughey, told him that very many people were interested in his welfare and that the general attitude he detected in a recent tour of the country was that he was very much missed.[52] Another journalist, the editor of the *Irish Independent*, Louis McRedmond, wrote to Haughey sympathising with him on his accident and his subsequent absence from the rest of the referendum campaign, and noting that he was missed not only by his party 'but here at the Independent where we would have been glad of a sharper mind to do battle with than some of those on offer'.[53] This was a not-so-subtle nod to the paucity of talent in the Fianna Fáil ministerial ranks when it came to defending the referendum proposals. The editor of the *Irish Press*, Tim Pat Coogan, also referenced the referendum when writing to Haughey in its aftermath, declaring that he hoped Haughey would not get too much worry or pressure on him over the defeat as 'good men are scarce and whether in politics or any other field you follow you will come out at or near the top.[54] Coogan wisely noted that while 'the welter of politics was always boiling', none of Haughey's achievements would be lasting if he could not share them with his family. This hit a nerve with Haughey, who thanked Coogan for his thoughtful letter, which came as a 'tonic'.[55]

Haughey left hospital and returned to Grangemore on 1 November to continue his recovery. He was ordered off all work by his doctors and although O'Donnell was over and back to Grangemore the material he brought Haughey from his office was of an insignificant nature. Haughey followed the 1968 American presidential election closely and was disappointed that the Democratic candidate Hubert Humphrey lost narrowly to the Republican Richard Nixon. Humphrey's campaign manager, Larry O'Brien, escaped to Ireland soon after the campaign and paid Haughey a brief visit where they talked about the difficulties he had to contend with in battling Nixon. Haughey also followed the racing press closely in his convalescence. He was particularly interested in the thoroughbred Sir Ivor, owned by the recently departed American ambassador to Ireland, Raymond Guest. Earlier that summer Sir Ivor had won the 2,000 Guineas and the Epsom Derby. During Haughey's illness he followed the horse's fortunes as it finished second in the Prix de l'Arc de Triomphe, before winning the Champion Stakes at Newmarket and the Washington, DC, International in Maryland. Haughey told Guest that he was absolutely thrilled with Sir Ivor's performance but that his own recovery from the accident was fairly slow.[56]

By Christmas 1968 Haughey was nearly fully recovered. In another indicator of how close he was to the journalistic community, the editor of the *Sunday Independent*, Hector Legge, wrote to Haughey in mid-December inquiring about his health and asking whether he would like any reference to him in the following Sunday's paper. Haughey declined, saying it would be better not to say anything for the moment but that he was almost a hundred per cent fit again and looking forward to getting back to the office.[57] He remained, however, in a thoughtful and contemplative mood. In a revealing three-part profile on Haughey published just before the June 1969 general election, headlined 'Horseman, Pass By!', the *Irish Times* stated that friends of the minister felt that the accident had changed him; it had made him look differently at life, and at his own limitations, bringing a new maturity. One unnamed associate said it was as if he 'had undergone some kind of mental plastic surgery'.[58] While the profile was anonymised in the newspaper it was actually written by Michael Viney, who had alerted Haughey to it and sought his co-oper-ation. Prior to its publication Viney thanked Haughey for co-operating in a project he did not really care for while telling him that his original profile had been 'subject to extensive additions and interpolations by other hands: it is now the product of "a team"'.[59]

Whatever about the mental anguish of the accident, Haughey cer-tainly remained in physical pain but was determined to regain his fitness. One of the first things he did on his return home was to indulge in his favourite pastime of riding horses. At the beginning of 1969 he told Bill Stanhope, the Earl of Harrington, and Master of the Limerick Hounds, that he was 'almost completely fit again and am actually riding. However, I did promise my doctors that I would not hunt this season. They tell me that it would be quite detrimental if I were to get a fall!'[60] His doctors recommended a sun holiday and cleared him to travel to Jamaica later in January with Maureen and their friends Pat and Joan O'Connor. At this stage the Caribbean was a favourite holiday destination for the Haugheys and O'Connors – later that year, in October, they would visit Antigua and Anguilla for nine days. Haughey was back from his January holidays for the opening of Ballymun church on the first Sunday of February, performed by the Archbishop of Dublin, John Charles McQuaid.

He was then faced with preparing for the budget a few months later and a widely predicted general election at some stage in the summer or autumn. Key to that election would be Fianna Fáil's legendary ability to get out the vote. This brought the question of its organisational abilities back to Haughey's agenda. During his recuperation Frank Ryan told him that if the party aimed to win another term in office, something would have to be done about its organisation at both a national and constituency level. It was 'indisputable that headquarters conveys an image of leth-argy and inefficiency'.[61] The Minister for Transport and Power, Erskine

Childers, had similar worries and wondered how the party could connect with the floating voter given that it did no opinion polling and had
no proper public relations organisation. He told Haughey that Fianna
Fáil could not win the election 'without a much deeper penetration of
the electorate' and the party needed 'more indoctrination'.[62] Both men
were worried about Fianna Fáil's lack of vision in communicating to the
people what the party actually stood for. Childers told Haughey that the
party needed a statement of philosophy, which he was trying to write.

Notwithstanding its spectacular success as a political movement,
which was copperfastened by its results in the 1969 general election,
what Fianna Fáil stood for remained an ongoing issue for its supporters
and members alike. At the end of March 1970, Des O'Kennedy, of the
O'Kennedy and Brindley advertising and marketing agency, who handled
a lot of public relations material for Fianna Fáil in this period, advised
Haughey that the party should provide a fact sheet for all cumann members. They should also give a concise statement of Fianna Fáil policy
and achievements to all new members, as these were the people who
did the arguing in the pubs and should thus be armed with facts to
'propagandise' with. He despaired of the literature the party issued to
new members, lamenting to Haughey it was 'mainly devoted to Dev's
speech in 1926, plus obituaries of dead warriors'.[63] Yet if paid advisers
like O'Kennedy, and party stalwarts like Childers, and indeed Haughey,
struggled to convey what Fianna Fáil actually meant, it certainly did not
affect its electoral results. When Childers wrote in January 1969 that
Fianna Fáil would not win the next election unless it did something
about understanding the electorate, he was reflecting an attitude widely
felt across the party. It would fall to Haughey as Minister for Finance to
present a budget in May that would allow Fianna Fáil to go to the country
with a reason to keep the party in power.

AN ELECTION BUDGET

The budget Haughey delivered on 7 May 1969 was described in the *Irish
Press* as a 'Share and Care Alike' one.[64] Writing over three decades later,
Tim Pat Coogan, editor of the newspaper at the time, called the budget

blatantly election-slanted; it increased social welfare benefits across a range of services to the underprivileged, but was clearly a vote-buying exercise. He added that it was to his 'shame' that the *Irish Press* headlined the budget as it did.[65] The budget saw the most comprehensive package of social benefits ever produced for the weaker sections of society and bore, as Michael Mills, the political correspondent of the *Irish Press*, put it, 'Mister Haughey's own personal stamp in his oft-expressed concern for those who are not in a position to provide for themselves'.[66] Haughey set aside £12.5 million for increased children's allowances, social welfare supports, tax reliefs, and public service pensions. Taxes on tobacco, alcohol and petrol were raised. Haughey argued that it was a budget designed to eliminate injustice and poverty, and to bring everyone in the community a little further along the road to prosperity and the good life. He ended his speech by proclaiming that he dared to hope that the budget would be regarded as 'enlightened and that it will take its place in the financial calendar as one which made a real contribution to improving the present, and safeguarding the future, for the ordinary people of Ireland'.[67]

Reaction to the budget was varied. The NFA bemoaned the fact that farmers would only see infinitesimal increases, while publicans, cigarette manufacturers and petrol companies complained about increases in taxes, arguing that they were unoriginal and unimaginative. The Federation of Irish Industries did, however, say that Haughey had brought in a responsible budget because he had placed its emphasis on social welfare. The trade union movement offered a cautious welcome but warned there was much more to be done to ensure a more equal Ireland. On the journalistic front the *Irish Independent* led with the headline 'Robin Hood Haughey'.[68] It noted that the budget had met with a mixed reaction. The *Cork Examiner* decided to mix its own metaphors by stating that Haughey had assumed the mantle of Robin Hood rather than that of the Fairy Godmother in clamping down on luxury spending so that the less affluent could be given more.[69] Why this should have been a matter of shame to anyone is rather perplexing. The *Irish Independent*, under the headline 'Budget gave no pointer to election date', suggested that whether this was or was not an election budget depended on whether one believed Jack Lynch would go to the country in June or wait until later in the year.[70] There was the usual charge from the Labour Party that Fianna Fáil was doing what was best for itself rather than the country and from Fine Gael that it was a cynical exercise in vote-catching. Yet, rather than being cowed by the budget, both opposition parties called for the immediate end of the Dáil and an election.[71]

Correspondence to Haughey concentrated on his innovative artists' tax exemption scheme, tax reliefs, and the social solidarity elements associated with the budget. It came from all quarters including political colleagues, the civil service, the private sector and the arts community. From one of the country's main employers, Waterford Glass, the managing director Noel Griffin congratulated Haughey on a superb budget, noting that the extension of export tax reliefs was a great inducement for Irish industry to continue its export drive. Yet in a significant nod to its social solidarity elements he said that many of the budget's impositions were necessary to keep down luxury spending and reduce the country's balance of payments. He finally noted that the increase in children's allowance went a long way towards meeting the many social aspects of the state's financial policies that needed looking after.[72] Haughey replied that Griffin would have the satisfaction of knowing that the submission he had put forward contributed in a large degree to the adoption of the proposal extending export tax relief.[73] His former civil servant in Justice, Paddy Terry, wrote on behalf of the Association of Higher Civil Servants to thank him for bringing parity to civil service pensioners and the granting of pensions to widows of civil servants, which had long been a bone of contention for civil servants.[74] Dozens of widows of civil servants also wrote to thank him for this gesture. There were many comments about the social solidarity elements of the budget. These were summed up on the day of the budget by the first-time Fianna Fáil TD David Andrews, later to become a bitter enemy of Haughey, who thanked him for a really great budget, stating that he had 'done a great service in a practical fashion to the concept of social justice'.[75] From another legendary Fianna Fáil family, Terry de Valera, then Taxing Master of the Supreme and High Courts, and a son of President Éamon de Valera, told Haughey he spoke with such clarity, dignity and consideration on the night of the budget on RTÉ that it was his finest performance.[76]

It was, however, Haughey's proposal that painters, sculptors, writers and composers living and working in Ireland would be exempt from income tax on all earnings derived from works of cultural merit that brought the largest and most positive response. On the day of the budget it was immediately welcomed as being both magnificent and tremendous by Maurice MacGonigal, the president of the Royal Hibernian Academy, who stated that it was the kind of thing that could save an artist from a tremendous amount of anxiety and would give great encouragement to all artists.[77] MacGonigal would later change his mind, describing the scheme as benefiting only the 'art nits of Dublin and the art parasites of Europe'.[78] David Andrews's father, Todd, at that stage chairman of the RTÉ Authority, told Haughey that it was 'a wonderful stroke of positive genius' to recognise writers and painters so handsomely in the budget, but that had not yet dawned on the media, including RTÉ.[79] From the Supreme Court, Haughey's close friend Justice Brian Walsh humorously quipped, 'needless to say all my judgements in the future will be of cultural and artistic merit', to which Haughey replied, 'I will read your judgements with even greater care in the future.'[80] From the *Irish Times*, the literary editor Terence de Vere White told Haughey, 'Your cultural proposals have sent all the bells ringing. Seán Ó Faoláin is on the phone to say it is world-pioneering.'[81] Ó Faoláin was quoted in the following day's *Irish Times* as saying that the scheme would lead to a marvellous cultural renaissance in Ireland. For his part, de Vere White said that he had written six novels in ten years and had been described as the most prolific of Irish writers, plaintively adding, 'Who could live on that?'[82]

From London, the broadcaster and former chairman of the RTÉ Authority Eamonn Andrews reported to Haughey that 'there was a great buzz of comment over here about the Budget nod you gave in the general direction of the arts. What a great idea. Whether it can be worked out without spilling a lot of blood over a lot of statues, I don't know, but the principle is such a refreshingly civilised one in this materialistic world of ours that it must be applauded. I do so.'[83] The playwright and author Hugh Leonard was also supportive, writing to tell Haughey what a marvellous precedent he had created: 'You have made an immeasurable contribution to the arts in Ireland and people such as myself are very much in your debt.'[84] On Haughey's death over three and a half decades later Leonard was far less effusive, describing him as a fantasist and a noble statesman who set no law except his own. He lamented what he saw as Haughey's failure to follow through on the artists' scheme, despite telling the Revenue to give the benefit of the doubt to writers: 'I never got nor ever asked for a penny out of that.'[85] He did seek Haughey's help to get a telephone line installed to his Dalkey home before he returned to Dublin from England in April 1970 to take advantage of the artists' tax exemption scheme.[86] He quickly turned against Haughey after the arms trial, and unmercifully satirised him over a decade later in his 1982 play *Kill*, mocking his patronage of the arts.[87]

In the United States, the arts magazine *Saturday Review* welcomed the initiative, editorialising that there was something rather wonderful about a country willing to give a substantial tax break to writers, painters, composers, and others of their ilk. It further noted that Ireland evidently intended to show that it considered the creators of art as worthy beneficiaries of tax incentives.[88] The *New York Times* declared that Haughey had shown an enlightened and sympathetic attitude towards the arts and that he had placed Ireland in a unique position, but it warned that it was too early to say whether Ireland was to become a modern Athens for the world's artists, or a tatty paradise for Europe's parasites, or both.[89] A number of months after the Finance Act had placed the scheme on the statute book, the screenwriter and film producer Kevin McClory wrote to Haughey that many of his friends were already in the process of finalising arrangements to move to Ireland and others were investigating the possibility of doing so. He stated the evidence was clear that the Act was attracting creative talent from all parts of the world daily and that this would bring about great cultural benefits to the country.[90] Another correspondent, Nancy Latimer, painted a different picture, after she had been turned down by the Revenue Commissioners, lambasting Haughey for turning it into a scheme for the famous and well-established which

treated some citizens as more equal than others. In late 1972 she excoriated it as 'a gimmick for well-heeled foreigners to come here and enjoy
tax privilege but "No Irish Need Apply"'.[91] Haughey replied that there
was nothing he could do as the scheme was administered by the Revenue
Commissioners, but he did offer to contact them on her behalf. He did,
however, take exception to her use of the phrase 'well-heeled foreigners',
maintaining, 'It is not a gimmick and the overwhelming majority of
those who have so far qualified for exemption are Irish.'[92]

Haughey's initiative on the arts has been both lauded and criticised
ever since. One of his most vociferous critics, the journalist Bruce Arnold,
later complained that it was constitutionally questionable to leave the
rest of the population without the selective benefit that Haughey gave
to artists. In an overblown exercise of intellectual casuistry he accused
Haughey of being to a large extent in the hands of a set of instincts that
Haughey did not in some way understand himself and that he was led
by others, most notably Anthony Cronin, who would later become his
cultural adviser when he was Taoiseach, in respect of the tax benefit.[93]
A more generous approach was offered by the painter Robert Ballagh,
who painted a famous portrait of Haughey in 1980, titled *The Decade
of Endeavour*, but fell out with him over the design of a government-is-
sued stamp commemorating the bicentenary of the French Revolution
in 1989. Ballagh felt that when politicians intervened in the arts it was
nearly always in negative and censorious terms. The tax exemption for
artists, on the contrary, he maintained, was a remarkable intervention
on a practical and philosophical level, saying that this state valued what
artists do in society.[94] This was a theme the actress Fionnula Flanagan
alluded to some twenty years after the introduction of the scheme, when
she told Haughey that 'Politicians of course are notorious for their "token"
support of the arts – but in your case this is not true. Your record in
support of the arts is splendid and bespeaks a dimension in your states-
manship which alas, is all too uncommon.'[95]

THE 1969 GENERAL ELECTION

The general welcome for the May budget encouraged Jack Lynch to go to the country in June 1969 to seek his own mandate as Taoiseach. On Wednesday 21 May, just before 11 p.m., he travelled to Áras an Uachtaráin to advise President de Valera to dissolve the Dáil. Polling day was set for Thursday 18 June, which left four weeks for hectic campaigning. Lynch had been contemplating calling an election since before the budget. Haughey had been doing the same, and just before the budget he commissioned a report on voting intentions and issues from Conrad Jameson Associates in London, which specialised in survey research.[96] The report surveyed 1,000 respondents on the basis of a national quota sample of the population during April 1969. It sought to glean information on three specific issues: whether Fianna Fáil should seek to call an election in the following few weeks; how the party compared to what the report called its main potential rival, Labour; and an examination of the main target group that Fianna Fáil needed to win – the youth vote. The emphasis on Labour, rather than Fine Gael, as the main rival to Fianna Fáil reflected a growing belief in political circles that Labour was the coming force in Irish politics and that Fine Gael, notwithstanding its 'Just Society' wing, was stagnating.

Labour was better resourced than it had ever been before, had a well-staffed head office, was running ninety-nine candidates, over double the number it had run just four years earlier in 1965, and had a raft of candidates with a national profile, such as the academics and broadcasters Justin Keating and David Thornley. Perhaps its most exciting candidate was Conor Cruise O'Brien, the internationally renowned writer, academic and former diplomat, who was chosen to run in Haughey's constituency of Dublin North East, one of no fewer than three Labour candidates. It was a sign of Labour's optimism. Labour was also boosted by a specially commissioned Gallup poll of 2,000 respondents on political attitudes, which put its support at 29 per cent in Dublin, up ten points on its 1965 showing, and a more modest 18 per cent in the rest of the country.[97] Its heady ambition to break the two-party monopoly was summed up by its anti-coalitionist stance and its slogan 'The Seventies will be Socialist'. Meanwhile, Fine Gael was seen, particularly in the media, as old and unfashionable. It was particularly contemptuous of the Labour manifesto, with Liam Cosgrave describing it as something for 1984 rather than 1969.[98]

The Jameson report claimed that perhaps the strongest argument against Labour was the socialist nature of its policies and their tinge of communism. Of those who had complaints or dislikes to express about Labour some 25 per cent complained of its socialism and its possible association with communism. It stated that the recruitment of someone like Conor Cruise O'Brien had only increased those fears. Fifty-seven per cent of the people polled agreed with the statement that Labour would get the support of a lot of people if only it wasn't quite so strongly socialist. Crucially, the report offered the view that such widespread fear would form a good platform for arguments that could be used to reassure the potential anti-Labour vote, and to dissuade the Labour sympathisers. Another worry for Fianna Fáil was that 44 per cent of the sample agreed that Labour TDs seemed to take more trouble for their constituents than TDs of other parties. Given that 86 per cent of respondents agreed that they would like a TD who would spend more time in the constituency helping people with their problems, this seemed clearly to concur with the view that Labour was on the verge of a major breakthrough. The pithy phrase used by Jameson: 'Labour, it seems, is nearer to the people' was enough to chill the blood of any member of any Fianna Fáil, including everyone in its cabinet.[99]

And that cabinet was the object of the sample's ire. Young people in particular were reported as having a comparatively low opinion of Fianna Fáil and its ministers. The report clearly elucidated an ongoing worry in Fianna Fáil that when it came to voting intentions young people were well below average in their support of the governing party. When young people were asked to rate each of the three parties on their characteristics, Fianna Fáil received below average ratings from young people on each of the three qualities: go-ahead; good at their job; honest. In the latter category Fianna Fáil received 47 per cent; the average was 60 per cent. This was the lowest score for all of the three traits and was made worse by the fact that when asked to list three out of a list of twelve adjectives which they felt described each of the four leading cabinet ministers, including Haughey, young people, particularly those in the 25–34 age bracket tended, much more than the average, to choose derogatory rather than laudatory words. One of the most important adjectives offered was honest/dishonest. The average score for the four leading ministers Lynch, Haughey, Colley and Blaney was 38 per cent, and this fell to 30 per cent for young people. Lynch alone, reflecting the widely used journalistic nickname 'Honest Jack', had a rate of 76 per cent for the honesty category. Haughey's rating in this category was just 7 per cent among young people, despite the fact that overall support for him came mainly from this sector of the community.

In putting the case for an early election the Jameson report put Labour support on 21.8 per cent nationwide, Fine Gael on 32.5 per cent and Fianna Fáil on 44.4 per cent. It also noted that the mood of the country remained emphatically optimistic and there was general satisfaction with the state of the economy. It crucially pointed to the fact that Fianna Fáil supporters were more confident of the outcome than either Fine Gael or Labour supporters and in that context it was likely that there would be a good turnout of Fianna Fáil voters at election time. To maximise an even greater Fianna Fáil turnout it advocated that guilt-ridden non-voters from the last election should be a key target group who must be made to feel that this was a critical election where every vote counted. Against the calling of an early election was the widely shared view that Labour would increase its vote quite considerably and a significant portion of that vote would come from Fianna Fáil defectors. More time would be needed to stem the leakage and build up an anti-Labour case in the minds of the electorate. Moreover, the report counselled, the message that needed to be aimed at the key target group of young voters who were interested in housing and the administration of welfare benefits might be difficult to develop in a short space of time.

Other minor irritants the report considered Fianna Fáil should be concerned about was the widely felt sense that the government was guilty in not making sufficient efforts to negotiate with the farmers; that it was becoming more autocratic and out of touch; that the medical and social services operated by the local authorities were not being administered properly; and that the recent salary raises for TDs had caused widespread ill will, coming as they did at a time when the nation's belt was being tightened. One of the most intriguing aspects of the report was the view expressed by young people that they felt themselves to be a type of 'proletariat'; they were either ignored or left out of a political system that neither encouraged their participation nor educated them to understand it. In fact, 65 per cent of all respondents agreed with the view that politics and government are so complicated that 'people like me' can't really understand what's going on. Fianna Fáil, as the party in power, it warned, was most to blame for this situation.

The most extraordinary of the findings and solutions offered by the report, however, related to Haughey. Assuming that an election provided the best opportunity for individual politicians to increase their personal stature, it said, it might be worth leaving time to allow him to establish a greater popular following. Considering that Haughey had been a minister since 1961 and that an election had to be held by 1970 at the latest, it is hard to see how much more time he actually needed to build up a public profile. He was possibly the best-known member of the cabinet apart from Jack Lynch. He was, however, behind Colley in terms of popularity in the country at large: 37 per cent of people said they would like to see Colley succeeding Lynch as Taoiseach, compared to only 27 per cent who preferred Haughey. Haughey was more respected for his abilities, while it was considered that Colley had done more for Ireland. Among Fianna Fáil supporters, Haughey and Colley were neck and neck in relation to succeeding Lynch, while Haughey was considered both abler and to have done more for Ireland. The report concluded that no cabinet minister had a clear and radiant image, and none could count on a large popular following. This situation, it was considered, could work either for or against Haughey; but, the report argued, it might be well to allow time in which to build up an image, particularly within the party, so that it would be clear after the forthcoming election that victory was primarily due to him. Again, it is difficult to see how Haughey could have done any more since he was first elected to build up an image or profile in the party. Both prior to and after his first election to the Dáil he had been stumping around the country reporting on the state of the Fianna Fáil organisation and meeting its members. As a minister he was widely considered by other parliamentarians and indeed the wider Fianna Fáil family to be among the most approachable members of the cabinet. He held the crucial Finance portfolio and was constantly in demand for party events.

It might simply have been the case that Conrad Jameson was unaware of Haughey's position within Fianna Fáil or of the general nature of Irish politics and the fact that an election was due within the year. After the election had been called Jameson wrote to Haughey reinforcing the general message of his report. He strongly reiterated the point that the enemy was Labour, not just because it was gaining a disproportionate number of defectors from both Fianna Fáil and Fine Gael and was a threat to the future, but mostly because it presented a youthful image which Fianna Fáil needed to win back. One way of doing this, he argued, was to show that Labour's policies were essentially old-fashioned, not that its doctrines were foreign or morally wrong. This just seemed to fall on deaf ears among the public: 'Fianna Fáil by contrast stands for up-to-the-minute computerized, supercritical critical path analysis, management techniques, etc., while Labour has no such skills and is too old hat to take an interest in what these skills can do.'[100] What Haughey thought of the phrase 'supercritical critical path analysis' can only be guessed at but it must surely have led to a lifting of those famous hooded eyes and the emission of an expletive or even two. Jameson cautioned Haughey that he 'should at all costs avoid getting into the role of hatchet man who defends the Fianna Fáil record as this role could be construed as cynical and complacent'.[101] He urged Haughey to attack Labour on the grounds that it was a danger to rising standards of living but to stress that materialism in itself came with obligations, while in the same breath raising hopes for material aplenty. He believed that Fianna Fáil's best electoral hope was to honour its history by mentioning past achievements almost backhandedly by way of benchmark references to what was still to be done. Jameson ended by telling Haughey that his image could best be developed by showing terrific moral conviction and seriousness in everything he did.

In light of his report's findings that none of the ministers had a genuinely national following, Jameson asked Haughey whether the time was ripe in Ireland for 'projecting a new style of authority in a shirt-sleeves image of a political leader, a man who (during an election at least!) makes his own telephone calls, visits people in their homes, talks in an easy vernacular etc.'[102] That image summed up Jack Lynch as much as it did Haughey. Haughey, as Fianna Fáil's director of elections, was wise enough to base the party's campaign and whole electoral strategy around its leader in a manner befitting an American presidential election, complete with helicopter trips, mass rallies and the clever campaign slogan 'Let's Back Jack'. Haughey took Jameson's advice on board when it came to Labour, and missed no opportunity to accuse them of offering the electorate a form of extreme socialism which was old hat and had failed everywhere it had been tried. He particularly enjoyed attacking the new breed of Labour politicians, asking why Irish people should turn the clock back and adopt such socialism just to satisfy 'the whims of a small coterie of left-wing intellectuals. The Labour Party wants controls, regulation, regimentation. That is what extreme left-wing socialism means. It is a joyless, soul-destroying, materialistic concept of life.'[103] Haughey was but one of many Fianna Fáil politicians who enthusiastically embraced the 'red scare', attacking Labour as extreme socialists and crypto-communists. In a final note to every director of elections and every candidate in Dublin he stated Fianna Fáil's canvass showed that there were deep divisions among former supporters of the Labour Party. Ordinary members in the constituencies were deeply suspicious and resentful of the extreme left-wing intellectuals who had been forced upon them from outside. It was, he said, a battle between the party of Bill Norton and of those who wanted extreme socialism. He urged every Fianna Fáil activist to stress the point that there was now two Labour parties, with left-wing extremists trying to take over the traditional party.[104] This message was to prove brutally effective. Labour's unexpectedly poor showing, after putting forward an ill-judged multiplicity of candidates, fatally fracturing its electoral support, led some cynics to suggest that Labour rephrase their party's slogan 'The Seventies Will be Socialist' as 'The Socialists Will be Seventy'.

While Fianna Fáil put most of its resources into Jack Lynch's nation-wide tour, Haughey's individual efforts were no less vigorous. He appeared regularly on RTÉ radio and television. After one appearance on RTÉ's flagship programme *Seven Days*, its producer Muiris Mac Conghail, who Haughey had sparred with during the farmers' strike of 1966, fore-cast that he would gain a record poll in Dublin North East.[105] The same programme brought an enthusiastic response from within Fianna Fáil itself. Niall Andrews proclaimed that Haughey had put the heart back into the grassroots, who would be making a great effort in the coming week, and endorsed a colleague's comment: 'There's no doubt but it's Haughey I want to lead me into the '70s.'[106] A confidential report on the programme carried out by the audience research division of RTÉ found its way to Haughey. It noted that of the three participants, Haughey, Gerard Sweetman of Fine Gael, and Labour's Michael O'Leary, it was Haughey who was the most popular. He received remarkably little criticism and his confident and business-like approach was highly com-mended by many of the viewers.[107] Haughey put significant time and effort into his television and radio appearances and was always seeking to improve his performances. A year earlier he thanked one of his regu-lar correspondents, Frank Roe, who, while congratulating Haughey on a television appearance, warned him that on occasion he was prone to slipping into saying the word 'the' as 'de', just as Roe's Cork-born mother warned him against relapsing into the Corkman's 'dis, dhat, dhese, and dhose'.[108] Being accused of having a Cork accent would have been one of the cruellest jibes against Haughey, but he simply reassured Roe that he was especially grateful for his criticisms, which were very valuable and useful to get.

Haughey also had to deal with disgruntled potential candidates who did not make it onto the Fianna Fáil ticket, resignations from various cumainn officers over the selection of various candidates, and complaints of canvassers overstepping the mark in their enthusiasm for particular candidates. In Dublin North Central he received a complaint that canvassers for the party were advocating that voters should vote Colley number 1, Ryan number 2, which was not normal Fianna Fáil practice. Haughey replied, 'To say the least of it there are things happening in that constituency which are not in accordance with Fianna Fáil practices and traditions.'[109] It was a clear sign that he believed Colley was not above reproach in the robust game of electoral politics. Early in the campaign Haughey became ill after presiding over the selection of candidates for the Limerick East convention. He complained of stomach pains and was moved to hospital by the doctor who attended him. This was another attack of Haughey's recurring kidney stone problems. He stayed overnight in Barrington's Hospital before being released the following morning, later complaining that reports of his illness were exaggerated and that the doctor who attended to him was a bit 'over-fussy' in keeping him in overnight.[110] Nevertheless, it was a telling sign of a problem that would cause him much pain during the rest of his life.

In February 1969 Haughey purchased Abbeville, consisting of a twelve-bedroom house, an uninhabitable cottage and 270 acres of land, at Kinsaley for £146,977. He sold his house in Grangemore for £204,500. Haughey had been in negotiation with Franz Zielkowski, a German industrialist, for a number of months before finally buying the house and lands.[111] Zielkowski had bought Abbeville from Percy Reynolds, a horse breeder and former chairman of CIÉ, in 1963 and added extra land to the estate. Haughey had become aware through a friend, Standish Collen, that Zielkowski wanted to sell the house and lands and was open to offers. Ingrid Lauterbach, who managed his stud farm in Ashbourne, acted as an interpreter in the negotiations. Abbeville had been on the market for some considerable time before the Haugheys decided to buy it.

In December 1968 he told one of his correspondents that his plans for Abbeville were still at a very tentative stage and had not yet been finalised.[112] The row that erupted over Grangemore arose in the middle of the 1969 election campaign when the *Evening Herald* revealed details of its sale by Haughey to the Gallagher Group with the eye-catching headline

'£204,500 for Home of Minister'.[113] Notwithstanding the vociferous complaints of Conor Cruise O'Brien of Labour and Gerard Sweetman of Fine Gael about what they alleged to be, in effect, insider dealing, it had no impact on the campaign itself or its final outcome. Haughey, having referred the complaint to the Revenue Commissioners, simply declared it to be a private business matter, and dismissed the claims of his opponents that it was a sordid example of the unhealthy links between some in Fianna Fáil and rapacious property speculators. In reality, Cruise O'Brien was blissfully unaware that referring in caustic terms to Haughey's wealth, with the implication that this was a valid criticism, betrayed his own patrician ignorance of the fact that large swathes of the Irish electorate were imbued with an unshakeable reverence for wealth, and cared little about its origins or propriety. In his one statement on the controversy Haughey stated that he was 'totally committed to public life and to serving the people to the best of my ability and will not be deflected from doing so by this campaign'.[114] He expressed confidence that the people he had the honour to serve would not turn away from him, and he was right. He was elected with a massive 31.5 per cent of the vote, having received 11,677 first preferences, and he brought one of his two running mates, Eugene Timmons, with him. The other two candidates elected were Paddy Belton for Fine Gael and Labour's Cruise O'Brien, who polled 7,591 first preferences and was also elected on the first count alongside Haughey.

While Haughey had the satisfaction of comfortably exceeding Cruise O'Brien's vote, the attacks on his wealth clearly stung him. A week after the election, Haughey's solicitor and election agent Pat O'Connor wrote to RTÉ complaining about its coverage of the count in Dublin North East involving Haughey and Cruise O'Brien. He noted that RTÉ's newsmen covering the count reported that Cruise O'Brien was either ahead of Haughey or that they were in a very close contest to top the poll. O'Connor stated that it was obvious from tallies that Haughey was well ahead by a very large majority and that ultimately the public received a very prejudiced and one-sided view of the count. He finished by demanding that RTÉ apologise to Haughey for its incorrect reporting and the insinuation that he was being beaten by Cruise O'Brien.[115] In response,

RTÉ's deputy director general, John Irvine, argued the station's belief that the count was close was shared by the Dublin evening papers. He pointed to the vast scale of RTÉ's coverage and stated that given its size it was inevitable that in some instances the situation would not accurately reflect the subsequent counted votes. In the case of Dublin North East, Irvine stated that RTÉ was sorry that the likely outcome of the first count did not manifest itself to the station earlier but was adamant that its reports reflected the situation that it believed existed at the relevant times.[116] The contretemps between Pat O'Connor and RTÉ over a relatively minor matter was indicative of the extent to which Cruise O'Brien had rattled the Haughey camp, although it was of little consequence to Haughey himself.

The 1969 election was Jack Lynch's triumph. Fianna Fáil won seventy-five seats, a majority of five, on 45.7 per cent of the vote. Fine Gael held its own, while the Labour Party breakthrough never materialised. Its vote went up slightly to 17 per cent but it lost one seat to return with eighteen. Fine Gael won four extra seats, returning with fifty on 34.1 per cent of the vote, the same percentage it had received in 1965. The final percentages were very close to those offered by Conrad Jameson in his report of just over a month earlier; he had Fianna Fáil on 44.4 per cent, Fine Gael on 32.5 per cent and Labour on 21.8 per cent. He was not alone in overselling the Labour threat to Fianna Fáil and indeed Fine Gael. The scale of Fianna Fáil's success and the failure of Labour to make any sort of surge surprised RTÉ, the newspapers, political commentators and many in Fianna Fáil. In the aftermath of the results, Des O'Kennedy of O'Kennedy Brindley, who were responsible for Fianna Fáil's advertising, told Haughey that he was 'still a bit rocked and delirious with the extent of our success'.[117] The congratulatory letters rolled in over the following weeks and continued when Haughey was rewarded by Jack Lynch for his role in the election by being reappointed Minister for Finance when the new Dáil convened on 2 July. One of his close friends, the public relations specialist Frank Ryan, told him, 'It must have given you great personal satisfaction to note that all the political pundits and politicians – friend and foe alike were agreed on the occupant of one ministry only.'[118] From the world of finance, Bunny O'Reilly of the Bank of Ireland remarked that he could not 'think of anybody who could fill the post with equal efficiency, dignity and courtesy'.[119]

Jack Lynch shared the election victory with his wife, Máirín. Her presence on the campaign trail had fortified her husband and delighted the crowds who thronged to his appearances. The week after the election Haughey arranged a presentation of flowers and a gold and sapphire bracelet and watch to Máirín Lynch on behalf of Fianna Fáil. She thanked him in warm and exuberant tones a few days later saying the presentation was one of the most exciting days in her life because of the unexpected thoughtfulness, beauty and generosity that it represented. She played down her own role, as was her general style, telling Haughey that she was just an actor playing a role in a good play which had been written by Fianna Fáil four and a half years earlier, and had excellent production and direction, supported by an equally excellent cast. She declared herself happy that the audience was appreciative and pronounced the play a success. The truth was that she had played an important role in a close-fought election in which the opposition thought they had a good chance of beating Fianna Fáil. The presentation was in recognition that as a very shy and private woman she had had to step well outside her comfort zone to support her husband on the campaign trail. In that role she added to 'Honest Jack's' cross-over appeal among middle-class voters. She signed off by saying that she knew 'Jack is even happier than I am at this misplaced kindness and thoughtfulness.'[120] Jack Lynch had written to Haughey a few days earlier to thank him, his team in Fianna Fáil headquarters, constituency directors, directors of elections and the thousands of voluntary workers throughout the country for all they had done to bring the party victory in the general election. He stated that it was a tremendous exercise in efficient and well-coordinated teamwork and 'augurs well for the future of our organisation and of the country'.[121] This prophecy, however, would prove to be dramatically inaccurate. The following eighteen months would bring both the organisation and the country to the precipice of disaster and change the life of Charles Haughey, and indeed the internal politics of Fianna Fáil, for ever.

CHAPTER 10

MR HAUGHEY'S ATTITUDE TO ILLEGAL ORGANISATIONS AND ACTIVITIES

A TIDE IN THE AFFAIRS OF MEN

The period between the eruption of violence in Northern Ireland in August 1969 and Haughey's acquittal by the jury in October 1970 in his trial on conspiracy to import arms illegally into the state was among the darkest of his life. In under twelve months he went from the zenith of masterminding Fianna Fáil's June 1969 election victory, and his reappointment as Minister for Finance, to the nadir and humiliation of being sacked from office and arrested and charged in May 1970 of what effectively amounted to treasonous activity against the state. He faced the very real possibility that he would be sent to jail for up to a decade, leaving a wife and four children of school-going age to fend for themselves. He was sustained and fortified at this time by the support of his wife Maureen and a tight circle of friends.

In Haughey's private papers there is a list of both printed and hand-written notes from the 1970s which are evidently jottings in relation to speeches and interview preparation. In one of these notes the question is asked, 'What is your personal position in relation to the events of the last twelve months?' Haughey gives the following answer: 'I am fully recovering and enjoying good health. I have had an opportunity to do some thinking. I haven't lost the friendship of one single person that I care about. In fact the last year has been a great period in my life from that point of view. I have had a remarkable demonstration of what friendship and loyalty can mean.' The reference to health relates to Haughey's serious injuries resulting from a fall from a horse at his home in April 1970 on the day he was due to deliver the budget. This, in itself, was the subject of baseless rumour and innuendo for years. Haughey needed the support of his friends as his liberty and career were at grave peril when he stood trial for the second time on 6 October 1970 after the first trial in September was aborted after just a week.

Fourteen months earlier, Haughey, like all his government colleagues, was shocked by the attacks on nationalist areas in Northern Ireland on the nights of 12 and 13 August 1969. He was particularly taken aback by the violence in Derry, a place he knew well, had holidayed in as a child and teenager, and had great affection for given his parents' roots in the county. Rioting in the Bogside of Derry on 12 August after the ending of an Apprentice Boys parade in the city spread to other parts of Northern Ireland the following day. It led to fierce fighting between nationalists and the Royal Ulster Constabulary (RUC) that lasted the whole day of 13 August. Nationalists in Derry called on supporters elsewhere in Northern Ireland to rise and relieve the pressure on the Bogside and for the Irish government, and indeed all Irish people, to do something about the intolerable situation they were facing. From the safety of Cork one of Haughey's correspondents, the Mallow solicitor Richard Moylan, expressed the anguish many nationalists were feeling when he wrote on 13 August, 'The events of last night in Derry fill me with frustration and compel me to write to you to suggest that we appear to be sitting back, afraid to say or do anything ... and are allowing our fellow Irishmen to be driven completely into the ground.' Moylan, like pretty much everyone else, did not have a solution but told Haughey that there was a 'tide in the affairs of men … and if ever action on a National level was needed, it is needed at the present time'.[2]

Like Moylan, the government did not have a workable solution. What it did have were words. After an exhausting cabinet meeting which began at 2.30 p.m. on 13 August, the Taoiseach, Jack Lynch went on RTÉ television that night to state that his government would not simply stand by and see innocent people injured, although he did not use the phrase 'idly', as has often been assumed. The gravity of the situation was summed up by the fact that there were continuous changes to the text up to the time Lynch delivered his address. He did not even have a typescript; rather incredibly, it seems he was going to read from practically illegible notes. RTÉ's deputy head of news, Desmond Fisher, insisted that his notes be typed up, and gave Lynch a drop of whiskey to fortify him.[3] Lynch eventually read his statement in sound and firm tones. He did not hold back in his condemnation of the Stormont government and in his view that the British army could not provide a long-term solution. His statement further called for UN action to calm the situation. It also reiterated for many that what Fianna Fáil stood for, its very raison d'être – its insistence on the reunification of the national territory – was the only permanent solution to the problem:

> It is evident, also, that the Stormont government is no longer in control of the situation. Indeed, the present situation is the inevitable outcome of the policies pursued for decades by successive Stormont governments. It is clear, also, that the Irish government can no longer stand by and see innocent people injured and perhaps worse. It is obvious that the R.U.C. is no longer accepted as an impartial police force. Neither would the employment of British troops be acceptable nor would they be likely to restore peaceful conditions – certainly not in the long term. The Irish government, have therefore requested the British government to apply immediately to the United Nations for an urgent despatch of a peace-keeping force to the six counties of Northern Ireland.[4]

Over the following chaotic days, hundreds of refugees from the violence fled across the border into the Republic. The Fianna Fáil government was in crisis mode as it sought how best to respond to the unrest engulfing Northern Ireland. Lynch's statement, with its implicit threat of Irish army intervention, and its lack of any faith in the Northern Ireland administration, the RUC, and the British army, certainly raised the hopes of nationalists that the Irish government was about to do something about the intolerable situation. Lynch and the rest of his cabinet, including Haughey, rejected the urgings of the Minister for Agriculture, Neil Blaney, to send the Irish army over the border to create an international incident which, Blaney hoped, would force the UN to intervene. This would almost certainly have made things much worse: no one could possibly have predicted what sort of opposition Irish troops would have been faced with. British army troops had arrived in Northern Ireland on 14 August, the day after Lynch expressed no confidence in them. It was later revealed that they were ordered not to engage if they encountered Irish troops.[5] Given the extremely fraught situation on the ground, however, any incursion into Northern Ireland by the Irish army had the potential to gravely escalate matters, particularly since the army did not have the equipment, weapons, knowledge, men or organisation to mount any significant operations in Northern Ireland.[6]

The government ultimately agreed to order the building of camps and field hospitals along the border and assigned the army to protect them. One thousand five hundred soldiers were deployed to the border and stayed there for close to three months.[7] Blaney's own defence of his idea – it could scarcely be called a plan – was that it was in essence a holding position. He insisted some two decades later that the army's role went well beyond guarding field hospitals and that intervention would still have been possible if circumstances had deteriorated into the so-called doomsday scenario. He noted that once the government rejected his idea it then agreed 'to send the army to the border, under the cover of field hospitals ... The field hospitals idea we went along with. I didn't give a goddamn how they went up as long as the army went up and were there to go in. And that was what was in the minds of, I'd say,

The family home of Johnnie Haughey in Stranagone, in south Derry. (*Courtesy of the Charles J. Haughey Papers, Dublin City University*)

12 Belton Park Road in Donnycarney, where the Haughey family moved to in 1933, when Charles Haughey was seven. His mother, Sarah, lived there until her death in 1989. (*Courtesy of the Charles J. Haughey family*)

Haughey's parents, Johnnie Haughey and Sarah McWilliams. (*Courtesy of the Charles J. Haughey Papers, Dublin City University*)

Johnnie and Sarah Haughey with their newly born first child, Maureen. The Haugheys had seven children in all. They christened their third child Charles James but called him Cathal throughout his childhood. (*Courtesy of the Charles J. Haughey Papers, Dublin City University*)

Scoil Mhuire, Marino, 1937 Dublin Primary Junior Gaelic Football champions. Cathal Haughey is in the back row at the extreme left. (*Courtesy of the Charles J. Haughey Papers, Dublin City University*)

First Of 500

★ **Twelve and a half years old** ★ Cathal Haughey, of Belton Park, Dublin, who won first place among 500 entrants in this year's Dublin Corporation Scholarships to Secondary Schools. He is a pupil of the C.B.S., Marino.

A month before his thirteenth birthday, Cathal Haughey comes first of five hundred in the Dublin Corporation Primary School scholarship examination, allowing him to attend St. Joseph's Secondary School in Marino. (*Courtesy of the Charles J. Haughey Papers, Dublin City University*)

Platoon leader Cathal Haughey leads his 'A' Company, North Dublin Battalion, on training manoeuvres during the Emergency. (*Courtesy of the Charles J. Haughey Papers, Dublin City University*)

Haughey as a student in UCD, complete with pens in his jacket pocket.
(*Courtesy of the Charles J. Haughey Papers, Dublin City University*)

Haughey graduates as a barrister-at-law from King's Inns in September 1949. He is congratulated by his mother, Sarah, as his then girlfriend Maureen and sister Bridie look on. (*Courtesy of the Charles J. Haughey family*)

Charles Haughey and Maureen Lemass on their wedding day in September 1951. They were married in the Church of the Holy Name on Beechwood Avenue in Ranelagh. (*Courtesy of the Charles J. Haughey family*)

ꝼɪᴀɴɴᴀ ꝼáɪʟ
The Republican Party

HAUGHEY, Charles J., B.L., B.Comm.; F.C.A.

A message from
EAMON DE VALERA

Facts For Your Consideration

POLLING DAY, MONDAY, 30th APRIL
9.0 a.m. to 9.0 p.m.

VOTE

1 | HAUGHEY

Leaflet for Haughey in the Dublin North East by-election on 30 April 1956. He was defeated by the independent candidate Patrick Byrne. It was the third time he had been rejected by the constituency's voters. (*Courtesy of the Charles J. Haughey Papers, Dublin City University*)

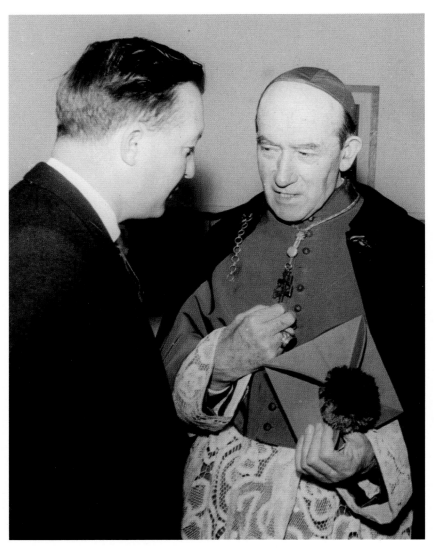

Haughey speaks with the Catholic Archbishop of Dublin, John Charles McQuaid. Haughey regularly consulted with McQuaid on various issues during his time as minister in three different departments in the 1960s. (*Courtesy of the Charles J. Haughey Papers, Dublin City University*)

The ambitious young minister in typical pose at the chess board as he plots his next political move.

Haughey at the Galway races. Horses were one of Haughey's major pastimes for over five decades. He was a keen owner and breeder and went to the races as often as he could. (© *The Irish Times*)

For decades Haughey enjoyed the isolation that the sea gave him. Sailing was one of his main pastimes. (© *The Irish Times*)

The Taoiseach, Seán Lemass, Minister for Finance, Jack Lynch, and Minister for Agriculture board the plane to London to negotiate the Anglo-Irish Free Trade Agreement. (© *The Irish Times*)

Haughey posing for the camera before presenting his budget in May 1969.
The budget introduced a tax exemption scheme for artists. (© *RTÉ*)

Haughey and Neil Blaney outside the Four Courts during the most famous trial in the history of the Irish state. Blaney had earlier been cleared of all charges, leaving Haughey the only parliamentarian to face trial. (© *Independent News and Media/ Getty Images*)

Haughey and his solicitor Patrick O'Connor hold a press conference in the Four Courts after his acquittal (© *Eddie Kelly/The Irish Times*)

The Fianna Fáil front bench meets in 1975. Haughey, brought back as spokesman on Health, remains a somewhat isolated figure. (© *Independent News and Media/ Getty Images*)

Haughey at Éamon de Valera's funeral in September 1975, behind the veteran Fianna Fáil politician Seán MacEntee. To his right are Máirín Lynch and Jack Lynch. (© *Independent News and Media/Getty Images*)

A jubilant Haughey prepares to speak to the press after winning the Fianna Fáil leadership election in December 1979. The party's chief whip Dr Michael Woods gets proceedings underway. (*Courtesy of the Charles J. Haughey Papers, Dublin City University*)

Haughey gives the thumbs up to the Fianna Fáil faithful at the party's 1980 Ard Fheis. (© *Paddy Whelan/The Irish Times*)

Haughey addresses the delegates at the 50th Fianna Fáil Ard Fheis in the RDS in April 1981. The Ard Fheis had been reconvened after the original was postponed in the aftermath of the Stardust fire two months earlier. (*Courtesy of the Charles J. Haughey Papers, Dublin City University*)

the majority of our cabinet that day.'[8] It was not the opinion, however, of at least three members of the cabinet; Patrick Hillery, Pádraig Faulkner or even the ultra-hawkish Kevin Boland. And neither was it the view of Des O'Malley, who, as the government's chief whip, was entitled to attend cabinet.[9] All took the view that only in the direst of circumstances would the government even contemplate any crossing of the border. Boland later claimed that opponents in the cabinet kept talking irrelevant nonsense about the inadequacy of the Irish army in comparison to its British counterpart and how it would be wiped out within hours, but 'No one contemplated war with the British army.'[10] The thorny problem remained the lack of knowledge of how the British might react to any intervention by the forces of the Irish state into Northern Ireland. This was something no Irish minister had any idea of at the time, given that they knew very little of events on the ground in the first place, and had no concept or foresight of the emerging crisis.

Some commentators, most notably Angela Clifford, Michael Kennedy, Donnacha Ó Beacháin, and more recently Michael Heney, have all suggested to some degree that the movement of troops and artillery to the border was part of a generally shared cabinet view that some sort of cross-border intervention to protect Northern nationalists from sectarian assault might be necessary if the circumstances did indeed become dire.[11] The problem was that no one could clearly say when the cross-over point into the doomsday scenario might actually be reached. By late August the government was painfully aware of its military inferiority along the border when Garda intelligence reported that there were some 9,000 British ground and air forces, and B Specials along the border region.[12] This far outweighed anything the Irish state could muster. There were only 8,000 full-time members of the entire Irish army and much of its equipment was outdated and in poor condition.[13] On Saturday 16 August the government met again and established a Northern Ireland sub-committee comprising Haughey, Blaney, Joseph Brennan, also from Donegal, and Pádraig Faulkner from Louth, another border county. The sub-committee had ill-defined terms of reference and would meet only once. Faulkner recalled that they had 'an informal discussion about the

North and how to counter misleading publicity from Unionist sources so we could clarify the factual position.'[14] A date for a second meeting was set but neither Blaney nor Haughey turned up and the committee effectively ceased to exist. Its establishment, however, allowed Blaney and Haughey the ability to use its implied authority to develop policy as they saw fit, away from the cabinet table, and without the full knowledge of Lynch.[15]

Ó Beacháin claims that at this stage Jack Lynch was delegating policy on Northern Ireland to ministers with whom he had fundamental differences of opinion. Yet Faulkner was a loyal and staunch supporter of Lynch, and it is not at all clear that Haughey was seen by his colleagues in cabinet as being 'synonymous with hard-line republican views' as Ó Beacháin describes him.[16] In fact, there was no difference on Northern Ireland policy between Lynch and Haughey when the Troubles erupted. Haughey and the Minister for Defence, Jim Gibbons, were then given responsibility to prepare the army to deal with the possibility of a contingency situation, although what that contingency might be was not elucidated. The responsibility was entrusted to the two ministers by an agreement at cabinet level, rather than by a full decision of the government.[17] This symbolised the general chaos that the Fianna Fáil government found itself in during these hectic few days. It was caught completely unaware by the crisis and had little idea of how to respond to it.

In developing its ad hoc contingency plans the government also decided that 'a sum of money – the amount and the channel of the disbursement of which would be determined by the Minister for Finance – should be made available from the exchequer to provide aid for the victims of the current unrest in the six counties.'[18] Charles Murray, the secretary of the Department of Finance, who had replaced T.K. Whitaker in March 1969, later maintained that he had never seen a government decision drafted in such wide terms.[19] Haughey was in effect given elastic powers to help nationalists in Northern Ireland as and how he saw fit. This was the money that would eventually be used for the procurement of arms that led to the arms crisis of May 1970 and the subsequent arms trials of a few months later. It was agreed that the Irish Red Cross would be the vehicle through which the majority of the funds would be disbursed.

That same day Haughey rang Leslie de Barra, the president of the Irish Red Cross, and invited her to meet with him the following Monday to discuss relief for the victims of the disturbances. De Barra, wife of the legendary War of Independence stalwart Tom Barry, immediately left her Cork home and travelled to Dublin. When they met, Haughey told her that the government had decided to supply every possible aid to the victims, that the Irish army was opening up field hospitals and refugee centres, and that the help of the Red Cross was needed. She replied that a significant amount of cash and relief supplies had already been donated to Red Cross headquarters and its various centres around the country and the organisation would leave no stone unturned in operating the relief venture successfully.[20] She continued to report directly to Haughey on the relief position over the following months. And indeed the donations were flooding in, including one of £1,000 from the Archbishop of Dublin, John Charles McQuaid, from the charitable funds at his disposal, who sent it directly to Lynch on 16 August. Three days later McQuaid sent a handwritten note to Haughey saying that had he known that Haughey was looking after the relief fund he would have sent it to him directly. Haughey replied that McQuaid's generous and timely contribution was already helping to relieve distress through the machinery of the Irish Red Cross.[21] A large donation of $10,000 payable to Irish Red Cross to be used in helping the 'distressed people of Northern Ireland' came from Mayor Richard Daley of Chicago, who sent similar amounts to the Northern Ireland Inter-Denominational Distress Organization and the Ancient Order of Hibernians Relief Fund.[22] After the feverish activity of the early days of the Troubles, an eerie calm had descended on the border by September 1969. The field hospitals and the refugee camps emptied as it became apparent that there would be no mass exodus of wounded nationalists into the Republic.

SUBJECT TO EVERY SPITEFUL RUMOUR

Haughey's role in the events of the months from August 1969 to April 1970, when Jack Lynch visited him in hospital and accused him of disloyalty to the Taoiseach, the government and the state, has been the subject of much speculation, innuendo and allegation. Haughey's motives in this period have generally been seen as malign. He has been accused of running a quasi-alternate secret government in a plot to force Lynch out of office and become Taoiseach himself; of using the crisis in Northern Ireland as a means to advance a united Ireland; of arming the Provisional IRA; and of recklessly endangering the stability and safety of the Irish state. Haughey rejected all these allegations. In notes he took some time after the arms trials he noted bitterly: 'Had to endure a great deal. Arrested. Sacked by Telephone. Savaged in the Dáil. Subject to every spiteful rumour.'[23] Such iniquities, as he clearly saw them, would only become more pronounced over the following years and indeed decades.

Once his trial was over in October 1970, Haughey displayed lifelong reluctance to discuss the events of the arms crisis and trials. Beyond his witness statement, the evidence he gave at his trial, and his evidence at the later investigation of the Public Accounts Committee, Haughey never spoke publicly, or even privately to his family, about the events between August 1969 and his acquittal some fourteen months later in October 1970. What he did do was categorically deny, in his response to Lynch from his hospital bed, and for evermore, that he was ever disloyal to Lynch personally or the Fianna Fáil government he had the privilege to serve in. The wider story of the arms crisis and indeed the arms trial itself is shrouded in secrecy, half-truths and untruths. Recent scholarship, most notably by Michael Heney, David Burke, and Conor Lenihan, has forcefully challenged the dominant, although not universally accepted, narrative that Jack Lynch uncovered a dangerous and illegal conspiracy within his own government. The essence of the traditional view is that after a period of some vacillation, Lynch ultimately and decisively acted to secure Irish democracy by sacking two of the most powerful ministers in his government, Charles Haughey and Neil Blaney, who were at the heart of the conspiracy or plot to import arms. This narrative has been espoused by a number of historians and commentators, most notably Lynch's most comprehensive biographer, Dermot Keogh, and an array of others, including Bruce Arnold, T. Ryle Dwyer, and T.P. O'Mahony, all of whom have written sympathetic biographies of Lynch.[24] It has also been strongly reinforced by some who served with Lynch, including Des O'Malley, Pádraig Faulkner and Patrick Hillery.

The alternative narrative argues that Lynch clearly knew to some degree about the arms importation, that it had been substantially authorised, whether officially or unofficially, and that there was in effect no plot or conspiracy. Lynch, along with the Minister for Defence, Jim Gibbons, is the guilty party in these accounts, denying, as he did, any and all knowledge of arms importation, and thus responsibility, while clearly knowing a large part of what was happening. Lenihan insists that Lynch threw Haughey, Blaney and Captain James Kelly (the key army intelligence officer involved in the purchase of arms) 'to the wolves'.[25] Burke bluntly accuses Lynch of a 'cover up'.[26] Heney, in the most comprehensive account of the arms crisis so far, criticises Lynch's 'subterfuges, deceptions and a terminal reluctance to discuss in detail the events of the period'.[27] In turn, Heney and Burke were bitterly criticised by Des O'Malley, the last surviving member of the Fianna Fáil government of the period, and a close ally of Lynch, as purveying fiction rather than fact.[28]

Haughey's defence of his position and actions in the crucial period between August 1969 and April 1970 was that he always acted in accordance with government policy. Notes made with his legal team for his trial show that Haughey believed that Jim Gibbons never gave him the slightest indication that Captain Kelly was anything other than a first-class officer in whom Gibbons had complete confidence. In any meeting Kelly had with either Haughey or Anthony Fagan, the Department of Finance civil servant who acted as Haughey's assistant, Haughey understood that Kelly was acting in his official capacity as an army intelligence officer who carried out his duties with the full authority of his superiors and his minister.[29] Haughey had brought Fagan with him from the Department of Agriculture when he moved to Finance. Beyond Blaney, Haughey knew very little about his fellow accused: Captain James Kelly, the army officer who organised the arms importation; John Kelly, a Northern nationalist and key member of the Northern Defence Committees; and Albert Luykx, an expatriate Belgian businessman who acted as an interpreter during arms-buying trips to the continent, having been recruited for that task by Neil Blaney.

During this period Haughey was kept informed of ongoing developments in nationalist circles in Northern Ireland by Captain James Kelly, although they only met on a handful of occasions; Haughey reckoned it was only three or four. Haughey, as Minister for Finance, had to decide who would get the Northern relief funds allocated by the government on 16 August 1969 and how they should be disbursed. Kelly had a key role in recommending and determining who on the ground in Northern Ireland would get Irish government assistance. Haughey never met Albert Luykx during the period of the arms crisis. Haughey did think it might be possible that they met socially; but even if they had they would have exchanged only the briefest of social courtesies. Haughey never met John Kelly individually but did meet him as part of various delegations of nationalists who came to Dublin as part of the Northern Defence Committee to seek assistance from the Fianna Fáil government. Haughey met Captain James Kelly on a number of occasions with other deputations of nationalists. At these meetings Kelly would brief Haughey on developments in Northern Ireland, which Haughey saw as being entirely in keeping with his official duties as an officer of army intelligence.[30] When nationalist groups of various hues wanted to see members of the government, including Haughey, Kelly was the person who brought them to Dublin, arranged the meetings and introduced the participants.

THE ALTERNATIVE LEADER?

Among the accusations of disloyalty levelled at Haughey in this period is that he acted as a sort of alternative leader of Fianna Fáil, and Taoiseach, by meeting at his home in Kinsaley with the British Ambassador to Ireland, Andrew Gilchrist, on Saturday 4 October 1969. Stephen Kelly, for instance, has labelled this meeting as evidence of Haughey's 'utter contempt for the Taoiseach's authority and more generally cabinet collective responsibility'.[31] David Burke has rather luridly claimed that Haughey lured Gilchrist to Abbeville after failing to develop a back-channel to London through the writer Constantine FitzGibbon, with whom Haughey was friendly, and who Burke claims was a British agent.[32] Haughey and FitzGibbon met the day before Haughey's meeting with Gilchrist and Haughey briefed the writer on the government's stance on Northern Ireland. According to Michael Heney, Haughey had gathered that FitzGibbon intended to report back on what was said to the British embassy and that Gilchrist was about to travel to London to brief the British Foreign Secretary, Michael Stewart, on current Irish government thinking.[33] In that context Haughey wanted to brief Gilchrist personally without having his views reported for him. This was something Haughey did not think unusual. In notes for his trial Haughey stated that the Taoiseach expected him to take care of things that cropped up at weekends, when Haughey was one of the few government members in Dublin.[34] Moreover, Haughey was continually hosting all sorts of diplomats at his home and had been doing so for a number of years. It is extremely unlikely that he considered himself an alternative Taoiseach at this meeting and it is clear that Gilchrist did not think he was talking to one.

Gilchrist's account of his meeting at Abbeville noted that he could not know how Haughey's view differed from the government's, given his view of the rivalry between Haughey and Lynch. He also reported on Haughey's clear passion for Irish unity. He further reported that Haughey stated that there was nothing he would not sacrifice in order to obtain a united Ireland including Irish neutrality, membership of the North Atlantic Treaty Organization (NATO), the position of the Catholic Church, Ireland's return to the British Commonwealth, and the use of Irish military bases for the Royal Navy, all wrapped up in a possible federal solution.[35] It would have been a very odd Fianna Fáil politician in October 1969 who did not have a passion for unity, given that the reunification of the island was one of the party's core founding tenets. The desperate events of the previous weeks in Northern Ireland would certainly have made such passions stronger among elected Fianna Fáil politicians and the party's supporters. Moreover, Gilchrist did not find Haughey's unity position terribly unusual and it certainly did not stop them becoming friendly.

On the same day as the Haughey–Gilchrist meeting in Abbeville, Captain James Kelly convened a meeting of the Northern Defence Committees in Bailieboro, County Cavan, where the plan to import arms was born. Five days later Haughey and his wife left for a nine-day vacation in the Caribbean. When Gilchrist retired in March 1970 he wrote to Haughey with the salutation 'Dear Charlie, (if a nearly ex-ambassador may be so familiar!)'. He went on to give Haughey a present of a travel guide of the British Isles and finished by saying that it had 'been very nice to work with you and I will be sorry not to see you again'.[36] Gilchrist added directions to his home at Arthur's Crag, Lanarkshire, Scotland, telling Haughey it would be a good staging post for a holiday in these islands. Haughey replied saying that it was a great personal pleasure for him to have known and worked closely with Gilchrist during the ambassador's all too short a time in Dublin, that Maureen and himself wished the Gilchrists every happiness in their retirement and hoped one day to follow the excellent directions to Arthur's Crag. He ended with the laconic comment, 'The ducks at Abbeville will quack gleefully as your departing aeroplane roars overhead but the rest of us will all be sad.'[37]

Other accusations that Haughey wilfully disobeyed Lynch in this period include the allegation that he refused a demand from the Taoiseach that funding be withdrawn from the propaganda newspaper *Voice of the North*, edited by Seamus Brady, which had been funded by the government and was widely distributed in Northern Ireland. Lynch had been upset by hostile comments in the paper towards Fianna Fáil and wanted it shut down. While Heney has claimed that the funding, once it had been given, remained for the Northern account holders who ran the paper to do with as they saw fit, there is no doubt but that Haughey, as the man in charge of the money, could have demanded that the newspaper change tack.[38] That Haughey did not seek any changes certainly left him open to the charge that he was casual in the extreme in his efforts to see Lynch's wishes followed. It hardly amounts, however, to a wilful attempt at directing an alternative Northern Ireland strategy from Dublin.

The final allegation that speaks to Haughey's supposed campaign of duplicity against Lynch, and indeed the government, is that he made a private deal with the IRA chief of staff, Cathal Goulding, in the autumn of 1969 allowing the IRA to move arms freely across the border in return for halting its attacks on foreign-owned property in the Irish Republic. This allegation was based on a memorandum written by Peter Berry in June 1970 after Haughey had been charged with conspiracy to illegally import arms and there is some confusion as to whether Haughey supposedly met Goulding or Mick Ryan, the officer commanding of the Dublin Brigade of the IRA, later to become quartermaster general of the IRA. These have been rightly described by Heney as a 'jumble of unsubstantiated, incoherent and unverifiable claims'.[39]

The idea that Haughey, the scourge of the IRA just a few years earlier, when he was Minister for Justice, would have met with the chief of staff of the IRA and sought a deal with an organisation that he viscerally loathed, just a few weeks after the outbreak of the Troubles, in order to stop illegal activity in the Irish state is outlandish in the extreme. In January 1980, just weeks after Haughey became Taoiseach, Constantine FitzGibbon sent him a newspaper clipping of a profile of Haughey by the journalist Max Hastings in the *Evening Standard* entitled 'Haughey: the bogeyman cometh'. FitzGibbon attached a letter from Hastings to himself thanking him for his help with the profile, leading FitzGibbon to tell Haughey that the piece 'was largely inspired by myself' and he hoped that it conveyed the image Haughey wanted to project to the British public.[40] In that piece Hastings described Haughey as 'the most formidable figure to come out of Ireland for many years' and went on: 'It is unthinkable that a man as strongly entrenched as himself in the new professional business class can feel any affinity for the young Marxists of the IRA.'[31] That comment could well have been written in 1969, such was Haughey's antipathy to the IRA in both its Marxist and traditional forms as the Troubles began. There is no real evidence that Haughey ever met Cathal Goulding and it seems that the meeting to which Berry alluded to may well have been with Haughey's younger brother, Pádraig, or Jock, as he was known. According to John Kelly, Jock Haughey reportedly supplied Goulding with two boxes of weapons in this period.[42]

IMPORTING ARMS

By June 1970, when Peter Berry wrote his memorandum, Haughey's life had undergone a shattering metamorphosis. In the space of less than a year he had gone from masterminding Fianna Fáil's general election triumph and being reappointed Minister for Finance, to being sacked and charged with a serious criminal offence and of effectively betraying the state. When Haughey was charged, his legal team prepared extensive notes on the main protagonists involved. The note on Berry states that he was always preoccupied with Secret Service matters, illegal organisations and the Special Branch, and had no interest in any of the ordinary activities of the Department of Justice. It adds that Berry was secretary of the department when Haughey was Minister for Justice, and that Berry considered Haughey the most capable of all the ministers he worked with during his long career of over four decades. It forcefully made the point that the two men worked together in stopping the cross-border campaign by the IRA and that Berry was 'fully aware of Haughey's attitude to illegal organisations and activities'.[43]

When Berry was ill in hospital in the autumn of 1969 Haughey went to see him on Saturday 4 October at Mount Carmel Nursing Home. This was the same day Haughey met Ambassador Andrew Gilchrist. Earlier that day Berry had had a visit from the head of the Special Branch, Chief Superintendent John Fleming. Fleming told him that an army intelligence officer, Captain James Kelly, had been in contact with the chief of staff of the IRA, Cathal Goulding, and that he had arranged a meeting for that afternoon at Bailieboro with known subversive elements from Northern Ireland. Berry was worried about this as there had already been intelligence reports of Kelly liaising with subversives and suggestions that he had promised them money and arms. When Berry could not reach either the Minister for Justice, Micheál Ó Móráin, or the Taoiseach, Jack Lynch, he called Haughey, who answered the phone at Abbeville and immediately went to Mount Carmel. Berry then told Haughey about the information he had received relating to Kelly's meetings with IRA leaders and the Bailieboro meeting, which was taking place that very afternoon. Haughey wanted to know more about the reliability of the information Berry had but nothing more was forthcoming. The two men then talked about Berry's illness and reminisced about their days in the Department of Justice.[44]

In the notes for the trial Haughey recalled that Berry was very bitter about the fact that the government had let him down in his confrontation with the comptroller and auditor general.[45] This related to an incident the previous year, 1968, when the Public Accounts Committee protested to the Dáil that the comptroller and auditor general had been refused access to certain files in the Department of Justice. Berry had refused to release the files on the grounds that they contained high-security information. Berry was outraged by the failure of Minister for Justice Brian Lenihan and Taoiseach Jack Lynch to support him.[46] As a result of the conversation between Haughey and Berry in Mount Carmel, Haughey reported back to the establishment officer, and the secretary of the Department of Finance, that in his view 'Berry was no longer physically and mentally capable of running the Department of Justice, particularly in times of stress, and delicate situations.' The secretary agreed and said that the best thing would be to get Berry to take twelve months' leave. Haughey mentioned this view of his informally at a government meeting.[47]

What Haughey did not tell Berry was that just two days before, on Thursday 2 October 1969, he had held a meeting at his home in Abbeville with Kelly and the then head of Military Intelligence, Colonel Michael Hefferon, at which they discussed the forthcoming Bailieboro meeting and the payment of expenses, although Haughey later denied that he had arranged a payment of £500 to Kelly for the Bailieboro meeting.[48] In his notes for the trial Haughey claimed that 'Berry's alter ego is the I.R.A', that he had lived with them throughout his career, personally ran the Special Branch and the Secret Service Fund and that the containment of illegal organisations inside the twenty-six counties had been his life's work. Haughey maintained that Berry could not in effect come to terms with the fact that developments in the six counties after the outbreak of violence in August 1969 brought a new dimension to his work which he clearly did not allow for. In that context Haughey was of the view that Berry resented the use of army intelligence by the government in the new situation that had emerged since the onset of violence in Northern

Ireland and 'it was clear that he was out to get Capt. Kelly. He failed to distinguish between illegal organisations on this side of the border and groups inside the six counties who are in a completely different category politically and otherwise.'[49] This explains why Haughey did not tell Berry on 4 October 1969 of his earlier meeting with Kelly and Hefferon. Haughey may well have been naive or wilfully ignorant as to who Kelly was meeting and of their intentions but it is abundantly clear that he was wary of Berry in these early months of the Troubles.

Between November 1969 and April 1970 a number of attempts were made to import arms into the Irish state. After two failed attempts to procure weapons, arrangements were finally made with Otto Schlueter, a professional arms dealer based in Hamburg, to ship a cargo consisting of 200 submachine guns, 84 light machine guns, 50 general purpose machine guns, 50 rifles, 200 grenades, 70 flak jackets, 250,000 rounds of ammunition and 200 pistols into Dublin Port from Antwerp in March 1970. This attempt, under the control of Colonel Michael Hefferon of Military Intelligence, failed when the consignment was impounded in Antwerp owing to the lack of an end user's certificate. In his notes for the arms trial, Haughey claimed not to know anything of this shipment. He had held a meeting on 22 January 1970 with Jim Gibbons and officials from their two departments to discuss the estimate for the Department of Defence for 1970/71. After the officials left, Haughey stated, Gibbons had stayed behind to discuss special requirements for any contingencies that might arise, and Haughey assured him that everything possible would be done to help him. Haughey then reported that when in March 1970 his official, Anthony Fagan, asked him to direct customs to clear consignments for army intelligence without opening them, Haughey 'had no doubt whatever the request related to these requirements'.[50] This related to a meeting between Captain Kelly and Fagan on Thursday 19 March 1970 in Haughey's office in Government Buildings. Haughey was not there when Kelly arrived and, in the minister's absence, Kelly told Fagan that he wanted Haughey to provide clearance through customs for an expected consignment of goods due to arrive at Dublin Port. Kelly did not specify that they were arms. When, later that day, Fagan told

Haughey of the meeting, Haughey's first thought was that it was all very dubious and he wondered who in the Revenue Commissioners he could talk to about it. Fagan told him he had already spoken to an officer there, Bartholomew Culligan, who confirmed that Haughey had the power as minister to direct that the consignment be customs-free. In that context Haughey told Fagan to contact Culligan again and say that was fine.[51] Fagan reported later that Captain Kelly came to see Haughey the following day, 20 March 1970, after which Haughey in effect instructed Fagan that customs clearance without a check was to be given to a cargo described as 'mild steel plate'. Haughey strongly denied this. In a handwritten note on a copy of a document in his archive, 'The Attorney General – v – Luykx and Others', which outlined the charges and witness statements, he states: 'N.B. not in the Dáil on a Friday.'[52]

THE TYPE OF THING THE TAOISEACH WOULD EXPECT ME TO DO

Given that this consignment never arrived, the customs clearance became moot, but it provides the crucial context for the dramatic events of Saturday 18 April 1970 when Haughey had his fateful phone call with Peter Berry about the arrival of a shipment of arms into Dublin Airport. Haughey always denied that he knew that this shipment was arms. Earlier that day Haughey and his family were at the Curragh races. Anthony Fagan had tried to ring him in the afternoon but could get no answer at Abbeville. At 6 p.m. he finally reached Haughey and told him there were difficulties with an incoming shipment on an unknown flight and that Chief Superintendent Fleming wished to get clearance from a minister for the consignment.[53] Fagan's own memory of this conversation was that he told Haughey that Chief Superintendent Fleming intended to seize the consignment unless Haughey, or some other government minister, contacted him in the meantime.[54] Haughey told Fagan that he could not understand why Chief Superintendent Fleming was mentioned. He then added that if Fleming wanted to speak to Haughey he could ring him at home but he would not be ringing Fleming. That was when Haughey decided to ring Berry.

In the notes with his legal team for his trial, Haughey stated that the first he heard about this was on receiving Fagan's call, which provided no further details. He claimed that any details he learned about the consignment came from his later phone call with Berry. That phone call was made at 6.25 p.m. when Haughey rang Berry to inquire if he knew anything about a consignment supposed to be arriving at Dublin Airport. The first thing Berry said, according to Haughey, was 'Have you a scrambled telephone?', to which Haughey replied 'No.'[55] Haughey then asked Berry if he knew what this consignment to Dublin Airport was about. Berry said that an alleged consignment or cargo of some seven or eight tonnes was coming into Dublin Airport and that he, Berry, knew all about it: 'It was the most stupidly handled affair he had ever come across in his career, that he had every port in the country under observation and that anything that came into the country would be seized. Mr. Berry did all the talking.'[56]

Haughey's view of the telephone call was that it was entirely natural and the sort of thing he would normally do as a senior member of the government when learning of some impending development, particularly at weekends, when he was likely to be one of the few members of the government in Dublin. He stated that it was the type of thing that the Taoiseach would expect him to take care of if he was out of town. He added that Berry gave no impression that this was a dramatic event involving the security of the state but rather was a routine security matter which he was handling in his usual competent manner. Haughey claimed that it quickly became evident to him that the Special Branch under Berry and Military Intelligence were at cross purposes, and there was a danger of this being disclosed to the public. This was what led him to state: 'It had better be called off whatever it is'.[57] Haughey was also insistent that he did not use the words 'bad decision' as claimed in Berry's statement, or the word 'guarantee' – as in asking whether Berry would let the cargo through if a guarantee was given that it would go straight to the North.[58] He also denied ever asking the question, 'Does the man from Mayo know about this?', claiming that he would never have described a ministerial colleague in this way to a civil servant like Berry.

He stated that what he said was 'Does your minister know about it?'[59] The question as to what the minister, or the man from Mayo (Micheál Ó Móráin, the Minister for Justice), was actually supposed to know is in itself problematic. Berry assumed it was whether Ó Móráin knew of the consignment; the writers Angela Clifford and Michael Heney suggest that the question was whether he knew that the Special Branch intended to seize it.[60]

Berry's statement has long been seen as the crucial evidence against Haughey, containing as it does the supposedly damning words attributed to Haughey that he had asked if the cargo could be let through if it would go directly to the North. Its importance is summed up by the fact that at the first arms trial, counsel for the state Seamus McKenna opened the prosecution's case with his account of the Haughey–Berry phone call. Any suggestion that the consignment was bound for Northern Ireland would clearly put it outside the use of the agents of the state and thus make it an illegal importation. That is how the state portrayed the phone call in both trials. This raises perhaps the most crucial question of all in relation to the arms crisis and trials: why would Charles Haughey ring Peter Berry and essentially incriminate himself if he was indeed secretly plotting to import arms into the country? Haughey knew Berry distrusted army intelligence. He knew Berry hated the IRA. He knew Berry had no fear of politicians, including himself. He knew that if Berry felt there was any type of threat to the Irish state he would use every resource at his disposal to crush it and nobody, including Haughey, could stop him.

If Haughey was aware that there were arms in the proposed shipment to Dublin on that crucial Saturday of 18 April, and if he was trying to import them to illegally fund the IRA, surely the last person he would have tried to persuade to let the arms into the country was Peter Berry. Haughey's argument was that during this whole period he always acted as a government minister following government policy. In relation to the crucial events of March and April 1970, the notes for his legal team point out that when it came to authorising shipments into the country he was adamant that he was acting solely in his official capacity as a minister to authorise customs clearance for the importation of 'bona fide consignments by army intelligence. Mr. Haughey had no contact with anyone outside the official administrative machinery … It is inconceivable that if he were engaging in a secret conspiracy he would act openly through official Channels, especially the Revenue Commissioners.[61]

At his trial Haughey insisted that after he had his phone call with Berry he called Fagan back and told him that as a result of his conversation with Berry 'it was better to have the whole thing called off.'[62] He did not explicitly tell Fagan to arrange for this, given that in his view it was a Ministry of Defence operation, but he assumed that the word would get back to Military Intelligence. He denied that on the morning of Monday 20 April he told Fagan that he had been talking to Jim Gibbons, that the operation was off, and that Fagan should ring Captain Kelly in Vienna to that effect. He stated that he did not see Gibbons until that afternoon, that he did not know Captain Kelly was in Vienna, and that he had already informed Fagan the previous Saturday night that the operation should be called off. Yet Fagan, on that day, Monday 20 April 1970, did telephone Captain Kelly in Vienna at just before midday to tell him Haughey and Gibbons had discussed the matter and they had both agreed the importation could not and would not go ahead.

Haughey said that Fagan's statement was simply not correct. He stated that Gibbons phoned him early that day asking to come and see him and the two men met in Haughey's office between 4.30 p.m. and 5 p.m. Haughey recalled this conversation as being very brief and did not recollect using the words 'dogs in the street are barking it' as alleged by Gibbons; his legal team said, 'It is not a typical phrase that would be used by him.' He also denied ever saying the words 'I will stop it for a month' and stated that there was no mention of what the consignment was and that the word 'arms' was never mentioned.[63] This was a crucial point in Haughey's whole defence. He and his legal team felt strongly that if Gibbons really thought Haughey was bringing in illegal cargo, would not the obvious thing be for Gibbons to go to the Taoiseach and inform him? Moreover, given what Berry had told Haughey about a ring of steel being placed around all the state's airports and ports the previous Saturday to stop that particular importation, how did Haughey think he would be able to get a similar consignment into the state at any time in the immediate future? Haughey might have suffered from a certain hubris during this whole period – he was, after all, in control of the state's finances – but no matter how severe that hubris was he was smart enough to know that there could be no importation in a month's time, or indeed any time, given what Berry had told him on Saturday 18 April. By the end of their meeting on Monday 20 April the ministers for Finance and Defence had agreed that the importation be called off.

At roughly the same time Haughey and Gibbons were meeting that afternoon, Peter Berry was telling Jack Lynch about the arms importation and how it had been foiled. Haughey could not explain how the importation could have been cancelled by Fagan calling Kelly that morning, considering that Gibbons and Haughey did not meet until a few hours later. Fagan was adamant that Haughey told him at about 10 a.m. on Monday 20 April that he had already had a conversation with Gibbons. Heney has speculated that there was an earlier meeting between the two ministers on Monday 20 April 1970; Fagan, in a statement to Gardaí, said that he had told Haughey on that day that Captain Kelly had been on to him the previous day, Sunday 19 April, looking for instructions about what to do with the consignment. Fagan stated that Haughey then told him that he had consulted the Minister for Defence on the morning of Monday 20 April and that they both agreed that the whole project should be abandoned.[64] Fagan then phoned Captain Kelly in Vienna. In Jim Gibbons's witness statement he maintained that he spoke to Haughey on the phone that day and told him that a telephone call had come to the Department of Defence from Dublin Airport asking if the army expected delivery of a consignment of arms. Gibbons went on to say that Haughey replied, 'The dogs in the street are barking it.' Gibbons then asked Haughey if he could stop the operation, to which Haughey replied, 'I will stop it for a month.' An exasperated Gibbons pleaded with Haughey: 'For God's sake stop it altogether.'[65] But at the trial it was clear that the meeting where this disputed conversation took place, was held in person in Haughey's office, not on the telephone; so perhaps there were indeed two meetings, one on the telephone in the morning and one in person later in the afternoon.

Fagan made a variety of statements to the Gardaí and had been interviewed for between eight and nine hours by the Special Branch. His comments were heavily criticised by Haughey and his legal team. According to Haughey, Fagan was responsible for press and television relations, protocol, looking after visiting dignitaries, travel arrangements and duties of that nature. In notes for his legal team Haughey stated that Fagan had his 'complete confidence and very often acted in my name on his own responsibility'.[66] Haughey stated that he knew Captain Kelly had a special mission in relation to the six counties situation but that the two men had only met on a few occasions, no more than three or four times in Haughey's estimation. On one occasion, Haughey recalled, Captain Kelly brought a group including John Kelly to see him and he arranged for them to see the Taoiseach. In one of his statements Fagan told gardaí that Haughey was 'disturbed' when Fagan told him he had the authority to provide clearance to customs for imported consignments. Haughey maintained that he was 'surprised' he could give a directive to the Revenue Commissioners as he had always thought they were completely in charge of customs and independent in the exercise of their authority.[67] A number of years earlier a Fianna Fáil colleague had passed to Haughey a complaint that the motor car businessman Sonny Linders, who had provided fleets of cars for Fianna Fáil at election time, had relating to a demand from the Revenue Commissioners for turnover tax. Haughey replied that he had great admiration for Linders as a businessman, and affection for him as a person, but his complaint was 'quite daft ... In no country in the world are the customs authorities ever particularly noted for their courtesy or politeness.[68] It is a telling indication that Haughey considered the Revenue Commissioners to be independent in their work. In the context of importing shipments he had assumed that he had no authority over the actions of the Revenue Commissioners until he was told differently by Fagan.

Haughey reiterated his view that Fagan was mistaken in his belief that Haughey met Captain Kelly in his office on Friday 20 March 1970 because he would not be in Leinster House on a Friday. Haughey's defence rested on the view that he told Fagan 'if army intelligence wished to import a consignment through customs with a maximum of secrecy they were to be facilitated. This was a general cover not relating to any particular consignment.[69] Finally, Haughey stated that Fagan's reference to the events of Monday 20 April 1970 were erroneous: Haughey insisted that he did not see Gibbons until 4.30 p.m. that day and the conversation that Fagan said took place between the two ministers that morning did not happen. While Haughey was critical of parts of Fagan's statement, he noted with approval that Fagan confirmed that anything that was done in relation to the importation was official, routine, and an army intelligence operation. He said that Fagan 'confirmed my own view that I never had any knowledge of what army intelligence might wish to import. Arms were never referred to.'[70]

Haughey's account to his legal team, and indeed his evidence at the trial, as to what he knew about the arms importation, and when he knew it, has long been subjected to ridicule and scorn by a range of his contemporaries and subsequent writers, historians and commentators of various hues. A common narrative is that he simply committed perjury on the stand and, by implication, told lies to his legal team in his own accounts of what happened. Kevin Boland told the historian Donnacha Ó Beacháin that Haughey had informed Boland privately of the arms shipment. Boland maintained that Haughey's motivation in arms procurement was driven by a desire to enhance his republican credentials in Fianna Fáil at a time when Lynch was vulnerable on the national question; Haughey was laying the groundwork for a heave. Boland finally speculated that Haughey was determined that his role in the venture would not go unacknowledged.[71] How Haughey would go about ensuring this acknowledgement is never properly explained by Boland. It is difficult to see how any heave against Lynch based on the illegal importation of arms could have had any hope of succeeding. Questions in relation to how this illegality would have been announced, who would have announced it, and what the reactions from within Fianna Fáil, and from the British and the Irish people would have been, remained unasked and unanswered by those who supported such a theory.

Most accounts of Haughey's alleged perjury point to naked self-interest, although the eminent political scientist and historian Paul Bew had maintained that Haughey might well have unleashed a tidal wave of naked nationalism if he had proclaimed that he had acted in the best interests of Ireland. Instead, he preferred to perjure himself and in the process revealed the unfolding hypocrisy of the Irish political class when it came to Northern Ireland.[72] Another eminent historian, Diarmaid Ferriter, maintains that Haughey's actions were based on not risking his career and underlined his lack of conviction on the Northern question.[73] Yet there was far more at stake for Haughey than his career as his trial loomed.

The consistency of Haughey's account and its simple narrative was that he had acted properly at all times in carrying out his ministerial duties. At its heart these duties consisted of him being in essence the minister who signed the cheques but left the details of what army intelligence wanted to army intelligence itself. In that context his defence was that he met Captain Kelly only intermittently for vague and generic updates of what was happening in Northern Ireland, and was happy to meet delegations of Northern nationalists to assure them that the government was conscious of their plight and would seek to help them as best it could. The trouble for Haughey is that, given how on top of his brief he had been in every ministerial position he had held, the idea that he would not be fully aware of the details of any particular importation or policy over which he had financial control seems beyond naive and illogical for a politician of his standing. It was, however, a theory he insisted was correct. His other insistence – that he knew nothing about arms importation but was happy to provide ministerial orders to Customs to allow proper army intelligence shipments into the country – put him at odds with the other defendants in the trial. Captain James Kelly, John Kelly and Albert Luykx all admitted to attempting to import arms but claimed they did so in the knowledge that it was a fully legal Irish government-sanctioned operation; and Captain Kelly claimed that he had kept Jim Gibbons updated about his activities at all times.[74]

Haughey was of course unique in being the only public representative among the defendants. The charges against Neil Blaney were dramatically, and rather surprisingly, withdrawn on the orders of Judge Donal Kearney at a preliminary hearing in the Dublin District Court in early

July. Kearney stated that there was no direct evidence of Blaney's involvement in the importation scheme. Blaney's acquittal came despite the fact that he was in direct control of all operations to buy arms on the European continent and it was he who had brought Albert Luykx into the arms procurement scheme.[75] Haughey's account of his own activities in the period between August 1969 and April 1970 would be put to the ultimate test in his own trial, scheduled to begin in September 1970. By the time Haughey went home to Abbeville on the evening of Monday 20 April 1970, after a day spent preparing for the budget he was to present just two days later, meeting with Jim Gibbons, and calling off the consignment of arms into the state, he could have been forgiven if he hoped that things might begin to ease off once the budget had been delivered. If so, he could not have been more wrong.

CHAPTER 11

THIS TIRESOME BUSINESS OF THE TRIAL

I'VE BEEN SACKED

On the morning of Wednesday 22 April 1970, Charles Haughey rose at 6 a.m. and decided to ride one of his horses around the grounds at Abbeville in order to clear his head for the busy day ahead. His first budget since Fianna Fáil's election victory was an opportunity for him to set out his and the government's priorities for the years ahead. At the end of his ride Haughey put his hand on a drainpipe at the back end of the house to jump off the horse and the drainpipe broke. He fell heavily, suffering a number of injuries including a fractured skull, a broken right collar bone, a torn right eardrum, a fractured vertebra and severe concussion.[1] It was a simple accident – later lurid allegations that he was beaten up in a public house have no basis in fact. Ruth Young, a nineteen-year-old groom employed by Haughey, witnessed the accident. She helped Haughey up off the ground and into the house, where Maureen and their fifteen-year-old daughter Eimear saw him stumble to the floor. Ruth Young attended a press conference called by Haughey's solicitor, Pat O'Connor, on 11 May, at which O'Connor outlined the severity of Haughey's injuries.

Young then told the assembled media about how she had witnessed Haughey's fall and helped him into the house.[2]

After being helped off the floor, Haughey kept repeating 'It's my budget day, it's my budget day.'[3] Maureen Haughey called the family GP, Tony Hederman, who arrived at the house and promptly took Haughey to the Mater. Maureen then rang the hospital. When he arrived, Haughey was met by a family friend, Dr Bryan Alton, who immediately took charge of his admission and treatment.

A week later Haughey was still in hospital when Jack Lynch came to interview him in suite number 47 of the Mater Private, at 9 a.m. on Wednesday 29 April 1970. Bryan Alton had not wanted Lynch to talk to Haughey until Haughey was fully recovered, but relented when Haughey said he would be happy to see the Taoiseach. Alton warned Lynch not to say anything that would upset Haughey and was shocked to hear from Haughey later the tenor of the conversation and Haughey's expectation that he expected to be sacked as soon as he was out of hospital.[4] Haughey, in his notes for his trial, said that Lynch accused him of disloyalty to the Taoiseach in not informing him that he had given customs clearance for a consignment arriving into the country. Lynch then asked Haughey for his resignation. Haughey assured Lynch that there was no disloyalty at any time and that he was not prepared to resign.[5] Lynch, at this stage, did not accuse Haughey of complicity in the proposed importation. He said that he would go away to think the matter over and would do nothing until he had spoken to Haughey again.[6] He did not go to see Haughey either at the Mater or at Abbeville before sacking him over the phone six days later. From his perspective, Lynch stated that he was not given permission to speak to Haughey for several days after his first request and that when he eventually did see him, Haughey was not in a position where Lynch could question him at any length.[7] Maureen Haughey went to see her husband after Lynch's visit. He told her that Lynch had put it to him that he was involved in the illegal importation of arms, and had been disloyal to Lynch and the government. Haughey denied the charge and then told Maureen that he was sure Lynch was going to sack him as soon as he possibly could.[8]

That sacking officially came the following week, at 2 a.m. on Wednesday 6 May 1970. Haughey had been released from hospital two days earlier. Alton had told him to rest for a significant period and not to become stressed. At 8 p.m. on 5 May 1970, while Charles and Maureen Haughey were having dinner at the house of a friend, Brian Dennis, Liam Cosgrave was visiting Jack Lynch and presenting him with evidence, in the form of an anonymous leaked document on Garda-headed notepaper, that cabinet ministers were allegedly involved in illegal efforts to bring in guns for Northern nationalists. A couple of hours later, Lynch phoned Abbeville and was told that Haughey was out having dinner. He finally reached Haughey in Brian Dennis's house. After a brief telephone conversation, in which Lynch asked Haughey to resign and Haughey refused, Lynch dismissed his Minister for Finance. Haughey returned to the dinner table and said, 'That's it. I've been sacked.'[9]

News of the sackings of Haughey and Blaney sent shockwaves across Ireland, both North and South, and further afield. Haughey did not attend the Dáil debate on the sackings or the installation of new ministers, which took place on 7 and 8 May 1970. On the advice of Bryan Alton, he stayed cocooned in Abbeville. Alton would keep a close eye on Haughey over the next five hectic months as Haughey dealt first with his sacking, then his arrest and charge, and finally his two trials. For a man with a range of ailments, including painful periodic bouts of kidney stones, and who had been ordered by his doctor to avoid stress, this period would put Haughey's equanimity to a severe test.

Haughey's sacking brought with it a large volume of correspondence. It was summed up by Paddy Connolly, who would act as one of Haughey's barristers during the arms trial, and would later become one of his most controversial Attorneys General, when he told Haughey that it seemed 'an appropriate time for a man to receive letters from his friends; a time of physical and public setback'.[10] In urging Haughey not to be tempted to abandon politics, Connolly expressed a widely held sentiment among Haughey's correspondents. Another important figure in Haughey's later life as Taoiseach, P.J. Mara, wrote to offer his support, saying that as far as he was concerned, 'a Fianna Fáil government without Charlie Haughey is just not on.'[11] Bruce Arnold, one of his most vituperative critics in later years, wrote to him five days after his sacking. His letter got straight to the point in its very first line: 'I regret very much your departure from the Department of Finance and hope your absence from the government won't be too prolonged.'[12] Arnold went on to say that if he could be of any help in the future, Haughey should get in touch. Haughey replied close to a month later thanking Arnold for all the help he had given him when he was in the Department of Finance and said he would like to have a talk with Arnold's uncle, who had expressed an interest in seeing Abbeville.[13] Another trenchant critic in later years, Hugh Leonard, wrote to say that he was sorry that Haughey was being plagued by his present difficulties and hoped that things would work out well for him, noting that 'the political wilderness seems (vide Churchill and others) to be an essential ingredient for future high achievement and I hope you can regard what is happening now as no more than a hiatus.'[14] Also from the world of the arts, Hilton Edwards and Micheál Mac Liammóir told Haughey, 'whatever way any cat in the world may jump we will both be forever grateful for all you have tried to do for us and beg that you will consider us your sincere friends.'[15] From RTÉ, John Feeney, who worked for *7 Days*, told Haughey that his removal from Finance was a great disappointment and that his abilities would be sadly missed by the government.[16]

At the Department of Finance there was also much disappointment at Haughey's dismissal. One of his civil servants, Mary Morrissey, wrote, 'I don't think I'm wrong in saying that the feeling in the department is one of enormous loss. We have lost a great minister but one who was never too great to be human … the country can ill afford the loss of its most competent minister.'[17] Charles Kennedy, the President of the Retired Civil Servants Association, praised Haughey for introducing a variety of 'realistic and humane provisions' which created civil service history of the highest order and with which his name would also be associated.[18] The most famous of those former civil servants, the Governor of the Central Bank, and former secretary of the Department of Finance, T.K. Whitaker, voiced the hope that Haughey was on the road to recovery and not 'dispirited', adding that he and his wife, Nora, deeply appreciated 'your many kindnesses for me and my family ... I shall always retain the happiest of memories of working for you as Minister for Finance.'[19]

Two days after his sacking as Minister for Finance, and as the debate on the unfolding crisis was winding its way through the Dáil, Haughey made his first public comment on the tumultuous events of the previous few days. In a statement on 8 May 1970 he regretted that because of his accident he could not make a personal address to the Dáil on the termination of his office as a member of the government. He stated that since his appointment as a minister he had endeavoured to the best of his ability to serve his country, Dáil Éireann and the government and had never acted in breach of the trust placed in him. He said that the Taoiseach had requested his resignation on the grounds that not even the slightest suspicion must attach itself to any member of the government, a view to which Haughey himself fully subscribed. Haughey noted that Jack Lynch had received information that, in the Taoiseach's opinion, had cast some suspicion on his Minister for Finance. Haughey then complained that he had not had the opportunity to examine or test this information or the quality of its source or sources. He finished his statement by adamantly insisting that at no time had he 'taken part in any illegal importation or attempted importation of arms into this country. At present I do not propose to say anything further except that I have fully accepted the Taoiseach's decision as I believe that the unity of the Fianna Fáil party is of greater importance to the welfare of the nation than my political career.'[20]

NO QUESTION OF A PROSECUTION

At 11 a.m. on Monday 25 May 1970 the head of Garda Special Branch, Detective Chief Superintendent John Fleming, and his colleague Detective Inspector Patrick Doocey arrived at Abbeville to interview Haughey in the company of his solicitor, Pat O'Connor. Haughey offered the two detectives tea. They refused. Haughey said he was having some anyway, so tea was brought for all four men. After some small talk about the weather, O'Connor said that before the meeting began he wanted to reiterate what had been said to the press and radio about Haughey's health. He handed Fleming the original medical report from Bryan

Alton, and recommended the detective read it, which he did. Fleming apologised for having to disturb Haughey and hoped that he was fit and well. Haughey stated that his mind still became a little tired if he was speaking and concentrating on a particular item for any great length of time, to which Fleming replied that he would not be there long.

Haughey asked the detectives the purpose of their visit. Fleming responded that they were investigating the alleged importation of arms into the country and were taking statements from a number of people. He then stated that Haughey's name had been mentioned a number of times and kept reappearing in these statements so in that context he would like to discuss the matter with him. Haughey asked on whose authority Fleming was making these inquiries and the superintendent told him that his instructions had come directly from the Attorney General, Colm Condon. Haughey said he would help as much as he could, but the detectives had to realise that as a former member of the government, he could not possibly answer questions which would breach the trust and confidence placed on him by virtue of that position.

Haughey then asked the crucial question: was there any question or possibility of a prosecution being brought against him? Fleming replied that there was no question of that at this stage. Haughey said that because it was a delicate matter and might involve government policy and decisions, he would like Fleming to put any questions in writing so that Haughey and his solicitor could decide what questions could be answered without breaking any confidences. Fleming agreed. He said he would report to the Attorney General immediately and seek his advice, but he would like to have Haughey's answers as soon as possible. O'Connor said that the questions could be submitted to him at Ormond Quay, while Haughey said he would be in bed for the afternoon. When O'Connor showed the detectives to the door, he informed them of a robbery in his offices between Saturday and Sunday 2 and 3 May during which the file of 'Kelly, deceased' was tampered with, along with some others. The whole meeting lasted for about twenty minutes.[21]

Fleming's own report of the meeting states that when he mentioned Haughey's name had come up frequently in the replies of other people he had interviewed, Haughey replied: 'My name comes up in a lot of things', adding that it was his duty as a citizen and a former minister to give every possible assistance. Haughey then asked that because of the delicate nature of the issue he wanted to see the questions in writing so that he could look them over and see which he could answer without disclosing government policy and decisions. He added that the questions could either be delivered to his solicitor or sent to his home in Abbeville. In response to Haughey's query as to whether there was any question of a prosecution at this stage, Fleming replied that the matter had not yet been fully investigated; but his own report did not mention him saying that there was no question of a prosecution being brought at this point. The meeting ended, according to Fleming, with Haughey giving him a copy of his (Haughey's) public statement on the matter, which had received wide publicity, and suggesting that Fleming would like to have it for his files.[22]

Fleming certainly must have planned on returning to Kinsaley to question Haughey. He never got the opportunity because the Attorney General, Colm Condon, decided to charge Haughey. He was arrested on the morning of 28 May. As Michael Heney points out, Condon's decision pre-empted whatever conclusions or recommendations on prosecution Fleming might have contemplated.[23] Fleming had clearly told Haughey that there was no question of a prosecution being taken against him at this stage; so Haughey must have assumed that he would at least have the opportunity of replying to Fleming's questions before any arrest or charge. This was to prove a costly mistake for Haughey. When he discovered he was to be charged both he and his solicitor Pat O'Connor were shocked.[24]

Haughey was arrested at his home at Abbeville just before 10.30 a.m. on Thursday 28 May 1970 and taken to Bridewell Garda Station where, along with Neil Blaney, he was charged with conspiring with John Kelly, Captain James Kelly, Albert A. Luykx and others unknown to import arms and ammunition into the country between 1 March and 24 April 1970 in contravention of Section 17 of the Firearms Act, amended by Section 21 of the Firearms Act 1924. On the night before, as Leinster

House swirled with rumours of the imminent arrests of a number of unnamed politicians, a group of Fianna Fáil deputies including Haughey, Blaney and Kevin Boland, Senator Bernard McGlinchey, who was close to Blaney, and a number of legal advisers, met from 8 p.m. to 9.30 p.m.[25] Haughey and Blaney then talked on their own for another thirty minutes. John Kelly, Captain James Kelly and Albert Luykx had all been arrested, charged and released on bail earlier in the day in relation to the alleged conspiracy to import arms. The following morning Maureen Haughey took her son Ciarán to the dentist for a nine o'clock appointment. On their return home just over an hour later, she found a number of gardaí in the hall. She immediately brought Ciarán upstairs. Charles Haughey told her, 'They're arresting me for something I didn't do and I don't know when I'll be back. Bye.'[26] Maureen's sister Peggy O'Brien, an asthma sufferer who was recovering from TB and had given birth to a baby not long before, was recuperating at Abbeville. Supreme Court Justice Brian Walsh, a close friend of both Haugheys, had come out to Abbeville that morning to give Charles advice and to support Maureen. Walsh and Peggy O'Brien watched from the landing as Haughey was taken away. He was kept in the Bridewell for close to an hour as the charge sheets were being prepared. Just before noon Haughey and Blaney were brought through the underground passage from the Bridewell up the steps into court number 4 to face the crowded courtroom.[27]

Assistant State Solicitor E.J. Durnin opposed bail for Haughey on the grounds that he would interfere with witnesses. Justice Herman Good, however, decided to grant bail on the basis that a man was innocent until proven guilty. Both Blaney and Haughey were remanded to the District Court on 4 June on their own bail of £500 and an independent surety of £1,000. Henry Bernard Dennis, a company director from the Howth Road, and a close friend of Haughey's, put himself forward as bailsman for Haughey and Blaney, who left the courts and returned home.

That night, as Haughey and Maureen pondered their next steps, Máirín Lynch was speaking in Cork at a dinner to mark that year's Harty Cup and All-Ireland victories of North Monastery CBS, where her husband had been a past pupil. In her speech she said, 'Patriotism very often demands sacrifices and true patriotism very often requires the submerging of natural inclinations to think only of the good of sectional interests. The road to true patriotism never has been and never will be an easy one.'[28] She told reporters that she was expressing her husband's sentiments when she said that the practice of true patriotism was meant to work for the overall good of all the people of the country. Eleven months earlier, Máirín Lynch had told Haughey that she was just an actor with an easy part to play during the general election campaign. She was now playing another role as her husband's closest confidante and chief adviser and she would stand steadfastly by him during the tumultuous months to follow. That same night Maureen Haughey was also standing steadfastly by her husband, but she had far more to be worried about. The trial to come would place her husband's liberty, and their future, in grave peril.

For Haughey, the period between being charged on 28 May 1970 and the beginning of his trial four months later on 22 September was a strange twilight zone. The recovery from his injuries was slow and he was faced with serious preparation for his trial. He refused to speak publicly or, indeed, privately about the trial except with his legal advisers. His solicitor Pat O'Connor retained two of the finest senior counsel practising at the Bar, Niall McCarthy and Peter Maguire, and a junior counsel, Patrick Connolly, to defend him. In July Haughey inadvertently received an entreaty from a member of the public meant for the Minister for Agriculture. He forwarded it on to Jim Gibbons, who had been moved from Defence in Lynch's reshuffle after Haughey's and Blaney's sacking, pithily writing, with a hint of gallows humour, 'I am sure you will let the poor man have his grant!'[29]

The Haughey family prepared for Eimear to go on a showjumping trip to St Moritz in August, and they holidayed together in Wexford and Kerry later in the month. Haughey also had a large amount of positive correspondence in advance of his trial. He still had his supporters in Jack Lynch's new cabinet; the Minister for Lands, Seán Flanagan from Mayo, wrote to him in late July: 'Maybe being dismissed and put on trial has its compensations. It is about the only way to find out what people think of you. It must be some consolation that you have the affection of about

3 million people … In the meantime the petty meanness & jealousies of "life at the top" go on.'[30] Outside the cabinet there were many letters of support from people in Fianna Fáil who were supporters of Lynch, including the party organiser Padraic O'Halpin, who a month before the trial reassured Haughey, 'You will be back before long, where you are needed.'[31] Of course, there was no guarantee that he would be back, such were the severity of the charges and the power of the state ranged against him when he presented himself for trial at the Four Courts on the morning of Tuesday 22 September 1970.

IN THE BEAR PIT

The great chronicler of the arms trials, Tom McIntyre, described Haughey on the second day of his trial as 'small, reasonably trim for his mid-forties, immaculately dressed – always … Not one to shake hands readily – a bow suffices. The vanity is near his centre all right but beneath the patrician hauteur – for mass consumption – that he is one of the boys. Maybe.'[32] This evocative description summed up the enigma that was Haughey as the trial began. Exactly who were these 'boys'? His correspondents and friends came from many different walks of life. Many Northern nationalists viewed him as one of theirs. A few weeks before the trial the Derry nationalist Paddy Doherty wrote to him in connection with a meeting held in March 1970, some six months before, between Doherty and three ministers of the government, Haughey, Blaney and Gibbons. In his letter Doherty offered to testify on behalf of Haughey to the effect that 'there was never any suggestion at the meeting of procuring same by illegitimate means.'[33] The 'same' being 'means of defence', which Doherty had requested. Four days before Haughey's trial began, his friend, the theatre impresario, actor and writer Micheál Mac Liammóir touchingly invited him to lunch or dinner with Hilton Edwards and himself 'next week', asking Haughey what day would suit him best.[34] Replying on the first day of the trial, Haughey politely declined, but '[as] soon as this tiresome business of the trial is out of the way I shall get in touch with you.'[35] It was perhaps a sign of optimism that Haughey himself thought he would be acquitted. Many of those who would have considered him 'one of the boys' were of the same view. Two days before the beginning of the trial, John Healy wrote Haughey a letter of support, noting that 'on this rather lonely morning' he still had many friends. Observing that it was a 'lonely spot in the centre of the bear pit', Healy compared the trial to a good election contest and expressed his confidence that 'you'll pin down those twelve votes. I'll always take my chances with twelve Dublin men.'[36]

Haughey followed a similar routine in that first week of the trial. He woke early, dealt with correspondence, took a walk around Abbeville, then put on a suit and waited for Pat O'Connor to drive him into the Bridewell. He seemed to both his family and his solicitor to be relaxed enough about the proceedings.[37] He was certainly worried, however, about the toll the trial would take on his family, particularly his daughter Eimear, who decades later recalled the strain involved: 'I hated the notoriety. With the arms trial it was awful. I blocked it out. I just pulled down a blind.'[38] Once in the courtroom Haughey, like everyone else in attendance, was absorbed by the proceedings. Haughey's legendary hauteur slipped as the first trial collapsed. At 2 p.m. on Tuesday 29 September 1970 Judge Aindrias Ó Caoimh withdrew after what he considered an attack on the conduct of the trial by Ernest Wood, counsel for Albert Luykx. Tom McIntyre captured the picture: 'Hissing with frustration the accused Charles Haughey half-rises from his seat – "Resign from the Front Bench." Making for his chambers, Mr Justice Aindreas O'Keefe [sic] President of the High Court does not break his determined stride.'[39] There was no precedent in Irish legal history for the abrupt discharge of a jury in a criminal trial, which gave rise to rumours that the state might enter a *nolle prosequi*.[40] The state had, however, come too far and the second trial was set for the following Tuesday, 6 October 1970.

Haughey gave his evidence on the morning of Monday 19 October. When he had made himself comfortable in the witness box the packed court, as McIntyre eloquently described it, gave itself to the witness. He painted Haughey as having 'a tongue in his head too … years of experience in the House behind his finesse in handling answers, qualification, elaboration; and this gruesome control, and of course the vanity.'[41]

Haughey spent the day in the witness box, giving precise, clipped answers to the questions he was asked. To the crucial question – had he given customs clearance knowing that a consignment of arms and ammunition was involved – he confidently asserted 'No'. He did not know, he said, that customs clearance was directed to a specific consignment but thought it was rather a general arrangement whereby army intelligence would be absolved from customs examination for any consignment they wanted to bring in. He insisted it was a very normal routine procedure as far as he was concerned but he did not exclude the possibility that the consignment might have contained arms and ammunition. He gave his side of his conversations with Berry on the evening of Saturday 18 April and with Gibbons on the afternoon of Monday 20 April. He never wavered. On the following morning Haughey briefly took the stand again to answer some minor cross-examination points and within an hour his evidence was over. He was the last witness to testify at the trial.

On Friday 23 October 1970 Justice Séamus Henchy charged the jury in the most famous trial in the history of the Irish state. He reviewed the cases of both the state and defence and made clear his belief that the prosecution had been properly brought by the Attorney General. Given the vehemence with which every lawyer for the accused had deemed the prosecution both unfair and unnecessary, Henchy felt forced to give his view, but stated that he was not expressing in the least an opinion on whether or not that prosecution should succeed. That was a matter for the jury alone. Haughey watched him impassively. At 3.28 p.m. the jury retired. Just over two hours and fifteen minutes later they were back with four not guilty verdicts. The court erupted into cheers. Haughey nodded at his family and supporters and gave a wry smile. Minutes after the verdict was announced, chants of 'We want Charlie!' began to echo around the dome of the Four Courts.[42]

Haughey's relief at the verdict quickly gave way to the fury that had been seething inside him ever since Jack Lynch had come to the Mater Hospital to question him six months earlier. After accepting the boisterous well wishes of countless supporters who thronged the lobby of the Four Courts, Haughey appeared at a press conference at the Four Courts

Hotel. On behalf of himself, his wife and his co-defendants, whom he described as 'fellow patriots', he expressed gratitude for the loyalty and devotion of his supporters in recent weeks. He rejoiced that he had been 'vindicated by twelve fellow-citizens of Dublin'. At this stage the stresses of the trial got the better of him. Those 'responsible for the debacle have no option but to take the honourable course open to them'. When journalists asked him what this course was, he replied cryptically, 'I think it is pretty evident.'[43] During his press conference Haughey stated that: he would never lead a breakaway from Fianna Fáil; could not see any reason for a mini-budget that had been mooted by his successor, George Colley; a position in the present government did not arise; there was no need for a general election; the case had done a great deal of damage to the country with repercussions at home and abroad; and a top priority was to set about restoring the damage done to the party and the country. He was described as being 'specific, vague, serious, humorous but at all times, apparently, confident'.[44] His confidence that he had the backing of his party was, however, vastly misplaced. When asked if he had any idea of the extent of his support in the parliamentary party, Haughey replied that he had been surprised at the tremendous support not only from his own constituency but from all over the country. This, he declared, had been for him the most satisfying aspect of the whole affair. That support, however, did not become apparent; over the next few days the cabinet and the Fianna Fáil parliamentary party rallied around Jack Lynch. That was still in the future, though. For now, Haughey finished his press conference and he and his supporters adjourned to the bar, where the atmosphere was described as like an All-Ireland final.[45]

THE GHOSTS OF THE ARMS TRIAL: I INTEND TO STAY AND FIGHT

The ghosts of the arms trial never left Charles Haughey. On 9 November 1971, Fine Gael moved a Dáil motion arguing that on 8 May 1970 Jim Gibbons, then Minister for Defence, had misled the Dáil, and that his conduct was unworthy of a member of the government and of a member of Dáil Éireann.[46] The day before, Haughey, much to the surprise of many, stated that he would vote with the government against this motion of censure in Gibbons, who had in effect been the prosecution's main witness in the arms trial. Haughey said that the 'time has now come to leave the events of May 1970 and their sequel behind us and to let history judge all those who played any part in them. I know there will be some to whom this decision of mine will come as a disappointment. To them I say that the unity of Fianna Fáil is of the greatest importance to the welfare of this nation, and I have followed that belief consistently since my statement of May 8 1970.[47]

Jack Lynch had widened the debate beyond a simple vote of confidence in Gibbons by essentially declaring that any Fianna Fáil deputy who did not vote with him would have the parliamentary party whip removed and he would propose to the national executive that they not be ratified as a candidate in the next election. This was effectively a 'vote with us or get out' ultimatum. Blaney was not willing to back Lynch and was duly expelled from the Fianna Fáil parliamentary party after abstaining on the motion. In June 1972 he was expelled from Fianna Fáil by a vote of the national executive for conduct unbecoming a member of the organisation, after it was found that his supporters had been organising the party's national collection in his constituency without reference to its national headquarters.

Haughey's closest friend and business partner, Harry Boland, claimed that Haughey's decision to back Gibbons was one of the lowest points of their friendship, which dated back to their schooldays.[48] Yet the reality was that if Haughey wanted to achieve anything in politics, Fianna Fáil was the only vehicle in which he could do so. Not for him the fantasy of Kevin Boland's essentially one-man party, Aontacht Éireann, or Neil Blaney's equally one-man Independent Fianna Fáil. In May 1971, Kevin Boland resigned from Fianna Fáil. Four months later, on 19 September 1971, he launched his new political party before an audience of over a thousand delegates. Aontacht Éireann was in essence a vanity project. Its initial application for registration with the state as a political party was rejected but granted on appeal in October 1971. It performed spectacularly badly in the 1973 general election, none of its thirteen candidates coming anywhere near winning a seat. Boland polled just over two thousand first preference votes on 6 per cent of the vote in Dublin County South. Aontacht Éireann did not put itself forward as a party for election again, although Boland did unsuccessfully fight a by-election in 1976 in Dublin South West where he polled just 1,187 first preferences, 4.75 per cent of the votes cast.[49]

Boland had completely misread the political scene when he set about establishing Aontacht Éireann. He genuinely saw it as a replacement for Fianna Fáil and believed that it could overcome any organisational challenges it might face. Much of the newspaper commentary of the time shared his optimism. Michael Mills, the respected political correspondent of the *Irish Press*, reported on its launch that it would be very foolish for any of the existing political parties to write it off as presenting no threat.[50] Boland's problem was that he could see no policy beyond the 'six counties'. His combination of rigid arrogance and strange innocence, in Patrick Maume's characterisation, was a very far cry from Haughey's much wider intellectual stance.[51] The only thing that worried Boland before the formation of the new party was the position of Haughey and Blaney. He expected both men to break with Fianna Fáil, and did not want to officially announce the new party until they were on board. He felt that it would be a great pity if, after all that had happened in the last two years, Haughey, Blaney and himself could not find it possible to act in unison now. Boland had, however, spectacularly misread Haughey when he asked him to 'accept that it is your national duty to be in on this at the outset, which is now'.[52] Given that over nine months had passed since Haughey's acquittal, any possible momentum he might have given to a new party had long since passed.

Supporting Gibbons was the bitterest pill for Haughey to swallow, and there was no guarantee that it would have long-term benefits. The alternative, however, was far worse. Since entering public life, Haughey had held a special scorn for independents; neither was he particularly enamoured of small parties. He wanted to be in government so that he could get things done. He also wanted to be back in government, and ultimately he wanted to be Taoiseach. In the Ireland of 1971, the only way he could aspire to either of those positions was to remain in Fianna Fáil. It was a price he was prepared, however reluctantly, to pay.

Haughey never had any intention of leaving Fianna Fáil. On the first day of the trial in September 1970, when his bitterness towards Lynch must surely have been at its strongest, and as he faced the potential loss of his liberty, he told Tras Honan, a regular correspondent, that he agreed with her that 'any suggestion of a second party is completely out of the question.'[53] He repeated this in his press conference after his acquittal. A few months later, in February 1971, after he had been found not guilty in the second trial, Gordon Colleary, the founder of the USIT student travel agency, wrote to Haughey demanding to know what he planned to do politically. Colleary said that unless he was sure that Haughey intended to get back into office at the top, which was something worth fighting for, he would leave the party and join Labour. Fianna Fáil, he said, was led 'by the most lazy lacklustre leader in our history'.[54] Haughey replied: 'I intend to stay and fight.'[55] Some months later in August 1971 one of Haughey's correspondents, Louis O'Connor, rather naively urged him to 'make a bid for the position of Taoiseach right now' so that he could take some action about Northern Ireland.[56] Haughey replied that he was following the situation with deep anxiety and 'if an opportunity presents itself to do anything worthwhile I will not hesitate.'[57]

Haughey's decision to support Gibbons three months later was the epitome of that intention to stay and fight, but many of his supporters were aghast. In urging him to abstain, one of his correspondents, Mary Wilson, no doubt spoke for many when she told him that if he supported the party which had put him in this dilemma, his personal standing would be 'eroded beyond redemption throughout the country and the cynicism with which most people now regard politicians will be confirmed'.[58] An alternative view came from the Cathal Brugha branch in Haughey's own constituency of Dublin North East: in supporting the Gibbons motion the position he faced was an extremely unenviable one and the vote he cast was 'in support of the Fianna Fáil party, the organisation which has been your prime concern for many years and whose success is a tribute to your unstinting efforts on its behalf'.[59]

At its heart Haughey's decision was the ultimate expression of pragmatic politics. One of his supporters, Kevin Barry, praised him for overcoming 'what must have been one of the toughest personal, family and political problems of your life and career'.[60] And indeed it was, but it was a decision Haughey took on his own. His wife, Maureen, daughter of the legendary Seán Lemass, played no part in it. She noted that 1971 was an extremely tough year for Haughey; he had survived the arms trial, but was in political purgatory when the party rallied around Lynch.[61] Haughey's daughter Eimear, at that stage sixteen years of age, recalled her father, who was like a lost soul in the year after the arms trial, looking out the window of the house in Abbeville and her mother laughing and saying, 'Leave him alone, only he can make the decision and he'll make the right one. He's just waiting for his country to call him.'[62] In choosing to support Jim Gibbons just a year after his criminal trial Haughey was playing the long game. It was an extremely risky one but at its heart it was the right strategy. Fianna Fáil would eventually come calling close to a decade later.

THE GHOSTS OF THE ARMS TRIAL: AN EVENT BEST FORGOTTEN

The ghosts of the arms trial would haunt Haughey for the rest of his life. On becoming Taoiseach in December 1979 his first row with RTÉ came about because of the arms trial.

One of the staple diets of the Ard Fheiseanna of the main political parties was an interview of the party leader on RTÉ's flagship current affairs radio programme *This Week* at Sunday lunchtime. In preparation for Haughey's first major sit-down RTÉ interview, one of the programme's presenters, Kevin Healy, went to see the new Taoiseach at Government Buildings. Healy and his co-presenter Gerald Barry had decided that they would have to make some reference to the arms crisis and trial. When Healy broached the subject, the new Taoiseach exploded: 'How dare you, Healy, why do we have to bring that stuff up? If you ask me that on air, I'll tell you to fuck off.' Healy replied, 'I don't think you realise where I'm coming from, Taoiseach, and you'll have to trust my bona fides on this as a journalist,' but before he could say another word, Haughey roared: 'I know where you're coming from all right! You're one of Jack Lynch's fucking henchmen from Cork and you want to hang me from the nearest fucking lamp post, well you'll not fucking hang me.'[63] Healy tried to reassure Haughey that this wouldn't happen, but the new Taoiseach was not for turning. For the first time ever, RTÉ did not have an interview with the Taoiseach at his party's Ard Fheis. Haughey appeared on numerous other RTÉ programmes but he would not appear on *This Week*. Barry and Healy decided it was a matter of principle that no politician they interviewed could dictate what questions they asked. Haughey eventually did appear on the programme later that summer when Barry and Healy were both on holiday.

A year later the issue re-emerged when Healy and Barry met Haughey and the government press secretary Frank Dunlop in Government Buildings in January 1981. At this meeting, in which Haughey was in ebullient form, the two journalists said that they would have to ask Haughey about the recent debate in the Dáil on *Magill*'s series on the arms trial and the revelations in the Peter Berry diaries. Haughey's mood quickly darkened. 'If you ask me about that I'll tell you to fuck off.' Healy replied that Haughey's answers were up to him but he had to ask the questions. Haughey said that he could not understand Healy's continuing obsession with the arms trial and that the story would descend into 'Here I am again in a public row with RTÉ … Taoiseach refuses to do interview, etc.' Healy said that the interview would have no integrity if the *Magill* revelations and the Dáil debate were not referred to. He pointed out that the BBC investigative programme *Panorama* had already aired an interview with Haughey in which he was asked some of the questions Healy wanted to ask. Haughey replied that *Panorama* had cheated and he would never do anything for them again. He finished by telling Healy that he had decided not to talk about these issues and offered the programme the Minister for Finance, Gene Fitzgerald, instead.[64] Thus once more Haughey and *This Week* failed to come to an arrangement about an interview.

The arms crisis was a bottom-line 'no interview' area for Haughey. Journalists would constantly seek to ask him about it, but he never spoke of it. The academic and writer Justin O'Brien did meet with Haughey in Abbeville in 2000 before the publication of his book on the arms trial. In the book he advanced the theory that the arms crisis had essentially been a battle for the soul of Fianna Fáil, and that Haughey and Blaney were operating a type of a shadow administration during the period. He argued that the ultimate aim of the two ministers was to topple Lynch, allowing one or the other to become leader of the party, although he does argue that Lynch was aware of efforts to import arms long before April 1970. Haughey and O'Brien discussed Fianna Fáil's view of itself as the guardian of the nation, but not the specifics of the arms crisis or the trial itself.[65] O'Brien's view that Haughey and Blaney helped to finance the emergence of the IRA would certainly not have pleased Haughey, who always abhorred the use of violence in Northern Ireland, notwithstanding various lurid claims to the contrary. O'Brien sought another interview with Haughey in 2000 in relation to a PhD thesis he was working on, but was rebuffed.

One journalist who was close to Haughey was Vincent Browne. In May 1971 Browne was stationed in Belfast as Northern news editor of the *Irish Press* group. He wrote to Haughey in May that year to offer condolences to him on the death of his father-in-law, Seán Lemass. Browne said that being in the North was very interesting journalistically but deadly dull socially and went on to 'note with interest and pleasure the gradual rehabilitation of your political fortunes and I hope that you are shortly restored to your former public prominence.'[66] Haughey replied telling Browne that he had been following carefully his reports from Belfast and wanted him to know that he thought them of 'exceptional quality' and would very much like to meet him to discuss the situation in general.[67] Thus began a relationship between the two men that would have many ups and downs over the following three and a half decades; Browne would veer from investigating the state of Haughey's wealth and finances to sharing hospitality with him.

Like every other journalist, Browne could not, try as he might, get the truth of the arms crisis and trials out of Haughey, or even Haughey's version of it. From his early days in Northern Ireland, Browne made a significant impression on a wide range of people. In August 1971 one of Haughey's correspondents, Gordon Colleary, who considered himself an expert on Northern Ireland, advised Haughey that the best way to rehabilitate himself with both Fianna Fáil and the country at large was to concentrate on Northern Ireland. He should call for a massive influx of aid and borrowing as the best way to reassure the business community, which was the backbone of unionism. 'The best man to help you is Vincent Browne … His analysis of the situation is up to date and superb … Only drawback is that he cannot be trusted fully – only because he talks too much. He may help on a personal basis because he admires you … He would be best for an assessment of the right-wing Unionist position as well as the Provisionals.'[68] And Haughey did seek Browne's counsel on Northern Ireland in this period. Some eighteen months later, in January 1973, Haughey wrote to a number of his friends in the United States, asking them to give Browne any assistance they could on a visit he was due to undertake there: '[He] is a very good friend of mine and a journalist of the highest integrity'.[69]

On 15 September 1978, a year after he had launched *Magill* magazine, Browne went to see Haughey in his office at the Department of Health. (Haughey had been appointed Minister for Health and Social Welfare after Fianna Fáil's landslide victory in the June 1977 general election.) The topic of conversation was the arms trial. When the meeting ended Haughey handwrote a note to himself:

Vincent Browne in the course of a conversation stated that in his view the two interesting things about the arms trial were Berry's evidence and the army directive. Peter Berry told him that he was sitting naked about to go into this sauna on the Saturday evening when I phoned him. His thoughts were as follows: Here we have a conspiracy to import arms in which the Ministers for Finance, Agriculture and Defence are involved, the Minister for Justice and Taoiseach don't wish to hear about. What am I to do. He phoned Dev – Dev told him to phone the Taoiseach and tell him that he had been in touch with him (Dev) about it. Vincent Browne states that Berry also recalled Fleming calling to see him in Mount Carmel in November 1969 as a result of which he arranged for Jack Lynch to call to see him. JL came through the garden. He told JL of the attempt to import arms and was flabbergasted to hear the following April JL in the Dáil say the first he heard of it was when he received the reports in the previous few days.[70]

Browne wrote an account of the Berry–Lynch conversation in his 1980 *Magill* series on the Berry diaries, which featured exactly what he said to Haughey at their September 1978 meeting, including the detail about Berry being naked and about to go into the sauna. Given the liberal use of pronouns in Haughey's account this text takes some decoding, but it seems clear that Berry told Browne that he (Berry) was sitting naked getting ready to go into the sauna when Haughey phoned him (Berry) on Saturday 18 April 1970. Berry's thoughts then were that there was a conspiracy to import arms with which the Ministers for Finance, Agriculture, and Defence were involved in but which the Taoiseach did not want to know about. Berry pondered what to do and then phoned President de Valera, who told him to tell Lynch that Berry had spoken to him (de Valera). The second point is easier to decode: Berry told Browne that after he had met John Fleming during his stay in hospital in November 1969, he arranged for Jack Lynch to call to see him. In the course of that conversation in Mount Carmel Hospital, Berry told Lynch about the plot to import arms and was thus shocked when some six months later – in April 1970 – he heard Lynch tell the Dáil that the first he had heard of the alleged importation was when he received the reports in the previous few days.

The November 1969 date is problematic because according to Berry's own account it was 17 October 1969 when Berry told Lynch that Captain James Kelly had promised money to members of the IRA for the purchase of arms.[71] It is most likely here that Browne simply mixed up October and November in the course of the conversation, or that Haughey wrote November instead of October. Lynch's claim that he had not heard of the arms importation before April 1970 rested on a suggestion that Berry was drugged and on a nose drip during their conversation in the hospital and might have retrospectively confused what he meant to say with what he had actually said. Berry specifically stated that this claim by Lynch was itself mistaken.[72]

There has long been controversy about the Lynch–Berry conversation. Who was telling the truth? Was it a mixed-up jumble of forgetfulness and misremembering? Michael Heney, in a forensic deconstruction of the meeting, its historiography, and its relevance to later events, offers a devastating critique. He sides with Berry's account, arguing that Lynch and his Minister for Defence not only failed to act at the time but later pretended that they had never got the warning.[73] By September 1978 Haughey deemed it important enough to write himself an aide-memoire and put it in his safe after his conversation with Browne. Browne and Haughey were quite friendly in this period. Three months later, in December 1978, Browne thanked Haughey for his hospitality after a dinner at Abbeville: 'Next time I'm doing a Haughey profile I think I'll just talk to Maureen – I might actually get some information.'[74] Notwithstanding the joke, Maureen Haughey was unlikely to tell any journalist, no matter how friendly, anything about her husband. Her view of the arms trial was that it was an unjustified attack by the state not only on her husband but on her family too.[75] When her father, Seán Lemass, died in May 1971, a steady stream of sympathisers called to her parents' home in Palmerston Road. One of them was Jack Lynch. When he knocked on the door, it was answered by Maureen Haughey. She looked at him, turned around without speaking and alerted her mother that the Taoiseach was on the doorstep.[76] Lynch was brought into the house, sympathised with Lemass's widow, Kathleen, and left immediately.

Close to a year after writing down his recollection of the meeting with Browne, Haughey met the former Chief of Staff of the Defence Forces Seán MacEoin, at a social event at the Burlington Hotel on 5 July 1979. The famous army directive of 6 February 1970 came up in conversation. In that spoken directive, Jim Gibbons ordered MacEoin to prepare for possible military intervention by the Irish army across the border into Northern Ireland. Eleven days after their conversation, at 3 p.m. on Monday 16 July 1979, MacEoin went to see Haughey in his office. Less than five months later Haughey was Taoiseach. After the meeting, Haughey wrote an aide-memoire to himself which began by stating that since they had last spoken at the Burlington Hotel, General MacEoin had an opportunity to check the situation about the government directive in which Haughey was interested. MacEoin stated that the position was as follows:

> On the 6th February 1970 he, General MacEoin, received a government directive from the Minister for Defence, Jim Gibbons, verbally. Colonel Hefferon, Director of Intelligence, was present but his presence was accidental. The directive was to the effect that should the British Army be unwilling or unable to offer protection cross the border where possible to offer such protection to the extent that their resources permitted. The Irish army were to bring with them arms and ammunition for issue to members of the minority in Northern Ireland capable of using them for their own protection.

> Having received this directive General MacEoin conveyed its terms to Colonel Adams, the staff officer involved. Colonel Adams reduced the directive to writing in his own hand. He made three copies, one of which was placed in a file entitled Government Directive in the Plans and Operations section. This copy remained on the file and was still there when Colonel Adams retired in June 1972. Colonel Adams raised a number of questions on the implementation of the directive. The most important of these questions was whether the British government would be informed in advance of the border crossings by the Irish army. Three days after the verbal directive of the 6th February General MacEoin went back to the Minister for Defence for instructions and clarifications on the various questions raised by Colonel Adams. On the question about informing the British in advance the Minister's reply was a clear indication that they would not be so informed.

General MacEoin stated that subsequently the directive of the 6th February was followed up with a military directive, this was confined to headquarters, that is the Adjutant General, Q.M.G, Assistant Chief of Staff, and the Brigade Commanders, six in number. The General was of the opinion that this consequent military directive may have been the reason Kevin Boland came to the conclusion that there were two government directives, the latter one being substituted for the first. The General was satisfied that the original directive was not changed or superseded certainly before July 1972 and in all probability was still in its original form on the file. General MacEoin undertook to let me have a written account of this affair as soon as possible.[77]

Haughey initialled the aide-memoire and dated it 16 July 1979. Five days later, MacEoin sent Haughey a handwritten account of his own recollection of the directive. He began by saying that Gibbons had given him the directive in his (the minister's) office in Parkgate Street and it was 'very brief and in the most general of terms'.[78] The order was, in effect, that in the event of a 'doomsday situation', the Defence Forces would be prepared to send detachments across the border for the relief of those in danger. No places were identified; neither was there a directive on the strengths or equipment of units formed for this purpose. MacEoin continued that he was ordered by Gibbons that units of Defence Forces sent on the mission across the border would take with them arms and ammunition for distribution to members of the minority population for their protection. Quantities and types of weapons were not specified. The directive was then drafted for General MacEoin by Lieutenant Colonel Joe Adams. Having studied the directive, MacEoin went back to Gibbons seeking clarification on a number of issues dealing with strengths, equipment, and some administrative issues such as housing and feeding troops. He also asked Gibbons if the British would be informed of the movement of contingents of Irish troops into the six counties. The answer was 'No'. No reply was given to the question of who should receive the arms, 'other than to the minority'.[79]

MacEoin recalled in his memorandum an instruction he received from the then Minister for Defence, Jerry Cronin, to claim privilege over the directive and not to give evidence in relation to it when he was summoned to appear in private before the Committee of Public Accounts on 2 February 1971. This committee was investigating the spending of public monies for Northern Ireland relief. It had summoned MacEoin to appear before it and produce all documents relevant to the matter being examined. In particular, MacEoin was asked to produce the directive issued by Gibbons on 6 February 1970. He did not do so, having been ordered by Cronin to claim privilege over it. Cronin's reasoning was that the document should remain private, having regard to the public interest and the safety of the state.

MacEoin made two other observations in his recollection to Haughey. The first was that a military directive based on the 6 February directive was issued in June 1970 but was limited in circulation and was delayed because the Minister for Defence was reluctant to have the instructions in the directive circulated beyond the general staff. On 5 June 1970 MacEoin had a briefing paper prepared for him in advance of a meeting with the Taoiseach, Jack Lynch, which took place on 9 June 1970. That briefing paper describes discussions between MacEoin and Gibbons in the days after 6 February that aimed to clarify exactly what the directive entailed. The briefing paper begins by stating that the lack of a clear-cut government directive on the form that defence policy should take had created a considerable degree of uncertainty and frustration within the Defence Forces. No long-term procurement policy in regard to personnel or equipment could be drawn up in such a climate.[80] According to MacEoin's note to Haughey, the June directive seemed to have given rise to the thinking in some quarters that a directive later than 6 February had been issued by the Minister for Defence.

The second issue MacEoin raised related to the movement of army lorries containing weapons and ammunition to the Military Barracks in Dundalk on 2 April 1970, as violent rioting in Ballymurphy, Belfast threatened to get out of control. MacEoin said that Gibbons ordered him to send rifles, ammunition and gas masks to Dundalk and that

Gibbons told him he 'was acting under pressure from Mr. Blaney'. The consignment consisted of 500 rifles, 80,000 rounds of ammunition and 3,000 respirators. Gibbons gave no instruction about what was to be done with these weapons when they reached Dundalk. The rifles and ammunition were taken back from Dundalk about a week later because of the insecurity of the barracks in Dundalk and a 'belief that O'Bradaigh was planning a raid on Dundalk [Barracks]'.[81]

The army directive of 6 February, like the Lynch–Berry conversation, has spawned one of the great historiographical controversies of modern Irish history. The directive clearly does show that Jack Lynch's government was prepared to make incursions into Northern Ireland if there was a complete breakdown of law and order and if Irish nationalists were not being protected by the British army. In that context there was no plot or conspiracy; the government simply agreed to urgent demands by various delegations from the north for respirators, ammunition and weapons.[82] There were two distinct elements to the directive. One involved preparation for cross-border incursions. The other made specific provision for supplying guns to nationalists in Northern Ireland. An alternative reading of this directive suggests that this was a legal movement of state arms to the border, as Des O'Malley has described it.[83] Some in the army thought this oral order was ambiguous, and sought clarification about how arms would be handed over, when, and to whom. Gibbons's response – that he had no idea how the directive should be operationalised – could suggest that the government had not taken any decision about how to implement the directive but merely wanted to plan in the case of a doomsday scenario in Northern Ireland.[84] Haughey considered MacEoin's memorandum important enough to make a note of it and keep it safe, but like everything else to do with the arms trial he did nothing with it.

In the days after Haughey was elected leader of Fianna Fáil in December 1979 he received a large amount of correspondence, which took his office some time to work through. One of the more intriguing of these letters came from a businessman, John G. Lyons. After congratulating Haughey, he wrote that he hoped he was not presuming on an event best forgotten when he raised the subject of the arms trial. Lyons had been a juror in the first trial and enclosed a jury exemption certificate dated 1 October (after the trial collapsed when, as we have seen, the presiding judge Aindrias Ó Caoimh withdrew after being accused of bias by Ernest Wood, senior counsel for Albert Luykx). Lyons went on to ask Haughey if he remembered that the two men had met at the back of the Four Courts when Haughey was accompanied by his barrister, Niall McCarthy, and Haughey congratulated Lyons on being discharged. Then Lyons reflected that he had expressed the opinion that 'there was no way you could be convicted' and Haughey thanked him for the 'first ray of hope' in quite some time.[85] A week after receiving the letter, Haughey told Lyons that he was very interested in his recollections of their 'brief conversation in the Four Courts and the events of that time'.[86] Lyons was one of many who believed that Haughey would not be convicted.

In August 1980 James Kelly wrote to Haughey asking for his commission in the Defence Forces to be reinstated from the time he retired on 1 May 1970 with appropriate upward adjustment in rank. He claimed that it was now clear to the vast majority of Irish people, and interested people abroad, that the arms conspiracy charge was based on false and contrived evidence and that the time had come to resolve the matter. He stated that he had been forced to resign from the army by Jim Gibbons's attempt to absolve himself from responsibility for the arms importation at a meeting in Neil Blaney's office on 23 April 1970 when Gibbons told Kelly that he was in the 'hot seat'. Kelly further added that his arrest, by two of his fellow officers, on 28 April on the instructions of Gibbons, and Gibbons's cancellation of Kelly's leave on the following day, also left him no choice but to resign. Only by resigning could he preserve his integrity and effectively challenge what he described as the false evidence of the former Minister for Defence. Now, a decade later, and with a fellow arms trial defendant in the Taoiseach's office, Kelly was seeking reinstatement. He had suffered a significant cost in his career with no possibility of reaching the highest rank in the Defence Forces.[87] Haughey replied that he had referred Kelly's letter to the Attorney General for his advice and observations on the matter.[88] Kelly in turn sent a warm handwritten note to Haughey to say that he would be happy to meet if the Taoiseach thought it desirable and that he and his wife, Sheila, were looking forward to Haughey 'holding the fort' for many years.[89] Four months later, the Attorney General, Anthony Hederman, wrote to Haughey to say there was no statutory or other authority that empowered the Minister for Defence, or the government, or the president (acting on the advice of the government) to accede to Captain Kelly's request.[90] Five days after receiving Hederman's communication, Haughey wrote to Kelly informing him of the Attorney General's opinion and added no further comment.[91]

Captain Kelly was disappointed but philosophical. He knew that Haughey had put the events of the arms crisis and trials behind him and that, after Jack Lynch had brought him back to the Fianna Fáil frontbench in 1975, he just wanted to forget about them. Kelly did not blame Haughey for his own difficulties in 1970 and he believed that Haughey had himself received a raw deal from the Fianna Fáil aristocracy associated with Frank Aiken and George Colley. Kelly's bitterness was aimed specifically at Jack Lynch and Jim Gibbons. He suffered years of penury and his family were publicly insulted and shunned on the streets of Bailieboro.[92] He became a vice-president of Kevin Boland's Aontacht Éireann and contested the 1973 general election for the party in the Cavan constituency, winning 8 per cent of the vote. He later stood as an independent in Cavan–Monaghan in the 1977 and the February 1982 elections, in which he polled negligibly. He then joined Fianna Fáil, believing that under Haughey it had reverted to its constitutional republican outlook. Kelly sought a Fianna Fáil European election nomination for Connacht Ulster in 1984 but was too late putting forward his nomination papers; Haughey rejected a plea from Sheila Kelly that her husband be added to the ticket, saying that there was nothing he could do about it.[93] In 1985 Kelly was elected to Fianna Fáil's national executive, holding this position until he resigned from the party early in 1989, disappointed with Haughey's Northern Ireland policy and in particular with its policy on extradition.[94] After Haughey essentially rejected Kelly's plea for reinstatement into the Defence Forces, James and Sheila Kelly would periodically write to him offering advice and encouragement on a whole range of issues. Haughey would always send polite replies saying he welcomed their advice and would take it into account. He never did.

One final arms trial ghost came to Abbeville as Haughey was on the verge of ending his remarkable public life. It came in the form of a letter from Circuit Court judge Diarmuid Sheridan. On the eve of Haughey's exit from the office of Taoiseach in early 1992 Sheridan wrote complimenting him on the dignified and graceful manner of his exit. He went on to say that he was saddened by the campaign of vilification which had constantly been waged against Haughey since he had been elected leader of the party. Then Sheridan added, intriguingly, that he had in his possession a letter 'written by Jack Lynch to me after the events of 1970 which even at this remove may surprise you'. This passage is underlined in red ink. Sheridan had, he said, hesitated to bring it to Haughey's attention because of both their offices but would gladly do so now, if Haughey wished to see it. He noted that it was 'very complimentary to you in its real context and reflects my feelings expressed at the time'.[95] There is no reply in Haughey's papers, but this in itself is not terribly surprising as Haughey was prone to replying to sensitive correspondence by either telephoning or arranging to meet the correspondent, or both. There is also the possibility that Haughey simply did not want to know what Lynch had thought over two decades earlier, given that his own career as Taoiseach was now at an end. For many years after Haughey's retirement from public life various journalists and academics would write to Haughey urging him to comment about the arms trial, while other correspondents urged him to clear Kelly's name. He never replied to such entreaties.

CHAPTER 12

ISOLATION

THE FIANNA FÁIL CONUNDRUM

In the days and weeks after his acquittal Charles Haughey's post box at Abbeville bulged. From all across the globe people wrote to congratulate him. Many of his correspondents told him that they looked forward to seeing him back at the forefront of political life in a very short period of time. James Croke wrote: 'I do not doubt that you have the strength of character to rise above this recent unpleasantness and to resume your proper place in Irish life … your political star has shone brightly in the dull sky of Irish politics for many years – I trust we will see it back in orbit again and very soon.'[1] The reference to strength of character was telling. On the night of his acquittal, Haughey hosted a large party in Abbeville. Muiris Mac Conghail, at the time editor of RTÉ's *7 Days* current affairs programme, was in attendance, and was reported to be staggered by the number of senior members of the judiciary, senior gardaí, senior civil servants and heads of semi-state bodies who were there. Also present was Haughey's brother-in-law, Jack O'Brien, who was Jack Lynch's aide-de-camp. Anyone who was anybody in public life was there, according to Mac Conghail.[2] Yet after the euphoria of the acquittal, Haughey was faced with an, at best, uncertain future. Politics was his life. Yet his place at the centre of Fianna Fáil was now unceremoniously gone. The show of strength given by Fianna Fáil to Jack Lynch on his return from New York in the immediate aftermath of the trial fortified the Taoiseach. It also had the effect of completely side-lining Haughey. A week later Lynch won a vote of no confidence in the Dáil by 74 votes to 67 with Haughey joining every other Fianna Fáil deputy, except Kevin Boland, in voting for the Taoiseach. Haughey was now a backbencher with no prospect of returning to government any time soon.

Haughey also continued to have health worries. A few days after he was acquitted, he received a letter from Bryan Alton: 'I know your mind is on other things at the minute, but I do not want you to get a recurrence of your sinusitis and bronchitis.'[3] While neither illness in itself was overly worrying, Haughey's injuries from his horse fall six months earlier still lingered. In June 1972 he sympathised with a correspondent's illness: 'I have had a fair amount of hospitalisation myself and know what it is like. However, the human body has wonderful recuperative powers and it is really amazing how one recovers.'[4]

Haughey spent much of the months after the arms trial at home in Abbeville. He walked its grounds and the neighbouring beaches of Malahide and Portmarnock, thinking about his next steps in a barren political landscape. Haughey and Maureen went to the Virgin Islands for a holiday in January 1971. On his return he told one of his regular correspondents, Sr Mary Leontia of the Sisters of Charity, that she could be 'assured I have no intention whatsoever of leaving politics' after she told him how worried she was by rumours in the press that he was considering exiting public life. She bluntly told him, 'You can't let us down – 1970 has proved how strong and true your friends are.'[5] By now, however, the flood of good wishes had dried up and the postman's bag became lighter. The Haughey children were persistently jeered at in their schoolyards, but, like their father, they had good friends who stuck by them. The children of Neil Blaney and Captain James Kelly suffered similar indignities.[6]

Friendships did indeed sustain Haughey over the following years. After he was brought back to the cabinet by Jack Lynch in the aftermath of Fianna Fáil's victory in the 1977 general election, Haughey wrote to Tomás Mac Anna, the artistic director of the Abbey Theatre, that he had not forgotten his and his wife, Caroline's, visit in May 1970, 'and I shall always remember with gratitude your encouragement and support in the lean years that followed'.[7] At the same time he told his close friend, the general secretary of the Irish Transport and General Workers' Union, Michael Mullen, 'how much your friendship and encouragement has meant to me in these recent difficult years'.[8] And indeed the years after the arms trial were politically lean and difficult for Haughey once Jack Lynch took full control of the party after its 1971 Ard Fheis.

In February 1971, Kevin Boland tried to organise a grassroots revolt of Fianna Fáil activists at the Ard Fheis. He, and a small group of his supporters, had been plotting how best to do this for some months. They were outmanoeuvred by the leadership, who used the machinery of the party to isolate both Boland and Blaney by manipulating the accreditation rules to ensure that Lynch's supporters dominated the attendance and votes.[9] Blaney was one of the casualties and was ousted as the party's joint treasurer. Events came to a head on Saturday 21 February when Boland interrupted the Minister for External Affairs, Patrick Hillery, who was speaking from a podium on the platform. Boland appeared at the side of the platform and started shouting at Hillery. Stewards intervened and tried to remove Boland from the main hall of the RDS. Boland, all shoulders and gestures, tried to bait Hillery by curling his index figure at him, at which Hillery famously shouted at Boland and his supporters, 'You can have Boland, but you can't have Fianna Fáil.'[10] This led to more jostling and a bout of fisticuffs between supporters and opponents of Boland before the man who considered himself the true heir of the party's republican tradition left the hall and disappeared from Fianna Fáil for ever. On the day, Haughey was very keen to dissociate himself from Blaney's antics and from the dissidents' howls of 'Union Jack' aimed at the Taoiseach. He told Paddy Hillery that he had nothing to do with it. Hillery believed him.[11]

Just before Lynch gave his speech Haughey made his way on to the stage from behind a curtain on right-hand side and was escorted to a vacant seat. Despite the predominance of Lynch supporters in the hall there was significant cheering from the packed audience. Erskine Childers looked at Haughey aghast and placed his head in his hands. Lynch and Haughey rose simultaneously and shook hands. Then Jim Gibbons crossed the stage from the other side, tapped Haughey on the shoulder, and the two bitter antagonists of the arms trial shook hands.[12] Yet for all the drama of the Ard Fheis, once it was over Lynch was immeasurably strengthened and Haughey considerably weakened. The Fianna Fáil cabinet was now united behind Lynch, as was the party's organisational structure, including its Committee of 15, national executive and officer board. The 1971 Ard Fheis was a defining moment for Fianna Fáil. Its radical republican wing had been routed and its leader had complete control of both his government and the party itself. Meanwhile Haughey's future in Fianna Fáil looked very bleak indeed. He was determined to stay in the party but seemingly had nowhere to go within it.

That 1971 Ard Fheis came in the wake of a Dáil decision in December 1970 that the Committee of Public Accounts was to conduct hearings into the expenditure of money voted for Northern Ireland relief. Sir John Peck, who had replaced Andrew Gilchrist as British ambassador in Dublin, reported back to London that it was widely believed that Jack Lynch's government saw the enquiry 'as tantamount to a re-run of the Arm[s] Trial, getting the verdict right this time'.[13] Haughey viewed it in the same terms.[14] The week after the Fianna Fáil Ard Fheis he gave evidence to the Committee of Public Accounts and faced a range of questions from its members, pretty much all of them hostile. He stuck rigidly to reiterating the testimony he had given in his trial. He was never going to do otherwise. His aim was to give his evidence and move on. His answers to his interrogators were short, precise and clipped.

Over the following months, after the euphoria of his acquittal subsided, and the reality that Jack Lynch was in control of the party became even clearer, Haughey was faced with an important decision. He was at his lowest ebb in the six-month period between September 1970 and March 1971. His acquittal by a jury of his peers was followed by what he saw as a trial of a different sort, one in which his political peers would make their judgement. When he finished giving his evidence to the Committee of Public Accounts, Haughey had to decide what to do politically. His decision to remain in Fianna Fáil and rehabilitate himself from within was the only plausible course of action to take. The form that rehabilitation would take was, however, a much trickier proposition. Given his banishment to the backbenches, and the fact that many of his former government colleagues would have been quite happy to see him leave Fianna Fáil, finding a route back to relevance in the party was always going to be difficult. While he was isolated within the parliamentary party, with the exception of a handful of supporters, he had the support of his own constituency and much of the wider Dublin network of the Fianna Fáil cumann structure. The support of the Fianna Fáil grassroots on the northside of Dublin was crucial to Haughey's comeback over the following half decade. That support soon spread across much of the capital and eventually to much, but not all, of the country. It was driven by Haughey's relentless acceptance of every invitation to speak at Fianna Fáil cumainn across the country, no matter the distance involved.

THE REHABILITATION BEGINS:
THE CENTRAL REMEDIAL CLINIC

In April 1951 Lady Valerie Goulding and Kathleen O'Rourke set up the Central Remedial Clinic (CRC) in O'Rourke's flat in Dublin's Pembroke Street with the aim of rehabilitating children and adults suffering from polio after outbreaks of the disease in 1948 and 1952. With the enthusiastic support of an orthopaedic surgeon, Dr Boyd Dunlop, the two women began providing an aftercare, remedial and rehabilitation service. Lady Goulding spent much of her time driving around the slums of Dublin collecting and delivering children for treatment in O'Rourke's flat. Goulding was an indefatigable campaigner who over the course of her three decades as chairman and managing director of the clinic from 1951 to 1984 persuaded a number of prominent celebrities and businesspeople to raise funds for it. Perhaps most famously she introduced the sponsored walk to Ireland which was led by the BBC disc jockey, the flamboyant Jimmy Savile (who was revealed after his death to have been a serial paedophile), and persuaded celebrities such as Princess Grace of Monaco, Louis Armstrong and Bing Crosby to help the clinic by coming to Dublin.[15] Until 1977 the CRC was entirely dependent on private donations.

In the summer of 1971 Lady Goulding approached Haughey to assist her with fundraising for the CRC. He had supported the clinic financially for some time and they knew each other socially.[16] Haughey was reluctant; he told Lady Goulding that he was not the right person as he was perceived as having a 'bad odour' about him.[17] Lady Goulding persevered and Haughey initially agreed to get involved 'once and once only' in a fundraising campaign Goulding was planning. Once Haughey began to help her, however, he stayed until 1975. He began work in September 1971 after returning from a holiday in Cannes in the south of France with Maureen, his solicitor Pat O'Connor, and his wife, Joan. Haughey first became chairman of the clinic's fundraising committee and later executive vice chairman of its development committee.

Haughey was an enthusiastic supporter and champion of Lady Goulding's work. One of the first things he did was to go to the clinic's bankers, Bank of Ireland, in early October with a fellow board member, John Good. They sought additional overdraft facilities up to £150,000 from the bank to see the clinic through before the fundraising campaign that Goulding had initially approached Haughey about came to fruition. The clinic proposed a target of £300,000 from the fundraising campaign, of which, they assured the bank, £100,000 had already been pledged, and devised a plan to reverse revenue deficits it had accumulated in the previous number of years.[18] By June 1972 the bank had given permission for an overdraft of £50,000 and had agreed to write £12,000 off an existing overdraft. For the first time since 1967 the CRC was in credit.[19]

At the same time as Haughey was negotiating with Bank of Ireland about the CRC's overdraft he was engaged in the same process with Allied Irish Banks (AIB) about his own personal financial situation. In March 1972, AIB fixed an upper limit of £250,000 on his overdraft with the condition that it be cleared within six months. It was reduced to just over £150,000 by June, after he lodged £100,000 he had borrowed from the Northern Bank Finance Corporation using his lands in Ashbourne as collateral. The overdraft had, however, gone up again to £183,000 by that November. Haughey gave commitments to the bank that it would be fully cleared by the end of February 1973 after he sold his Ashbourne lands, and parts of Abbeville. The last day of February saw Haughey re-elected in the 1973 general election, again decisively topping the poll in Dublin North East, winning over 30 per cent of the first preference vote. Tom FitzGerald, his personal bank manager at AIB in Dame Street, wrote to offer his 'heartiest congratulations on the very fine voted polled by you yesterday. It was a magnificent personal tribute.'[20] Yet, a year later, by February 1974, when he was still spearheading the CRC's fundraising efforts, Haughey's personal financial situation was more chaotic than ever. He borrowed a further £160,000 from the Northern Finance Bank and reduced his debt to AIB to £120,000 after selling seventeen and a half acres of land at Abbeville to Cement Roadstone for £140,000.[21] Despite the bank's optimism that he would soon pay off the rest of his debt, his overdraft was allowed to mushroom substantially in the following five years. When he became Taoiseach in December 1979, he owed AIB the staggering amount of over £1 million.

At the heart of the initiatives to erase the CRC's deficits, and upgrade its resources and capabilities, was a proposal by Haughey that individual members of the clinic's development committee, including himself, would approach individual firms for support. The Irish Banks standing committee gave a cheque to the clinic for £5,000 after a personal appeal by Haughey in December 1971. The previous month he had put together a list of over a hundred potential donor firms, from semi-state bodies to merchant banks, to be contacted and proposed that he would approach over twenty himself.[22] Haughey's enthusiasm for his work even extended to giving the annual CRC radio appeal which aired on Radio Éireann on Sunday 21 November 1971. In April 1972 Haughey and Lady Goulding travelled to the United States and raised around £45,000 for the clinic.[23] Over the following three years, until he was brought back to the Fianna Fáil frontbench in January 1975, Haughey spearheaded the CRC's various fundraising campaigns, including the redevelopment of St Patrick's psychiatric hospital in James Street.[24] He also used his own grounds at Abbeville to run an annual gymkhana every summer on behalf of the CRC where the great and good of polite Dublin society mingled with the equine community. Haughey was comfortable with both social sets. He offered his grounds and facilities to the army's equitation school over many years. Ward Union hunts and Irish horse trials were also held at Abbeville.

Much of the commentary around Haughey's work with the CRC is based on the idea that it helped rehabilitate him after the arms trial and that it led him to meet Jimmy Savile, who was a prominent campaigner for the clinic.[25] But Haughey's fundraising efforts at the CRC had nothing to do with increasing his profile in the aftermath of his sacking from government and office. He rarely spoke of this work either publicly or privately. His interest in the CRC was driven by memories of his father's illness, and the pain and poverty it had caused his mother and her children in the family home in Donnycarney. His intention had simply been to help out with one fundraising initiative for a cause he was personally interested in, and Lady Goulding persuaded him to stay on. During his time as chairman of the CRC fundraising committee Haughey took on very few other obligations, telling one correspondent in January 1972 that he was not taking on any business or commercial commitments for the present.[26] The following year he told an American correspondent, the publisher Thomas Collins, who wished to open an editorial office in Ireland and use Haughey as a consultant, that he had a policy 'not to involve myself in any commercial or business activities so that I may devote myself exclusively to politics'.[27] A number of months earlier Collins had tried to persuade Haughey to write what seemed essentially a picture book about Ireland for which he promised editorial and research assistance. The concept of the book was that it would consist of photographs and excerpted material, controlled by a running text originating from Haughey, who would have final control on content. Collins came to Abbeville in October 1972 to talk to Haughey about it and was convinced he had a deal. Haughey, however, opted out in early 1973 without offering any reasons. He may have begun to have doubts when, in the course of their meeting in Abbeville, Collins suggested to him that he was 'associated in the minds of many outside the country with the gun-running episode'.[28] Haughey's response that he doubted this was the case was the forerunner to his exiting the project.

Haughey certainly met Jimmy Savile on a number of occasions in the 1970s, at the sponsored walk and, most likely, also at Abbeville. In May 1980, five months after he became Taoiseach, Haughey hosted Savile and Lady Goulding in Government Buildings when Savile was in Ireland for one his many fundraising visits. The day after the meeting Lady Goulding wrote to Haughey saying that Savile was thrilled to have met him and adding, intriguingly, 'as you say, he could be a good mediator as he really is very well in with Mrs. Thatcher and members of the Opposition as well'.[29] Haughey no doubt said this to Lady Goulding, but the idea that he in any way viewed Savile as a mediator on anything to do with Anglo-Irish relations is implausible. His private secretary at the time of the visit, Seán Aylward, recalled that Savile showed up in the Taoiseach's office wearing his trademark tracksuit, and that afterwards one of the department service officers observed that Savile was as 'phony as a three-bob note'.[30] By the time he became Taoiseach, Haughey had cultivated many contacts across British society, including people in both the Conservative and Labour parties. As early as 1973 he told an English correspondent that he was very anxious to keep open as many lines as he could with British politicians.[31] He also had the weight of his own office behind him for any initiatives he wanted to undertake. He certainly did not need Jimmy Savile to act as a mediator on anything. Savile was an important fundraiser for the CRC, and a good friend of Lady Goulding. In that context Haughey was happy to host him and show him the trappings of his own power. Haughey simply viewed Savile as a fundraiser. Two years later, in May 1982, he regretted that Savile could not lead the clinic's fundraising walk that year, noting that his efforts had been outstanding over the years and that he would be missed.[32]

In November 1987 Haughey opened the CRC's new research building in Clontarf. In that year Lady Goulding was reported to have said, 'But for Charlie, we'd have no centre today.'[33] That was the year Haughey became Taoiseach for the third time. As he faced that daunting task, with an economy on its knees, and a society bruised from the abortion and divorce referendums of the 1980s, which he himself had contributed to, he would have welcomed that comment from Goulding.

Lady Goulding was not the only person involved in medical issues to be grateful to Haughey. On another November, this time in 1971, a new Department of Obstetrics and Gynaecology of University College, Dublin was opened at the National Maternity Hospital in Holles Street. On the day of its opening Professor Éamon de Valera, consultant gynae-cologist at the hospital, and son of the then President de Valera, wrote to Haughey: 'I cannot let the day go by without writing to thank you for what you did to assist me in this matter. Unfortunately, only a very few will know of your help but without you the whole scheme would have been forgotten.'[34]

THE REHABILITATION CONTINUES

In the aftermath of Haughey's work with the CRC he was often approached by organisations looking for help and advice on fundraising. In January 1977, the Irish Society for the Prevention of Cruelty to Animals wrote to him on the understanding that he was an 'authority' on fundraising and would be grateful if he could come up with any ideas by which they could raise money. He replied that he had 'no particular expertise in fund raising' and suggested they consider employing a professional firm.[35] In reality, the only fundraising Haughey was worried about, beyond the CRC, was his own. Once he was finished at the CRC, he turned down pretty much all invitations to help organisations fundraise.

Haughey was, however, constantly beseeched by ordinary citizens to help them with their problems. Many wrote directly asking for money; others asked for help with claiming social welfare benefits and pensions. The pain and poverty of many of his constituents was summed up by one who wrote of having lived 'through the seas of sorrow' when she appealed for him to help her with a widow's pension.[36] More wrote of being in hopeless situations, dire poverty and desperate straits. Haughey made small donations to some correspondents; others he could only offer sympathy. More asked him to use his political influence to help them move up the social housing list or to get jobs for their children. Some he offered to help and asked them to give him a call. He gave short shrift to others. One who asked for help in securing her son a job told him, 'You have the pull, so what can you do for a man that wants to return to work here?' He replied that he did not really care who she voted for but it would have helped if she had given some details beyond telling him that she did not vote for his party.[37] It was not just ordinary people who had great faith in Haughey's ability to get things done. His long-time friend, the senior trade unionist Michael Mullen, approached him in late 1972 wondering whether he could help prevent the prosecution of one of Mullen's union officials for a 'slight mishap' of a traffic accident. Mullen said that he would consider it a 'personal favour' if Haughey could help. Haughey replied that he had Mullen's 'representation' on the issue but did not know if there was any way in which he could be of assistance, although he was making enquiries about the case.[38] Haughey considered all these requests, whether plaintive appeals from people in desperate poverty or from friends wanting help for themselves or their colleagues, as part of his representative mission.

The CRC was not, however, the only organisation that came calling to Haughey in the summer of 1971. On 9 June the general secretary of the Garda Síochána Representative Body for Inspectors, Station-Sergeants and Sergeants, Thomas Mark Muldoon, wrote to him asking if he would be interested in helping their body in an advisory capacity.[39] This invitation came after the appointment of a professional consultant to the body was raised at one of its meetings. Haughey replied that he would be 'honoured to be of any assistance' he could offer.[40] On 22 June a three-man deputation from this body, including Muldoon, met Haughey in Abbeville, and he agreed to act for them as a consultant on an honorary basis.[41] The day after this meeting the representative body wrote to Garda Commissioner Michael Wymes seeking authority to employ Haughey as a consultant. Just under three months later Wymes replied that he had considered the matter fully but was not satisfied that it was appropriate under the Garda Síochána regulations of 1962 and therefore he was not in a position to grant the application.[42] Wymes specifically referred to Article 18:2 of the regulations which stated that if '(a) a Joint Representative Body or a Representative Body considers that the services of a particular person who is not a member of the Garda Síochána are necessary to assist it in the formulation of claims or proposals for determination under conciliation or arbitration machinery, and (b) an application to employ that person is made to the Commissioner – the Commissioner, if satisfied that to do so would not be prejudicial to discipline and would be in the interests or the welfare of the rank or ranks concerned, shall grant the application.[43] Those regulations were signed when Charles Haughey was Minister for Justice.

Wymes's refusal to let the representative body employ Haughey led to 'serious disquiet, disturbance, and sadness' among its membership. Muldoon, in his response to Wymes, wrote that the membership deeply resented the fact that it had taken him twelve weeks to respond. Muldoon maintained that the proposed appointment of Haughey had been greeted with enthusiasm from members and ex-members alike, who had contacted the body to voice their congratulations and wholehearted approval. He maintained that the commissioner had to be satisfied that the employment of Haughey would be prejudicial to discipline and welfare in the force and 'it is absolutely inconceivable to the Body that you would be so satisfied'.[44] But the idea of Haughey, who had faced the rigours of the Irish legal apparatus just over a year before, having been arrested and charged by the Gardaí, acting as a consultant to a representative body of the Gardaí, was too much for Commissioner Wymes, who had led the force during the arms crisis, and no doubt for the Minister for Justice, Des O'Malley. He refused to change his mind and in a curt reply to Muldoon just before Christmas told him that the decision still stood.[45]

Over the next three years Haughey offered advice to the Garda Representative Body for Inspectors, Station-Sergeants and Sergeants. The body forwarded him copies of pay claims with the Garda Conciliation Council, letters to the Minister for Justice, correspondence with the Department of Justice, correspondence with the Garda commissioner, and various communications to their members.[46] When Jack Lynch reappointed Haughey to the Fianna Fáil frontbench he ceased his involvement with the representative body. Their attempt to hire him as a consultant was yet more evidence that Haughey was seen as a man who could get things done.

THE GRASSROOTS

Getting things done within Fianna Fáil was, however, a much more difficult matter for Haughey. In December 1972, a Fianna Fáil activist from the Donogh O'Malley cumann in Limerick wanted to initiate a 'Bring Charlie Back' campaign at the Ard Fheis, but such was Haughey's isolation in the parliamentary party that he replied, 'I think on the whole it would be better not to initiate it and to let events take their course.'[47] At the February 1972 Ard Fheis he had been elected as one the party's five vice-presidents, which, while a slight embarrassment to the leadership of the party, did not indicate great support for Haughey, particularly within the parliamentary party. There was little Haughey could do about government events, but there was something he could do about the party and that was to visit its members all around the country. Those visits, accompanied by a variety of friends, most notably P.J. Mara, were sometimes soul-destroying and sometimes exhilarating. What they did do was bring Haughey to the grassroots; and the grassroots never forgot him.

Once Haughey decided to stay in Fianna Fáil he vowed that he needed to get to know its members better. This was particularly the case when it came to younger members, with whom Haughey thought he was somewhat out of touch. He asked P.J. Mara, who had been a key helper in Haughey's constituency machine since the mid-1960s, to help.[48] In 1965 Mara had suggested to Haughey that he needed a personal assistant. Now, less than a decade later, Mara essentially took on the role when Haughey was at his most isolated.[49] Mara, like another Haughey supporter and constituency organiser, Séamus Puirséil, had attended most days of the arms trial and was convinced that Haughey had received a raw deal in being charged. For five years, from 1972 until he returned to government after Fianna Fáil's landslide victory in the 1977 election, Haughey toured the country attending dinners and giving relatively anodyne after-dinner speeches to the Fianna Fáil faithful. In the early stages the invitations sometimes came somewhat furtively from local cumann members without the input of the local TD, and sometimes from one TD who had an intra-Fianna Fáil constituency rivalry with another TD. These dinners, and the fact that Haughey came to them, were deeply important to those Fianna Fáilers in rural Ireland who considered that the 'great party', as they saw it, had become too gentrified and urban under Cork-City-born Jack Lynch and the genteel Dubliner George Colley. Haughey, while also of course city-born and bred, had developed an affinity with rural Ireland dating back to his holidays as teenager in south Derry, and his tour of Fianna Fáil constituencies on behalf of Seán Lemass in the 1950s. Crucially, he knew the importance of rural Ireland to Fianna Fáil itself. He knew that rural Ireland felt urban Ireland looked down on it and he knew how slighted many rural Fianna Fáil members felt by their counterparts in Fine Gael. In small-town Ireland the vast majority of solicitors and shop-keepers gave their political allegiance to Fine Gael; and many in Fianna Fáil, whether justified or not, felt they were seen as second-class citizens by these 'Blueshirts'.[50] In that context Haughey's attendance at their dinners was seen by the locals as much more than a visit by a senior politician, even one who had been ostracised by the party. It was, instead, an affirmation of what they stood for as people, and what their party stood for.

Haughey's tour of the cumainn became even more pronounced after Fianna Fáil lost the 1973 general election and found itself back in opposition for the first time in sixteen years. After that election defeat, Haughey was much more open in his attendances at party dinners right across the country. In contrast, the party leader had no interest in these dinners and the locals favoured Haughey over any of Fianna Fáil's frontbench. He was particularly popular in the border counties where there had been no mass exodus to Kevin Boland's new party, as some in Fianna Fáil had feared, but where Haughey, after his trial, was seen as more sympathetic than the leadership to the republican position.[51] It was also known throughout the grassroots that if Haughey was invited he would almost certainly come. He rejected an invitation to become the patron-in-chief of a literary dinner club that the restaurateur Mike

Butt wanted to develop, telling him that it was his 'intention to be very active politically in the years ahead'.[52] In 1956 Butt had opened the first Indian restaurant in Ireland, the Golden Orient on Lower Leeson Street. In 1970 he opened at the same premises the luxurious Tandoori Rooms, which became one of Dublin's leading restaurants and earned international recognition. When Haughey began his affair with the socialite Terry Keane in 1972 they would often socialise at the Tandoori Rooms. It was the ideal place because Butt never publicised those who ate at his restaurants, giving his customers complete privacy.[53]

There was certainly no Indian food on offer at the Fianna Fáil cumann dances of the 1970s, where the fare was usually chicken and ham. At times there were more than three hundred people at these dinners, and Haughey might attend two a week. He tried to avoid going to events on successive nights, particularly at weekends, but at times judged them important enough to do so. The problem for Haughey was that many cumainn wanted to host their dinners at the weekend, so he sometimes attended one event on a Friday night and another, in a different part of the country, on Saturday night. He would set off with P.J. Mara on Friday afternoon, return to Abbeville in the early hours of Saturday morning, and head off again in the early evening. He would always return home on the Saturday night, steadfastly refusing to stay in any of the local hotels that the party organisation would offer to arrange for him. Mara went with him at least once a week; at other times local party dignitaries would ferry him to and from the dinners. Longford's Albert Reynolds, another regular attendee at the arms trial, was one of these.[54] The usual routine was that Mara drove to the dinner and Haughey drove back, allowing Mara to enjoy the hospitality of the local organisation while Haughey – refusing the ubiquitous chicken and ham – would eat Dover sole and sip from a glass of white wine. For these years in the 1970s, the Haughey–Mara drives and constituency dinners became an important part of the lives of both men. They had no Machiavellian plan to take down Jack Lynch either immediately or in the short term. Mara claimed that their conversation on the long drives on bad roads was about general political events both in Ireland and internationally. The unspoken understanding between them was that they both wanted Haughey ultimately to lead the party and that they were playing a long game.[55]

Haughey's overdraft woes with AIB in the early 1970s did not stop him living the lifestyle he had become accustomed to. He redeveloped the grounds at Abbeville, putting in a swimming pool, which he viewed as the best money he ever spent.[56] He introduced mallards and pheasant to his estate in the autumn of 1971, which, an inspector in the Department of Lands told him, would give him 'many hours of environmental enjoyment in addition to some pleasant shooting'.[57] The lake at Abbeville had been polluted since he bought the lands and he had it drained and restocked with rainbow trout in mid-1972. He began keeping bees and would give jars of his Abbeville honey to various visitors. He grew tomatoes in a greenhouse just inside the Victorian walled garden at the front end of the estate. It was in these early years of the 1970s that he started thinking about broader questions of conservation. He struck up a correspondence and friendship with an American academic and environmentalist, David Cabot, who had completed a PhD in University College, Galway in 1967 and worked on preparing environmental impact assessments for An Foras Forbartha, the National Institute for Physical Planning and Construction Research in Dublin. Cabot told Haughey that he liked his approach to the environment and his emphasis on the necessity of a comprehensive national policy for planning economic development and protecting and conserving the natural environment.[58] Two decades later, Haughey appointed Cabot as his personal adviser on the environment in the lead-up to Ireland's six-month presidency of the EC from January 1990. Haughey rang Cabot, summoned him to Dublin and told him that he wanted the environment to be one of the features of his presidency. Cabot later described Haughey as 'a great man to work with, having tremendous intelligence, vision, foresight and the perception to think clearly in terms of doing more, particularly when it came to the environment which he was interested in from when I first got to know him in the 1970s'.[59] Cabot stayed on as Haughey's adviser on the environment until he left the office of Taoiseach in 1992, and continued in that position under Albert Reynolds.

HARVARD

In January 1972, William Howard Adams, director of the National Program for the National Gallery of Art in Washington, DC, wrote to Haughey and invited him to spend a few days at Harvard University in July, as a guest of the University's Institute in Arts Administration summer school which was to be devoted to 'Arts and the Majority'. The Institute, Adams told Haughey, was particularly interested in hearing about 'the tax policy you initiated and other reflections on public policy and the arts'.[60] Initially Haughey hesitated, but his friend Anthony Cronin told him he had to go and started working on a draft of the speech. Adams asked Haughey to deliver an hour-long lecture that would cover his personal philosophy and his accomplishments, both from the Arts Council's standpoint and the 'revolutionary reform you initiated'.[61] He also wanted to hear Haughey's views on what a modern democratic government's role and responsibilities ought to be in the field of the arts. Cronin submitted a first draft in late May, but he was worried that Haughey would not like it because it came definitively down on the side of the individual; Haughey, he said, could throw the whole thing aside if he wanted.[62] Haughey told him it was superb, precisely what he hoped he would deliver, and he had been immersed in it since it arrived.[63]

By the time Haughey gave his lecture there had been 789 applications for tax exemption by artists, of which 574 had succeeded, 68 were under consideration, and 147 had not been determined because of insufficient evidence. Of the 574 who had been granted the exemption, 69 per cent were writers, 21 per cent painters, 6 per cent sculptors, and 3 per cent composers. It was estimated that about half of the successful applicants came from abroad. These included the writers Leslie Charteris, J.P. Donleavy, Len Deighton, Frederick Forsyth, Catherine Gaskin, Leon Uris, Gordon Thomas and Wolf Mankowitz.

After a number of changes and emendations that Haughey and Cronin made before the final draft, the main thrust of the lecture Haughey gave on Wednesday 12 July 1972 was that his scheme was an attempt to halt the intellectual drain of Ireland's most creative people leaving the country.[64] His aim was to underline the importance of the artist to the community in which they lived and the value of the contribution they made. In that context, the taxation and financial aspects of the scheme were of relatively minor importance. The primary purpose of the legislation was not to confer any great financial benefit on creative people but to help create a climate in which art would flourish. He was concerned with indicating to creative people that the Irish state valued their contribution to the community and that he intended the scheme to be a stepping-stone to a comprehensive and appropriately financed national cultural policy. He viewed the scheme's early years a success in helping to keep at home quite a number of young artists who would otherwise have emigrated and in attracting significant writers from abroad, although he was disappointed that only a few painters or sculptors had settled in Ireland. He dismissed as absurd criticisms that the scheme had simply conferred tax exemption rights on rich foreign authors, making the point that if the concessions had not existed, these authors would not have come to Ireland and there would be no incomes to tax. There was, he maintained, no loss to the Irish exchequer; if anything, there was a net gain as most of these authors received the bulk of their earnings abroad, and yet paid taxes of some sort in the Irish community. One of the difficulties the arts faced, Haughey argued, was that because some creative processes take a long time to mature, society at large was unwilling to support individual artists without any strings attached. He cited the poets Tennyson and Rilke, who were unproductive for years, and Rimbaud, who gave up poetry altogether, as examples. He also referenced Coleridge, whose 'Kubla Khan became one of the most beautiful pieces of unfinished poetry in the English language', Kavanagh, Yeats and Samuel Johnson in the course of his wide-ranging address.[65]

Before finalising his script, Haughey had written to the chairman of the Revenue Commissioners, J.C. Duignan, to inquire about the operation of the scheme. Duignan had told him that the only problem that had arisen in its administration related to the question of an appeal by a person who was aggrieved by the refusal of the Revenue to make a determination in their favour. Revenue's approach was to ask the claimant to produce evidence on their behalf from an authoritative person or body of persons.[66] Ever attuned to publicity, Haughey wrote to the editors of the main Irish newspapers enclosing a copy of his lecture before he travelled to Harvard. While he was in the United States, Bord Fáilte's general manager in North America, Joe Malone, issued a press release to the major newspapers and broadcast outlets highlighting the fact that Haughey called for impartial government patronage to foster, but not control, the arts.[67] Haughey was very proud of both his tax exemption scheme and his lecture. In Harvard he mentioned that when he went abroad the scheme was what people wanted to hear about, being the one thing that Ireland had done in the modern world that was unique. When it was over he told his regular correspondent Mother Bernard that he was particularly pleased that she had liked his paper so much as he had put a lot of work into it.[68] Another correspondent, commenting on how well-thought-out and 'beautifully clean' it was, suggested that he continue in the literary vein and write an autobiographical work for people like herself who never voted Fianna Fáil but thought he had suffered an injustice in the arms trial.[69]

Before he left Boston, Haughey dined at the famous Anthony's Pier 4 restaurant, one of the most successful and busiest in the United States, owned by the world-renowned restaurateur and Albanian immigrant Anthony Athanas. That night Haughey was served by Agnes Breathnach, a UCC student from Waterford who was in Boston on a J1 student visa. On hearing Breathnach's Irish accent, Haughey asked her how she had come to work in the famous restaurant, where she was studying, and how her summer was going. He then ordered the lobster, the keynote dish of Pier 4, and when the sommelier had taken Haughey's wine order, Athanas came onto the restaurant floor, a rare enough event in itself, and asked Breathnach, 'Who is that man at your table?' Haughey had ordered such a rare and expensive wine that the sommelier had felt he had better notify the restaurant's owner. Not having the time to give Athanas a complex Irish history lesson, Breathnach replied, 'That man could be a future prime minister of my country.' Athanas later went over to Haughey and had a pleasant conversation with him; and Breathnach received a tip of ten dollars, ten times her hourly wage.[70] From then on

Haughey always dined in Pier 4 when he was in Boston, including on a number of occasions when he was Taoiseach, and became friendly with Athanas. Over a decade after his first visit to Pier 4, he went missing from his hotel one morning in Boston on an official visit as Taoiseach, and his worried civil servants eventually found him in Pier 4 having lunch with a friend, the Fianna Fáil fundraiser Paul Kavanagh, sitting at a table with Athanas discussing the finer points of French wine.[71]

HORSEMAN

In the early 1970s, Haughey holidayed with Maureen in Biarritz in the south of France and went to Longchamp Racecourse in Paris to watch the Prix de l'Arc de Triomphe, with Arthur Gibney, Sam Stephenson and their wives. Horseracing and hunting was a huge part of Haughey's life. Image had nothing to do with it. He was a horse owner, took a four-person box at Leopardstown racecourse annually, and went to the racing every Saturday if he could. His love of racing extended to his family, his daughter, Eimear, and son Conor both developing a strong interest in the sport. Eimear Haughey's prowess as a showjumper in her teenage years brought her into conflict with her school, Manor House in Raheny, in 1971 when the headmistress, Sister Margaret, wrote to Charles and Maureen about her significant absences from school. Haughey replied that all her absences were because she was taking part in competitions both at home and abroad. Both Charles and Maureen considered this to be part of her education, so much so that they said they would endeavour to keep her absences to a minimum – consistent with her being able to continue her showjumping career.[72] Conor Haughey was also an accomplished showjumper and was selected for the Irish team to compete in junior internationals at Lucerne in 1974.

During the whole of his public career Haughey was a keen advocate for developing the equine industry. In April 1971 one of his correspondents told him, 'One would have to be very much out of touch not to realise the great stimulus you have given, both officially and personally to equitation and horse-breeding in Ireland.'[73] In 1972, Goffs Bloodstocks Sales wrote to him to say that his 'efforts [had] helped the Irish bloodstock industry to attract, in increasing numbers, buyers from all over the world'.[74] Those efforts were based in the first place on Haughey's decision in 1969, as Minister for Finance, to introduce a tax exemption for stallion fees in the Finance Act, for which he gained cross-party support. At the time there were only four stallions in the National Stud, which was woefully inadequate to cater for the demands of breeders. The idea was to induce foreign owners to send their more valuable horses to Ireland. This decision had the effect of making Ireland a prime location to stand some of the best racehorses in the world, and for some four decades Ireland became the destination of choice for many stallion owners. The incentive, which basically exempted profits from horse and greyhound stud fees from tax, applied to all breeds of horse, but mainly underpinned the growth of a world-class thoroughbred industry, whose players included a mix of Irish operators such as Coolmore and Rathbarry studs, and overseas investors including the Aga Khan and Dubai's ruling family, the Al Maktoums.

In introducing the bill in the Seanad, Haughey also made the point that the concession, as he described it, would also be no small boon to the breeder of limited means.[75] More significantly, however, some of the world's most influential breeders bought substantial stud farms in Ireland. The result was that some of the best broodmares in the world were sent to Ireland to be covered, and many of the best racehorses in the world carried the IRE suffix in their name. The tax exemption contributed to a burgeoning stallion business in Ireland, with John Magnier's Coolmore Stud becoming a world leader, and Sheikh Mohammed choosing Ireland's Kildangan Stud as home to many of his best sires. The decision to introduce the stallion fee exemption was made following strong lobbying by Captain Tim Rogers, owner at the time of Airlie Stud in Lucan, County Dublin.[76] Airlie Stud was largely a stallion farm and had up to fifteen stallions at any one time at various stud farms. Rogers had been Winston Churchill's aide-de-camp during the Second World War and became Churchill's principal adviser on bloodstock matters. He later became a vocal member of the Commission of Inquiry into the Thoroughbred Horse Breeding Industry, which had been established during Haughey's second term as Taoiseach in September 1982 under the chairmanship of Lord Killanin, the former president of the International Olympic Committee. The Killanin Report, issued in 1986, recommended the establishment of a Thoroughbred Industry Board which would have responsibility for all areas of racing except those relating to making and administering the rules of racing. In 1998 *Magill* magazine claimed that Haughey personally received financial contributions from Captain Rogers in the late 1960s. It quoted a reliable but unnamed source in the bloodstock industry, who purported to have been present at several meetings between Haughey and Rogers, to substantiate this claim. *Magill* did not state how much money Rogers allegedly gave Haughey, but reiterated that it was Rogers who persuaded Haughey to introduce tax exemptions for the horse breeding industry.[77]

Another of Haughey's horse racing initiatives as Minister for Finance was his decision in 1970 to raise on-course betting tax from 2.5 per cent to 7.5 per cent by extending the turnover tax to cover on-course betting. An on-course betting levy had been introduced as part of the new Racing Board legislation introduced in 1945 and for many years it was levied at 5 per cent. It dipped to half that amount before Haughey trebled it in 1970. As it turned out, the bookmakers appreciated the need for the levy to fund racing, and acquiesced to the rise, which ultimately benefited them, and they also secured a seat on Ireland's Racing Board.

Haughey was also at the heart of the establishment of Bord na gCapall (the Irish Horse Board), which was an essential part of the Horse Industry Act of 1970, introduced at a time when the horse racing industry was in great difficulty. Haughey was a keen supporter of the legislation when it was introduced in April 1970 but was out of government when it was finally passed the following July. When he was Minister for Agriculture in 1966, Haughey formed a special committee to examine the sector and identify its needs. It recommended the establishment of an Irish Horse Board to co-ordinate the activities of the various associations dealing with equestrian matters and to set up a national training centre for riders and instructors. As a result, Bord na gCapall was established with the remit to promote and develop the non-thoroughbred horse industry and to advise the minister on matters relating to the breeding, sale and export of horses. One of its novel schemes was the introduction of a farriery apprenticeship scheme, which enabled young people interested in the care and welfare of horses to become qualified farriers. Perhaps Bord ns gCapall's most significant achievement was the foundation of the Irish Horse Register in 1974, which incorporated the approval of stallions for breeding and was essential for maintaining the high standard of the Irish sporting horse. In the same year Haughey became a director of Ballsbridge International Bloodstock Sales. Over the following two years he was first a board member of the Ballsbridge Sales Advisory Committee, and later chaired the Ballsbridge Breeders Committee.[78]

Haughey found some success as an owner in this period when one of his horses, an eight-year-old gelding named Vulforo, won the Powers Gold Cup at the Easter meeting at Fairyhouse in 1973. Trained by Jim Dreaper and ridden by Sean Barker, the gelding was a 10/1 shot on the day. In all, Vulforo won thirteen races. Haughey did not enjoy the same level of success with his runners on the flat, but he did have one significant winner with a horse named Aristocracy. A son of the Irish National Stud stallion Lord Gayle, Aristocracy had his biggest success in 1977 at the Phoenix Park racecourse, in a Group 3 Whitehall Stakes. The Irish champion jockey Wally Swinburn was riding the three-year-old, who was trained by Richard McCormick, son of Haughey's first trainer, Dick McCormick. Aristocracy raced for four seasons and retired to stud as the winner of five flat races and three hurdle races.[79]

Horse racing and breeding did not come cheap. In 1978 Haughey moved Aristocracy to be trained by Vincent O'Brien at his world-famous Ballydoyle stables in Tipperary. Haughey had become friendly with O'Brien a decade earlier. Haughey and Maureen had spent a weekend with O'Brien and his wife, Jacqueline, just a few weeks before he was sacked as Minister for Finance in May 1970. Following that visit, Haughey told O'Brien that he would be happy to do what he could in relation to a site near the river in Ballydoyle that O'Brien had shown him on his visit.[80] O'Brien's monthly charge for Aristocracy in September 1978 was as follows: keep charge £10 a day (30 days for £300); veterinary charges to Demi O'Byrne amounting to some £62; expenses to the Curragh, where the colt won the Liam Flood Autumn Handicap, which had a total purse of £3,670, was £69; a 2 per cent cut of the prize fund for O'Brien £73.40; and finally 7 per cent of the purse for the jockey, Lester Piggott, £256.90; giving a total of £761.30.[81] A couple of months earlier, in July 1978, the Haugheys attended the wedding of O'Brien's daughter, Jane, to the horse breeder Philip Myerscough. Just over a week after getting his September bill, Haughey sent O'Brien a gift of a bronze bust of Lester Piggott.[82] Aristocracy also enjoyed some success as a stallion when he was put out to stud.

The financial outgoings of buying and running a stud were significant. In July 1971, Haughey's nephew Seán Lemass wrote to him from New York asking for details of the capital outlay and running costs involved in owning a stud farm; one of the chief executives in his firm was thinking of investing in one, given Ireland's proposed entry to the Common Market. Haughey replied that first-class stud farms usually ran to between three and four hundred acres and that buying and running a stud would be a major financial undertaking, costing somewhere between two and three hundred thousand pounds.[83] As Haughey's overdraft problems with AIB in the 1970s continued, his passion for horse racing and breeding, and the concomitant costs, continued unabated.

In January 1972 after a dinner of the Central Remedial Clinic board, Haughey met the journalist Terry Keane at the Club Elizabeth nightclub in Leeson Street.[84] At that time Keane was the fashion editor of the *Sunday Press*, and Haughey was languishing in the purgatory that had followed the arms trial. They began a twenty-seven-year affair which would end painfully with Keane telling her side of the story to Gay Byrne on the *Late Late Show* in May 1999. That explosive interview on Ireland's most-watched television show was followed by a four-week serialisation of her memoirs in the *Sunday Times*. The catalyst for the revelations was Keane's belief that a tell-all book about her that would prominently feature the affair was about to be published. She intended that her own serialisation in the *Sunday Times* would be turned into a book. As it turned out, neither book was published.[85] Keane claimed that her television appearance had the blessing of Haughey and her husband, the former Chief Justice of the Supreme Court, Ronan Keane, from whom she had separated in 1983. In fact, the day before she did the interview, Keane and Haughey met for lunch at Le Coq Hardi, and he pleaded with her not to go through with it.[86]

Haughey never spoke of the affair and many of his supporters remained permanently affronted by its revelations. Some, including Haughey's long-time ally P.J. Mara, claimed that Keane was not as significant in his life as she maintained she was, and ridiculed the idea that Haughey ever took political advice from her, or was on the verge of leaving public life and emigrating to France with her in 1982, during one of the heaves against his leadership, as she claimed in the *Sunday Times*.[87] There are many others, however, who argue that Keane was a very important figure in Haughey's life both politically and personally. Her long-time editor at the *Sunday Independent*, Anne Harris, who assembled and edited Keane's famous column, 'The Keane Edge', trenchantly made the point that since Keane spent twenty-seven years with Haughey, 'Of course, she influenced him. How could she not? By all the rules of common sense she must have had some influence. Terry was very bright, very intelligent, very quick to pick things up. She was very well read, fast and witty in conversation with a wicked sense of humour.'[88] The journalist Sarah Carey, a family friend of Terry Keane's children, also maintained that Keane had a huge influence on Haughey. She noted that 'he was referred to openly and fondly by them all. His relationship with their mother, and themselves, was a normal part of their life.'[89] In contrast, none of Haughey's children had any idea of their father's extra-marital affair, and the revelation hurt them all deeply.

ISLANDER

Although Haughey's financial position at the beginning of his relationship with Keane remained extremely precarious, he started investigating the possibility of acquiring an off-shore island. In October 1971, the artist Maria Simonds-Gooding sent Haughey a photograph that she had recently taken from the island of Inishvickillane looking towards its sister island of An Tiaracht. Two months later, she told him that she would be looking into the island for him.[90] She had spent three weeks in the summer of 1968 alone on Inishvickillane, painting and living off rabbits, limpets and periwinkles.[91] She was not the first acquaintance of Haughey to have spent time alone on the island. In 1965 the *Irish Times* journalist Michael Viney stayed there for a week for a series he produced for the paper, copies of which he sent to Haughey when he bought the island. Haughey, who spent many holidays in Dingle in the 1960s, had become acquainted with Simonds-Gooding, who lived in Dunquin, west Kerry. In June 1970, on finishing a painting he had commissioned from her, she was one of the many who offered him sympathy on his arrest and charge, hoping 'everything would soon be back to normal'.[92]

Inishvickillane is one of the five Blasket Islands, the others being the Great Blasket, Inis Tuaisceart, An Tiaracht and Beiginis. Inishvickillane was second in importance to the Great Blasket, which was inhabited until 1953. By contrast, the last inhabitants of Inishvickillane, the Ó Dálaigh family, had left in 1904. The island was bare, yet capable of growing reasonably good crops, and the Ó Dálaighs kept sheep on it after they relocated to the Great Blasket. In 1973, Haughey agreed to buy the island from the three surviving Ó Dálaigh brothers, Tomás, Paddy and Muiris.[93] After some negotiation, in April 1974 he paid £25,000 to become the legal owner of Inishvickillane, which, as he described it, was an island of some 200 acres with large areas of good mountain-type pasture, about a hundred sheep, a very important habitat for sea birds, completely isolated from the mainland, never had any artificial fertiliser applied to it, and free of the usual diseases. He asked the director of the Agricultural Institute to assess the island to see if it was possible to establish some interesting agricultural or horticultural project on it.[94]

Haughey's purchase of Inishvickillane has led to all sorts of speculation. As he told one of his correspondents who wanted to use it in June 1974 to explore wave energy: 'I do not think … that Inishvickillane would be of any use as a base for your work. There are no facilities or amenities of any sort available there.'[95] The historian Diarmaid Ferriter has seen it as evidence of his 'fiefdom' approach to public life.[96] The cultural critic Declan Kiberd argued that the attraction of island life to Haughey was the notion of absolute solitude, of sanctuary and withdrawal; somewhere he could wall himself away, first in Abbeville, and then in Inishvickillane; places where others could not get at him.[97] This was something alluded to by his son Conor, who noted that it was a place where Haughey had no hassle and no one could get to him.[98] It was also perhaps the one place where he could be himself. As Terry Prone, who came to know him well in the 1980s, observed, 'When he talked of nature, the environment, deer, eagles, bees, honey, and the like, he was real and he was passionate.'[99] No one could get to the island if Haughey did not want to see them. There was no telephone connection, no visitors, no journalists, no one seeking either his advice or some personal advantage.

Haughey was very interested in the natural world and many conservation observers and activists were very glad to hear that he had bought the island. These included, J.P. Kane of the Westmeath Longford branch of An Taisce, the National Trust, who welcomed the announcement of the purchase and said it was even better than if An Taisce itself had got hold of the island.[100] Inishvickillane was home to about 10,000 pairs of storm petrel, a small black seabird. The Kerry islands held the largest known colonies of the birds in the world. The Irish Wildbird Conservancy was anxious that its members would still be allowed to visit the island, and that any building Haughey did on it would not have a negative impact on the birds. He told them that he was anxious to facilitate their visits; and that the importance of the island as a habitat for wild birds was, for him, one of its most attractive features, which should not be diminished in any way.[101] In August 1974, Haughey went to Inishvickillane to camp out with his four children for two weeks, an experience he described as 'absolutely wonderful'.[102] After that he would holiday there every August. Maureen Haughey refused to go. Camping was not for her.[103] Over the following decade, Haughey had a house built on the island, and installed solar panels, a French Arrowatt wind turbine and a diesel generator, all of which made the island much more habitable. In the late summer of 1977, after Haughey was back in cabinet, as Minister for Health and Social Welfare, he asked Gerry Wrixon of UCC to visit him. Wrixon was a young but renowned microelectronics expert who had returned to Ireland from the United States to take up a lecturing position in Cork. Haughey told him about Inishvickillane and asked him if renewable energy could work on the island. Wrixon found the island ideal for solar energy when the sun shone, and he designed and oversaw the installation of solar panels on the house Haughey had built.[104]

The building of the house was not without its complications for Haughey. He had a wine cellar installed and stocked it with Château Margaux (Premier Grand Cru Classé), an extremely expensive wine. He employed local labour from Dingle to build and furnish the house, and left instructions that the men should feel free to have a drink at the end of their working day. To that end he also stocked the house with beer. Once the beer was gone the men came across the wine and helped themselves liberally to the contents of Haughey's carefully chosen cellar. Having finished their work, the men thoughtfully replaced the wine they had consumed with an equivalent number of bottles of wine of the same colour from a supermarket in Dingle. This particular vintage was, however, Bull's Blood from Hungary, at the opposite end of the market in quality and price from the Château Margaux. When Haughey returned for his August holiday and checked the contents of his cellar, all he could really do was laugh.[105]

With all the physical improvements on the island, Haughey did not neglect its natural development. In March of 1980 he arranged for four wild deer from Killarney National Park to be brought to the island. He was concerned about the genetic purity of the red deer living in the mountains close to Killarney National Park, which were at risk from interbreeding with sika deer that had been introduced into the national park. After discussing it with his environmental adviser David Cabot, and other experts, Haughey introduced a small herd of red deer to the island, where they thrived.[106] By 1987, he was able to report to Professor Bob McCabe of the Department of Wildlife Ecology at the University of Wisconsin-Madison, who advised him on their development, that 'the deer on the Inis are doing wonderfully well. We now have a total of eighteen.'[107]

In 1981 Haughey began to examine the possibility of breeding sea eagles on the island and commissioned a report from the Irish Wildbird Conservancy to see how a similar breeding scheme operated in Scotland.[108] A decade later he asked David Cabot to examine the possibility of introducing white-tailed sea eagles to the island to see if the birds would breed, in what Cabot considered ideal conditions. Cabot found a source of sea eagles from the German Raptor Centre and travelled to Berlin with Haughey and Seán McKeown of Fota Wildlife Park to view the eagles. In 1992 two sea eagles were sourced from the German Raptor Centre and another two birds were set up for breeding in Fota Wildlife Park, under the direction of McKeon. The captive Fota birds were intended to provide young for subsequent release into the wild, but they did not breed and were eventually returned to Germany. The other two German eagles, named Maeve and Aillil, were released on Inishvickillane under the watch of Claus Fentzloff, a noted German eagle expert, but soon disappeared.[109] A number of years later, Maeve returned, but Aillil was never seen again.

Over the years a number of Haughey's international political friends including Senator Ted Kennedy and President François Mitterrand were guests of the island. Maureen Haughey started going when the house was built. Terry Keane was an intermittent visitor. Ultimately, though, it was a place of isolation. Inishvickillane, perhaps, was the one place where Haughey could be himself. A year after he bought the island, one of Haughey's correspondents, C.J. Falconer, told him that looking from Valentia Island, the sun tended to set immediately behind the Blasket Islands, giving the impression of the islands being raised above sea level as though they were floating in air. This reminded him of the mythological Hy Brasil. Haughey was delighted with the description: 'We often think of Inishvickillane as Hy Brasil.'[110] The reference to the phantom isle, said to be visible only every seven years, would have appealed to Haughey's sense of the dramatic. The isle had appeared on maps and charts from as early as 1325 up to the late 1800s. In 1674, John Nisbet, a Scottish sea captain, claimed to have seen the island while travelling from France to Ireland. Four members of his crew went ashore and were met by a 'wise old man' who gave them gold and silver.[111] In buying Inishvickillane, Haughey acquired not only the island but the aura of the mysterious 'wise old man' of the island; solitary, melancholy, a donor of largesse who needed the affirmation of the people. When he bought Inishvickillane, that political affirmation was still to come, but, like Hy Brasil, it loomed in the distance.

CHAPTER 13

A CORINTHIAN, A LAD OF METTLE, A GOOD BOY

THE 1973 GENERAL ELECTION

On 28 February 1973, a majority of the Irish electorate decided that sixteen years of Fianna Fáil in power was enough and voted the party out of office. A few weeks earlier, on Sunday evening 4 February, the day before Lynch called the election, a small cabal of Charles Haughey's closest constituency supporters met in Pat O'Connor's home in Malahide. Their specific aim was to ensure that Haughey topped the poll. Their target was that he would receive more than 13,000 first preference votes. Haughey had received 12,415 votes in the 1965 election and 11,677 in the 1969 election, although his percentage was significantly higher in 1969 given that the constituency had been reduced from five seats to four. The group estimated that 13,000 votes would be about 30 per cent of the overall poll. The figure of 13,000 votes was psychologically important because it would allow Haughey, and his supporters, to claim that notwithstanding the travails he had undergone since the 1969 election he had received a larger mandate from the people of his constituency than ever before.[1] There was one other reason – Jack Lynch. Lynch had received just short of 13,000 votes in the 1965 election in a five-seater in Cork, and just over 11,000 votes in a three-seater in 1969. The overriding aim of Haughey's people was that their man would poll more than Lynch. They estimated that Lynch, again standing in a three-seater, would likely have to poll in the region of 45 per cent of the vote to get close to 13,000 votes. The psychology of Haughey receiving more first preference votes than Lynch was something they considered well worth fighting for.

When the votes were counted the day after the election, Haughey, in Dublin North East, received 12,901 first preference votes, topping the poll with just over 30 per cent of the vote. Lynch, in Cork City North, received 12,427 votes on just over 46 per cent of the vote. The Haughey group were relatively satisfied. Their man had received more votes than Lynch, notwithstanding that he was in a larger constituency. The fact that he fell just 99 votes short of the magical 13,000 figure they put down to the bad weather. On the night of the count, Haughey held a gathering in Abbeville for friends and supporters. A few of his closest friends and family watched the results coming in on the television in the kitchen. It was a strange night for Fianna Fáil. The party's vote went up by half a percentage point to 46.2 per cent, but it lost five seats. Before the count was complete, Jack Lynch, in a live interview with Brian Farrell, became the first Taoiseach to concede defeat in a general election on television. When Lynch conceded, Haughey's brother Jock jumped up and shouted delightedly: 'That fucker Lynch has got what he deserved.' His brother, however, had a very different, and more muted reaction: 'We're out.'[2] Haughey had never served on the opposition benches.

Jock Haughey's animus towards Lynch was, if anything, more hostile than his brother's. Just two years earlier, Jock Haughey had been called before the Committee of Public Accounts into its hearing into the £100,000 grant-in-aid for Northern Ireland relief. He made a brief statement rebutting the evidence of Chief Superintendent John Fleming that he had been deeply involved in dealings with the IRA leader Cathal Goulding in 1969, and that he had arranged for the arrival of a consignment of arms at Dublin Airport in October of that year. Fleming also claimed that Jock Haughey had later travelled to London to purchase arms, which he again denied. Jock Haughey further stated that he had never directly or indirectly got in touch with his brother Charles about the authorisation of customs clearance of any guns, ammunition or material of any nature or description.[3] The committee referred his case to the High Court, which sentenced him to six months in prison for contempt for refusing to answer questions. He appealed to the Supreme Court, which held that the offence was not one of contempt and that evidence against him had been given on affidavit, instead of orally, and he had been denied an opportunity to cross-examine. It thus allowed his appeal on the grounds that the legislation empowering the committee to find him in contempt was unconstitutional.

Notwithstanding Jock Haughey's jubilation on election night in 1973, the common consensus in Abbeville that evening was, that while no tears were shed for Jack Lynch, a coalition government of Liam Cosgrave and Brendan Corish was unlikely to do much for the country. There was, however, the satisfaction of a job well done in Dublin North East. Haughey described it to Joe Malone, Bord Fáilte's manager in North America, as a 'considerable victory'.[4] Malone had been close to Haughey for a number of years and had flown back to Ireland to campaign for him in the constituency. The comment of the barrister Peter Maguire, who told Haughey that he could 'well imagine how happy it must make you to have got such a magnificent endorsement from your constituents at the first election since the traumatic events of 1969/1970' was apt.[5] There was silence, however, from the Fianna Fáil parliamentary party. A rare exception was Senator Michael Yeats, who told Haughey that since Fianna Fáil were now in opposition he hoped 'you will be able to play a major front bench role in the Dáil. Lord knows they could do with a bit of strengthening.'[6] That call from Jack Lynch did not come. A correspondent who told Haughey that his support among professional people was 'very great although it might not be evident in public' summed up a particular problem for Haughey.[7] His party was out of office. He was out of favour with its leadership, and there was no easy route back in. He might well have had support from the professional classes and, as his close to 13,000 votes showed, he was clearly hugely popular in his constituency, yet if he could not have an impact on public policy that popularity could well wane. His political rehabilitation still depended on the party's leadership and Jack Lynch seemed, as yet, in no mood to welcome back Fianna Fáil's prodigal son. When Fianna Fáil lost office, Jack Lynch decided to stay on and rebuild the party in opposition. Charles Haughey was not part of his plans.

The day after the count, Haughey received a letter from the journalist Alan Hart, who worked for the BBC's current affairs programme *Panorama*. Hart had made a name for himself as a courageous reporter for ITN in the Middle East during the Arab–Israeli Six-Day War in 1967. When he moved to *Panorama* he covered events in Northern Ireland. In his letter to Haughey, Hart told him that an intelligent reading of the result would be that Lynch and Haughey would work together to bring Fianna Fáil back to power as soon as possible and that if Fianna Fáil were back in power within a year, 'Jack to be Taoiseach for one year – and then over to you ... I also know that Jack doesn't want more than another two years.'[8] This was a spectacular misreading of the situation and Haughey well knew it. First, there was very little chance that the Fine Gael–Labour government would implode in the short term, given that it had not seen power for sixteen years. Second, the decision of the veteran Fianna Fáil politician Frank Aiken not to contest the election in protest at Haughey being ratified as a candidate was a more accurate reflection of how many in the Fianna Fáil parliamentary party viewed Haughey. It was easier for Aiken to make the decision not to stand than many others, as he was now seventy-five years of age. He was outraged when Lynch did not interfere with Haughey's ratification, and some other veteran members of the party had to talk him out of writing to the newspapers. He was so disillusioned that he never attended another Fianna Fáil event. He felt that Haughey was somehow not worthy of being in Fianna Fáil, and that only people like himself, stern and austere, deserved the mantle of 'soldier of destiny'. He did, however, represent a point of view, shared by some within the party, that Haughey, in the words of Evans and Kelly, was 'power-hungry, ruthless, and ostentatious'.[9] Haughey was wise enough to know that Hart's analysis of the situation was clearly misconceived, and that Aiken's withdrawal from the scene would have no long-term consequences for the party itself.

POLITICAL PURGATORY

Haughey might have been re-elected, but he was still looking for a role. The following month, a twenty-eight-year-old Canadian student named Ken Carty wrote to Haughey seeking to interview him for his doctoral research into political parties.[10] A week later, Carty spent an afternoon in the company of Haughey at Abbeville. Their conversation ranged over a wide variety of subjects, but Carty was struck by Haughey's description of the importance of Fianna Fáil's grassroots to its overall success as a party. For Haughey, the democratic genius of the grassroots lay in the fact that they expected to be consulted and listened to, and any potential candidate who did not do that would soon find themselves out of favour when it came to selection. He told Carty that the local organisation jealously guarded their rights of candidate selection and by controlling this gateway into the system helped control the governments and personnel that Fianna Fáil produced. Haughey felt that the continuous consultation process also fed into the decision to choose a leader, with TDs sensitive to what their local activists wanted.[11] This point was the key to Haughey's grassroots tour in the 1970s. He saw cultivation of the grassroots as the way to their TDs, and those TDs as the route to the leadership.

At the 1973 election Haughey complained that the director of elections, George Colley, and, by extension, Jack Lynch ignored the views of constituency organisations who, in turn, protested that they were not being listened to by the leadership. He placed the responsibility for defeat squarely on the shoulders of Colley, who, he believed, had pushed Lynch into an early election in the hope of coming out of it as the architect of a great victory. Instead, Colley, who had placed himself at the centre of the campaign, presided over an electoral disaster. The centralisation of the Fianna Fáil campaign at its headquarters in Mount Street led to allegations from constituencies that it was inefficient and unresponsive to their needs and would not listen to their concerns. In that context party headquarters undid much of the good work of its superior field organisation. Haughey thought Colley was too casual and unprepared in 1973. Six years later, when the two men duelled it out for the leadership of the party, Haughey was convinced that Colley carried the same traits. While Haughey spoke eloquently and freely to Carty, he gave the Canadian doctoral student the impression that he was a smart and cunning man. When Haughey was asked a question that piqued his interest, and challenged him to think about how he wanted to answer it, Carty could see him almost come alive. When less interested, he seemed to be going through the motions. Carty left Abbeville happy with his afternoon's work but amazed that Haughey had given him so much time, and puzzled at Haughey's changing moods during their talk. His overriding impression was that Haughey knew he was in a kind of political purgatory but was prepared to wait it out.[12]

Haughey was indeed in political purgatory but his unparalleled instinct as to the role of the grassroots in the Fianna Fáil organisation would stand him in good stead over the next number of years. The grassroots were the key to his return to the frontbench, the gateway back to ministerial office, and ultimately the artery to his leadership of Fianna Fáil. It was, however a very slow process and Haughey was susceptible to periods of serious self-doubt. In February 1974, one of his correspondents told him that 'the thought of Churchill's long years in the political pre-war wilderness should be an inspiration when you feel low.'[13] The reference to Winston Churchill was apt. Churchill, like Haughey, had seen himself as the man destined to lead his people to greatness, was sustained in his lifestyle by wealthy supporters, complained of an ungrateful electorate, and of intellectual pygmies in his own party, and suffered bouts of melancholy and self-doubt. Haughey was the same in all respects.

Haughey remained extremely frustrated by what he saw as the weakness of the Fianna Fáil frontbench in failing to hold the Fine Gael–Labour coalition government to account. He was critical of the party's centralisation under Lynch, telling one correspondent in late 1974 that it seemed 'almost impossible to get anything moving at headquarters level'.[14] In an act of supreme irony, when he became leader he would centralise headquarters to a much greater degree. For all Haughey's criticisms of the party's performance in opposition, he was often stung by criticism himself. Usually he simply disregarded pieces about him, having long become used to attacks from all quarters in the media. When he was annoyed about what he considered particularly egregious falsehoods about him in the print media, he would complain to editors, but he never sued. An opinion piece in the *Kerryman* newspaper in November 1974 by the celebrated journalist Con Houlihan particularly annoyed him. Houlihan criticised a speech Haughey had given on the spirit of republicanism in the Mount Brandon Hotel in Tralee a few weeks earlier. Haughey was in Kerry to launch the Kerry leg of the Tom McEllistrim memorial fund, celebrating the life of one of the founders of Fianna Fáil, who had been a deputy for some forty-six years and had died the previous December. McEllistrim's son, also named Tom, would play a crucial role in Haughey's election as Fianna Fáil leader some five years later. In Haughey's speech in Kerry, his first on Northern Ireland since the arms trial, he complained that there was a full-scale attempt under way to deny the people of the country 'any pride in our past or faith in our future'.[15]

In response, Houlihan painted Haughey as a 'capitalist-extraordinary and pseudo-republican', and proclaimed that to 'hear Charles Haughey restating the principles of republicanism is akin to hearing someone suffering from colour blindness discussing impressionistic painting'. He further argued that anyone who was deceived by Haughey was 'either a willing dupe or an incorrigible ignoramus'.[16] Haughey told his friend Sam Stephenson that 'a number of people have been in touch with me deploring this particular piece of objectivity' including the newspaper's former proprietor, Dan Nolan.[17] The *Kerryman* had been sold to Independent Newspapers in 1972, who Haughey was convinced were hostile to him. This was a rare example of Haughey complaining about his critics. More typical was his reaction to a piece on him, in a book published a couple of years earlier, by the then twenty-four-year-old journalist Rosita Sweetman, called *On Our Knees: Ireland 1972*, a collection of profiles of twenty-four prominent Irish people from north and south of the island. Sweetman's portrait of Haughey was called 'A Decent Man' and in it she portrayed him as the epitome of the new breed of Fianna Fáil men in the 1960s: 'slick, rich, clever, international, mohair-suited and silver-tongued', who had subsequently, in the aftermath of the arms trial, learned to keep his temper in control and when to say absolutely nothing about anything.[18] This led Tony Gallagher, the public relations officer of the Irish Farmers' Association (IFA), to tell Haughey that it was the 'most scurrilous piece of writing I have read in my many years in journalism'.[19] Haughey replied that fortunately he had 'long since learned to ignore this sort of thing'.[20]

Another book published the same year was *States of Ireland* by Haughey's constituency rival, Conor Cruise O'Brien. In August 1972, before the book was published, the publisher and editor of the magazine *Hibernia*, John Mulcahy, sent Haughey some pages which referred to him with the pithy comment: 'it should amuse you.'[21] In the book Cruise O'Brien wrote of Haughey that his admirers thought he resembled the Emperor Napoleon, some of whose better-known mannerisms he cultivated; that he obviously enjoyed spending his money in a rakish eighteenth-century style, of which horses were particular symbols; and that, as a small man when he dismounted, he strutted. Cruise O'Brien further argued that if the 'conditions ever became ripe for a characteristically Irish Catholic form of Fascism, Charles J. Haughey would make a plausible enough Taoiseach/Duce'.[22] Haughey told Mulcahy that the extract was indeed very amusing and it was 'hard to understand why people bother to write this sort of bull, or, perish the thought, could it be simply for the money?'[23]

By the time of Houlihan's article in late 1974, however, the route for Haughey's return to front-line politics was beginning to open up. In a long piece for *Magill* magazine in January 1980, the month after Haughey became Taoiseach, Vincent Browne wrote that a private meeting was held between Lynch and Haughey at some point before the Taoiseach brought Haughey back to the frontbench. At this meeting Lynch reputedly asked Haughey whether he would agree to issue a statement affirming his support for the party's Northern Ireland policy, in advance of his return to the frontbench. Haughey, according to Browne, demurred, pointing out that this would look as though he was buying his way back.[24] Lynch ultimately turned the timeline on its head and agreed to restore Haughey to the frontbench, after which Haughey did make a statement agreeing with the party's Northern Ireland policy. On the day of his acquittal in the arms trial, Haughey had stated that there was a fundamental difference of policy between Lynch and himself on Northern Ireland, but refused to elaborate on it. In the intervening four years he had never issued any statement in relation to Fianna Fáil's policy on Northern Ireland, creating the impression that the difference remained and was central to his continuing but unstated challenge to Lynch's leadership of the party. A declaration of loyalty on Northern Ireland was now the defining issue for Haughey's return to the Fianna Fáil bench.

ON THE FRONTBENCH

On Thursday 30 January 1975, Jack Lynch carried out a major reshuffle of his frontbench and brought Haughey back to his team as spokesman on health. Lynch also brought Jim Gibbons back from the European Parliament and made him spokesman on agriculture, although Gibbons had previously stated that he would not serve with Haughey. Lynch told a press conference that Haughey had given him his personal assurance that he fully supported, and was committed to, party policy on Northern Ireland. He then added that the party decision in relation to the events of 1970 surrounding the departure of Haughey from the cabinet remained the same in that it was his prerogative as leader to make appointments, and the right of the leader to do so had not been in question at any time. Haughey, for his part, stated that it was basic Fianna Fáil policy to seek the reunification of the country by peaceful means and he had always adopted and supported that position. He reiterated that he was a pacifist who was completely opposed to violence in any shape or form; he rejected any attempt to reunify the country through violence as this would be doomed to fail. Asked about the leadership of the party, Haughey stated that he would like to think he would be in the running to lead Fianna Fáil when that position arose but there was no issue at that particular time.

Later that night Lynch spoke to a crowd of five hundred people at a Cairde Fáil dinner in Dublin. He stated that his party was completely united in its aim to take government at the first available opportunity. After Lynch had finished his speech, the *Irish Press* reported, many of the guests stood up and applauded him. Then Haughey, who was at the same table as the Taoiseach, and was sitting beside Máirín Lynch, stood up and also applauded. At this, the entire attendance rose to their feet and delivered a standing ovation.[25] The following day, Haughey made his way to Claremorris in Mayo, where he was guest of honour at the local party's annual dinner dance. He was back on the frontbench, but the tour of the grassroots did not stop.

In handwritten notes he took after the arms trial, which look as if they were the basis of a speech he intended to make, but never did, Haughey argued that it was his right to criticise both the government and the Taoiseach, and to suggest change in a democratic party. He wrote that in the aftermath of the trial, the Taoiseach said support him or cause a general election, but that an alternative course was to let the party choose a new leader. Lynch had always conveyed the impression that if he was not wanted he would go, and had in fact only come to the position reluctantly in the first place. Haughey continued that he was prepared to find solutions to give the party time. In the most interesting of his jottings he writes: 'T. at airport said no compromising on fundamental policy. But who has? I have always subscribed to it. A vicious, prejudiced attempt to distort. Either for Lynch or you favour force. Just not true.'[26] He stated that every army in the world had contingency plans and he knew the Irish army was the same – it had to be. In that context, he claimed, it was monstrous to label him a fanatic, and he was neither inflexible nor a diehard. He was simply following the long tradition and fundamental position of Fianna Fáil that the British had no more right to the six counties than the twenty-six. If the national organisation let go of that principle, then, to Haughey, there was no difference between Fianna Fáil and Fine Gael. Some four years after these musings, Haughey reiterated that he had always supported the party's position on Northern Ireland and unity. He had at least persuaded himself that this was the case. Now he had to decide how to play his frontbench return, knowing, as he did, that most of the men on it, including Colley, Gibbons and O'Malley, did not want him.

CARING ABOUT POWER

In July 1975, RTÉ aired *People and Power*, a twelve-part series of interviews with prominent people in Irish public life, with Brian Farrell as the interrogator. Haughey agreed to take part in the programme a couple of months earlier and his interview appeared on 22 July. In preparation, Haughey spoke with the RTÉ broadcaster Donncha Ó Dúlaing, who later sent him a note advising him to use one or, at most, two quotations with discretion. He gave him a list that included quotations from Shakespeare (some of the sonnets and *All's Well That Ends Well*), Tennyson, Wordsworth, Pope, Dryden, Aristotle and Lord Acton's 'Power tends to corrupt, and absolute power corrupts absolutely. Great men are almost always bad men', adding in parentheses, 'most people don't know the last line.' Ó Dúlaing urged Haughey to permit himself to smile once or twice 'in the boyish way that only those who know you well are allowed to see'. If he conveyed the impression of being intensely interested in the interviewer's questions, who he presumed would be Brian Farrell, so much the better. He told Haughey to take the events of 1970 on the chin, that he had to leave the strong impression that he cared about power and did not shirk it. He argued that the question of vast wealth would scarcely arise. What could be more difficult was the apparent contrast between Haughey's right of centre attitude on wealth taxes and the radical reform policies of Fianna Fáil in the 1930s, which were much beloved of Dick Walsh, probably Michael Mills, and he suspected the grass, though not the concrete, roots of the present party. Ó Dúlaing ended by telling Haughey how important it was that he emerge from the interview a greater man than he was seen before, that he had to keep in the forefront of his mind that 'we are led by little men and deserve or at least crave better. So show yourself a Corinthian, a lad of mettle, a good boy.'[27]

In a trial question and answer session, Haughey answered the question, 'Will you stay in politics?' with a yes: it is 'my way of life now and

I am fully committed to it. In political life one can find a fundamental intellectual satisfaction which no other vocation can offer.'[28] In answer to the question, 'What does the word "Republican" mean to you?' Haughey argued that it was a noble and selfless concept and that bigotry and sectarianism were totally alien to it. In the interview itself, Haughey told Farrell that a person was only justified in having power if they used it and he had absolutely no time for people who 'seek power, get power, and then are quite content with the trappings. And I'm afraid there is a fair amount of that.'[29] After the interview was shown, one of Haughey's correspondents told him that his 'image of calm reflective dynamism was just briefly marred once or twice by some darting of the eyes which could be mistaken for unease, furtiveness or some other unflattering ascription', but that this small caveat did not diminish the comforting message of the programme that all Irish politicians were not inarticulate reactors devoid of the sustaining font of strong personal philosophies.[30] And, indeed, Haughey remained one of the few Irish politicians who did not see politics as beginning and ending in his own constituency.

Parochialism, and the focus on the constituency, remained the hallmark of Irish politics when Haughey was brought back to the frontbench. Ken Carty, who interviewed many Fianna Fáil politicians on his visit to Ireland, was constantly struck by how much tending of the constituency they had to do; many told him that they had never been to party headquarters in Mount Street, or had anything to do with it.[31] Haughey, of course, did vigorously tend his own constituency, and with a zeal that was unmatched by most of his peers. Notwithstanding his own peripatetic tour of the constituencies of other TDs, Haughey remained very protective of his own patch. In 1975 Fianna Fáil established a party journal for members. A member of the party's national executive, Liam Lawlor, wrote to Haughey in late July to say that he had been given the responsibility of raising the number of subscribers in Dublin Artane. Haughey was having none of it. He told Lawlor that it 'would be better if you devote yourself to the affairs of West County Dublin and let us look after Dublin Artane'.[32] He was not going to let any outsiders into his particular bailiwick, no matter what party headquarters had ordered them to do.

On Monday 22 September 1975, Haughey was fined £102 when he was found guilty of dangerous driving and assault at the Dublin District Court for an incident in Molesworth Street the previous October. Justice John McCarthy fined him £100 for dangerous driving and £2 for the assault on Noel O'Loughlin, which was based on the allegation that he had driven his car, a Daimler, at O'Loughlin. Haughey, who was with his solicitor Pat O'Connor at the time of the accident, gave evidence that it was one of those minor incidents that took place every day, and that he had not been driving at excess speed, or at the man. A few months later, when it became clear that the case would go to court, he told his long-time correspondent Mother Bernard that it was a very minor, insignificant traffic incident 'but of course it was seized upon'.[33]

Haughey's barrister, John Murray, said the case should be dismissed as there was no intention on the part of Haughey to assault O'Loughlin by driving his car towards him. The judge disagreed, however, preferring the evidence of O'Loughlin and of a witness, Catherine Cranley, who said she saw O'Loughlin stumbling over a moving car while trying to get out of its way.[34] After the case, Haughey's old friend Tony Gallagher of the IFA wrote to him in colourful terms: 'Bejasus if you had nicked an apple your man would have had you hanged, drawn and quartered. A disgraceful and bigoted conviction.' Haughey lamented that he 'did not have much of a chance with the District Justice in question'.[35] McCarthy had been appointed to the District Court in 1974 by the Cosgrave government and had been a Fine Gael candidate in Mayo South in the 1948 general election.

Haughey's motoring problems continued into 1976 when he was involved in yet another car crash on the night of 6 July of that year. He had chartered a plane from Iona Airways to take his two younger sons, Ciarán and Seán, and their friend Graham Turley, with him from Dublin to Farranfore Airport to bring supplies ahead of their annual August holiday on Inishvickillane. Foggy weather had forced the plane to divert to Shannon, where Haughey hired a taxi to complete the journey to Farranfore, where he was being collected for the onward journey to the island.[36] On the Adare–Patrickswell road there was a head-on collision between the taxi and a van containing a man and two children. All eight people were taken to hospital by ambulance but it was Haughey who came off the worst, being the only one who was kept in overnight after suffering a number of cuts and bruises.[37] A few months after the crash, the Fianna Fáil TD for Clare, Dr Bill Loughnane, wrote to Haughey to tell him that the driver of the taxi, a man named Vincent Flanagan, had called to him and asked Loughnane to put in a word with Haughey, 'not to be too hard with him'. Haughey replied that he had every sympathy for the driver who, he reckoned, had suffered enough with the accident and that he had already written to him to say how lucky everyone was to get off as lightly as they did.[38]

NOT JUST AN ELECTION VICTORY

On the evening of Friday 17 February 1978, Haughey told the Fianna Fáil Ard Fheis that the party's resounding general election triumph the previous year was 'not just an election victory. It was an historic assertion of national identity by the people of Ireland who came forward in overwhelming numbers to make a declaration of faith in themselves and in their ability to solve their own problems.'[39] He certainly did not feel this way the previous year when Fianna Fáil unveiled its historic manifesto. In May 1977, Martin O'Donoghue, then a relatively obscure Trinity College economics professor, and Fianna Fáil Dáil candidate, deliberately introduced a splash of communism into Irish politics when he brought the word 'manifesto' directly to the Irish people. Officially known as the 'Action Plan for National Reconstruction', but ever since as simply the Fianna Fáil manifesto of 1977, the party's programme remains the most famous and contentious election document in modern Irish history. O'Donoghue, who had been advising Jack Lynch since 1970, later recalled that the use of the word 'manifesto' was specific: 'I was even deliberately borrowing Maoist and other communist language. I picked the word for it, it was originally going to be a programme for government, and I said no, it's going to be a manifesto. They asked me why, and I said that every kid knows the Communist Manifesto, that's the revolution. They've all heard of Che Guevara and all the others. If you want to appeal to the young kids, it's the manifesto.'[40]

There were 400,000 first-time voters on an electoral register of just over 2.77 million at the 1977 election. The voting age had been reduced to eighteen for the first time and a quarter of the electorate was aged under twenty-six. In an era when there were no influential small parties, and very few successful independents, this was a significant tranche of new voters for Fianna Fáil, Fine Gael and Labour to chase.[41] Fianna Fáil was determined to get back into office and to offer both new and existing voters a specific policy platform on which to vote. It was not going to simply rely on party loyalty. The manifesto opened with the words, 'The real threat to the future of our country lies in the economy', and with that Fianna Fáil committed itself to a full employment strategy.[42] O'Donoghue also insisted on calling the programme one of 'national reconstruction': 'a good communist word as well. I learned it from dealing with Maoist students, they were always confronting the concrete realities of the situation, a wonderful phrase, never forgot it, never knew what it meant. As part of confronting concrete realities, I said right we're going to have to reconstruct this thing, so that's what the programme was going to be, national reconstruction.[43] The fact that employment and the economy were central to this document, with Northern Ireland, for instance, relegated to two brief paragraphs at the end, shows clearly where Fianna Fáil's priorities lay.

Continuing with the communistic theme, O'Donoghue argued that a new government department of economic planning and development would be needed to drive the economy forward. He had, however, underestimated the civil service bureaucratic machine. In his memoir the former government press secretary Frank Dunlop argued that the new department was heading for impending disaster from its inception, as there was no way any secretary of the Department of Finance would allow a new department to usurp any of the powers of Finance, no matter how trivial. The strength of the administration's bureaucracy is summed up in Dunlop's recollection of a conversation he had with Haughey a few days after the formation of the government in 1977: 'I had lunch with Charlie Haughey in the Dáil restaurant and he was scathing about the move. In his opinion the mandarins in the Department of Finance would take a long view and gradually strangle O'Donoghue's ministry to death.[44]

The Fianna Fáil manifesto has gone down in history as the epitome of auction politics. It was the first example of an Irish political party making specific promises of what it would do once it was in government. The 1973 Fine Gael–Labour alternative coalition government had a four-teen-point plan, but that was written on a single A4 sheet and could best be described as a statement of intent. It promised a variety of reforms, all of which were suitably vague and which Fianna Fáil dismissed as a collection of pious aspirations and platitudes.[45] This may well have been the case, but the fourteen-point plan did prove useful as a type of pro-gramme for the coalition government for the next four years. By contrast, Fianna Fáil's 1977 document was a much more specific forty-seven-page affair in which the party made an array of spending promises, most spec-tacularly pledging to abolish car tax and local government rates (the two most famous giveaways), unlike any other in the history of the state. Such promises were based on the government's proposals to pump prime the economy through a form of deficit-financing fiscal policy which was to achieve significant growth rates and bring about full employment by 1983.

Fianna Fáil's 1977 campaign had been years in the planning. Although its frontbench had performed lamentably for most of its period in opposi-tion since 1973, which was one of the reasons for bringing Haughey back, Lynch made a number of important internal appointments to reorganise the structure of the party. Three young men who would prove crucial to the party's success in the 1977 election were brought into the party fold. Séamus Brennan was appointed general secretary, Frank Dunlop was given the job of party press secretary, and Esmond Smyth became director of research.[46] By the time Cosgrave called the 1977 election, all three had Fianna Fáil in a position to run the most professional cam-paign seen in Irish politics since the foundation of the state. Brennan was acutely aware of the importance of the vastly increased young vote and was responsible for the establishment of a specific youth wing of the party, Ógra Fianna Fáil, which he considered a vehicle to attract newer members, and thus votes, to the party at the subsequent general election.[47]

By early 1974 many of the essential elements that would make up the 1977 manifesto were being discussed and formulated by an informal cabal of party members and supporters established by Lynch and known as the 'Saturday Group'.[48] Much of the manifesto was given an early airing in September 1976 by Fianna Fáil's press and information service, under the leadership of Dunlop, when it issued the party's economic proposals under the heading *The Economic Emergency*. These proposals included increased government spending of £100 million in 1977, tax cuts to the order of another £100 million in the same year, and some modest wage rises. All this was to be paid for through a strange concoction of increased borrowing, good old-fashioned Keynesian demand management, and a certain dash of neoliberal trickle-down entrepreneurial job creation by the private sector. This was a fatal mistake in that it ignored an important lesson of Irish history: there was no justification for having such confidence in Irish business, most of which had survived since independence only through the Fianna Fáil policy of protection.[49]

The manifesto was at the heart of the Fianna Fáil campaign, which was run with almost military-style planning based mainly on the successful 1976 Democratic presidential campaign of Jimmy Carter in the United States. It featured Jack Lynch touring the country in an election battle bus replete with theme song, baby kissing, and mass torchlight rallies reminiscent of a bygone age. It attracted enormous media and public interest. Fianna Fáil had set the agenda for the campaign and never let it go. Brennan went to the United States in the spring and summer of 1976 to study the campaign techniques of the Carter campaign. He brought back a variety of lessons, none more important than the need to centre any campaign on the personality and leadership of Jack Lynch.[50] Lynch became the cornerstone of the campaign as the party's main electoral asset and he preached the gospel of the manifesto, which was to put more money into people's pockets.[51] It was a winning combination. While Haughey had very little input into the manifesto or the campaign, its success was not lost on him. According to Frank Dunlop, Haughey's reaction was to simply raise his eyes to heaven and mutter 'Oh dear, oh dear' when he first saw it, while suggesting that the document was the amalgam of some drunken economists in Doheny and Nesbitt's, the favoured Baggot Street watering hole of the chattering classes.[52] His scepticism extended to not attending the manifesto's launch. After close to two and a half years on the party's frontbench Haughey remained very much a semi-detached member of Lynch's team.

Fianna Fáil gained the largest seat share in its history with 84 TDs elected from 148 seats, a twenty-seat majority, and its second largest ever percentage of the vote share with just over 50 per cent. It was the zenith of Lynch's political career. But the nadir was in sight. The 1977 manifesto, and the electoral success attached to it, did nothing for Lynch's leadership, which soon came under intense pressure. The ominously large majority from the 1977 general election led to a situation in Fianna Fáil where, once the economy began to decline, various jealousies emerged and many of the twenty-eight new deputies, and fifty-seven backbenchers, became susceptible to the argument that the party needed a new and dynamic leader if their seats were to be made safe.[53] Much of the grief emerged because of Lynch's own laconic leadership style. In his memoirs, Bertie Ahern, who was first elected at the 1977 election, noted that he never actually ever spoke to Lynch, recalling a non-incident in the Dáil where the two passed one another silently in a corridor.[54]

Michael Woods, another first-time TD, had a similar experience. Woods had been appointed by Lynch to the committee on resurrecting the party when Fianna Fáil lost the 1973 election, and was on the selection panel that appointed Seamus Brennan as general secretary. He ran as George Colley's running mate in the constituency of Dublin Clontarf in 1977 and had been a conduit for Lynch in finding out what was happening in the grass roots of Fianna Fáil on the northside of Dublin, something Colley had little insight into. Yet when Woods entered the Dáil he had very few dealings with Lynch, noting that this was a common complaint among pretty much all first-time TDs. Woods took the third seat in Dublin Clontarf on Colley's transfers, knocking out Labour's Conor Cruise O'Brien in the process. After his somewhat unexpected victory over Cruise O'Brien, Haughey congratulated Woods, joking, 'What have you done, my foil is gone.'[55] Five days into the campaign, Cruise O'Brien, then Minister for Posts and Telegraphs, attacked Haughey in an interview with the *Times* of London, and in a BBC radio interview on the issue of the state's security. In that interview he claimed that Haughey was a 'dangerous force with a lot of mystery surrounding him' and that the policies of Fianna Fáil and the IRA in relation to Northern Ireland were a distinction without a difference.[56] Given that very few people in Ireland listened to the BBC, or even had the capacity to, and practically no one read the *Times*, Cruise O'Brien's choice of broadcast medium was odd, but RTÉ Radio picked up on the remarks and broadcast a report on his comments, giving them a national audience.

P.J. Mara suggested to Haughey that he should simply ignore the comments, but given that RTÉ had picked up on the remarks Haughey felt he should respond.[57] He also sensed an opportunity to shore up his own vote in the constituency. He issued a statement in which he stated that the unfounded allegations made against him by Cruise O'Brien were simply a repetition of those on which he had based his campaign back in 1973. In that election the voters of Dublin North East had responded by giving Haughey the second largest vote in the country. He believed they would react in a similar way at this election. He continued that it was not surprising that O'Brien would go to the London *Times* to launch such a piece of character assassination against a fellow Irishman, given the newspaper's role in Irish history, but what was astounding was that RTÉ should, 'within a matter of minutes, rebroadcast verbatim the vicious personal attack made on me by Dr O'Brien on BBC radio'.[58]

The following day Cruise O'Brien stepped up his attack on Haughey, asking whether the people of Ireland could trust an alternative government, which would include Haughey, on security, the IRA, Northern Ireland and Anglo-Irish relations. He asked whether the Irish people were prepared to entrust their security to a government that might turn out to be led by a person with the record of Haughey, given it was widely believed that he would succeed Lynch as the leader of Fianna Fail party in the near future. He asserted that these were matters that affected lives, property, jobs, tourism and the country's reputation.[59] Haughey refused to react on this occasion and Cruise O'Brien was ultimately reined in by

Fine Gael's two main strategists, Richie Ryan and Garret FitzGerald, who felt that the attack had played into Fianna Fáil's hands. Cruise O'Brien later recalled to Stephen Collins that the coalition would have lost anyway but by a smaller margin if it had concentrated on a 'Haughey is not a safe man' type of charge, which, he argued, would have diverted some attention from the promises of Fianna Fáil and for which a good case could have been made.[60] This was a self-serving and spectacular mis-reading of the political realities of the campaign. Haughey's situation had had little impact on the 1973 election and, even though he was now on the frontbench, he was a relatively peripheral figure in the 1977 national campaign. Cruise O'Brien's obsession with Haughey and his supposed threat to the stability of the state had no impact on the voters on the northside of Dublin or indeed anywhere else. It is far more likely that had the attacks continued, Haughey's vote would actually have increased.

Haughey ran in the constituency of Dublin Artane. The old Dublin North East constituency was split in 1974 when the constituency bound-aries were infamously redrawn by Minister for Local Government Jimmy Tully, giving rise to the colloquialism 'Tullymander'. Tully's boundary revision was a clearly naked redrawing of the constituencies in favour of the government parties and was reckoned by most political commenta-tors to be worth at least half a dozen extra seats for the coalition.[61] The Tullymander provided for more three-seater constituencies in Dublin and more four-seaters in rural parts of the country. However, it failed spectacularly when the coalition government failed to observe the first law of Irish elections under PRSTV – get enough first preference votes. The Tullymander ultimately ended up giving Fianna Fáil a far greater seat bonus than its first preference vote warranted. Despite consumer confidence in an improving economy and the sleight of hand of bound-ary manipulation, the Fine Gael–Labour coalition ran one of the most anaemic campaigns of modern electoral history. They were not helped when a strangely uninterested Liam Cosgrave decided halfway through not to continue campaigning, pleading a bad bout of laryngitis.[62] Pretty much all the pundits expected a coalition victory, but Fine Gael and Labour quickly found themselves bowled over by Fianna Fáil's relentless machine. Long before polling day, both government and opposition knew a change was inevitable. Haughey polled just over 11,000 votes on 36.7 per cent of the vote in the new three-seat constituency and brought one of his running mates, Timothy Killeen, with him. The other seat was taken by the veteran socialist Noël Browne, who had crossed the river for the first time ever to specifically challenge Haughey and polled a very respectable 5,601 votes. Fine Gael failed to take a seat.

THE MINISTER FOR HEALTH AND SOCIAL WELFARE

Given his frontbench position, there was no surprise when Haughey was duly appointed Minister for Health by Jack Lynch when the 21st Dáil met on 5 July 1977. The surprise was that Haughey was also given the responsibility of social welfare. Neville Keery wrote the manifesto's section on social security, which promised to maintain the living standards of social welfare recipients by regular adjustments of the level of payments in line with the cost of living; to work towards the elimination of discrimination against single, married and widowed women; and to simplify all social security forms.[63] In health the manifesto committed to preventive medical and health education, the provision of as many health services as possible in the local community and a complete reorganisation of the mental health service

More than most TDs, Haughey was acutely aware of the poverty that afflicted large swathes of Dublin's northside and he was also familiar with the difficulties of rural Ireland from his journeys around the country. Two days before the election, while Haughey was out canvassing, a man showed up at Abbeville whose landlord had given him seven days' notice to quit his home. He had nowhere to go. He had first gone to the Dublin Corporation offices and arrived at Abbeville saying that a man from the corporation had told him to contact Mr Haughey. He was informed that Haughey was not at home, that as he did not even live in the constituency there was probably very little that could probably be done for him, but that Haughey's office would try and find out the position for him.[64] The man was eventually placed on the housing list, but he was one of thousands who looked to Haughey for help.

Haughey was constantly bombarded with entreaties for medical cards, housing allocations and improvements, and oftentimes appeals for money from constituents in desperate financial straits. A few months before the election, the chairman of the National Trust Archive, Nick Robinson, husband of the crusading lawyer Mary Robinson, informed him that it was establishing a visual record of Irish architecture, was in the process of forming a committee to ensure the archive's financial well-being, and did he want to be involved? Haughey wished Robinson every success, but pointedly added, 'please don't ask me for a financial contribution as I am absolutely inundated locally.'[65] Haughey knew both what it was like to be poor and what many of his constituents had to endure in their own lives. He considered the bureaucracy around health and social welfare to be dehumanising and demoralising for citizens.

On the day Haughey was appointed Minister for Health and Social Welfare, he rang Brendan O'Donnell, his private secretary from his Agriculture and Finance days, and asked him to come to see him in Abbeville. He told O'Donnell he had two goals, one short term, the other long term. In the short term he wanted to humanise the whole health and social welfare system, to make it more accessible, and to ensure that people got their just entitlements. The long-term goal was far more exhilarating. Looking at O'Donnell with those famous hooded eyes, Haughey said in a steely voice, 'I want to be Taoiseach of this country and I want you to help me get there. You've always had a good rapport with the deputies and also I've two departments and I don't want a parliamentary secretary because they only get in the way. I want you to ensure the new deputies are provided with a first-class service from my office, vet representations, and if there is anything sensitive bring it to me.'[66] There were fifty-seven backbenchers in Fianna Fáil after the election and they would play the central role in Haughey's rise to the leadership of Fianna Fáil and to the office of Taoiseach.

In early 1978 Haughey had another bad bout of kidney stones. By the first week of March it was becoming increasingly uncomfortable. He went to the Longford Chamber of Commerce dinner as a guest of Albert and Kathleen Reynolds on Friday 3 March but was clearly in pain and had to leave early. Two days later the Reynoldses wrote to thank him for keeping the appointment and expressed hope that the visit would not result in any lasting damage to his health.[67] The following week, Haughey was hospitalised and had an operation to remove the troublesome stone. Earlier that week his friend Micheál Mac Liammóir had died peacefully at his home in Harcourt Street after a short illness. Haughey missed the funeral because he remained in hospital, but in attendance were President Patrick Hillery, Taoiseach Jack Lynch, a number of other ministers, and various opposition politicians, including the leaders of Fine Gael, Garret FitzGerald, and Labour, Frank Cluskey, and a host of other luminaries. The flag at Dublin City Hall flew at half-mast. A few days later, Mac Liammóir's partner, Hilton Edwards, wrote to Haughey. Edwards's first thought was not of Mac Liammóir but of Haughey's illness, which, he said, he was most distressed to hear about. He poignantly added, '[I have] lost Micheál and with him I fear I have lost my way; but I will do my best to deserve the faith that you had in us both. It is going to be hard and I am praying for your indulgence, but send you assurances of my good intentions.'[68] Another artist worried about Haughey was the painter Edward McGuire. Haughey had commissioned McGuire to paint a portrait of him but was rarely around to sit for it. When the painting was finally finished it featured a bowler-hatted Haughey mounted on a hunting horse outside Abbeville. Once Haughey came out of hospital he caught up with his correspondence telling Maguire he had been suffering greatly for about a month before getting the kidney stone removed. To the Reynoldses he wrote that he was 'so depressed at having to disappoint everybody and present such a dismal spectacle'. He told Edwards that he had been looking forward to having him and Mac Liammóir out to Inishvickillane later in the year and sympathised with him on his grievous personal loss.[69]

Haughey's own health problems informed much of his thinking about his new department. In his view, increased spending was badly needed to bring the health service up to modern European norms, and he became a vociferous advocate at cabinet for the allocation of more resources to the health and social welfare services. Increased spending would also, of course, provide plenty of opportunities for Haughey to deliver largesse to Fianna Fáil backbenchers. Health spending increased at a rapid rate during Haughey's time as minister, doubling between 1977 and 1980. By the time he became Taoiseach, overall spending on health had risen to 7.8 per cent of national income. It had been less than 4 per cent just a decade earlier.[70] He announced plans for new hospitals in Beaumont, in his own constituency, which would replace the Jervis Street and St Laurence's hospitals, and in Tallaght in west Dublin. He committed to having six hospitals in Dublin, three on the northside and three on the southside. The 1977 manifesto had pledged to preserve the role of the county hospital in providing the necessary level of services for the local community. Provision for the building of hospitals at either end of the country, in Letterkenny and Tralee, were also announced. The emphasis on localism and the importance of the county hospital put the manifesto at odds with the Fitzgerald report of 1968 which advocated the rationalisation of local hospitals and recommended that there be four regional and twelve general hospitals across the state. Haughey, and Fianna Fáil, were not alone in their disregard for this report; it aroused enormous hostility among politicians of all hues, furious at what they considered to be the downgrading of health services in their native regions.

To fast-track the building of Beaumont, Haughey proposed that the plans for the Cork Regional Hospital, which was then nearing completion, could be applied to Beaumont with little alteration.[71] When Beaumont finally opened in 1987 it was an almost exact replica of the hospital in the Cork suburb of Wilton. Haughey cut the first sod to begin the building of Beaumont Hospital in March 1978 after his kidney stone operation. Some fifteen years later he revisited Beaumont and presented the spade with which he had cut that first sod to the hospital. Its then chairman, Niall Weldon, said that he had done more to mastermind and put in place Beaumont than any other person.[72] Another letter that Haughey received in retirement came from his old sometime friend, sometime adversary Vincent Browne. In November 1997, a few months after the publication of the McCracken report, and the establishment of the Moriarty Tribunal, Browne wrote to Haughey suggesting they meet for dinner. He reassured him that in the aftermath of the McCracken report, he believed that almost everything written and said about the former Taoiseach was unfair. He particularly made the point that Haughey, in his view, more than almost any other person who had held senior public office, sought to look after the disadvantaged: 'I was in St. Ita's Portrane on Tuesday and saw the deplorable conditions in which 350 mentally handicapped people are kept. The last Minister for Health to visit the place was yourself in 1977 and that is very much remembered there.'[73] Haughey took the mental health section of the 1977 manifesto seriously but significant increases in the budget failed to dramatically improve the service.

The care for the disadvantaged that Browne alluded to was certainly a feature of Haughey's tenure in Social Welfare. The February 1978 budget provided for a 10 per cent increase in social welfare payments. It gave single women and widows full access to unemployment assistance, eased the five-year residence requirement for old age and other pensions, made provision for those who qualified to get free gas in lieu of electricity, granted a scheme of allowances for bottled gas, and gave free telephone rental to old age pensioners who lived alone. Haughey had made the point that the telephone was often the only panacea for loneliness among those who were on their own in their later years. In health, he honoured the Fianna Fáil manifesto by strengthening the role of the Health Promotion Unit in the department, including giving free toothbrushes to all primary schoolchildren, and introduced reforming legislation to control tobacco advertising and sponsorship as the party had promised during its campaign.[74] The 1979 budget saw a further increase of 16 per cent for old age pensioners and other long-term social welfare claimants, and of 12 per cent for short-term claimants. He announced free access to hospitals for those earning less than £5,550 a year, on an income-related health contribution basis, and generally went about his business in the robust and flamboyant style he had adopted as a minister throughout the 1960s.

THE IRISH SOLUTION

Haughey faced his biggest test when tackling the complex question of family planning, which had eluded the Fine Gael–Labour coalition in 1974, and which many in his own party found intractable. The Fianna Fáil manifesto pledged to 'ensure the widest possible acceptance of a positive policy for family planning and enact the necessary legislation'.[75] This was the party's delayed reaction to the 1973 Supreme Court decision in the McGee case. That case found that married couples had the constitutional right to make private decisions on family planning, and specifically that May McGee's right to marital privacy had been denied by the 1935 Criminal Law (Amendment) Act, which prohibited the importation of contraceptive devices into the state.[76] When Fianna Fáil returned to power, responsibility for the contraceptive issue was moved from the Department of Justice to the Department of Health, and the new minister viewed it as a health matter.

Introducing the second stage of the Health (Family Planning Bill) in the Dáil in February 1979, Haughey stated that before bringing to this stage a bill that was bound to be contentious and had been the subject of concern and controversy for so many years, he deemed it prudent to make every effort to inform himself of the views and attitudes of those professional bodies who would be affected by the provisions of family planning legislation. These included the health boards, Church leaders, community organisations, vocational bodies and individuals who he thought could help to convey to him the range of views held throughout the country. During the consultative process, eighteen organisations discussed with him the provisions that might appropriately be included in a family planning bill. Many more wrote to share their views. He had little time for those traditional Catholic interest groups, such as the Irish Family League, who demanded a return to the status quo. While he was more sympathetic to the position of liberal groups, such as the Irish Family Planning Association, whom he met in July 1978, he knew that the vast majority of his parliamentary party colleagues, and indeed Fianna Fáil's support in the country, was conservative on the issue.

The party had imposed a whip to oppose the coalition's Control of Importation, Sale and Manufacture of Contraception Bill in 1974, which provided for the sale of contraceptives through pharmacies to married people only. It is likely, however, that the overwhelming majority of Fianna Fáil TDs were opposed to liberalising the law on contraception and would have voted against the government's legislation, whether there was a whip in place or not. Notwithstanding his own complicated personal life, Haughey also had a somewhat conservative streak on moral issues and certainly was not in favour of the widespread availability of contraception when he piloted his own legislation through the Dáil.[77] In this he was reflecting the beliefs of most people in his own party. He also believed that he was reflecting the values of wider Irish society.

By the time Haughey started to think carefully about the issue, polls showed that 43 per cent of the people supported access to contraceptives for married couples only, while fully a third continued to oppose any legalisation at all.[78] The latter situation was not feasible. The Supreme Court decision in the McGee case effectively undermined the existing regulatory regime and contraceptives were widely available. Notwithstanding that they had voted against the coalition's bill a few years earlier, Jack Lynch and Haughey were both of the view that legislation was necessary to restrict access to contraception so that young unmarried people could not obtain it.

From Haughey's perspective the key to passing any legislation was to get the Catholic Church onside. Before he set out on his consultation exercise he told Brendan O'Donnell that the greatest difficulty would be persuading what he described as Fianna Fáil's antediluvian backbenchers to support it. He fully believed that if he could persuade the Catholic Church to support his legislation, or at least not to oppose it, he would be able to obtain the support of the parliamentary party. A number of years earlier Haughey had completed a questionnaire by an American Fulbright exchange student at UCD, A.S. Cohan, about political elites and leadership. He replied 'nonsense' to a question that asked whether he agreed with the statement that the most powerful institution in Ireland was the Roman Catholic Church.[79] He was also not averse to letting individual priests know of his displeasure with them, particularly when it came to how they proposed to vote. As Fianna Fáil's spokesman on health, he received a letter from one of the Oblate Fathers in Inchicore, where his own brother Eoghan was a member, complaining about Jack Lynch's stand on contraception. The writer, Fr Joseph Horan, told him that Lynch had put himself outside the possibility of getting the clerical vote at the next election. It was Liam Cosgrave and Dick Burke, both of whom had voted against their own government's legislation on contraception the previous year, who stood with the feelings of the people. Haughey replied that he found the argument confusing in that it was Cosgrave's government who introduced the bill, and Fianna Fáil that defeated it, and to vote for Cosgrave and Dick Burke was to vote for Conor Cruise O'Brien, Garret FitzGerald, Justin Keating and all that they stood for, before caustically adding, 'maybe there is some sophisticated way which I do not understand in which it is possible for the clerical vote to have its coalition cake and eat it.'[80]

By the time Haughey went to Inishvickillane in August 1978 he was confident that he could get his legislation through in the following Dáil session, and that it reflected the majority view of those groups he had consulted. As Diarmaid Ferriter has convincingly argued, he was most certainly not in the pocket of the bishops, but he had played a delicate balancing act in persuading them that his legislation would provide for a more restrictive situation than that which currently existed, and that his proposals were essentially conservative in nature.[81] The final draft of the legislation restricted access to contraception to 'bona fide' couples – there had been legal and constitutional worries about the use of the term 'married couples' as had been originally intended. Brian Girvin has persuasively argued that while Haughey got the political balance right, he was able to do this by essentially agreeing to a position that the bishops could accept.[82] The leaders of the Catholic Church remained opposed to contraception but had accepted the constitutional situation as set out in the McGee judgment. What they wanted to see, however, was as restrictive a position as possible in the legislation that gave effect to the Supreme Court's decision. Haughey's proposals essentially did this. The night before he introduced the bill in the Dáil he went to the Archbishop's palace in Drumcondra to get the Catholic Church's final approval for his proposals from the Archbishop of Dublin, Dermot Ryan.[83]

Some conservative elements in Fianna Fáil were still not satisfied. The Minister for Agriculture, Jim Gibbons, threatened to resign from cabinet when the legislation was discussed. In the vote on the second stage of the bill in April 1979, Gibbons and two backbenchers defied the three-line whip and refused to vote at all. In a party that had not allowed a free vote on the coalition's bill in 1974, Jack Lynch rather amazingly allowed Gibbons to suffer no consequences, accepting that there was a genuine issue of conscience involved, and that there would be no requirement on Gibbons to vote on the subsequent stages of the bill. This was an extraordinary tolerance of a lack of discipline by a senior minister. It reinforced a view Haughey had long held that Gibbons had some sort of hold over Lynch dating from the arms trial.[84]

In his February 1979 Dáil speech on his family planning bill, Haughey ended his remarks calling for support of the bill by maintaining that it sought to 'provide an Irish solution to an Irish problem. I have not regarded it as necessary that we should conform to the position obtaining in any other country.'[85] When Haughey's Department of Health civil service team were putting the final touches to his speech, a young female administrative officer told him it was an Irish solution to an Irish problem. His looked at her with those hooded eyes, and said 'Yes, it is.'[86] Two decades later, and long into retirement, he maintained that it was a very sensible phrase. He couldn't 'see anything wrong with propounding an Irish solution to an Irish problem and I think every country in the world does it. I know enough about France to know the French have their own way of doing things. They present themselves with problems that are unique to them, and they solve them in their own way.'[87] And indeed this particular solution was unique. Haughey had piloted the bill through his own parliamentary party and the Dáil. He had kept the clergy and his own party relatively happy, and while the legislation did not lead to a more liberal society into the 1980s, that had never been its aim.

Five months later, on 17 July 1979, Haughey had the final word in relation to the long and complex family planning legislation when he spoke last in the bill's final hearing in Seanad Éireann. He attacked Senator Mary Robinson when she said that the Houses of the Oireachtas were divorced from the public in the debate. He maintained that, on the contrary, in the twenty-two years he had been in the Dáil he had never seen a debate in the Oireachtas in which the different segments of passionately held opinions of members of the general public were as accurately reflected as they were in relation to family planning. One criticism that could not be made of the Oireachtas, and indeed of Haughey himself, was a lack of consultation. He apologised to the Seanad if he ever demonstrated impatience, irritation, tedium or boredom, but he attributed these traits to the long-drawn-out debate on the measure that had taken place. Haughey finished his remarks by stating that he was not terribly fond of the proposition that he kept to the middle of the road in the legislation. The great Welsh Labour politician, Aneurin Bevan, had said that the man who kept to the middle of the road invariably got knocked down by the traffic.[88] For Haughey, the legislation was the starting point for the inauguration of an adequate and comprehensive family planning service for the people, given that it was something that affected the lives and happiness of ordinary men and women in such a fundamental way.[89] He did not add that these ordinary men and women had to be in 'bona fide' relationships. It did not matter. He had finally steered his legislation through the Oireachtas. It was signed into law by President Patrick Hillery the following week.

On the first week of August 1979, Haughey decamped to Inishvickillane, where he stayed for the whole month, apart from one trip to the mainland for the Dingle Regatta. While on the island he decided to provide £3,000 to the Department of Civil Engineering at UCC to conduct research into wave-powered generators.[90] Five years after buying the island he considered it the one place he could be on his own with the time to think. That August, his mind was consumed with the future of Fianna Fáil and his own position in the party. Two months earlier, the June election to the European Parliament had been an unmitigated disaster for the party, which had won just five of the fifteen seats on offer and received less than 35 per cent of the popular vote. The local elections were not much better. Fianna Fáil lost twenty-four seats and polled 39 per cent of the vote. The huge majority of 1977 and the 50 per cent of the vote seemed very far away. The backbench TDs were getting restless about their seats. Jack Lynch had never been interested in them and was far removed from their concerns.

His cabinet had quickly grown stale. Haughey, meanwhile, remained the repository for the backbenchers' complaints. He was in no position to challenge Lynch for the leadership, but in the two years since he had returned to cabinet he had accumulated significant backbench support. When Haughey made his way back from Inishvickillane at the end of the month, he could not have known that within a hundred days that support would manifest itself in a leadership battle that would make him Taoiseach and would split Fianna Fáil for the following decade and a half.

CHAPTER 14

I HAVE THE VOTES

PLOT

On Tuesday 11 December 1979, the day Charles Haughey was elected Taoiseach, the editor of *Magill*, Vincent Browne, wrote to him seeking an immediate interview for a background briefing for a large story that Browne was planning on 'The Making of a Taoiseach'. Browne's plan was to deal with everything that had happened politically since the 1977 election. He had a long list of topics he wanted to cover including how the 1977 election was won, how the economy had prospered throughout 1978, entry into the European Monetary System, the National Understanding negotiations and how they fell apart, the farmers' levy, the PAYE revolt, the postal strike, the oil crisis, the local and European elections, the Fianna Fáil caucus meeting of backbenchers to discuss the leadership of Jack Lynch, the Síle de Valera speech, the air corridor row, the American trip, the Bill Loughnane affair, Lynch's resignation, the canvassing for the election, the running of the Haughey and Colley campaigns for leadership, and finally the making of the cabinet.[1] The exhaustive list of topics was indicative of the dramatic change in politics in the two and a half years since Lynch's landslide general election victory.

Browne had spoken with Haughey about the article the day after the dramatic Fianna Fáil leadership election, which had seen Haughey, with the overwhelming support of the backbenchers, win the leadership of the party. Browne told Haughey he needed to speak with him urgently because of the looming deadline; *Magill* intended to publish the leadership article before Christmas. Haughey refused to do the interview and the article did not appear until the January 1980 edition. It was a stunning piece of reportage. It outlined in over 12,500 words of tremendous detail how Haughey won the leadership with thirty-nine of the fifty-seven backbench votes. It charted Haughey's recovery from the dark days of 1970 when he was fired as Minister for Finance, arrested at his home and taken to the Bridewell in a Garda car, held for the morning before being bailed, and subsequently prosecuted in the courts on a charge of conspiracy to illegally import arms, to the day when he was elected Taoiseach. What was perhaps most extraordinary for those reading the riveting account was that Haughey's election had been orchestrated by a handful of rural backbenchers referred to as the 'gang of five'. Seán Doherty, Jackie Fahey, Mark Killilea, Tom McEllistrim and Albert Reynolds were the leaders of a group who had schemed for months to oust an administration which, they believed, would be routed at the next election. The only thing more extraordinary than this revelation was that Haughey himself had played little part in the removal of Lynch. As Browne accurately put it, 'the eventual benefactor of that revolt, Charles Haughey, had little involvement in and indeed, little knowledge of what was going on.'[2] That was true, but only to a certain extent. Certainly Haughey was very aware of the discontent with Lynch on the backbenches and the fact that many were anxious for a change of leadership. He also knew who they were. In his personal papers there is a photocopy of a page with sixteen signatures on it under the small-type heading: 'It is our view that the interest of the party can best be served by the early retirement of Jack Lynch and the election of a new leader of the party.' The first signatory is Jackie Fahey. Of the gang of five, Doherty, Killilea and McEllistrim all appear in the list. The other signatories are Liam Aylward, Lorcan Allen, Chub O'Connor, Joe Fox, Paddy Power, Eileen Lemass, John Callinan, Charlie

McCreevy, Seán Calleary, Seán Keegan, Ger Connolly and Síle de Valera. There is no date and a small yellow Post-it with the date 1979 is attached to the sheet.[3] All voted for Haughey in the leadership election.

When Haughey returned from Inishvickillane at the end of August 1979, two events were convulsing the Irish people. One was the heinous IRA murder of Queen Elizabeth II's distant cousin Lord Louis Mountbatten, in a bomb attack on his boat, *Shadow V*, just outside the harbour at Mullaghmore in County Sligo on Tuesday 27 August. The other victims were the Dowager Lady Brabourne, and two teenage boys, Mountbatten's grandson, Nicholas Knatchbull, and Paul Maxwell, from Fermanagh, who was working as a local boat boy for the summer. On the same day eighteen British soldiers were killed in an IRA attack at Warrenpoint, County Down, the British army's greatest loss of life in a single incident in Northern Ireland. On a more hopeful note, Pope John Paul II would visit Ireland at the end of September.

Jack Lynch was on holiday in Portugal with his wife, Máirín, at the time of the Mountbatten bomb attack. He did not return home immediately, although at least one person in his private office thought he should. Instead he was persuaded that he should stay on holiday until all arrangements had been made. He was widely criticised by the Irish and British press, and eventually returned home a day later. His return coincided with the removal of Mountbatten's body by air to London from Baldonnel Airport. The special representative of the Queen sent over to accompany the body back refused to salute when Lynch offered him the Irish government's condolences. This was interpreted by the Irish military present as an official indication of the fury in British government and royal circles at Ireland's failure to protect Mountbatten.[4] Lynch, and by extension his government, was deeply embarrassed that the Irish security forces had failed to protect Mountbatten. The newly installed British Prime Minister, Margaret Thatcher, who had come to office after an emphatic victory in the May 1979 British general election, visited Northern Ireland to hold discussions on security two days after the bombing. Following her visit, the British government increased the size of the Royal Ulster Constabulary by 1,000 officers to 7,500. Meanwhile, in Rome it was announced that Pope John Paul II would not travel to Armagh during his forthcoming visit to Ireland, as had previously been planned. On 5 September, Lynch, on behalf of his government, attended the funeral service in Westminster Abbey. He cut a sombre, downbeat figure.

After the service Lynch met Thatcher for what was billed a summit between the two prime ministers. In advance of the summit Lynch had stated that a British initiative was needed to tackle the cause rather than the effects of the violence in Northern Ireland and that he would be pressing for such a move at his meeting with Thatcher.[5] The reality turned out somewhat differently; Lynch spent the five-hour meeting on the defensive as Thatcher attacked him over what she saw as his government's failure to properly police the border. In her view, this made the Republic of Ireland a safe haven for murderers. She wanted an immediate strengthening of security and asked Lynch to make practical concessions in this regard. One of these was to review and slightly modify overflight arrangements for British helicopters to cross the border for a limited distance in cases of so-called hot pursuit.[6] Lynch did not concede to British demands for unlimited overflight rights over the border, or on unlimited rights of pursuit. The modification on control of air activities on the border referred to the fact that a British helicopter flying at several hundred feet on the northern side would be able to observe what might be going on over a considerable swathe of Irish territory; some five kilometres in all directions. The Irish team had a prepared position based on international law that so-called hot pursuit was a purely naval concept. In a naval conflict, if a hostile vessel sought refuge in the national waters of another state it could be pursued and engaged in those waters. In that context the Irish view was that hot pursuit could never relate to a military cross-border incursion. Margaret Thatcher's Attorney General, Sir Michael Havers, was summoned to the meeting and made it clear by a silent signal to the prime minister that the Irish could not concede in any major way on these issues or on the general question of extradition. He was then summarily dismissed by Thatcher.[7]

Lynch at this stage was politically extremely vulnerable. After Mountbatten's funeral rumours began circulating in political and journalistic circles that there had been a stepping up in the security arrangements between North and South, but there was no confirmation from the government of what the changes actually were. A few weeks later Michael Mills revealed in the *Irish Press* that the new security arrangement apparently defined an air corridor of ten kilometres – five kilometres on either side of the border – that could be used by helicopters or light aircraft from the North or South in cases of hot pursuit of suspected terrorists.[8] This was not strictly the case and was instantly denied by government sources, but it set off an intense bout of introspection and loudhailing from those who considered themselves to be on the green wing of Fianna Fáil.

A month earlier, Fianna Fáil's youngest TD, twenty-four-year-old Síle de Valera, a granddaughter of the party's founder, Éamon de Valera, had delivered an inflammatory speech in Cork. Speaking in Lynch's home place, de Valera railed against her Taoiseach and urged him to demonstrate his republican leadership. She opposed what she described as so-called solutions such as a Council of Ireland or devolved government in Northern Ireland. In effect, her argument was that Jack Lynch was not strong enough on the national question and was leading the party away from its traditional aim of seeking a united Ireland, the reason for which her grandfather had founded the party. Her speech was all the more extraordinary because she had been called in by Lynch beforehand and he had told her that it was contrary to government policy, wrong, unhelpful, and untimely.[9] De Valera was in no doubt that her speech was unacceptable to the leader of Fianna Fáil. Yet she felt in no way intimidated by Lynch, who was forced to condemn her speech on the day it was delivered, which meant that both the speech and his criticism of it was front page news in all the newspapers. Lynch only had himself to blame for the breakdown in party discipline. His failure to punish Jim Gibbons the previous year over Haughey's family planning bill had shown that there were no consequences for disobeying the party line. By allowing Gibbons to dissent on an issue of conscience, he essentially allowed any member the leeway to do the same on any issue that they claimed was a matter of conscience. De Valera was simply the first to take advantage of Lynch's casual attitude to his backbenchers and his failure to insist on party discipline when he had the opportunity.

Things soon became worse for Lynch. Following the disclosures in the *Irish Press* about the cross-border air corridor, the backbench Clare TD Bill Loughnane asked the Taoiseach whether there had been any change in such policy. Lynch assured him that there had been no change in the sovereignty exercised by the state over Irish airspace. This was true – the government retained the sovereign right to permit or deny access to Irish airspace – but Lynch did not say whether the Irish were willing to let the British use Irish airspace. The following month, on a trip to the United States, Lynch spoke to the National Press Club in Washington. It was a routine enough affair; Lynch had made many such speeches. But then the *Irish Times*' Seán Cronin, a former IRA chief of staff during the border campaign, asked what new arrangements had been made about over-flying national territory. The history of his questioner would not have been lost on Lynch, but he seemed quite unprepared for the question. He replied that the regulations under the Air Navigation Act remained unchanged, except in one slight respect, and went on to explain the change in the regulations that would have the effect, although Lynch did not phrase it like that, of letting the British enter Irish airspace.[10]

An enterprising *Irish Independent* journalist, Ray Managh, phoned Bill Loughnane to get his opinion on Lynch's comments. Loughnane promptly called Lynch a liar; the Taoiseach, he said, was either lying to his own TDs or to his American hosts. On 12 November the *Irish Independent* led with the headline 'North: Jack Lying Says T.D.'[11] At the bottom of the page was a story by Chris Glennon, who was travelling with the Taoiseach, that many readers might have missed. In it Glennon noted that although they were four thousand miles apart Lynch and Haughey were involved in an argument over the legacy of Pádraig Pearse. On the hundredth anniversary of Pearse's death, Haughey had given a speech in Dublin in which he had said that partition would have been completely inconceivable to Pearse, who had viewed Ireland as one indissoluble nation in every aspect of its emotional, spiritual, intellectual and political life. In response to Haughey's old-style rallying cry of nation and nationhood, Lynch instead insisted that the paradox of Pearse's message to the Irish people was that they should live and work for Ireland, not die and kill for it. In Glennon's interpretation, both Lynch and Haughey, but particularly Haughey, were outlining their views not just on Pearse's legacy but on their own qualifications to lead Fianna Fáil, the party that had always claimed to have special ownership of republican ide-als.[12] Haughey had not known of either Síle de Valera's speech or of Loughnane's accusation against Lynch, but he judged that the time was right to put forward his own republican vision at a time when Lynch was out of the country and considerably weakened.

Glennon began his piece by noting that many people considered Haughey's speech the first round in the Fianna Fáil leadership battle. Lynch's next step would provide Haughey with another opportunity to make known, subtly but decisively, his opposition to the Taoiseach, gaining him yet more significant support from the backbenches, weakening Lynch, and ultimately damaging the Taoiseach's preferred successor, George Colley. When Lynch reached Houston, he phoned Colley, who was nominally in charge of the Fianna Fáil party during the Taoiseach's absence, and they agreed to remove the party whip from Loughnane. Haughey and, ironically, one of his archenemies, Martin O'Donoghue, dissented from the majority view in cabinet that Loughnane should be disciplined.[13] Not for the first or the last time, Lynch and Colley had misread the mood of the parliamentary party, which refused to remove the whip from Loughnane. Various other backbench TDs voiced their opposition to giving the British increased access to Irish airspace. Loughnane withdrew his reported statements calling the Taoiseach a liar and remained in the parliamentary party. It was, however, a resounding defeat for Lynch and indeed for Colley.

Lynch had also been badly damaged by Fianna Fáil's defeat in a by-election in his heartland of Cork City on 7 November, the same day he left for his trip to the United States, when its candidate John Dennehy had lost to Fine Gael's Liam Burke. Fine Gael also won the by-election in Cork North East on the same day. The Cork City defeat was particularly humiliating for Lynch as he had been campaigning in Cork on four successive weekends. Fianna Fáil losing in the Taoiseach's native city, where he was held in something approaching awe, was something that no observer had predicted. Yet a number of shrewd political journalists knew all was not well in Lynch's Fianna Fáil. Michael Mills, of the *Irish Press*, recalled that as he watched Lynch's final rally in Cork City on the eve of the elections, it seemed to him that the Taoiseach's extraordinary personal appeal to voters, which had seen him win the 1977 general election with the biggest majority in the party's history, had lost much of its magnetism. Gone was the old enthusiasm of the crowds, to be replaced by a dull apathy.[14] Lynch received the news of the Cork by-election defeats when he was standing on the White House lawn with President Jimmy Carter. He was clearly shaken by the scale of the defeat in Cork City in particular. In the 1977 election Fianna Fáil had won over 58 per cent of the first preference vote. Now, less than two and a half years later, Dennehy had polled just under 36 per cent. Kevin Healy of RTÉ described Lynch as ashen-faced, very subdued and almost resigned to his fate when they had a one-to-one interview in Boston a few days later. This interview took place just before Loughnane's accusation that Lynch was a liar. When Lynch heard that comment his lethargic resignation turned to fury.[15]

Yet when the Fianna Fáil parliamentary party failed to discipline Loughnane, the lethargy returned. Lynch raised a final attack on the Irish newspapers, saying that he had been misinterpreted and was both surprised and disappointed by the claim that he had revealed details to the media that he had not given to the Dáil.[16]

ELECTION

Lynch flew back to Ireland on the morning of 16 November. He was met in Dublin Airport by Colley, and up to forty other ministers, TDs and senators. The greeting was far more subdued than that of some nine years previously when he returned from the United States in the week of Haughey's acquittal in the arms trial. Haughey did not show up. This was seen by some as an indication of the opening salvo of a leadership challenge to Lynch, but at this stage Haughey had no intention of challenging Lynch for the leadership. He was willing to bide his time, to wait for Lynch to resign and to take his chances against the party elite's preferred candidate, George Colley. As November ended he judged that the contest was very close, but would probably not happen until well into 1980, although some in his inner circle thought it would be January. None of them considered that Lynch would go in December.[17] Lynch told his parliamentary party on Wednesday 5 December that he was stepping down as Taoiseach and leader of Fianna Fáil. The contest to replace him would take place two days later and the new Taoiseach would be installed the following Tuesday. Just two days before his announcement the *Irish Independent* led with a story that Lynch was on the brink of making a decision on his leadership, but if he thought that Haughey would replace him, he would stay until the new year.[18]

On the day before Lynch's announcement, Haughey was engaged in his normal humdrum work as Minister for Health and Social Welfare, and local TD for Dublin Artane. That afternoon he met a three-person delegation from the Coolock Community Law Centre who were looking for a grant of £37,000 from the Department of Justice to continue operating into 1980. The Coolock Community Law Centre was the first such law centre in Ireland and was opened under the auspices of the Free Legal Aid Centre, which had been established in 1969. On 1 April 1975 the Coolock Community Law Centre opened its doors at the Northside Shopping Centre in Coolock. It was originally managed by a full-time solicitor, George Gill, and Máire Bates took over the management of the centre the following year.[19] Operating in the heart of Haughey's constituency, it provided a free legal aid service for those who needed it, but by the end of 1979 it was worried that its funding would cease given the development of the state's own scheme of civic and legal aid; it was anticipated that voluntary bodies would not continue to be assisted. At the meeting on 4 December, Haughey explained to the three members of the community centre, including Bates, that he could do nothing for them in his ministerial capacity because their operation as a law centre came under the functions of the Minister for Justice, but he would make representations on their behalf as a TD for the local area.[20] Given that Haughey had found Bates to be unduly aggressive at a previous meeting, he declined an invitation to appear at a public meeting the centre planned to hold in January 1980.[21] He finished work for the day, still with no idea that Lynch would announce his resignation the following day.

On the day of the parliamentary party meeting, Geraldine Kennedy reported in the *Irish Times* that it was not certain if Lynch would tell the party of his plans but that he was unlikely to step down in the short term. She did point out, though, that if there was a leadership contest anytime soon, Haughey was likely to have thirty-eight votes, with thirty-six for Colley, and eight undecideds.[22] This was remarkably prescient. Kennedy had long considered that Haughey would win a two-way contest against Colley. She recalled a conversation she had with a delighted Haughey in the RDS on the night of the 1977 election. She said to him: 'I don't know what you're so pleased about given that Jack Lynch is going to get a strong overall majority,' and he replied, 'Yes, but they're all my people. Now I know I'll be leader.'[23] Lynch's announcement that he was stepping down and the short time period for the contest was essentially designed to ensure a Colley victory. The then Tánaiste was convinced he had the necessary support, notwithstanding what Kennedy had written about the tight numbers in a two-way contest.

The Haughey–Colley leadership contest of December 1979 pitted the maverick of the cabinet, and the darling of the backbenchers, against the candidate of the party's establishment, and one seen by that establishment as epitomising its traditions. It was the quintessential contest between the outsider with no Fianna Fáil bloodline and the insider whose family was steeped in the party. When it was over, those on the defeated side could not understand how they had lost. They felt that it must have been due to the nefarious tactics of the victor. According to Dermot Keogh, Jack Lynch's most comprehensive biographer, in the autumn of 1979 Haughey had one major tactical advantage: that his opponents felt a Haughey victory was unthinkable. They 'could not conceive of a campaign in which there would be no rules, no boundaries, no depths to which their opponents would not sink to secure victory for their candidate'.[24] There is, however, no description or assessment of what these rules, boundaries or depths were. The then Fine Gael leader, Garret FitzGerald, wrote in his autobiography that several Fine Gael TDs told him that many Fianna Fáil TDs had told them they were being intimidated by people in Haughey's camp and that the ballot to elect the leader would not be conducted in secret. Some deputies claimed that they had been told that unless, as they walked to deposit their votes in the ballot box, they showed them to members of the Haughey camp they would be assumed to have voted for Colley and would subsequently be treated accordingly.[25] It is not clear what 'treated accordingly' means, given that if Haughey had lost he would have had no spoils of office to distribute and very likely no other chance to become leader, certainly not in the short to medium term. In his autobiography, Des O'Malley, one of Colley's chief supporters, and at that stage Minister for Industry and Commerce, writes that he was shocked by the number of people who voted for Haughey on the grounds that by not voting for him he would have smashed the party; O'Malley asserts that this was a 'perversion of democracy'.[26] The irony that both Colley and O'Malley themselves refused to accept the result, or their own tactics in the contest, is not commented upon.

After the fiasco of the failure to remove the whip from Bill Loughnane, Colley went to Lynch and told him that unless he went quickly there was every chance that Colley himself would lose support and that the unthinkable, a Haughey victory, could happen. In the three weeks since his return home in mid-November until he announced his retirement on 5 December, a number of backbenchers were summoned to Lynch's office in Leinster House while Colley was there. At least a dozen more were not contacted at all because the Colley camp assumed that their votes were secure. This was a terrible misjudgement. It was not just Lynch who had no relationship with the backbenchers; the same was true of Colley, O'Malley and Martin O'Donoghue. The fear of giving Haughey more time to build up his support base was what, in essence, led Lynch to announce his resignation so quickly. He was not forced out by Haughey and could have stayed on if he wanted to. The Colley camp ultimately pushed him to go several months early because they felt they were losing ground. Those hectic meetings with backbenchers in late November were a late bid to stave off the tragedy of a Colley defeat. It was too late. The same backbenchers had long since decided it was time for a new direction. The day before the vote, Colley and O'Donoghue made a frantic round of last-minute phone calls from the Taoiseach's office to every minister and minister for state to shore up their support. The tenor of those calls was extremely blunt: stay with Colley or face not being in cabinet. Some of the calls were made right in front of Lynch's deputy private secretary, Seán Aylward.[27] All pretence of Jack Lynch being in any way neutral in the contest to succeed him had been dropped.

Symptomatic of the miscalculation in the Colley camp was its view that it could count on the votes of the Minister for Foreign Affairs, Michael O'Kennedy, and the Minister for State at the Department of Finance, Ray MacSharry. MacSharry had been contacted as early as October by some confidants of Colley who told him they suspected that Lynch would be retiring in the next number of months and they were setting up a team to support Colley. Given that MacSharry was Colley's junior in Finance, they reckoned that they could count on his support. MacSharry rebuffed them, stating that he would not be involved in any leadership contest at this stage given that there was no vacancy, that he had been appointed by Jack Lynch, and that he did not know who the other candidates might be. He later phoned Haughey and told him that he'd better get on his bike if he intended to be leader of Fianna Fáil because Colley already had his team set up and was ready to go. Haughey told him he was talking out of his backside. MacSharry replied that Haughey could think what he liked but that was the situation.[28]

Notwithstanding MacSharry's original refusal to support Colley, the Tánaiste's camp still considered that he would vote for their candidate. In the end, however, like pretty much all the undecideds, he went for Haughey on the grounds that Haughey would be more progressive and would protect Fianna Fail's republicanism. He also considered Colley to be too conservative. By contrast, MacSharry considered Haughey's genuine interest in people would make a real difference. For many, Haughey was interested in the backbenchers, as naturally they were the ones who could make him Taoiseach, but he was also interested in what politics could do for ordinary people.

On the night before the election, Colley invited MacSharry to his office in Leinster House to make a last-ditch attempt to get his vote. Their conversation was short and to the point. Colley asked MacSharry for his vote and MacSharry refused, saying he had decided to vote for Haughey. Just before midnight, Ray Burke and Brian Lenihan came to see MacSharry and asked for his vote for Colley. Once again, he refused and set off to the house he shared with Mark Killilea, Flor Crowley, and Bernard McGlinchey in Harold's Cross.[29] On his way out of Leinster House, Seán Duignan of RTÉ asked MacSharry who was going to propose Haughey for the leadership. MacSharry replied that if Haughey was stuck for someone the following morning he would do it himself. RTÉ duly reported this in its hourly bulletins. At 7 a.m. on the morning of the vote, Haughey rang MacSharry. Close to four decades later, the conversation was still imprinted in MacSharry's mind:

> CJH – Who the fuck said you were proposing me?
> RMacS – Well, if you're having trouble finding someone, I'll do it. How many votes do you have?
> CJH – Fifty-two.
> RMacS – Fifty-two? If you have forty-two you'll be doing well.
> CJH – What the fuck do you mean? I have the votes.
> RMacS – Two of your bankers are supporting Colley.
> CJH – Who?
> RMacS – Lenihan and Burke, your two neighbours. You still have work to do.
> CJH – Fuck. Well if you want to propose me go ahead.[30]

With that Haughey slammed down the phone. Another phone call shortly afterwards, however, put Haughey in a much better mood. The Minister for Foreign Affairs, Michael O'Kennedy, rang him to tell him that he would be voting for him.[31] As was typical, Haughey neither promised him anything for his vote nor even asked him for it. O'Kennedy knew, however, that in deciding to vote for Haughey he was either guaranteeing himself a senior role in Haughey's government or potentially banishing himself to isolation in a Colley government, as had been intimated in the calls from the Taoiseach's office the previous day. Haughey was absolutely ecstatic that O'Kennedy switched to him at the last minute. O'Kennedy was the most prominent defection from the rump of Fianna Fáil Munster deputies who were regarded as most heavily influenced by Lynch, and his decision clearly swayed at least one other deputy from the region. In a tight contest every vote counted. Haughey immediately rang Brendan O'Donnell and told him to spread the word that O'Kennedy was voting for him.[32] He rang Frank Dunlop with a similar message.[33] O'Kennedy was closer to Haughey than Colley on the Northern Ireland question, and while some of the hardcore backbenchers saw him as a late convert, it was a brilliant political judgement call, guaranteeing him a senior ministry, and later the EU commissionership, where, ironically, he was extremely unhappy.

O'Kennedy's decision to vote for Haughey came as a major surprise, particularly to the Colley camp, which considered that it had every vote in the cabinet. O'Kennedy was, however, disconcerted by the phone call he received from Colley. He was also angered by what he considered a very aggressive approach by Colley's chief canvasser, the Minister for Defence, Bobby Molloy, demanding to know which way he was going to vote. O'Kennedy was also bitter about a row he had with Colley the previous year over funding for the Department of Foreign Affairs, in which, he felt, he had been humiliated by his government colleague.[34] His defection to the Haughey camp certainly persuaded a number of undecideds to join him. Among them was a former Minister for Defence, Jerry Cronin, who had replaced Jim Gibbons after Haughey's sacking in 1970, but was not reappointed to cabinet by Lynch in 1977 and seethed for two and a half years before voting for Haughey. Both O'Kennedy and Cronin came under significant pressure again later that morning from Colley's camp to change their vote, but they were not for turning.

Just after 11.15 a.m. on Friday 7 December 1979 in the Fianna Fáil parliamentary room of Leinster House, Des O'Malley proposed George Colley for the leadership of Fianna Fáil and he was seconded by Seán Browne. Ray MacSharry then proposed Haughey, with Jerry Cronin seconding him. No speeches were allowed. Over the next forty minutes the eighty-two TDs voted. When they were finished the votes were counted by the official tellers, Michael Woods and Ben Briscoe. When the counting was finished Woods handed the result to the party chairman, Willie Kenneally from Waterford, a strong Colley supporter. A shocked Kenneally then read out the result; forty-four for Haughey, thirty-eight for Colley. Immediately, Haughey shook hands with both Colley and Lynch. He made a brief speech to the stunned gathering saying there was no animosity between himself and his 'old school pal', ending by telling the deputies, 'You can be sure of one thing; I will give it my very, very best.'[35]

Haughey had genuinely believed that he would win more than fifty votes. He had asked Michael Mills of the *Irish Press* how many votes Mills thought he would get. Mills told him that the estimate of the political correspondents was that he would get forty-five or forty-six. Haughey expressed disappointment as his own estimate put him at more than fifty votes.[36] Haughey had been extremely confident that he had the backbench vote sewn up and, once O'Kennedy declared for him, he was sure he had fifty votes in the bag. He was very much mistaken. MacSharry, who acted as his teller on the day of the count, reckoned he would win by just about reaching the magic number of forty-two that he needed. Haughey's other teller was a young backbencher from Kildare, Charlie McCreevy, who, like many in the party, felt that the country was on its knees and a new visionary leader was needed. A vote for Colley was, for McCreevy and others, a vote for a dreary continuation of the status quo and they were not going to countenance that.[37] McCreevy was unclear how many votes Haughey would get but, like MacSharry, he thought that it was likely he would win just enough to take the leadership. So it proved.

Haughey retired to his office on the first floor of Leinster House to prepare for his live press conference that afternoon. P.J. Mara and

Brendan O'Donnell made brief visits, but otherwise he was alone.[38] It was an apt metaphor. For all the jubilation his victory brought to the backbenchers, and to the grassroots of Fianna Fáil, Haughey essentially remained a solitary figure. At that press conference he was surrounded by the party whips, Michael Woods and Ben Briscoe, and about thirty of his supporters. Right behind him were Síle de Valera and Bill Loughnane, the two TDs who, by their criticism of Lynch, had ensured the contest took place much sooner than Haughey thought it would. Of all the supporters around him, none could be in any way classified as a close friend. In his speech Haughey emphasised that his chief priority was the 'peaceful unification of the people of Ireland', a very unusual but carefully chosen phrase, stressing as it did that unity was about people. He also stated that he had a very clear priority to promote the economic development of the country and to provide the best possible social welfare arrangements for people who needed it. He condemned the IRA, and refused to be drawn on the arms trial, saying that he was leaving it to the historians. He swatted away questions about his wealth with the witty but essentially true response that the questioner had 'a simple false assumption … that I am a wealthy man. I wouldn't necessarily assume that if I was you. Ask my bank manager.'[39] He also declared that George Colley had promised him his full support and loyalty, which was not true. When the press conference ended he made his way home to Abbeville, and that night hosted a party for a large number of friends. There were few politicians in attendance. Both MacSharry and O'Kennedy went home to their constituencies. Burke and Lenihan were not invited.

CABINET

Over the weekend Haughey began putting his cabinet together. He made up his mind early in relation to at least twelve members of the cabinet. O'Kennedy and MacSharry were summoned to Abbeville on the Sunday morning and given the jobs of Finance and Agriculture. In Haughey's private papers there are lists of names jotted in his own handwriting of who he was considering putting in his cabinet. He had decided that, of his opponents, he had to have Colley and O'Malley in the cabinet. Both were simply too senior in the party not to be in government. They would also have been rallying figures for Haughey's opponents in Fianna Fáil if they were not in government. Sacking Colley would have been seen by the party and the wider public as an unprecedented act of political savagery, and it was just not politically feasible. The trouble for Haughey was that he then conceded too much to Colley. He had legitimately won the office of Fianna Fáil leader and Taoiseach. In the context of being the democratically elected leader of the party and the government he undermined himself from the off by giving Colley the power of veto over who could be appointed to the position of Minister for Justice.

Less than two weeks after Haughey's election as leader Colley gave a speech in Baldoyle where he gave, at best, qualified support for Haughey's leadership. Events over the last twelve months, he said, had shown that Jack Lynch had not received full loyalty from a number of deputies and senators, which was both wrong and reprehensible. He maintained that these Fianna Fáil members had broken a core tenet of the party; that every member owed full loyalty and support to the elected leader. He finished his speech with the ambiguous remark that the question now arose for the members of Fianna Fáil who agreed with his analysis to decide what rule one would follow now. His own answer was that the Taoiseach was 'entitled to our conscientious and diligent support in all his efforts in the national interest'.[40] This was about as lukewarm an endorsement a Tánaiste could give to a Taoiseach. Another problem was that when cuts had to be made at the very beginning of Haughey's tenure as Taoiseach, O'Malley in the Department of Industry and Commerce refused to countenance any reduction in the budget of his own department.[41] Haughey could do nothing about it.

While Colley and O'Malley were too powerful in the party to be removed from cabinet, the same could not be said of Gibbons or O'Donoghue. Gibbons had shown in his abstention on Haughey's family planning legislation that he could not be trusted in cabinet. Haughey also had an intense hatred of Gibbons going back to the arms trial. He was cast aside without a thought. Given that O'Donoghue had only been elected a TD at the 1977 election he could be dismissed without rousing the enmity of half the party. Most of the backbenchers elected with him in 1977 had no sense of what he was like, and he was clearly not one of them. His total devotion to Lynch meant that he was entirely expendable. Haughey had never liked the idea of a separate department responsible for economic planning and development and had resolved to be rid of it as soon as he could. O'Donoghue, as its head, was discarded with it.

The other two ministers dropped were Bobby Molloy from Galway and Denis Gallagher from Mayo. Haughey was far more enamoured by Máire Geoghegan-Quinn, the twenty-nine-year-old Minister for State at the Department of Industry, Commerce and Energy, than her constituency colleague, Molloy. He had been impressed with Geoghegan-Quinn since she had entered the Dáil at the by-election in 1975 caused by the death of her father. Her youth and gender would also have the advantage of freshening up his cabinet. Molloy, who had upset O'Kennedy and others in the Haughey camp with his strong-arm tactics during the election, was also expendable. Denis Gallagher was probably the least well-known member of Lynch's cabinet. Haughey had decided to appoint Geoghegan-Quinn to the Gaeltacht portfolio and had no place for Gallagher. His omission was not going to cause any wider ructions in the party. Any worries about geographical bias against the west of Ireland were countered by the fact that MacSharry and Geoghegan-Quinn were from the same region. Three other ministers he considered dropping were Gene Fitzgerald, Gerry Collins and Pádraig Faulkner, but he decided to keep them on, judging that five new cabinet members was enough.

Haughey had to find space for his own supporters. There was not much point in the backbenchers scheming for months to change the leader if their candidate was going to make minimal changes. Haughey had five positions open to him, a full third of the cabinet. MacSharry's public support meant that he had to be in cabinet. Geoghegan-Quinn was a natural second. After considering various options he finally settled on Paddy Power from Kildare, his fellow northside Dubliner Michael Woods, and the Longford entrepreneur Albert Reynolds. After dropping O'Donoghue he wanted to keep a Dubliner at the cabinet table and chose Lynch's chief whip over Bertie Ahern and Ray Burke. Judging by Haughey's cabinet jottings, Albert Reynolds was the last to be included. In various iterations of Haughey's thinking, the other four members of the gang of five, Fahey, Killilea, McEllistrim and Doherty are all mentioned. Of the four dropped ministers only Bobby Molloy is considered as a possibility in Haughey's notes.[42] Others thought worthy of inclusion were Charlie McCreevy, Bertie Ahern, Ray Burke and Pádraig Flynn, all of whom would later play significant roles in Haughey's various periods in power.

On the morning that he was to be elected Taoiseach, Haughey summoned various TDs to his office to tell them that they were going to be either in or out of his cabinet. At 10.50, Haughey told Albert Reynolds, one of the gang of five, that he was to be the new Minister for Posts and Telegraphs. He was the last to be told he was in the new cabinet. Máire Geoghegan-Quinn had been summoned by Haughey earlier that morning to his office on the fifth floor of Leinster House. Haughey, on his own, and normally so formal, was more laid-back than she had ever seen him before, with his hands behind his back and his feet on the desk. He offered her tea from what she later described as a beautiful silver tray and pot and then said: 'Máire, I think you and I are going to make history. I want you to be in cabinet.' Although the weekend's newspapers had speculated that she would be appointed to cabinet, Geoghegan-Quinn had told her husband, John, on the way to Leinster House that she did not think she would be offered a position. Haughey had caught her somewhat off guard and in a moment she always regretted, she replied, 'Do you think I'm good enough?' Haughey's feet immediately came off the table. He stood up rigidly and said, 'Do you think I would have offered you the position if you weren't?' He then offered her the position of Minister for the Gaeltacht, told her she could tell her husband and mother, and summarily dismissed her saying, 'Walk out there now like you got bad news.'[43] Just over five months earlier, after the birth of her second child, he had told her not to worry about the Dáil session to come and assured her he would personally answer all her questions and put through any legislation she had if it was necessary.[44] At that time, TDs had no right to statutory maternity leave; and Geoghegan-Quinn had decided to breast-feed her child, which, she told him, 'may cause some problems in the next Dáil session but with a little patience and understanding on everyone's part I'm sure I can overcome the problems'.[45] Haughey felt the same about her problem-solving abilities and made her Ireland's first female minister since the appointment of Countess Markievicz in the first Dáil of 1919.

PEDIGREE

The day Haughey had longed for all his adult life began early, as it always did at Abbeville. Haughey rose before 6 a.m. He walked the grounds of his estate before having his normal spartan breakfast and readying himself for the day. The postman came early, bearing a deluge of congratulatory mail. His driver, Max Webster, collected him and drove him into Leinster House. His family followed him some hours later. His brother Eoghan collected their mother and drove her in. She had bought a new hat for the day.[46] Sarah Haughey's proudest day was, however, soon to be marred by the vehemence of the attacks on her son by his political opponents. The speeches from the opposition that greeted Haughey's nomination as Taoiseach were among the most aggressive seen in Dáil Éireann since its foundation. In opposing Haughey, the Fine Gael leader, Garret FitzGerald, quite early in his speech, famously said that Haughey 'presents himself here, seeking to be invested in office as the seventh in this line, but he comes with a flawed pedigree'.[47] FitzGerald's point, he insisted ever afterwards, was that all previous holders of the office had the full confidence of their own parties and indeed a degree of respect from their opponents in the Dáil. That confidence did not exist when it came to Haughey, who, he claimed, did not have the support of almost three-quarters of the Dáil; it was in that respect, he said, that Haughey's pedigree was flawed. He blamed the use of the phrase on the late hour at which he had drafted his speech the night before.[48]

Up in the VIP gallery, Sarah and Eoghan Haughey bristled with shock and indignation. What right did Garret FitzGerald, a man brought up in privilege, have to cast aspersions on their son and brother? Charles Haughey had earlier warned his mother that she should expect that he would be subject to what he described as predictable attacks, but none of the Haugheys was prepared for FitzGerald's particular line of assault.[49] As Martin Mansergh, later to become one of Haughey's most trusted advisers, pointed out, the word 'pedigree' reeked of social snobbery.[50] What made it even worse was that it came from a man who had had a private education and every advantage that the Irish social class system could give. FitzGerald would never have used such a word about George Colley, if Colley had achieved just four more votes and won the Fianna Fáil leadership election, even though half of his own party would have voted against him. He also would never have expected such a word to be used against himself, except perhaps to indicate in a positive way his own social standing. The phrase rankled with Haughey on the day and was one he never forgave FitzGerald for using, primarily because it had been made in front of his mother, a woman who, with virtually nothing, had raised a son who had risen to the office of Taoiseach. A son who, she was aware, had flaws, like all sons, but a son who nevertheless had overcome a childhood of deprivation to become Taoiseach. The good of that historic achievement had been taken away from her by a man with no conception of what it was like to be poor, and to have struggled the way she did when she was raising her seven children in Donnycarney. Haughey seethed with resentment against FitzGerald through all their battles over the course of the next seven years.[51] There was more to their dislike of each other than the 'flawed pedigree' remark, but to Haughey, FitzGerald had crossed a line.

For six hours, Haughey listened to attacks on his character from the opposition. Noël Browne told the Dáil that in his own nightmare Haughey was a dreadful cross between Richard Nixon and the Portuguese dictator António Salazar. He basically accused Haughey of being a quasi-dictator by asking whether, when Haughey found himself faced with defeat in the Dáil, he would obey the words of the Chair and relinquish his position. The leader of the Labour Party, Frank Cluskey, implored Fianna Fáil deputies not to vote for a man who they knew better than him was 'totally unfit for that position'. Fine Gael's John Kelly told the Dáil that it would be well for the *Irish Times* to bear in mind that 'this is Dáil Éireann not the Reichstag' after the paper's editorial that morning had counselled the opposition to treat the motion with reserve and play it down. Kelly insisted that he would not play it down; the Dáil was about to elect a man who since his ascension to the leadership of Fianna Fáil the previous Friday had generated a depth of dismay, consternation and fear in hundreds of thousands of Irish people.[52]

At 5.06 p.m. Haughey replaced Jack Lynch as Taoiseach, the man who had sacked him from office over nine and a half years earlier and who Haughey had long suspected was the cause of his trial for conspiracy to illegally import arms. He then went to Áras an Uachtaráin to receive his seal of office from President Patrick Hillery before returning to the Dáil to unveil his ministerial team. He had a very quick briefing with the secretary of the Department of the Taoiseach, Dan O'Sullivan, and told him he wanted all the offices from Economic Planning and Development to be reassigned to the Taoiseach's office. When O'Sullivan asked what they should do with the civil servants who worked there, he said to send them all back to Finance. When O'Sullivan said that not all of them came originally from Finance, Haughey harrumphed and said they would sort it in the next few weeks. O'Sullivan then went to see Noel Whelan, the young secretary of that department, and said 'He's like a roaring lion with a mission but doesn't know what to do with you yet.'[53]

After the Dáil rose for the night Haughey returned home to Abbeville where a select group of friends and family met him to celebrate his historic achievement. One of them was the merchant banker Patrick Gallagher. Haughey's announcement as Taoiseach had reached the Gulf States and the Middle East where it was announced on the news that 'Today millionaire Charles Haughey was elected Prime Minister of the Republic of Ireland.'[54] The truth was that Haughey owed AIB over £1 million when he was elected Taoiseach. At the gathering in Abbeville to celebrate his election, Gallagher told Haughey he would give him a third of the money.[55] Like all of Haughey's benefactors he knew the money he gave came with no conditions.

Haughey had an uncanny ability to compartmentalise the various facets of his public and private lives. Within a month of becoming

Taoiseach he would go on television to tell the country it was living beyond its means, notwithstanding the fact that he was in serious, eye-watering debt. When he was introducing family planning legislation for married couples, he was involved in an extramarital affair. While Haughey would often claim that his entire life bound up in politics, the reality was that he had an unparalleled ability to divorce his private life from his political decisions. When the revelations about his financial and private lives became public two decades later, he was widely reviled as a byword for hypocrisy. Yet in real time Haughey never saw it that way. Politically, he made decisions that he thought would work. There were times when he would have liked to have gone further but was restrained by various factors including opinion within Fianna Fáil and indeed among the public at large. That was the public Haughey and it was a persona that was far removed from the private Haughey. The great advantage the public Haughey held was that he was able to keep the private Haughey out of his decision-making on public policy. The private Haughey would, however, go on to haunt the public Haughey in the aftermath of the Taoiseach years, when his secret life was revealed.

Haughey's four children were not among those in Abbeville that night. They had stayed in the city centre after the ending of the Dáil proceedings and went to Peter's Pub, just off St Stephen's Green, to celebrate with their friends. Haughey had given them just one piece of advice earlier in the day: 'Whatever you do, don't get arrested.'[56] Haughey's own party was a much more subdued affair than the one he had held the previous Friday night. He had to be up early the following morning. There was work to be done.

On the day after his election Haughey again woke early, walked at home, ate breakfast and arrived at Government Buildings at 9 a.m., where he was met by Lynch's deputy private secretary, Seán Aylward. Aylward had been told to expect him at 10 a.m. but decided he would be ready earlier given Haughey's own legendary reputation for punctuality, and he had been waiting outside Government Buildings since half past eight. On being shown around the building, Haughey said to Aylward, 'It's very quiet here, isn't it? A right sleepy hollow.'[57] That would change. Later that day Haughey took on as his private secretary Seán O'Riordan, who had been recommended to him by the Department of the Taoiseach, as the senior assistant principal officer in the department. Early the following year O'Riordan moved on to the administrative side of the department when he was promoted to principal officer. Aylward was Haughey's personal choice to take over the private secretary role; by then a rapport of sorts had been struck between this still relatively junior staffer and the Taoiseach. Aylward retained the role of private secretary for the remainder of Haughey's first two terms as Taoiseach. He was described by Frank Dunlop as being the ideal private secretary for Haughey. He did not suffer fools gladly and had an innate ability to second-guess Haughey. He was very protective of who was allowed to see or talk to the Taoiseach when he was in his office.[58] For the two periods Haughey was in office, Aylward had almost continuous access to him, and Haughey trusted him implicitly.

As Declan Kiberd has suggested, the almost moralistic language used about Haughey in the debate on his election as Taoiseach conditioned the sense he had of himself as an outsider.[59] He was not the only child of poverty to make it to the Dáil, but the language of condemnation that he faced on that day had never been used so venomously about any other member. The criticism of Haughey triggered another voluminous postbag. As the congratulatory letters on his appointment as Taoiseach continued to flood in to both Government Buildings and Abbeville, a large amount of correspondence complained about the attacks on him. Vincent Browne, in his letter seeking an interview with Haughey, ended his request by stating that he was 'delighted for yourself, for the country and the wild men on the backbenches who put you there ... PS I thought Garret's behaviour was disgraceful but from your point of view it's just as well to get these matters out of the way and let you get on with things.'[60]

There was outrage from the Fianna Fáil grassroots, but many of Haughey's correspondents were not rabid Fianna Fáil republicans. One told him that he felt 'less a grass roots, and more a noxious weed roots, supporter of the Fine Gael party' and complimented him for his disdainful yet dignified treatment of the attack, which was utterly admirable.[61]

Another stated that her political philosophy was opposed to Fianna Fáil, and she was not a republican, but was 'appalled and ashamed at the virulence of your attackers in the Dáil yesterday. Every man has the right to show what he can do before the vultures descend.'[62] The congratulatory messages, however, outweighed anything else. Some of the letters were simple and some pages in length. They came from all corners of the world, from rich and poor, the famous and unknown, from the worlds of arts and sport, and from both the political world and the plain people of Ireland. Aidan Lehane, the President of Blackrock College, de Valera's alma mater, told him that another former president of the college, John Charles McQuaid, had said twice in the months leading up to his death that 'Charlie Haughey will be Taoiseach. He was the most competent minister I ever dealt with.'[63]

The American author Gore Vidal, who a decade earlier had sought Haughey's help in inquiring how to gain Irish citizenship, telegrammed to say he could not be more delighted: 'Finally, in life as in drama, the best man wins.'[64] He then sent Haughey a personally inscribed volume of his works. The spy novelist Len Deighton, who had availed of Haughey's artists' tax exemption scheme was another writer who routinely sent him inscribed copies of his books. A telegram from the art collector Garech Browne, misquoting Dickens, expressed delight: 'Great Expectation. Miss Haversham [sic] says good news is rare. I agree with her.'[65] The Irish actress and producer Phyllis Ryan complained that the country had become a 'depressed version of the "Non-Workers Paradise"' but his election had given it renewed hope.[66] From a porter in Mallow County Hospital came the simple but profound message of congratulations and best wishes 'from one horseman to another'.[67] There were thousands of other messages of goodwill.

On the last day of 1979 Jack Lynch wrote to Haughey to say that he did not wish for 'any function to be held or any presentation to be made to me', saying it would be entirely inappropriate for the party to make such a presentation in the circumstances, which he did not specify.[68] He had heard from Seán Browne, who himself had seconded Colley in the leadership election, that his successor as Taoiseach was planning some sort of function. The man Lynch hoped would succeed him, George Colley, had suggested at the meeting of 5 December, at which Lynch had announced that he would be stepping down, that such a presentation be made. This was greeted with widespread acclaim, and it was widely accepted across the parliamentary party that such a presentation would happen, no matter who succeeded Lynch. The result changed Lynch's attitude. There could be nothing inappropriate about Lynch being thanked by the party, and he well knew this to be the case. Given his long service to the party, it would have been entirely fitting, and Haughey also knew this. Haughey's victory was what made Lynch go quietly. He had made his mark on Irish politics, and after Haughey's victory he was happy to leave it behind. He simply did not want Haughey presenting him with any gift at a function. His decision, however, denied Haughey any opportunity to stress that there was continuity within Fianna Fáil. Haughey was, in fact, quite willing to acknowledge Lynch's contribution to the party. Lynch spurned the opportunity but stayed in the background, supporting the deposed old guard of Colley, O'Malley, and O'Donoghue.

Lynch's refusal to accept any form of official farewell, however, exacerbated the trenchantly held opinion of his supporters that he had been cruelly treated by Haughey. His shadow would stalk the party for some considerable time as many within it thought that his successor had somehow forced him from office. Some of them had difficulty accepting the result. More never did. It was summed up by the attitude of the chairman of the parliamentary party, Willie Kenneally. In the great vaulted front lobby of Leinster House one morning in March 1980 Frank Cluskey, the Labour leader, told Kenneally that his Taoiseach was at that moment speaking in the Dáil chamber, and he should probably go in and support him. Kenneally looked at Cluskey and replied: 'He's not my fucking Taoiseach, and well he knows it.'[69] That refusal by some in the party to consider Haughey the legitimate leader of Fianna Fáil would traumatise his leadership and haunt him for the rest of his public career.

Haughey would go on to make plenty of mistakes as Taoiseach, and indeed as leader of the Fianna Fáil party. He was, however, severely constricted by the deep divisions within his party; divisions that would not heal until his third election as Taoiseach in 1987. Even then, the unity of the party would only last for just over two years until coalition with Des O'Malley and his band of apostates in the Progressive Democrats opened up yet more divisions. Yet when Haughey had his first cabinet meeting on Thursday 13 December 1979, he had high hopes that his administration would reshape Ireland's politics, society and economy into the 1980s. He was to be sorely disappointed. He arrived into the cabinet room in Government Buildings five minutes early. He was the first to arrive. By 10.30, when the meeting was due to begin, he was still on his own. The five newcomers came in together just after the scheduled starting time. Haughey began to drum the table with his fingers. The rest of the cabinet arrived over the next quarter of an hour. Haughey kept drumming until everyone was in place. He was used to the laid-back style of Jack Lynch's cabinets but was determined to set down a different marker. He was coldly resolute as he told his cabinet that meetings would start at exactly at 10.30 a.m., and end at 12.45 p.m., and anyone who was not on time should not bother coming at all.[70] The tone was set.

CHAPTER 15

TAOISEACH

THE REALITY OF OFFICE

Haughey's first order to Seán Aylward when he became Taoiseach was that he wanted a set of battery-driven brass carriage clocks for the desk and side tables in the Taoiseach's office both in Government Buildings and at Leinster House, so that he could check the time whether seated at his desk or at the head of the conference table.[1] Haughey never wore a watch but was obsessed with punctuality and timekeeping. For his whole working life, Haughey seemed to be a man always racing against the clock. He hated time-wasters and had no interest in small talk. He was generally interested in people when he was out of the office, but in the office he talked nothing but business. He wanted solutions, not excuses. All his private secretaries quickly learned how to keep the time-wasters away because they ruined Haughey's temper for the day.[2] The next major purchase for the new Taoiseach was a Burco boiler. His private secretarial team had swiftly burned out three electric kettles making Haughey endless pots of tea. While Haughey was a fussy eater, due to his constant kidney problems, tea was his staple drink during the day. He drank it black, strong, and in copious amounts.

Haughey's first few weeks involved a hectic round of civil service briefings on the economy, Northern Ireland, and planning initiatives in various departments. There were constant demands from home and abroad to get the first sit-down interview with the new Taoiseach. The BBC even contacted him seeking clarification on how to pronounce his name: was it 'hochi' (o as in hot; -ch as in Scottish loch) or 'hawchi' (aw as in law)? An exasperated civil servant, Seán O'Riordan, replied saying it would be better if the BBC rang him so he could give them the correct pronunciation.[3]

One of Haughey's first actions was to restructure the staffing in his own department. Having abolished the Department of Economic Planning and Development, he now had to decide what to do with the civil servants who staffed it. He eventually integrated its economic and social policy functions into his own department. Noel Whelan, after spending three weeks in civil service limbo, was ultimately appointed deputy secretary in the Department of the Taoiseach on 1 January 1980. When appointing Whelan to this position Haughey set out his views on how he worked with his senior civil servants. He told Whelan he was very demanding of public servants and civil servants, but only so that he could get the best out of people who worked for him, and with him, and he was thus willing to be equally demanding of himself. He demanded and expected results from his civil servants and himself. Then, narrowing his eyes, he said, 'I may be rough and demanding of public servants and civil servants, but I'm never ruthless. I'm ruthless with my political enemies because I have to be to survive but I'm never ever ruthless with public servants and civil servants.'[4] It was a revealing insight into his working method. He could be extremely dismissive of his political colleagues but, while he was demanding of his civil servants, and could be sharp with them if he thought they were not coming to the point quickly enough, he was never dismissive of them or rude to them. The same could not be said of his attitude to his political colleagues.

Six other civil servants – an assistant secretary, Pádraig Ó hUig-inn, and five principal officers – were also transferred to the Taoiseach's department. Over the following decade Ó hUiginn was to become

Haughey's chief economic adviser, and would play a crucial role in driving various public policies to completion, all with Haughey's imprimatur. By Haughey's third government in 1987 he was one of the most influential people in the country, and certainly had the most impact of any civil servant since T.K. Whitaker. Dan O'Sullivan retired as secretary of the Department of the Taoiseach in late June 1980, and on 2 July Haughey split O'Sullivan's functions into two by appointing Whelan secretary of the department, and Dermot Nally (the other deputy secretary in the department) secretary to the government. This was unheard of in the civil service and came as a surprise to most insiders, who expected Nally to simply replace O'Sullivan. There had been speculation that Haughey distrusted Nally as he was seen as having been close to Lynch, and to Liam Cosgrave before him.

One of Haughey's closest confidants, Pádraig Ó hAnnracháin, was believed to be particularly suspicious of the close relationship between Nally and Lynch.[5] In his first day on the job Haughey issued orders that Ó hAnnracháin be moved from the Department of Education to the Taoiseach's department and be given the title of deputy secretary. Ó hAnnracháin had been a Haughey loyalist since the mid-1960s and his duties in his new position seemed to consist of being the Taoiseach's point man in government with a brief to watch out for potential trouble. He certainly had no policy brief. While the decision to make Whelan and Nally co-equal secretaries worked relatively well in that they had discrete responsibilities, Haughey quickly wearied of Whelan's detailed style of presenting various options for dealing with policy difficulties. He came to prefer the solution-oriented, though often not overly in-depth, style of Pádraig Ó hUiginn. He also grew to trust Dermot Nally as a shrewd provider of dispassionate advice and came to rely on him as a highly valued repository of ideas and information. One of the first things Haughey asked Nally to do was to bring him the documents relating to the Lynch–Thatcher meeting that followed Mountbatten's funeral. On reading them he broke out in sardonic laughter. A major part of Haughey's attraction to the Fianna Fáil backbenches was that he would be stronger than Lynch on the national question, with the overflight issue being brandished as proof. Haughey laughed when he saw how little there actually was in it.[6] He must have remained puzzled as to why Lynch had found himself in so much trouble over a relatively minor modification of border overflights; one that would never have allowed any infringement of Irish sovereignty. The overflights issues had been the focus of a series of parliamentary questions by the Labour leader, Frank Cluskey, not because he was a rabid republican, but because he shrewdly knew that this was the best way of unsettling Fianna Fáil generally.[7] He certainly succeeded in that aim.

On the night of the 1977 election, when Haughey told Geraldine Kennedy he would be Taoiseach, he promised her that when it happened she would get his first face-to-face interview. Once he became Taoiseach, Kennedy came calling for that interview. Haughey had retained Lynch's press secretary, Frank Dunlop. Dunlop told Kennedy that while Haughey was glad to grant her an interview he could not give her the exclusive first interview as she was too junior and it would annoy the other political correspondents. Kennedy was very unimpressed. She was invited to meet Dunlop and Haughey in the Taoiseach's office to discuss a possible interview at some undisclosed future date. She bluntly told Haughey that if he went back on his word to give her the exclusive first interview, it would be proof that all those who called him a liar were right all along. Haughey, as Kennedy recounted some four decades later, went ballistic, accusing her of unprofessionalism. When he calmed down he eventually agreed to do the interview, but when she said she would have to ask him about the arms crisis he again lost his temper and said he would not answer any questions on 'that arms business'. She replied that she would have to ask them but he did not have to answer.[8]

Like Kevin Healy's interview for the *This Week* programme at the February 1980 Fianna Fáil Ard Fheis, any mention of the events of close to a decade earlier were off limits for Haughey. Kennedy eventually met Haughey for that sit-down interview in mid-January but reckoned afterwards it was one of the worst of her long career. Haughey had recently given his state of the nation broadcast on RTÉ. He had told the public that the situation he had to describe to them was not a cheerful one, that the country was living way beyond its means, and that the state's excessive rate of borrowing could not continue.[9] His address had to a certain extent robbed Kennedy of any exclusive. Now in his interview with her, the normally verbose Haughey was quiet, introspective and had something of a haunted look. It was as if the tumultuous journey back from the dark days of the arms trial to become Taoiseach had left a man who did not know what to do with the power he now had. The overriding aim of becoming Taoiseach had been so all-consuming that he appeared to Kennedy unsure of what to do when he finally assumed that great office. The man of great charisma, great ability, great ideas was spooked by the economic mess he had inherited, and the reality that his party, hopelessly split over his own leadership, would not unite behind him in the hard decisions that had to be taken. Kennedy formed the impression that, notwithstanding what Haughey had said in his RTÉ broadcast, and that he knew what needed to be done, he would not be able to do it.[10] The reasons were twofold. First, there was his own economic philosophy. Second, there was the divided party.

THE DECADE OF ENDEAVOUR

In February 1980, Haughey spoke to his first Fianna Fáil Ard Fheis as leader on the theme of making the 1980s the decade of endeavour. Over the previous weeks his team had coined a number of potential slogans including the rather anodyne 'Into the Eighties with Fianna Fáil', and 'Fianna Fáil – The Party of Progress'. They settled on using the phrase 'Decade of', but could not decide what the decade would actually stand for. Various iterations were tried: of Development; of Decision; with a Difference under Fianna Fáil; of Recovery under Fianna Fáil; of Distinction; of Drive; of Determination; of Dynamism; of Progress. Haughey finally settled on the Decade of Endeavour.[11] To the dismay of some in the trade union movement, he was piped into the auditorium by the ITGWU band playing 'A Nation Once Again'.[12] The Labour TD, and ITGWU member, John Horgan later wrote to the union's general secretary Michael Mullen to enquire why the union band had performed what seemed a pretty nakedly political act. He received the sardonic reply: 'They were paid.'[13]

Haughey began his speech by paying tribute to his predecessors, de Valera, Lemass and Lynch. Contrary to the received wisdom that Haughey immediately erased Lynch from the party's history, he stated that Lynch had brought the party and country through difficult times with patience and wisdom, with personal qualities that endeared him to the entire nation in a way rarely achieved by political leaders.[14] While there was wild enthusiasm in the RDS for his leadership, the cabal of those who opposed him remained large and significant. Their fears about his leadership, and what they considered to be his narcissism, were copperfastened when, as he arrived on stage, his most fervent supporters in the front rows of the audience held up icons and portraits of Haughey. Their actions were mirrored by the enormous picture of Haughey that served as the backdrop to the stage, with Des O'Malley saying he had never seen anything like it, and that it foreshadowed a worrying merging of the party with a leader who would brook no dissent.[15]

Haughey's speech continued with the themes of Northern Ireland and economic progress that he had mentioned in his press conference after winning the Fianna Fáil leadership. His rhetoric on Northern Ireland was particularly strong. He argued that Northern Ireland was a failed political entity, that a new beginning was needed, and that the issue had to be raised to another plane by the two sovereign governments involved. This was sure to rankle with the unionist community, who believed that the Irish government should have no involvement in a state that it had nothing to do with. Given his arms trial past, they also viewed Haughey as the ultimate southern bogeyman. The other major plank of Haughey's speech was devoted to the economy. He asserted that Ireland could only maintain its place in the world if the state mobilised all its resources and utilised them to the full. In that context, he told the enraptured crowd that in 'the boardroom, on the factory floor, on the farm, in the public service, and in state companies a new sense of commitment to the job is required.'[16] To achieve economic progress and social stability, he knew he would need industrial peace and would have to develop harmonious relations with the various sectional interest groups of trade unions, farmers and business organisations. This was much easier said than done.

Haughey had strong links with both the trade unions and business communities, but many farmers had distrusted him since the bitter days of the strike of 1966. He had, however, long cultivated relations both with business and union leaders and was not averse to using them in situations which were not in his direct line of responsibility. When he was Minister for Health and Social Welfare he used his ministerial position to intervene in, and ultimately resolve, a nationwide postal strike, although as minister he was responsible for neither the postal service nor industrial relations. The strike by the Irish Post Office Workers' Union, which lasted for eighteen weeks from February to June 1979, was eventually settled for a modest pay increase, much less than the 30 per cent originally sought. Haughey mediated a solution with his old friend Michael Mullen of the ITGWU, who, while his own union was not involved in the dispute, had influence with a range of Dublin trade unionists.[17] In his memoir, Des O'Malley complained that when the postal workers went on strike Haughey ensured that they were paid social welfare immediately, maintaining that this was a move intended not merely to ease the burden on the strikers.[18] Thirty-five years after the resolution of the strike, Stephen Collins revealed in the *Irish Times* that striking postal workers had their bar bills paid by Haughey.[19] According to Collins, a copy of the cheque, drawn on Haughey's account, and used to settle the bill, was given by a senior garda, who was concerned that Haughey was attempting to sabotage the policy of his own government, to the Department of Justice, although no account is given of how the unnamed garda got hold of the cheque in the first place. Yet the idea of Haughey sabotaging his own government makes no sense. If Haughey had wanted to do this, he would not have involved himself at all in the strike. The idea that Haughey agreed to pay for strikers' meals and drink in an effort to prolong the strike is equally absurd. Some militant Irish trade unionists were used to long strikes and were hardly going to be manipulated into extending this strike by having soup and sandwiches paid for by a government minister. It is also not clear how much Haughey actually contributed to what was in effect a strikers' fund. The reality was that Haughey was able, through Mullen, to secure an agreement to end the strike and he had received agreement for his discussions with Mullen from his cabinet colleagues, including O'Malley. No matter how unconventional this approach was, the problem was at least solved and it demonstrated Haughey's ability to get things done. It also gave a firm clue as to the action on industrial relations he would take as Taoiseach.

Haughey's links to both the trade union movement and the business community served to act as a kind of bulwark to the weakness of his political position. He met the Irish Congress of Trade Unions (ICTU) in January 1970 to assure them of his full commitment to the National Understanding for Economic and Social Development, as long as pay discipline was maintained. He also asserted that he would develop a policy of tripartism with the unions and employers beyond what all parties agreed was the uncoordinated approach of the last Lynch government. He contrasted his approach with what was happening in Britain under Margaret Thatcher, who had made no secret that one of her main economic aims was to break trade union power. Instead, Haughey proposed to combat the deterioration of the economic situation by combining prudent fiscal management with industrial expansion. In that context he urged ICTU to think in terms of a growth formula as distinct from what he considered to be sterile employment targets. At his first Ard Fheis as leader, Haughey stated that there was a better way to manage the economy and he wanted to develop the National Understanding into a new type of partnership between workers, employers, and government which could show the outside world that the Irish state had at last found the way to handle a difficult, complex, but vitally important aspect of national life.[20]

The trouble for Haughey, however, was there was a massive and growing gap between what the state was producing, and taking in from taxation, with what it was spending. Within six months of his doomsday address about the state of the economy, Haughey received a missive from the Department of Finance which left no doubt as to the perilous state of the economy. Maurice Doyle, the deputy secretary of the Department of Finance, whom he had known since the early 1960s, told him that Ireland's public spending was out of control and the country was between stages one and two of a potential six stages of economic disintegration. Stage one was where a government's freedom of manoeuvre was lost and the rapid rate of foreign indebtedness destroyed freedom of action in monetary policy. High interest rates had to be maintained, while business and industry had to be encouraged to raise loans abroad. Stage two was where international respect and influence was lost. In stages three and four it became difficult to borrow commercially, assistance had to be sought from international agencies like the IMF or the EEC, and a reform programme approved by the political authorities governing the international agency had to be adopted and followed. Finally, in stages five and six, creditors would form a consortium to insist on a scheme of net repayment of debts at the expense not only of external reserves, but of a marked deterioration of living standards. Ultimately the welfare state and political stability disintegrated. Doyle cautioned him that nobody should imagine 'it can't happen here' in a country where all government expenditure was financed at the margin by foreign borrowing.[21]

In the decade since 1970, government borrowing had grown from 5–6 per cent of gross national product (GNP) to 13.7 per cent. This was in the context of two decades of public expenditure which, in Doyle's words, had been large, continuous and accelerating. Taking 1960 as an index of 100, GNP in 1980 would be approximately 1,300, while current public expenditure was 2,500 and the public capital programme was 2,250. In two decades, public expenditure had risen from just under 30 per cent of GNP to 55 per cent. Haughey was warned that overconsumption in the economy was encouraged by government policies, which actually fostered it, and was further fuelled by government expenditure, which in itself was being financed by foreign borrowing at an unsustainable rate. All this was happening when the government seemed happy to contemplate overruns on public expenditure, was taking on new commitments, and was succumbing too easily to pressures from 'every lame duck and pressure group in the country'. Doyle ended his grim description of the country's finances by citing the haunting words of the great French political scientist Alexis de Tocqueville that democracy was the best form of government because one could always rely on democratic governments taking the right decisions after they had exhausted every other possibility.[22]

The difficulty was that Haughey remained an instinctive Keynesian. Although he had had no input into the 1977 manifesto, and considered some of its public spending promises ludicrous, he believed in the power of the state to transform people's lives. The election of Margaret Thatcher in Britain in May 1979 and Ronald Reagan in the United States in November 1980 ushered in a decade of neoliberal economics and a rolling back of the state in many western democracies. At its core was a belief that, above all, inflation had to be defeated. Haughey was at best sceptical about this approach. In March 1981 the industrialist Colm Barnes wrote to him recalling that when the leadership battle was under way he had been hoping Haughey would win for he believed he had the steel for the Northern issue and the courage to fight excessive inflation. He told Haughey that he was doing well on the North but was shocked to hear him recently, at a meeting with the Confederation of Irish Industry (CII), express a defeatist attitude towards excessive inflation. Barnes reminded Haughey that during his period as Minister for Finance he had denounced inflation 'with all its works and pomps. It was a cancer then and a bigger one now.'[23] Haughey replied that he was 'not defeatist about inflation. I am afraid, however, I do not award it the same absolute priority over economic development and jobs as is fashionable in other countries at present.'[24] He reminded Barnes that the objective of the meeting with the CII was to discuss what practical steps they could come up with to improve output, productivity and competitiveness. Instead, Haughey was concerned that the CII was preoccupied with inflation and there were enough economists and commentators lecturing him about that already. In his memorandum Maurice Doyle had warned Haughey that under no circumstances should any settlement on the National Understanding be bought by commitments to job creation in the public sector, which he considered to be a most unfortunate and misleading phrase; neither should there be any commitment to higher government outlays in 1980 or 1981.

WOUNDS

Haughey's attempts to get to grips with the economic situation were continually hampered by the divisions in Fianna Fáil. In the same month as Doyle's grim prognosis about the state of the economy, he had to go to Waterford to try to resolve an internal dispute over who would replace Jackie Fahey, one of the original gang of five, on Waterford County Council. Haughey had appointed Fahey to the position of Minister for State in the Department of the Environment and Fahey's son had been proposed to succeed him on the council, which brought a ferocious reaction from Fahey's opponents in the party. When his son eventually withdrew from the contest to succeed him, Fahey claimed he was the victim of a vendetta. This led the *Irish Times* in an editorial to accurately state that the wounds of the December leadership contest had not been healed by time but were as sore and raw as ever. It argued that the incident painted a picture of a Taoiseach less in control of his cabinet than Lynch had been before the arms crisis a decade before and there were no signs that Haughey was either in control of his cabinet or knew where he was going.[25]

A month earlier Haughey had been involved in a dispute with his old adversary from the arms trial, Jim Gibbons, when remarks Gibbons had made allegedly purporting to be about Haughey appeared in the *Kilkenny People* newspaper. Gibbons had been a significant dissident voice on government proposals to tax farmers throughout 1980 but went much further in the interview with his local paper. He was quoted as saying that there was 'a great need for leadership from someone universally looked up to and respected. That person must himself be a man of the highest character, and not merely motivated by political gain or personal ambition. The tuppence ha'penny politician is no good to the country.'[26] Haughey summoned him to a meeting a number of days later, after which Gibbons issued a statement stating that he was simply reiterating his own long-held and well-known personal views and that his remarks were not intended as a personal attack on the Taoiseach. Insofar as his remarks could be construed as such, he withdrew any such implication. Haughey issued his own statement saying that Gibbons had given him his unequivocal assurance that his reported views were not intended as a criticism of the Taoiseach personally, or of his leadership of the party and government, but were of a general nature that were not related to any existing situation. He also stated that Gibbons had given him a guarantee of his loyalty and support as Taoiseach and leader of the party and government for its work in the national interest.[27] Gibbons had told the *Kilkenny People* after his meeting with Haughey that there was no question of retracting any statements he had made in his original interview.[28] Notwithstanding Haughey's statement, the damage had been done. His leadership and personal qualities had clearly been challenged and the comments had been allowed to stand. The idea that Gibbons was talking in general terms was nonsensical, but Haughey clearly felt that he could not sanction him in any meaningful way. It was another blow to his authority as leader.

Haughey did rein in his Keynesian instincts in his first year as Taoiseach by introducing expenditure cuts, which led to a reduction in current spending deficits. While unemployment continued to rise, there remained general optimism that the economy was recovering. Haughey continued to use stimulus measures to drive the Irish economy. Foreign direct investment continued to be secured, with Apple becoming the first American computer firm to establish itself in Ireland when it opened a manufacturing plant in Hollyhill on the disadvantaged northside of Cork City. Haughey also saw opportunities for Irish firms and semi-state companies abroad. He was instrumental in securing health and engineering consultancies for semi-states and helped to increase beef sales to the Middle East, through making a declaration that aligned Irish policy with Arab opinion on the Palestine conflict, and made Ireland the first EEC state to recognise the Palestine Liberation Organisation.[29] He had travelled to Iraq in April of 1978 with a number of semi-state companies and private business operators in an attempt to seek out new markets. Industrial conflict fell to its lowest level since Fianna Fáil had returned to power in 1977 and Haughey was convinced that his government was well on the way to being the innovating, transforming agent of change in the Irish economy that he envisaged it would be on his election as leader.

Haughey's work ethic was, however, taking its toll. He had another painful attack of kidney stones after his August holiday in Inishvickillane. At the same time, in September 1980, his friend, the journalist John Healy, told him that he was working himself into the ground: 'I was shocked the other night to see how the task had got you down. The loss of ebullience, of confidence. The weariness which I recognise comes from trying to be Minister for Everything. I'm sorry, friend – BUT IT IS SHOWING.'[30] Healy added that the cabinet dissidents must be exultant that Haughey was so bogged down in detail that it looked like he might break his own neck. In a supreme irony he finished his letter by telling Haughey that even 'Honest Jack' could be ruthless in a steely way when it suited him, and Haughey should soon do the same with his own cabinet.

THE NORTH

Immediately after his leadership victory Haughey claimed that a solution to the Northern Ireland problem was his top priority, and he devoted a significant section of his first Ard Fheis speech to the issue. He continued with the approach he had taken at his first press conference by stressing that in seeking a solution to the national question that put people first he wanted the Ard Fheis to mark a new departure in the history of Fianna Fáil and the country. That new departure was to strive towards the idea of a united Ireland that was not the reintegration of de Valera's fourth green field, but rather a solution that could accommodate all the people of the island. This was Haughey's theory of unity by consent. It was a de facto rejection of de Valera's insistence that Britain alone had the responsibility of solving the problem and in fact mirrored quite closely the relatively softer approach of both Lemass and Lynch. Haughey now had to figure out how to put it into practice. He believed that after the outbreak of the Troubles, Lynch had basically given up on any idea of pursuing a positive agenda for unity and he wanted to rectify that.

From the time he was brought back on to the frontbench in January 1975 until he became leader close to five years later, Haughey had not uttered one word in public about Northern Ireland. His last speech about Northern Ireland was in Tralee in November 1974. After that reaffirmation of Haughey's republican principles he was challenged by the then Minister for Posts and Telegraphs, Conor Cruise O'Brien, to a television debate. He refused, saying that the merits of his and Cruise O'Brien's arguments had already been judged by their constituents. This led the American embassy to suggest that Jack Lynch had set Haughey up and was delighted by Cruise O'Brien's attack and Haughey's retreat, since Lynch considered Haughey a dangerous man both for Fianna Fáil and for the country. The American embassy was almost always wrong when it reported on Haughey. This time its view was that he would have lost any such debate as the inconsistencies of republicanism would have been hard to defend against an opponent of Cruise O'Brien's talents, and that Haughey's speech in Tralee had given Lynch the excuse he needed not to promote Haughey to the frontbench. Two months later Lynch brought Fianna Fáil's prodigal son back to the frontline of Irish politics. About the only thing the American embassy was right about was that it could not predict how things would work out because Cruise O'Brien was disliked by so many people there were advantages in being attacked by him.[31] Now, half a decade later, Haughey's republicanism was back on show for the first time since that Tralee speech. Haughey's silence in the years between January 1975 and December 1979 was seen by his opponents as ambivalence towards the activities of the IRA. The reality was different. His return to the frontbench was predicated on the fact that he would not speak about the North. He stuck rigidly to this, noting that he had no authority within the party to speak on the subject. Involving himself in trade union disputes was one thing; speaking about an issue as sensitive in Fianna Fáil as Northern Ireland was quite another.

Yet from the time of his acquittal in the arms trial, Haughey had kept a close watch on events in Northern Ireland and continued to talk to various contacts about the ongoing violence of the Troubles, and how it could be resolved. In the aftermath of the events of Bloody Sunday in Derry on 30 January 1972, Haughey went north and discussed the crisis with the civil rights leader John Hume. He was in Hume's house on the morning of 2 February, when eleven of the thirteen victims were buried, to pay his respects.[32] He was but one of the thousands across Ireland who made their way to Derry for the funerals. In Dublin there were work stoppages and a crowd estimated at 100,000 marched to the British embassy carrying thirteen coffins and black flags. Later the building was attacked and razed to the ground. The following year, after the 1973 election, he told his long-time correspondent Mother Bernard that 'this seemingly hopeless Northern situation overshadows everything else.'[33] A few years later, in January 1976, he lamented to one of his American namesakes, Robert Haughey, that 'in the North things seem to be almost hopeless.'[34]

Haughey's condemnation of the Provisional IRA in his introductory press conference as leader, and again at the Ard Fheis, was welcomed by the British. They viewed him as the only possible hope of securing the support of the more republican wing of the party for any solution that could be devised for the North. Hector Legge, the former editor of the *Sunday Independent*, welcomed Haughey's Ard Fheis speech, telling him that the people were open to change in so many areas including Northern Ireland but that the ultimate solution was to 'keep at the British. They got out of Cyprus, Malta, Aden and other places. There'll be no peace here till they go.'[35] Vincent Browne was another correspondent who advised him that Britain leaving was the best hope of a solution. The British should be persuaded to say they would withdraw and a new constitution drafted which would get over the problem of the unionist veto: 'I emphasise that we need to break out of the current deadlock and you are the person to make some progress and exert some pressure.'[36] What this had in common with de Valera's view, but not with Lemass's or Lynch's, was that the opinion, votes and capacity of Northern Ireland's unionists to make mischief, or stop any progress, was irrelevant.

And indeed that was the attitude Haughey took as he prepared to meet Margaret Thatcher in Downing Street for the summit between the two leaders on 21 May 1980. In a confidential report before that meeting he was seen by the British embassy in Dublin as 'no friend of ours, but not, perhaps, actively hostile'; in his short period in office he had not harmed security co-operation between the Gardaí and the RUC. In fact, it had actually improved. Like everyone else, however, the embassy could not speculate as to Haughey's real intentions as his 'cards were held very close to his chest'.[37] The reality was that Haughey saw Northern Ireland as both a historical anomaly and an equally historical absurdity. It was, to him, an artificial entity, artificially maintained, and it did not help the unionists in the North who, he claimed, he did not want to uproot, destroy in any way, or change. He just wanted them to live in a united Ireland. It was revolutionary talk for any Irish leader to describe Northern Ireland as a failed entity and a historical absurdity, but Haughey was absolutely convinced that he could break down barriers, and prepared diligently for his meeting with Thatcher in that frame of mind. At the same time, describing Northern Ireland in these terms was hardly an approach guaranteed to win over unionists of any stripe.

In the run-up to his historic meeting with Thatcher, Haughey was keen to get a sense of Britain's Iron Lady and how he should deal with her. He had been fascinated by the impact she had made in her short time as prime minister, and what he saw as her almost quasi-religious mission to transform Britain.[38] He was keen to make a similar impression on her. It also suited his own view of himself as a man of destiny. In the week prior to the meeting he hosted a small lunch with the group who were to make up the official Irish diplomatic party to Downing Street. It included Andy O'Rourke and Noel Dorr, from Foreign Affairs; the ambassador in London, Eamon Kennedy; the deputy secretary in his own department, Dermot Nally, whose advice he was becoming increasingly trustful of; and Pádraig Ó hAnnracháin, his civil servant without portfolio, who was there to act as a sort of republican keeper of the flame, given that Haughey's distrust of the mandarins in Foreign Affairs was almost an article of faith. Dorr's view was that Haughey should think of the meeting as a possible new opening in Anglo-Irish relations between two recently elected leaders. Haughey decided that he would present Thatcher with a gift. Dorr strongly advised him against it, pointing out that gifts were usually something given by heads of state on official visits.[39] Haughey dismissed his objections and asked Mary Preece in his department to locate a suitable gift, and it was she, with her husband, John Taylor, who came up with the idea of a Georgian Dublin silver teapot and strainer.

They located it from a local artist, Kurt Ticher, from Roebuck Road in South Dublin.[40] It was then examined and approved by an independent expert on Irish silver, Ronnie le Bas, the assay master in Dublin Castle.[41]

It was Haughey himself who decided to have the strainer inscribed with the famous words of St Francis of Assisi that Thatcher had quoted on the night of her election as prime minister: 'Where there is discord, may we bring harmony.' The quotation continues, 'Where there is error, may we bring truth. Where there is doubt, may we bring faith. And where there is despair, may we bring hope.' Haughey thought it an apt line for his discussion with Thatcher as he was correctly of the view that there was no conceivable possibility of any type of diplomatic breakthrough if she could not be convinced of a solution. Like Thatcher, Haughey had faith that he would be the one to finally broker peace and pave the way to unity. He was realistic enough to know that this was no short-term project, but he was determined to show her that he wanted to achieve something concrete. He also knew he did not have much time to accomplish something of lasting merit. The complexities of his own position within Fianna Fáil, and the vagaries of Ireland's fluid electoral politics, with no guarantee that he would win the next election, made the situation all the more urgent. In that context, although Thatcher saw the meeting as a 'getting to know you' exercise, Haughey wanted her to know that nothing that advanced the situation would be ruled out, no matter how revolutionary or implausible. He had told a group of British MPs visiting Dublin in April 1979 that the man who ultimately solved the North would be seen as a saint, and that he rather fancied canonisation.[42] While said in jest, it had the kernel of truth.

In the Irish embassy in London the night before the meeting, Dorr asked the Minister for Foreign Affairs, Brian Lenihan, to prevail upon Haughey not to make his presentation, but the Taoiseach was not for turning. He was furious the following morning, however, when Geraldine Kennedy reported in the *Irish Times* that he would be presenting a gift of a silver Georgian teapot to Mrs Thatcher later that day. While the element of surprise was gone, the meeting itself was regarded as a success by Haughey. Thatcher was delighted with her gift. She first stated that it was far too valuable, and she could not possibly accept it, but was assured by one of her civil servants that she could in fact receive it on behalf of the British state. Prior to the meeting Haughey had sought and was granted a private meeting with her, but much to his surprise, when the time came, Thatcher had a note-taker with her. Dermot Nally had tried to dissuade Haughey from this course of action, telling him it was not a good idea to have a meeting without any civil service input, but again he overruled the official advice.[43] There was no damage done on that occasion, but Haughey never again attended any meeting as Taoiseach without at least one official with him. Both leaders agreed to enhanced co-operation between the states in economic, political and security fields and recognised that the relationship between their countries was unique. For Haughey, the key point was that he had stressed it was the wish of his government to secure the unity of the island by agreement and in peace. He felt it important to lay down from the off what his position was. He invited Thatcher to visit Ireland and she responded positively. Haughey left London delighted that the meeting had gone so well. The second summit in Dublin was to turn out somewhat differently.

Haughey's ability to control his own government and the state's administrative organs was again brought into question when, in the month following his trip to Downing Street, he tried and failed to reassign Ireland's ambassador to the United States, Seán Donlon. Donlon had been in the position since July 1978 and had built up an impressive array of contacts on Capitol Hill, including the so-called 'four horsemen', Senators Ted Kennedy and Pat Moynihan, the Speaker of the House of Representatives Tip O'Neill, and Governor Hugh Carey of New York. Donlon's mission had explicitly been to reduce American financial, political and logistical support for the IRA, and to work closely with the IDA to encourage foreign direct investment into the country by American multinationals.

When Haughey was elected Taoiseach, Neil Blaney, the independent Fianna Fáil TD for Donegal, was in the United States as a guest of the Irish National Caucus (INC), an Irish-American lobby group founded in 1974 by Fr Seán McManus, and deeply distrusted by Donlon for not condemning the IRA's campaign of violence. Blaney issued a statement saying that with the formation of a new government under Haughey, 'it is the wish of all the friends of Ireland that the government will work with the INC in the important task it has undertaken ... it is doing the job that our embassy in Washington should be doing but is not doing.'[44] McManus followed up Blaney's statement by calling for Donlon's removal and the appointment of an ambassador who would reflect Haughey's views. Blaney and McManus were but two of many who believed that they knew what Haughey wanted, which of course reflected their own views. Yet they did not know what Haughey wanted; beyond his long-held notion of a united Ireland he did not know himself in any detail what he wanted. He was hardly alone in that. He also knew that great goal could not be achieved by violence and had indeed said so in his remarks at his press conference on becoming Taoiseach. Another Irish-American lobby group, Noraid, the American fundraising arm of the Provisional IRA, also started making noises about changing the ambassador.[45] Both lobby groups had found a supporter in Mario Biaggi of New York who in turn had created in the US Congress an informal ad hoc committee on Irish affairs. The four horsemen distrusted Biaggi and let Donlon know that they could not be involved in influencing US policy and, indirectly, British policy on Ireland, if there was any change of direction coming from the new administration in Dublin. Donlon later intimated that their concerns were based on Haughey's involvement in the arms trial, the divisions within Fianna Fáil, and the fact that Blaney and the INC had warmly welcomed the change in leadership in Dublin.[46]

It seemed that no matter what Haughey did, the ghosts of the arms trial followed him everywhere. He had been found innocent of all the charges he faced, but pretty much everyone in public life felt they could ascertain what his views were on the basis of what had happened a decade earlier. This was particularly the case in relation to Northern Ireland. The truth was that there was something almost naive in Haughey's views on Northern Ireland. Essentially, he believed that the Irish state needed to gain as much external support as possible for the concept of unity and that the ultimate goal was to get the British to declare their own interest in the unification of Ireland. This was in effect a carbon copy of de Valera's policy on Northern Ireland but not really reflective of the policy of Lemass or Lynch.

No British prime minister had ever expressed such a belief and it was difficult to see Margaret Thatcher taking a different path. Haughey had told Donlon in mid-December to inform the four horsemen that he did not know the INC, had never met them and had nothing to do with them. Any of the horsemen could phone him at any time if they wanted clarification on any point or a general talk on the situation. He then reiterated his view that no solution could be found without Irish government input and that he hoped to continue the good working relationship with Margaret Thatcher that Jack Lynch had enjoyed. At the end of the year, and after a few tumultuous weeks, the Minister for Foreign Affairs, Brian Lenihan, issued a statement declaring confidence in Donlon. Yet three months later, Lenihan met Biaggi at a White House reception to mark St Patrick's Day, giving Biaggi the opportunity to say, quite inaccurately, that the INC was now officially recognised by the Irish government and was working with them.

Irish-American opinion, however, was not just associated with the four horsemen on one side, and the militant INC and Noraid on the other. At the end of January 1980, Haughey wrote to Justice John P. Flaherty of the Supreme Court of Pennsylvania to assure him that both he and his government had full confidence in Ambassador Donlon and his staff.[47] Haughey's declaration of confidence came the week after he hosted an intensive two-day meeting of various senior officials from his own department and the Department of Foreign Affairs, and the ambassadors to Britain and the United States, Eamon Kennedy and Donlon. It was Haughey's first opportunity to have a fully fledged discussion on Northern Ireland and he encouraged a frank discussion. This was dangerous enough territory for the officials in Foreign Affairs in particular as there was a widely held view in that department, and across the civil service, that Haughey distrusted the lot of them. Haughey had made it clear that he wanted to see a unity of opinion in Irish-American circles. Donlon warned him against this approach, pointing out that there was a wide chasm between the four horsemen on one side, and Noraid and the INC on the other. He was supported in his views by his civil service colleagues in both the Taoiseach's department and in Foreign Affairs.[48]

Donlon was called back to Dublin in June 1980. Lenihan told him that although he had been doing a good job he was being moved out of Washington due to his involvement in US politics. In a brief meeting later that day, in which Donlon stated he was not invited to sit down, Haughey told him that he was being appointed as Ireland's permanent representative to the UN in New York. Donlon may not have been invited by Haughey to sit down, but then few people were. There was always a seat placed in front of Haughey's desk for one-to-one meetings and his private secretarial team advised visitors not to wait to be asked to sit down. Haughey did not like to have people standing over him, given his diminutive height, even when he was seated.[49] Donlon, of course, may have felt that he had no choice but to stand. He told the Taoiseach that his move out of Washington would be seen as a snub by the four horsemen, which most likely copperfastened Haughey's view that Donlon had indeed become too close to the American political scene. Haughey did not want a discussion and summarily terminated the conversation.

On 5 July the *Irish Press* led with a story of changes to the diplomatic service. It speculated that the INC, Biaggi's ad hoc Committee of the US Congress, and Blaney might seek to claim that Donlon's exit from the Washington scene was the direct result of their influence and an indication, perhaps, of a change in emphasis in the US on the Irish government's policy on Northern Ireland.[50] The four horsemen contacted Donlon, who told them that the story was essentially true but that he did not want to be drawn into controversy.[51] Then Ted Kennedy phoned Haughey. After the call Haughey called Dermot Nally into his office and simply said: 'I have never been spoken to in that way before.' Kennedy had told him unequivocally that the four horsemen would never ride again if Donlon was moved.[52] On 10 July 1980, the *Irish Independent* reported that Haughey had told Donlon to 'keep the job' and added that Senator Kennedy was happy that Donlon would keep his present post. He had been an effective voice in discouraging American support for violence in Ireland, and an equally effective voice for Irish unity as the only realistic avenue to genuine and lasting peace and reconciliation.[53] Noel Dorr was sent to New York as Ireland's representative to the UN. Five weeks later, in a speech in Cork, Haughey appealed to all those in America who had Ireland's good at heart not to support Noraid or indeed the INC, and to unite behind the position of the Irish government. He had opened the Siamsa Cois Laoi music festival in Páirc Uí Chaoimh on the same day and was in relaxed form as the sun beat down on the American folk singer Joan Baez, the Dubliners, and the Wolfe Tones, noted for the republican flavour they brought to their concerts, on the last Sunday in July.

It had, however, been a hellish month for Haughey. The Donlon case had seen him accused by Garret FitzGerald as being ambivalent towards 'provo front' organisations in the United States. On the day he finally issued his denunciation of such organisations, Jim Gibbons had issued yet another quasi-challenge to his leadership by demanding on RTÉ's *This Week* that Haughey publicly clarify the position regarding their conflicting testimonies at the arms trial a decade previously and reiterated that during the whole saga he told Haughey: 'For God's sake, stop it completely.' Then, surreally, he stated that he recognised there had been 'a democratic decision of Fianna Fáil to elect Charlie Haughey as successor to Jack Lynch, but there was no question of the personal oath of allegiance which the German Army took to the person of Adolf Hitler late in the war. Fianna Fáil, who were democratic, did not have that.'[54] Earlier in the month the country had been convulsed, not by the Donlon controversy, but by the heinous killing of two gardaí, John Morley and Henry Byrne, in Ballaghaderreen, County Roscommon after a bank raid by republican subversives. Haughey immediately travelled to Roscommon, and declared that no expense would be spared in efforts to catch the murderers. He attended the removal of Garda Morley on the same evening it was made clear that Donlon would not after all be moving from Washington. It was a stark reminder for him, and indeed for the Irish people, that serving the state and its people sometimes came at the cost of life. The following week, the Fianna Fáil TD for Donegal, and Ceann Comhairle, Joseph Brennan, died suddenly. The by-election to replace him would be Haughey's first electoral test as leader.

The Donlon affair was never about Blaney's continued exile from the party and getting him back into the Fianna Fáil fold, as various journalists speculated at the time. Haughey was in fact quite happy to have Blaney outside the party. He was only six months in the job, had a split party, and the last thing he needed was as divisive a figure as Blaney seeking entry back into the party, and demanding, as he inevitably would, a cabinet seat with it. Haughey also viewed Blaney's irredentist nationalism and republican rhetoric as completely unsuitable to the circumstances of the 1980s. Throughout his leadership he routinely received entreaties from Fianna Fáil members and supporters demanding he bring Blaney back. All were acknowledged and ignored. He was, however, wounded politically by the Donlon controversy. Haughey clearly did want rid of Donlon, who he considered not republican enough. He was encouraged in this view by Pádraig Ó hAnnracháin.[55] There was more to it than that, though. Haughey had wanted a more ecumenical approach to the unity issue, one that would bring people into his wider republican family, rather than simply repudiating them. That was the context of his thinking on Donlon. He thought he could reach out a bit more widely and bring people in rather than keeping them on the outside.[56] Fundamental to Haughey's view of himself was that he could find solutions. He essentially thought that when it came to the USA, he could bring the INC, Noraid and Marco Biaggi together with the four horsemen. The SDLP leader John Hume told him that this was an impossible task.[57] Donlon believed that Biaggi and the INC had a romanticised view of Ireland. Noraid were unreconstructed supporters of the Provisional IRA. The four horsemen could never associate themselves with these groups. Hume held a similar view. He had long held that his own work was best served by not embroiling himself in the internecine workings of politics in the Republic of Ireland, but in this instance he sided with Donlon, issuing a statement that it had to be made abundantly clear that the activities of Biaggi, and those organisations he associated himself with, enjoyed no support whatsoever among substantial sections of Irish opinion.[58]

Haughey was prey to a certain naivety in his approach to the various Irish-American groups. He was excoriated on the green wing of Irish nationalism for not being republican enough, and on the moderate wing for being far too republican in his supposed willingness to be associated with those who advocated physical force as the solution to the Northern problem. Ultimately the Donlon affair made Haughey look weak. He could have insisted on moving Donlon, as would have been his right, and he could still have made a statement condemning the INC and Noraid. He had badly miscalculated and was spooked by the hostile reaction, particularly from what might be considered the official USA, in the guise of the four horsemen. Once they turned on him, however, he had no realistic alternative but to retain Donlon. He could not afford a hostile USA when he was looking for both foreign direct investment and external involvement in his efforts to advance the cause of Irish unity. It was a valuable lesson and he quickly moved on from it.

Donlon returned to Dublin as the secretary of the Department of Foreign Affairs in October 1981 when Haughey was in opposition. Four months later, in February 1982, they would work together again during Haughey's brief second term as Taoiseach and face an even greater storm during the Falklands conflict. Haughey was not one to bear a grudge against civil servants, but he strongly believed that Donlon had overstepped the mark in the summer of 1980. Outside the Department of Foreign Affairs, this was a view many across the wider civil service shared. In that context Haughey's relations with Donlon during his second term as Taoiseach were never less than professional and never more than chilly. Haughey also never resiled from the view that the Irish Embassy in Washington cleaved too closely to the British line on the North. Haughey's relationship with the Department of Foreign Affairs would come under severe stress during the pressure of the Falklands conflict when he once again fundamentally disagreed with the view of the Department of Foreign Affairs and indeed many others in his team of senior civil servants. The result was to substantially rupture his relationship with Margaret Thatcher.

Haughey might well have found himself blindsided by the support the four horsemen had given Donlon, and by the phone calls he received in support of the ambassador, but it did not stop him becoming firm friends with Ted Kennedy and Hugh Carey in the aftermath of the whole affair. Haughey visited Kennedy's home in Hyannis Port on a number of occasions over the following two decades, while Kennedy stayed at both Abbeville and Inishvickillane. At Christmas 1989, Hugh Carey wrote to Charles and Maureen Haughey to tell them that 'your friendship is our greatest gift.'[59]

THE IRON LADY

One relationship that would go in the other direction, however, was Haughey's with Margaret Thatcher. The positive vibes from the May 1980 visit with Thatcher began to dissipate after the second summit in Dublin just over six months later. The month before the summit, Haughey spent a significant amount of time in Donegal campaigning for Fianna Fáil's candidate in the Donegal by-election, Clem Coughlan. This was the first test of Haughey's electoral appeal since becoming party leader and it took place in the worst possible place. Donegal was Blaney heartland, and the by-election took place in the darkest of circumstances. With two weeks to go, seven republican prisoners began a hunger strike seeking the right not to wear the prison uniform and not to do prison work, among other demands. Haughey viewed it as his first real political trial of strength. He invested significant time in the contest, travelling to Donegal five weekends in a row to canvass. The consequences of a loss for Haughey's leadership were unthinkable, given that the two by-election defeats in Cork just a year earlier had effectively marked the demise of Jack Lynch.

His natural enthusiasm for campaigning waned on occasions and it fell to Brendan O'Donnell and Ray MacSharry to keep him motivated during a gruelling campaign. O'Donnell accompanied him everywhere during that campaign. Haughey was desperate to win but was worried about the effect of the hunger strike, the potential strength of the Blaney vote, the fact that Donegal had always had a very strong Fine Gael presence, and that there were some 7,000 Protestant votes in the constituency. One wet Sunday in the middle of the campaign he was anxious to get back to Dublin and decided he had enough of visiting small towns and villages, despite having a few more on his list. He declared that he wanted to be taken straight home. Coughlan's director of elections, Ray MacSharry, bluntly asked him: 'Look, Taoiseach, do you want to win this fucking by-election or don't you? If you do, you'll have to visit these places and if you don't, go back to Dublin and we'll see how we get on.'[60] He stayed. He was also helped by the fact that Coughlan, a thirty-eight-year-old teacher, was a superb campaigner in his own right, traversing the county at a rapid pace generating representations on behalf of the voters using a battery-powered dictaphone. His representations got priority attention during the campaign and it came as a certain shock to him after his election that he could not secure the same ease of access for his later letters and phone calls to the Taoiseach's office.

By the final weekend the Fianna Fáil team were quite confident of a victory. On Saturday 1 November, Haughey spoke at Fianna Fáil's final large-scale rally in Letterkenny and promised government support for an airport at Big Isle; fish processing in Killybegs; harbour development in Burtonport; the pier at Greencastle; and industrial development in Gweedore, Letterkenny and Buncrana.[61] It was the warm-up speech that provoked all the controversy, however. Síle de Valera delivered a broadside against the British government and Margaret Thatcher in particular, proclaiming that as a woman she was deeply shocked at Thatcher's lack of compassion on the issue of the H-Blocks. 'The Iron Lady image of which the British Prime Minister seems so proud is little less than a mask for an inflexible and insensitive lack of common humanity.'[62] Haughey sat stony-faced next to her. After he had finished, a hasty meeting was held in the Golden Grill in Letterkenny, which was owned by Bernard McGlinchey. In attendance were Haughey, MacSharry, O'Donnell and Gerry Collins, the Minister for Justice. The only topic up for discussion was what to do with de Valera. After much angst, Haughey asked O'Donnell what he thought. His long-time adviser replied that she was best ignored: 'We'll just say you're on your way back to Dublin and not available for comment, that's the best way to approach it.'[63] Haughey agreed but he also immediately instructed the Irish ambassador in London, Eamon

Kennedy, to contact Thatcher and say the views expressed by de Valera were personal, and not those of Fianna Fáil, or indeed Haughey himself, who had been personally distressed by them.[64]

Haughey, however, had had enough of de Valera, and ordered MacSharry to brief journalists that she would not be allowed to make any further speeches without them being vetted by him in the first place.[65] Haughey's personal efforts paid off when Clem Coughlan comfortably won the by-election, receiving some 3,400 first preferences more than Fine Gael's Dinny McGinley. Neil Blaney's candidate, Paddy Kelly, was some 9,000 votes behind Coughlan. Haughey was ecstatic with the result. The *Irish Independent* summed up his mood and that of the party faithful with the headline: 'FF Homage to King Charlie'.[66] He received numerous congratulations on Fianna Fáil's success. One was from Senator Paddy McGowan, who praised Haughey's son Ciarán for his canvassing. Haughey passed on the message, signing off as 'Da'.[67] Another was from the journalist Bruce Arnold, who would soon become perhaps Haughey's most vociferous critic. In a handwritten note congratulating Haughey, Arnold told him: 'I have to say your singleness of purpose is a huge strength. It's an economical use of resources that others could emulate elsewhere.'[68]

That singleness of purpose was on show when Margaret Thatcher flew into Dublin at lunchtime on Monday 8 December 1980 for her meeting with Haughey. It would, however, prove a significant drawback to the overselling of what was achieved in the short few hours before the British Prime Minister flew back to London that evening. Haughey was keen to discuss the whole gamut of Anglo-Irish relations, including the constitutional status of Northern Ireland, the H-Block hunger strike, cross-border security, and co-operation on economic issues. It was by some distance the most high-powered British delegation to come to Dublin for talks with an Irish government, and included Foreign Secretary Lord Carrington, Chancellor of the Exchequer Sir Geoffrey Howe, Northern Secretary Humphrey Atkins and a number of senior officials. There was massive security around Dublin. The two leaders had met for about thirty minutes the previous Monday in Luxembourg at the end of the first day of the gathering of the EEC heads of government. The situation in the H-Blocks was raised specifically at the Luxembourg meeting by Haughey, who expressed his deep concern to Thatcher, and told the Irish political correspondents afterwards that he thought she felt the same way. The arrangements for the Dublin meeting were finally agreed in Luxembourg. Thatcher had been anxious to fulfil the Dublin engagement ever since the May summit. Notwithstanding the mounting tensions in Northern Ireland, with the H-Block hunger strike, and fears of a major protest in Dublin by its supporters, Thatcher was still keen to come to Dublin; not to do so might be seen as a victory for the Provisional IRA.[69] Haughey was accompanied by the Minister for Foreign Affairs, Brian Lenihan, the Minister for Finance, Michael O'Kennedy, in one of his last acts before becoming Ireland's European Commissioner, and the Minister for Justice, Gerry Collins.

While Haughey saw the meeting as a historic summit of the two leaders who could solve the Northern Ireland problem, Thatcher saw it as more of a routine discussion of Anglo-Irish relations; hence the high-powered team and wide agenda. Haughey was also happy with the big agenda but was keen to make some breakthrough on his quest for unity. The two leaders repeated their individual discussion from the London summit, and they met for eighty minutes. This time Haughey had a note-taker, Dermot Nally, with him. In keeping with his idea of himself as someone who had solutions to historical and deep-rooted problems, Haughey suggested that what was needed was 'a great historic move'.[70] By contrast, Thatcher had no interest in any such grand gestures. The two leaders agreed to the setting up of a series of studies conducted jointly by the Irish and British governments to examine possible new institutional structures within the islands. The studies were intended to embrace security matters, economic co-operation, and measures to encourage mutual understanding throughout the islands. A joint communiqué issued after the meeting said that the next summit between the two governments would consider the totality of relationships within these islands.[71]

In an unusual change to the normal way of writing up the results of summits, the communiqué had been pre-prepared by officials. After several sessions with British officials in advance of the summit, a situation had been reached where the British side had pointed out passages that they could not accept. In the final preparatory meeting between Haughey and his officials he was told that it was up to him to raise these points with Mrs Thatcher in their face-to-face encounter and to seek her agreement. Haughey never did. At the end of the summit, before the communiqué was issued, and as Thatcher was mulling over it, Lord Carrington intervened to respond to Thatcher's questioning of the content of the communiqué by saying that the text was agreed and had been worked on by British officials. She fell silent.[72] She later rebuked herself for not being sufficiently involved in the preparation and ultimate drafting of the communiqué and allowing a commitment to review the totality of relationships at the next Anglo-Irish summit.[73]

The difficulties began after the meeting. A strong difference in emphasis by the two governments emerged at their subsequent press conferences in Dublin and London over what might emerge from the joint studies. According to Haughey, it was a historic breakthrough that did not rule out any possibility, including a new type of federal or confederal arrangement involving Ireland, Britain and Northern Ireland. Citizenship rights as well as constitutional and legal arrangements would all be considered in the joint government studies which were to commence in the new year at ministerial and official level. At her press conference, Thatcher said there was absolutely no possibility of a confederation flowing from agreements reached in Dublin Castle. She stressed that there was a unique relationship between Britain and the Republic of Ireland because of the common land border and that the joint aim of the two countries was continuity of co-operation between them.[74] This was about as far away from Haughey's interpretation as it was possible to be.

Things quickly became worse. Haughey and Lenihan saw the totality of relationships as a sort of open-ended discussion on the constitutional future of Northern Ireland, and the joint studies as a potential blueprint for fundamental change.[75] The British saw them as nothing of the sort. Thatcher considered the joint studies a modest vehicle for civil service recommendations which could then be ignored by politicians. On the Irish administrative side, Dermot Nally saw them in much the same way.[76] Yet Wally Kirwan, also from the Department of the Taoiseach, saw in them the potential to move the intractable problem of Northern Ireland forward. This is how Haughey himself saw it; Kirwan described him as 'cock a hoop' in the days afterwards.[77]

Two days after the summit, the British Foreign Office contacted its embassy in Dublin to say that although they appreciated that Haughey had what they called presentational problems with the communiqué, they wanted the Irish government to know that any suggestions that new institutional arrangements might include federal or confederal arrangements caused great problems in London. In that context they asked that Dublin be notified that the British government hoped the Taoiseach would take great care, when talking to the press and in the Dáil, to say nothing that would encourage speculation about any federal or confederal solutions. The embassy replied that they had spoken to Dermot Nally, who had stated, with the Taoiseach's approval, that Dublin was fully aware of the difficulties the British had, and would do nothing to exacerbate them.[78] Haughey, however, had both his own audience, and his belief that he had achieved something worthwhile, to consider. The belief, as expressed in his original press conference, that a major breakthrough had been achieved was allowed to stand. Thatcher wrote to him on 11 December, three days after the summit, thanking him for his hospitality and asking for her appreciation to be passed on to those involved in ensuring the success of the summit, particularly on the security side. Her fury was only ever slightly masked when she added that although they had carried the relationships between the two countries a stage further, the 'reactions to the communiqué have already shown how great the difficulties are going to be but I believe that the path on which we have set out is the right one.' Haughey replied that he agreed that the development of relations had been brought forward and also wished to continue along the path, 'despite the difficulties which the reactions you mention have shown to exist'.[79] This overtly polite exchange barely concealed the reality that the goodwill that emanated from the May summit had been shattered and the consequences as 1981 loomed would be very grave indeed.

The following March, at a European Council meeting in Maastricht, a furious Thatcher assailed Haughey, accusing him of overselling the summit's results. Prior to the meeting Brian Lenihan had claimed that although Northern Ireland's constitutional position was not under active discussion, the results of the ongoing Anglo-Irish talks could be Irish unity in ten years. After a side meeting with Haughey, Thatcher, dressed in green, found Ireland's Minister for Foreign Affairs at a reception, and pointedly said to him, 'Mr Lenihan, the Irish don't have a monopoly on green.' Haughey came in, and was described as never having been so pissed off, and berated Lenihan in front of his team of civil servants.[80] At this stage Bobby Sands was three weeks into his hunger strike.

CHAPTER 16

RISE AND FOLLOW

THE FOURTH ESTATE

In the first week of January 1981, Haughey told the Donegal businessman Michael MacGinty, 'A great deal of political reporting in this country is of a fictional nature and a corresponding amount of political comment is pure rubbish.'[1] This attack on the political press came in the context of what Haughey felt was unfair comment in relation to the National Understanding he and his government had agreed with the trade union movement and the employers just a few months before. But Haughey's antipathy to the press went way beyond economic comment. He was convinced that the political lobby in Leinster House had wanted George Colley to win the Fianna Fáil leadership and had never got over the fact that their favoured candidate had lost. He also believed that every single political correspondent in the country, with the exception of Liam O'Neill of the *Cork Examiner*, was antipathetic towards him.[2] Even then, his inner circle believed that O'Neill's even-handed approach was neutered by the paper's anti-Haughey agenda at editorial level.[3] This was not simply paranoia on Haughey's part. Within the political lobby itself, there was wide distrust of Haughey dating back to the arms trial. Even those who came to political journalism after that seminal event in the history of the state were influenced by their more senior contemporaries' perception of Haughey. The widespread view in the political lobby was that Haughey could not be trusted.[4]

The corresponding view in Haughey's camp was that the hostility towards him of the political lobby and indeed journalists generally was so desperate, and so thinly disguised, that it tainted their capacity to report on him fairly.[5] This was made worse as the decade continued and Haughey, an unwelcome victor in the Fianna Fáil leadership stakes in the first place, continued, despite the wishful thinking of the political lobby, to survive the various heaves that were launched against him, much to the puzzlement of those journalists who had predicted his downfall. When Haughey finally fell in early 1992 his long-time press secretary P.J. Mara remarked that he found it 'quite extraordinary that there shouldn't be one or two or three out of twenty, thirty, forty working journalists who wouldn't have a different view of Haughey and would stand slightly apart'.[6] After his first year in office, the tension between Haughey and the political lobby was set. He was underwhelmed by the reportage of his Dublin summit with Thatcher, and considered it typical of the political lobby not to give him any credit. Their scepticism on this particular occasion was perhaps justified, given the differing noises emanating from London on what the outcome of the summit actually meant.

Haughey was also unhappy with what he saw as the media's failure to properly credit his administration's economic successes, particularly the National Understanding with the trade unions and the employers of September 1980. From taking office as Taoiseach, Haughey had made it clear that he was keen to see a new national pay deal in place when the original National Understanding ended in the autumn of 1980.[7] He told both the unions and the employers that successfully negotiating such a new National Understanding was a major priority for his government. He viewed pay deals as an essential element in providing macroeconomic stability and ensuring Irish competitiveness internationally in an increasingly unstable world. Key to this was securing the support of the trade unions. In its annual report for 1980, the Irish Congress of Trade

Unions (ICTU) asserted that Haughey considered meeting Congress a fundamental part of the role of Taoiseach.[8] He met Congress on no fewer than five occasions in his first year as Taoiseach. Maintaining trade union movement support was vital to Haughey's plans for winning the next general election; one he considered essential to prove his authority to a divided party. This need appeared to colour the approach his government adopted to trade union pressure on pay and other issues. Haughey was reluctant to adopt measures that could prove politically unpopular. Although high levels of current expenditure produced a budgetary over-run in 1979 and 1980, his government continued its expansionary policies in 1980 and 1981.

Haughey defended this approach as being appropriate in the worsening international economic situation resulting from the second oil crisis and the sharply accelerating increases in Irish unemployment and emigration. However, this situation was in itself bringing renewed inflationary expectations among Irish workers. That caused the Federated Union of Employers (FUE) to change its own views on central bargaining. In September, as the National Understanding talks entered their final stages, they collapsed twice in ten days. This resulted in significant intervention by the government. Haughey eventually persuaded the national executive of the FUE to resume negotiations by pledging guarantees on the content of the 1981 budget. By the end of September executives of both ICTU and the FUE had agreed to a text and the second National Understanding was finally ratified by both organisations in November 1980. The conclusion of this second understanding, however, drew the resentment of the FUE over what it saw as the unwarranted political pressure brought to bear upon it.[9]

On the morning of Tuesday 16 September, when the negotiations were at their most difficult, Haughey had made an unscheduled and unprecedented visit to the FUE headquarters in Baggot Street, where its General Council was meeting.[10] He argued that the merits of partnership consensus over confrontational monetarism would best suit Ireland. He vowed to maintain prudent financial management but argued that some slippage on borrowing was a price worth paying to prevent the economy collapsing. He would include business reform demands in his 1981 budget, but warned the employers that if they rejected the agreement he would conclude a public sector one anyway that would set a benchmark for the private sector.[11] The outcome led Joseph O'Malley from the *Sunday Independent* to argue that 'with a seat in the cabinet, the trade unions could hardly have done better or secured more from Fianna Fáil.'[12] It was perhaps in that context that the political lobby looked with a jaundiced eye at Haughey's economic achievements. On the same day that Haughey was describing political reporting in the country as rubbish, Paul Tansey in the *Irish Times* was detailing how even before the formal pay negotiations between the government, the FUE and ICTU had got under way in July of 1980, the employers were having the rug gently pulled from under them by the unlikely and implicit partnership of Fianna Fáil and ICTU. Tansey argued that the consequences of this were that the trade union movement was freed from the consequences for employment of their 20 per cent pay demand, and they could get on with the job of extracting from the employers as much as possible in the form of pay increases.[13] Haughey simply viewed such commentary as biased. After the Minister of Finance, Michael O'Kennedy, went to the European Commission, Haughey replaced him, to the surprise of pretty much everyone who knew anything about Irish politics, with Gene Fitzgerald, the genial but generally ineffective Minister for Labour. It was widely seen as a centralisation of power by Haughey. In the run-up to the 1981 budget it was Haughey who took control of the government's spending and taxing parameters. Accompanied by Fitzgerald, Haughey met his other ministers to discuss their departmental plans, but routinely ignored his own Minister for Finance during the discussions.[14]

Haughey was comfortable with the result of his National Understanding negotiations and considered them a confirmation of his ability to find solutions to problems. This was the attitude he brought to his budgetary preparations as well, but it led many in his party to distrust him even more. The National Understanding affirmed the government's commitment to full employment and to achieving a 15,000 net increase in jobs in 1981. While the employers were sceptical participants, the unions were delighted with the outcome, and Haughey very much wanted the trade union movement on his side. He always worried when the unions threatened to uproot their relationship with Fianna Fáil. In the Seanad elections of August 1981, Haughey's old friend Michael Mullen of the Irish Transport and General Workers' Union (ITGWU) wrote to him seeking his influence in getting the union's president, John Carroll, elected on the Labour panel. Haughey did not reply. Just over a week later, after Carroll had failed to get elected, Mullen penned another letter to Haughey, complaining that Fianna Fáil had colluded with Fine Gael to ensure Carroll's defeat and warning him that 'eaten bread is soon forgotten and you and your party's offhand treatment of this union will be remembered.'[15] Haughey replied that Mullen was completely wrong in his interpretation of the result, and that Carroll's defeat was due to the unfathomable intricacies of the Seanad electoral system. He told Mullen he remained convinced that it was important for the general welfare of the country and its people that the traditionally friendly relations that had always prevailed between 'the greatest trade union in this country and the greatest political party should continue'.[16] Hyperbolic, certainly, but also an accurate reflection of Haughey's view of the relationship between the two organisations. The Mullen letter has, however, the tone of fake injury and of being written for an internal union audience. Mullen well knew that Haughey had no power to direct his TDs, senators and councillors to vote for Carroll. If he really wanted something done, he would most likely have just picked up the phone to Haughey.

STARDUST

Notwithstanding the difficulties he had with the press, the Donegal by-election victory and the Anglo-Irish Dublin summit had put Haughey in an ebullient mood at Christmas 1980. In the new year, however, he struggled with a viral infection throughout January. Just prior to the Fianna Fáil Ard Fheis his doctor, Bryan Alton, prescribed a new tablet, manufactured in Germany, to clear away the residual lethargy he had been suffering from. He had also been prescribed a supplemental tonic and vitamin tablets, and Alton wanted him to have a chest X-ray, blood tests and a cardiograph after the Ard Fheis.[17] Haughey's physical ailments aside, he was preoccupied by one enormous political decision; when to call a general election. There had already been preliminary preparations for a snap election campaign. In January, the advertising executive Peter Owens, who was involved in planning the Ard Fheis, and was close to Haughey, wrote to the architect Arthur Gibney, another confidant of the Taoiseach, about the visuals he wanted in the RDS. Owens stressed the importance of coming up with slogans and themes that gave a hard edge to the potentially tough years and struggles that lay ahead, as they were 'almost certain to see an election before mid-year 1981'.[18] Yet, as the Ard Fheis opened on Friday 14 February, Haughey had not definitively made the decision on when to go to the country. What he had decided was that it would be by the end of the summer.[19]

That night over eight thousand people packed into the RDS for Fianna Fáil's annual gathering. It had a capacity of less than half of that. A few hours later, and just a few miles away, north of the River Liffey, eight hundred young people were at the Stardust nightclub in Artane, in the heart of Haughey's constituency, for a night out. Forty-eight of them would never come home.[20] The Stardust fire tragedy had a huge effect on the northside of the city, devastating lives and the close-knit working-class communities of Coolock and Artane. Haughey was on his way home to Abbeville, accompanied by P.J. Mara, when he learned of the tragedy.[21] He went home, changed his clothes, got up-to-date news from his officials and the Gardaí and then went to the Mater Hospital just before 6 a.m., where he met Bertie Ahern, who had worked there as an administrator.[22] Haughey and Ahern visited the accident and emergency room but quickly left, given the chaotic scene, and then went to some of the wards where the injured were being treated. The Taoiseach gave his first reaction to the shocked nation on the 7.30 a.m. RTÉ radio bulletin. He was in shock himself. Distressed and ashen-faced, he spoke to the press later that morning, expressing his heartfelt sympathies to the families and friends of all the victims, many of whom he knew as friends and neighbours. After visiting the hospitals, Haughey held an impromptu cabinet meeting in the RDS and adjourned the Ard Fheis. He then went to visit the burnt-out shell of the Stardust. A few hours later he returned to the RDS, and at 3.30 p.m. told the hushed crowd that the rest of the Ard Fheis was cancelled. A day of mourning was announced for the following Tuesday.

The appalling loss of life at the Stardust had a devastating impact on Haughey. He knew many of the victims personally. One of the injured was nineteen-year-old Walter Byrne, a stable boy at Abbeville. Over the next week Haughey visited Byrne and dozens of other survivors, and also called to the homes of the bereaved to sympathise.[23] In most of the homes he was welcomed as a native son and mourner of friends and family, as much as he was the Taoiseach.

The immediate political consequence of the tragedy was that Haughey postponed any idea of calling a general election. Barely fourteen months in power, Haughey was desperate to call and win a general election. He had to a very large extent been living on his nerves since winning the Fianna Fáil leadership. The cabinet was divided, and his opponents within it made little secret of the fact that they wanted him gone. He was trapped in a form of political insecurity that he believed he could only resolve by going to the country to win his own mandate.[24]

Over the next three months he pondered when to call the election while his government suffered from political drift. The Stardust tragedy had taken a significant amount out of Haughey, both physically and emotionally. He always became somewhat tetchy and apprehensive in the lead-up to big Ard Fheis speeches, television debates and important Dáil speeches. Once he was in the moment, though, he relaxed and he was a formidable speaker and debater. For a few weeks after the Stardust tragedy, however, he became more tempestuous and impatient, particularly when it came to party business.[25] He had badly wanted a general election and was frustrated that he could not call one, and win it. That would give him the opportunity to reshape his cabinet; he felt that Colley and O'Malley were becoming increasingly insufferable. He found the days of the Stardust funerals particularly difficult given that the victims were his constituents and he had known their families for decades.[26]

Just over a fortnight later, republicans in the Maze prison began a staged hunger strike, seeking the same five demands as those from the first strike the previous October: the right of prisoners to wear their own clothes; the right not to do prison work; free association with fellow prisoners; 50 per cent remission of sentences; and normal visits, parcels, educational and recreational facilities.[27] Haughey was dismayed. Coming so soon after the previous aborted strike, he was concerned that nothing beyond the full acceptance of the demands by the British government would satisfy the hunger strikers and the wider republican movement. He had, however, come to know Margaret Thatcher's temperament, and doubted that she would accede to any of the demands – to do so would, in her view, legitimise the armed struggle. This was the ultimate goal of the hunger strikers, and she was unlikely to yield. Since becoming Taoiseach, Haughey had developed his own source for insight into the thinking and attitude of republican prisoners in the Maze. Fr Denis Faul would say mass to the prisoners on Sunday and occasionally met with Ray MacSharry in either Enniskillen or Letterkenny afterwards to give him an indication of the mood of the prisoners and what their thought process was. At the beginning of the hunger strike, Haughey was in no doubt that the attitude of IRA prisoners had hardened considerably since the end of the 1980 strike, and they were determined to see their demands met or make the ultimate sacrifice.[28]

AOSDÁNA

As the hunger strikes were beginning, Haughey unveiled his Aosdána scheme for artists. On 5 March 1981, Aosdána was launched as an initiative which would allow artists to devote their energies fully to their art through the payment of a state stipend. It was the brainchild of Haughey's adviser on the arts, Anthony Cronin, and appealed to Haughey's long-held view that the state had an obligation to support the arts community and to honour artists whose work was making an outstanding contribution to the arts in Ireland. A few months after being appointed Taoiseach, Haughey had asked Cronin to become his cultural and artistic adviser. On the Aosdána scheme, Haughey stressed to Cronin that he wanted whatever emerged to have an honours dimension that would involve state recognition of artists and their importance, as well as being a means by which artists' financial circumstances might be improved. The idea was to increase respect as well as provide subsistence.[29] Haughey wanted a system of bursary schemes and scholarships which would ensure that artists did not have to endure the rather demeaning procedure of constantly filling in application forms for state assistance.[30]

Prior to the announcement, the artist Robert Ballagh congratulated Haughey on what he described as the proposed imaginative Aosdána scheme, stating that he suspected its effects would certainly be far-reaching.[31] Cronin and Haughey had tentatively discussed the issue as far back as Haughey's Harvard speech in the summer of 1972 on what a modern state's arts policy should be. Both men felt that there was a peculiarity in Ireland about the way state bodies looked at the arts, which was to concern themselves with performance and distribution, rather than with the actual creative process. When they provided money for the arts, governments and government agencies tended to favour organisations over individuals and performances over creativity. Another problem was that Ireland did not have the economy of scale of larger countries, where artists could live off the earnings from their works.[32]

A decade later there was some controversy about the origins of Aosdána when Brian P. Kennedy, in a book on the state and the arts published in 1990, maintained that it was the Arts Council that had driven the scheme after an initial suggestion by Haughey and Cronin. Kennedy quoted the then director of the Arts Council, Colm Ó Briain, that Aosdána represented the culmination of six years' work by the council.[33] Cronin wrote to the chairman of the Arts Council in October 1990 to state that the book's account of the origination of Aosdána was quite inaccurate and that while it was not his purpose to perpetuate controversy he wrote as a matter of a record and in a private capacity.[34] In a review of the book for the *Irish Times* he pointed out his belief that Kennedy was mistaken about Aosdána's beginning but said no more in what was generally a critical review.[35]

It was Haughey, according to Cronin, who told his arts adviser that he needed to work through the Arts Council, the body charged with devising and administering arts policy in the state, to get the scheme

established. Cronin then met with Ó Briain, and the scheme was formulated. It was due to be announced at the Fianna Fáil Ard Fheis, but
when that was postponed, the launch was delayed until early March.[36]
A year after the publication of Kennedy's book, in November 1991, two
hundred copies of it were shredded on the instructions of the director of
the Arts Council, Adrian Munnelly, giving rise to rumours that Haughey,
now Taoiseach again, had somehow brought influence to bear on the
decision. The reality was more prosaic. A year and half after publication
of the book, and embroiled in various controversies, Haughey could not
have cared one whit about it. The reality was that 1,500 copies of the book
were printed. Three hundred were sold; eight hundred given away to
libraries and other institutions; two hundred, which had been returned
unsold from booksellers were shredded; and two hundred remained
in stock and could be bought from the Arts Council. It was a small
but revealing example of the strange phenomenon that any controversy
at all to which Haughey was even tangentially related was widely perceived to be due to his malign influence. From its foundation Aosdána
would rescue many Irish writers and artists from penury, something
that greatly pleased Haughey. He had a genuine love of the arts, notwithstanding the view of some that his support for the arts was part of
an image-building exercise.[37] On the contrary, Haughey, as a republican,
had, as the poet Michael O'Loughlin wrote in 2017, an idea of the vital
relationship between a nation's image of itself and the contribution of
the arts.[38] He populated Abbeville with various pieces of art and considered himself a patron of Irish artists. He owned works by the sculptors
and painters, John Behan, John Haugh, Ruth Brandt, Patrick Hickey,
Louis le Brocquy and Maria Simmonds-Gooding. In 1987 he received
two watercolours of Inishvickillane from le Brocquy. He told the famed
artist that they arrived like messengers from another world, bringing
together two things that were very precious to him: 'the art of Louis le
Brocquy and the magical beauty of the Blaskets'.[39] Haughey and Cronin
wanted Aosdána to be a sort of Irish version of the Académie Française.
They saw the value of the Arts Council administering Aosdána, but they
also wanted to ensure that it would be self-governing, and not some sort

of socialist Valhalla for the politically correct literati who, they feared, would be favoured by the Arts Council bureaucracy.

HUNGER STRIKE

A different facet of Haughey's republicanism was on show by the time the rescheduled Fianna Fáil Ard Fheis took place on the weekend of 10 and 11 April 1981. The hunger strike was into its sixth week and Haughey was filled with a sense of foreboding. The previous day, the first of the hunger strikers, Bobby Sands, had won the Fermanagh–South Tyrone by-election, beating the Ulster Unionist candidate, Harry West, whom Haughey had known well in the 1960s. Haughey had by this stage all but made his mind up to go to the country in June. He told the Ard Fheis that the National Understanding had restored discipline to the public finances, reduced industrial disputes to their lowest level since 1975, particularly in the public sector, and averted the social confrontation and dislocation which was widespread elsewhere. This was a not-so-subtle reference to affairs in Britain and the consequences of Thatcher's policy of monetarism. Notwithstanding Thatcher's hostile reaction to Haughey's interpretation of their December summit, he told the Ard Fheis that joint studies were now being used by the two governments, covering, in the words of the communiqué issued at the time, 'the totality of relationships between the people of these islands'. He went on to say that the inauguration of the process represented by the studies had been welcomed by responsible opinion all over Ireland, and among Ireland's friends around the world. He said nothing about Britain. He repeated his view that he wanted an Ireland united and at peace based on arrangements acceptable to the different traditions on the island. But he then asked loyalists to recognise the hopelessness of the present situation, and to look positively at what a united Ireland would have to offer them.[40] This was cheered jubilantly in the crowded auditorium. The reaction from the leaders of unionism, afterwards, was predictably hostile.[41]

After Haughey's two-hour address the song 'Rise and Follow Charlie' by the Tipperary folk group the Morrisseys was played to wild enthusiasm. The Morrisseys were due to perform the song later that evening on

The Late Late Show, but the show's producer, Peter Feeney, was ordered by John Kelleher, RTÉ's controller of programmes, not to go ahead with it in case RTÉ was charged with favouritism in the run-up to the putative general election to come. The producers and composers of the song protested that as there was no political party mentioned there could be no possibility of bias, but RTÉ was unmoved. The lyrics of the song, written by Pete St John and Donie Cassidy, are:

> From southern glens to western shores, the ancient cry of freedom roars;
> From northern hills to Leinster's shores, we'll rise and follow Charlie.
> Charlie's song we'll sing as one, Charlie's song we'll sing along;
> Charlie's song, we'll march along, we'll rise and follow Charlie.
> Hail the leader, hail the man, with freedom's call it all began;
> With Irish pride in every man, we'll rise and follow Charlie;
> Young and old we all approve, he's kept the country on the move;
> He's helped the nation to improve, so rise and follow Charlie.

It was easy to see why RTÉ would feel it best not to broadcast the song on its most-watched television programme, but the CMR Records label claimed that RTÉ had allowed Frank Kelly's parody song 'Learning to Dance for Fianna Fáil' to be played on every major television and radio show. While amusing to some, the song was deeply offensive to others.[42]

After the Ard Fheis, Haughey went for a few days' rest and recuperation to Inishvickillane. The horse trainer Vincent O'Brien wrote to him inviting him to call in at Ballydoyle on the way back, offering food and hospitality for the Taoiseach and, rather cryptically, 'for whoever may be with you'. Haughey was, however, already back from what he described as a 'a few wonderful days' on his island.[43] By then he had made up his mind to go to the country, and started to think about the date. His preference was for a June election. While the Fianna Fáil grassroots, like Haughey, were enthusiastic for an election, some more cautious voices counselled against it. Fianna Fáil had a large majority and there was no requirement to call an election for at least another year. Ray MacSharry was one who urged him to wait: 'We are up to our eyes in Provos and hunger strikes. Why would we go to the country now?[44] Bertie Ahern was also doubtful about an early election, pointing out that the economy was relatively weak. Fianna Fáil's 1981 budget had reduced current spending but considerably increased short-term welfare benefits and committed £1.5 billion to the state's capital programme. By the beginning of May, the spending targets of that budget were spiralling out of control and Haughey felt that things would only get worse if he did not go to the country. A strike in the troubled Talbot car plant in Santry, in Haughey's own constituency, which involved an around-the-clock picket, was symptomatic of the difficulties in the economy. For Ahern, things could hardly be worse in the North, with the hunger strikes in full swing and the likelihood of deaths coming in the middle of the campaign if it was held in May or June. He also urged Haughey to wait.[45] Haughey was aware of the potential difficulty of having an election in the middle of the hunger strikes. After the death of the second hunger striker, Francis Hughes, Dermot Nally communicated to London Haughey's fear that in a general election up to half a dozen IRA sympathisers might be elected and hold the balance of power.[46]

The problem was that the majority was Jack Lynch's and nothing could dissuade Haughey from the entirely rational desire to have a majority of his own. It was, however, to some within Fianna Fáil, entirely irrational because it was impossible to predict how an election campaign would go. As Bobby Sands had contested the Fermanagh–South Tyrone by-election, there was every likelihood that hunger strikers, or at the very least their supporters, would contest the general election to highlight both their demands and the plight of the men who were dying. This was likely to have an impact on Fianna Fáil's vote in the border counties. That was what happened, and it cost Haughey, not only his overall majority, but his position as Taoiseach.

On the night of Thursday 23 April, when Bobby Sands was in the fifty-fourth day of his hunger strike, Haughey met his father, Jim, his mother, Rosaleen, and his sister, Marcella, at Abbeville. He was impressed by what he considered their humility and was of the opinion that they were people who would be law-abiding pillars of society in any other setting but Northern Ireland.[47] The previous day he had summoned the British ambassador, Leonard Figg, to his office to express his concern at the likely consequences of Sands' death and his fears about violence in the North spilling over into the Republic.[48] On the Monday of that week, Neil Blaney, Síle de Valera and Dr John O'Connell, members of both the Dáil and the European Parliament, had visited Sands in the Maze. O'Connell urged Sands to give up his strike, saying that dying would achieve nothing. He was rebuffed. Margaret Thatcher refused the three Irish politicians' request to meet with her. After his meetings with the Sands family and the British ambassador, Haughey was more dismayed than at any time since the strike began. The British would not budge. The Sands family knew their son would not budge. Haughey also knew it.

Two days after his meeting with the Sands family, Haughey said that the best chance of saving Sands' life lay in his family making a complaint to the European Commission of Human Rights. That same day Marcella Sands made such an application. When her brother found out he was furious; he believed that Haughey could have influenced the British government by supporting the prisoners' five demands.[49] Sands went into a coma on Sunday 3 May, and the following day the Irish government asked Marcella to make a new complaint to the European Court of Human Rights. She refused, believing that Haughey's gesture was an empty one, given that he had not supported the hunger strikers' demands. The following day Bobby Sands died. Haughey was criticised by the wider republican movement for not having done enough to save his life. The reality was somewhat different. Haughey could not publicly support the hunger strikers' demands. To do so would in effect place him on the same side as the provisional movement and thus make a mockery of his call to unionists in his Ard Fheis speech that a united Ireland would be a welcoming place for them. It would also have clearly legitimised the Provisional IRA view of the conflict in Northern Ireland, and Haughey could certainly not do that. Any progress that had been made with the British since he had become Taoiseach would have been immediately halted if he had made any sort of statement supporting the aims of the hunger strikers. As it was, the joint studies offered some tangible hope to Haughey of some sort of breakthrough, no matter how distant.

As the leader of constitutional republicanism in the Republic, as he saw it, Haughey believed that he and his party were the barrier between the state and its possible collapse into anarchy.[50] Again, he was not going to let that happen. He was, however, seriously distressed by the attitude of Margaret Thatcher towards the hunger strikers, and indeed towards his own position as the leader of Ireland's real republican party, and one that could help engineer a solution to the most intractable of problems. It was an attitude he would not forget. Months later, when in opposition, he wrote to the British ambassador to Ireland, Leonard Figg, to thank him for the very real contribution he had made personally to the improvement of Anglo-Irish relations during Haughey's period in office and his constant efforts to overcome difficulties and problems.[51] He did not think the same of the British prime minister. He was deeply frustrated by her simplistic hard line of 'no concessions to the prisoners', which, he feared, would lead to the deaths of the hunger strikers and plunge the politics on both sides of the island of Ireland into unknown territory.

ELECTION '81

On the afternoon of Thursday 21 May 1981, sixteen days after the death of Bobby Sands, Haughey went to Áras an Uachtaráin to ask President Hillery to dissolve the Dáil. The writs for the forty-one constituencies were issued later that evening to allow the election to take place on 11 June. A few hours later, Patsy O'Hara became the fourth of the hunger strikers to die. It was an election that both main parties were prepared for. Fine Gael had concluded from early in the year that Haughey would plump for a June election as they believed he was a poor decision-maker, naturally indecisive, and afraid to offend the warring factions in his party and important interest groups. This was gleaned from a report by two psychologists hired by the party to assess Haughey's personality. It is not quite clear how calling an election in June, a full year before one was needed, indicated that Haughey was irresolute, but Fine Gael was

convinced that it could plan for an election based on Haughey's inde-
cisiveness.[52] It was also convinced from at least February that Haughey
could not win an overall majority. One of Haughey's correspondents, the
solicitor Bruce St John Blake, wrote to him in late February 1981, enclosing what he described as a detailed commentary on a recent Fine Gael
analysis outlining how Fianna Fáil could not secure an overall majority.[53]
Haughey thought differently.

Having decided to go to the country in the middle of the hunger
strikes, and in an increasingly difficult economic situation, Haughey
campaigned energetically for his longed-for overall majority. Fianna Fáil
spared no expense. It spent £150,000 on press advertising.[54] It had a fully
manned general election information centre, open from 8 a.m. to midnight, that covered every aspect of the campaign, from the Taoiseach's
tour to providing speakers for after-mass meetings to daily reports on
the results of the canvas in every constituency. It was planned to the last
detail to ensure that directors of elections, candidates, the party's election
committee and the Taoiseach himself had up-to-the-minute information
throughout the campaign.[55]

Haughey's main message was that only Fianna Fáil could provide
stable government and that the Fine Gael and Labour programmes were
essentially monetarism with socialist trimmings, which would require
a series of rather aimless compromises, leading to drift.[56] Fianna Fáil
argued that the opposition had scarcely anyone in its ranks who had had
a successful ministerial career. In his own handwritten emendations on
how his team compared to Fine Gael's and Labour's, Haughey noted that
he led a government that was agreed and united on all major issues; the
alternative was a 'coalition in which diametrical opposite policies will
have to be bartered'.[57] In a press conference on 3 June, just over a week
from the election, Haughey maintained that the Fine Gael programme
introduced the 'economics of wonderland where everything is promised
but nothing is paid for', pointing out that Fine Gael's platform containing
140 new expenditure proposals covering all areas of the economy had
almost no costings.[58] The problem was that Fianna Fáil's own costings
were based on a booming economy operating in a pristine industrial

relations landscape. The reality was that tax protests, a fragile National Understanding agreement and lavish spending promises meant that the economy was already in crisis.

Haughey's campaign was ultimately fought on two fronts. On one side he was fighting Garret FitzGerald and Fine Gael on the economy. On the other he was fighting the H-Block candidates on the hunger strikes. He was certainly happy to campaign on the economy, but the continuing hunger strikes and the nomination of nine republican prisoners, including four hunger strikers, to run in the election turned into the nightmare Ray MacSharry had warned him about. Wherever he canvassed across the country Haughey was followed by small unruly groups of republican protesters waving black flags and hurling abuse at him. He remained frustrated over the hunger strike and concerned about the black flags and youth protests proliferating around the country. The black flags that were tacked on every telegraph pole and the potent graffiti accompanying them would, he knew, feed into electoral problems for Fianna Fáil. And yet he had insisted on calling the election. He had underestimated the influence that the H-Block candidates would have in the battle for the last seats in marginal constituencies. He was not alone. The consensus view across the parties, and indeed the political journalists, was that the H-Block candidates would have a negligible influence on the outcome. The coverage on RTÉ's election results programmes on both radio and television, and the commentary in the press after the election, all pointed to the surprising success of the H-Block candidates.[59]

That political consensus was shattered when two H-Block candidates, the hunger striker Kieran Doherty in Cavan–Monaghan, and Paddy Agnew in Louth, took seats. Another hunger striker, Joe McDonnell, just failed to take a seat in Sligo-Leitrim and the other H-Block candidates polled well enough to eat into the traditional Fianna Fáil republican vote. In August the polling company IMS conducted a post-mortem review of the campaign for Fianna Fáil. It came to the conclusion that many of the voters had made their mind up whether to vote for or against Fianna Fáil well in advance of the election and that the key factor determining their vote was the management of the economy; the feeling was that tough decisions were called for but were not forthcoming. The report did not shy away from criticising Haughey, noting that there was widespread agreement that when he came to power he was expected to take tough decisions and be an equally tough manager of the economy. In that context a 'feeling of disappointment permeated reactions throughout group discussions that he had not reacted in this manner: he is suspected [of] having taken soft options over the twelve months before the election.'[60] It went on to point to: the attraction of Garret FitzGerald as a candidate for young people; weakening party loyalties, particularly among the young; the fact that while Fianna Fáil's main strategy was to stand on its record, the problem was that the record itself was not considered adequate; and a belief that the Fianna Fáil canvas was weaker than in other elections, particularly when compared to Fine Gael's. The H-Block candidates were not mentioned. The party's general secretary, Frank Wall, however, was in no doubt that a few hundred votes in a number of constituencies that moved from Fianna Fáil to the H-Block candidates cost it about eight seats and, with them, Haughey's cherished overall majority.[61]

Fianna Fáil won 78 of the 166 seats on 45.3 per cent of the vote. In the face of a rejuvenated Fine Gael, in which Garret FitzGerald matched Haughey's enthusiasm on the stump, and was a far more attractive leader than Liam Cosgrave in 1977, and the spectre of the hunger strikes, the Fianna Fáil vote held up remarkably well. The scale of Jack Lynch's win in 1977 meant that losses for Fianna Fáil were almost inevitable whenever Haughey went to the country. In a worldwide economic downturn, the international trend was against incumbent governments. A month earlier, François Mitterrand had defeated the incumbent Valéry Giscard d'Estaing in the French presidential election, and the year before, Ronald Reagan had ousted Jimmy Carter in the USA. Margaret Thatcher's rout of Labour in Britain in 1979 had begun the trend.

While Haughey polled over two quotas in Dublin North Central, the overall result was that his gamble had failed. Fine Gael had an astounding election, winning sixty-five seats, a gain of twenty-two on 1977, on 36.5 per cent of the vote. Labour stagnated, coming back with fifteen seats, the same number they had going into the election. Its leader, Frank

Cluskey, lost his seat, as did one of the party's more impressive Dáil performers, John Horgan, both losing out to a significant Fine Gael increase on the southside of Dublin. Notwithstanding Haughey's accurate claim that Fine Gael and Labour had very little in common, Garret FitzGerald and the new Labour leader, Michael O'Leary, quickly formed a minority government with the support of a number of independents. Their friendship and the antipathy of their parties to Haughey was enough of a common denominator to send him to the opposition benches.

OPPOSITION

Haughey's loss of office hurt him badly. Despite the IMS report that many of the voters had their minds made up from a long way out, and that it was the economy more than anything else which caused Fianna Fáil to lose just enough support to cost it the election, Haughey remained convinced that it was the hunger strike that had caused his defeat. He found this particularly hard to take because of his own republicanism.[62] He also felt his own efforts at resolving the strikes had not been appreciated. The editor of the *Irish Press*, Tim Pat Coogan, wrote to sympathise; he was sorry that 'your efforts to end the hunger strike met with so little recognition or success – they certainly deserve better, given the time and effort you put into trying.' Coogan added that he hoped and expected that Haughey would be back in power before too long. If 'you got any kind of fair play on the North and the economy I think you could bring lasting benefit and improvement to the country'.[63] The Bishop of Derry, Edward Daly, was also appreciative of Haughey's efforts, telling him that he must have been as frustrated as Daly himself was with the intransigence on both sides and the fact that they both had to 'take stick from both sides involved in it'. He asked Haughey to 'keep up your interest in our situation here, despite the frustrations you may have experienced. We will almost certainly need a lot of support, encouragement and friendship in the future.'[64] Haughey replied that the hunger strike situation was one of the most 'agonising and difficult' that he had ever had to face.[65] The consequences of that agony was that in his electoral defeat he became ever more vocal in opposition to any suggestion by the new government of how to move the Northern Ireland issue forward. In his view any plan that deviated from the results of his summits with Thatcher was doomed to fail and an abandonment of the goal of Irish unity. This was particularly the case when the new Taoiseach, Garret FitzGerald, launched his constitutional crusade to convince the unionist community in Northern Ireland that the Republic was not a sectarian state. Haughey accused him of, in effect, giving unionists a veto over a united Ireland and abandoning those nationalists in every part of the island who cherished that goal.

Fianna Fáil's loss of power gave significant succour to Haughey's opponents in the party, who blamed him for the its defeat. The eighteen months since his election as Taoiseach had been bruising for Haughey. Borrowing, direct and indirect taxation, inflation and the national debt all soared, leaving him somewhat bewildered. The hunger strikes only added to the general sense of dismay in the country. The decision to call the election had been his alone and in its aftermath his party was still divided, but now he had no spoils of office to divest, making matters much worse than they had been in December 1979. Haughey took some considerable time to accept the defeat and for a full six months he left his former ministerial team in place, shadowing FitzGerald's cabinet. This was the first time he had led the opposition and he found it difficult to come to terms with his new position. The last time Fianna Fáil had been in opposition after an election he had been in the political wilderness. The stakes were far higher now. The revelation by the new government that the state of the country's finances was immeasurably worse than Haughey had stated at the general election put him in a quandary. He opposed the emergency budget introduced in July by the new Minister for Finance, John Bruton, as unnecessary and monetarist. He painted Fine Gael as Ireland's equivalent of the heartless Tories, hell-bent on conquering inflation to the detriment of people's jobs and livelihoods. He was conscious, however, of the need to get the public finances under control. He had taken note of the IMS findings that the public had expected him to take hard decisions when he was appointed Taoiseach and that he had not. The result had been that some voters had lost confidence in him and in Fianna Fáil. He needed to get that confidence back.

Many in Fianna Fáil felt that the party needed to show a responsible attitude to the public finances while it was in opposition. It was
not just Colley, O'Malley and O'Donoghue who were advocating this
approach; Ray MacSharry and Albert Reynolds were of a similar view.[66]
Haughey was quietly dismissive of the so-called financial rectitude of
the Colley wing of the party. None of them would accept cuts to their
own departments during his brief tenure as Taoiseach, and all of them
were enthusiastic advocates of the giveaway 1977 manifesto. Yet Gene
Fitzgerald had inspired nobody during his stint as Minister for Finance.
It was in that context that Haughey finally named a new frontbench
in January 1982, taking the apparently extraordinary decision to make
Martin O'Donoghue, architect of the 1977 manifesto, which Haughey
had privately derided, his spokesman on finance. He had, of course, also
excluded O'Donoghue from his cabinet just eighteen months earlier.
O'Donoghue was one of the few people who Haughey considered intellectually able within Fianna Fáil.[67] He also liked that O'Donoghue was
of humble stock and had worked as a waiter to put himself through
college. Whatever doubts Haughey had about the 1977 manifesto, he
knew O'Donoghue's abilities and he needed someone in the Dáil to mark
John Bruton. Haughey thought that O'Donoghue was a technocrat who
could defend Fianna Fáil's position. He also believed it might help to heal
the deep divisions which still haunted Fianna Fáil if he had his known
enemies on his frontbench. He was very much wrong in that view as he
utterly failed to realise how deeply entrenched O'Donoghue was in the
Colley–O'Malley camp. In any event, O'Donoghue never got any chance
to make his mark as opposition finance spokesman as the government
failed to get its January budget through the Dáil.

The one sliver of consolation Haughey had when he went into opposition was that the coalition was inherently unstable, with the two parties
holding polar opposite positions on pretty much all aspects of public
policy. This was particularly the case when it came to the public finances.
Another less visible but equally problematic issue was that, from the
beginning, the Taoiseach, Garret FitzGerald, governed as if he had a
strong majority. Haughey considered the government to be made up

of inept, if well-meaning, amateurs and viewed its attitude towards the independents keeping it in office as proof of this.[68] When the government fell in late January 1982, having failed to get its budget passed in the Dáil, Haughey was unsurprised. Proposals to extend VAT to clothing and footwear were too much for the independent socialist TD Jim Kemmy, and he let the coalition know that he could not support the budget. The majoritarian attitude of the government was on full display during this episode. FitzGerald simply assumed that the logic of his proposals would win out and he did not consider it plausible that Kemmy and another independent, Seán Dublin Bay Loftus, would vote against the budget and thus cause an election. He was later reduced to begging for Kemmy's vote on the floor of the chamber when he realised that the Limerick TD would indeed vote against the budget.[69] A compromise proposal to exempt children's clothing and shoes was rejected by the Department of Finance for the absurd reason that women with small feet might be able to avoid the tax by buying children's shoes.[70] Maurice O'Connell, second secretary in the department, having received advice from Treasury officials in Britain, insisted that the exclusion for children would probably be unworkable and open to abuse.[71] This was indeed a long way from Haughey facing down his secretary of finance T.K. Whitaker on free electricity for pensioners in his April 1967 budget. Now, some fifteen years later, a Fine Gael Minister for Finance, John Bruton, was captive to his own officials. The result was that his government became the first in the history of the state not to pass its own budget.

There was confusion in the Dáil when the government was defeated. Given that a budget defeat is the equivalent of losing a vote of no confidence it dawned on the assembled deputies and journalists that the government had indeed lost the confidence of the house and the result would be a general election. Haughey had a different view. He issued a statement saying that the President should consider the situation that had arisen when the Taoiseach ceased to retain the support of a majority of the Dáil, and he was 'available for consultation by the President should he so wish'.[72] At the same time, Loftus felt that there was no need for a general election and he tried to stop FitzGerald going to the Áras to seek the dissolution of the Dáil. He rang the president's aide-de-camp to pass on the message that he was willing to meet Fine Gael and discuss the situation. He had been ignored by the party in the lead-up to the budget and felt slighted. He then telegrammed the Áras to reiterate his message. He received no reply. His thinking seems to have been that Hillery should have summoned the Council of State, and convened a joint meeting of the Houses of the Oireachtas to form a national government.[73] Loftus considered FitzGerald an amateur in the game of politics, but he could be accused of the same himself, as he seemed confused about the impact of his vote on the fateful night.[74] It was rather late to believe he could rescue the situation by trying to stop FitzGerald meeting the president to ask for a dissolution of the Dáil. Hillery and FitzGerald both wisely ignored his call to the Áras.

Following Haughey's statement that he was willing to meet with the president, two of his frontbenchers, Brian Lenihan and Sylvester Barrett, tried to phone their former colleague, Patrick Hillery, to ask him to talk formally to Haughey about the possibility of Fianna Fáil forming an alternative administration before he agreed to dissolve the Dáil. Haughey called once himself at 8.15 p.m. on 27 January. It certainly would have been possible for Haughey to form a minority government, but its numbers would have been much tighter than the outgoing coalition's and in reality it would never have been able to govern for any plausible length of time and it would have had no mandate from the people. While there was no constitutional barrier stopping Hillery asking Haughey to see if he could form a government, Hillery himself certainly did not want to be put in that position. He knew that Jim Kemmy would never vote for Haughey and was worried that if he refused a dissolution and Haughey could not form a government, as was probable, a real constitutional crisis was likely. Ultimately, as his biographer John Walsh points out, Hillery did not want to embroil the presidency in a party political conflict. This was central to his thinking on the night of 27 January 1982.[75] He told his aide-de-camp that he would not speak to anyone who phoned that night, with the exception of the Taoiseach. FitzGerald made matters worse by delaying going to the Áras, having first chaired an emergency cabinet meeting. The preparation of the necessary papers was then delayed, giving Haughey the time he needed to call the Áras seeking to speak to the President.

This was a serious miscalculation on Haughey's part. It was one thing to issue a statement saying he was available to speak to the president. It was quite another to ring the Áras demanding to see the president to try and persuade him that he could form a – very unlikely – alternative arrangement. Haughey should have known that Hillery would not want to see him and be dragged into a political controversy in which there could be no winners. Haughey should also have known that he did not have the numbers to form a government. If the president had agreed to see him, Haughey would in fact have been in a much worse position. Hillery would certainly have refused his request to form an alternative government as it would have been a hopeless task. Haughey would then have been in the extremely difficult position of trying to explain his own stance and motives. Hillery eventually saw FitzGerald at 10 p.m. that night and agreed to a dissolution of the Dáil. Attention quickly turned to the second election in eight months. Haughey's frantic machinations had come to nothing. Yet the night of 27 January 1982 would come back to haunt Haughey. His long-drawn-out exit from public life began when the fateful phone calls were brought up in the 1990 presidential election, to devastating effect for Haughey, Lenihan and Fianna Fáil.

THE FEBRUARY 1982 ELECTION

With the hunger strikes over and the emotion of June 1981 a distant memory, the three-week campaign in 1982 was fought primarily on the economy. An important sub-theme was Haughey himself. The Fianna Fáil campaign was again presidential in nature, with Haughey as its primary focus. The emphasis on the leader had been the party's strategy in general elections since its foundation, but Haughey's opponents saw it as an extension of his cult of personality. They had not seen it in those terms when the party ran a similar campaign based around Jack Lynch just five years earlier. Fine Gael and Labour, while defending their own positions, basically an extension of the defeated budget, also sought to persuade the electorate that Haughey was a dangerous megalomaniac. The irony was that Fine Gael's campaign was also based on idealising its own leader, Garret FitzGerald.

Haughey soon regretted appointing Martin O'Donoghue as Fianna Fáil finance spokesman. The two men clashed over the necessary financial adjustments needed to tackle the country's dire economic circumstances, resulting in mixed messages coming from the party in the crucial first week of the campaign. Haughey was forced to face the reality that the country could not borrow itself out of recession, notwithstanding an early attack on the coalition over its obsession with government debt. O'Donoghue pointedly contradicted him on radio a week into the campaign, and then refused to answer questions about whether he supported Haughey's leadership at all.[76] Haughey was put on the back foot and faced a torrent of questions from journalists as to what he was going to do about his finance spokesperson. Reports then started to come back from Fianna Fáil canvassers that there was a so-called 'Haughey effect' on the ground, and it was not positive. Many in Haughey's camp believed it was being orchestrated by Fine Gael and Labour, and gleefully reported by hostile journalists. After the election one of his correspondents told Haughey that he had heard from reliable sources that the smear campaign was 'a well planned and organised conspiracy amongst the hierarchy of Fine Gael to split Fianna Fáil' in order that Fine Gael would become the strongest political party in the country.[77] The attacks on Haughey during the campaign would be deemed by the public as evidence of a party in decline, disunited and losing its way. There was more than a hint of truth in the perception that Fianna Fáil was divided, but an election victory, and an overall majority, would, Haughey felt, give him the opportunity to unite the party. His opponents had a different view; that it would give him the opportunity to purge them and write the Colley wing out of the party altogether.

One other issue which came up in the campaign was the thorny question of abortion. The day before the government fell, Garret FitzGerald told the Dáil that his government was strongly opposed to abortion and in favour of ensuring that the Constitution provided protection for all life, including the life of the unborn child. He added that he would 'deprecate any attempt to make this a political issue in the House because there are certain things that the parties in the House are united on and this is one.'[78] Haughey replied that he wanted FitzGerald to accept his assurance that Fianna Fáil had no intention of making abortion a party issue. Whatever steps the government took would receive full and expeditious co-operation from his side of the house; but in his view that legislation and the proposed amendment on abortion should be advanced without reference to any other matter. This was a reference to FitzGerald's constitutional crusade and his idea of linking a referendum on abortion with a wider constitutional review which he had asked his Attorney General, Peter Sutherland, to undertake. Fianna Fáil's view was that in coupling the issue of an abortion referendum with other unspecified constitutional issues, FitzGerald was taking away from the importance of the pro-life campaign and essentially reneging on another election promise.

The Pro-Life Amendment Campaign (PLAC) had sprung up completely unannounced the previous year and on the same day in April 1981 met with both Haughey, then Taoiseach, and FitzGerald, the leader of the opposition, to try to persuade them to call a referendum that would, in effect, guarantee the rights of the unborn child and constitutionally outlaw abortion.[79] It anticipated that abortion might become legal either through parliamentary action or the courts, or both. Its basic premise was that there was a strong possibility that the Irish Supreme Court might copy its American counterpart's decision in the case of *Roe v Wade*, which eight years earlier had declared state legislation against abortion to be unconstitutional in the USA. In Ireland, restrictive abortion legislation had remained intact and virtually unchallenged since 1861 under Section 58 of the Offences against the Person Act. Section 59 of the same Act also provided that anyone helping a woman have an abortion would be liable to considerable penalties.

Yet PLAC seemed to fear that a simple amendment of the existing Act could legalise abortion, despite the fact that replacing the existing Act with a more permissive or liberal Act was simply not an option that any government would be willing to sign up to, or even want to do, in this period. Second, the pro-life campaign feared that if abortion was not constitutionally prohibited, there was a danger that an action could be taken in the Irish courts to challenge the legislative prohibition of abortion in an attempt to have it declared unconstitutional. Again, the likelihood of this in a state noted for its social conservatism since its foundation was virtually nil. No liberal cadre of jurists or constitutional lawyers were advocating for such a judgment. In fact, Haughey's own advice from the office of the Attorney General was that a constitutional change was not necessary and that a Supreme Court ruling legalising abortion, like that of *Roe v Wade*, was a very remote possibility. Moreover, as medical science advanced and evolved, legislation was a better way to deal with complex medical issues as they emerged, for example the life chances of a pregnant woman and the foetus she was carrying in cases where the mother was ill.

One of PLAC's members, the gynaecologist Professor Eamon O'Dwyer, summed up the fears of those advocating for a referendum when he wrote to Haughey in April 1981 to say that the weight of legal advice PLAC had was that the law as it stood might not afford absolute protection to the unborn. PLAC could see the 1861 Act being challenged as unconstitutional and perhaps being overturned 'in the case of rape (especially involving a very young person), incest, and in the case of a gross cognitive imperfection like anencephaly'. O'Dwyer went on to tell Haughey for 'your own private ear' that Fine Gael was interested in such a referendum and that Garret FitzGerald had indicated his interest in and sympathy for such an amendment, which he would be prepared to sponsor.[80] Two days later this view was confirmed when PLAC met with both Fine Gael and the Taoiseach. On that day, 30 April 1981, Haughey, as Taoiseach, met with representatives of PLAC, who explained to him the dangers they felt were inherent in the legal situation. He described his meeting with them as very satisfactory and responded positively to their submission.[81] Prior to their meeting with Haughey, PLAC met with the leader of the opposition, Garret FitzGerald, to present its arguments.[82] After that meeting, a member of the PLAC committee who was friendly to Fianna Fáil, rang the Taoiseach's office to say that they had just met FitzGerald in Leinster House, and he had agreed 'with alacrity' to their suggestion of a constitutional referendum.[83] Haughey was now armed with two pieces of evidence that Fine Gael was going to commit to a referendum. He thus felt that Fianna Fáil had no option but to do the same. Any previous advice from the Attorney General's office was quickly forgotten and the die was cast for a constitutional referendum on abortion.

Two weeks later Haughey met with PLAC again and this time he committed Fianna Fáil to a referendum, conveying to Julia Vaughan, PLAC's chairperson, 'a solemn assurance that an appropriate constitutional amendment to give effect' to Fianna Fáil's total opposition to abortion would be brought forward as soon as circumstances permitted. He declared that the government was examining the form such an amendment would take so as to ensure it would be fully constitutionally and legally effective.[84] Garret FitzGerald met with PLAC in December 1981 to tell them that a constitutional change in relation to abortion would be incorporated into a general constitutional review that he had proposed. They were dissatisfied with his response and continued to demand a single referendum to outlaw abortion.[85]

When the February 1982 election was called Haughey confirmed that Fianna Fáil was committed to the idea of presenting just one referendum to the people. He wrote to PLAC to confirm that when elected to office the new Fianna Fáil government 'will arrange to have the necessary legislation for a proposed constitutional amendment to guarantee the right of the life of the foetus initiated in Dáil Éireann during the course of this year, 1982, without reference to any other aspect of constitutional change'.[86] And indeed, on returning to office, Haughey immediately asked his new Attorney General, Paddy Connolly, for his advice on an appropriate form of wording of the amendment, which he wanted submitted to the government at the earliest date possible.[87] That was the position Haughey took when questioning FitzGerald the day before the government fell. FitzGerald also committed to a referendum as part of his wider crusade. The issue cropped up intermittently on the campaign, with Fianna Fáil attempting to outdo Fine Gael in its social conservatism, but the fact that both parties had promised a referendum of some sort took the heat out of the issue. It would, however, return, bringing significant consequences, over the next eighteen months.

On the night of Tuesday 16 February, with just over a full day to go in the campaign, Haughey and FitzGerald faced off in the first ever television debate between the leaders of the two main parties that had dominated the state since its inception. Fianna Fáil, conscious that many voters in the July 1981 election had made their minds up early in that campaign, had sought an earlier date, but Fine Gael had refused. In the days leading up to the debate, Haughey practised in Kinsaley with Fianna Fáil's general secretary, Frank Wall, and its director of elections, Albert Reynolds, who had made a big impression on Haughey in his short period of time as Minister for Posts and Telegraphs, and whose political advice he trusted.[88] The former director of the Government Information Bureau in the late 1960s, Eoin Neeson, had written to Haughey the previous week advising him to remember the lessons of the famous Kennedy–Nixon debate in the 1960 US presidential election. The viewers of that debate were impressed by Kennedy's manner and appearance but not by Nixon's. Neeson counselled Haughey that visual impact was what mattered, that he should make his points as lightly as possible without diminishing them and that he should smile and laugh where it was reasonable to do so. Neeson ended with the ringing endorsement that FitzGerald could be made to seem confused and by contrast Haughey could 'appear almost benign with advantage'.[89] Yet, for his final preparations, Haughey went to the communications team of Terry Prone and Tom Savage of Carr Communications with whom he went through a very detailed simulation on the day before the debate in their studio. He was much amused when Prone told him that Neeson's advice about smiling was 'shite' and that the most important thing was to remain calm, focused and keep his points simple for the average undecided voter.[90]

On the night itself, it was clear that there was no warmth between Haughey and FitzGerald. Their handshake prior to the contest, which was chaired by Brian Farrell, was stiff and formal and neither made any effort to be cordial to the other. As Raymond Smith in the *Irish*

Independent observed, 'they were on the eve of a moment of destiny in Irish politics when a heavy defeat for either one of them could mean the end of the line.'[91] The debate itself proved a dull enough affair. The only excitement came when FitzGerald waved a document in the air that, he claimed, was proof that Fianna Fáil had in effect cooked the books to the sum of £130 million. What the exact proof was, he never said. In his autobiography, published close to a decade later, he still claimed he had the documentary evidence but again did not say what it was.[92] Haughey replied that it was all nonsense, a figment of FitzGerald's imagination; it was simply a list of figures that meant nothing. Nine months later, in the teeth of the November 1982 election campaign, Haughey asked the secretary of the Department of Finance, Maurice Doyle, for a note on the events surrounding the statement by FitzGerald in the February debate on the refusal of the Central Bank to lend funds to the exchequer in 1981. On the afternoon of the February debate, FitzGerald's adviser Patrick Honohan had sought Doyle's confirmation that the Central Bank had indeed refused the exchequer the sum of £350 million. On discovering that Honohan's inquiry was directed to briefing FitzGerald for the election television debate that night, Doyle warned Honohan that no mention should be made of these events in the debate as they were highly sensitive, could damage Ireland's credit standing, and that it was unlikely that Haughey was aware of the transaction. Doyle told Haughey that it was his understanding that the document used by FitzGerald in the debate that night was in fact a table indicating that expenditure was running ahead of the 1981 budget estimate.[93]

It was reported in the following day's papers that Haughey won the debate, that he made his points more cleverly, and was more easily understood than FitzGerald – as both Neeson and Prone had advised him to do. According to Michael Mills in the *Irish Press*, Haughey won hands down on style; he was cool, where FitzGerald was excited.[94] The problem for Haughey was that his victory was not considered to be by a significant enough margin to make a noticeable difference at the polling booths. In fact, an immediate Lansdowne Market Research poll for the *Irish Independent* stated that although Haughey was judged the winner, it did not translate into any increase in support for Fianna Fáil.[95] On the night the ESB reported a big rise in electricity consumption at the halfway stage, but not at the end, which the *Irish Press* took as a sign that most voters did not stay to the end of the ninety-minute marathon.[96] Haughey, who was desperate for an overall majority, having fallen short the previous July, had not, it seemed, done enough to sway the undecideds his way. The week after the election he received a video tape recording of the debate from the chairman of the RTÉ Authority, Fred O'Donovan, who hoped Haughey would consider it a memento of a historic occasion in Irish broadcasting.[97] And indeed it was a historic occasion, but Haughey was not satisfied that he had done enough. He went home to Abbeville in a downbeat mood. He had one last full day on the canvas to persuade the Irish people to give him an overall majority.

The campaign ended in high farce when, on the morning of the election, Haughey's own election agent Pat O'Connor was alleged to have attempted to vote twice, in Kinsealy national school (where Haughey and his family voted) at 9.35 a.m., and in Pope John Paul II national school in Malahide at 10.30 a.m. On receipt of complaints by Fine Gael personation agents, the Gardaí began an investigation. The *Evening Herald* ran with the story on its front page that evening, under the headline 'Garda Probe at Kinsealy Booth', when there was still hours left to vote.[98] Later that evening Haughey met O'Connor at the Fianna Fáil constituency headquarters in Killester and was described as being incandescent with rage.[99] Just over two months later the summons against O'Connor, and his daughter Niamh, was dismissed at Swords District Court. Judge Donal Kearney ruled that the prosecution had not proved, and as the law stood could not prove, that the defendants, or indeed any defendant, had 'committed this offence of double-voting or whatever the word is'.[100] Haughey was at this stage two months into his short-lived chaotic government of 1982 and already embroiled in various controversies that would follow him for the rest of his public life.

CHAPTER 17

1982

The results of the February 1982 election were again inconclusive. Fianna Fáil gained three seats, winning eighty-one of the 166 on offer, an agonising three short of an overall majority. Its share of the vote also went up 2 per cent to 47.3 per cent. It has never been as high since. It was not enough, however, to guarantee Haughey a return to power. Fine Gael's percentage of the vote went up to 37.3 per cent but it lost two seats, to return with sixty-three. Labour once again returned with fifteen seats. Sinn Féin – The Workers' Party (SFWP) won three seats and there were four independents. Seán Dublin Bay Loftus lost his seat in Haughey's constituency and would never be elected to the Dáil again. Kemmy was re-elected in Limerick, and the other independents were Neil Blaney in Donegal, who could be expected to vote for Haughey, and the automatically returned Ceann Comhairle, Dr John O'Connell. With three more seats than the outgoing coalition government, Haughey was in prime position to form a government.

Yet, in the immediate aftermath of the election, Haughey's biggest difficulty remained an internal one. Although both Fianna Fáil's seat share and its percentage of the vote had gone up, Haughey's enemies in the party, including George Colley, Des O'Malley, Martin O'Donoghue and Séamus Brennan, gathered the day after the results to plot a way to oust Haughey from the leadership. Over two years after Colley's defeat in the Fianna Fáil leadership campaign, none of them had come to terms with Haughey's victory. They had never accepted his leadership, never given him any loyalty, and never would. To P.J. Mara, they wanted to restore an 'old order that was gone, shattered, never to return'.[1] In the election, 786,951 people had voted for Fianna Fáil. Now a group of four malcontents were trying to oust the party's leader before the new Dáil had even met. The problem was that beyond their general objective of forcing Haughey from the leadership they had little idea of what they were doing, and no obvious reason for replacing Haughey beyond the fact that they did not like him. They seemed disappointed that in two elections in a row Haughey had failed to obtain an overall majority for Fianna Fáil and harked back for the glory days of the 1977 election, won under a manifesto whose lavish spending promises they would, had Haughey written it, have decried.

The group of four first toyed with the idea of putting down a motion of no confidence in Haughey, which they thought would force him out, thus necessitating a new leadership contest. O'Donoghue then favoured forming a group to include former unnamed Haughey loyalists which would go to Haughey and prevail upon him the need to step down.[2] He seemed convinced that there was a significant majority in the party who were opposed to Haughey's leadership. If Haughey had badly stumbled by appointing O'Donoghue as the party's spokesman on finance, O'Donoghue had in turn misinterpreted how Haughey might react to such a delegation visiting him and calling on him to step down. Haughey had not spent a decade in the wilderness after the arms trial and won a party leadership election against the odds to meekly surrender it after a general election in which he had come so close to an overall majority. The anti-Haughey camp eventually settled on a third strategy. O'Malley would challenge Haughey at the parliamentary party meeting at which it would vote on its nomination for Taoiseach. The trouble with this particular strategy was that O'Malley was a reluctant challenger. He claimed that he had no interest in being the leader of Fianna Fáil and

Taoiseach and was only persuaded to put himself forward out of a fear of what he saw as Haughey's malignant nature.[3] In reality this was a power struggle in Fianna Fáil. It was a good old-fashioned plot to take out the leader. The newspapers certainly saw it this way, with Dick Walsh in the *Irish Times* writing of the 'dissidents' in Fianna Fáil claiming a majority. The *Cork Examiner* dubbed those opposed to Haughey 'plotters'. Neither newspaper could be seen in any way as sympathetic to Haughey.[4]

On the day before the parliamentary party meeting the newspapers reported that O'Malley was saying that he had over forty votes and would win. This was more wishful thinking than anything else. The make-up of the parliamentary party had changed since 1979 and Haughey loyalists like Flor Crowley, Mark Killilea, Eileen Lemass, Tom Nolan and Seán Moore had all lost their seats in the election. Bruce Arnold, in a spectacular misreading of the Fianna Fáil landscape, reported that O'Malley had forty-six votes, Haughey only twenty, and the fifteen undecideds were leaning towards O'Malley.[5] Haughey's uncanny ability to survive came to the fore and three of his most foremost supporters, Ray MacSharry, Albert Reynolds and Seán Doherty, launched a concerted lobbying effort in the final forty-eight hours to firm up support for Haughey and take it away from O'Malley – who had said that he never wanted the leadership in the first place. Haughey, by contrast, desperately wanted to remain as leader. He could see the prize of Taoiseach looming once more. In reality, all he needed was the votes of Neil Blaney and Tony Gregory to become Taoiseach. He had already reached out to Gregory and met him for an hour the night before the parliamentary party meeting to listen to his demands in return for supporting a Fianna Fáil minority government. On the afternoon of the vote it was O'Malley's staunchest supporter, Martin O'Donoghue, who changed the temperature of the entire meeting right from the off when he called for no vote to be taken. O'Malley was taken aback, ruefully remarking after the meeting that he and a number of those who he assumed were in his camp 'may have been on a different wavelength'.[6] O'Donoghue had wanted a broad-based campaign to oust Haughey, but not for the first time had miscalculated the support there was in the anti-Haughey camp. The *Irish Times* reported that O'Malley suspected he was the victim of a 'set-up', although, he told reporters, there was no evidence of it. On RTÉ television later that evening O'Donoghue angrily rejected suggestions that he had played a 'Judas role' in the O'Malley campaign, saying that such a notion was extremely insulting and extremely incorrect. He admitted that he had attended a number of so-called caucus meetings for O'Malley but insisted he had made it known all along that he was only in favour of a change of leader if that was the general wish of the party.[7] It clearly was not.

As always, Haughey's postbag bulged with the weight of correspondence in the uncertain post-election atmosphere. The aristocrat Randal Dunsany wrote to him to wish him luck in the leadership battle and to suggest that once he came through it, he should consider coalescing with Fine Gael. This dramatic suggestion was dismissed by Haughey on the grounds that this would in effect be a national government. The combined strength of both parties would leave no effective opposition in the Dáil, which he considered a necessity in the Irish democratic system. He added that there were also fundamental differences between the parties' policies, which would make an alliance between them difficult to envisage. Dunsany had, however, made an insightful point when he said neither Fianna Fáil nor Fine Gael could 'govern effectively in the present situation with the dubious support of four or five independents'.[8] Another regular correspondent of Haughey's, the writer Desmond Fennell, congratulated him on seeing off the dissidents but urged him to take a different approach to the task of Taoiseach than he had on the first occasion he held the post. Fennell's view was that in that first term Haughey was suffering from a crisis of confidence in himself and that on becoming Taoiseach this time he should 'do us all a favour and follow your instincts absolutely. Act and speak according to what you most personally feel to be right.'[9] The problem was that Haughey's confidence issues were bound up with his internal difficulties within the party and his failure to win the elusive overall majority. Moreover, at the time of Fennell's letter he still had to negotiate a government.

Key to getting back in government was doing a deal with either the three SFWP TDs or the self-styled republican socialist independent Tony

Gregory, who had taken a seat in Dublin Central, and represented one of the most deprived areas in the whole of the state. Yet many of Haughey's correspondents were hostile to any arrangement being reached with Gregory, Kemmy or the SFWP. The businessman Donal Flinn warned Haughey against being forced to accept a government which would 'accommodate political and social ideologies and philosophies which were entirely alien' to his own beliefs.[10] He added that any leader who departed from the fundamental beliefs of the majority of the electorate in order to secure government would be betraying the trust of the electorate. Perhaps feeling the pressure of the situation, Haughey replied that he found Flinn's 'advice gratuitous and your suggestion I might betray the trust of the electorate insulting'.[11]

Haughey had to deal in political realities in the weeks following the election. He met both Gregory and representatives of SFWP, and exchanged various documents. By the final few days he felt that there were too many difficulties and individuals to satisfy within the SFWP group. All negotiations were conducted by its general secretary Seán Garland and leader Tomás Mac Giolla, and Haughey remained convinced that they would never sign up to any deal. Instead, he concentrated on getting an agreement with Gregory, a thirty-four-year-old teacher with republican sentiments who had long campaigned for improvements in inner-city Dublin. He had been elected to Dublin City Council in 1979 as a Dublin Community candidate and polled credibly in the 1981 general election before taking a seat in February 1982.[12] When all the results were in it became clear Gregory's vote could be crucial for Haughey in particular. With Neil Blaney expected to vote for Haughey, Gregory's vote would give the Fianna Fáil leader 83 of the 166 votes. If John O'Connell were reappointed Ceann Comhairle, Haughey would have a bare working majority. In that context, if Gregory voted for Haughey, the Fianna Fáil leader would almost be guaranteed to be elected Taoiseach and would not need the votes of the SFWP deputies. Haughey did not take Blaney's vote for granted but given Blaney's heritage he would either vote for Haughey or abstain. Haughey met a six-man delegation from Blaney's team, who demanded state supports for the construction industry, a reiteration of the traditional Fianna Fáil position of seeking Irish unity and a withdrawal of the British from Northern Ireland.[13] Haughey readily agreed. He also appointed Blaney's director of elections, James Larkin, to the Seanad. This was too much for many in Fianna Fáil, with the Donegal North East organisation telling him not only of their opposition to Larkin's appointment but also of their hostility to any return of Blaney to Fianna Fáil.[14]

In a profile prepared for Haughey for his discussions with Gregory, the new TD was described as an 'articulate, well-mannered, and principled young man and is certainly no fool'.[15] The profile went on to say that Gregory's overriding priority was inner-city redevelopment, with the emphasis on housing and the recreation of a living community. He saw building local authority housing as the solution and claimed that local authorities had had their budgets cut in real terms over the past few years. He was also a strong believer in public works as an employment provider and was, the profile stated, interested in Fianna Fáil's proposed public works programme as a contribution to both jobs and the environment. It was expected that among his demands would be strict controls on prices, and no extra VAT on food or essentials. Haughey was advised that Gregory might be interested in participating in government at ministerial level and it was suggested that he be offered a junior ministry in Social Welfare or Environment, with special responsibility for urban renewal. Haughey rejected this from the off. Giving a junior ministry to a non-member of Fianna Fáil, in a minority government, was something he was not prepared to do. Moreover, Gregory did not want a junior ministry, preferring to support the government on a case-by-case basis. The profile ended by suggesting that although Gregory saw the dangers of being identified with one party, he was shrewd enough to realise that if he succeeded in getting his inner-city redevelopment project off the ground he could go back to the electorate with his head held high. Haughey was finally advised to try Gregory on the Irish language, Irish culture, his distrust and dislike for the SFWP, and Fianna Fáil's excellent record on social welfare and the inner city.[16]

The latter point was stretching the bounds of credulity given the fact that Dublin Central was among the most deprived in the city, ravaged by heroin, poverty, and neglect from politicians of all hues. These were the very reasons Gregory had been elected. Haughey went to see Gregory in his inner-city office and agreed with him in the first instance that a more proactive approach to housing, the drug problem and economic deprivation was necessary. The difficulty would be how to counteract such long-standing and endemic poverty. Garret FitzGerald also went to see Gregory, hoping to engineer his own deal which would see him reappointed Taoiseach. There was pressure on everyone, including Gregory, who, as the Fianna Fáil profile pointed out, had a historic opportunity to revitalise the inner city. Many people counselled Gregory to support Haughey. One was the solicitor Vincent Shannon, who had previously given free legal advice to Gregory and his colleagues on the Inner City Housing Action Group in 1979 and 1980. Shannon wrote to urge Gregory to support Haughey for Taoiseach arguing that the very issues that were close to Gregory's heart, such as housing in the inner city, were much more likely to be understood, appreciated and acted upon by a Fianna Fáil government than a Fine Gael one.[17] This was a point that Haughey himself had stressed to Gregory.

After close to two weeks' negotiation, a deal was still not in place. On the morning of Sunday 7 February, just two days before the Dáil vote to elect a new Taoiseach, Haughey again went to Gregory's office at Summerhill Parade. He drove himself and went alone. The previous Wednesday he had delivered a forty-page document to Gregory outlining what a Fianna Fáil government would do to ensure his vote. On that Sunday morning Haughey negotiated on his own with Gregory and his team, which comprised his brother, Noel, Mick Rafferty and Fergus McCabe. After a meeting lasting a few hours, Haughey ultimately agreed to Gregory's final proposals, although some of them would have to be phased in over a number of years. The so-called Gregory deal was then signed and witnessed by Haughey's old ITGWU friend Michael Mullen. It included commitments to create a separate fund for the creation of 3,700 jobs in the inner city, 440 new local authority houses in the inner city and 1,600 across Dublin, the building of a new community school in the inner city, free medical cards for all pensioners, the nationalisation of Clondalkin Paper

Mills in the west of the city, and the acquisition of a twenty-seven-acre site in the Sherriff Street–Amiens Street area from Dublin Port and Docks.

The day after Gregory voted for Haughey in the election for Taoiseach he was hailed as the £57 million man in the front-page headline of the *Irish Independent*. The *Irish Press* reckoned the cost would be £120 million, while the *Irish Times* suggested £150 million.[18] The all-encompassing nature of the deal showed Gregory to be much more than a parish pump politician.[19] Yet Gregory was heckled throughout his maiden Dáil speech and Garret FitzGerald reportedly muttered that perhaps 'we should have transferred Knock airport to Fairview.'[20] The fact that Haughey did the deal himself confirmed his long-held belief that he was better at finding solutions to problems than any of his party colleagues. As he would have to sign off on it anyway he might as well undertake the negotiations. It certainly annoyed Gregory's constituency rival, Bertie Ahern, who believed it set a bad precedent for future leaders who might be involved in similar government formation talks.[21]

At 3.30 p.m. on Tuesday 9 March 1982, Haughey was elected Taoiseach for the second time, by eighty-six votes to seventy-nine. It was a deceptively large victory. The three SFWP deputies voted for him but certainly could not be relied upon – as the next hectic eight months would prove. Gregory retained the right to vote for the government on a case-by-case basis. He insisted that his programme, as he always called it, was just to vote for Haughey as Taoiseach, but he added the proviso that his single vote would never bring the government down on its own. The internal divisions that racked Fianna Fáil were soon evident when George Colley refused Haughey's offer of a cabinet seat. In a statement issued shortly after Haughey had announced his cabinet, Colley said that the Taoiseach's refusal to make him Tánaiste had caused him to turn down a ministerial post. Colley maintained that Haughey had offered him the position of Tánaiste in the immediate aftermath of the election but had then changed his mind because of Colley's recent activity in the party; a reference to O'Malley's aborted leadership challenge. Colley added that the 'refusal to appoint me as Tánaiste was, in my opinion, designed to reduce my influence on government policy and would, in fact, have done so. In all of the circumstances, I consider that I can best serve the interests of the country and the party on the backbenches.'[22] Haughey's supporters countered that no offer to make Colley Tánaiste was ever made and that in any event Haughey had no obligation to make Colley Tánaiste given that he had received no loyalty from him since becoming party leader.

It was far better for Haughey to have one of his main allies as Tánaiste and into that role he put Ray MacSharry, whom he also appointed Minister for Finance. Given the wide divisions in the party and the grim nature of the country's financial position it was an onerous position of dual responsibility. Martin O'Donoghue's role in ensuring there was no vote for leader in the aftermath of the election saw Haughey bring him back to cabinet as Minister for Education. Haughey never entirely trusted O'Donoghue, and he knew that O'Donoghue felt the same about him, but he nevertheless felt it better to have him in cabinet. The eventual challenger to Haughey's leadership, Des O'Malley, considered not accepting his ministerial invitation to serve in Tourism, Trade, and Commerce out of solidarity with Colley, but ultimately felt it was better to be inside the cabinet to keep what he described as a watching brief on Haughey.[23] The problem for Haughey was that he now had a situation where his opponents had figureheads both within and outside the cabinet.

Another noticeable absentee from the cabinet was Michael O'Kennedy. After an unhappy tenure as Ireland's European Commissioner he had returned, much to Haughey's unhappiness, to fight and win a seat in Tipperary. But the man whose vote probably swung the 1979 leadership election for Haughey was now out of favour and went to the backbenches. Another of that 1979 cabinet not to be reappointed was Máire Geoghegan-Quinn, who was not told by Haughey that she would not be getting a cabinet position but took the setback stoically, noting that Haughey wanted two of his 'spear carriers', Seán Doherty and Pádraig Flynn, in cabinet.[24] Haughey appointed Doherty to the Justice portfolio, and Flynn to the Gaeltacht. These were two appointments that Haughey would in time come to regret.

Haughey's 1982 government was mired in difficulties from the beginning and has gone down in history as perhaps the state's most controversial administration. On taking up office, Haughey received the usual innumerable congratulatory letters, and requests for interview. One was from the journalist Nell McCafferty, who wanted to interview him about the role of women and suggested that their conversation would range over the philosophical as well as the factual. Playing on his Derry heritage, she told him that in Derry when someone made a statement that everyone else found hard to believe, they expressed scepticism in the phrase 'A how'ye Burke.' She added that she did not know the provenance of the phrase or its grammatical translation but declared that he was no doubt a happy man on becoming Taoiseach again.[25] Some weeks later in late April, Haughey replied in similar tones, rejecting her request on the grounds that he just would not have the time. He said that in Swatragh they would say 'Thon's a grand wee girl but her head's astray.'[26] At this stage he was becoming increasingly concerned about the ongoing tensions in the Falklands.

THE FALKLANDS

When war broke out in April 1982 between Britain and Argentina over the Falkland Islands, Haughey was as bemused as most world leaders about Margaret Thatcher's decision to send an armada eight thousand miles to retake the islands after the Argentinian military junta had invaded and seized them. Even the United States was unsure about Thatcher's course of action. The four weeks between the Argentinian invasion of the Falklands on 2 April 1982 and the USA's declaration of support for the British response saw frenzied efforts by the USA, through its Secretary of State Al Haig, to mediate a peaceful solution. President Reagan himself was torn between an instinctive pro-British attitude and a realisation that Argentina was the USA's closest ally in South America and a strong bulwark against communism. Reagan's own attitude to the Falklands crisis can probably best be termed as unsure. Even as late as the National Security Council meeting of 30 April, at which the decision was taken to tilt towards outright support of the British through various sanctions, the official minute notes that at one stage 'the President interjected that he had no objection to giving materiel support but wondered if that would not significantly undercut any future role for the US as mediator.'²⁷ On the same day Reagan wrote in his diary that 'Al H. has announced the turn-down of our plan by Argentina and that we now must come down on the side of Britain.'²⁸

Haughey was not quite the bogeyman in Conservative Party circles that many assumed he was. One of the congratulatory letters to him after his election came from the Tory MP Michael Mates, who told Haughey that if he could be of any help to him 'over here' he only had to ask.²⁹ Haughey had kept up correspondence with a myriad of British politicians and observers since he first entered politics. Over the next three months he was to disappoint all of them. From mid-April to 4 May, Haughey's government supported the European Community's (EC) policy of sanctions against Argentina. Immediately after the invasion, the British called for a meeting of the Security Council of the United Nations on which Ireland then held one of the elective, non-permanent seats. Thatcher asked for, and received, a UN resolution condemning Argentina and demanding that it withdraw its troops. The Irish government supported an EC statement condemning the invasion, and Noel Dorr, the Irish permanent representative at the UN, spoke in the Security Council debate condemning the flouting of the Council's earlier call to avoid the use of force. Ireland then voted for UN Resolution 502 calling for an Argentinian withdrawal.³⁰ While Haughey disliked having to identify with the British position, he felt he had no choice but to support the Community's supportive approach. Thatcher had written to him four days after the invasion seeking his support and personal help to bring about the urgent introduction of economic and financial measures against Argentina. Haughey replied that he was ready to help in any way he could in advancing a resolution of the conflict.³¹ His government did not engage in any unilateral action but simply continued its policy of supporting the European sanctions.

In those tense April weeks, Haughey had been warned by the Irish embassy in London of the dangers of rejecting the British request to impose sanctions against Argentina. Patriotism was at fever pitch in the United Kingdom and Haughey was cautioned as to the detrimental effects on Anglo-Irish relations if Ireland did not support British efforts. There was also the unpredictable effect that opposing the British could have on the Irish community there, who might become the target of ugly hostility. Irish exports could be affected and there was the possibility of boycotts.[32] At the same time there was a large volume of post coming into the Taoiseach's department in Dublin, most of which was critical of the British.[33]

The sinking of the Argentinian cruiser the *General Belgrano* by a British submarine, HMS *Conqueror*, on 2 May 1982 fundamentally changed Haughey's attitude. The loss of 323 lives caused widespread revulsion across Ireland, especially since the attack had taken place outside the British-declared 370 km total exclusion zone established only days earlier. For the more republican elements in Fianna Fáil it copper-fastened their view, held since the hunger strikes, that Margaret Thatcher would stop at nothing to get her own way. This view manifested itself in the form of the Minister for Defence, Paddy Power. In a speech in the Copper Beech Lounge in Edenderry, County Offaly, just after the news of the sinking emerged, Power declared that the British were very much now the aggressors. According to both Frank Dunlop and Power's son, J.J. Power, Haughey summoned Paddy Power to his office the following day and told his Minister of Defence that he wanted him to withdraw his remark. Power refused to do so, returned to his own office in the Phoenix Park and heard no more about it.[34] All Haughey would say about it was it was a personal statement by Power and did not represent government policy but that he would be taking no action against the minister.[35]

On Tuesday 4 May, the government, under Haughey's direct orders, issued its fateful statement that it would seek an immediate meeting of the UN Security Council calling for a cessation of hostilities in the Falklands and for the withdrawal of the EC's economic sanctions against Argentina.[36] The statement caused widespread offence in Britain for failing to mention the British-sponsored UN Resolution 502, which called for the withdrawal of Argentinian forces, and came the day before both sides were to respond to proposals from UN Secretary General Javier Pérez de Cuéllar, who was desperately seeking a solution to the conflict.

The British immediately branded Ireland's move 'a mistake', and a senior Whitehall official was quoted as describing Ireland as 'a fair-weather friend turned disloyal in foul weather'.[37] The change was Haughey's decision alone and was regarded with dismay by the mandarins in the Department of Foreign Affairs, and by Dermot Nally in the Taoiseach's own department. It was also a surprise to Noel Dorr and his team at the Irish UN mission in New York, who only received the change in policy as a press release and were not given any instruction as to what to do about it.[38] The Minister for Foreign Affairs, Gerry Collins, was kept wholly in the dark about Haughey's intentions.[39] There was no memorandum to the government on the change in its policy. It was all done with extraordinary speed, unusually for Haughey, who was normally very good at thinking through the long-term ramifications of policy decisions and was not inclined to take them in haste. Even among Haughey's own close confidants there was deep unease at the change in position. Brendan O'Donnell, who had been at his side in government since his days in the Department of Agriculture, told Haughey it was a mistake to leave himself isolated on the Falklands within the EC, but he would not listen: 'Well, he'd listen, but it wasn't registering.'[40]

Haughey's decision, as the official British historian of the Falklands campaign, Lawrence Freedman, noted, marked the decisive shift in Irish policy.[41] The diplomatic concern of Foreign Affairs was communicated to Haughey in a meeting in Abbeville on the night of Tuesday 4 May 1982, when he met with officials to discuss how best to communicate the decision he had made. Its political director, Paddy McKernan, told Haughey the proposed change of stance on sanctions would damage Ireland's standing in the EC. Dermot Nally went further, arguing that it would seriously damage Anglo-Irish relations as well. As Michael Lillis, then a senior official in the Department of Foreign Affairs later pointed out, the stance implied a degree of acceptance of Argentina's illegal occupation of the territory of another country by force.[42] This might have been the view of some in Foreign Affairs, but it certainly was not Haughey's. Neither was it shared by the wider public, among whom there was significant support for Haughey's change to the Irish line on sanctions, and his instruction to the Irish UN delegation to propose an immediate ceasefire, not an Argentinian withdrawal. Dorr, at the United Nations, also seemed to think that Ireland could make a difference on the Security Council and that there was a chance of averting a fight to the finish. This proved illusory.[43]

A week later, on 11 May, in a statement to the Dáil, Haughey remarked that it was important to 'make it clear that we have not acted in any spirit of animosity towards our closest neighbour but rather in a desire to help. We believe that we can see the Falklands crisis objectively and separate it from other issues as a mature and responsible member of the community of nations. We have given every support to a diplomatic solution to the conflict based on Resolution 502. In trying to halt the conflict and prevent further loss of life we are acting in a way that seems to us the only sane and reasonable course to take.[44]

Yet, for Thatcher, Haughey had by his actions put himself on the wrong side of that community of nations. Haughey's volte face poisoned relationships between himself and Thatcher for a number of years, although as both were reaching the end of their tenures towards the end of the decade, a type of rapprochement was reached. It certainly damaged Anglo-Irish relations in the short term and ended any hope Haughey could have had for a diplomatic breakthrough on Northern Ireland. Thatcher, already lukewarm over the December 1980 summit, and the overselling, as she saw it, of the totality of relationships idea basically shut down all communication with Haughey. The result was her statement of 29 July 1982 that 'no commitment exists for Her Majesty's government to consult the Irish government on matters affecting Northern Ireland. That has always been our position. We reiterate it and emphasise it, so that everyone is clear about it.[45] She made it clear that she had no intention of having any further bilateral meetings with the Taoiseach. She felt that the Irish had tried to impede British victory in the Falklands. She was indeed not for turning.[46] After the dramatic events of 4 May, the next few weeks saw the British inexorably move towards military victory. The Irish position at the UN remained in abeyance; Dorr had moved to immediately seek a meeting of the UN Security Council, but he knew that this would not necessarily mean an immediate meeting and could take the weeks that it actually did.[47] And there it stayed until the Irish resolution, reduced to calling for a seventy-two-hour truce, came before the Security Council on 25 May and quickly evaporated as British troops had already landed in the Falklands. All six non-aligned members of the Security Council then proposed deleting the call for a truce and the resolution became so meaningless that it was adopted unanimously, with even the British being able to vote for it.

The very swiftness of the British military victory saved the Irish government any further international embarrassment, but the issue certainly led to significant issues for the Irish living in Britain, and for companies trading there. No less a brand than Guinness was affected. Edward Guinness told the Irish embassy in London in August 1982 that while 'an association with Ireland was part of the Guinness image ... he was no longer sure that this association with Ireland was helpful. They were encountering a lot of reaction to the Irish angle and this could force them to emphasise facts such as that Guinness was an English company which had its base at Park Royal. Indeed, they had publicity material of this kind ready during the Falkland Crisis but had not used it.[48] Guinness refused to accept the diplomats' view that British attitudes to Ireland went through cycles and that opinions would improve. Haughey believed that no great harm had been done to Anglo-Irish relations or to the Irish in Britain. In late June he wrote to Peter McKimm, the chairperson of the Irish Exporters' Association, that he deplored the lies and misrepresentations of his government's position on the Falklands that had been such a feature of the British popular press. This was in response to a claim by the Exporters' Association that the trade backlash in Britain resulting from Ireland's policy of opposing EEC sanctions was the most severe since at least 1969. Haughey insisted that his government was doing all it could to counteract such misconceptions and mistaken views as to the motivation of its approach over the Falklands and would take whatever remedial actions were necessary and possible to help Irish exporters.[49] Still, there were tales of Irish-labelled beef, lamb and butter being swept off the supermarket shelves of Britain.

Haughey must have known that Thatcher would react with fury to his alteration of the Irish position, so why did he, alone among the EC leaders, change tack and jeopardise the breakthrough, as he originally saw it, of the December 1980 summit? After Britain's victory in June 1982, Haughey had no ability whatsoever to influence British policy. He was certainly resentful of Thatcher's attitude towards the hunger strikes of the previous year, which he continued to believe had cost him the July 1981 election. Thatcher's official biographer, Charles Moore, claimed that Haughey saw the Falklands as a chance for revenge.[50] This is too simplistic. The Falklands might well have been the colonial anachronism that Haughey thought it, and he was quoted as saying that it was a ridiculous war, but once Thatcher made the decision to send ships to the South Atlantic it became something far more important than a minor colonial scuffle to the British.[51] If Haughey's reaction was an overtly nationalistic, even visceral, one made for domestic reasons, as Michael Lillis, for instance, saw it, Thatcher's decision to order her navy south was somewhat similar.[52] Both decisions were legitimate assertions of international sovereignty and Haughey's was in line with Ireland's long history of neutrality in international relations. Dáithí Ó Ceallaigh of the Irish embassy in London believed that Haughey was certainly piqued by having to support the original EC sanctions, but before the sinking of the *Belgrano* he had resigned himself to supporting the Community's decision.[53] Once the *Belgrano* was sunk, with the appalling loss of life, Haughey's calculations changed. In part Haughey was reacting to public opinion, but it was ruinous to what he had achieved with Thatcher up to then. The period between the hunger strikes and the Falklands was a dark time in Anglo-Irish relations and Haughey's frustration from the terrible months of May to July 1981, when the hunger strikers started to die and he lost the election, carried on into the Falklands affair.[54]

Yet, in viewing the Falklands as a historical, colonial anachronism, as indeed did many other European leaders, Haughey, according to his long-time adviser Martin Mansergh, also saw it as a chance to assist in Margaret Thatcher's potential demise, given that many of her own cabinet thought it a foolhardy exercise. He gambled that the fall of Thatcher after the sinking of the *Belgrano* might produce a more amenable partner. Instead, her position was immeasurably strengthened in victory.[55] Haughey seems to have hoped that his decision to seek the withdrawal of sanctions would lead to a similar reaction in other EC capitals because of the shock caused by the sinking of the *Belgrano*. It is not clear who this amenable partner could have been. Thatcher certainly had her enemies in her own cabinet, and on the Tory backbenches, but Conservative Party thinking on Northern Ireland was unlikely to change dramatically in the short term, no matter who led the party. If Thatcher had fallen in 1982 there would not have been any major change in Tory thinking and none of her possible successors would have been enamoured by Haughey's dramatic change of Irish policy. In that context, and on the major international stage, Haughey had miscalculated the mindset of Thatcher, the Conservative Party and, indeed, the British people. Indeed, by the time of the British victory Haughey had come to realise very well the weak position he had got himself into internationally.[56] The decision, in the eyes of the British, put Haughey on the same side as the bloodthirsty Argentinian junta. Haughey, normally so sure-footed on the international stage ever since his time as Minister for Justice two decades earlier, had somewhat lost his compass. No other EC state, beyond Italy, which was exempt from the original sanctions decision, felt the need to diverge from the Community's policy after the sinking of the *Belgrano*. There were many, however, who thought Haughey had clearly taken the right approach. In *Magill*, Vincent Browne argued that given Ireland's own history, it was quite right that we should be unashamedly suspicious of any British assertions of sovereignty anywhere in the world, especially over islands eight thousand miles away.[57] A year after the conflict, Todd Andrews wrote to Haughey: 'Aren't you proud to have stood up to the Brits on Argentina? Nemesis is bound to overtake them.'[58]

It is most likely that Haughey's calculations were influenced by the fragility of his minority government, and his need to keep Neil Blaney, the three SFWP deputies (who were beholden to Garland and Mac Giolla) and Tony Gregory onside. All were strong republicans who loathed Thatcher, and felt that the war was unjust. Haughey also had a divided party, with elements within cabinet, such as Power, who were willing to speak out about the conflict, and outside it people like Síle de Valera who had been complaining since the war began that Ireland's support for sanctions had eroded the country's proud neutral stance. On 14 June 1982, the Argentinian decision to surrender was greeted with exultation all across Britain. Ten days later the Fianna Fáil TD Niall Andrews wrote to Haughey to say that there had been an intensive propaganda campaign against the Fianna Fáil party with allegation after allegation made in Leinster House, and to the correspondents of the newspapers, which had been taken up without any denial of any kind. He complained that the Fianna Fáil 'organisation is suffering great demoralisation' from the unrelenting venom from columnists such as Bruce Arnold and Conor Cruise O'Brien, which was 'having a subliminal effect on the minds of our members'.[59] Haughey had been in office for only just over three months and already his party and support were fraying severely. The mood in Fianna Fáil had been poisonous since the party lost the Dublin West by-election on 25 May, the day the UN Security Council finally heard the rather pointless Irish resolution calling for a seventy-two-hour truce in the Falklands.

PATRONAGE

Immediately on assuming office in February, Haughey approached the Fine Gael TD for Dublin West, Dick Burke, and offered him the vacant position of European commissioner. This caused consternation throughout the political system. It was designed to give Fianna Fáil an extra vote in the Dáil and take one from Fine Gael – since Haughey assumed he would win the subsequent by-election. This was a serious miscalculation. Haughey could not nominate any of his own TDs because of the Dáil numbers and did not seem too enamoured of any prospective Fianna Fáil candidates outside the Dáil. He could sell Burke's nomination as being in the national interest given that Burke had already proved to be a capable and competent commissioner between 1977 and early 1981. Yet Fine Gael had taken three of the five seats in Dublin West in the February election and had marginally outpolled Fianna Fáil in the popular vote. In that context there was no guarantee that Fianna Fáil would win the by-election. The presence of the Workers' Party leader Tomás Mac Giolla, who had polled over three thousand votes in the February election and could expect to do considerably better in a by-election, complicated matters further. Although Burke had enjoyed his time as European commissioner, he was initially suspicious of Haughey's approach. He first rejected Haughey's advances, telling him on 14 March 1982 that while he was appreciative of the great honour Haughey proposed to confer on him, he had decided to decline.[60] Haughey was persistent, however, and ten days after initially turning the new Taoiseach down, Burke changed his mind and decided to accept the offer. He did so without consulting his party leader, Garret FitzGerald, in the hope of keeping it secret until it was announced at the first full meeting of the new Dáil session, when Haughey could declare the appointment to be in the national interest. On 24 March, just a few hours before Haughey was to announce the appointment in the Dáil, the news leaked from Brussels as the Fine Gael parliamentary party was meeting and Burke came under significant attack from his fellow Fine Gael TDs for what they saw as his treachery. He was so shocked by the forcefulness with which he was assailed that he agreed to turn down the Haughey offer to which he had already given his full agreement. He sent a note to Haughey to the effect that he had reconsidered his position and was now declining the offer. This was now the second time that Burke had turned Haughey down, but it was far more public. Garret FitzGerald recorded that Burke was emotionally shattered by the reaction he received from his fellow Fine Gael TDs.[61] Haughey, meanwhile, was humiliated at having his deal rejected.

Yet the prize of weakening Fine Gael and strengthening his own position saw Haughey persevere with the idea of persuading Burke to take the position. Burke, somewhat alienated following the reaction he had received from his own parliamentary party, eventually succumbed and on Tuesday 30 March decided to accept Haughey's offer. He promptly resigned as a TD. A somewhat dejected Garret FitzGerald described Burke's decision as unhelpful, while his deputy leader, Peter Barry, said Burke had let down the party that had been so good to him.[62] Meanwhile, the Fianna Fáil benches were exultant at what they saw as a decisive blow to Fine Gael's morale. It was a pyrrhic victory. The party was fully confident that Eileen Lemass would win the resulting by-election. She had narrowly lost out in February and was popular within the party. The belief in her ability to win was wildly misplaced. Fianna Fáil mounted a typically energetic campaign, but the increase in PRSI contributions for workers, which the FitzGerald government had introduced in its January budget, and had been retained in Ray MacSharry's March budget, became the dominant issue of the campaign. Local issues, typically a feature of by-elections, only added to Fianna Fáil's woes. Its canvassers reported complaints about the lack of schools and jobs, waiting lists for telephones, and delayed hospital appointments.[63] Yet on the day of the election Fianna Fáil was extremely confident that it would prevail. The defeat was crushing. Liam Skelly, a candidate Garret FitzGerald did not even know before he was nominated to run for the party, brought Fine Gael one of its most historic by-election victories. The Lemass name, Fianna Fáil royalty, was not enough for Eileen Lemass. She was just over three hundred votes ahead of Skelly on the first count but was swamped on transfers, and he was eventually elected with over two thousand votes to spare. It was one of the most devastating by-election defeats ever suffered by Fianna Fáil. The verdict of Ray MacSharry summed it up: 'We just did not see it coming.'[64] Both Lemass and Skelly would win seats in the November election, but in an ironic twist, Skelly would leave Fine Gael and sit as an independent for part of that Dáil.

The by-election defeat was catastrophic for Haughey. He had lost valuable patronage in nominating Burke to the European Commission, and all for naught. The Fianna Fáil deputies who had exulted in Garret FitzGerald's discomfort at Burke's appointment were subdued. For some of them, that crestfallen air changed to all-out anger at their leader. The week after the by-election George Colley made yet another speech criticising the standard of political leadership in the country. He was followed in quick succession by Bobby Molloy and Jim Gibbons, with Molloy complaining that 'the traditional philosophy underlying the policies of our major political parties is now seen by some of our leaders to be dispensable in the interests of their achieving and holding on to power.'[65]

The death of the Galway East deputy Johnny Callinan the following month narrowed Fianna Fáil's position in the Dáil even further. It was followed by the revelation of the Talbot workers' agreement. This in effect guaranteed the eighty-eight assembly line workers a job for life by ensuring that if they did not find employment within the same industry in six months, they would be provided with an income for life adjusted in line with national pay agreements. The Labour TD Barry Desmond read the agreement between the government, Talbot Ireland, the Amalgamated Transport and General Workers' Union (ATGWU) and ICTU into the Dáil record, to astonishment from the opposition benches. When faced with hostile questioning on the deal, Haughey told the Dáil he had no apology to make for the agreement. The *Irish Independent* called it the 'deal of a lifetime'.[66] It emerged during the debate that Haughey had met senior executives from Talbot at his home in Kinsaley just three days before the June 1981 election, but he dismissed this as being of no consequence. He told the Dáil that it was much more convenient to meet them at his home to discuss the situation: 'I do not for one moment apologise to the House for holding meetings in Kinsealy. It is a very pleasant place to hold a meeting. I will continue to hold meetings in Kinsealy, any meeting I feel like and as often as I feel like.'[67] Haughey received much, mostly hostile, correspondence on the agreement. He would routinely state that it was not a deal but an agreement and that the language used showed 'how effective our opponent's propaganda has been'.[68] He stressed that the kernel of the agreement was the provision of alternative employment, which the men involved were very keen to acquire. This might well have been the case, but there is no doubt that the agreement hurt him in the court of public opinion. The reality was that Haughey did not want to lose trade union support in the middle of an election campaign and thus arranged a special grant from the Department of the Taoiseach, and AnCo, the state's agency for assisting workers to get back to employment, to be paid through the ATGWU, which kept the Talbot workers on full pay.[69]

There was some respite for Haughey when on 20 July Noel Treacy comfortably won the Galway East by-election for Fianna Fáil on the first count. The dull campaign was notable for yet another internal Fianna Fáil attack on Haughey. Jim Gibbons appeared on the RTÉ radio programme *This Week* the Sunday before the vote to slam Haughey for the Talbot agreement. He stated that the general handling of the country over the previous two years had left it in a deplorable condition and rather oddly called for likeminded people in both Fianna Fáil and Fine Gael to come together to tackle the country's economic problems before it was too late.[70] This was certainly not going to happen. At the same time, Haughey and MacSharry, along with Pádraig Ó hUiginn, who had brokered the Talbot agreement, had begun working on a new national economic plan to eliminate the budget deficit and restore growth in the economy.[71]

Haughey had come to believe that the corrective action needed in the public finances was possible only in the context of a comprehensive and balanced economic and fiscal plan with the support of the main social partners: the trade unions, the business organisations and the farmers. Such a plan would need to contain positive proposals for economic growth as well as some essentially negative measures to contain public expenditure. This is how Haughey described his eureka moment when it came to social partnership:

> I vividly recall the occasion that, in all probability, was the first time I began to think along the lines of this concept of social partnership. A European summit in Brussels on 28th/29th June 1982 had just concluded and Chancellor Schmidt of Germany and I were chatting together when I asked him what he would spend the forthcoming weekend on. He said: 'This weekend is the most important one in my annual calendar – I meet with the employers and the trade unions to hammer out an agreement on the rates of pay and salaries appropriate for the coming year in the light of the economic situation anticipated.' I was immediately struck with this common-sense approach and began, in my mind, as I listened to Chancellor Schmidt, to develop and expand the concept.[72]

It was specified by Haughey from the outset that the social partners should be consulted in the preparation of the national plan. Following his meeting with Schmidt, Haughey was insistent that this new plan would be written in such a way as to obtain the agreement of the social partners, who, he believed, would sign up to it and to the new concept of social partnership. He was assisted by a steering committee composed of civil servants from the economic departments and agencies with some outside expert assistance. One of these experts, Kieran Kennedy, the director of the Economic and Social Research Institute, played a crucial role in its formulation.[73] At its heart, however, was Ó hUiginn, who lived and breathed it for months, working on it at his kitchen table in his home in Templeogue on the southside of Dublin.

GUBU

As July 1982 ended Haughey was looking forward to some relaxation on Inishvickillane. He had endured a few torrid months, but he was in power, and had his national plan idea as a guide to tackle the country's economic circumstances. Given the difficult arithmetic in the Dáil he was also aware that the plan, as yet unnamed, would be the basis for Fianna Fáil's next election manifesto.

The week before Haughey went on holiday the country was convulsed by the heinous murder of a young nurse, Bridie Gargan, who, while sunbathing beside her car in the Phoenix Park, was brutally attacked by a man with a hammer who then drove off with Bridie lying fatally injured in the back seat of the car. She was from the Riggins in Dunshaughlin, where Haughey had lived as a young boy. She lived for four days before finally succumbing to her injuries. Three days after the attack on Gargan, an Offaly farmer, Donal Dunne, was shot dead in Edenderry. Two other murders were committed in the country over the course of that week. Patricia Furlong, a twenty-year-old from Dundrum, was strangled and her body found in the Dublin mountains; and Robert Belton, a fifty-five-year-old post office sub-master was shot in a raid on Donnycarney post office. The Gardaí initially assumed they were looking for four separate killers.[74] They did not know for sure that the killings of Gargan and

Dunne had been committed by the same man until after his arrest on the evening of Friday 13 August.

In the early morning of Saturday 14 August, Haughey's private secretary Seán Aylward was phoned by a Garda contact and informed that a man had been arrested in a luxury apartment block the night before on suspicion of the murders of Gargan and Dunne and that the story would be in that morning's newspapers. The story would state that the Attorney General, Patrick Connolly, lived in the penthouse suite in the same block. Aylward was told that the suspect, later named as Malcolm MacArthur, was indeed found in the Attorney General's apartment and that Connolly was there at the time of the arrest. Aylward rang the Department of Justice, was updated on events, and then rang Haughey, who was still in Inishvickillane. After being routed through the exchange in Dingle, Aylward finally reached Haughey, who he described as being thunderstruck.[75] Connolly had rung Haughey at about 10 p.m. on the night of MacArthur's arrest but Haughey had not grasped the fact that Connolly was in attendance when the Gardaí made the arrest and that it had taken place in Connolly's flat.[76] After Aylward's revelatory call Haughey immediately made plans to return to Dublin. He did so the following day, having been collected by the Air Corps at 12.30 p.m., after a delay caused by fog. [77]

Despite the extraordinary events of that Friday night when MacArthur was arrested, Connolly decided to proceed with a holiday to New York. He first flew to London on the 9.30 a.m. Saturday flight to Heathrow, where he was met by an official from the Irish embassy. In the meantime, Aylward was trying to reach Connolly at his brother's home in Carlow. He was informed that Connolly had gone to London. Aylward then contacted the secretary of the Department of Foreign Affairs, who ascertained that Connolly was staying at the Cavendish Hotel. Aylward eventually reached Connolly and told him that while the Taoiseach did not say he could not go on holiday it might be wise to postpone it for a couple of days. He also told Connolly that he was to ring the Taoiseach at ten o'clock the following morning, even if it meant missing his flight to the USA. At about 10 p.m. on the Saturday evening Connolly rang

Haughey with Margaret Thatcher outside the door of Number 10 Downing Street at their first summit in May 1980. It was at this summit that Haughey famously presented Thatcher with a gift of a silver Georgian teapot. (© *Keystone Press/ Alamy Stock Photo*)

Haughey with Ronald and Nancy Reagan during a visit to the White House for the St Patrick's Day festivities in March 1982. (© *Maidun Collection/Alamy Stock Photo*)

Haughey meets with Ted Kennedy during a visit to the US in 1982. The two politicians were firm friends and visited each other's homes regularly. (*Courtesy of the Charles J. Haughey Papers, Dublin City University*)

Implacable enemies within Fianna Fáil, Charles Haughey and George Colley share a confidence in January 1982. A quizzical Brian Lenihan looks on. (© *Pat Langan/The Irish Times*)

Haughey faces off against Garret FitzGerald in the first ever television debate between the leaders of Fianna Fáil and Fine Gael in February 1982. The ever-calm Brian Farrell acts as the moderator. (© *RTÉ*)

Haughey, flanked by Albert Reynolds and a voluble Martin O'Donoghue, during the February 1982 general election campaign. (© *Peter Jordan/Alamy Stock Photo*)

Haughey with the independent TD for Dublin Central Tony Gregory in the heart of the inner city in April 1982 before he started a sponsored cycle from Dublin to Kilnacrott, Co. Cavan, to raise money for a holiday home for inner-city children. The famous Haughey–Gregory deal ensured Haughey's election as Taoiseach for the second time after the February 1982 general election. (© *Peter Thursfield/The Irish Times*)

Haughey gives his first sit-down interview as Taoiseach with the journalist Geraldine Kennedy, of the *Irish Times*. Kennedy's phone was tapped on an order from the Minister for Justice, Seán Doherty, in 1982. Doherty's accusation that Haughey was aware of the tap on Kennedy's phone and on that of her fellow journalist Bruce Arnold precipitated his downfall a decade later. Haughey always denied that he knew of the taps. (© *Peter Thursfield/The Irish Times*)

Haughey and his wife Maureen vote in the divorce referendum of June 1986. Ray Burke looks on. (© *Independent News And Media/Getty Images*)

Brian Lenihan shakes hands with a youthful Ben Dunne. Haughey looks on with a baleful eye. The revelations that Dunne had given Haughey over £1 million between 1987 and 1991 put in train a series of events that effectively ruined Haughey. (© *Eamonn Farrell/RollingNews.ie*)

Haughey, Dick Spring and Garret FitzGerald at the opening of the RTÉ Dáil studios in 1986. FitzGerald and Spring provided effective opposition to Haughey in the Dáil throughout his periods as Taoiseach. (© *Independent News and Media/Getty Images*)

Haughey celebrates with Stephen Roche on the Champs-Élysées after the Dublin cyclist's famous victory in the 1987 Tour de France. (© *Michel Lipchitz/ AP/Shutterstock*)

Haughey greets French President Francois Mitterrand at Dublin Airport in February 1988. Mitterrand later was a guest of Haughey's at Inishvickillane. (© *Peter Thursfield/The Irish Times*)

Haughey with the Soviet Premier, Mikhail Gorbachev on 2 April 1989 in Shannon. Gorbachev made a brief stopover in Ireland on his way from Moscow to Cuba. (© *Shutterstock)*

Haughey meets with the members of U2. Bono was an enthusiastic supporter of the plans to renovate Temple Bar in the early 1990s. (© *Irish Photo Archive)*

Haughey and Brian Lenihan in ebullient form at the beginning of the 1990 presidential campaign. The smiles would quickly fade after Haughey sacked Lenihan from Cabinet. (© *Matt Kavanagh/The Irish Times*)

Haughey with Ray MacSharry, Ireland's European Commissioner, in 1990. MacSharry had been a Haughey loyalist since proposing him as Taoiseach in 1979. As Minister for Finance between 1987 and 1989, MacSharry oversaw Ireland's economic recovery from the deep recession of the 1980s. (© *RTÉ*)

Haughey and Lenihan are grim-faced as Mary Robinson is elected President of Ireland. (*Courtesy of The National Library, Ireland*)

As the Republic of Ireland football team bow out of the 1990 world cup in Rome, Haughey salutes the crowd. (© *Ray McManus/Getty Images*)

Haughey's last cabinet. The two Progressive Democrat members, Des O'Malley and Bobby Molloy, sit resolutely side by side. Albert Reynolds is notable by his absence, having been sacked by Haughey. (© *Hulton Archive/Getty Image*s)

Haughey at Abbeville. (© *Photocall Ireland*)

Haughey at home in Abbeville, the James Gandon-designed mansion in Kinsaley that he bought in 1969. He died there in June 2006. (© *RTÉ*)

Haughey receives an honorary doctorate from the University of Notre Dame, in South Bend, Indiana, in May 1991. (*Courtesy of the Charles J. Haughey Papers, Dublin City University*)

Terry Keane speaks to Gay Byrne on the *Late Late Show* in May 1999 of their twenty-seven-year affair. At the same time, Haughey was having dinner with his wife Maureen and friends in Malahide. (© *RTÉ*)

A visibly frail Haughey waves to the crowd after giving evidence to the Moriarty Tribunal, which was investigating payments to him. He appeared before the tribunal on a total of 33 occasions between July 2000 and March 2001. (© *Alan Betson/The Irish Times*)

Haughey is driven away from the Moriarty Tribunal in September 2000, having completed his evidence for the day. (© *David Sleator/The Irish Times*)

Haughey's coffin is brought to the Church of Our Lady of Consolation in Donnycarney. His wife of 54 years, Maureen, leads the cortege. (© *Maxwells-Pool/Getty Images*)

Maureen Haughey and her children, Eimear, Conor, Ciarán and Seán, enter the church for Haughey's funeral mass. (© *Maxwells-Pool/Getty Images*)

Haughey's official Oireachtas portrait hangs in the gallery above the entrance to the Dáil chamber in Leinster House. Haughey personally chose the artist John F. Kelly. Critics have described it as showing Haughey as both imperial and sphinx-like. (*Courtesy of Leinster House*)

Haughey to tell him he was on the point of going to the USA and that he was entitled to go on his long-planned holiday. Haughey seemingly thought that this meant Connolly was about to board the plane and let him go.[78] This was to prove the biggest mistake of the whole affair.

In the meantime, MacArthur had been charged with the murders of Gargan and Dunne. Connolly, however, decided to continue with his journey and flew to New York from London on Sunday morning. At this stage the Sunday newspapers had revealed that MacArthur had been arrested in Connolly's flat. On his arrival in the USA on Sunday Connolly was met by the deputy consul general in New York, Donal Hamill, and driven to his hotel, the Roosevelt, on Madison Avenue and 45th Street. He arrived to a stack of messages from the Taoiseach's office, which he studiously avoided, before finally being advised by Hamill to take a call from Aylward. Acting on instructions from Haughey, Aylward ordered him home.[79] Aylward gave Connolly the Taoiseach's number. When Connolly rang it he was told by Haughey that it was imperative he return immediately. That evening Garda Commissioner Patrick McLaughlin and the senior officer on the case, Detective Superintendent John Courtney, were summoned to Abbeville to give Haughey a full report.[80]

On Monday 16 August, Connolly flew Concorde from New York to London and then onwards to Dublin, where he went straight to Haughey's house in Kinsaley. After a difficult and terse meeting both men eventually agreed that the Attorney General would have to resign, although Connolly had initially rejected the suggestion.[81] Connolly's resignation statement was sent to the newspapers in the early hours of Tuesday 17 August. It stated that he was taking this course of action having regard to 'the embarrassment which, however unwittingly, must inevitably be caused to the government'.[82] He added that at no time did he ever have any knowledge of the fact that the Gardaí were trying to find MacArthur in relation to the offences with which he was charged; neither had he any occasion to entertain such a suspicion. Later that day, at a chaotic press conference, Haughey rejected any suggestion that he had mishandled the affair, which he described as unprecedented, an unbelievable mischance, grotesque, bizarre and tragic, giving rise to Conor Cruise

O'Brien's famous GUBU acronym. Haughey then inadvertently congratulated the Gardaí on their painstaking work, which had resulted in finding
'the right man'. The government's press secretary, Frank Dunlop, immediately knew that Haughey had made a mistake. At this stage, that man,
MacArthur, had not been tried. He was innocent until proven guilty. A
number of journalists had also picked up on Haughey's words. He was
not interrupted at the time, but later, on being told by Dunlop what he
had said, he replied, 'Oh, God. I didn't, did I?'[83] In later briefings Dunlop
told journalists that it was merely a slip of the tongue, but many seemed
to believe that it was a deliberate attempt to pervert the course of justice.
This was arrant nonsense. MacArthur's lawyers later attempted to have
Haughey cited for contempt in the High Court. This failed when the
judge accepted that Haughey had made a simple mistake.[84]

Connolly and Haughey had known each other for quite some time.
Connolly had been Haughey's junior counsel during the arms trial.
Connolly was a classic legal counsel of the old school – discreet, reticent
and cautious. He was an intensely focused man, buttoned-up, dark-suited,
and with a polished manner when at work, but he had a relaxed social
side to him as well. He was profoundly affected by the events that brought
about his resignation. He was in total shock. Haughey was right when
he said in his statement accepting Connolly's resignation that he was a
'kind and compassionate man of the highest integrity'.[85] Connolly would
periodically write to Haughey over the next few years with congratulatory messages and suggestions on various events. In May of 1984, for
instance, he sent Haughey, by then back in opposition, a note with some
ideas on the appointments of judges to the High and Supreme Courts.
He was sending his ideas to the Bar Council to have them forwarded
to the Minister for Justice, but wanted Haughey to know of his views.
Connolly was worried that a person who had never practised at the Bar
on any regular basis, 'save to seek involvement in types of political cause
celebre might be considered'.[86] He was also concerned that, seeing as the
note came from himself, there was an element of confidentiality involved.
Haughey replied that he was fully in agreement that persons of the right
calibre and status would be appointed to these positions.[87]

Haughey was also shocked by the events of the MacArthur affair, but in that phlegmatic way of his he quickly adjusted back to the normality of everyday life. He appointed John Murray, the son-in-law of his close friend Brian Walsh, as Attorney General, and went back to working on his economic plan. Yet his government had gained the reputation of being ridden with scandal, and that would not go away. Various salacious stories about the Minister for Justice, Seán Doherty, were particularly damaging given that he held such a sensitive portfolio. They would plague Haughey for ever.

THE WAY FORWARD

On Friday 1 October 1982 the Kildare backbencher Charlie McCreevy wrote to Haughey at his Abbeville address under the heading 'VERY IMPORTANT'. His letter simply said: 'Enclosed please find photocopy of letter and motion which I have today submitted to the chief whip.'[88] The photocopy was of a letter to Bertie Ahern which set out the following motion: 'That the Fianna Fáil members of Dáil Éireann have no confidence in Charles J. Haughey as leader and Taoiseach.'[89] Bertie Ahern had for some time been worried about such a motion as the Dáil was beset by rumours of plots and counter-plots. On receiving McCreevy's motion, he asked him, 'What are you doing this now for?', but McCreevy was not for turning.[90] Ahern then rang Haughey at Abbeville to impart the bad news, but Haughey had already received his copy of the motion.

Less than three years earlier, McCreevy had been a staunch advocate for Haughey's leadership challenge. He had supported Haughey as far back as the arms trial. He had, however, become quickly disillusioned with Haughey's first government and after Haughey lost power he grew increasingly restless at what he saw as Fianna Fáil's drift. By December 1981 he was a hostile and vocal critic of Haughey and he gave full vent to those feelings in an interview with Geraldine Kennedy in the *Sunday Tribune*. When Haughey called for his expulsion from the parliamentary party, he resigned the whip. This did him no harm in his own constituency and he was elected on the first count with nearly a quota and a half in the February 1982 election. Haughey was quite happy to have him on the Fianna Fáil ticket as he knew McCreevy was a proven vote-winner, and both men thought that Fianna Fáil could take three of the five seats in the constituency. In June 1981, the party had only won two. Seats were everything for Haughey in February 1982 and McCreevy duly topped the poll and brought two of his running mates with him. The return of Fianna Fáil to power did not placate McCreevy, however, and after just six months of Haughey's government, he had decided that the party had fatally lost its way and it was time for action.[91] There were, however, two problems: timing and numbers. The national economic plan was nearly ready for publication and with the numbers so tight in the Dáil, there was no predicting the impact such a contest would have on the party. Bertie Ahern, as the chief whip, could not be sure how those who had been disaffected with Haughey since he won the leadership would react, particularly if they lost, as he thought likely. He could not even be sure that they would support the government in subsequent Dáil votes. He started to ring various deputies but was surprised at the depth of ill-feeling towards Haughey, with many complaining about the Gregory deal and how they could not get to see Haughey when the Workers' Party TDs could walk in on him whenever they liked.[92] While this was more apocryphal than true – the list of those who could get to see Haughey at short notice was kept very tight by his private secretarial team – he was certainly disconnected from many within the parliamentary party.

The no confidence motion was heard on Wednesday 6 October. Two nights previously the party's national executive overwhelmingly backed a motion giving 'total support to An Taoiseach, and the government in their endeavours to bring our country safely through these difficult times'.[93] The general consensus was that the vast majority of Fianna Fáil supporters wanted Haughey to continue on for the moment – while the economic situation was so bad, was the view of one delegate. George Colley said that it would look extremely bad for the national executive if it backed a leader and then had to support a different leader the following day if the parliamentary party chose differently. This was a rather Jesuitical argument and in the end only Colley and one other delegate, Eoghan Fitzsimons, of the seventy-eight-member executive voted against the motion. The following day, Colley stated that he would vote for the McCreevy motion. Later that night Des O'Malley and Martin O'Donoghue signalled that they would resign from cabinet on the day of the vote. On the night before the vote, O'Donoghue and his wife attended the premiere of Hugh Leonard's political allegory *Kill*, a thinly veiled attack on Haughey, at the Olympia Theatre.[94] Leonard had moved a long way from his support of Haughey in the pre-arms trial period. If O'Donoghue thought *Kill* an omen for the following day's events he was to be mistaken.

Bertie Ahern described the parliamentary party no confidence motion meeting as 'carnage'.[95] Haughey succeeded in his insistence that the vote be taken by open roll call. His rationale was this was not a leadership contest and it was appropriate that local cumann members would know which way their TD voted. His opponents wanted a secret ballot, and if they succeeded Haughey would almost certainly be defeated. Haughey remained wildly popular with the grassroots and vast amounts of correspondence started arriving at Fianna Fáil headquarters, the Department of the Taoiseach and Abbeville in support of him. Perhaps the letter most likely to have raised a smile from Haughey was one from two members of the Ógra Fianna Fáil Dublin South East branch who, in deploring both the timing and content of McCreevy's motion, said that they awaited 'with interest the publication of Bruce Arnold's list of anti-Haugheyites so that we can divide by five and subtract four to gauge the true strength of the prima donnas in the party!'[96]

Despite vociferous objections, the meeting decided to accept the public roll call and the motion against was duly defeated by 58 votes to 22. The scenes after the announcement were the most shameful witnessed in the long and proud history of Leinster House. Drunken supporters of Haughey manhandled and jeered those Fianna Fáil TDs who had supported McCreevy's motion. McCreevy himself was jostled and verbally abused as he went to his car. Jim Gibbons was physically attacked and pushed to the ground. He had first been elected to the Dáil in 1957 in the same general election as Haughey. He had given long and distinguished service to Fianna Fáil and to the country. Yes, he was a trenchant opponent of Haughey and made no secret of it, but he did not deserve the treatment meted out to him by Haughey's so-called supporters that night. In fact, no one did. The shameful scenes tarnished both Haughey and Fianna Fáil for some time to come. Gibbons suffered a heart attack a few weeks later and was unable to attend the Dáil. One of Haughey's most trenchant supporters, Dr Bill Loughnane, whose outburst about British overflights had played such a key role in bringing about the end of the Lynch era, died suddenly of a heart attack on 18 October and Haughey's hold on power was severely diminished. He could now only count on the votes of 79 TDs. If the Workers' Party deserted him, he would be gone.

Fianna Fáil's national economic plan, *The Way Forward*, was published on 21 October. It drew on the admiration both Haughey and Ó hUiginn had for Seán Lemass, who had originally devised a type of proto-corporate state in the 1960s by being the first politician to bring the social partners into the charmed circle of power. *The Way Forward* also drew on the experience of other small European states both as a development model for the future and as a reference point on the need for social consensus. Many of its economic assumptions were dismissed by a cadre of economic commentators, who were sympathetic to Fine Gael and its more traditional approach to free market economics, but the cuts that were proposed were of a magnitude to turn the Workers' Party fully away from Fianna Fáil. They would not be long in signalling that they would no longer support the government. Those cuts were among the toughest ever put forward by any government. They involved eliminating the current budget deficit over the following four years, withdrawing at least £900 million from public expenditure, limiting public sector pay increases, and introducing substantial changes in the social welfare system with regard to unemployment and disability benefits.

The Way Forward was derided by official Ireland. The Department of Finance, still sore over the whole idea of the Department of Economic Development and Planning, contemptuously dismissed it as 'The Way Backwards' and briefed incessantly against it, insisting that it alone was the repository from which economic policy should derive and that anything else was to be treated with suspicion. It was not impressed with so-called national economic plans. Two weeks after *The Way Forward* was published the government fell and the document seemed destined to become a historical artefact. It was written off by the then press secretary Frank Dunlop as 'a one-day wonder ... the document that had caused so much sound and fury signified little and was largely forgotten.'[97] But it was certainly not forgotten by either Haughey or Ó hUiginn, who would return to its basic premise in 1987.

The death of *The Way Forward*, and the end of Haughey's second government was inflicted by the Workers' Party after they agreed to support a motion of no confidence in the government proposed by Garret FitzGerald. In a series of meetings between representatives of the parties in the days leading up to the vote, the Minister for Finance, Ray MacSharry, came to the view that no matter what Fianna Fáil promised, Tomás Mac Giolla wanted to be in the Dáil and the best way to achieve that was for an immediate election. Mac Giolla and Seán Garland were as well briefed as the government on the economic issues facing the country, feeding into the widespread and accurate belief that the party had many supporters at senior levels not only in RTÉ, but also in the civil service, and the Revenue Commissioners as well.[98] The Workers' Party's three deputies were split about the upcoming Dáil vote. Paddy Gallagher from Waterford and Joe Sherlock from Cork were anxious to avoid an election. While both were livid with Mac Giolla's insistence on voting against the government and thus bringing it down, they would not pit themselves against the leadership. Both paid a heavy price when they lost their seats in the subsequent general election. Mac Giolla took a seat in Dublin West, and Proinsias de Rossa held on in Dublin North West, but reduced to two deputies the party found itself without any influence after the election.

Haughey was almost paranoid when it came to the Workers' Party and their cadre of influential supporters across the public service. When Bertie Ahern, who had been involved in the discussions to keep the Workers' Party on board, told Haughey that there was no hope of changing their minds when it came to the Dáil vote, and that the result would almost inevitably be a defeat, and yet another general election, Haughey was almost relieved, describing them as nothing but a bunch of amateurs.[99] He was particularly dismissive of those who were not in the Dáil – Mac Giolla and Garland – but controlled everything the party's deputies did and said. On Thursday 4 November 1982, Haughey lost a no confidence motion in the Dáil by eighty-two votes to eighty. The Workers' Party voted against him. Tony Gregory abstained. Elaborate last minute plans to try and bring Jim Gibbons to the Dáil from St Luke's Hospital in Kilkenny to support the government were finally abandoned. The Twenty-Third Dáil, which had lasted just 240 days, ended on a dark, dank November night. Haughey went straight to the Áras to seek a dissolution of the Dáil and a weary Irish people were headed back to the polls for a third time in eighteen months. Haughey was weary too. His government had been tarnished by scandal, poor decision-making and sheer bad luck. The political omens did not look particularly good for him as he once more boarded his battle bus and toured the country looking for votes and another chance to gain that elusive overall majority. Once again, he was to be denied.

CHAPTER 18

PHONE TAPPING

THE DOC

The November 1982 general election campaign was dispiriting for Fianna Fáil and for Haughey. The electorate was tired of canvassers and voting. The most common message fed back to election headquarters from Fianna Fáil canvassers was one of apathy: 'the general reaction is that the response is very dead', wrote one director of elections.[1] Haughey still led a divided party seeking a mandate for an overall majority when the electorate was fully aware that a significant rump neither wanted him nor trusted him as leader. The conundrum was summed up in a letter Haughey received in the immediate aftermath of the October heave when the former senator Professor Richard Conroy told him, 'the time for magnanimity has passed. Those who have declared no confidence should neither be retained or invited to return to the government.'[2] The problem was that if he took this approach he would certainly split the party even further. He knew he would have to face a general election sometime soon and was determined to put this latest heave behind him and present a united front to the electorate. Haughey's personality once again became a dominant theme of the campaign. There were differing reports on the leadership question from the canvass, some constituencies noting that strong and stable leadership was a theme, others stating that there was some concern over Haughey's control of the party. In the aftermath of the Falklands crisis, Haughey, emboldened by public support for his position, tried to make Anglo-Irish relations a main plank of the campaign. Various Fianna Fáil candidates expressed the view that Thatcher wanted Garret FitzGerald back in office, and Haughey out.

The international press continued to be attracted to Haughey. The mass-circulation *Sunday Times* in Britain published a long focus piece on him on the Sunday before the election. A supporter told Haughey that he had complained to the paper about the scurrilous and inaccurate nature of the piece but had received the reply that they 'had to take account of the extraordinary flow of rumour concerning him'.[3] Closer to home, Fianna Fáil's general secretary, Frank Wall, felt compelled to write to the *Irish Times* after the election about a letter they had printed from the noted travel writer Dervla Murphy on the Duke of Norfolk, formerly head of intelligence at the British Ministry of Defence. During the campaign Haughey had insisted that FitzGerald, in dining with Norfolk, had met with a trained British spy. In her letter Murphy claimed that Haughey's 'vicious attempts to conjure up the vision of the Noble spy subtly manipulating a naive Dr FitzGerald over lunch would be hilarious if it were not proof that Irish domestic politics had sunk to sewer level.[4] This led Wall to retort that if Murphy would really like to do some research on the topic of sewerage in Irish politics, she should 'do a survey on the campaign of scurrility against Mr Haughey conducted by Fine Gael canvassers on the doorsteps in every constituency'.[5] This reflected a common view in Haughey's inner circle that he had been deliberately targeted and demonised by Fine Gael, aided and abetted by malcontents in Fianna Fáil. It was perhaps best summed up by the editor of the *Irish Press*, Tim Pat Coogan, who in 1984 told the *Crane Bag* journal that 'a group of Fine Gael people got together and decided the way to take out Fianna Fáil was to take out Charlie Haughey and they made that settled policy. Nothing was bad enough to say about him, or to let drop through the lobby system, and of course they were aided in this by splits in the

Fianna Fáil party itself. The enemies within conspired with the enemies without.[6]

Ultimately, the difficult economic situation was too much for Haughey to overcome. Fianna Fáil's vote went down by just over 2 per cent to 45.2 per cent and the party lost six seats, falling to seventy-five. The election was a triumph for Garret FitzGerald; Fine Gael won seventy seats on 39.2 per cent, its best ever performance. It seemed on the verge of overtaking Fianna Fáil. Labour, under its new leader, Dick Spring, won sixteen seats, which meant that the numbers were there for a stable majority Fine Gael–Labour coalition. Haughey was destined for opposition. He was relatively sanguine about the result, writing to his brother Eoghan, then on a mission to the United States, that even though the outcome of the election was very disappointing there was general agreement that having regard to the difficult circumstances, Fianna Fáil had done very well.[7]

The Fine Gael–Labour coalition proved more difficult to negotiate than anticipated, which presaged a difficult four years in office. Haughey would find it equally problematic in opposition. Seán Doherty was the catalyst for many of Haughey's problems. During his short stay as Minister for Justice, Doherty, a former Garda, was involved in a number of controversies. Principal among them was the so-called Dowra affair. Early one morning in September 1982, a witness from Northern Ireland was held by the RUC in Fermanagh and thus prevented from testifying in an Irish court on an assault charge against Doherty's brother-in-law, Tom Nangle, who was a member of the Gardaí.[8] This was not just a story orchestrated by the media, although Doherty described allegations of interference with the RUC as 'total bullshit'.[9] The reports of the story worried plenty of people in Fianna Fáil, in government, on the backbenches, and at the grassroots. One letter from the local cumann in Blacklion, just a few miles from Dowra, told Haughey that the incident cast a serious reflection on the government and on Fianna Fáil and called on him to 'clear the air and expose the people responsible for preventing justice being done in this case'.[10]

Doherty was also involved in another case involving a Garda, when Sergeant Tom Tully successfully resisted an attempt to have him transferred from Boyle in Roscommon to Ballyconnell in Cavan. Tully saw the move as victimisation by Doherty because he would not yield to political pressure to overlook serious violations of the law. After originally being ordered to move by the Garda commissioner, Tully appealed to the Garda review body on transfers and was successful. This was the first successful transfer appeal by a member of the Association of Garda Sergeants and Inspectors. Doherty was reported to be furious at the decision and castigated the deputy commissioner, Lawrence Wren, who had been a member of the review committee, and Liam Breathnach, an assistant secretary in the Department of Justice.[11]

Doherty also had a four-foot perimeter wall built around his house in Cootehill. When the RTÉ current affairs programme *Today Tonight* showed up to ask about its purpose and cost, Doherty told them that it was to 'stop Séamus Brennan looking in over it'.[12] Brennan, of course, was a long-standing opponent of the Haughey wing of the party. On 9 December, as the new Fine Gael–Labour government was about to be formed, *Today Tonig*ht broadcast a long-planned show alleging that Doherty had used his position as Minister for Justice to interfere directly in Garda activities in his own constituency. The Tom Tully case was the centre of the piece, which produced evidence of Doherty's interference in drunk driving and other cases. He later rejected all the claims, stating that they were evidence of RTÉ bias, and that all he was guilty of was petitioning on behalf of his constituents. He would make no apology for that. One of Haughey's correspondents got to the kernel of the issue in February 1983, the day after Haughey survived his most serious leadership challenge: 'A Minister of Justice who makes representations – as a TD – to the police is – to say the least – not suited for a minister's post.'[13] Unfortunately for Haughey, it took him some considerable time to recognise this.

As his 1982 administration was coming to a close, Haughey was becoming increasingly worried by Doherty's performance as Minister for Justice. Close to a decade later, in the context of Doherty's allegations that Haughey knew about the tapping of journalists' phones, Haughey stated that he was sufficiently concerned by Doherty's conduct in 1982, and by the serious allegations of political interference with the Gardaí, to set in train arrangements for setting up a judicial inquiry, which was the best means of independently and impartially ascertaining the truth, until his government fell. His press secretary, P.J. Mara, also claimed many years later that Haughey was exasperated by Doherty's performance as Minister for Justice, but that once he had been appointed, he was not easy to get rid of. That would have handed more ammunition to Haughey's opponents in Fianna Fáil.[14] Another close adviser to Haughey, Martin Mansergh, took the view that by the end of that government Haughey had come to realise that Doherty was a serious political liability and a loose cannon.[15]

In the week after the *Today Tonight* show things got much worse for Doherty, and for Haughey. On Saturday 18 December 1982, Peter Murtagh, the security correspondent of the *Irish Times*, published a front-page piece which began: 'The telephones of two prominent polit-ical journalists were being tapped by Mr Haughey's government.'[16] He named the journalists as Bruce Arnold and Geraldine Kennedy. Both were known to be hostile to Haughey. The new Minister for Justice, Michael Noonan, who had been in office for less than a week, ordered an investigation to find out whether there had indeed been taps and whether they were ordered for improper reasons. On appointing Noonan to office, the new Taoiseach, Garret FitzGerald, told him that he had come into information that the phones of Arnold and Kennedy had been tapped, and ordered Noonan to find out if that was indeed the case. On his first day in office, Noonan was told by the secretary of the department, Andy Ward, that indeed there had been taps.[17] Three days after Murtagh's revelations, Haughey, at a dinner in Johnny Oppermann's restaurant in Malahide for the Fianna Fáil ministers of the outgoing administration, claimed he had asked Doherty about the revelations and received general assurances that there was nothing of significance involved.[18]

That Christmas, Haughey was facing the prospect of a significant period in opposition. His disappointment was eased temporarily by the gift of a hand-carved casket filled with cigars from the Cuban leader, Fidel Castro, who had stopped over in Shannon on a recent trip, although Haughey was unable to meet him on the occasion.[19] He read Len

Deighton's Second World War novel *Goodbye, Mickey Mouse* and told him it was his best yet; an 'incomparable novel'.[20] That novel dealt with war in the air. As 1983 dawned, the storm clouds were gathering over Kinsaley and would soon bring with them the most serious challenge yet to Haughey's leadership of Fianna Fáil.

ANOTHER HEAVE

On 20 January 1983, Michael Noonan announced that the phones of the two journalists had indeed been illegally tapped at the instigation of the then minister Seán Doherty, and that there was no justification for such taps. Noonan revealed that the taps were put on the two journalists' phones on the basis that Doherty wanted to detect and put an end to leaks from the media from within the government. Doherty had not, however, mentioned any such leaks or given any indication that either Arnold or Kennedy had actually published any leaks. In case there was any doubt about the explosive political nature of his statement Noonan made it clear that in normal circumstances the procedure for tapping telephones lay in the hands of the Garda commissioner, who would seek approval from the minister. In this case the procedure was reversed. The phones had been tapped at Doherty's behest, and Commissioner Patrick McLaughlin and Deputy Commissioner Joe Ainsworth felt they had no option but to comply with the minister's wishes.

In a rather surreal twist, Noonan also revealed that Doherty had provided Minister for Finance Ray MacSharry with bugging equipment to enable him to record a conversation with the Minister for Education, Martin O'Donoghue, in October, when O'Donoghue tried to persuade MacSharry to switch allegiance from Haughey. While this conversation came in the aftermath of the McCreevy motion it was symptomatic of the ongoing attempts by Haughey's opponents to undermine him. The transcript of the tape made it clear that O'Donoghue took the initiative in a discussion of the persistent leadership problems and the future of the party. He expressed concern that as long as the present leadership held, 'people are going to be very jittery because some will not like going into the next election with him.'[21] This was an obvious reference to Haughey, and MacSharry then made it clear that as far as he was concerned the matter had been settled by the confidence vote earlier that month. MacSharry had initially sought the recording equipment because he was concerned about the rumours sweeping through the party that he could in effect be bought to change sides, and he wanted to record any attempt that might be made to bribe him. He was long known to have had money problems. In an interview over three and a half decades later he described his thought process: 'I thought this was terrible that money would be used to overthrow the democratically elected leader. I did have a tape recorder when I met O'Donoghue. But unfortunately, some of the main points were not transcribed because I couldn't change the tape around to get the second part of the tape in there. There was rumours that Haughey bailed me out but I can tell you no one bailed me out only myself and I was down at the bottom.'[22] O'Donoghue never broached money at all in the conversation.

Noonan's revelations set off a firestorm in political circles and ignited the third heave against Haughey in the space of a year. It took place over the following three weeks, and this time all the expectations were that Haughey would inevitably be deposed after just over three tumultuous years as leader. After Noonan's announcement, Haughey immediately said that he had known nothing about the phone tapping. He regarded it as an abuse of a procedure which was only justified to combat crime or subversion, and he would never countenance such an action. He then established a four-man committee, consisting of the party chairman Jim Tunney, David Andrews, Bertie Ahern and Michael O'Kennedy, to inquire into the scandal. He said that he was happy to appear before the committee himself. Haughey's difficulties were eased somewhat when Doherty stated that he alone was responsible for the phone tapping and had never discussed it with Haughey. In an interview with RTÉ's *This Week* radio programme on Sunday 23 January 1983, he said, 'Mr Haughey did not know that I was tapping these journalists' phones.' Nine years later he was to tell a different story, and made sure everyone knew about it. In the immediate aftermath of Doherty's statement that he had acted alone, a meeting of the Fianna Fáil parliamentary party was held at which support for Haughey seemed to be holding firm. There was no support for Doherty's actions.[23]

The following week was a difficult one for Haughey. The newspapers revealed extensive details of the O'Donoghue–MacSharry taped conversation and disquiet within the party grew. By Wednesday 26 January, Bertie Ahern had decided it was time to tell Haughey that the numbers in the parliamentary party were against him. George Colley had impressed upon Ahern that it was no less than his duty to go to Kinsaley and inform Haughey that 'the game was up'.[24] That evening Ahern went to Kinsaley to see Haughey and told him that if there were a vote today, he would lose, and Michael O'Kennedy, not Des O'Malley, would have a clear path to victory. (O'Kennedy had, of course, supported Haughey in 1979, and was not associated with the Colley–O'Malley wing of the party.) That piece of information told Haughey that the situation could be rescued. In one way it was very bad news for him in that his opponents were not just the gang of twenty-two who had supported the McCreevy motion the previous October. The fact that those newly disaffected TDs were not going to the dissident wing of the party gave Haughey the belief that he could persuade enough of those who were against him to change their minds.[25] Haughey told Ahern that the deputies could do what they liked but he was staying. Like Thatcher in Britain, Haughey was not for turning.

The following day Haughey woke up to read his own obituary in the *Irish Press*.[26] Things were so bad for him that he was even taken out of the betting odds as to who would be Fianna Fáil leader by the end of the month. A day later the *Irish Independent* reported that Haughey was in his 'final days'.[27] This view was widespread across the party. Discussion then turned to who would succeed Haughey. At least three candidates, Des O'Malley, Michael O'Kennedy and Gerry Collins, declared that they would be prepared to stand. Haughey, however, was not gone. The more candidates in the race the better was Haughey's attitude, and also that of P.J. Mara, who told him 'We need confusion.'[28] If there were a number of candidates in the race, it would potentially shore up Haughey's own position, and make it clear that none of those who wanted to succeed him would have a majority of support within the parliamentary party.

On 1 February, the day before the parliamentary party was to meet and take a decision on the leadership, Clem Coughlan, the victor in Haughey's first electoral test, the Donegal by-election of December 1980, was tragically killed in a car crash on his way from Galway to Leinster House. At the subsequent parliamentary party meeting, Haughey paid tribute to Coughlan. Then, to the surprise of many, after a minute's silence, the chairperson, Jim Tunney, adjourned the meeting. Many attendees were so desperate to get rid of Haughey that they wanted the meeting to continue. Bertie Ahern and Jim Tunney were having none of it. At their meeting in Kinsaley the previous week, Ahern had advised Haughey to play for time.[29] Now, in the most desperate of circumstances, the untimely death of Coughlan had given Haughey that time.

As the challenge to Haughey's leadership seemed unstoppable within the parliamentary party, he took the unusual step of appealing directly to the party's grassroots. Once again they rallied round him. The telephone calls, to Fianna Fáil's office in Mount Street, and the letters flowed in. They urged him to stay and not to yield to plotters and malcontents. Many said it was nonsense that he should know what his underlings were doing. One suggested that if he did indeed yield to the campaign to oust him, he would 'open a sluice gate of media activity which will alter the character of our democracy and endanger the position of every subsequent Taoiseach and party leader. Government by TV and editorial will succeed.'[30]

On the day that letter was written, Haughey issued a statement to the Fianna Fáil faithful calling 'on all members to rally behind me as their democratically elected leader and give me that total support that I need to restore unity and stability, to reorganise the party, to give it a new sense of purpose, to restate our policies, to re-establish and implement the traditional code of discipline, and to make it clear that those who bring the party into disrepute, cause dissension or refuse to accept decisions democratically arrived at can no longer remain in the party.' It was a clever tactic. Haughey stated that he already had received a lot of support from members and supporters asking him to stay on, and that he was deeply moved by the faith they had placed in him 'despite everything that a largely hostile media and political opponents at home and abroad could do to damage not only me but the great party and traditions of Fianna Fáil'.[31] Pointing to outside influences who were trying to tarnish the good name of the party also played well with the grassroots. Haughey was essentially moving the battleground away from the parliamentary party and into the sphere of local politics.

Within the parliamentary party, Ben Briscoe, once a firm Haughey supporter, submitted a motion to the chief whip, Bertie Ahern: 'The Fianna Fáil members of Dáil Éireann request the resignation of Charles J. Haughey as leader now.' The word 'now' was so that Haughey would not be able to use any procedural issues or further postponements to delay what his opponents saw as the inevitable. Moreover, they wanted to call on him to resign immediately, at the beginning of the meeting scheduled for Monday 7 February. On the weekend before the meeting, the newspapers were reporting that votes were slipping away from O'Kennedy and moving towards Collins, who was seen as the clear favourite. Collins issued a rebuke to Haughey's appeal to the grassroots. The parliamentary party, he said, would not be intimidated out of doing their duty; many TDs had reported having received phone calls urging them to vote for Haughey.[32] The battle for the very soul of Fianna Fáil was fought out at that meeting of 7 February. Ben Briscoe felt that the party had lost its soul, lost what it stood for. 'Give us back our soul', he told the parliamentary party.[33] Haughey, on the contrary, was of the view that he was the very soul of Fianna Fáil.

From the start of the meeting at 11 a.m., it became clear that Haughey was not going to instantly resign. He sat silently as the first item on the agenda, the report of the sub-committee on the Doherty leaks, was discussed. Those who were anti-Haughey did not want the report debated at all as they were anxious to get straight to the Briscoe motion. A vote on whether to discuss the report was accepted by fifty-nine votes to thirty-five – the party's MEPs and Senators were entitled to vote in this ballot. The report was more a summary of the interviews the committee had undertaken than a forensic analysis of the issues involved. It concluded that Haughey was unaware of the tapping. David Andrews, long a critic of Haughey's, inserted his own opinion into the report that although Haughey was unaware of the tapping, he should have known – he was the Taoiseach and the party leader, with whom ultimate responsibility lay.[34] Haughey then announced that he would be proposing a motion to expel both Seán Doherty and Martin O'Donoghue from the parliamentary party at its meeting the following week. It was well into the evening before Briscoe's motion, to be voted on by TDs only, was debated. The omens first looked bad for Haughey, as the principle of the secret ballot was upheld. Haughey proposed that since this was not a leadership vote it was important that the grassroots should be able to know which way their TD voted. This was rejected by the meeting.

The rebels needed thirty-seven votes to prevail. After hours of rancorous speechmaking it was announced at 11.15 p.m. that the no confidence motion had been defeated by forty votes to thirty-three. Just the previous week, forty-one members of the parliamentary party had signed a motion seeking a special meeting on the leadership. Eight of them had changed their minds. There seemed to be three main reasons for Haughey's remarkable victory. The main one was the exoneration of Haughey by the sub-committee. Then there was Haughey's decisive action in seeking the expulsion of Doherty and O'Donoghue which, it seemed, had swayed some votes. Finally, it was believed that Michael O'Kennedy would only contest the leadership if Haughey signalled his intention of leaving voluntarily. He did not wish to be involved in a purge of the leader, or to be associated with the Colley–O'Malley wing. He did not speak in the debate, which many deputies took as tacit acceptance that he was voting for Haughey. For the second time in four years O'Kennedy's vote for Haughey was vital.

The result was that Haughey had held on, against all the odds. The significance of his win was that his leadership was as secure as it had ever been. He had in effect won three battles in the space of a year. The cartoonist in the following day's *Irish Press* captured the mood: 'Houdini was only in the Ha'penny Place'. But the comment of one deputy on the losing side offered a more sombre take on the implications for the party: 'We simply all filed out past the coffin of Fianna Fail.'[35] That was not quite the case, but it does reveal how many members viewed Haughey's unlikely victory.

Later that night, Haughey, back in Kinsaley, suffered a severe attack of his recurring kidney stone problem. This was always more acute at times of high stress. A late-night injection eventually relieved the pain and the kidney stone that caused it.[36] The stress of these times for Fianna Fáil took a heavy toll on many TDs. Within a year both George Colley and Ber Cowen would die of heart attacks. Liam Hyland also had a heart attack after hearing the news of Clem Coughlan's death. Gerry Collins was only out of hospital a matter of days before the February 1983 vote, having suffered a serious gall bladder problem. Others also became ill. Bertie Ahern, who as chief whip was at the heart of the action, was in no doubt that these illnesses were politically related.[37] Haughey was not immune to the stress either, and would suffer increased bouts of kidney stones over the remaining nine years of his public life. When George Colley died suddenly in September 1983 at Guy's Hospital in London after undergoing tests for a heart condition, Haughey was meeting Fianna Fáil's chief fundraiser, Paul Kavanagh, in his office in Leinster House. On hearing the news, Haughey was described by Kavanagh as being in 'deep shock. He was just stunned. He literally couldn't move.'[38] Colley was only fifty-seven years of age. Haughey had just turned fifty-eight the previous day.

On the day after Haughey's victory, Seán Doherty, with 'deep regret', resigned from the Fianna Fáil parliamentary party. He stated that he had acted properly at all times in the discharge of his duties and responsibilities as minister but was sorry that not all his party colleagues had accepted his view. He ended his letter of resignation to Haughey saying he knew 'there was no need to assure you of my constant loyalty to Fianna Fáil and my wish to continue to serve the organisation in any way open to me at all times in the future'.[39] Martin O'Donoghue quickly followed him. His handwritten letter was short and to the point: 'In order to avoid any further discussion of a contentious nature on matters relating to me, I hereby resign from the Fianna Fáil Parliamentary Party.'[40] Notwithstanding Haughey's threat in his message to the grassroots that those who caused dissension should be removed from the party he took no steps to discipline any other member. This was a shrewd and appropriate move given the turmoil of the three heaves against him in the space of a year. The leadership issue was now settled and there was nothing to be gained from a triumphant attitude in victory. This was particularly the case since Fianna Fáil looked set for a long period in opposition.

THE 1992 REVELATION

The question of whether Charles Haughey knew about the tapping of Bruce Arnold's and Geraldine Kennedy's phones in 1982 remains one of the great controversies of Irish politics. Both Arnold and Kennedy were convinced that Haughey had indeed orchestrated the tapping. After close to a decade of saying nothing about it, Doherty, in early January 1992, chose a relatively obscure late-night RTÉ television programme called *Nighthawks* to tell the nation that Haughey had in fact known about the phone tapping. Talking casually to the show's presenter, Shay Healy, in Hell's Kitchen, a public house in Castlerea, County Roscommon, Doherty said that there was a cabinet decision to stop the leaks from cabinet and that as Minister for Justice he had a job to do. He then said he was let down by the fact that people knew what he was doing and that he had a constitutional obligation to find out who was taking information out of the most important boardroom in the country and making it available without authority to the national media and others. He felt this was wrong and his cabinet colleagues felt the same way. He added that he was required to ensure that the leaking would be stopped, that he consulted with the authorities, and that one of the methods decided upon was tapping phones. Off air after the programme, Doherty wanted to make sure that Healy understood the importance of what he had said: 'Don't forget, I've said something very significant that I've never said before in my life.'[31] Doherty did not mention Haughey by name and stated that the cabinet had agreed that he get to the bottom of the leaks. The latter point was certainly news to those who had served in cabinet with Doherty.

The day after the programme was aired, both Ray MacSharry and Des O'Malley, who were members of that government, denied that there was any cabinet decision to tap any journalists' phones. Within two weeks Doherty had changed his story. In an explosive press conference on 21 January 1992 he said he was confirming that the Taoiseach, Mr Haughey, was fully aware, in 1982, that two journalists' phones were being tapped, and that he at no stage expressed any reservations about this action. He then went on to say that he 'did not seek, nor did I get, any instruction from any member of the cabinet in this regard. Nor did I tell the cabinet that this action had been taken. Telephone tapping was never discussed in cabinet.[42] This was of course completely at odds with what he had told Shay Healy only two weeks earlier. He was very specific that he had handed Haughey transcripts of the tapes and that out of loyalty to the leader and the party he had taken the blame and accepted the consequences in 1982. Doherty claimed to be motivated by the publication in December 1991 of a telephone tapping bill, introduced by Minister for Justice Ray Burke, which, Doherty stated, would have forced him to tell lies to the Seanad about what had happened in 1982, and this he would not do. Lying might have been appropriate in 1982, but it was not appropriate a decade later. Doherty had become somewhat religious over the course of the decade, which many took to be the reason for his volte face. Haughey immediately issued a denial, quite reasonably pointing out that he had always been consistent in his view; it was Doherty who had fundamentally changed his story in the intervening years. Yet, as Terry Prone, who advised Doherty about his press conference, pointed out, he had nothing to gain by telling all, other than personal ignominy, loss of his senate seat and extrusion by Fianna Fáil, something he alluded to in his speech that night.[43]

At his own press conference the following day, Haughey asked the attendant journalists where the transcripts were, if they existed, because they were not and never had been in his offices. On Doherty's motivation, he asked whether Doherty was serious that the then Fianna Fáil–Progressive Democrat government should have refrained from carrying out its clear public duty to protect the rights of the citizen out of regard for his position as Cathaoirleach of the Seanad. He went on to say that he found it ironic that Doherty, in what he claimed was his

desire to protect the Fianna Fáil government of 1982, and Haughey as
Taoiseach, had singlehandedly done more than anyone else to damage
the reputation of both. In essence Haughey's view was that 'Doherty did
not dare inform me of what he had authorised' until his actions were
on the verge of being exposed by the Fine Gael–Labour coalition.[44] In
Haughey's papers there is a copy of the *Irish Times* of 22 January 1992, the
day Haughey gave his press conference. In that the edition of the paper,
Haughey has handwritten some emendations on the verbatim statement
issued by Doherty the previous day. He jotted down three points:

1   'Who recommended' – This was in relation to Doherty's state-
     ment that Deputy Garda Commissioner Joe Ainsworth, who
     was also head of security, agreed that the leaks were posing a
     national problem. Doherty maintained that at a later meeting
     Ainsworth said it would be difficult to prevent such leaks by
     most methods, and recommended the option of tapping the
     phone of journalist Bruce Arnold.
2   'Best advice' – This related to Doherty's statement that he took
     the best advice available to him, which was that tapping was
     the recommended action.
3   'Over months' – This was in connection with Doherty's
     statement that in 1983 not only did he take the blame for the
     tapping, but when Haughey claimed not to have been aware
     of the tapping while it was in progress, Doherty did not cor-
     rect the claim and indeed supported it. Doherty went on to
     say that Haughey had known about the tapping and had not
     expressed any 'reservation during the several months in which
     he received from my hands copies of the transcripts of the
     taped telephone conversations'. The final phrase is underlined
     in Haughey's copy of the *Irish Times*.[45]

These were the issues that Haughey finished his own press conference
with. He maintained that it was quite clear that, despite Doherty's claim
to the contrary, Joe Ainsworth did not recommend the option of tapping

the telephone of Bruce Arnold. Haughey claimed that in the course of the Fine Gael–Labour government's investigation Ainsworth stated that it was Doherty who put it to him that in the interests of the security of the state there should be an intercept on Bruce Arnold's telephone; and that far from being advised to do this, Doherty was specifically advised against it. Doherty's suggestion that a further tap should be put on Arnold's phone in October some months after the first had been removed was rejected. Second, Haughey asserted that Doherty's claims that the transcripts were taken to him as Taoiseach over a period of time was contradicted by all the evidence. Again he cited Ainsworth's evidence to the original inquiry that he, Ainsworth, had shown the intercepts to Doherty on one specific occasion. Doherty then gave the intercepts back to him and Ainsworth later shredded the copies. On that defiant note Haughey ended his press conference, and then took questions for over an hour, unlike Doherty, who had answered no questions at his own conference the previous day.

After Haughey's press conference, Ainsworth was quoted as saying that decisions on the tapping were arrived at spontaneously, taps were put on the telephones only for the shortest possible times, and 'I stand apart from the whole damn lot of them. I do not want to become involved in any controversy on anything they might say.[46] Ainsworth had had a slightly different view five years earlier when he congratulated Haughey on his performance in the 1987 general election. Two days after the election, when the results were becoming clear, he wrote to Haughey expressing delight at Haughey's victory, and complimenting him on his performance – despite the begrudgers, and despite an adverse media at home and abroad, including the usual foreign subtle interference in the country's domestic affairs. He went on to say that, looking back, he doubted 'if the short political gain has helped the politicians who set out to destroy yourself, Seán Doherty and myself and our families in such a calculated and determined way.[47] This was a reference to various allegations and rumours that British intelligence wanted to unseat Haughey and had tried to do so, particularly in 1982.

PLOT?

The theory that British intelligence was involved in nefarious activities relating to Haughey was put forward most notably by the publisher Captain John Feehan of Mercier Press. In 1984 he published a book entitled *Operation Brogue: A Study of the Vilification of Charles Haughey*, which alleged an anti-Haughey plot by various British agencies. Feehan wrote to Haughey looking for help with the work and enclosing the first few pages.[48] He followed this up the following year with a hagiographical account of Haughey's qualities in *The Statesman*.[49] In 1988, a year after Haughey was back in power, Feehan took a completely different view. In another book, he denounced Haughey as a collaborator with the British occupation in Ireland. In *An Apology to the Irish People* he argued that Haughey had been fraudulently anti-British in opposition. In 1987, Feehan had told Haughey that he did not wish to write such a book but would be compelled to do so unless Haughey threw out the Extradition Act, which was basically a test in 'showing to the nations of the world who is the effective Taoiseach in Ireland – you or Margaret Thatcher.'[50] He had already written to Haughey earlier that year after the Revenue Commissioners had turned down a number of his books for the artists' tax exemption and alluded to rumours that the Revenue Commissioners had been given a political directive that would nullify the benefits of tax exemption for writers. Haughey told him he 'would not be party to any such subterfuge', and that the Revenue Commissioners had to discharge their responsibilities in this scheme as they would in any other.[51]

The belief that British intelligence had tried to destabilise Haughey was widespread in those with republican views. The veteran civil rights activist Seán MacBride, a regular correspondent, wrote to Haughey in 1985 to say that from his own personal and direct experience of British secret service operations relating to Ireland, he had no doubt that Feehan's Operation Brogue was well-founded and that 'many of the sustained and systematic efforts to destabilise your leadership and the influence of Fianna Fáil, have their origins in British secret service operations.'[52] The renowned UCD archaeologist George Eogan, another regular correspondent, whom Haughey appointed to the Seanad in 1987, was also suspicious of British intelligence, and what he considered the propaganda campaign against the Fianna Fáil leader. After the 1987 election, Eogan told Haughey that his electoral achievement was all the more impressive 'when one remembers the intense propaganda you had to overcome'.[53] In July 1984, Haughey had spent a day visiting the Neolithic passage grave in Knowth, which Eogan had begun excavating as far back as 1962. Eogan was a strong supporter of Haughey. In 1983 he wrote to Fianna Fáil headquarters before the leadership vote: 'In Mr Haughey your party has an experienced intelligent and independently minded leader. Surely that is what your party and the country needs.'[54]

On 18 January 1992, in the period between Seán Doherty's *Nighthawks* appearance and his fateful press conference, Joe Ainsworth wrote to Haughey that he was 'satisfied, as I always have been, that a plan to destabilise the lawful government of 1982 was well organised from July 1982, and the use made by politicians of the leaked information of the tap was, I believe, the king link which was deliberate in approach and politically managed in the progress of intrigue to the lead-up to the election and the following events including character assassination tactics used so successfully'.[55] Ainsworth attached three pages of notes he had taken on the date of his letter. This was the same day Michael Noonan spoke on RTÉ radio about the events of nine years before. These notes outlined Ainsworth's version of the events of the publication of the phone taps in December 1982. In particular, he wanted Haughey to know that he was carrying out an investigation into planned leaks about phone tapping until, on 7 January 1983, he was ordered to stop by the Minister for Justice, Michael Noonan, via the secretary of the Department of Justice and the Garda commissioner. In his notes, Ainsworth added that at no time did he ever discuss any leaks with Haughey and that at any time he met Haughey there was always someone else present. He did discuss phone tapping with Seán Doherty but stated that the government did not give him a direction to tap a phone or phones, and neither did Doherty. This was an allusion to his later comments in the press that decisions on the tapping were arrived at spontaneously. He ended his note to Haughey by stating that when he left the force in 1983 he was furious about a lot of things, including that 'righteous politicians who were investigating the phone matters were careful and selective to avoid any shadow on themselves ... The mole had to be protected.'[56] This was a reference to whoever leaked the fact that there had been phone tapping in the first place, which Ainsworth assumed was someone in Fine Gael. Two decades later, in an opinion piece in the *Irish Times* on the events of 1982, he stated that there were 'dark forces operating from the shadows who were pumping out carefully tailored propaganda'.[57] He always insisted that the taps were for security reasons and in no way political.

THE HAUGHEY DEFENCE

Haughey's family, and some of his close confidants, have always believed that he did not know about Doherty's phone-tapping exercise. His wife, Maureen, recalled how in January 1983 he had been completely shocked by the revelations.[58] P.J. Mara maintained that over dinner one night in 1983, when the affair was fresh in both men's memory, he asked Doherty what the real story was. 'Doherty used to stay with me in Clontarf and I said to him once, "What the fuck were you at with the tapes and did you ever tell Haughey about that?" and he said "No, I never told him."'[59] Mara recounted the same story to his biographer, Tim Ryan, adding that Doherty told him: 'On my oath Haughey knew nothing whatever about the tappings.'[60] Mara went on to say that he had discussed Doherty's revelations with various unnamed members of the 1982 government, all of whom had confirmed to him that Doherty's story of 1983, not 1992, was the correct one. In the week of Doherty's revelations, Martin Mansergh, Haughey's long-term special adviser, wrote, 'Like others of the small group of people, both civil servants and political appointees, who worked closely with Mr. Haughey in 1982 or since, in government and in opposition, and who were privileged to enjoy his confidence, I can testify that there was never the slightest hint or sight by anyone of phone tappings or of the existence of transcripts ... I can also testify that when Mr. Haughey learned of the truth of the reports in January he was absolutely shattered. It was he that felt badly let down.'[61]

Haughey must take the blame, however, for appointing Doherty Minister for Justice in the first place. As a successful minister in that

department himself two decades earlier he was aware of the crucial sensi-
tivity of the post. His difficulties with Justice at the time of the arms crisis
were well known. He had agreed to a veto by George Colley in the department when he first became Taoiseach in 1979, and retained Gerry Collins
in the role. In February 1982, when he had the unencumbered opportunity to appoint his own minister, he chose an ex-Garda. This in itself
showed extremely poor judgement. He was also leader when Doherty
was brought back to the parliamentary party in December 1984, and was
reported as giving his personal backing to Doherty's return. It certainly
would not have happened if he was opposed. Doherty's readmittance to
the parliamentary party occurred at a routine meeting at which Haughey
himself was not present. There were few people at the meeting when
Doherty's readmission was proposed by Brian Lenihan. There was no
discussion, no disagreement from anyone in attendance that Doherty
be readmitted, and the chairman, Jim Tunney, immediately moved the
agenda along.[62] By this time Haughey had almost complete control of
the parliamentary party. The death of George Colley in September 1983,
and the expulsion of Des O'Malley from the parliamentary party in May
1984 over a dispute with Haughey about Fianna Fáil's reaction to the New
Ireland Forum report, had consolidated Haughey's position.

When Fianna Fáil returned to power in 1987, Doherty expected a
recall to cabinet and was disappointed when he was not even made a
minister for state. In the run-up to the 1987 general election, he had made
it privately known to journalists that he would expect a ministerial post
from Haughey if Fianna Fáil returned to power, hinting darkly that his
exclusion from office might encourage him to talk more freely about the
events of 1982 and 1983.[63] When he received no post in that government
Haughey wrote to one of his correspondents: 'I do not need to tell you
how highly I regard Seán Doherty and I regret very much that it was
not possible to include him among my recent appointments because he
would certainly be quite capable of holding down any one of a number
of posts. You can rest assured that I intend to keep Seán's talents and
experience in mind for the future'.[64] Two years later Doherty lost his
Roscommon seat in the June 1989 general election. He took a seat in

the subsequent Seanad election and sought to become Cathaoirleach of the Seanad that November. Haughey, however, refused to support either Doherty or the other candidate, Des Hanafin, who was an avowed anti-Haugheyite. The fact that Haughey remained neutral was perhaps indicative of his real view of Doherty.

Despite its inconsistencies, Doherty's January 1992 statement has become the dominant narrative of the phone tapping controversy. In a book on Haughey written in the immediate aftermath of the affair, the historian T. Ryle Dwyer argued that Doherty's revelations were to do with the leadership struggle in Fianna Fáil and that Doherty knew he had the power to 'deliver a fatal blow by telling what he knew about the events of 1982'.[65] Des O'Malley always asserted that 'it was obvious Doherty was telling the truth.'[66] When the presenter of *Nighthawks*, Shay Healy, died in April 2021 his obituarist wrote that few doubted Doherty was telling the truth during his phone-tapping revelations, 'but Haughey had always lied about it, blaming Doherty as a lone transgressor'.[67] The inconsistencies in Haughey's own career, and the subsequent revelations about his finances after he left public office meant that pretty much anything could be said about him. It seems quite clear now that the Doherty intervention in January 1992 was orchestrated by opponents of Haughey within Fianna Fáil. O'Malley claimed in his memoir that he had 'no doubt the intervention was orchestrated'.[68] In his own political memoir, the veteran Fianna Fáil politician John O'Leary, no friend of Haughey, placed Pádraig Flynn at the centre of the intrigue, while also speculating that Albert Reynolds was fully aware of a plan to essentially take Haughey down. O'Leary stated that on the night in 1991 when a party was being held to celebrate O'Leary's twenty-five-year unbroken stint in the Dáil he 'was told that Flynn and Doherty were in cahoots and plotting the downfall of Haughey ... The plan was to get Doherty to come out straight and name Haughey as one of those who knew about the phone tapping, something he hadn't done yet. I'd be very much surprised if Albert Reynolds didn't know what was happening behind the scenes.'[69] Reynolds, in his own autobiography, argued that Haughey, in denying Doherty's revelation, 'made some spurious claim that it was all part of some plot thought up by my supporters. He convinced no one.'[70] Given Reynolds's ruthlessness when he became Taoiseach and sacked half of Haughey's cabinet, his own challenge to Haughey just a number of months earlier, and his desperation to become Fianna Fáil leader, it would be difficult to think that he would stand aloof and let either events take their course or others plot to take Haughey down without his knowledge. Yet the public relations specialist Tom Savage, who was an adviser to Reynolds at this stage, had given Reynolds a heads-up that Doherty was going to appear on television and reveal his view of the phone tapping. He reported Reynolds as going berserk and telling him to stop Doherty; he was concerned that the Roscommon man would wreck his plans to eventually oust Haughey, which were based on an understanding Dr John O'Connell had with Haughey as to when he would resign, of which Reynolds was aware, but Savage was not.[71]

In any event, Doherty's phone-tapping actions of 1982 were the catalyst for Haughey's downfall a decade later. That decade between January 1983 and February 1992, when Haughey finally stood down, was one in which he would eventually unite Fianna Fáil, but only at the cost of significant defections from the party, including Des O'Malley, and the establishment of the Progressive Democrats. Haughey would then break one of Fianna Fáil's core values by agreeing to coalesce with O'Malley. The decision in June 1989 to form a coalition with the Progressive Democrats was the major underlying factor in Haughey's exit from public life just over two and a half years later because a significant minority in Fianna Fáil, associated with Albert Reynolds, never agreed with it. It was also a time of major developments in Northern Ireland and the economy, and divisions in the country's social fabric over abortion and divorce. For Haughey it was a decade of triumph and failure. He came close to losing his life on three occasions and faced a severe crisis in his personal finances. He would reach the zenith of his career on the European stage, but would plunge uncontrollably and crushingly to the nadir of his exit from public life.

CHAPTER 19

HAUGHEY'S IRELAND

THE NEW IRELAND FORUM

While Haughey's narrow leadership win in February 1983 secured his position, it did not heal the divisions within the party. These emerged again with some force in the wake of the report of the New Ireland Forum in May 1984. The forum, which ran from May 1983 until February 1984, was initially convened by the Taoiseach, Garret FitzGerald, in an attempt to forge a common consensus among constitutional nationalists on the island of Ireland. The preface to the final report outlined that the forum was 'established for consultations on the manner in which lasting peace and stability could be achieved in a new Ireland through the democratic process and to report on possible new structures and processes through which this objective could be achieved.'[1] It was also an attempt to counteract the growing support in Northern Ireland for Sinn Féin, at the expense of the Social Democratic and Labour Party (SDLP).

Given the control Haughey had within Fianna Fáil, and the fact that he considered himself its one true voice on Northern Ireland policy, he was never likely to countenance any dissent from within its ranks when it came to the party's position on the forum. Just before the forum began, one of his correspondents complained about the appointment of Ray MacSharry as a Fianna Fáil representative: 'I was stunned to learn that you had appointed MacSharry to the New Forum. His bugging activities have, I know, been whitewashed by the Parliamentary Party but not I daresay by the Fianna Fáil party. After all it is the party which gives you all the jobs – not the other way around.'[2]

At the conclusion of the public session of the forum on 21 September 1983, Haughey said that Northern Ireland was a political anachronism which was 'neither a viable political nor a viable economic entity'.[3] That day, two academic economists, Charles Carter and Louden Ryan, had presented to the forum on the economic cost of a united Ireland. Haughey began his statement by thanking both academics but added that while it was the job of academics to advise, it was that of politicians to decide. In a critique of their presentation he argued: 'If economics is the dismal science, politics must be the profession of hope.' He found it hard to accept, he said, that the two economists could not formulate a prospect of an all-island economic entity capable of developing its own inherent dynamic for progress, provided the political structures were right. This statement succinctly summed up Haughey's attitude to both the forum and Northern Ireland itself. His sole thought process was based on the idea that a united Ireland could be a success.

The forum's final report put forward three options: a unitary state; a federal or confederal state; and joint British-Irish authority. Haughey, although he signed the document on behalf of Fianna Fáil, quickly advocated the unitary state structure and dismissed the other two options as not feasible. The unitary state was defined in the final report as a state that would embrace the island of Ireland. It would be governed as a single unit under one government and one parliament elected by all the people of the island. It would seek to unite in agreement the two major identities and traditions in Ireland. In a private document entitled 'The Case for a Unitary State', Haughey set out his views on why the unitary state was the best possible solution for progress on Northern Ireland. As for the other possibilities, he considered that northern nationalists would still be under unionist domination in a federal/confederal solution, while the problem with joint sovereignty was there would still be a British military and political presence, which Haughey considered one of the main problems afflicting Northern Ireland. He was also sure that any departure from the unitary model would be eagerly portrayed by the British media as an abandonment of the aim of a united Ireland, which would have a destabilising effect both North and South, and lead to a growth in support for republican extremists.[4]

After the final report was published, Haughey went on RTÉ radio and stated that it was dangerous and foolish to put a whole range of alternatives to the British government. He argued that the forum had reached a valuable degree of agreement; that all the parties wished to see a unitary state established because it offered the best possible way of achieving lasting peace and stability; and it was thus essential that the report be put clearly and specifically to the British government to get its response. To do otherwise would, he argued, be dangerous and defeatist. He added that his comments represented the official policy of his party.[5] Haughey's remarks were made in the context of a decision by the Fine Gael–Labour government to seek talks with the British government on the section of the document dealing with the realities of the present situation and the requirements for devising a framework for a solution. Fianna Fáil issued an immediate statement saying that it was the government's duty to put the case for Irish unity and that it could not support the government if it adopted a position that specifically went against the arguments and conclusions of the Forum in favour of Irish unity and the unitary state.[6]

After his radio interview Haughey was taken to task by Des O'Malley and Senator Eoin Ryan, both of whom argued that the party had not been given the opportunity of considering the forum report from a policy point of view. Ryan stated that the report had been negotiated by a delegation from the party, not the party leader, and he specifically reserved the right to comment on it afterwards, as he did indeed in a speech in Wexford after the report had been issued. Ryan and O'Malley were critical of Haughey's over-emphasis on the unitary state option, arguing that it would frighten the British away.[7] They wanted to broaden the party's platform on ways of seeking to resolve the Northern conflict and argued that all political options in line with the overall tenor of the forum's report should be discussed by the parliamentary party, not simply decided by diktat from the party leader. O'Malley made the point that from a nationalist point of view the unitary state would be the preferable or desired solution but that the forum's federal option was the most practical suggestion. It was one that could bring about substantial progress and in time lead to further developments. There was a lot of caveats in his statement, but he argued that what was important in the short term was that the present situation could not go on and some way had to be found to change it. If a federal state was a way of achieving that kind of objective, it would have very widespread public support. He insisted that the full report needed to be debated both in the Fianna Fáil parliamentary party and in the Dáil. Haughey asserted that as leader he had to defend the party's position.

The battle lines were once again drawn over Haughey's leadership. This time, however, Haughey's victory was quick and decisive. Within a week of O'Malley's comments, he had been expelled from the parliamentary party on a vote of fifty-six to sixteen after another marathon six-hour parliamentary party meeting. Haughey had moved the expulsion motion following a charge by O'Malley that party policy on Northern Ireland, as enunciated by Haughey, had never been discussed by the parliamentary party. The expulsion of O'Malley saw the beginning of the fissure in the party that led to the formation of the Progressive Democrats with Mary Harney, the young TD from Dublin South West, telling the meeting that 'if there was no room in the party for the ideas expressed by Mr. O'Malley there was no room in it for her.'[8] Harney, and a number of others, considered resigning the party whip but were persuaded against this action by O'Malley.[9] It would not be long, however, before O'Malley's supporters decided that they would be better off outside Fianna Fáil. P.J. Mara's later 'uno duce, una voce' comment, although said in jest, summed up for many the problem of Fianna Fáil under Haughey. He would brook little or no dissent, and certainly none on the question of Northern Ireland. Haughey was outraged by Mara's comments and fired him instantly, but a few hours later had calmed down enough to simply warn his press adviser about such remarks. He felt that they played into the hands of a media that already distrusted him and had long sought to turn anything he said or did against him. He also believed the media had the same attitude towards all his advisers. He detested the 1983 book *The Boss* by the journalists Joe Joyce and Peter Murtagh, which portrayed him as venal and thuggish, and refused to read it or have it mentioned in his company. He also viewed it as wildly inaccurate.[10]

Des O'Malley was expelled from Fianna Fáil on 26 February 1985 by a vote of seventy-three to nine of the party's national executive. The motion called for his expulsion 'for conduct unbecoming a member'. In the hour after his late-night expulsion he told RTÉ that he was going to give strong consideration to establishing a new party.[11] Haughey told the national executive that he had 'done everything possible' to accommodate the deputy from Limerick East, but O'Malley's decision not to support the party in its opposition to the government's family planning legislation the previous week was indeed conduct unbecoming a member of the party. After a stirring speech in the Dáil, basically in support of the government's bill, O'Malley then decided to abstain on the curious grounds that he hoped his speech would prevent a parting of the ways with Fianna Fáil, or out of deference to some of his colleagues.[12] He was not quite sure himself. O'Malley had never accepted Haughey's position as leader of Fianna Fáil and felt trapped within the party. His expulsion produced a storm of correspondence to Haughey and to Fianna Fáil. Most of it was supportive, making the point that O'Malley's behaviour had been disruptive to the party for years, but Haughey had little interest in those voices who saw it as the ideal opportunity to bring Neil Blaney back into the fold. There were also many who took a different view. Some complained that O'Malley's behaviour could in no way be compared to Seán Doherty's, yet Doherty was brought back to the fold while O'Malley was quickly ushered out. A telling commentary on O'Malley's exit came from one correspondent who complained that in the eyes of the voters Haughey had taken the guise of a latter-day Caesar and that O'Malley's expulsion had left the 'ranks of the Fianna Fáil front bench a veritable intellectual desert'.[13] O'Malley might have had his own Caesar-like pretensions, but no one in Fianna Fáil or the wider political arena was in any doubt that his departure from the party had left it significantly poorer intellectually.

Fianna Fáil policy on Northern Ireland was now fully controlled by Haughey. It was from this position of strength that Haughey would come to make one of the most serious mistakes of his career, and one that weakened him in the long run. That mistake was overplaying his and Fianna Fáil's opposition to the Anglo-Irish Agreement signed by Garret FitzGerald and Margaret Thatcher in November 1985. Haughey's instinctive, visceral opposition brought with it charges of national treachery and claims that he was attempting to sabotage the painstaking efforts of the coalition government to bring peace to Northern Ireland. He paid little heed to such viewpoints. His opposition, however, was also the catalyst for the formation of the Progressive Democrats, and that was to haunt him until his retirement.

THE ANGLO-IRISH AGREEMENT

The Anglo-Irish Agreement established an inter-governmental conference comprising officials from both the British and Irish governments. While it had no decision-making powers, the fact that it had a permanent secretariat and was based in Maryfield, close to Belfast, underscored the fact that the Irish government now had a legitimate concern in the affairs of Northern Ireland. Another innovative feature was that the Irish government could propose various policy initiatives, although the final decision on any such policies rested with the British. The fact that the agreement was to be lodged at the United Nations gave it an international focus that previous initiatives had lacked. While there was outrage in unionist communities at what they saw, in Ó Beacháin's words, as 'creeping Dublin annexation of the North', and in Sinn Féin, which claimed that the Irish government, and the SDLP, had made the lives of northern nationalists much worse by effectively copperfastening partition, the reaction in the Republic of Ireland and internationally was overwhelmingly positive.[14] At its heart the agreement was a very serious attempt made by the Irish government to represent Irish nationalist concerns, and that is how it was sold.[15]

The main exception to the broad welcome for the agreement in constitutional nationalist circles came from Fianna Fáil. When it was signed, Haughey immediately declared that Fianna Fáil was opposed to the agreement. This was haste on an unprecedented scale. On the Friday the Anglo-Irish Agreement was signed the Fianna Fáil front-bench watched the ceremony together in Haughey's room in Leinster House and on his recommendation made a quick collective decision to oppose it.[16] After O'Malley's expulsion from the parliamentary party it was clear that Haughey's opinion was the one that would decide party policy on Northern Ireland. As Máire Geoghegan-Quinn pointed out, 'There was no discussion in the parliamentary party about the Anglo-Irish Agreement. Haughey did Northern Ireland himself and gave no updates about it until the very end.'[17]

Haughey was very much against the agreement being lodged at the UN. Just four days after it was signed he told the Dáil that this would 'elevate this very insubstantial document into something of major importance and significance. It would help the British government to create the impression that the problem of Northern Ireland has been finally solved, that everybody now recognises Northern Ireland as an integral part of the United Kingdom, that British sovereignty is not disputed and that the community of nations, of which Ireland for so long [has been] a devoted and dedicated member, now accepts and endorses the position of Northern Ireland as part of the United Kingdom.'[18] Haughey complained that the agreement created an unacceptable and unconstitutional recognition of partition, which would lead any Irish government into the impossible position of accepting responsibility for actions over which it had no control. This would particularly be the case in the security field. He told the Dáil:

> We are deeply concerned that by signing this agreement the Irish
> government are acting in a manner repugnant to the Constitution
> of Ireland by fully accepting British sovereignty over a part of
> the national territory and by purporting to give legitimacy to a
> British administration in Ireland. By confirming what is called the

constitutional status of Northern Ireland as an integral part of the
United Kingdom in this agreement we will do serious damage in
the eyes of the world to Ireland's historic and legitimate claim to
the unity of her territory.[19]

As a basic restatement of Fianna Fáil policy of Northern Ireland this was
a traditional enough response. After all, the British government itself
claimed that the union had been strengthened by the agreement.

It was at this stage that Haughey miscalculated. In attempting to
internationalise his opposition to the agreement, he sent Fianna Fáil's
spokesman on foreign affairs, Brian Lenihan, to the United States to drum
up support for the party's position and in effect denounce the agreement.
This was a new departure in the politics of opposition. It was one thing to
oppose policy domestically; it was quite another thing to do it on a foreign stage, particularly when the agreement would be an internationally
binding one. Once he arrived in the United States, Lenihan made no real
effort at articulating the Fianna Fáil position. He had advised Haughey
not to oppose the agreement in the first place.[20] Lenihan, a very well-read
and erudite man with a keen political brain, quickly decided that there
was no mileage in advocating his leader's and his party's official position.
According to his son Conor, Lenihan spent the week drinking with his
old friend Ted Kennedy and catching up with his Irish-American coterie.
They already had their minds made up about the agreement, having been
briefed on it by the SDLP leader, John Hume.[21]

Haughey's reaction to the Anglo-Irish Agreement had three elements.
One was certainly the classic adversarial approach so common in Irish
politics since the foundation of the state. As Rory O'Hanlon pointed out,
many in Fianna Fáil, including himself, would have supported Haughey
at the time simply because that is what oppositions did. When Haughey,
back in power after the 1987 election, decided to work with the agreement, his TDs again followed his lead.[22] The second factor was the fact
that Garret FitzGerald had negotiated it and he was certainly annoyed
by that. Haughey essentially viewed FitzGerald as an amateur on the
international stage who was not able to stand up to Thatcher and had

been humiliated by her 'Out, Out, Out' response to the New Ireland Forum's three proposed solutions. Haughey's view was that any agreement signed by FitzGerald with Thatcher was not going to work. The final element was certainly intellectual. The fact that the agreement was institutionalised and recognised by the UN as an international agreement convinced Haughey that it had to be opposed because it constituted a legal recognition of Northern Ireland and was thus in contravention of the Irish Constitution.

This was the position Haughey outlined in the Dáil debate on the agreement four days after it had been signed. In that debate the government simply proposed a motion that Dáil Éireann approve the terms of the Anglo-Irish Agreement. Haughey tabled a detailed amendment to the motion requesting that the government 'call upon the British government to join in convening, under the auspices of both governments, a constitutional conference representative of all traditions in Ireland to formulate new constitutional arrangements which would lead to uniting all the people of Ireland in peace and harmony.'[23] This was rejected by Garret FitzGerald, using the words of Éamon de Valera in a debate in 1949; Fianna Fáil's first leader had maintained that if just one member of such a conference said, 'No, I will not accept that', the end of the conference would obviously be worse than the beginning. Given the hostility of unionists of all hues to the agreement it was clear that they would not sign up to any such constitutional conference. As they had not joined the New Ireland Forum, they were certainly not going to join any immediate alternative. Haughey's motion was inevitably defeated, but he would return to the constitutional argument in the 1987 general election campaign. Haughey ended his Dáil speech with an impassioned assertion that as a responsible political party, Fianna Fáil, regardless of whether it cost the party votes or popularity, was not 'prepared to surrender by desertion the constitutional nationalist position. Any other stance would be to turn away from the deepest aspirations of the Irish people and represent a massive psychological blow to their self-confidence and their self-esteem.'[24] This was a nod to the widespread acclaim with which the agreement had been greeted by the public. An MRBI poll showed that over 59 per cent of people in the Republic of Ireland had voiced approval for it just two days after it had been signed, while 56 per cent disagreed with Haughey's stance.[25]

Haughey's position had brought him into serious conflict with the SDLP. It was a particularly sensitive issue given that the two parties had closely co-operated during the New Ireland Forum. Haughey originally thought he had more support from the SDLP than he actually had.[26] Some SDLP members were unhappy with aspects of the agreement but were determined to make it work because it addressed serious nationalist concerns and was both a concrete and coherent sign of constitutional progress through exclusively political means. The fact that Sinn Féin was against it crystallised the choice on offer for nationalists in Northern Ireland. In that context, Haughey's opposition was deeply felt by the SDLP leadership. In his Dáil speech on the agreement, Gerry Collins stated that Fianna Fáil's political objection to it was that 'Irish sovereignty over the whole island is not merely shelved but effectively abandoned. Partition has thus been copperfastened and the credibility of constitutional nationalists severely undermined.'[27] The reference to the credibility of constitutional nationalists clearly stung the SDLP and its supporters. Haughey's claim that the agreement was a rejection of constitutional nationalism was quickly repudiated by John Hume, who said that perhaps the difference between his vision and Haughey's was that he had 'grown up in the North, represented the North, and judged things from a Northern standpoint'.[28] That standpoint had now seen the British recognise that there was a valid nationalist position, when only ten years previously the British government had told Jack Lynch that the North was none of his business. Hume's reply was certain to annoy Haughey, who had always played up his own Northern background and claimed to understand unionists as he had 'lived among them as a boy'.[29]

Hume's deputy leader, Seamus Mallon, whom Haughey had appointed to the Seanad in 1982, was also dismayed by Fianna Fáil's position on the agreement. Mallon had defended Haughey's advocacy of the unitary state position in his response to the New Ireland Forum as being a perfectly legitimate position. He also disagreed strongly with

Garret FitzGerald over how a forum consisting of constitutional nationalist parties could come to a series of conclusions that did not include
Irish unity. Mallon also felt that at times in the mid-1980s the SDLP itself
was in danger of losing its core belief in unity. Given that Mallon was
widely recognised as being on the greener or more republican wing of
the SDLP, and had long been committed to the idea of Irish unity, his
support for the Anglo-Irish Agreement was crucial. It dealt a severe blow
to Fianna Fáil's position that the agreement somehow copperfastened
partition. Mallon was critical of Haughey's instant rejection of the agreement, making the point in his memoir that any agreement, including
both Sunningdale and the Good Friday Agreements, that fell short of
unity could be seen as copperfastening partition. Mallon's support for
the agreement caused such a schism with Haughey that they had no
more contact ever again.[30] He did, however, send a handwritten note
to Haughey on the occasion of Haughey's retirement telling him that
he had been proud to work with him to try to bring peace and unity to
Ireland: 'I simply cannot conceive of a situation where you are not there
helping us and guiding us in our search for a solution in N.I. Please
understand that the nationalist people here are forever grateful for your
support and leadership. You were the rock of strength we all focused on
through the dark days. Your going has left both a personal and political
void for all of us.'[31]

Mallon's anger about Haughey's stance on the Anglo-Irish Agreement
was shared by other influential constitutional nationalists in Northern
Ireland. One was Edward Daly, the Bishop of Derry, who had praised
Haughey's efforts to try to resolve the hunger strikes. Two days after the
agreement was signed Daly wrote a long letter to Haughey stating that
it grieved him deeply that Haughey had expressed opposition to it. Daly
told Haughey that Éamon de Valera had been his father's political hero,
and his own, and that his family was steeped in Fianna Fáil. He wrote
of Haughey's family in Swatragh, how much he admired him, and how
grateful he was to Haughey for 'your own personal kindness to me in
the past'. Daly then told Haughey that he considered the agreement had
the potential to be a great step forward for the nationalist community in

the North; that it did not copperfasten partition in any form, but rather was a positive step forward for Irish unity in the long term. He added that there was a widespread feeling of positivity towards the agreement from people he knew in the North, but that there was an equal feeling of 'great annoyance and distress at your opposition to it … a feeling here this weekend that you are not acting in our best long term interests'. Daly pleaded with Haughey to reconsider his assessment of the agreement, adding that Haughey's support for it would be of vital importance. He pointed to the reaction of Ian Paisley as proof of the agreement's worth: 'I think they see this agreement in the same light I see it. Their race is run. Their total control and their absolute hold on power and privilege is beginning to slip away.' Daly finished by telling Haughey that he was writing as a friend and did not want Haughey to interpret the letter in any way 'as a crosier-bashing exercise. I see my crosier more as a weapon of defence than attack! It is a confidential letter. I do not wish it to become any kind of obstacle to our continued friendship … I care very deeply about the community here as you do.'[32] It was in that context that Daly asked Haughey to reconsider his approach to the agreement. Haughey did not.

Daly's letter was just one of thousands that poured into Fianna Fáil headquarters and to Abbeville. While most praised Haughey's position and predicted that he would be vindicated, some told him that although they were hardcore Fianna Fáil members his attitude was simply wrong. One cumann in Cork was outraged: 'Your immediate condemnation of the agreement was embarrassing for our party … it was a sad day for us to be on the same side as Ian Paisley and against people like John Hume.'[33] There were letters asking that Fianna Fáil consider the possibility of taking a case against the agreement to the courts to test its constitutionality. To one cumann in Waterford, Haughey replied that Fianna Fáil believed 'our efforts should be made in the political arena and that pursuing political objectives through the courts is neither appropriate nor satisfactory.'[34] He also made the point that Fianna Fáil felt that if the ministerial conference could help alleviate the situation of the nationalist community in Northern Ireland, it should not inhibit or oppose its efforts in that connection; and challenging the agreement in the courts could have that effect. At this stage Haughey was in the very early and tentative stage of dialogue with the Redemptorist priest Fr Alec Reid about the possibility of dialogue with Sinn Féin, and an IRA ceasefire.

RUPTURE AND DIVISION

Despite Haughey's original vociferous condemnation of the Anglo-Irish Agreement being sent to the UN, he was able to use the fact that it was an internationally binding agreement to his advantage when he became Taoiseach in March 1987. For those on the republican wing of the party he kept to the idea that the best approach to Northern Ireland was to work with the agreement until Fianna Fáil could negotiate something better. It was the ultimate in pragmatic politics. It had, however, significant consequences when the party's opposition to the agreement resulted in yet more of its members deciding that Fianna Fáil was not the party for them. Five weeks after the Anglo-Irish Agreement was signed, the Progressive Democrats was formed.[35] Mary Harney, who had been expelled from Fianna Fáil for voting for the agreement, was, with O'Malley, one of its founding members. There was no mass exodus from Fianna Fáil but it suffered a severe jolt a month later when, in a surprise move, Bobby Molloy, the long-serving TD for Galway West, and frontbench spokesman on the environment, resigned and joined O'Malley's new party. On Thursday 23 January 1986 the Fianna Fáil frontbench was meeting in Leinster House. Molloy was absent. Just the previous weekend he had received an award from his constituency for twenty-one years' service in the Dáil, having been first elected in 1965, and he had received a rousing reception from the Fianna Fáil faithful.[36] There was no indication that he was on the verge of resigning. He had been in Cork a week earlier to try to persuade the Cork South Central TD Pearse Wyse not to leave the party. Frank Wall interrupted the frontbench meeting and passed a note to Haughey. It was a sixteen-word handwritten resignation letter from Molloy. Haughey looked at the letter and then told the meeting: 'I believe we won't have Mr Molloy for company today.'[37] He then had

Wall read out the letter. The meeting was aghast. Bertie Ahern, who had previously shared an office with Molloy and had had a drink with him the previous night, had no inkling he was thinking of leaving the party.[38] Haughey did have some indication Molloy might defect to the Progressive Democrats. That morning he rang Carr Communications looking for Tom Savage for advice on how to handle a lunchtime event at which he expected that he might be doorstepped about the possibility of Molloy leaving Fianna Fáil. As it turned out, Haughey spoke to Terry Prone, who gave her usual blunt advice.[39]

Molloy was seen as hardcore Fianna Fáil. While he was known as a staunch opponent of Haughey, nobody in the party could quite believe that he had left it. This was the defection that really rocked Fianna Fáil, and Haughey. Mary Harney had only been a TD since 1981. Pearse Wyse had previously been a minister for state under Jack Lynch but was not a significant figure in the party. Molloy's resignation was of a different calibre altogether, and set off rumours that a series of further defections was imminent, with names like Charlie McCreevy and David Andrews mentioned most often. None transpired, but it was a tense time for Haughey and the party.

Fianna Fáil had been riven with factions since the arms crisis. In some form the divisions all revolved around Haughey. Yet, in the year between February 1986 and January 1987, it united behind him. After three years in opposition, the prize of government after the next general election loomed. Notwithstanding the wide public support for the Anglo-Irish Agreement, the Fine Gael–Labour coalition government had never been a harmonious one. It was divided over the abortion referendum of September 1983, and hopelessly split on the worsening economic situation.

Within two months of its foundation an *Irish Times*/MRBI poll had the Progressive Democrats at 25 per cent, two points ahead of Fine Gael. Fianna Fáil was at 42 per cent. Haughey knew that he was unlikely to get an overall majority on that figure. Just a few months earlier Fianna Fáil was polling at over 50 per cent. Polls could, of course, be wrong. On the same day the *Irish Times* revealed its startling opinion poll numbers for the Progressive Democrats, it had another poll showing support for removing the restrictions on divorce from the Constitution at 52 per cent.

Defending the Constitution had been at the heart of Fianna Fáil since its introduction in a plebiscite in 1937. As Haughey pointed out in October 1986: 'Fianna Fáil today is more than ever left alone as the guardian of the republican tradition and the Constitution of this state, in which that transition is enshrined. We are a constitutional party in the fullest sense in that we support totally and unequivocally the Constitution of our country. Fianna Fáil see that Constitution as giving substance and meaning to Irish national life and to our freedom and independence.'[40] The Constitution was the weapon in the vicious morality wars that stoked divisions all across the country between 1983 and 1986.

The wording of the 1983 abortion referendum was Fianna Fáil's, though there had been reservations in the government, particularly from Attorney General Peter Sutherland, who was opposed to the final text used for the vote.[41] When the proposed wordings from both parties were issued, Fianna Fáil viewed the Fine Gael wording as negative and minimalist and one that would still allow the Oireachtas to legislate for abortion. It argued that the Fine Gael wording did not recognise the right to life of the unborn and in that context was in no sense a pro-life amendment. For Fianna Fáil, the right to life of the unborn had to be explicitly and positively stated; otherwise the 1861 Act that prohibited abortion could be overturned by the European Human Rights Convention.[42] Fine Gael's own wording was rejected by enough of its own TDs (and by PLAC) to ensure that the Fianna Fáil wording was the one presented to the electorate in September 1983. Haughey told one of his correspondents that Fianna Fáil was: 'of the opinion that the wording contained in the present bill is satisfactory and that it should be put before the people by way of referendum at the earliest possible opportunity'.[43]

While the government did not campaign on the referendum at all, Fianna Fáil made some efforts, but these were localised and not driven by head office. Haughey's inaction on the matter was criticised by many within his own party. One member noted that the officers of various cumainn in his area were 'amazed, confused and dismayed by your silence'.[44] Many supporters of the amendment encouraged him to speak out more loudly in its favour. He told one correspondent in the week before the vote that he had been 'endeavouring to ensure that the national consensus which exists on the issue of abortion will be reflected in a vote in favour of the amendment.[45] To that end, he did not want to make it a party-political issue. He was concerned, however, when a number of Fianna Fáil supporters who opposed the amendment wrote to him complaining that they had received letters, signed by Senator Des Hanafin, seeking donations for PLAC. The only way they could have received such solicitations from PLAC was through the Fianna Fáil mailing list. One complained that the only conclusion he could draw was that 'Mr. Hanafin was kicked out the front door, and came in through the back door.[46] This was a reference to the fact that when he became leader Haughey had dismissed Hanafin from his position as the party's chief fundraiser. Haughey told one of the complainants that neither Hanafin nor anyone else had any authority whatsoever to approach Fianna Fáil supporters or contributors in this way.[47] The referendum was comfortably carried by a margin of two to one, but the low turnout of just under 54 per cent reflected the fact that the issue was not as important as some thought. It did, however, have substantial support from the vast majority of Fianna Fáil supporters. Those supporters were again on show when it came to the referendum on divorce in the summer of 1986.

Both the Labour Party and the liberal wing of Fine Gael had long been in support of removing the constitutional prohibition on divorce. The Divorce Action Group, formed in 1980, proved very effective in attracting support from the Labour Party and the liberal wing of Fine Gael, but found no appetite for its cause in Fianna Fáil. The introduction of divorce was one of the core tenets of Garret FitzGerald's constitutional crusade and he was personally willing to put his own intellectual heft behind a referendum to achieve this aim. In July 1983, the government established an all-party joint committee on marital breakdown with a view to obtaining cross-party consensus on a family law agenda, including divorce. This committee received over seven hundred written and twenty-four oral submissions including the views of AIM, the

Divorce Action Group, the Free Legal Aid Centres, the Catholic Marriage Advisory Council and the Irish Council for Civil Liberties.[48]

When the committee finally reported in 1985 it stopped short of recommending the removal of the ban on divorce because the then opposition Fianna Fáil members opposed such a move. However, the government, buoyed by a series of opinion polls, decided that the time was right to tackle the issue of divorce. Yet after the decision to hold a referendum was taken, FitzGerald procrastinated for months while he attempted to convince the churches, particularly the Catholic Church, that the time was right to introduce a modest measure of reform. The delaying of the referendum, however, also delayed the preparation of the necessary background papers to enable the government to deal with any issues that might arise in the course of a referendum campaign. The result was that when the referendum was called, with little advance public or political discussion, the government, as one of its senior advisers later admitted, was woefully unprepared.[49] So desperate was FitzGerald to bring all groups together after the division of the abortion referendum that his vacillation made him appear weak. His cherished aim of a civilised debate and an overwhelming Yes vote dissipated and after the referendum was over his beloved constitutional crusade was in ruins. The referendum, held on 26 June 1986, was rejected, with over 63 per cent voting No on a turnout of just over 60 per cent. Fianna Fáil did not officially campaign or take a position on the referendum, but many of its parliamentary party members and ordinary members, advocated for a No vote. As Collins and Meehan point out, the Fianna Fáil party organisation was the backbone of the No campaign in many constituencies.[50]

The opposition of the Catholic Church had proved crucial. FitzGerald at the outset of the campaign had assumed that given the Catholic Church's stated position that it would not seek to impose its theological views on the civil law of the state, then the only relevant consideration would be whether the balance of social good would or would not be served by a restricted form of divorce. When the Catholic hierarchy then came out and called on the people to vote no he seemed more saddened than anything else.[51] Furthermore, in a country where ownership of property means so much, doubts raised in the public mind by those on the No side as to the equitable distribution of property proved hugely influential in returning a No vote.

Prior to the referendum Haughey told one of his correspondents that 'our party came to the conclusion that this was an issue which should be left to the people to decide in a calm, objective non-political atmosphere.'[52] In a society still bruised from the abortion referendum, that was never likely to be the case. Both FitzGerald and Haughey were mistaken in their view that any referendum on a matter of morality could take place in such an atmosphere. Haughey had supported the recommendations of the Oireachtas All-Party Committee on Marital Breakdown and its measures to help alleviate the suffering and hardship caused by marital breakdown. Many of his constituents were in such a position; and many of them wrote to tell him their woes. Yet, in a statement made in the closing stages of the campaign, Haughey said that he came to the issue of divorce from the perspective of the family, and expressed his 'unshakeable belief in the importance of having the family as the basic unit of our society'.[53] He added that divorce itself would create many problems of its own. This left no one in any doubt as to where he stood on the referendum. Over a decade later, the revelation of his affair with Terry Keane led to allegations of hypocrisy. His critics said that Haughey was quite happy to espouse family values while condemning thousands of others to misery in loveless marriages.[54] This is obviously true on one level, but on the other hand it is also clear that Haughey never intended to leave his own wife. He certainly had no interest in getting divorced and he did believe that the family unit was best organisational structure for society. He was also reflecting the widespread anti-divorce view across Fianna Fáil. In that context he was never going to advocate a Yes vote. At the 1986 Fianna Fáil Ard Fheis he told the audience: 'the family as the basic unit of our society is under severe pressure today from many directions ... in the last three years a new right-wing philosophy has taken hold in Irish political life.'[55] This was in essence characterising divorce as an attack on the family while also giving it a political angle. And there was base politics at play during the referendum. A No vote would clearly damage both coalition parties, but particularly Fine Gael. Haughey was well aware of the internal tensions on the economy within the coalition. He was not going to throw them any sort of lifeline when an election could come within a matter of months.

A number of months after the referendum, Haughey received a letter from the Dublin Council of Churches, a fellowship of parishes and congregations of all churches in Dublin outside the Catholic Church. In it the council told him they would find 'abhorrent and repugnant' a suggestion which they associated with him; that of extending the existing law of civil nullity into line with the nullity practices of the Catholic Church.[56] Haughey replied that he had no idea why the council should think that such an idea was particularly associated with him, and that he found it 'abhorrent and repugnant' that anyone would make such a suggestion about him. He added that he was 'unfortunately, accustomed to offensive accusations of this kind from politicians, journalists and others but it is a new kind of experience for me to find this sort of thing emanating from a Council of Churches.'[57] The Haughey instinct of defending himself from what he saw as unwarranted attacks was on full display. At this stage Haughey was on the verge of contesting his fourth general election as leader of Fianna Fáil. The coalition government was about to implode in recriminations. His poll numbers were above 50 per cent and an overall majority was again in sight. Opposition had been difficult for him, but he could sense that it was at an end.

The period between December 1982 and January 1987 saw Haughey overcome serious threats to his position as leader of Fianna Fáil, the fracturing of the party, and a schism with the SDLP over Northern Ireland, resulting in Fianna Fáil standing alone among the constitutional nationalist parties in opposition to the Anglo-Irish Agreement. It also saw two traumatic referendums which deepened and entrenched social division across the state. The country went through a prolonged recession which saw mass emigration and unemployment return to levels not experienced since the 1950s when Haughey first entered Dáil Éireann.

LIFE RAFT

It was also a strange personal time for Haughey. In the space of a couple of days in late September 1985 Haughey survived two accidents, one in the air and one at sea, that could have killed him. During the last week of September, Haughey was a passenger in a twin-engine Cessna small aircraft which flew him from Dublin to Farranfore Airport in Kerry a few days before he was due to sail his boat, the *Taurima*, from Kerry back to Dublin. As the plane was coming in to land, the undercarriage gave way, it burst a tyre, and slid along the runway. Haughey was shaken but completely unscathed. He told Maureen that he had had a lucky escape.[58]

The events of a few nights later were far more life-threatening. At 5.30 p.m. on Saturday 28 September, Haughey was collected at Dunquin harbour by his son Conor and three others; Brian Stafford, the boat's skipper, Paul Devaney and Vivian Nangle, who had sailed the boat from Dingle. Their final destination was Dublin. When they left Dunquin they were waved off by Graham Turley and Veronica Guerin, who were on their honeymoon at the time, and had been friends of the Haugheys since childhood. Veronica Guerin also worked in Fianna Fáil. The *Taurima* was a 52-foot ketch rigged yacht that Haughey had bought in 1977. At the beginning of the voyage, Stafford had laid a course to clear Mizen Head before taking a path between Fastnet Rock and Cape Clear to Crosshaven. Yet, as night came, so did a dense mist. The *Taurima* was soon depending entirely on radar, and that radar proved faulty. At 1.15 the boat hit the rocks underneath the Mizen Head lighthouse at the southwestern tip of the country. The *Taurima* was a mile off course. Haughey, who was asleep, heard a 'shuddering crunch', immediately jumped up, put on some clothes, including a sailing jacket that had been a gift from the Fianna Fáil staff at Leinster House, and went to see what had happened. He knew the boat was in trouble. Conor Haughey quickly sent out a distress call on the ship's VHF radio. Brian Stafford, on hearing the crash, rushed to the engine room and saw water boiling up from the bilges. Paul Devaney and Vivian Nagle confirmed that the boat was taking on water. Stafford gave the order to abandon ship.

Conor Haughey's mayday signal was clear and to the point. There were five people aboard and they were preparing to board the life raft. The keepers in the lighthouse signal station, Richard Cummins and Richard Foran, immediately called both Baltimore and Valentia lifeboats, and then went to the sailors' aid, shining lights on them and keeping them up to date with the progress of their rescuers. The preparedness of the *Taurima*'s crew was crucial. They had a rubber dinghy, which had been inflated and lashed to the deck, as well as a life raft. They also had a working radio. Within fifteen minutes the *Taurima* had sunk. Conor Haughey and Brian Stafford took the dinghy, while the other three men went into the canopied life raft, which was linked to the dinghy by a towrope. Prior to the voyage, Senator Tom Fitzgerald from Dingle was doing some building work on Inishvickillane. Before the party left Dingle, Fitzgerald had asked if he could borrow the dinghy to land materials on the island. The initial reaction of the boating party was to give it to him, but Brian Stafford spoke up: 'The dinghy is part of the boat's equipment and must stay on the boat.'[59] Charles Haughey agreed. The dinghy stayed on board. Twelve hours later the dinghy was the only thing that prevented the life raft being smashed on to the rocks. Conor Haughey then rowed the boats around the edge of the Mizen and into a pocket underneath the cliffs.

At this stage, the principal lighthouse keeper, Richard Foran, was lowered down the side of the lighthouse to wait for the Baltimore lifeboat and guide it to the men in the boats directly beneath him. While he waited, Foran became fearful that the dinghy would strike the jagged rocks and sweep the men to their deaths. There was also a strong smell of diesel – the *Taurima*'s fuel was bubbling up from her ruptured tanks. Stafford moved into the life raft and over the next three tense hours Conor Haughey managed to keep the dinghy off the rocks until the Baltimore lifeboat, piloted by coxswain Christy Collins, arrived and plucked the men to safety just after 4 a.m. While it was clear that the Baltimore lifeboat was going to get to the stricken party first, Richard Foran, who was from Valentia, insisted that the Valentia boat continue on its journey as well as he knew they had a RIB dinghy on board which he thought might be needed to get into the narrow cove where the sailing party were sheltering. When the Baltimore lifeboat rescued the men, they were given blankets and tea and brought to Baltimore, where they were put up in Bushe's public house. Haughey was a regular visitor to Baltimore and frequented Youen Jacob's restaurant every summer during his visits to Inishvickillane. The day after the accident Collins told reporters that the men were in 'a very bad spot and in real danger. I would say that they are lucky to be alive.'[60] Four years later, Richard Cummins wrote to Haughey seeking a character reference. He was being made redundant from the lighthouse service due to automation and was going to emigrate to America. Haughey replied that he was sorry to hear that Cummins was emigrating and sent him a reference saying how Cummins had served with distinction, and was of excellent character, reliable and trustworthy.[61]

In the weeks following the sinking of the *Taurima* Haughey received numerous sympathetic letters. A postcard addressed from New York from the Dáil's other sailor, Fine Gael's Hugh Coveney, said, 'I know how it feels!' Haughey replied that it was a bit tense for a while but fortunately everything worked out but that he was 'very saddened at the loss of our grand old boat'.[62] He had a similar response for the Israeli ambassador, Yehuda Avner, who had sympathised with him; the whole event was all a bit traumatic, he said, but he was heartbroken to have lost his family boat.[63] He was, however, alive, and he could continue with an intriguing project with the British television company Channel Four.

Charles Haughey's Ireland, a one-hour documentary narrated by Haughey, was aired on Channel 4 on the evening of Sunday 23 March 1986. It was watched by 969,000 people in Britain in a slot that usually received an audience of 700,000 viewers. Channel 4 was delighted with its reception and reckoned that including Irish viewers it had been seen by at least 1.5 million people.[64] It was later shown by RTÉ on 11 May of that year. The programme begins with Haughey sailing the *Taurima* and speaking of Ireland's historic traditions of resisting invaders since the dawn of history and sending its people to enact change all across the world. He paints Ireland as a nation that coupled strong historical traditions with a desire for change and progress. Haughey then speaks of the sinking of the *Taurima*, blaming it on a navigational error, and intones that through a long and troubled history the Irish had shown ourselves to be a race of survivors. Over the next fifty minutes Haughey took his viewers on a quixotic journey from Newgrange to Croke Park; from Dáil Éireann to the National Microelectronics Centre in UCC; from Inishvickillane to Swatragh in a tour of Ireland where he expounded on his views of sport, history, culture, economic development and the country's future. He finished by excoriating the very idea of the border, saying that its very existence was preposterous to him, asserted that the term Londonderry meant nothing at all, and with visible annoyance noted that every time he came to the border he experienced deep feelings of anger and resentment. The border, in his view, was an artificial line of economic, social and geographic nonsense and that as long as it remained, relations between Britain and Ireland would regrettably never be as close as they should be. He ended on an overtly nationalist note: 'When I talk about my Ireland I'm talking about something that is not yet a complete reality, it is a dream that has not yet been fulfilled.'[65]

The programme was made over the summer of 1985. The script was written by Anthony Cronin, who was assisted by the executive producer, John Kelleher. It was directed and produced for Channel 4 by Michele Kurland, who had spent over a year trying to persuade Haughey to front a documentary. After discussions with Cronin and P.J. Mara, Haughey eventually agreed to do it but refused to take a fee from Channel 4. This was unheard of for the television station, but eventually Haughey agreed to sign a contract on condition that his fee go to charity. Kurland described hearing about Haughey's difficult and explosive moods but found him relatively easy to work with. She was surprised at his patience and good humour, particularly when her cameraman dropped his camera into the sea. After seven months of persuasion, Kurland eventually convinced Haughey to let her film on Inishvickillane. Haughey had jealously guarded his privacy on the island in the decade since he had bought it, but Kurland told him that a documentary called *Charles Haughey's Ireland* that did not feature the island would simply not work. He only wanted to refer to it, but after much cajoling he relented and let her film him and his family there. Kurland recalled that at one stage Haughey's patience eventually snapped and he started to tell everyone involved with the project, including herself, that they were fired. She retorted that as she worked for Channel 4 he could not fire her or any of her crew. After calming down Haughey resorted to calling her 'the Holy Terror' for the rest of the filming. Kurland was amazed at what she described as Haughey's ceaseless ability to have a real rapport in rural Ireland and to know minute details of the lives of people they met on their travels.[66]

Charles Haughey's Ireland is a revealing insight into Haughey's persona. He saw politics as a way of changing things – that was why he went into politics. He pointed to some successes in redressing certain social imbalances. He commented on his affection for Dáil Éireann, although his comment in the draft script that he could be found in the chamber more often than most deputies was cut from the final programme. Haughey's remarkable ability to connect with people that Kurland found so amazing on her trip around the country with him was also alluded to. Haughey said that through liking people he had become a good judge of character. He asserted that while some of his critics and even friends remarked that he was too sentimental and even romantic in his loyalties to people, 'As yet, the iron hasn't entered into my soul.' Perhaps the two most important aspects of Haughey's character that did not make it into the final cut, but were in a draft script, were his comments on sports and politics. In the section on horse racing he noted that horse racing attracted him 'because it's competitive, a matter of win or lose. And I'm a competitor. I like win or lose activities.' In his comments on politics, Haughey said the following:

> I'm not the cloistered academic type who shrinks from human contact and thinks there's something demeaning about looking for the vote. Nor am I the Coriolanus type, too proud to go out and get it. I love all that side of things and when people vote for me I feel really good. In the dark days after the arms trial, when the future was uncertain, it was a wonderful deep-down feeling for me

that the people of my own constituency (here) were unwavering in their support, that I got the biggest individual first preference vote that anybody got in any constituency in Ireland. And of course I love to win.[67]

Haughey's penchant for quoting Shakespeare was instructive. In the play *Coriolanus*, the eponymous hero cannot hide his contempt for the plebeians of Rome when he seeks its highest office of consulship and is ultimately banished from the city. By January 1987, when Garret FitzGerald's coalition government fell, Haughey was ready one more time to go to the Irish people to again seek the highest elected office. Having been banished to opposition for four years he was desperate to win. It had been a long four years for him. He was tired of opposition.

CHAPTER 20

NATIONAL RECOVERY

1987: THE APPALLING STATE OF THE PUBLIC FINANCES

The 1987 election campaign revolved around the grim state of the Irish economy. The coalition partners, which had never really united during the administration, finally split when the four Labour ministers decided they could not support the upcoming budget being prepared by Fine Gael's Minister for Finance, John Bruton. The coalition had been all but sundered the previous year when the Minister for Health, Barry Desmond, refused to move in a proposed reshuffle by Garret FitzGerald, fatally undermining the Taoiseach's authority. The government limped towards an inevitable end as emigration and unemployment inexorably increased. Polling day was set for 17 February, with FitzGerald deciding that a longer campaign of four weeks would give him more time to explain his party's economic position and fend off attacks from Fianna Fáil and the Progressive Democrats. Towards the end of the campaign FitzGerald proposed the idea of a national economic forum along the lines of the New Ireland Forum to deal with the country's economic problems. This was completely unrealisable; there were genuine differences between all the parties about how best to tackle the worsening situation. The previous four years had seen those differences on full show in the coalition. The Progressive Democrats wanted a weakening of the state and vast reductions in public spending. Fianna Fáil in opposition had railed against what it saw as the monetarism of Fine Gael. In Haughey's mind, the Progressive Democrats were offering a similar prognosis. He had a very different approach. The idea of a long campaign also had the faint air of a desperate bid by FitzGerald to hold on to some form of power in post-election Ireland. Fianna Fáil had never been keen on the idea of national governments to deal with economic problems. Having been in the purgatory of opposition for four long years, Haughey was in no mood to share office, or even ideas, on how to overcome the state's continuing economic difficulties, especially when his solution was very different from Fine Gael's. In particular, he saw the idea of a national government as an affront to the democracy of the ballot box.

Once FitzGerald's national economic forum idea went nowhere, he resolved to try to keep Haughey out of power. In the last week of the campaign he encouraged all Fine Gael voters to give their second preferences to the Progressive Democrats. This was certainly an audacious move to stay in power and was in effect a repudiation of the government he had led for four years. The Progressive Democrats were not convinced. Des O'Malley refused to advise his supporters on who to give their second preferences to beyond an anodyne statement that they should vote for candidates whose principles and policies were closest to their own. The evangelical stance of the Progressive Democrats as mould-breakers would have been immediately plunged into jeopardy if they had aligned themselves too closely to Fine Gael. Also, despite relatively good poll numbers, nobody could say for sure how well the Progressive Democrats would do when the voters entered the ballot box. The last MRBI poll of the campaign found that 34 per cent of Fine Gael and Progressive Democrat voters would transfer to one another but that 21 per cent of Progressive Democrat voters would transfer to Fianna Fáil. There were plenty of would-be Progressive Democrat voters who were more comfortable with Fianna Fáil than they were with Fine Gael.[1]

Fine Gael and the Progressive Democrats offered the electorate deep cuts in public spending, reform of the tax structure, and a rolling back of the state. Labour advocated opposition to the cuts proposed by their former government partners but were basically in survival mode. Haughey, by contrast, proposed a new model of social partnership. Returning to the principles of *The Way Forward*, the Fianna Fáil manifesto specifically said that its national goals could best be achieved through a forum in which the social partners could negotiate the terms of a national plan based on agreed medium-term objectives. Since his June 1982 meeting with Helmut Schmidt, Haughey had never let go of the social partnership idea. Not everyone in his party was convinced. Ray MacSharry was particularly sceptical on the grounds that it would be all but impossible to get the trade union movement united in the first place. Given the difficulties the two groups had experienced with each other back in 1981, it would be equally difficult to get the unions and employers to agree on a model.[2] In opposition, Haughey sent his frontbench to Austria to examine its model of social partnership. As Bertie Ahern recalled, this was because Haughey believed it was why Austria, with its small open economy and consensus approach, had risen from the ashes of a world war to rank well above the OECD average on most indices.[3]

In late 1986, when Fianna Fáil was preparing for what it knew would be the upcoming election, Haughey brought his frontbench to Raglan Road to meet the ICTU. This was the first time any political party had gone into the bear pit of Congress. Two years earlier, in 1984, ICTU had issued a document called *Confronting the Jobs Crisis: Framework for a National Plan*. Haughey had been impressed with it. The meeting of the Fianna Fáil frontbench and ICTU's representatives, Peter Cassells, Bill Attley, John Carroll and Eddie Browne, was the vital step in finally persuading sceptics on both sides of the need for the unions to come onside with Haughey's idea of social partnership. *Confronting the Jobs Crisis* was basically ICTU sending a signal that they believed the provision of jobs was the absolute priority and that if a new government was prepared to engage in a positive way, the unions would be willing to seriously address the question of the public finances. Peter Cassells described it as 'a classic Haughey gesture. He came to Raglan Road to meet the Executive Council of Congress. Now that had never happened before and instead of meeting somewhere quietly he did a very public show of let's go and meet them and show them we mean business. And he did. He impressed on us that he was serious he could get the economy growing but he needed us and the employers with him.'[4]

On the political side, there was also scepticism on Fianna Fáil's frontbench, but Bertie Ahern had been keeping in regular touch with the unions and he believed that they would be receptive to a political initiative. He organised the frontbench meeting with ICTU and drafted the party's response endorsing it. It was Haughey who laid out the party's strategy at the meeting, but that the meeting took place at all was noteworthy. As Ahern recalled, 'It was a big decision and it took bravery for him to go down there. He believed if you're going to implement these things, you have to carry the trade unions with you and not tax marchers. Once we were finished that meeting he was very bullish about the election to come and getting back to government to make it work.'[5] The Department of Finance were unconvinced, as were the vast majority of professional economists and pundits, but Haughey had never paid much notice to them anyway. Traditional bureaucracy and economic orthodoxy did not believe that a government could get low pay increases for a sustained period, in lieu of tax cuts, that would allow it to cut public expenditure and grow the economy. Haughey and Ahern were convinced they could, and in turn persuaded MacSharry, who was earmarked to become Minister for Finance in a new Fianna Fáil administration in which he would insist on having control of budgetary strategy.

During the election campaign the media mostly ignored Haughey's social partnership idea, and concentrated on how Fianna Fáil would pay for its promise not to cut back on public spending, particularly in health, after it revealed the devastating slogan 'Health cuts hurt the old, the sick, and the handicapped.' Haughey's fitness for office once again became a major theme of the campaign with a mostly hostile media still disinclined to give him any sort of positive coverage. The *Irish Press* had never taken to Haughey, having long seen George Colley as the most appropriate successor to Jack Lynch. The *Irish Independent, Cork Examiner* and *Irish Times* were all reliably anti-Haughey. Yet during the campaign the editor of the *Irish Times*, Conor Brady, traditionally a Fine Gael supporter, went to Abbeville for a private working dinner with Haughey, accompanied by the newspaper's long-serving political columnist John Healy, who himself had long had Haughey's ear. Brady listened with an open mind to Haughey's economic strategy based on his social partnership concept. He left Abbeville impressed and began to editorialise favourably on it. Brady praised Haughey's partnership strategy as coherent and pointed to the international view that Ireland lacked a clear strategy for growth. This led to indignant outrage in the *Irish Times* staff room where Haughey, who was known to them in private as 'El Diablo', was viewed with outright hostility.[6] Brady did not advocate a vote for either Haughey or Fianna Fáil, as he clearly was not in any position to do so. Neither his staff nor his readers would countenance such a prospect. Yet, in the interregnum between counting the votes and the election of a Taoiseach in the Dáil, he asserted in an editorial on 2 March that a Fianna Fáil government dependent on the vote of Tony Gregory was an appalling prospect. He stated that since Haughey was the only party leader with any credible chance of forming a government the other parties should consider what a Fianna Fáil minority government propped up by Gregory would mean for the country.[7]

Another person impressed with Haughey's approach towards the 1987 election was the stockbroker Dermot Desmond. Desmond and P.J. Mara were friends and used to drink together in Scruffy Murphy's public house close to Lower Mount Street and Merrion Square. Coming up to the election Mara suggested that Desmond meet Haughey to discuss Fianna Fáil's economic policy. Haughey was keen to get the input of a number of economists and successful businessmen on solutions for the Irish economy. Desmond was sceptical. He had already been to Abbeville to discuss his proposals for an international financial services centre, to be located in Dublin's docklands. Desmond had at one stage suggested this idea to the coalition government but it went nowhere. One night in late 1986, again in Scruffy Murphy's, Desmond mentioned his idea to

Paul Kavanagh. Kavanagh passed it on to Haughey, and showed him a document that Desmond had had commissioned on the feasibility of such a project. Haughey read it and on a Sunday evening, rang Kavanagh and told him to have Desmond out to Abbeville in the hour to present his idea. After a frantic search Kavanagh eventually tracked Desmond down and they made their way to Abbeville.[8]

Haughey listened but was initially sceptical. At this stage he still had no idea of when the election would take place but considered it would be a matter of months at most. While the financial services centre was Desmond's key idea, and was certainly both radical and innovative, his other panaceas to the Irish economy were the simple ones of cutting public spending and cutting both personal and business taxes. He also suggested that the public debt had to be managed much better. These were the solutions both Fine Gael and the Progressive Democrats were proposing. Haughey needed something different. Over the previous year, Desmond had been in contact with Haughey with various ideas about how to make the country more attractive for international business. In February 1986 he had sent Haughey notes about the potential of Ireland becoming a leader in the development of a global data communications centre and further ideas on shaking up the Irish stock exchange.[9] A few months later, in May, he sent Haughey a proposal for the development of Irish capital markets.[10]

Despite Desmond's scepticism he went to the dinner in Abbeville in early January of 1987. At this stage he still was not sure whether his financial services idea would be adopted by Haughey and Fianna Fáil. Paul Kavanagh was in attendance, as was the economist Colm McCarthy. Haughey listened attentively to their relatively predictable solutions, but he said that the economists were men who were thinking in theoretical terms and asked what their cuts would mean for ordinary people. Then he told Desmond that his solutions were socially, morally and politically wrong, leaving the financier both astounded that his advice would be so easily dismissed and heartened that Haughey did not simply nod his head in agreement. Haughey then outlined his own social partnership idea and said he was conscious of the need for cutting public spending but that the public also needed a growth agenda to believe in.[11] At this stage Haughey was in the middle of leading the drafting of the election manifesto. After dinner he asked Desmond to examine the economic and financial parts of the manifesto. Desmond in turn asked one of his staff, Michael Buckley, who had recently joined the firm from the civil service, to help him out. Haughey was concerned about the coalition's deposit interest retention tax (DIRT) policy and had considered abolishing it. Desmond cautioned against this, saying that any hint during the campaign that the tax would be abolished would create huge difficulties, while making up for the loss of the tax would require gross expenditure cuts in the region of over £500 million. His advice was that the overall budget picture should be perfected right before any tax abolitions or reductions, and strongly recommended that the Fianna Fáil election platform should only commit itself to reviewing the collection process and ensuring that the tax operated fairly across all savings institutions.[12] Haughey took the advice on board. Michael Buckley provided an assessment of the expenditure implications of the current budget deficit scenarios and advised Haughey throughout the campaign on managing the debt and general budgetary issues.[13]

The International Financial Services Centre (IFSC) eventually became the flagship project of the Fianna Fáil manifesto, although, like social partnership, it would be greeted with scepticism by the Department of Finance. Desmond brought Haughey to talk to the economists in his stockbroking firm, NCB. They stressed that growth could only be achieved if public expenditure was brought under control and international confidence in the Irish economy restored. Haughey agreed, but also reiterated that people needed to see that there was a strategy for growth beyond simply cutting public expenditure. He also knew that any new government he would lead would have to face up to what he described to the teaching unions as 'the appalling state of the public finances' when they wrote to him in December 1986 seeking the payment of outstanding monies from a 1985 arbitration award.[14] During the campaign he told Kieran Mulvey, the general secretary of the Association of Secondary Teachers in Ireland, that it was not possible for Fianna Fáil 'in view of the state of the public finances to make specific commitments involving additional public expenditure.'[15]

Haughey, now sixty-one years of age, had come to realise that this was his last chance to leave a strong economic legacy. To do this he would have to be in power. The problem was that the electorate of 1987 was the most volatile Ireland had seen since the Second World War. The entry into the mix of the Progressive Democrats, who made the most impressive debut of any political party since Clann na Poblachta four decades previously, brought significant uncertainty to the political contest. When the votes were counted the three major political parties, Fianna Fáil, Fine Gael and Labour, all recorded their lowest first preference vote share in the modern era. Fianna Fáil's vote was its lowest since 1961. Nonetheless, it still received 44.2 per cent of the vote and won eighty-one seats, falling just two seats short of the holy grail of an overall majority. Fine Gael saw its vote slip to 27 per cent, its lowest since 1957, when it had last presided over an economy in severe recession. It lost twenty seats, falling to fifty-one. It had come within five seats of Fianna Fáil in the November 1982 election, but the voters had had enough of the party they had put into office to fix the economy and it now languished an astonishing thirty seats behind its great rivals. The Labour Party recorded its lowest vote since 1933. It managed to survive, however, coming back to the new Dáil with twelve TDs, a loss of four, on 6.5 per cent of the vote. Its leader, Dick Spring, hung on in Kerry North by just four votes. It looked as if the traditional two-and-a-half-party system was finally at an end. It had been broken by an ideologically right-wing party. The Progressive Democrats won fourteen seats on just under 12 per cent of the vote. Four of its TDs were former Fianna Fáil deputies. It was in every respect an astonishing achievement, and while much of its vote was taken from Fine Gael it also affected Fianna Fáil's performance. Haughey was once again denied an overall majority.

He was, however, able to put a minority government together. After the votes were counted Haughey declared that he believed he could form a government and would not do deals with any other parties or independents. This led Tony Gregory to say that he would vote against Haughey in the election for Taoiseach. As another independent, Seán Treacy from Tipperary, had agreed to Fianna Fáil's offer to take the position of Ceann Comhairle, and Neil Blaney had privately made it clear that he would support Haughey, he was now just one vote short of being voted Taoiseach for a third time. On the day the new Dáil reconvened, 10 March 1987, there was still no guarantee Haughey would be elected Taoiseach. As there was no possibility of anyone else being elected either, an air of uncertainty surrounded Leinster House. Haughey had even warned his own TDs to be ready for another election. This was the last thing any of them wanted. Over the previous fortnight Fianna Fáil had made it clear that there was no question of Haughey being removed to be replaced by someone who was more palatable to Fine Gael or the Progressive Democrats. The possibility of another election also concentrated the mind of Tony Gregory. He had been comfortably re-elected in Dublin Central for the third time in a row but he did not want another election after which the national results might look exactly the same. Gregory did not bring the Fianna Fáil government down in 1982 and believed that Haughey was living up to the deal they had signed when the Workers' Party TDs ended that government. Given that he could see no prospect of any government being formed if he did not do something, he decided to abstain on Haughey's nomination as Taoiseach. Haughey received eighty-two ballots in the vote for Taoiseach. Eighty-two TDs opposed him. With the casting vote of the new Ceann Comhairle he was Taoiseach once again.

AS WISE AS OLD SATAN HIMSELF

Given the tight numbers there was little expectation that this government would last any significant length, but Garret FitzGerald told the Dáil that Fine Gael would not oppose the government if the correct budgetary strategy was followed. Such noises had of course been made before in Irish politics. What was different this time was that, unlike pretty much any opposition in the history of the state, Fine Gael, under its new leader, Alan Dukes, actually did support the general thrust of the government's fiscal rectitude programme. This was something rather unique in Irish politics. Dukes vowed that Fine Gael would support the government in the broad thrust of its economic policy as long as Fianna Fáil was serious about tackling the mounting public debt. Dukes's so-called Tallaght Strategy speech of September 1987, in which he promised budgetary support for the government, was in essence formalising FitzGerald's Dáil speech of six months earlier. No one wanted a return to the chaos of the 1981–1982 electoral period, but Fine Gael also wanted to be sure that Fianna Fáil would abide by its promise to bring the public finances under control.[16] Haughey made two key decisions to ensure that this would happen. The first was to appoint Ray MacSharry Minister for Finance. The second was to support MacSharry in cabinet amid uproar once the new ministerial appointees realised that the government would have to cut expenditure dramatically. At the first cabinet meeting of the new government there was a tense standoff between Ray MacSharry and Pádraig Flynn, the new Minister for the Environment. At the beginning of the meeting Haughey asked MacSharry to give a summation of the state of the national finances. The news was not good. The national debt had soared to £22 billion during the coalition's term in office. Since 1977 there had been a spiral of high inflation and equally high interest rates, contracting output and unprecedented levels of unemployment (which had risen from 90,000 in 1980 to 227,000 in 1986, some 18 per cent of the workforce), resulting in a vastly increased social welfare budget.

The only plausible approach was to cut public spending, which would clearly impact significantly on public services, including the health services, which Fianna Fáil had placed so much store on protecting during the campaign. There was a shocked silence when MacSharry finished his presentation. Flynn was the first to speak up, telling Haughey that the people would simply not wear it and there had to be a better way. Haughey asked Ray MacSharry what he thought of Flynn's intervention. MacSharry replied: 'I've said my piece and I can say no more. There is no other way.'[17] MacSharry admitted to a worried wait before Haughey told Flynn that the Minister for Finance had said what he had said for a reason and that the government would implement his strategy. When Flynn intervened again, Haughey followed up by telling him that the decision has been made and if he did not like it he could leave, pointing to the door. Flynn stayed. MacSharry felt a marker had been set down and he could get on with the job of rectifying the public finances.

He was aided by Fine Gael's Tallaght Strategy, which he described as being 'designed to serve the party and the country. It combined altruism with a degree of political self-interest, and in fairness to Alan Dukes, perhaps more of the former than the latter.'[18] The strategy allowed Fine Gael to rebuild its tarnished reputation from the ashes of the horrors of the FitzGerald government, to have an input into the budgetary strategy being pursued by MacSharry and, perhaps most important of all, it allowed it to claim, perfectly legitimately, that it was putting the country first. For the rest of 1987 and into 1988, the two-pronged approach of the nascent social partnership process and the reduction of public expenditure dramatically improved the country's economic outlook.

In October 1987, at the launch of the Programme for National Recovery, Haughey described social partnership as a major achievement for the nation.[19] That first social partnership agreement was developed as a means of responding to a grave fiscal crisis. The previous year the social partners, acting in the tripartite National Economic and Social Council (NESC), chaired by Pádraig Ó hUiginn, agreed a strategy to overcome Ireland's economic difficulties. The document, *Strategy for Development*, formed the basis on which Haughey's new Fianna Fáil government and the social partners negotiated the Programme for National Recovery. It was essential that Haughey neutralise trade union opposition to the cuts in public spending his minority Fianna Fáil government had to implement.

Fianna Fáil's economic strategy in 1987 was to enhance international competitiveness through reduced taxation, cuts in public expenditure, and a drive for increased foreign direct investment through a consensual partnership approach. The 1987 Programme for National Recovery, with its commitment to low inflation and export-led growth, had immediate success. The NESC reported in 1990 that despite still significant unemployment the overall performance of the economy was impressive, given the grim nature of the recession of the 1980s. Haughey was the political agent around which macroeconomic policy in the state revolved. In the final frantic few weeks before the Programme for National Recovery was agreed he met with all the groups involved. He had personal discussions with representatives of all the major trade unionists, including John Carroll, Billy Attley and Christy Kirwan, explaining that rigorous measures would be necessary in public expenditure as there was very little scope for any further borrowing.

He was accompanied in everything he did and everywhere he went by Pádraig Ó hUiginn. The final text of the programme encompassed monetary and fiscal goals, indicative job targets, social policy initiatives and a tax–jobs trade-off. The FUE was a reluctant participant, but Haughey told them the day before the programme was to be launched that if they did not participate he would still do a deal with ICTU that would set the parameters for the private sector. The small farmers' group, the ICMSA, sought a variety of last-minute changes, all of which Haughey rejected, finally telling the organisation that he would solve its problems by eliminating it from the draft programme.[20]

On the afternoon of Friday 9 October 1987, Haughey and his full cabinet assembled with the leadership of the country's main business, union and farming groups at the Burlington Hotel for the launch of the Programme for National Recovery. Haughey's arrival was announced by Ó hUiginn, whose negotiation skills and hard bargaining had done so much to secure the programme's passage, particularly in its final stages. One of Haughey's first acts as Taoiseach in March was to restore Ó hUiginn to the heart of decision-making in the Department of the Taoiseach. Before the formation of the government, Ó hUiginn, as chairman of the NESC, where he had been banished by FitzGerald in 1982, had assured Haughey that the trade union endorsement of its 1986 report was a real commitment, not just empty rhetoric. He told Haughey he was confident he could deliver the essence of that report, recast as a comprehensive new centralised agreement negotiated between the social partners. His one condition was that he wanted control of the negotiations from the civil service side and that he would report directly to Haughey and MacSharry and take instructions from them.[21]

The day after Haughey was sworn in as Taoiseach for the third time he met with MacSharry and Ó hUiginn for what he described as a working lunch in his office. Haughey agreed that their economic outlook would centre on the following points:

1. A commitment to a National Economic Plan, based on the NESC Strategy, to be negotiated with the social partners by Ó hUiginn, who would be responsible directly to Ray MacSharry and myself ...;

2. As a first fiscal measure, the current budget deficit in the budget to be introduced by MacSharry would have to be lower than that proposed in the budget proposals of the outgoing Fine Gael government;

3. That we should introduce a voluntary redundancy scheme in the public service to help curtail the public sector pay bill;

4. That we establish an International Financial Services Centre in Dublin with attractive tax incentives, on the lines recommended to me by Dermot Desmond;

5. That we should take measures to reduce the leakage of €250 million a year in cross-border shopping even though the EEC would oppose them.

In addition, they would establish a National Treasury Management Agency to manage the national debt.[22]

So ambitious were these aims that Ó hUiginn felt he would get nothing done if he had to observe traditional civil service norms: 'I knew that unless I was firm with Mr Haughey and told him that it wouldn't work unless I was given a free hand, we would be in the same position years from now. So I told him, look, we haven't got much time. Let me get on with it. He looked at me and said, "You'd better get it right, Mr Ó hUiginn."'[23] Haughey thought Ó hUiginn 'as wise as old Satan himself'.[24] And perhaps a touch of the devil was needed to ensure social partnership got to the stage of a launch at all. The same could be said for the IFSC, which was opposed by the Department of Finance, by most economists, and by the existing financial services sector in Ireland. In April 1987, Haughey told the inaugural meeting of the IFSC Committee that not only were they an unusual mixture of both the public and private sectors and one of the most high-powered committees ever established by any government but that it was 'of national importance that you succeed'.[25]

Haughey had a similar attitude to the National Treasury Management Agency. One of the difficulties of the massive public debt was that the state's borrowing costs had soared to an almost unmanageable level. As Minister for Finance in the 1960s, Haughey came across a young official, Michael Somers, who worked in the pensions section of the department. With the encouragement of Haughey and T.K. Whitaker, Somers established the widows' and children's state pension scheme. Some twenty years later Somers was secretary of the Department of Defence when Haughey phoned him up in March 1987 and got straight to the point. Somers recalled that Haughey said, 'What are you doing over there playing soldiers? There's a financial emergency, we need you here.'[26] Somers readily agreed, but there were problems with his title and salary; and he was worried about working within Finance's notorious bureaucratic structure. Haughey and Ó hUiginn had to cut through various civil service structures to ensure that Somers could eventually take the job as secretary of national debt management at the department. Three years later he was appointed the first director of the state's National Treasury Management Agency (NTMA). While he had worked relatively independently within the Department of Finance, he was convinced that he could do a better job if his agency were fully autonomous. Haughey had to be persuaded. Despite his difficulties with Whitaker in the 1960s he held the department in fairly good regard, but both Ó hUiginn and Somers told him that the NTMA had to be a stand-alone arm of the state so that it would not be encumbered by civil service bureaucracy.[27] The legislation establishing the NTMA in December 1990 was designed in such a way that the agency reported to the minister rather than the department. That enabled Somers to do his job in the knowledge that he had the support of Haughey and, by then, Albert Reynolds, who had become Minister for Finance the previous year.

One of the crucial reasons for establishing the NTMA was related to pay. Somers had to persuade Haughey, Reynolds and Ó hUiginn that the only way to compete with the private sector to get the best and most qualified staff to deal with the complexities of bond markets was to pay well over established civil service rates. The department was not particularly happy about the new arrangement. It saw the establishment of the NTMA as threatening its bureaucratic power by taking over what it saw as a very important function while at the same time breaking civil service rules. But Haughey and Reynolds eventually agreed to Somers's idea, such was their commitment to lowering the debt as the ultimate barometer of international confidence in the Irish state. Somers travelled the world trying to persuade the international finance community to invest in Ireland. He was a regular visitor to the Middle East and Far East, carrying the message from Haughey that Ireland was open for business. The establishment of the NTMA was a classic example of Haughey's leadership style. He was willing to listen to an idea, mull it over and then take decisive action. By the time he became Taoiseach in 1987 this was his standard approach to a whole range of issues.

One good example was Haughey's approach to the state's marine policy. In 1986, Eoin Sweeney, a former trade union economist who was then with the National Board of Science and Technology, had called for an industrial strategy on maritime resources. He mentioned to Haughey the potential power of the marine for the state. Haughey had long been interested in marine resources and the potential of wave power as a form of energy. His experiences on windswept Inishvickillane had made him think about harnessing tidal energy. Haughey later telephoned Sweeney and said he had been thinking about their conversation and would Sweeney come to his office in Leinster House and talk him through it. After Sweeney explained it to him, Haughey told him that it sounded good and to write it up immediately. Haughey left his office and gave Sweeney twenty minutes to draft what would become a Fianna Fáil Ard Fheis promise to address the neglect of Ireland's marine resources. This ultimately led to the establishment of Ireland's first Department of the Marine.[28] In 1991, under the Marine Institute Act, the Marine Institute was established to promote and assist in marine research and development that would in turn promote economic development, create employment and protect the marine environment. When first published as a bill, Haughey's initiative received plaudits from the noted maritime historian John de Courcy Ireland, who told him that his foresight would be remembered with gratitude by future generations and that the plan presented many opportunities to make 'an exceptional contribution to the building of a new Europe'.[29]

Haughey had a similar attitude to the building of an airport in Knock. He had assigned government funding to the project during his short-lived 1982 government, having been persuaded of its merits by Monsignor James Horan. Derided by economists and civil servants, it was defunded by the Fine Gael–Labour coalition, but the airport was finally completed in 1986 using private funds. It was seen by many across rural Ireland as a gateway to the development of the west of Ireland. At Horan's invitation, Haughey formally opened the airport on Friday 30 May 1986. In his speech he noted that airports were one of the wonders of the modern world and that the opening of the Connacht Regional Airport would be a turning point of historic significance for the west. He commissioned the poet Paul Durcan to write a piece for the opening. Durcan recalled that the reason Haughey was invited to do the opening was because the people of Knock, and the people of Mayo, felt that Haughey had 'supported them through thick and thin to get Knock International Airport in the face of contemptuous opposition from every quarter, most especially from the pedigree economists, calculators and sophists of Dublin and the Pale.'[30] Durcan later wrote to Haughey that he hoped the rain at Knock that day 'did not make you regret the poetic side of the venture', saying he was deeply moved and grateful for the invitation to mark the occasion with his poem.[31]

Once Haughey had decided on an approach to a policy, he was relatively happy to let those he had appointed to the job to take it from there. As Michael Somers recalled: 'Haughey was a delegator and he expected you to get on with it. I never went back to him and said "Taoiseach, I've a problem." I was expected to sort it myself. Get on with it. That suited me fine. He could have fired me many times but he thought at least this guy is doing things.'[32] Somers had a similar approach to Ó hUiginn, who operated on the principle that if the Taoiseach wanted something done and to succeed it was his job to make that happen. When he introduced Haughey that afternoon in the Burlington Hotel he was convinced that between the two of them they had just delivered something that would have a significant impact on the country's economic fortunes. Haughey entered the auditorium in the Burlington to the strains of Seán Ó Riada's score for *Mise Éire*, the famous film celebrating the birth of the state.[33] In his speech Haughey stated that the Programme for National Recovery supplemented the development and employment policies already being carried out by the government in accordance with its own programme while adding greater precision and new possibilities.[34] The final Programme for National Recovery document had something for everyone, but as Brendan Keenan observed in the following day's *Irish Independent*, Haughey had given away a lot less than seemed to be case. He now had the promise of industrial peace in the public sector while not being knocked off his budgetary course to any significant degree.[35] Observing from a distance, T.K. Whitaker, who had always opposed Haughey's ideas on social partnership, seemed aghast and impressed in equal measure at Haughey's and Ó hUiginn's achievement.[36] In retirement, Haughey told one of his correspondents his view of Whitaker: 'I have always had an unbounded admiration for him and regard him as one of the great men of our time whose influence in the shaping of modern Ireland was of paramount importance.'[37] While this was true, social partnership would play an essential role in rescuing the Irish economy from the morass of the mid-1980s.

Haughey was the driving force behind social partnership. Its main aims were to bring some stability into the economy and political success to Fianna Fáil. Haughey thought that social partnership had contributed to initiating and sustaining the transformation of the economy from the disastrous situation in 1986 to a prosperous and progressive economy. He expressed mild amusement at attempts by others to claim ownership of this concept:

There were, of course, other factors which assisted that transformation but social partnership from its inception and for twenty years
has provided the essential bedrock on which sound public finances
and progressive fiscal, social and economic policies could be firmly
based. Should any proof of its basic soundness be required, it must
surely be the number of individuals and bodies who have laid
claim to its parenthood.'[38]

Haughey was very proud to have brought social partnership to fruition. He rightly believed that it played a major role in driving the Irish
economy forward, noting just before his death in 2006 that the Irish
economy was rescued from the dire position it was in by a determined
and patriotic combination of government, trade unions, employers and
farmers that he put together.

From his return to office in March 1987, Haughey was consumed by
getting the economy fixed. Once the Programme for National Recovery
was agreed, he became even more evangelical in looking for cuts in
expenditure. From the whole period of his government to June 1989,
when he called an election, Haughey received encouragement from various quarters that his cutting strategy was the correct decision. From
within the Dáil, Fine Gael's Hugh Coveney told Haughey in the summer
of 1987 that he could probably do with some encouragement from this
unexpected source: 'Thank God we have someone who is at last facing
up to our deep set problems in a resolute and single-minded fashion,'
adding that the 'painless cutters are a sham' and that Haughey was not
to be 'deflected for the country's sake'.[39] On Haughey's sixty-third birthday in 1988, Niall Crowley of AIB congratulated him on the 'remarkable
achievements of government in the past eighteen months – a virtual
transformation has been largely achieved.'[40]

But that transformation was not without its difficulties. Haughey
constantly wrote to ministers and ministers of state looking for realistic
expenditure cuts and detailed plans. Nothing was off limits. In March
1988, for instance, he told his ministers that they had to ensure that their
civil service officials gave their full co-operation in and commitment to

controlling expenditure: 'You should encourage them to adopt a radical innovative approach to regard no expenditure as sacrosanct.'[41] In April of 1989 he demanded yet more cuts, telling his ministers, 'despite the great progress in controlling expenditure ... I am convinced that there is still substantial scope for further improvement.'[42] By this stage many of his ministers were exhausted by his demands. Rory O'Hanlon, the Minister for Health, told him that not only had his department 'reached the end of the road in regard to further reductions in the existing exchequer support for our services but that some comparatively small increases in the existing levels of funding are necessary'.[43] O'Hanlon recalled that he kept telling Haughey that the health services could not take any more cuts, but Haughey was insistent, saying that there could be no special dispensations for any department.[44] O'Hanlon's views would prove extremely prophetic when health cuts became a major issue in the June 1989 general election.

Haughey was on the back foot from the off in that election; Fianna Fáil's promises on the health service from the 1987 election were repeatedly brought up by the opposition and on the doorsteps. The health cuts issue reached a nadir for Fianna Fáil when Haughey admitted that he personally had not been aware of 'the problems and difficulties and hardships' they had caused.[45] Many in the parliamentary party were outraged by Haughey's remark. The Meath backbencher Noel Dempsey was canvassing in Nobber when he heard Haughey's comments on RTÉ's one o'clock news. He was later lambasted by a constituent for being out of touch if he did not know about the impact of the cuts. He recalled his fury on hearing Haughey's remarks: 'That, to me, was treachery. First of all, against a minister, O'Hanlon, who was only carrying out orders, and secondly, we had all defended him as best we could no more than we tried to defend Mary O'Rourke in the education cuts. Now that didn't sit well at all with many in the party. I said to myself, what the hell are we even having this election for.'[46]

After his remark on the impact of the cuts, Haughey claimed that there would be no more expenditure cuts if Fianna Fáil was returned to office as all the necessary cuts had already been made. To an electorate who remembered Fianna Fáil's catchy slogan from just two years earlier that health cuts hurt the old, sick and handicapped, this was hardly reassuring. If health was a crucial issue for Fianna Fáil's core working-class vote, the decision to call an election seemed to have alienated its middle-class constituency. Haughey also constantly faced the question of why a country coming ever so slowly out of the grip of a grim recession had to tolerate an election at all.

1989: WHY ARE WE HAVING THIS ELECTION AT ALL?

On Thursday 25 May 1989, Haughey went to Áras an Uachtaráin to seek a dissolution of the Twenty-Fifth Dáil. A month earlier, on 26 April, returning from a visit to Japan, he had been told on his arrival at Dublin Airport that later that day his government was certain to lose a vote on a private member's motion proposed by the Labour Party on compensation for haemophiliacs suffering from the Aids virus. He was jetlagged after the long journey, but went straight to Government Buildings. Paddy Teahon, a senior civil servant in his department, advised him to go home and rest, but Haughey was insistent.[47] He met Pádraig Ó hUiginn and demanded to be updated on the financial implications of the vote, and what it would take to satisfy the opposition. Ó hUiginn gave him a rough figure of just about £9 million to which Haughey immediately replied, 'No, we'll not be giving in to the opposition on that, where will it stop?[48] Ó hUiginn cautioned him against doing anything rash. Haughey then met with his chief whip, Vincent Brady, and Bertie Ahern, the Minister for Labour, complaining that the government could not be held to ransom on issues of money and finance. Bertie Ahern told Haughey that in his view a minority government had to accept that it would lose some parliamentary votes during its tenure but that as long as these were not confidence votes it could govern effectively.[49] The government had already lost six Dáil votes during its two years in office and the opposition believed that a defeat on this issue would not necessarily mean an election. One of those defeats was on pupil–teacher ratios. Mary O'Rourke, Minister for Education, refused to accept a Fine Gael motion with the result that the vote was lost. At the next parliamentary meeting

Haughey was furious about the defeat and O'Rourke bore the brunt of his criticism. Ray MacSharry intervened, pointing out that Fianna Fáil was in power because of Fine Gael but it was O'Rourke's job to defend her department, herself and Fianna Fáil. It was likely that there would be several more defeats, so the parliamentary party had better get used to it.[50] Haughey, however, could never abide the idea of being Taoiseach and losing votes.

Before Haughey left for Japan, Rory O'Hanlon had told him that if the government did not settle and agree to finance a compensation fund, it would be defeated in the Dáil. Alan Dukes had already written to Haughey in March to state that Fine Gael would be supporting the Labour motion. That motion would establish a trust fund for haemophiliacs who had become HIV positive, and some of whom had the Aids virus, as a result of having received infected blood products. Dukes added, 'I think it fair to say – and I say it without the slightest mischievous intent – that a good many deputies and senators in your party agree with the proposal also.'[51] He urged Haughey to urgently reconsider the minister's and Department of Health's resistance to the proposal. Over the course of the next few weeks, however, Fianna Fáil made little attempt to accommodate the opposition's proposal and thus knew a defeat was looming. Politically, Haughey wanted a settlement, but O'Hanlon and the civil servants in the Department of Health were not able to reach a settlement with the Department of Finance and Haughey, in a major miscalculation, did not insist that a solution be found.

During Haughey's first two governments, when he wanted to come to an agreement with interest groups he simply ordered his ministers to find a solution, with little thought for the financial consequences. In 1980 he instructed his Minister for Education, John Wilson, to give a pay rise to teachers, which had originally been steadfastly refused by his government. The final award of 30 per cent was significantly higher than that offered by the arbitration board, an offer which itself had been rejected as too costly by his government. The arbitration board resigned in protest, but Haughey had his deal. He did something similar with the Minister for Health, Michael Woods, and a contract for hospital consultants in April 1981. This was a two-pronged approach. It involved allowing consultants in health board hospitals to engage in unlimited private practice for which they would be paid on a fee-for-service basis. Those in the voluntary hospitals, meanwhile, gained the security of pensionable state employment while not ceding their private practice rights. Maev-Ann Wren described it as a 'sweetheart deal'.[52] The Haughey of 1989, however, was a zealous cutter of public spending.

Now that Haughey had returned from Japan, he wanted the word spread that if the government was indeed defeated there would be a general election. It had been a tiring month for Haughey. He made a brief three-day visit to the USA for St Patrick's Day. His personal physician, Dr Paddy O'Brien, was part of the delegation. O'Brien had started accompanying Haughey on visits abroad since Haughey's tour of Australia and New Zealand in July 1988. He had been suffering from incessant kidney stone problems and bronchial issues since returning to office in 1987 and felt more comfortable taking O'Brien with him when he went abroad.

Just before he left for this tour he had spent a number of days in the Mater Private Hospital with a kidney stone problem. Four months later, on the night of Thursday 13 October 1988, Haughey suffered a severe bronchial attack and was rushed to hospital. He had suffered from periodic attacks of bronchitis for decades and was this time a victim of bronchospasm – a sudden constriction of the muscles in the walls of the bronchioles. This, combined with a concurrent attack of kidney stones, saw him fall gravely ill. He had been in hospital under anaesthetic on no less than three occasions the previous week for his recurrent kidney stone problem, which left him weakened and unable to fight off an attack of bronchitis. The independent senator from Northern Ireland, Dr John Robb, whom Haughey had twice appointed to the Seanad, wrote to tell him that the 'combination of renal calculi and bronchospasm is most unpleasant'.[53] Indeed it was very unpleasant and Haughey was hospitalised in the Mater Private for nearly three weeks. The *Cork Examiner* had reported that Haughey was suffering from heart problems as well; his heart had missed a beat, and 'may have stopped for an instant during his intensive care treatment'.[54] This was strenuously denied by the government's press secretary, P.J. Mara, who threatened to blacklist the newspaper from government briefings, and rejected by his consultant, Dr Bryan Alton, who said that while Haughey was seriously ill, at no time had he been critical or in danger of dying, and that his heart had been one of the strongest parts of his constitution over the years. He had, however, been given emergency supplies of oxygen to help him breathe when he was transported to hospital.[55] After eighteen days, Haughey was released from hospital on Tuesday 1 November. The previous week he had donned a suit to meet the European Commission President, Jacques Delors, who was in Dublin. Photographers at the event were reported as being shocked at the frailty of Haughey's voice and taken aback by his apparent loss of weight.[56]

Haughey spent the rest of 1988 in a strange twilight zone of recuperating in Abbeville interspersed with manic bouts of work including a trip to the Greek island of Rhodes in early December for the European Community summit of the Greek presidency. In a bilateral meeting on the fringes of the summit, he engaged in a furious row with Margaret Thatcher over extradition. Thatcher complained that the Irish government had failed to arrest the terrorist suspect Fr Patrick Ryan after he arrived in Ireland from Belgium the previous week, while Haughey told her that the British paperwork seeking Ryan's extradition was faulty.[57] The Tánaiste, and Minister for Foreign Affairs, Brian Lenihan, did much of the heavy lifting of government during Haughey's illness and recuperation.

Haughey met with Mikhail Gorbachev on Sunday 2 April 1989 when the then General Secretary of the Communist Party of the Soviet Union stopped over in Shannon on his way from Moscow to Cuba to meet Fidel Castro. On the previous day Haughey met with a small team consisting of his Minister for Foreign Affairs, Brian Lenihan, the Minister for Transport and Tourism, John Wilson, and a number of officials, including the assistant Garda commissioner. The agenda for the meeting with Gorbachev was agreed. The Irish hoped to discuss the internal economic and political restructuring in the Soviet Union, the Irish government's position on Northern Ireland, arms control and disarmament, the role of the UN, difficulties in the Middle East, EEC–Soviet Union relations, and bilateral relations between Ireland and the Soviet Union. The final item was to be an invitation to Gorbachev to return to Ireland and a reassurance that the Irish state would 'always be ready to support the efforts of yourself and the other major power, with which we already have very friendly relations – the USA – to improve relations and further dialogue between you' (a veiled reference to possible summit venue).[58] Given the time constraints, Haughey himself reduced the agenda to the UN, Northern Ireland and the Middle East. On their departure, Gorbachev was presented with a Waterford Glass bowl and his wife, Raisa, with a set of fine Irish linen.

The official purpose of Haughey's trip to Japan was to promote an intensification of the political, economic and cultural ties between the two countries. He was, however, specifically trying to persuade a number of Japanese corporations who were thinking of locating in the IFSC to commit to their investment. The highlight of his visit was a meeting with Emperor Akihito. The end of Haughey's trip coincided with the dramatic announcement by the Japanese Prime Minister, Noboru Takeshita, that he would resign over a bribery and influence-peddling scandal that had paralysed his government for more than six weeks. As Haughey was readying himself to depart, an emissary from Takeshita came to deliver a message that the prime minister was about to resign but that the agreements that had been made between the two leaders would be honoured on the Japanese side.[59]

By the day of the haemophiliac compensation vote there was no prospect of any settlement. Haughey, tired and jetlagged, brooded in Leinster House. The irony of his Japanese visit was that it had been due to take place the previous September but was postponed because of the illness of Emperor Hirohito, who died in January. Now, just back in Ireland and considering the resignation of Prime Minister Takeshita, he seemed resolved to go to the country and call an election. On hearing this, the Fine Gael whip, Jim Higgins, thought it was some kind of joke. A decade later, Garret FitzGerald told John Horgan that when Higgins went to see the Fianna Fáil people to find out what was going on, he found 'Charlie, Lenihan and Brennan effing and blinding each other and realised that it would be inappropriate to intervene: vote was lost, election, and C.J. lost seats.[60]

Haughey had had enough of minority government. This was no fit of pique but a serious calculation that he could win an overall majority. Thus he went to the country on a campaign based not on policy but on the more nebulous question of governance, and the necessity and goodness of strong, stable single-party government versus the evils of weak coalitions and minority-led governments. A series of minor parliamentary defeats, while uncomfortable for Haughey and Fianna Fáil, was not exactly debilitating in terms of actually governing. It was, however, sapping to morale and was breeding uncertainty and instability. Moreover, given that the government had now lost a vote on a financial matter the chances of passing deeply contested health estimates on the government's terms was unlikely. Having campaigned in 1987 with the promise to protect the health services, the minority Fianna Fáil government quickly went into austerity mode once in power and began cutting public spending in all ministries, including health. Having been defeated on providing additional funding on the haemophiliac issue it seemed unlikely that the government could persuade the opposition to accept its health estimates. Beyond that, passing another difficult budget would also inevitably prove problematic, given the emboldened nature of the opposition. In that context, those ministers in Haughey's cabinet who advocated continuing in government on the reasonable grounds that the electorate did not want an election, such as Albert Reynolds and Bertie Ahern, quickly found themselves drowned out. The thinking among those who favoured a dissolution of the Dáil and a snap election, like Ray Burke and, in particular, Pádraig Flynn, was based on two premises: public opinion favoured the party, the leader and its policies; and some in Fianna Fáil simply detested not being able to govern independently and balked at the idea of sharing power with any other party or individuals. Mary O'Rourke, who was firmly against an election, recalls Flynn as being particularly bullish about an election, saying, 'Oh you'll sweep the land, boss, you'll sweep the land.'[61] There was no discussion about an election within the parliamentary party.[62]

Fianna Fáil stood at just over 50 per cent in some polls in early 1989 and the thinking within the party was that if it could achieve 47 or 48 per cent in an election, with some slippage during the campaign being very likely, it would certainly gain a majority. Gaining an overall majority had for Haughey become almost an article of faith. Tiring of what he regarded as an artificial arrangement, Haughey lost his patience and gambled on a quick early summer election in the expectation of getting that elusive overall majority. For those who were against any notion of an early election, calling the election was an act of supreme folly. With an improving economy, the restoration of the public finances to some order, and the fear that calling an unnecessary election would prove unpopular with the voters, the majority of the cabinet attempted in vain to talk Haughey out of this course of action, but he was having none of it. According to Ahern, Haughey found it a personal affront to his dignity that he had to rely on the goodwill of the opposition to keep him Taoiseach.[63]

The campaign was disastrous for Fianna Fáil. It was attacked from the right by Fine Gael and the PDs and from the left by Labour and the Workers' Party. It quickly became apparent that it could not win an overall majority. Given that that was the only reason for calling the election, this came as a crushing blow to Haughey. He made a desperate attempt to stave off that scenario in the last days of the campaign, noting that Fianna Fáil was not looking for a landslide of 1977-style proportions but simply wanted 'a working majority that will give us the capacity to implement our policies on a long term basis without insecurity or instability'.[64] Given that these policies of fiscal rectitude were very much the same in macro terms as Fine Gael's and that the idea of Haughey making a grab for overall power by calling an early election gained traction throughout the campaign, the country was not willing to give him his prized overall majority, for the fifth election in a row.

The results were calamitous for Haughey. Fianna Fáil lost four seats, falling to seventy-seven, leaving Haughey not only without his overall majority, but now some six seats short of a working majority and virtually no chance of forming another minority administration. The electoral gods were not with him. The party received a similar share of the vote as it had in 1987, but he was now in an extremely difficult situation. The whole point of the election had been to win an overall majority and that had been decisively rebuffed. The only consolation was that there was no obvious alternative government. The Fine Gael–Progressive Democrat alliance had also been rejected by the electorate. Fine Gael had clawed its way back to respectability by winning four seats to come back with fifty-five, while the Progressive Democrats had a terrible election, losing eight of its fourteen seats. There was a serious post-election stalemate as the opposition to Fianna Fáil was divided between right and left and a smattering of independents who could not by themselves form a government.

Haughey immediately announced that it was his intention to form another minority government and that he would be consulting with other party leaders, including Alan Dukes and Des O'Malley. Haughey and Dukes met on 22 June, a week after the election. That morning Haughey received a letter from Kieran Mulvey of the Association of Secondary Teachers of Ireland outlining some observations that he hoped would be of some help to Haughey in the 'difficult and somewhat testy negotiations' he would have to endure to form a government. Mulvey was a former Workers' Party activist who had refused Haughey's request to stand for Fianna Fáil in the election and in return the promise of a minister of state position. In his letter he told Haughey that Fianna Fáil's campaign was too personalised and its candidates spent too much time fighting one another rather than the opposition, resulting in not enough vote management and the loss of seats. He maintained that the successes of the government did not come across during the campaign and that it could not overcome media bias, particularly on the radio. Now in the messy post-election quagmire he suggested that the best way for Haughey to continue in power was to form a medium-term arrangement with the Progressive Democrats, who, he speculated, needed some form of parliamentary status in view of their mere six seats. Mulvey said that Tom Foxe, who had been elected in Roscommon on a hospital action platform, and the Green TD, Roger Garland, would not want an immediate election. Thus he should be able to come to an arrangement with the Progressive Democrats, whose background was 'totally Fianna Fáil'.[65] Yet, such was the enmity between Haughey and O'Malley, this arrangement seemed unlikely.

Haughey's meeting with Dukes was a tense affair. Mulvey had warned Haughey against any arrangement with Fine Gael. The price for that would be too high; it would include senate seats and a policy shift to the right, which would create conflict between the trade union movement and Fianna Fáil. Dukes, however, was looking for far more than that. Haughey asked Dukes for a continuation of the Tallaght Strategy, but Dukes took the reasonable view that as Haughey had called an unnecessary election he would have to take the consequences. The first of these was that if he was hoping to rely on Fine Gael's help he would have to do it within a formal coalition government in which Fine Gael would have seven seats at the cabinet table and there would be a rotating Taoiseach. Haughey paled visibly, Dukes recalled, when this proposal was put to him. He immediately ruled it out, at which Dukes told him, 'You don't really have too many options, Charlie, it's me or Dessie. We're not doing another minority government.'[66] After the meeting, Haughey wrote Dukes a confidential and 'without prejudice' note stating that if Fine Gael was prepared to support a minority Fianna Fáil administration, he would establish a procedure whereby a number of selected estimates could be nominated by Fine Gael and would be accepted by Fianna Fáil.[67] Dukes was having none of this and repeated his original call for a coalition.

Coalition government of any type was anathema to Haughey, and indeed to Fianna Fáil. Coalition government with Fine Gael was the last of all possible options he would explore. The history of both parties practically forbade it. Given that Dukes had brutally rebuffed Haughey's opening gambit of another minority government, Haughey found himself in an extremely difficult position. His gamble on securing an overall majority was lost. His unrealistic alternative of another minority government had been quickly closed off by Dukes. Labour and the Workers' Party were implacably opposed to Fianna Fáil. That just left the apostates of the Progressive Democrats as potential supporters of a minority government or as coalition partners. Notwithstanding Mulvey's point about the Progressive Democrats needing a parliamentary role, the numbers were too tight for a minority government. In any event, what would be the point of the Progressive Democrats supporting Fianna Fáil when it would receive none of the spoils of office and most likely no credit for its support? Before the election any thought of a Fianna Fáil–Progressive Democrats coalition government seemed ludicrous. After the votes were counted it seemed equally far-fetched. Both parties had lost votes. The Progressive Democrats only existed at all because of the schism within Fianna Fáil, which revolved around Haughey. All six Progressive Democrats TDs had been in Fianna Fáil. Most important of all, no greater enmity existed on a personal level within Irish politics than that between Haughey and O'Malley.

It was Mary Harney who first publicly mooted the idea of a Fianna Fáil–Progressive Democrats coalition. She had discussed it with Charlie McCreevy, who felt that personal enmity could be overcome and a decent government could emerge out of the two parties: 'It seemed to me that overall majorities were likely gone and we should join with people who had much the same ideas as we had about the economy.'[68] McCreevy had long since reconciled himself to Haughey's leadership after the drama of his no confidence motion in October 1982. Despite intense media speculation he never had any intention of joining the Progressive Democrats. By the time of the 1987 government, McCreevy had become a source of ideas for Haughey. Their mutual interest in horses had led them to meet socially on numerous occasions since that first heave. The two men had then started discussing politics and policy options. McCreevy wrote numerous letters to Haughey on the state of the nation, the economy, the party and political tactics. In September 1987, he told Haughey: 'there may never be a greater political opportunity than the estimates of 1988 and 1989 to really make an impact on the public finances and in particular the current budget deficit ... The punter – especially our own – may not like the medicine we are dishing out but we have their respect and I would wager that it also pays off politically for us at the next general election.[69] By March 1988 he was telling Haughey: 'By your actions on the economy and on Northern Ireland we have achieved a remarkable level of public support and good will. This is shown in the opinion polls and comes as no great surprise – to me at least.'[70] He warned Haughey, however, that the electorate was extremely volatile, prone to shifts and the chances of obtaining an overall majority at any time were still slim. By the time the election was called in June 1989 he had become even firmer in these views and worried that the unnecessary nature of the election had seriously dissipated the electorate's goodwill.

After Harney's intervention Haughey agreed to open negotiations with the Progressive Democrats. His opening position of minority support was instantly dismissed by O'Malley, who stated that it was a coalition or nothing. Haughey proclaimed that he could not sell that to his party, leaving O'Malley to make the pithy riposte: 'Charlie, from my knowledge of you inside Fianna Fáil I wouldn't underestimate your selling ability.'[71] On the morning of Thursday 29 June, as the Dáil was set to reconvene to try to elect a government, Dukes wrote to Haughey repeating his coalition offer. Haughey immediately replied:

> I have already clearly indicated that the proposal that the two parties should form a coalition government with an equal number of ministers and with both parties providing a Taoiseach for half the period would be unworkable and is unacceptable. During the course of our discussions I outlined to you what I considered to be a very reasonable working arrangement on the basis of which as the principal opposition party you could offer support to the Fianna Fáil government. I regret, however, that my proposals on these lines were rejected by you.[72]

He then went to the Dáil chamber, where he knew he would face defeat in his efforts to be elected Taoiseach. On that morning the Dáil failed, for the first time in its history, to elect a Taoiseach. There was uproar and confusion in the chamber when Haughey announced that he intended to stay on as Taoiseach. Amid uncertainty about whether or not he had the right to do so, and a ferocious onslaught from the Labour leader, Dick Spring, that he certainly had not, Haughey, after an adjournment, eventually resigned the position of Taoiseach, but stated he would remain in office in an acting capacity until a new Taoiseach had been elected.

In the middle of negotiations between Bertie Ahern and Albert Reynolds for Fianna Fáil and Pat Cox and Bobby Molloy for the Progressive Democrats, the Fianna Fáil acting cabinet met to discuss its options. It was deeply divided and reached no decision. Two days later, Pádraig Flynn, one of the main proponents of an early general election, spoke on RTÉ radio: 'The government is very strong. All the members of the cabinet are unanimous for no coalition. The national executive, the parliamentary party and the grassroots have indicated that this is a core value which we must preserve.'[73] This missed the important point that the people had decided not to give Fianna Fáil its longed-for overall majority. Once Haughey, or anyone else in Fianna Fáil for that matter, could not persuade one of the smaller parties to support them in a minority government, coalition became the only alternative, no matter how abhorrent Fianna Fáil found the whole prospect. Flynn was right in his assessment of the response of the grassroots; the letters to Haughey on the issue overwhelmingly urged him not to compromise.

There was, however, no unanimity in the parliamentary party, or among the Fianna Fáil ministers, where the reality of coalition as the only option for forming a government was becoming ever clearer. This was particularly the case for the one man who was all-important in Fianna Fáil – Haughey. After the acting cabinet meeting again brought no unanimity, Haughey prepared for coalition by talking individually to each of his ministers to ascertain their own views.[74] Most were still naturally reluctant but could not see any alternative. The main dissident was Pádraig Flynn, who told Haughey he should step down as leader of the party and let someone else try to form a government rather than coalesce with the Progressive Democrats.[75] He accused Haughey of acting out of personal gain and a lust for power, and for putting himself above the needs of Fianna Fáil.[76] The problem for Flynn was that he had no alternative strategy. He did not offer an idea of what type of government anyone in Fianna Fáil could put together once Fine Gael and the Progressive Democrats rejected a minority government. That was not going to change, no matter who the leader was.

Haughey clearly wanted to remain Taoiseach above all else. Abstract theories about coalition were not much use to him if he could not operate a minority government. The idea of hanging tough and fighting another general election – as suggested by those in Fianna Fáil who had been most enthusiastic for an election in the first place – seemed spectacularly misplaced and Haughey gave it little credence. Having just denied Fianna Fáil a majority, the electorate was hardly going to reward it for calling a second election, potentially in a matter of weeks. Just two days after Flynn's statement on the sanctity of single-party government, Haughey told the Dáil that while such an option was his preferred view: 'If our entry into some form of political alliance is the only possible way forward at this stage, the only way in which a government can be formed in this Dáil without causing another immediate general election, then clearly in the higher national interest our duty is positively and constructively to explore the possibility of finding some agreed basis for government. This we intend to do. I believe sincerely that the Progressive Democrats intend to do the same.'[77]

That, in essence, was the Rubicon crossed. Now it was only a matter of agreeing the details. At the heart of this process was Haughey himself. He liked being Taoiseach. He liked the power, but he also enjoyed getting things done. He considered he had done as good a job as anyone possibly could in rescuing the country from the shambles of the Fine Gael–Labour coalition. He certainly was not going to let the loss of a number of seats threaten his desire to lead the next government. Whether Fianna Fáil could have governed in a minority with a different leader was a question he was not going to let even be posed, never mind answered. Fianna Fáil's insistence on single-party government would only have worked if they had a leader who was willing to let such a situation develop into another general election if necessary. There was no real appetite in the country for another general election, and Haughey understood this. His mistake was going to the country in the first place.

Haughey kept his own party and his chief negotiators, Albert Reynolds and Bertie Ahern, in the dark and essentially did his own deal with O'Malley. This infuriated both would-be successors. Reynolds noted that once he became aware of Haughey's own secret negotiations, 'I lost all faith and made up my mind – enough of Charlie Haughey!'[78] On the morning of 12 July Haughey finally ceded a second cabinet seat to the Progressive Democrats, thus ensuring the creation of the coalition. O'Malley was insistent that he had to have a partner with him around the cabinet table, otherwise he would be completely isolated. The fact that it went to Bobby Molloy, whose defection had caused such pain in Fianna Fáil, caused uproar in both the parliamentary party and the grassroots. Party activists threatened to resign, both before and after the announcement that the second seat at cabinet would go to Molloy. Haughey paid them no heed. Coalition theories, policy compatibility, personal animosity, articles of faith; none of these mattered to Haughey. What mattered was leading the government. On the fateful morning when the deal was done he beamed at the Progressive Democrats delegation: 'Nobody but myself could have done it.'[79]

CHAPTER 21

WE WILL BE RELYING ON YOU

OUR MUTUAL FRIEND

On 19 May 1991, at its 146th commencement, the University of Notre Dame conferred the degree of Doctor of Laws Honoris Causa on Charles J. Haughey. The citation asserted that Haughey was:

… a head of government whose career has been notable both for its statecraft and for its range of achievements. Born in the troubled aftermath of Irish partition, he was a member of parliament by age 31 and early on attracted notice with his deft handling of a series of ministerial portfolios. Elevated a number of times to the leadership of his nation, he has eased long-strained Anglo-Irish relations. While Ireland held the rotating presidency of the European Community, he completed accords on political and economic union and finalised the Community's first formal ties to the United States. Now aspiring to resolve the tragic conundrum of Northern Ireland, he has worked to achieve historic agreements in which the parties have pledged a new attempt at reconciliation. May his legacy be the gift his own generation has never known – Ireland at peace.[1]

Given Notre Dame's long connection with Ireland, the concentration on Haughey's efforts to contribute to an enduring solution to the Northern problem was understandable. Accepting the honorary doctorate, Haughey told the university's president, Edward A. Malloy, that he was proud to accept the award, which he considered had been bestowed on Ireland as well as himself, from the 'great University of Notre Dame where Yeats once lectured'.[2] Haughey's award was made on the recommendation of Donald Keough, chairman of the university's Board of Trustees and the president of Coca-Cola, whom Haughey later thanked for his part in the honour.[3]

Just before he left for the United States, Haughey was corresponding with the British Prime Minister, John Major, who had succeeded Margaret Thatcher in November 1990. The topic was the preliminary round of political talks involving the SDLP, the Ulster Unionist Party, the Democratic Unionist Party, and the Alliance Party on the political future of Northern Ireland. Those talks consisted of three strands: internal Northern Ireland matters; North–South relations; and Anglo-Irish relations in general. They began on 30 April 1991, but problems almost immediately arose over Strand One of the talks in relation to where the discussions would be held and who would chair the later stages of these negotiations. Haughey and Major were conscious of the need to ensure the talks would not undermine the Anglo-Irish Agreement and thus potentially harm Anglo-Irish relations. Haughey told Major that his government was very conscious of the need to get the talks started, and wanted to pay tribute to the 'patient and painstaking efforts' of the Secretary of State for Northern Ireland, Peter Brooke, and his own Minister for Foreign Affairs, Gerry Collins, to move the process forward.[4] Two months earlier the two leaders had exchanged letters on Brooke's initial efforts to get talks under way. Haughey had told Major that he fully agreed with the prime minister's view that the 'point has been reached when it is necessary to resolve matters'. The Irish government accepted Brooke's formula for the talks and it was a process which 'if we can get it off the ground carries the potential, I believe, to transcend the differences between all the parties involved and to bring major benefits to all the people of these islands'.[5] The references to timeliness and to getting it off the ground were telling. The Troubles in Northern Ireland had now been going on for over two decades and no initiatives had resolved the political difficulties or stopped the killing.

By the time Haughey returned to power in 1987, his chief adviser on Northern Ireland, Martin Mansergh, was convinced that the only way to bring about any resolution to the conflict was to engage in contact with the leadership of the republican movement.[6] The question was how best to do this while the IRA continued its armed struggle. The previous year, on 15 January 1986, the president of Sinn Féin, Gerry Adams, wrote to Haughey:

> A number of people over the last few years have made approaches to me intimating that you would be agreeable to dialogue between our two parties on a private basis, and/or that you would be open to discussions on a private or personal basis with me. As you are perhaps aware, because I am sure you have been similarly approached, I would be pleased to initiate a dialogue with you. While this may give both of us political difficulties, nevertheless as MP for West Belfast and leader of a party which represents 42% of nationalist voters in the six counties I believe it is in both our interests and more importantly the interests of Irish nationalism that we have the opportunity to talk. As leader of the largest party on the political island it is important that you are fully briefed on the view of those people I represent. I would be pleased therefore if the bearer of the note was used to deliver any further communication between us. Please excuse my hurried scribble.[7]

Six months later, on 17 June, Adams wrote to Haughey again to say that 'our mutual friend has been pressing me to put my thoughts on the current situation to you', but that he found the process difficult because writing was an inadequate form of communication: 'indeed it could not be properly described as a communication … I accept that you have political differences about a dialogue between us. I am sure you will understand also that I feel a real commitment to dialogue would overcome such obstacles. Whether the advantages would justify the risk is a matter of judgement for you to make.' Adams went on to raise the possibility of internment being introduced in Northern Ireland by what he described as the 'British and FitzGerald governments', that the 'Hillsborough Treaty is aimed at stabilising British interest in our country and at defeating Irish nationalism of even the "constitutional" variant'. Adams told Haughey that those who drafted the Anglo-Irish Agreement on the Irish side had shown how prepared they were to compromise with the British and how much they wished to dilute nationalist aspirations and lower nationalist expectations. He described the republican movement as the only major obstacle to this 'conspiracy' and said that internment should be resisted by all nationalists in the island. He ended, 'you may not consider my sources to be reliable. They are.'[8]

As it turned out, the sources were not reliable – internment was not introduced – but Adams's letters seeking dialogue with Haughey brought with them both opportunity and danger. The opportunity lay in a potential path to peace. The danger was that any public revelation that Haughey was engaged in dialogue with the political wing of the Provisional IRA, when in opposition, would almost certainly see his career come to a very abrupt end. This was only fifteen years after his acquittal in the arms trial. Many of his political opponents criticised him as being somehow responsible for the birth of the IRA by virtue of that trial and the allegations that he had helped to import arms for it. By 1986, the government's economic record was such that Haughey was almost certain to win the next election on the back of the coalition's unpopularity. Yet, in the eyes of many, the fact that Fianna Fáil continued to oppose the popular Anglo-Irish Agreement had already aligned them with Sinn Féin. In that context any dialogue with Sinn Féin carried enormous risk, notwithstanding Adams's view that Haughey would be in some way agreeable to dialogue between the two parties. Martin Mansergh was sceptical that Haughey would have risked a direct meeting while he was still in opposition, although Haughey did not rule it out in principle.[9]

Adams's letter to Haughey in January 1986 was not their first communication. During the hunger strikes of 1981, the two men had exchanged messages via Pádraig Ó hAnnracháin, who handled secret phone calls to and from Adams.[10] These two letters by Adams to Haughey in 1986 were written as part of the initiative of the Redemptorist priest Fr Alec Reid to persuade Haughey to engage with the republican movement. He was the 'mutual friend' to whom Adams referred in his letters.

It was on a Saturday morning in August 1986 that Reid met Haughey in Abbeville to outline his scenario about how the IRA could be persuaded to call a ceasefire, and thus open the way to a permanent peace, and possible Irish unity. This meeting had been long in the planning. Reid's intermediary with Haughey was the editor of the *Irish Press*, Tim Pat Coogan, who had delivered Adams's letters to Haughey in Abbeville. Reid had initially approached Coogan nearly a year previously to say that as a friend of Haughey's, Coogan was in a position to help end the killing and bring about Irish unity.[11] What was needed was the political initiative from Haughey to meet with Adams. Haughey and Coogan had disagreed over the Anglo-Irish Agreement, so Coogan asked Reid for some sort of written authorisation from Adams that the Sinn Féin leader was indeed serious about peace, which Coogan could then show to Haughey as proof of Adams's bona fides. Neither of Adams's two letters set out such a position, but rather sought a dialogue while giving nothing tangible to Haughey in return. Haughey was not impressed.

It was not until two months after the second Adams letter that Haughey agreed to meet Reid. The intermediary was again Coogan. This time there was a blueprint from Reid that outlined the republican leadership's thinking on a strategy for peace, but he told Coogan that it should not be sent to Haughey just yet. Rather, Reid wanted to meet with the Fianna Fáil leader and explain that there was now real potential for a breakthrough. Haughey agreed to a meeting but wanted to ensure that this time Adams's ideas, which Reid would be bringing, would consist of more than a simple wish for a dialogue and complaints about the Anglo-Irish Agreement. In essence, Haughey wanted a clear rationale for any future potential meeting with Adams and the reasons he should accept that Adams was prepared to redirect the republican movement to exclusively peaceful means. At the August 1986 meeting in Abbeville, Reid sought to persuade Haughey that Sinn Féin was different from the IRA, but that it needed to be brought in from its political isolation. Reid argued that if Haughey would meet with Adams it would show Sinn Féin, and its supporters, that a broad constitutional and nationalist family existed from within which they could pursue the objective of a united Ireland. Reid explained to Haughey that it was the Fianna Fáil leader's republican credentials that made him attractive to Adams as a man he could do business with: 'the right man, in the right place, at the right time', as Ed Moloney put it.[12]

While Haughey listened attentively to what Reid had to say, he refused to meet Adams. It was simply too risky. He was in opposition, with every chance of being in power after the next election, which, given the fragility of the coalition, could happen at almost any time. The chance of any meeting with Adams being made public would inevitably end his chance of being back in government and his political career would most likely also end in ignominy. There was also no guarantee of any success, particularly in the short to medium term. Haughey would have to be in government with the backup of the power of the state to make any inroads into reaching a settlement. That was the context for the two men's next interaction when Reid sent his fifteen-page letter to Haughey, now Taoiseach, in May 1987. After that first meeting Haughey often invited Reid back to Abbeville to update him on thinking in the republican movement. At their second meeting, Haughey introduced Reid to Martin Mansergh and told him, as Mansergh's biographer, Kevin Rafter, relates: 'You can say to him what you'd say to me.'[13] Both Reid and Mansergh would play a crucial role in the developing peace process when Haughey finally authorised a Fianna Fáil delegation to meet with Adams.

The letter that Reid sent Haughey dated 11 May 1987 was the first of many that the Redemptorist priest sent to the Taoiseach outlining the thinking of the republican movement and the wider nationalist movement, including the Catholic Church. As Ed Moloney, who first published it, pointed out, it was the first open expression on Gerry Adams's behalf of his wish to end the IRA's violence for good; handled properly, the initiative could remove the gun from Irish politics for ever. The letter showed that the leader of the Catholic Church in Ireland, Cardinal Tomás Ó Fiaich, had endorsed the Adams–Reid dialogue, and that the Catholic Church would facilitate and host dialogue between Fianna Fáil and Sinn Féin in an attempt to create a type of pan-nationalist axis whose political clout would be of sufficient strength to persuade the IRA to lay down their arms. Reid expounded at some length on how Adams was prepared to move on long-held republican shibboleths, including a physical British withdrawal from Ireland, as long as they promised not to interfere in a settlement that derived from negotiations between unionists and nationalists, even if it fell short of Irish unity.

Reid began his letter by telling Haughey he was writing to him to 'ask your advice with the following because it concerns what the Church may be able to do over the coming months to help the cause of peace'. In the next seven thousand words Reid asserted his view that there now existed an opportunity 'not just for a ceasefire but for making final peace with the IRA and taking the gun out of nationalist politics forever'. He ended his letter by expressing hope that because of its length Haughey had been patient with him, but as it dealt with life and death matters he was of the view that both the Taoiseach and Fianna Fáil 'can be of immense help in terms of the advice, guidance, and co-operation that you can give us'.[14]

While the letter from Reid to Haughey essentially contained the blueprint for the peace process, the IRA continued its armed campaign and the conflict persisted unrelentingly. Yet by late October 1987 Haughey was contemplating a three-way meeting between himself, John Hume and Gerry Adams, to be hosted by Cardinal Ó Fiaich. He was also considering not renewing the extradition legislation that the coalition government had signed off on just before the election of 1987.[15] Extradition was always a divisive issue in Fianna Fáil and many in the party were against the very idea in principle. Again, Haughey's postbag bulged with the grassroots demanding that he scrap the bill.

Just six months after Reid's letter to Haughey, on 8 November 1987 the IRA detonated a huge bomb at a Remembrance Day commemoration in Enniskillen, killing eleven innocent civilians and seriously wounding dozens of others on a day considered sacred in the unionist tradition. The revulsion all around Ireland, both North and South, after Enniskillen, made any meeting with Adams and any softening of the extradition legislation impossible for Haughey. Haughey was badly shaken by Enniskillen. He was first told of the bombing by the Department of Foreign Affairs official Seán Ó hUiginn, who recalled him being absolutely shocked and disbelieving that the IRA could have committed the atrocity. Ó hUiginn was himself puzzled at Haughey's initial reaction. Decades later, after the revelations of the beginnings of the peace process, and Haughey's role in it, he realised that at a time when the first intimations of the peace process were beginning to manifest themselves it was, for Haughey, a brutal reminder of the people he was dealing with and would have to deal with in the future.[16]

This was an extraordinarily tense time for Haughey. He was leading a minority government and while Fine Gael was happy to sign up to the government's economic strategy, its pride in the Anglo-Irish Agreement and hostility to everything associated with Gerry Adams and Sinn Féin meant that Haughey had to tread very carefully in the Dáil when it came to Northern Ireland.[17] The public revulsion after Enniskillen did not stop the killing, however, and the following year saw twice the number of deaths in the conflict as there had been in 1985.[18] Haughey sanctioned a continuation of the meetings between Mansergh and Reid, and ultimately proposed a compromise whereby John Hume was invited to talk to Adams and asked to report back to Haughey via Mansergh. As Mansergh later pointed out, Hume and the SDLP could do what Fianna Fáil and Haughey could not.[19] Mansergh and Reid persevered with their meetings over the course of Haughey's last two governments. The process was never easy and the killing continued.

In May and June 1988, Mansergh, Dermot Ahern and Richie Healy of Fianna Fáil met with Adams, Pat Doherty and Mitchel McLaughlin of Sinn Féin on three occasions in the Redemptorist House in Dundalk, with Reid in attendance. The talks were highly secret, even if, as Mansergh pointed out, it was a relatively low-level Fianna Fáil party delegation.[20]

Dermot Ahern was only thirty-one years of age and had been elected for the first time in Louth in the 1987 election. On being asked to be part of the delegation by Haughey, Ahern agreed but asked Haughey, 'How will you keep your fingerprints off this?' Haughey replied: 'I'll get over that, but if it ever gets out, you're on your own.' He also added that he didn't know whether he could trust Adams and Sinn Féin, but it had to be worth trying. Ahern described himself as 'the sacrificial lamb. I was dispensable, in my view. I was under no illusions. And at the same time, I think he probably felt that, you know, I had a good enough grasp of things. When they were finished it was Mansergh who reported to Haughey. I never did. I asked him afterwards what was happening and he didn't say it bluntly but from what I assumed Mansergh was still talking to the boys.'[21]

After three meetings in which Mansergh and Adams did most of the talking, Haughey had decided there was no point in continuing with them. He had become convinced that Adams's aim was to end Sinn Féin's isolation while not being drawn on a timeline of when the IRA would lay down its arms and renounce violence. There was also a serious element of danger involved. In December 1988, for instance, Reid wrote to Haughey outlining his views on where he thought the republican movement was at in its pursuit of an alternative political and diplomatic strategy for justice and peace. He ended by saying that it was a long road that has no turning and that he hoped 1989 would see the turning that would make all the difference. In an addendum to the letter Reid outlined his concerns about his friend, 'not the well-known one', whose influence was crucial to what they were trying to do. He went on, 'my friend has already, in accordance with my advice, expressed formal regret under oath, although this was against the advice of the experts guiding him because it exposed him to an examination, which in the event was relentlessly pursued.' Reid vouched for his friend's total support for the process of politicisation, one which could not have been effectively initiated or pursued without his kind of support. At the end of the note, Reid told Haughey he was 'writing this note because of the danger of delay but I suggest it be destroyed as soon as you have read it.'[22] It was a sobering reminder of the risks being taken for peace.

Haughey needed little reminding of the dangers involved in peace-making. In August 1987, the Department of the Taoiseach received a letter purporting to be from the loyalist terrorist group, the UVF, stating that British intelligence had launched a smear campaign against Haughey. It added that MI5 had asked it two years previously to kill Haughey and claim responsibility for it. The letter stated that the group was approached by an MI5 officer based in the Northern Ireland Office. Chillingly, it said: 'He asked us to execute you ... We refused to do it, we were asked would we accept responsibility if you were killed we refused ... We have no love for you but we are not going to carry out work for the Dirty Tricks Department of the British.'[23] The letter was not discussed with the Department of Justice or with the then Minister for Justice, Gerry Collins, who never came across it.[24] The authenticity of the note remains in question, but whether it was genuine or not, it showed the dangers in working for peace; the UVF told Haughey that the MI5 operative gave details of his cars, photographs of his home, Inishvickillane, and his yacht, the *Celtic Mist*, which he had bought to replace the *Taurima*. Haughey also received a Christmas card from the UDA in this period. The front of the card is illustrated with a festive holly wreath and the UDA's Red Hand of Ulster badge bearing its slogan *Quis separabit*. The message inside reads: 'A merry Christmas and a happy new year'. There was also a handwritten note reading 'Season's greetings from the Ulster Defence Association'. Printed at the bottom was a quotation by Sam Duddy, who was the UDA's public relations officer in the 1980s: 'If this should finish as it might/ On England's soil, as England's fight/ Will you say then, "Why, they were right/ That lot from the north".'[25]

Another letter of somewhat questionable authenticity was received by Haughey in Abbeville at about the same time. It purported to come from the 'Army Council, Irish Republican Army', and claimed that despite reports of possible internment of IRA suspects in the Republic, the IRA was 'totally committed to a policy of non-confrontation in the 26 counties. Our armed struggle is against the British presence in the North and is aimed at forcing Britain to an objective which all Irish nationalists support ... Peace will come only when Britain goes. You know this as well as us.'[26] Much of the content, according to Haughey's chief adviser on Northern Ireland, Martin Mansergh, was consistent in style and substance with the position of the republican movement at the time, with the exception of the sign-off and the casual way of addressing the Taoiseach of the day as 'Charlie Haughey'.[27] Such statements were usually drafted essentially by one person on instructions and subject to vetting and amendment, and we have no means of knowing, even if the message was broadly speaking genuine, whether it was in fact signed off by the Army Council, or just one or two individuals acting in its name. The reference to internment is also questionable as none of Haughey's governments ever seriously considered introducing internment.

In December 1989, Mansergh submitted a report to Haughey of a meeting between Dermot Gallagher of the Department of Foreign Affairs and John Hume about a document Reid and his fellow priest Raymond Murray had produced. The document, which they proposed to publish, called for 'a democratic overall political and diplomatic strategy for justice, peace, and reconciliation'. Gallagher noted that Hume complained about the proposals to publish the document, which he saw as putting unnecessary pressure on both the Taoiseach and himself, and on what he saw as 'a general tendency to use Provo-type language in the text', particularly a proposal which called on the British to plan for a democratic, peaceful withdrawal from Ireland over a determinate period of time. Mansergh told Haughey that Reid believed that 'Republican-type language is required if the Provisionals are to be attracted to an alternative political path,' although Hume believed it would alienate unionists.[28] Facilitating the Provisionals was a particular problem throughout the whole peace process and there was a constant fear in Irish government and SDLP circles that Sinn Féin would never be satisfied and that any concessions to them would be seized upon by critics in both the Republic of Ireland and Northern Ireland, of whom there were many.

The month after Haughey received his honorary doctorate from the University of Notre Dame he met with John Major in Downing Street on the evening of 21 June 1991. Four days earlier the Northern Ireland parties, with the exception of Sinn Féin, met at Stormont to begin talks on the future of Northern Ireland. Haughey had a brief one-to-one meeting with Major before a working dinner at which he was joined by the Minister for Foreign Affairs, Gerry Collins, Noel Dorr, and Dermot Gallagher of the Department of Foreign Affairs and the secretary to the government, Dermot Nally, who described the meeting as business-like and amicable. The meeting revolved around the Luxembourg Council meeting, scheduled to take place the following week, and Northern Ireland. Haughey told Major that in his view there was a major opportunity for something to be done now, for the two governments to take charge and get a lasting settlement. Nothing would happen if it was simply left to the parties in Northern Ireland and the situation in Northern Ireland was a constant irritant to relations between the two governments on the world stage. There would be great benefit to both countries from 'a clearing of the decks. Both countries could then settle down to some sort of normal relations. I hope in all this I am not teaching my grandmother to suck eggs.' Major replied, 'Indeed you are not.'[29] Haughey told Major that a working group of both governments could look at 'any way of bringing Sinn Féin into the process. I am constantly being approached by people who say that we should get Sinn Féin into the process … We could have the experts look at any feasible way in which Sinn Féin could be worked in with a way of ending the violence.' Major was hesitant, telling Haughey they needed to bring the unionists with them, to which Haughey replied that Major wasn't aware of his own strength, and 'I think you are beginning to speak like Mrs Thatcher. Maybe you have one of her briefs. We have bitten the bullet on extradition and the system is operating, despite some political trauma in the South. People concentrate on feelings and animosities but I have my own party to consider.'[30] Major ended the discussion by telling Haughey he would reflect on the group he suggested and his positive ideas. One of those ideas was the revisiting of the Unitary State proposal from the days of the New Ireland Forum.

Over the next six months, Haughey became increasingly frustrated by the lack of progress in the Northern Ireland talks, which had been postponed since July. It was not until October 1991 that a draft document penned by John Hume, *A Strategy for Peace and Justice in Ireland*, which outlined a putative declaration by the British and Irish governments, was shown to Haughey.[31] Hume told him that the proposal had Adams's full backing. It outlined a series of ways in which a solution to the historical problems associated with Northern Ireland could be resolved. As Mallie and McKittrick pointed out, its crucial point was one which addressed the republican demand for self-determination but recognised that this traditional objective of Irish nationalism could not be achieved without the agreement of the people of Northern Ireland. This entwined the principles of self-determination and consent, combining a recognition of the aspirations of nationalists with a realisation that majority opinion should prevail in Northern Ireland.[32]

After some redrafting work by three people intimately involved in the process, Mansergh, Dermot Nally and Seán Ó hUiginn, a more nuanced version of Hume's document was presented to John Major at the Anglo-Irish summit of 4 December of 1991 in Dublin, which he promised to consider and report back to Haughey his own and his government's position. That meeting was to be Haughey's last with the British prime minister. The two men agreed to hold biannual bilateral meetings on the North and other issues of mutual concern in London and Dublin alternately. A similar agreement was reached between Haughey and Thatcher in 1980 but was never followed through. Major indicated that the Brooke talks process was still the only initiative on the table but claimed the proposed bilateral meetings would add weight and authority to the process. But there was no proposal for restarting the talks other than urging the parties concerned to get back to the negotiating table. After the four-hour meeting Haughey told the assembled press that, as far as he and the British prime minister were concerned: 'What we can do is lend the weight of our respective authorities to the process and we do in the communiqué urge everybody concerned to make an effort to get the process under way again.'[33] It was a muted end to Haughey's efforts with the British government that dated back some twelve years to the 'teapot summit' in December 1980. Just over two months later he was neither Taoiseach nor leader of Fianna Fáil.

NO SCOPE FOR ANY RELAXATION

While the Seán Doherty tapes revelation was the catalyst for Haughey's end as leader of Fianna Fáil, the process had begun on the day he was elected Taoiseach for the fourth time in July 1989. His decision to coalesce with the Progressive Democrats opened up significant fissures among both the Fianna Fáil members of his new cabinet, particularly Albert Reynolds and Pádraig Flynn, and a large number of his backbenchers. Many of these backbenchers had been upset by the calling of the election in the first place, Haughey's insistence that he had not known about the impact of the cuts, and the ultimate decision to enter coalition. Haughey was also weakened by the loss of Ray MacSharry from his cabinet. MacSharry had been appointed Ireland's EU commissioner in late 1988, despite a plea from Alan Dukes that Peter Sutherland be retained in the position. MacSharry had told Haughey that he would take the job of Minister for Finance in 1987 with the proviso that when the EU commissionership became vacant he would be appointed to succeed Sutherland. Haughey agreed. After the Dick Burke fiasco of 1982, there was no way Haughey was going to reappoint a Fine Gael nominee. He wrote to Sutherland in November 1988 that he was not reappointing him as European Commissioner: 'you brought great credit to Ireland and there is widespread recognition of your achievements as Commissioner … I am personally grateful to you because of your willingness to give valuable advice to me and the government while maintaining your strict objectivity and independence as a member of the Commission.'[34] On the same day he wrote to European Commission President Jacques Delors informing him of MacSharry's nomination. MacSharry began his new position in Brussels in January 1989 and was replaced as Minister for Finance by Albert Reynolds. His loss was keenly felt by Haughey in the coalition government but was much appreciated in Brussels; Margaret Thatcher, for one, later told Haughey that he was doing a very good job.[35] The strangeness of Des O'Malley and Bobby Molloy being back in a cabinet chaired by Haughey did not stop the coalition governing relatively successfully, but tensions were evident in Fianna Fáil from the government's inception. Jackie Fahey, one of Haughey's original gang of five supporters in his leadership bid of 1979, resigned from the parliamentary party in July 1989 after not receiving a position of minister for state. Two years earlier he was equally embittered by being overlooked, telling Haughey he was 'disappointed, disillusioned, and hurt' by his omission and would have to reflect on his position in the party.[36] He was persuaded to stay on that occasion but his resignation from the parliamentary party after the coalition was announced presaged internal difficulties for Haughey that never went away.

The strategy Fianna Fáil had pursued since 1987 of enhancing international competitiveness through reduced taxation, cuts in public expenditure, and a drive for increased foreign direct investment through a consensual approach had the support, ideologically, of both Fine Gael and the Progressive Democrats. Now in government, Des O'Malley was to the fore in insisting on continuing to cut taxes and public expenditure. Fianna Fáil had a much wider constituency to address in remaining steadfast to their corporatist approach to macroeconomic planning. For Haughey, the key to continued growth and Fianna Fáil success at the ballot box was social partnership, and he was particularly anxious to keep both the trade union and the business communities happy. He also knew, however, that the state of the finances was still fragile. Notwithstanding his election statement that the public expenditure cuts were about to stop, he wrote to all ministers just two weeks after the government was formed to say that the country's economic and budgetary difficulties were not over and that 'any departure from a disciplined approach to public expenditure would be disastrous ... You should direct your officials to make every effort to reach agreement with Finance on savings and allocations.'[37] The direction to officials was to allow Haughey and his cabinet ministers to concentrate on what he described as major questions.

At the same time Haughey was telling Peter Cassells, the general secretary of ICTU, that he regarded the government's 'ongoing consultations with the trade union movement to be of vital importance to our economic and social development'.[38] It was a difficult balancing act. The austerity cuts implemented by his 1987 minority government, particularly in health, made the trade union movement increasingly wary of him. Over the course of the following eighteen months Haughey was forced to intervene on a number of occasions with both employers and unions to secure agreement on a successor to the Programme for National Recovery. Yet there was no stopping his zeal for public expenditure cuts. In June 1990, for example, he again wrote to all ministers that it was 'necessary to state categorically that there is no scope for any relaxation in our collective determination to maintain tight control on public spending'.[39]

Social partnership was driven from the Taoiseach's office and at times was held together by the sheer political will of Haughey. He was the political agent who kept the process going. The result was a new social partnership programme agreed in January 1991; the Programme for Economic and Social Progress. This programme had something for everyone. It was seen by the unions as underwriting growth and development, while the business and employers' groups were keen on its commitments to low taxation, low public spending and its strategy of pitching aggressively for foreign direct investment. Haughey used all the power available to him in seeking foreign direct investment. In June 1990, the head of the Industrial Development Authority (IDA), Kieran McGowan, thanked him for being 'generous with your own personal time given to IDA clients over the entire period. It has been extraordinarily helpful to our efforts with companies such as Seagate, Mistui and Intel.[40] When the agreement was finalised, Haughey wrote to Jacques Delors outlining its features on pay and the concomitant improvements in social services, including health, education and social welfare. He stressed that the whole agreement was underpinned by continued strict control of public expenditure, and a steady reduction in the national debt to GNP ratio with a target of 1:1 by 1993.[41]

Haughey had had a rather tempestuous relationship with Delors since returning to office in 1987. In February 1990, the European Commission had turned down Ireland's nomination of Andy O'Rourke as Director General of the Structural Funds and instead opted for Tom O'Dwyer, who was part of Ray MacSharry's cabinet. Haughey told Delors he was 'appalled by the decision made by the Commission' which, he said, was viewed in Ireland as a major affront to the Irish government and an insult to the views and proposals put forward by it.[42] A number of months earlier he had complained to Delors about what he saw as the Commission treating Ireland differently from Greece, Spain or Portugal with regard to structural funds. He told Delors that there would be 'a public outcry against this discrimination', and that the government would have to rethink its attitude towards European Monetary Union; a decision by the Commission to treat Ireland differently from other disadvantaged regions would represent a clear departure from the principle of social and economic cohesion.[43] Just three months earlier he had told Delors that his government fully accepted 'that an economic union requires closer co-ordination of macroeconomic policy'.[44] Haughey's various interactions with Delors and the European Commission made him somewhat of an unknown quantity for them when Ireland took the presidency of the European Council in January 1990 for a period of six months. At heart, Haughey was a pragmatic nationalist. His first instinct was to protect Irish interests above all else, and that is what drove his interactions with Delors.

THE EUROPEAN PRESIDENCY

Haughey prepared meticulously for the European presidency. His big idea was that it would be the 'green presidency', placing economic and social sustainability on a European footing.[45] Months of planning had gone into preparing a green agenda when the Berlin Wall fell and three months' work was changed immediately. Haughey realised that calls for German unification would be the dominant theme of the presidency.[46] After the Berlin Wall fell on 9 November 1989, the ministerial group on the European presidency met every weekend in Kinsaley to rework the agenda for the presidency. Notwithstanding the dramatic events in Eastern Europe, Haughey was still keen on pushing the green agenda, and Ireland's presidency came at a time of turmoil in Britain over its role in Europe. There would also be state and federal elections in West Germany, and what was expected to be significant French pressure to maintain the momentum on further European integration. The rapidly accelerating pace of events in Central and Eastern Europe would certainly raise fundamental questions about the direction of European Community policy, and Haughey would be at the centre of how it would respond.[47]

Haughey approached this huge challenge with what one of his civil servants described as a combination of 'good politics and grand gestures'.[48] The good politics was preparing the ground for his presidency by meeting with other European Community country leaders individually. The grand gesture was getting German unification on the agenda and ultimately gaining agreement, after an April 1990 meeting in Dublin, that this would be a positive factor in the overall development of the European Community. The presidency began with the European Commission visiting Dublin on the first weekend of January for a series of meetings to discuss with Haughey and his ministers the agenda for the following six months. The vice-president of the Commission, Sir Leon Brittan, described the organisation as faultless and the discussions as both practical and imaginative: 'everything seemed to contribute to a perfect start to the Irish presidency … the unique and happy combination of grandeur and informality was at its peak when the splendid dinner in the glorious setting of the Hospital Chapel culminated in us all singing "In Dublin's Fair City".[49] The period after the fall of the Berlin Wall was one of dramatic change in Europe. Prior to the beginning of the Irish presidency Haughey remarked that, coming from a divided country, many Irish people would have great sympathy with their German counterparts who wanted a united Germany. This was something that deeply divided the European Community. Margaret Thatcher was vehemently opposed to any concept of a united Germany, and France's François Mitterrand was no keener.

On 16 February 1990 Haughey wrote to each of the leaders of the member states of the European Community, and the Commission's president, Delors, to propose a special meeting of the European Council to consider the implications for the Community of developments in Central and Eastern Europe, in particular the unification of Germany, and for the Community's own integration process.[50] He had suggested this to the German chancellor, Helmut Kohl, three days earlier, telling him that he hoped the German people could regain their unity through free self-determination.[51] He then went on a tour of member state capitals, meeting with individual leaders to ascertain their views, before hosting a summit in Dublin on 28 April. In inviting the leaders to Dublin he told them that their main task would be to agree on broad guidelines and procedures to ensure that the integration of the territories of East Germany into the Community would be accomplished smoothly and harmoniously: 'We are all confident that unification will make a significant contribution to the development of Europe as a whole. I believe we should also make clear that the integration of the territories of the GDR will contribute to faster economic growth in the Community in conditions of economic balance and monetary security.'[52] At the end of that meeting it was agreed that the European Community issue 'an expression of political support for the unification of Germany under a European roof'.[53]

Two weeks after that April meeting of European leaders, Haughey spent an afternoon with the foreign editor of the *Irish Times*, Paul Gillespie, to discuss the European presidency and various Irish foreign policy initiatives. Hostility to Haughey in the *Irish Times* was still as pronounced as ever, but as part of Conor Brady's attempt to achieve greater balance he encouraged Gillespie to undertake a long interview with Haughey. Gillespie arranged the interview through P.J. Mara and sent over a list of questions a few days before meeting with Haughey on Tuesday 8 May. Haughey and Gillespie met on their own, without any officials, in his office in Government Buildings. Haughey replied to the questions spontaneously and without notes. They broke for leaders' questions and Haughey brought Gillespie with him to the Dáil chamber before they went back to Haughey's office to finish the interview.[54] The interview was published verbatim in the *Irish Times* on Saturday 12 May 1990 over two full pages. It is a clear account of Haughey's view of the presidency, the European Community, Ireland's foreign affairs, his leadership style, and his relations with his European counterparts. He described his relationship with Margaret Thatcher as always being good and that it was misleading to convey the impression that she was always seeking to be isolated. The *Irish Times* had devoted significant resources to Ireland's hosting of the European presidency and it was for Haughey the perfect outlet to articulate his views to a domestic audience as the presidency drew to a close.

The presidency ended with a major summit held in Dublin Castle on 25 and 26 June. It paved the way for the European Commission to negotiate the scale of an aid package for the economy of the Soviet Union, and produced a major declaration on the rights of all 320 million European Union citizens to a pollution-free environment. This was particularly important for Haughey, who had not completely forgotten about his green presidency. The summit also arranged for special inter-governmental conferences on economic and monetary union, and political union, to be held the following December and praised the achievements of the Irish presidency in making significant progress towards the abolition of all internal barriers to trade.[55] On the first night of the summit there was a major dinner in Malahide Castle where Haughey personally chose the menu and organised the seating plan. After the summit Margaret Thatcher wrote to Haughey to thank him for his hospitality during the summit and congratulated him on its success: 'Some of the discussion was fairly tough going. But once again, you showed a very sure touch as chairman and I thought your final press conference was masterly.' She also told him that she thought he would be glad of a rest and, in handwriting, thanked him for 'your thoughtful gifts especially the exquisite and unique porcelain flowers.'[56]

Haughey and Thatcher had met in Downing Street two weeks earlier on 13 June for a working lunch which lasted for three hours. It was Haughey's first time in Downing Street since the teapot summit of 1980. Described by the note-taker, Dermot Nally, as 'very relaxed and affable in tone', it was a bilateral meeting to discuss the upcoming summit. Haughey told Thatcher it would concentrate on political union, economic union, the environment, drugs, the seats of the institutions and, later, South Africa. Thatcher told him that sanctions against South Africa were totally irrelevant, to which Haughey replied that there was a general feeling that some sort of signal of support and encouragement for the South African Prime Minister, F.W. de Klerk was likely. In a sign of her growing resentment towards Europe, Thatcher described the European Commission as 'just a new Politburo' when it came to a discussion on structural funds. On economic and monetary union, she stated: 'If you give away your powers of taxation, you have lost your sovereignty. In talking of a single currency, Delors must have had a rush of blood to the head. We are not going to have a single currency.' But the crucial point for Haughey was that Thatcher had agreed with him that no further legislative powers should be given to the European Parliament. She was totally opposed to a Belgian/German proposal that powers of co-decision be given to the Parliament. Haughey considered this to be an appalling proposal and told Thatcher he did not want any more powers for the European Parliament, adding: 'We will be relying on you.'[57]

By the end of the European Council meeting, Haughey was in ebullient mood. Significant progress had been made on a whole range of issues and German reunification was in train. Helmut Kohl never forgot the input and help of Haughey. A few weeks after German unification, Kohl wrote to Haughey thanking him for his 'personal support' as acting president of the European Council and 'for the support of your government on our way to German unity'.[58] One of the last letters Haughey wrote as Taoiseach was to Kohl in February 1992, in which he told him that he felt privileged to be President of the European Council when there existed the possibility to facilitate the unity of Germany under the European roof. He added that the division of Ireland gave 'us Irish a particular understanding of the joy felt by the German people on the unification of their country. I myself, as the son of parents from the sundered part of our country, was especially conscious of how much unification by agreement and in peace can mean.'[59] Whatever about their joy at the prospect of German unification, the Irish people were themselves in ebullient mood during the European summit, when on its first day, the Irish football team beat Romania on penalties in the last sixteen of the World Cup. Thatcher had told Haughey he needed a rest. What better way than to go and support the team in the quarter final of the World Cup in Rome? It meant refusing the request of the President, Paddy Hillery, who also wanted to attend. Haughey was not going to be upstaged when millions across the globe, and practically the entire population of Ireland, would be watching.[60] On Saturday 30 June 1990, Haughey, basking in the glory of the Irish football team, seemed to be at the height of his power.

In preparing for the 1990 Fianna Fáil Ard Fheis held in March, P.J. Mara approached Terry Prone of Carr Communications, who had been advising Haughey and Fianna Fáil for a number of years, seeking some ideas for the leader's set piece speech. Prone replied that there was no need for their services as Haughey had everything he needed already at his disposal and knew 'bloody well the general public think he's basically playing a blinder'.[61] She pointed out that he had a lot in the plus column, including the economic strides out of the mud, the indication that something was beginning to happen in North–South relations, the European presidency, and the Environmental Action Plan. On the night Ireland lost 1-0 to Italy in Rome, Haughey was cheered wildly by the crowd. Progress on the variety of initiatives Prone had pointed to had transformed Haughey's fortunes from the disaster of the general election just a year previously. He was looking forward to the visit of Nelson Mandela to address the Oireachtas the following week. He had planned an evening's sailing with the American ambassador Richard Moore for later in the week.[62] His son Seán was completing a successful term as Lord Mayor of Dublin. Another of his sons, Conor, was getting married in October to Jackie McClafferty. At the end of August, Haughey led the welcoming party at Dublin Airport for the released hostage Brian Keenan, who had spent over 1,500 days in captivity in Lebanon and for whom Haughey and Gerry Collins as Minister for Foreign Affairs had spent months trying to negotiate his release. He was set to face the new Dáil term with confidence and expected that in just over two months' time he would be celebrating a Fianna Fáil win in the presidential election. He was, however, very much mistaken. By the time that election was over, his party had been split down the middle and a forty-year friendship with Brian Lenihan had been sundered as the events of the fall of the coalition government in late January 1982 erupted with a vengeance that set the scene for Haughey's eventual departure from Irish politics.

THE PRESIDENTIAL ELECTION

In January 1990 the Labour leader, Dick Spring, announced that there should be a contest for the presidency and he was prepared to be a candidate if necessary. This forced Haughey into a contest he did not want to fight. He would have been quite happy if the main parties could have agreed to a compromise candidate. The presidential elections of 1959, 1966 and 1973 were straightforward political contests between Fianna Fáil and Fine Gael, with the winner expected to play a 'father of the nation' ceremonial-type role. When Spring persuaded Mary Robinson to run it was clear that the 1990 contest would be different. She articulated a different vision for the presidency, forcing both Fianna Fáil and Fine Gael to advance their own concepts of the office. As Robinson was the first woman to run for the presidency it also brought a different dynamic to Ireland's first contest in seventeen years.

Robinson's entry into the fray was not initially seen by Fianna Fáil as a major threat to its hold on the presidency. When it became clear that there would be a contest, Brian Lenihan was anxious to run. Haughey was not so sure about the wisdom of this. Lenihan had missed the entirety of the 1989 general election campaign due to his hospitalisation in Minnesota for a successful liver transplant, and there were doubts in Fianna Fáil about whether he had the stamina for a campaign. Ray Burke and P.J. Mara were enthusiastic about a Lenihan candidacy and persuaded Haughey that he was unbeatable, given his long public service and appeal to neutrals.[63] Haughey was also keen to support his friend of many decades in his quest for the presidency, despite the view of some Lenihan supporters that he had encouraged John Wilson to seek the nomination. Wilson had his supporters in the party, including Rory O'Hanlon, but his late entry into the race put him at a serious disadvantage. On 17 September, Lenihan comfortably beat Wilson by fifty-one votes to nineteen for the party's nomination. Fianna Fáil expected him to win the presidency comfortably. So did the bookmakers, and for the first five weeks of the campaign he was an unbackable favourite. Fine Gael was in turmoil with both Garret FitzGerald and Peter Barry refusing invitations from the party leader, Alan Dukes, to stand. It eventually chose the former SDLP MP and Northern Ireland civil rights activist Austin Currie to be its candidate. Currie had only been elected a Fine Gael TD at the 1989 general election and his selection was widely seen as underwhelming. While Robinson was traversing the country advancing her alternative view of the presidency, the campaign was drifting towards what seemed the inevitable conclusion of a Lenihan victory. But his campaign was spectacularly derailed with just two weeks to go to polling day.

On what seemed to be a routine appearance on RTÉ's panel discussion programme *Questions and Answers*, Lenihan was blindsided when questioned about phone calls he was supposed to have made to President Hillery in his official residence at Áras an Uachtaráin on the night of the collapse of the Fine Gael–Labour coalition government in January 1982. On the programme Lenihan denied making calls to the president asking him not to dissolve the Dáil. Garret FitzGerald, a late replacement for Fine Gael on the panel, insisted that Lenihan did indeed make the calls. A UCD politics student, Jim Duffy, produced a recording of an interview he had conducted with Lenihan on 17 May 1990, in which Lenihan admitted making the calls. The Fianna Fáil campaign was in turmoil. Lenihan downplayed the controversy, describing it as a storm in a teacup.[64] In an ironic twist, Jim Duffy had actually written to Haughey in February 1990 seeking an interview for his research on the presidency at the same time as he contacted Lenihan. Haughey refused, pleading pressure of work.[65] On 4 October, a few weeks before the fateful programme, Duffy wrote to Lenihan with a list of quotes he was hoping to use in his thesis. He said that if there were any 'you would wish me not to use or else to use without giving the source's name in the footnotes please let me know'.[66] Now, just three weeks later, Duffy had made the tape available to the *Irish Times*.

An unsigned note prepared for Haughey outlined that Duffy had a background in Fine Gael, was well known to Garret FitzGerald, was close to Senator Maurice Manning, had worked as a speechwriter for Austin Currie and Mary Robinson, and was regarded by associates as both 'a bluffer and a boaster'.[67] It went on to say that Fine Gael had been pressuring Duffy to release the tape. The politics department in UCD was in turmoil over Duffy's recording, with two of its most senior members at odds. Maurice Manning advised him to publish it and Brian Farrell advised him against, as it was obtained for research and not for political purposes. The note gave the background to the existence of the tape, produced the relevant quotes, in which Lenihan stated that he had rung the Áras, and concluded that Duffy was said to be enjoying the notoriety of the affair. If this was perhaps unfair to the young student, the fact that the note was written at all and presented to Haughey reflected the panic in Fianna Fáil. Three days after *Questions and Answers*, Duffy appeared at a press conference organised by the *Irish Times*. A few hours later, Lenihan went on the *Six One* television news to deny making the calls. In a famous political moment he told the presenter, Seán Duignan, that on mature recollection he could confirm that he had not attempted to contact President Hillery and his statement to Duffy had been incorrect. He stared straight into the camera, as if appealing directly to the Irish people, much to the horror of his advisers.

Immense damage had, however, been done to Lenihan and Fianna Fáil by the contradiction between what Lenihan had told Duffy in May, and what he was telling the Irish people five months later. The day after his television interview Fine Gael put down a no confidence motion in the government and the Progressive Democrats decided that they could not continue in government if Lenihan remained a minister – it was a matter of standards in government.[68] Des O'Malley later said it was not a problem of his party's making but it was a very real problem.[69] It was certainly a real problem for Haughey, who was faced with the problem of backing Lenihan and going to the country, or sacrificing Lenihan and continuing his government. He chose the latter, having failed to persuade Lenihan to resign at a dramatic meeting in Abbeville, described by Bertie Ahern, who was also in attendance, as a stalemate where the strain on both men was telling.[70] According to his daughter, Eimear, Haughey was in total despair at this time.[71] He wanted to stand by Brian Lenihan, but doing so would result in a general election that would almost inevitably cost Fianna Fáil seats, and perhaps power as well. Haughey still had to persuade the Fianna Fáil parliamentary party to back his stance. After a tense meeting at which Fianna Fáil's divisions were laid bare, the parliamentary party agreed that to avoid an election Lenihan should be sacked as Tánaiste and Minister for Defence. Haughey duly exercised his constitutional prerogative and the government was saved. Some in Fianna Fáil, most notably Albert Reynolds and those who had not wanted to enter coalition in the first place, believed the party should back Lenihan and go to the country. But poor poll numbers for Lenihan persuaded the majority that fighting an election in a dank November over a candidate who was himself struggling would lead to disaster at the ballot box.

Self-preservation won out, but the long-term cost was high. Lenihan remained Fianna Fáil's candidate for president and polled credibly, topping the poll with 44 per cent of the vote, but Robinson comfortably beat him on transfers. Haughey had alienated many within Fianna Fáil by his brutal treatment of Lenihan at the behest of the hated Progressive Democrats. During that heated parliamentary party meeting which decided to back Haughey, the young Kildare TD Seán Power had asked him what would happen in six months' time when the Progressive Democrats came looking for the Taoiseach's head.[72] Power's timing was out, but only by a matter of months, and it was he who would deliver the first wounding blow on Haughey by tabling a motion of no confidence in the Taoiseach in November 1991, almost a year to the day since Fianna Fáil lost the presidency for the first time in its history.

ENDGAME

A post-mortem report for Fianna Fáil on its presidential defeat laid the reason for its defeat squarely at its inability to attract the youth vote. It noted that the party had no cohesive appeal to the younger half of the electorate. It warned that the result should not be dismissed as 'a once-off freak achievement by a rainbow coalition of desperate elements'.[73] A focus group of Ógra Fianna Fáil activists concluded that young people in general felt that Brian Lenihan was an ill politician, closely associated with Fianna Fáil, who wanted to retire to Áras an Uachtaráin. On the day of Brian Lenihan's defeat, Albert Reynolds, the most senior and most visceral opponent of coalition within Fianna Fáil, announced that once there was a vacancy for the leadership of the party he would be a candidate. It was an odd time to announce his intentions and was clearly aimed at Haughey. It initiated a year of practically open warfare within the party, with tension bordering on animosity, as Reynolds described it, between Haughey and himself.[74] Reynolds became much more truculent in his dealings with the Progressive Democrats and openly began to build support within Fianna Fáil for a leadership battle.

A report commissioned by Fianna Fáil from Peter Owens in the aftermath of its defeat recommended that Haughey would have to consider developing in the future a more collegial style of leadership. He should involve specific ministers with specific projects and he should encourage Fianna Fáil to initiate changes that would in any event be forced on him by societal pressures. Fianna Fáil should lead rather than follow. Owens made the point that on occasions, both publicly and privately, Haughey projected 'a stern forbidding image and perception', and he needed a warmer connection to the public.[75] But Haughey was sixty-five years of age and unlikely to change. The decision to coalesce with the Progressive Democrats had, if anything, made his own leadership style more presidential. He was not going to change his style at this stage on the advice of an advertising executive. He had just seen Margaret Thatcher resign in Britain. Both were the same age and had come to office within months of each other in 1979. Haughey was in Paris at a meeting of the Conference on Security and Co-operation in Europe, at which Ireland had observer status, when Thatcher beat off the challenge of Michael Heseltine for leadership of the Conservative Party on 20 November 1990. Her margin of victory was not large enough to avoid a second round. Haughey privately told a number of journalists who were with him in the Meurice Hotel, one of the most exclusive in Paris, where Haughey always stayed, that the result meant Thatcher was effectively gone. She would not have enough support to win a second round.[76] So it proved, and Thatcher resigned just two days later. Haughey had outlasted her, but her exit from the great stage of politics showed him how dangerous and unpredictable internal party politics could be. He had just come through his own bruising and losing battle and would soon have to prepare for another.

In 1991 electoral politics became worse for Fianna Fáil when it suffered significant losses in the June local elections. Its first preference vote share fell by seven points from its 1985 result to 37 per cent, well under the crucial 40 per cent it assumed was its bottom figure in any election. Moreover, its vote in Dublin fell from 42 per cent to 31 per cent. This was particularly ominous considering the importance of the capital in any general election contest. The party was becoming more heavily dependent on its traditional rural support to do well in elections as urban voters began to look elsewhere. Fianna Fáil's poor result was laid at the door of its Dublin Taoiseach by many of its members, while the rural Reynolds was increasingly seen as the man to bring the party back to the glory days of single-party government. Although Dublin would be a crucial battleground in the next general election, a groundswell of opinion in the party began to move away from Haughey being its leader in that election. The local elections were the third national elections in a row where the Fianna Fáil share of the vote had been worse than expected and the blame was being laid at the door of its leader.

Haughey's woes were not, however, consigned to electoral politics. His status as Taoiseach itself was becoming severely undermined by an increasingly worrying number of scandals in the late summer of 1991 in which the government he led was embroiled. Haughey was friendly with a number of senior businessmen such as the beef baron Larry Goodman, the chairman of the semi-state sugar company Greencore Bernie Cahill, and the paper tycoon and chairman of Telecom Éireann Michael Smurfit. All of them had easy access to the Taoiseach; and the government seemed readily helpful to all of them.[77]

At the end of May the government established a tribunal to inquire into malpractice in the Irish beef processing industry, mainly centred on Goodman International, owned and controlled by Larry Goodman. Haughey had been friendly with Goodman for some time and had used Goodman's private jet for a trip to London not long after becoming Taoiseach in March 1987.[78] The Goodman group, which had been backed by Haughey's government, with both IDA grants and an export credit insurance scheme, went into examinership following the Iraqi invasion of Kuwait in August 1990. Various departmental and media investigations following complaints by Goodman's competitors uncovered multiple irregularities, including the sourcing of non-commercial beef outside Ireland. This led to the establishment of the tribunal, which drove another wedge between Haughey and O'Malley. In January of 1989 Haughey had provided a letter of reference for Goodman to the presidents of Angola and the Congo, respectively, when Goodman was seeking new markets in Africa. Haughey stated that Goodman was 'a businessman of the highest integrity and ability. His company is one of our most important and successful agri-businesses and he is the largest exporter of meat in Europe.'[79]

Irregularities in relation to the establishment of Greencore, the state purchase of Carysfort Training College in Blackrock, for use by UCD, and the purchase of a site on the old Johnston, Mooney and O'Brien premises in Ballsbridge by Telecom Éireann, for what seemed a vastly over-inflated sum, brought allegations of a golden circle of crony capitalists into the public sphere. All were tangentially linked to Haughey. Although Haughey denied any impropriety he was placed on the political defensive. The reality was that Haughey was not involved in any of these transactions but he faced a hostile media which was quick to insinuate that he was somehow playing a central role in a corrupt golden circle enriching itself at the public's expense. He was not. Yet two electoral defeats in just over six months, and his name being linked to scandals involving cronyism, left Haughey very vulnerable. In late September 1991, on national radio, he called on the chairman of Telecom Éireann, Michael Smurfit, and the chairman of the Customs House Docks Authority, Séamus Paircéir, to step aside until the investigation into Telecom Éireann's property dealings was completed. Paircéir was a director of the private sector company United Property Holdings, which had originally bought the former Johnston, Mooney and O'Brien site at Ballsbridge and then sold it on to Telecom Éireann. Both Paircéir and Smurfit were outraged by Haughey's call for them to stand aside. They were not the only ones.

Haughey's actions raised the ire of Noel Dempsey, the backbench TD from Meath, who wrote to the Taoiseach to say it 'was a poor recompense to the two men in question who, as you admitted yourself, had contributed enormously to the state over the years.' He added that he found it inexplicable that Haughey felt the two men should be asked to step aside when he did not express the same opinion about Bernie Cahill.[80] Cahill was also chairman of a mining company called Feltrim, which was owned by Haughey's son Conor. The same day Dempsey, with three other Fianna Fáil backbenchers – Seán Power, Liam Fitzgerald and M.J. Nolan – issued a statement expressing their growing disquiet with Haughey's leadership and criticising him for what they termed his incomprehensible handling of the Telecom Éireann land deal controversy. Dempsey insisted they were not stalking horses for Albert Reynolds.[81] The following day, the *Irish Independent* published a poll showing Fianna Fáil support at 41 per cent and Haughey's personal satisfaction rating at just 35 per cent, down thirteen points since June.[82] The pressure on Haughey internally in Fianna Fáil was growing.

After a difficult renegotiation of the programme for government in October 1991, where the Progressive Democrats once more threatened to pull out of government, and Albert Reynolds said that they should be let go, an agreement was reached only after Bertie Ahern secured an uneasy compromise between the two government parties. By November of 1991, Reynolds had had enough and launched a rather strange leadership by proxy bid. The main positive of putting the Fianna Fáil party through another leadership challenge was that this time it was in essence organised by many of those who had actually supported Haughey in the 1979 leadership election and thus it could be painted as a 'saving the party' initiative. The main negative of the challenge was that its supporters were very much of the conservative, rural, country and western wing of the party. They were accused by Haughey's supporters of acting out of personal ambition and bitterness following the formation of the coalition government and were hardly likely to regain political support in the large cities, where Fianna Fáil's vote was most at risk. On Bertie Ahern's advice, Haughey revealed to a parliamentary party meeting that he would step down after overseeing the 1992 budget, but this was not enough for Reynolds.

On 6 November 1991, following an extremely bitter and acrimonious parliamentary party meeting, a no confidence motion in Haughey proposed by Seán Power was tabled and Reynolds immediately said he would support it. Haughey promptly sacked him from government and also brusquely dismissed Pádraig Flynn, the Minister for the Environment, and a number of junior ministers, including Máire Geoghegan-Quinn, all of whom stated they would support the motion. Geoghegan-Quinn believed that Haughey had simply gone on too long and was damaging the party.[83] One of the party's new TDs, Micheál Martin from Cork City, who had been elected for the first time in the 1989 general election, described the atmosphere in the parliamentary party as poisonous.[84] Haughey's legendary survival skills moved into gear again and he began to meet individual backbench TDs, including Martin, in a bid to shore up his support in the parliamentary party.

Haughey still had strong support from many senior figures, including Bertie Ahern, whose job it was to secure the votes for a Haughey victory; Brian Lenihan, now back in the Haughey fold after the humiliation of the presidential election; Mary O'Rourke; Ray Burke; and Gerry Collins, who made an emotional appeal on television to Albert Reynolds not to burst the party. On Saturday 9 November, in the last of the four unsuccessful heaves against his leadership, the no confidence motion in Haughey was defeated by fifty-five votes to twenty-two. It was another marathon session of the parliamentary party. It began at 11.30 a.m. in the Fianna Fáil party rooms on the fifth floor of Leinster House and did not end until after 3.15 the following morning. It was split into two sessions. The first debated whether there would be an open vote or a secret ballot. Much as in previous heaves, Haughey was successful in ensuring an open vote. The second half of the meeting debated Power's no confidence motion. It began at 4 p.m. Haughey, who was in agony with his recurrent kidney stone problem, sat through the eleven hours of debate and did not speak.[85] In the course of his speech, Albert Reynolds claimed dirty tricks had been used against him and he had been under surveillance, in particular by a white HiAce van, at his Ballsbridge home.[86] Notwithstanding Haughey's victory, none of his supporters felt that he could go on for much longer.[87]

This feeling became even stronger when Fianna Fáil, and the government, quickly lurched into another crisis. Haughey, in his reshuffle of ministers, decided to appoint Dr James McDaid, a relatively unknown Donegal backbencher, to the position of Minister for Defence. McDaid's appointment came as a shock all across Fianna Fáil, including to himself: 'I would have been overjoyed had I been promoted to a junior post but when Mr. Haughey told me that he was appointing me to the cabinet as Minister for Defence I was left speechless.'[88] Then a photograph, taken in March 1990, emerged. It showed a smiling McDaid alongside an IRA suspect and constituent of his, James Pius Clarke, outside the Four Courts after the Supreme Court ruled against extraditing Clarke to Northern Ireland. The Progressive Democrats once again threatened to leave the government unless the McDaid appointment was withdrawn. McDaid took the initiative and told Haughey that he wanted to withdraw his name before it went before the Dáil for what would in effect have been a confidence motion in the government. Why McDaid was promoted at all remained unanswered. P.J. Mara attributed it to Haughey, emboldened after his party win, being of the view that it was his cabinet and he would appoint who he wanted. McDaid was smart and from an important constituency, but once the Progressive Democrats came after him, Haughey once again was left with no choice but to succumb to their demands. The journalist John Waters, who had conducted a *Hot Press* interview with Haughey in 1984 famous for the then leader of the opposition's liberal use of expletives, thought that, like most of Haughey's promotions to cabinet, it was part of a pattern whereby people were promoted 'not on the basis of their abilities or personal qualities but precisely because they were the kind of people whom nobody else would have promoted. They owed their entire positions and standing to him and he hoped that this would be sufficient to buy off a form of pragmatic loyalty for as long as he needed it.'[89]

The government continued, but Haughey's credibility both in the parliamentary party and its grassroots was seriously diminished. He was seen as being unable to stand up to the Progressive Democrats, all in the name of keeping himself in office. Most of those who had voted for Haughey just four days earlier were dismayed by the latest turn of events.[90] It was clear that Haughey was nearing the end. As Waters pointed out, now that Haughey had been significantly wounded, 'the smell of blood from his political position means that the kill will not be long in coming.'[91] Haughey was losing support in the parliamentary party, and the grassroots, so long his most stable of crutches, was heartily sick of the Progressive Democrats. Two months later Seán Doherty dropped his tapes bombshell and Haughey was gone.

CHAPTER 22

THE PULSE OF THE NATION

I'VE HAD MY NINE LIVES

On 30 January 1992, Charles Haughey announced his intention to stand down as leader of Fianna Fáil and as Taoiseach. He had been the dominant figure in Irish politics for twelve years, but from the time of the Doherty revelations it was clear that his political journey was at an end. Despite his busy agenda on social partnership and Northern Ireland, the previous year had been a difficult one for him. He had a fraught relationship with Mary Robinson. Four days after her inauguration as president, she wrote to Haughey thanking him for the splendid arrangements made by the government for her inauguration, and 'for the many courtesies that you extended to me and my family on the day and in the period since my election'.[1] Denis Corboy, the former director of the Irish Council of the European Movement, had told him before the inauguration that Robinson was manageable during the days when Haughey was Chairman of the EEC Committee in the Dáil in the early 1970s because 'she is an admirer of yours and I tell you this on the best authority.'[2]

As far back as 1976, when Robinson was a member of the Seanad, she had written to Haughey asking him to become a member of the

Oireachtas lobby for the preservation of civil liberties. This was to be composed of members of all parties who shared a deep concern that despite the stresses and strains on the country at present, 'our civil liberties should not be diminished or eroded.'[3] He politely declined, saying, 'I do not as a matter of practice become a member of lobbies. I am, however, in sympathy with your purposes and I would hope you will not hesitate to let me know when my support might be of assistance in regard to any particular matter.'[4] Yet, during the first year of her presidency, Haughey and Robinson had a turbulent relationship. She would later state that the most difficult encounters with Taoisigh during her tenure as president were with Haughey.[5] These came to a head when the government asked her not to deliver the BBC Dimbleby Lecture on the position of women and the family in Ireland. She accepted this advice without forcing a confrontation but was resentful of it. As her authorised biographers, Helen Lucy Burke and Olivia O'Leary, pointed out, the Constitution says nothing about government vetoes over interviews or other speeches.[6] In June 1991, Robinson wrote to Haughey outlining her concern about publicity given to her invitation to deliver the Dimbleby lecture. She told him that she did not know how the matter came to be disclosed in the media: 'I am satisfied that no member of my staff was involved … At no time was any information given to the media by my staff about consultations with government, or even about whether such consultations took place.'[7] She felt it was time to reassess the procedures for dealing with invitations that required consultation with, and approval of, the government. She looked forward to considering any proposal he felt was appropriate in that regard. Haughey's reply was perfunctory. He said that he too was concerned about the recent publicity, and that they could discuss the matter at their next meeting.[8] Her activist approach to what the President could and could not do was certainly not to Haughey's liking. As far as he was concerned the Dimbleby lecture was a political one that had always been delivered by a political figure; it was unprecedented that a head of state would deliver such a talk.

The scandals that had engulfed the government in the second half of 1991 and the vote of no confidence motion that November had wearied

Haughey. By the time of Doherty's tapes allegation, he was becoming increasingly isolated. The two people who spent most time with him in the fortnight between the Doherty revelation and his decision to resign were P.J. Mara and the Fianna Fáil chief whip, Dermot Ahern. Both urged him to continue. On the eve of Haughey's press conference to deny Doherty's allegations, Ahern told him that he would contact his ministers and ensure a show of strength on the day. Haughey replied that he was going to do it on his own. Ahern told him it was a mistake not to have his ministers around him; it would be the normal thing to show unity and being on his own would project an image of isolation and siege. Haughey refused. Ahern later suggested to Haughey that he might consider a motion of censure against Doherty at the parliamentary party, but Haughey again said no. On the night before making his statement of resignation, Haughey summoned Ahern to his office and told him that he was going. Ahern just shook his head. When he went home to Dundalk he told his wife, Maeve: 'I can't quite believe it. The great survivor, the cat with the nine lives is gone.' A few days earlier, Bertie Ahern went to Abbeville to update him on the difficulties with the Progressive Democrats over the tapes and to discuss Haughey's intentions. Haughey, however, had had enough. He shook his head and told Ahern: 'I've had my nine lives.'[10]

In late October 1991, after the programme for government had been renegotiated, Haughey told the Fianna Fáil parliamentary party that one of the most difficult questions of leadership was to know the right time to pass on the baton. In his handwritten notes for that meeting Haughey said it would be unreal if he were to address the party and ignore what was being said about his own position as leader. He crossed out the word 'happening' and replaced it with 'being said'. He wrote that it was not an easy matter to talk about but he hoped to do it without emotion or ill-feeling or without personalising it in any way. He crossed out the word 'rancour'. He told his colleagues that he believed he had 'sufficient experience and objectivity garnered over many years to take that decision in the best interests of the party, not the media or anyone outside. I will also take advice and weigh all the factors. My decision will be taken calmly and objectively, entirely on the basis of what will be best for the party.'[11] Many of those watching him that day, including Albert Reynolds, believed that, notwithstanding those words, he would never go voluntarily. But by late January 1992, his experience told him that his time was indeed up.

In the early morning of 30 January, Haughey sat down at his desk at Abbeville and wrote in longhand block capitals the resignation speech he would give to the parliamentary party the following day. He wrote that in particular he needed to face the fact that there was a great deal of uncertainty and confusion, which was not doing the party or the country any good: 'It would be wrong of me to let it continue; drag on indefinitely or indeed much longer. I am deeply grateful to those thousands who have asked me to stay on.' He crossed out the words 'kept faith' twice, and did the same in a paragraph reading: 'Despite the massive, relentless, venomous campaign waged against me personally for such a long time.' He also deleted a reference to his own election in 1979, when outlining the timetable for choosing his successor. In his handwritten notes, Haughey went on to outline how he looked back on his tenure in Fianna Fáil with pride and a 'deep sense of history', how central to his life the Fianna Fáil parliamentary party meetings were: 'here one could feel the pulse of the nation.' He rejected the specious criticisms of the opposition and the media, writing that Fianna Fáil had 'always been better at economic management. Quicker to identify the need for and to pursue social reform.'[12] Yet, by the time he arrived in Government Buildings later that morning, Haughey had changed his mind on the speech he would give at the parliamentary party. He reduced it to a simple outline of the position since October, a declaration that he was standing down as leader and Taoiseach, an outline of the procedures to elect his successor, and a note of 'deep and sincere gratitude for your support and loyalty'. He finished by seeking unity within the party for his successor and a statement that although there were many difficulties as well as successes, overall an enormous amount had been achieved for the country and its people.[13] With that he was gone.

On the day after making his resignation statement, the Haughey family celebrated the wedding of Ciarán to Laura Daly at a marquee in the grounds of Abbeville, in the company of some three hundred guests. After the celebrations, Haughey had ten days left as Taoiseach before the power in which he had invested so heavily over the previous decades would be handed on to Fianna Fáil's new leader. Haughey was desperate that Albert Reynolds not succeed him and urged Bertie Ahern to run. His fellow Dubliner decided not to risk defeat and stayed out of the contest, having reached an understanding that Reynolds would serve for at most six years. Reynolds beat Mary O'Rourke and Michael Woods in a landslide and was duly elected leader of Fianna Fáil. Five days later, on 11 February 1992, he was elected Taoiseach. Haughey was dismayed, but he had one very important job to do – to brief Reynolds on the embryonic peace process and the fact that there had been talks with Sinn Féin. Right up until his last days as Taoiseach, Haughey was being briefed both by the Minister for Foreign Affairs, Gerry Collins, and various officials on how to resume the Northern Ireland party talks. Albert Reynolds recounted that the briefing between Haughey and himself was brief, efficient and to the point. On Northern Ireland, Haughey simply told him: 'Ask Mansergh.'[14]

The day after Reynolds was elected leader of Fianna Fáil, Haughey went west to Sligo to inspect progress on the Ballinamore and Ballyconnell Canal restoration project, which he had opened back in November 1990. In those last few days his office frantically sought to clear his correspondence. One of the final letters issued from his office was to British Prime Minister John Major, whom he thanked for his generous tribute to Ireland's presidency of the European Community in 1990. He ended by expressing hope that their paths would cross again.[15] The day before leaving office, Haughey received a comprehensive update from the secretary to the government, Dermot Nally, on ongoing discussions between British and Irish civil servants on developments in Northern Ireland. Nally told him that there was no likelihood of any progress in advance of the British general election, which was expected to take place in April. Nally added that the British were less than happy with the proposals in Draft 2, and that if any progress were to be made on those proposals they would need considerable modification. He told Haughey that the British said that 'this course could only be embarked on if there were a clear understanding that there would be no direct contact with the Provos, and that the process would lead to a secure and deliverable cessation of violence.'[16] It was a rather downbeat end to Haughey's efforts as Taoiseach to secure peace in Northern Ireland.

EXIT

After Haughey's announcement that he was stepping down, a torrent of letters arrived at Abbeville wishing him well. The RTÉ broadcaster Gay Byrne, who had long tried and failed to get Haughey to sit down with him on the *Late Late Show*, wrote to say how sorry he was to see him leaving office, especially since he thought 'the basis of your going seems to me to be all wrong. But then, when enough Lilliputians start heaving on the ropes.'[17] Byrne told Haughey that he suspected he was about to enter the most enjoyable period of his whole life, with time to savour the many things he had had to forego through the years. He could not have been more wrong. There were hundreds of other letters in a similar vein. The manager of U2, Paul McGuinness, told him: 'You must be quite annoyed to have been thwarted by a bunch of pygmies.'[18] One letter that would have particularly pleased Haughey was from the director of the National Gallery, Raymond Keaveney: 'Through your steadfast support for the arts and your insistence that they receive proper funding you have given back to the people of Ireland, a sense of pride in their heritage and their public institutions.'[19] He received a similar letter from Pat Wallace, the director of the National Museum of Ireland, who told him that his interest in and support for archaeology in Ireland was without parallel: 'Your knowledge of and sympathy for our material culture are also unique.'[20] Acknowledgement from people in the arts community was always appreciated by Haughey. On a visit to Harvard University in April of 1988 the great poet Seamus Heaney was unable to meet up with Haughey due to conflicting schedules but inscribed for him a copy of his anthology *The Sounds of Rain*: 'With high regard for your commitment to the arts in Ireland and for the place of writing.'[21] Another writer, UCD's professor of English, Gus Martin, who was a close friend of Haughey's, and whom he had appointed chair of the Abbey Theatre, told him that he must 'have a deep sense of loss, but your irrepressible spirits and your robust sense of irony won't allow you a long period of mourning'.[22]

From across the political aisle, Enda Kenny quoted *Paradise Lost*: 'What though the field be lost, all is not lost – the indomitable spirit and hatred for revenge and courage never to submit or yield.' He attached a copy of the W.B. Yeats poem 'The People', telling Haughey to remember that there would always be a place for him in the west of Ireland.[23] The Archbishop of Dublin, Desmond Connell, told Haughey that he 'greatly admired your dignified bearing in the midst of an unprecedented onslaught against an Irish head of government'.[24] Frank McDonald of the *Irish Times* reminded Haughey that whatever else he may have done or not done, 'There is one thing that cannot be taken away from you – viz. your decisive role in saving the Temple Bar area of Dublin.' In the 1987 general election Haughey had told a meeting of the steering committee of a group calling itself the Dublin Crisis Conference that Temple Bar was one of the oldest, most historic, most traditional parts of Dublin. It had to be preserved and he would not let CIÉ near the place.[25] The director of Temple Bar properties, Laura Magahy, paid tribute to the way he helped bring about the development of Temple Bar: 'Without your personal commitment and your enthusiasm for this project I feel that it would never have got off the ground.'[26] This was indeed true. A number of years earlier, U2's lead singer, Bono, had written to Haughey telling him to check out the Temple Bar area of Dublin, which he described as being Dublin's Left Bank, reminiscent of Greenwich Village in New York, and asking him not to let it be turned into an area which would be redeveloped for 'bus stations, shopping centre, etc, etc …. Yawn. This would be a great shame, indeed a tragedy at a time when Dubliners are starting to hold their heads high.'[27] Haughey replied that he was sorry that Bono's letter was very nearly swallowed by the bureaucracy and had, only now, just a few months later been retrieved. He told the singer that the government had ordered CIÉ not to proceed with their plans for a transport terminal and that he was very interested in Bono's description of Temple Bar as Ireland's Left Bank.[28] In retirement Haughey would look back at the redevelopment of Temple Bar as one of his government's major cultural achievements.

Peter Sutherland, whom he had known from as far back as the arms trial, told him that he was struck by a comment Haughey had made some years ago about being unable to imagine life without politics, and while he was sure politics would remain important for Haughey, he was also convinced that there were many other areas of life that Haughey could contribute to. Wishing him well in the next stage of his life, he added, 'I cannot imagine you spending it in the garden!'[29]

The immediate next stage for Haughey was his farewell speech as Taoiseach to the Dáil. He followed his usual routine that day of waking early and walking around the grounds at Abbeville before being collected by his driver, Max Webster, and driven into Government Buildings. Haughey had opened the building, refurbished throughout 1990 by the Office of Public Works with a budget of some £17.6 million, in January 1991. The refurbishment project won a number of awards, including the Silver Medal for Conservation from the Royal Institute of the Architects of Ireland for the period 1987–1992. Its citation read, 'The re-use of this existing building of acknowledged quality for this new, and entirely fitting, purpose has created a special identity of government, and has contributed considerably to Dublin's status as a European capital.'[30] After John Major visited Haughey in December 1991 he wrote that he was 'enormously impressed by, and jealous of, your accommodation'.[31] During its design and construction, furnishing and decoration, Haughey was very much involved in watching over the redevelopment of Government Buildings, insisting on the use of Irish materials, especially Irish timber, which, according to his friend, the architect Austin Dunphy, he particularly loved, and employing Irish artists and craftsmen, whenever possible.[32]

Now, less than two months later, at just before 11 a.m. on Tuesday 11 February 1992, Haughey took the short walk from his office in the magnificent building through an internal tunnel into the Dáil chamber to deliver his final speech in Dáil Éireann, after a career spanning some thirty-five years. In his brief speech, after saying that he had always sought to act solely and exclusively in the best interests of the Irish people, he continued: 'I might quote, perhaps, *Othello*. "I have done the state some service; they know't. No more of that."' He ended by saying that it was not the time to outline any special list of claims or achievements: 'Let the record speak for itself. If I were to seek any accolade as I leave office it would simply be he served the people, all the people, to the best of his ability.'[33] The speech in *Othello* that Haughey quoted ends with the great tragic hero killing himself with his own sword. And there was a sense in Haughey of being forced to fall on his sword before his time had come. It was, as Declan Kiberd pointed out, a statement of pride, but also of some bitterness.[34] After his speech he went back to his office, received a mass bouquet from the cleaning staff to have a mass said for him every day for the rest of his life, and shared a tear with his personal assistant, Catherine Butler.[35]

He then returned to Abbeville, where more piles of post arrived over the next few weeks. Perhaps the one that brought him most enjoyment was that from Joyce Andrews, wife of the late Todd Andrews, who praised a piece by Nuala O'Faolain in the *Irish Times* supplement on the day he announced his retirement. Andrews claimed that O'Faolain's piece summed up the problem many people had with Charles Haughey: 'what John Mitchel referred to as the "genteel dastards" in their villas in Foxrock who feel they should be running the country resenting bitterly the like of yourself.' She told him that there was a lot of Shakespeare floating around during your 'Götterdämmerung' and quoted Lear to Cordelia: 'and we'll live, and pray, and sing, and tell old tales, and laugh at gilded butterflies, and hear poor rogues talk of court news, and we'll talk with them too, who loses and who wins, who's in, who's out.'[36] Some days after he resigned Haughey hosted a dinner in Abbeville for some of the senior civil servants who had worked most closely with him over the years, including Dermot Nally, Pádraig Ó hUiginn and Noel Dorr. Dorr remarked, 'You, more than most, valued the sense of commitment which is still evident in senior ranks of the public service.'[37]

RETIREMENT

Once Haughey's postbag lightened, he settled down to what he hoped would be a relatively active retirement. In late 1995 he told one of his correspondents, 'My own recent experience has emphasised for me very clearly how important it is that everyone should endeavour from an early stage to build up an interest in things outside their principal occupation so that they can turn to them when they retire.'[38] He had been diagnosed with prostate cancer in late 1994 but was told that it would be manageable and that he would not need an operation. Notwithstanding the shock of that diagnosis, Haughey's retirement was centred on his pastimes of sailing, horse riding and horse racing, holidays in France, and time in Inishvickillane. And for four years he did enjoy this life. He particularly enjoyed going to the South of France, once telling Tony O'Reilly that he thought Cannes 'the most civilised place in our modern world'.[39] He had famously gone to Paris for an eight-hour trip on Sunday 26 July 1987 to see Dublin's Stephen Roche win the Tour de France. Haughey flew to Paris on Sunday morning, and enjoyed lunch at the Irish embassy. As the peloton entered the city, Haughey joined French Prime Minister Jacques Chirac in a car that followed the cyclists up and down the Champs-Élysées. Haughey later described it as 'one of the greatest experiences of my life. It is one of my favourite cities… the atmosphere, the excitement. It was just unbelievable.'[40] As Chirac pulled the winning yellow jersey over Roche's head on the podium, Haughey was on his other side clutching a toy lion before lifting the victorious cyclist's hand high in the air. Roche proclaimed that he felt 'very emotional when I met Mr. Haughey and heard our national anthem'.[41]

The birth of Haughey's first grandchild in 1993 brought him and Maureen great joy. On the sporting front, the crowning glory was the triumph of his horse Flashing Steel in the 1995 Irish Grand National at Fairyhouse. The previous year, Vincent O'Brien had remarked to Haughey that he was 'delighted that you have a horse of the calibre of Flashing Steel to carry your colours'.[42] In May 1995 he went to the Scottish FA Cup final at Hampden Park as a guest of Dermot Desmond to see Celtic beat Airdrie 1-0 and win their first trophy for six years.[43] He appeared on the

RTÉ television programme *Kenny Live* in December 1994 and received a rousing reception from the audience. He followed political events at home and abroad closely. He went to Washington in January 1993 to attend the inauguration of Bill Clinton. At home, he was dismayed by the fortunes in Fianna Fáil. He considered the result of the November 1992 election a disaster for Fianna Fáil and the country.[44] He was withering in his verdict on his successor, Albert Reynolds, telling one correspondent that he was 'observing current political developments with some detachment but also with a great deal of discouragement'.[45] At Christmas 1992, he had a card from Michael Healy-Rae and replied that he 'did not find the current scene very encouraging'.[46] The *Evening Herald* wanted him to write a regular column but he turned down the offer on the grounds that he was of 'too kindly a nature, too charitable a disposition, too restrained in judgement, too generous of spirit to make even a passable columnist'.[47]

When the IRA ceasefire was called in September 1994 Haughey received a letter from Bishop Edward Daly thanking him for his important contribution to the peace process: 'I know that you were very involved in its initiation. The "priest from Belfast" was in regular contact with me throughout the process and he advised me of your involvement and he deeply appreciated your constant encouragement and support at times when the process was not popular.[48] Haughey replied that he greatly appreciated Daly's generous words: 'I am very glad that I was able to play a part. I am very conscious of the crucial part played by Fr. Reid, your good self, both cardinals and a number of others.[49] John Hume was another who paid tribute to him for his role in the search for peace in Northern Ireland. On the occasion of Haughey's seventieth birthday in September 1995, Hume wrote to 'express my deep appreciation for all that you did for the North during your time as Taoiseach and in particular the very crucial role that you played in developing the present peace process'.[50] When Hume was jointly awarded the Nobel Peace Prize in 1998, Haughey wrote to warmly congratulate him; he was 'overjoyed for Pat and your good self at the news. After the long years of disappointments and setbacks your dedicated and sustained efforts have now been fully recognised by this historic award.'[51]

He was often called on by journalists and academics to assist with research for books and television documentaries and did so, sometimes on the basis of anonymity; at other times he was happy to be cited publicly. Among those he met with were John Horgan for his biographies of Seán Lemass and Noël Browne, Kevin Rafter for his biography of Martin Mansergh and Ed Moloney for various works. For Justin O'Brien's book on the arms trial, Haughey refused to talk about the trial but gave general background on Fianna Fáil. There were many others, including Finola Kennedy, for her ground-breaking work on family change in Ireland, and a number of research students working on various aspects of his career, including Des O'Malley's son, Eoin, who was working on a PhD on cabinet government at Trinity College, Dublin. He met with Eunan O'Halpin and Anne Dolan of Trinity about his archive. He eventually sent his constituency files to Trinity and donated his personal papers to Dublin City University. In December 1994, he spoke to John Ware from the BBC's *Panorama* programme, 'without details or attribution', for a documentary on Gerry Adams.[52] The month before, he launched a biography of Seán Lemass by Michael O'Sullivan, stating that Lemass's 'leadership was self-assured and confident. There was a certainty of purpose, clear lines of authority and action. You knew where you stood.'[53] He would have liked to believe that the same would have been said about himself.

A number of people encouraged him to write his autobiography. Others sought help from him with biographies they were thinking of writing or television and radio programmes they wished to make about him. In early 1994, the journalist Emily O'Reilly wrote to ask him whether he would be interested in co-operating with her on writing a book about his life. He replied that he was not ready to undertake such a project but would keep it in mind: 'I do appreciate the courtesy of your approach in contrast to that of others who went ahead without even deigning to mention their intentions to me.'[54] A number of months later he rejected a request from the film producer Emmet Power, who suggested that they work on a television film of his life.[55] In June 1998, Cathal O'Shannon visited Abbeville with Fred O'Donovan, the former chair of the RTÉ Authority, to try to persuade Haughey to take part in a full one-on-one sit-down interview with O'Shannon. O'Shannon said, 'It would be almost criminal if the television archives of this state did not include a long, well-thought-out programme in which you would comment on your life and times ... What we would attempt to achieve would be a revealing portrait of a man of huge stature whose imprint on life in Ireland during the latter party of this century is indelible.'[56] Haughey was interested but asked for some time to think about it. A year later O'Shannon returned, but Haughey had changed his mind. The RTÉ radio producer Kay Sheehy was next to try. She visited Abbeville in July 1999 to ask if Haughey would appear on a programme called *Powerful Shadows*, which would cover his life and times. Again, he refused. On the letter where Sheehy had outlined a number of options for the interview, Haughey jotted: 'Spoke to Kay and told her I didn't want to do it.'[57]

In early 2000 he had discussions with the renowned film and theatre producer Noel Pearson, about a proposed documentary of his life. Pearson wanted agreement from RTÉ on the documentary before filming began. In March that year, Pearson sent Haughey a detailed outline of how he expected the documentary to look. It was, in essence, to be a full treatment of Haughey's life from his birth to what Pearson described as his 'fall from grace'.[58] Pearson had a film researcher and a director of photography lined up, but the documentary never materialised. In early 2004, the Mint Productions team of Miriam O'Callaghan and Steve Carson contacted Haughey about a documentary they proposed to do on his life. They went out to Abbeville on a dozen occasions in the early months of 2004, always at 7.30 a.m., and had detailed discussions with him about appearing in front of the camera. O'Callaghan found him extremely witty and without bitterness. At one stage they were convinced that he would appear, but in the end, much to their disappointment, he decided not to participate.[59] Although Haughey himself refused to appear, he did encourage three of his children, Eimear, Conor, and Seán, and his brother, Fr Eoghan, to participate. Two of his assistants, Catherine Butler and Niamh O'Connor, also agreed to take part after first talking to him.[60] He wanted to get his side of his own story across.

The four-part documentary *Haughey* appeared on RTÉ in summer 2005 on RTÉ, achieving record viewing figures for a documentary. It featured interviews with friends, enemies, political supporters and opponents and managed to successfully capture the ambiguity that surrounded Haughey throughout his life, although many of his critics felt it was too soft on him.[61]

The one programme Haughey did agree to take part in was Seán Ó Mórdha's *Seven Ages*. In October 1998, Ó Mórdha visited Haughey in Abbeville to discuss his landmark seven-part series on the development of the independent Irish state. He then sent Haughey a detailed outline of the shape the documentary was to take. Haughey asked Pádraig Ó hUiginn for his views on Ó Mórdha's vision for the programme and his own contribution. Ó hUiginn told Haughey that Ó Mórdha was far too focused on political issues, and that any historic view of Ireland since independence should surely concentrate on economic and social achievements: 'Starting much later, we have caught up on Switzerland and Denmark by our ability and enlightened government.' He commented that the historian Joe Lee's seminal book on twentieth-century Ireland, published in 1989, was 'a most uninformed view of our achievements'.[62] Lee had been critical of Haughey's handling of the economy after the famous address to the nation in January 1980, claiming that in *The Way Forward* Haughey had finally determined to treat the disease he had diagnosed but whose spread he had been instrumental in assisting.[63] Haughey jotted down detailed and extensive handwritten notes about economic recovery in 1987; cultural aspects of the state, including the tax exemption for artists, and Aosdána; reform issues such as the Succession Act and free travel; and Northern Ireland, where, he believed, 'unionists never sought reconciliation'. To a question on whether he needed wealth, he wrote 'not at all'. Finally, on his personal philosophy, he simply wrote, 'Politics is my life.'[64] In February 2000, Ó Mórdha wrote to Haughey thanking him for his help and giving him details of the programme schedule.[65] Haughey did not reply. He was very unhappy at a question he was asked by the documentary team about his appearance before the McCracken Tribunal. After an awkwardly long pause to a question the viewer does not hear, he states: 'I'm not going into that.'[66] Ó Mórdha, however, in the draft outline he sent to Haughey, did ask him whether he needed wealth, and whether he felt he had let some people down and disappointed some of his followers. And it was the questions over Haughey's wealth that would have been asked that ultimately made him avoid any public interviews after the revelations about his finances became public in April 1997, and were confirmed at the McCracken Tribunal three months later.

Haughey had thought seriously about a sympathetic biography, or an autobiography, after he had left office and asked his long-time adviser Martin Mansergh if he would be interested in helping him. Mansergh was, however, working full-time on the peace process and declined. Haughey let the project go but a few years later, towards the end of 2000, after much of the details of Haughey's finances had come into the public domain, he again started to consider an autobiography based on his personal papers, which at this stage were gathered in an upstairs room in Abbeville. He invited Mansergh again to come to Abbeville and discuss the project. By March 2001, Mansergh had drafted a brief introduction, which he invited Haughey to consider as providing the rationale for a reflective book that might stimulate his own thoughts and for him to work on.[67] It was a ringing defence of Haughey's work as a Dáil deputy, minister and Taoiseach. Mansergh wrote that any impartial observer would have to concede that the foundations both of Ireland's extraordinary economic progress and of the peace process were largely laid by the governments that Haughey led between 1987 and 1992. The draft added that Haughey had decided not to write his own memoirs when he retired as he was influenced by those of other leaders that he knew. He thought that in normal circumstances the form lent itself too easily to endless self-praise and self-justification that not infrequently exaggerated, at the expense of others, the uniqueness and value of the author's own contribution. This could rapidly become tedious, even to the most sympathetic reader. He was thinking here particularly of former Australian Prime Minister Bob Hawke, whose memoirs, he told Kevin Rafter, made for 'turgid reading as the author sought to explain decisions that would have been better left to others to judge in the fullness of time'.[68] He suggested that at different times he had both benefited and suffered from the cult of personality, which throughout history had tended to project onto one person both the dynamic qualities and the defects of the society of one's time, or certainly that of its leading members. The introduction went on to discuss briefly the travails of his financial affairs and ended by declaring that, in uncertain health and for the sake of those who remained loyal to him, and those who thought he had something to say, he had decided to render some account of his life as a contribution to a better understanding of the Ireland of his time and the part he played in it.[69] Haughey, however, decided not to pursue the project. As Mansergh reflected, 'Getting no reaction, I wasn't encouraged to continue.'[70]

Some nine months later, in December 2001, Haughey asked the former senior civil servant John Travers to lunch in Abbeville and asked him if he would be interested in helping with a proposed autobiography. Travers had known Haughey for over two decades. As a principal officer in the Department of the Taoiseach, he wrote many of Haughey's economic speeches in 1987 and 1988 during the beginnings of the social partnership process. He had been a member of the secretariat that had worked with Pádraig Ó hUiginn in writing the national plan *The Way Forward* in 1982. He again worked closely with Ó hUiginn in the negotiations with the social partners on the Programme for National Recovery in 1987, of which he wrote much of the final text. When he was the chief economic adviser in the Department of Industry and Commerce, Travers was also involved in the team that negotiated the first tranche of EU structural funds to Ireland in 1989 and was part of the ministers and secretaries group who met in Haughey's office every Thursday morning to review, monitor and oversee Ireland's strategy for negotiations with the EU between 1989 and 1992.[71] At their lunch meeting, Travers listened to Haughey explain that he was working on organising his papers with a possible view to writing, or having written, something on them. He asked Travers whether he would be in a position to help. Some days later Travers declined. He had come to the conclusion that having worked as a non-partisan, non-political civil servant, it would be better if he did not get involved in a political project.[72] Haughey then turned to Eoin Neeson, but that did not work out and his autobiography remained unwritten. While Haughey was waiting for Mansergh's draft in early 2001 he appeared to be having second thoughts, as he told the journalist Kevin Rafter, then working on a biography of Mansergh. His thoughts on putting pen to paper on his life story were: 'Never justify. Never explain.'[73] Haughey spoke to Vincent Browne in 2004 about an autobiography, asking the veteran journalist, whom he had known for close to four decades, whether he would assist him and if he could find a researcher for the project. Browne introduced the journalist Colin Murphy to Haughey, but again nothing came of it.[74]

REVELATIONS

On Thursday 17 April 1997, RTÉ's *Prime Time* named Haughey as the politician to whom Ben Dunne had given over £1 million over a four-year period from 1987 to 1991. In a report previewing the McCracken (Dunnes Payments) Tribunal whose hearings were beginning the following week in Dublin Castle, *Prime Time* said that Haughey was the alleged beneficiary of the money. It stated that sources close to Ben Dunne claimed he would name Haughey when he gave evidence to the tribunal. It presaged an enormously difficult last decade of Haughey's life. In the *Irish Times*, Cliff Taylor revealed the intricate details of the payments.[75]

The main remit of the McCracken Tribunal was to inquire into the so-called 'Dunnes payments' episode. The immediate origin of the tribunal lay in a rather mysterious and often squalid family dispute about control of the most famous supermarket group in Ireland, Dunnes Stores. Ben Dunne's arrest in Florida in July 1992 brought into the public domain the conflict, which had been going on in private for some years, between Dunne and his sister Margaret Heffernan over ownership of the Dunnes Stores group. During this often rancorous dispute, it emerged that a whole host of payments had been made to a number of politicians. Dunne had sworn an affidavit revealing contributions to politicians, including Haughey and the former Fine Gael minister Michael Lowry. In late November 1996, the *Irish Independent* journalist Sam Smyth revealed the unorthodox business relationship between Dunne and Lowry, telling his readers that Dunne had paid over £200,000 for renovations to Lowry's home. A few months later, in February 1997, the Oireachtas established a tribunal under the chairmanship of Justice Brian McCracken. It saw this as the best way both to establish the facts of the Dunnes payments and to command public confidence in the openness and accountability of the political process. At this stage Ben Dunne's payments to Haughey had still not come to light but Smyth's revelation put in train a series of events that would, in effect, ruin Haughey.

When Haughey's name was outed two months later the extraordinary double life he had been leading was about to be exposed in the starkest of terms. He was forced to give evidence to the McCracken Tribunal in Dublin Castle in July 1997. He received a number of letters in the weeks leading up to his appearance. To a supportive letter from his old friend, Kevin McCourt, he replied: 'I have always valued our friendship and am gratified that it will continue undiminished through this difficult period and beyond. Our old friend Cicero regarded friendship as one of the greatest of human virtues and at times like this one cannot but agree with him.'[76] The poet Theo Dorgan offered words of consolation: 'I have been thinking about feeding frenzies about how the mob and their tribunes turn mindlessly on public figures, the ruthlessness and inevitability of it all. I had been thinking about what it could be in the make-up of certain figures that they evoke great passions in the minds of people who do not know them.' He added that while they barely knew each other he wanted Haughey to know that in his eyes, and those of many of his friends and colleagues, there was a sense that 'your dance with history has been the real thing.'[77] A few days after the revelations that he had indeed received a number of cheques from Ben Dunne totalling some £1.3 million, the constitutional lawyer William Binchy wrote to him: 'You may not have a sense of the very high regard in which you are held by so many people.'[78]

The months between April and July 1997 were Haughey's worst since his criminal trial in 1970. He had initially denied to his own legal team and the tribunal that he had received any payments at all from Ben

Dunne. But when documentary evidence from Dunne's solicitor, Noel Smyth, emerged, Haughey was forced to admit that he had essentially been living a lie in relation to his finances. Ben Dunne's sister, Margaret Heffernan, had visited Haughey in Abbeville in autumn 1993 to ascertain whether her brother had indeed given Haughey over £1 million which, she insisted, was money that belonged to the company.[79] Smyth had met Haughey on five occasions and they had dozens of conversations on the telephone. Smyth made notes of the conversations and then posted those notes to himself. They showed categorically that Ben Dunne's evidence to the tribunal on 21 April 1997 that he had given Haughey £1.3 million was correct.[80] Smyth's evidence to the tribunal four days later on 25 April caused a sensation and plunged Haughey into despair. Haughey had denied in writing that he had received donations from Dunne.

Haughey was now faced with the greatest crisis since he was under the threat of imprisonment at the arms trial, over a quarter of a century earlier. He had no choice but to admit that he had indeed received donations from Dunne. He misled his own legal team, led by senior counsel Eoin McGonigal, right up until he was due to give evidence. On Wednesday 9 July, McGonigal told the tribunal that Haughey now accepted that Ben Dunne had handed him three bank drafts totalling £210,000 at Abbeville in November 1991. This completely contradicted Haughey's claim in earlier correspondence with the tribunal that he had received no such monies. McGonigal also told the tribunal that Ben Dunne had offered to give Haughey a further £1 million the previous February to pay off a tax bill arising from the earlier payments. He said that Haughey had reacted with panic during a meeting with Ben Dunne's solicitor, Noel Smyth, at around the same time to discuss the bank drafts, which the former Taoiseach recognised as 'lethal pieces of paper'.[81] And indeed they were. Haughey gave his own evidence on Tuesday 15 July 1997. He arrived at Dublin Castle before 7 a.m. to avoid the press and the anticipated crowds. He gave evidence for an hour and a half, between 11 a.m. and 12.30 p.m., and left by the front gate at 1 p.m. After a few initial friendly cheers, the crowd turned hostile and started to boo Haughey. His son Conor ushered him into his car and he went back to Abbeville. Although he was confident and defiant in his evidence, Haughey was shattered by the whole experience. So were his family.[82]

Justice Brian McCracken wrapped up his hearings and report in six months. His team had uncovered the fact that for practically his whole political career, Haughey's financial and tax affairs had been handled by his close friend and practising accountant Des Traynor. Traynor controlled the so-called Ansbacher accounts, a complex and extensive tax-avoidance system, traces of which the tribunal, and a separate investigation into the Dunnes Stores group by the Department of Enterprise, Trade and Employment, had uncovered. Some £40 million in these accounts was held in a Cayman Islands bank. The tribunal also discovered that a commercial firm, Celtic Helicopters, run by Haughey's son Ciarán, had benefited from funds in these accounts.[83] In his report, McCracken castigated Haughey's evidence as 'unacceptable and untrue', citing eleven instances in which the former Taoiseach's evidence was 'not believable', 'quite unbelievable', 'most unlikely', 'beyond all credibility', and 'incomprehensible'.[84] He said he could not believe that Haughey was not aware of monies kept for him in the Ansbacher accounts by Traynor (who had died in 1994), or of the tax implications of the monies he received from Ben Dunne. He could, however, find no evidence that Ben Dunne had sought or Haughey had offered political favours.

In fact, there was no evidence of any political impropriety by Haughey in relation to the monies he received. As Charlie McCreevy, who visited Haughey on numerous occasions in his later years, remarked: 'That summed up Haughey's relationship with money. He would have been outraged if anyone asked him to do anything for them in return for money. I guarantee you the one way not to get a decision from him was to give him something.'[85] Noel Smyth was another who did not think Haughey corrupt. Smyth strongly encouraged Haughey to admit to receiving the monies from Dunne before he was forced to do so. While he felt that Haughey had created the circumstances for his own downfall, he did not think him corrupt. Asked by the journalist Maeve Sheehan in 2018 whether Haughey was corrupt, he replied: 'Not at all … Haughey was a great character, great bonhomie, he felt that if somebody wanted to give him money, you know he had a lifestyle to lead, why not?'[86] Dermot Desmond held a similar view, often asking journalists to tell him what Charles Haughey did wrong.[87] But there were huge dangers in Haughey's dependence on large private donations and he did not seem to grasp the significance of this. He never expected that the vast amounts of money donated to him would be revealed by what was essentially accidental means. It was a fatal flaw.

Concerned that Haughey's attitude to the tribunal could have amounted to an offence under the Tribunal of Inquiry Act, McCracken sent his report to the Director of Public Prosecutions with a view to seeing if Haughey should be prosecuted for obstructing its work. Charges were brought against Haughey, and he appeared in the Circuit Court in Chancery Street on Thursday 14 October 1999, where his prosecution was deferred. Again he arrived early to avoid the media and crowds and later expressed his gratitude to the Garda inspector on duty for the 'manner in which you organised my entering and leaving the Circuit Court on Thursday last. Your kind concern was greatly appreciated and the courtesy and efficiency of yourself and your team was exemplary.'[88]

Ten days later Haughey went south to Cork for Jack Lynch's funeral. It was an uncomfortable experience for Haughey. He felt that he should pay his respects to a man he had known for over four decades, whatever the difficulties he was currently undergoing and the complex nature of his relationship with Lynch. Haughey also had a complicated relationship with Cork itself.[89] In October 1980, he had received a gift of a Glen Rovers tie and had told the club's secretary, Tomás Ó Murchú, that he would wear it with pride on every suitable occasion.[90] Glen Rovers, in the northside of the city, was Jack Lynch's club. The tie was a peace offering of sorts after an incident when Haughey made a scheduled visit to the club's premises in Blackpool only to find no one there. He quickly left. In 1983, Mary O'Shea from the Fianna Fáil cumann in UCC told him that while she realised that 'Cork has never been your strongest support ground', the cumann was fully behind him in the heave of that year.[91] He was friendly with local politicians, such as Gene Fitzgerald and Flor Crowley, and with Gerry Wrixon of UCC, but was suspicious of special pleading from the city. In November 1986, on the cusp of the February 1987 general election, the economist Colm McCarthy expressed scepticism about plans for a tunnel under the River Lee, telling Haughey, 'the ability of Cork interests to come up with Rolls Royce solutions on all available occasions should never be underestimated'.[92]

In February 1988, Haughey had been given the title 'honorary Corkman' by Lord Mayor Tom Brosnan after a trip to what he described as the 'fascinating, stimulating and beautiful city of Cork'.[93] Now, over a decade later, he got out of his state car at the courtyard of the North Cathedral at the top of Shandon Street, and was greeted with stony silence by the crowd. He entered the church on his own. His son Conor later regretted that he had not gone with him on the day to give him support.[94] Due to an administrative mix-up, Haughey found himself sitting next to Des O'Malley, who would later give the graveside oration for Lynch. Once the service was over Haughey quickly returned to Dublin, but as his car made its way through the city he was subjected to intermittent boos and jeers.[95] A week later one of his correspondents wrote to say that he wished 'to salute courage and dignity shown in the face of animosity in Cork last Saturday'.[96] Two days after Haughey died in June 2006, his brother Fr Eoghan received a letter from Cardinal Cahal Daly expressing sympathy. Daly stated that he had a cousin in Cork who had worked all her life among the poor in Cork City: 'She assures me that there is great and very genuine grief among the less-well-off people in Cork, all of whom had a special affection for "Charlie" and regarded him as a special friend of the poor. The same kindly and grateful feeling towards him is to be found among the elderly all over Ireland.'[97] But Lynch's funeral was an extremely difficult day for Haughey. As Cork mourned one of her greatest sons, he told his friend, the journalist James Morrissey, that the past should be buried, but it certainly was not buried that day in Cork.[98]

TERRY

As the winter of 1999 set in, Haughey was faced with the prospect of a criminal trial in the new year at which he faced possible jail time if convicted. It was also certain that he would have to appear before the

Moriarty Tribunal – established in the wake of the McCracken tribunal to investigate whether substantial payments which might not have been ethical to receive were made to him and whether he had made any decisions benefiting a person making such a payment – sometime in the future. He told one of his correspondents, 'Maureen and all the family are taking things very philosophically and standing up very well to it.'[99] The reference to Maureen was telling. In May that year, the other great secret of Haughey's life was laid bare when the social diarist, Terry Keane, with whom he had been having a relationship since 1972, revealed it to Gay Byrne on the *Late Late Show*. In early May, at their regular lunch at the restaurant Le Coq Hardi, Haughey had told Keane that he wanted to return various mementoes of their time together, including photographs and some correspondence. This upset her greatly as she felt she was being erased from of his life. It is more likely that Haughey was in fact putting his affairs in order. He was extremely conscious of the ambiguities of his life and highly sensitive to its ambivalences. The revelations about his finances had already sent his life reeling in a direction he could not control and he did not want the same to happen with his extramarital affair. He was under investigation by the Moriarty Tribunal, which was seeking to account for all monies he was given and looking at his various expenditures. It was certainly not beyond the bounds of possibility that money Haughey spent on Keane might have been investigated. The tribunal would indeed later reveal significant payments to Le Coq Hardi and to the exclusive Parisian shirtmaker and designer store Charvet, to which Keane claimed she introduced Haughey.[100]

After that initial meeting, Haughey and Keane met again for lunch at Le Coq Hardi, on Thursday 13 May 1999, when she told him she was publishing her memoirs, that it would be serialised in the *Sunday Times*, and that she was going to appear on the *Late Late Show* the following night. Haughey asked her not to go through with it, but she refused, although she would later tell Byrne that Haughey did not ask her not to do the interview or, indeed, the newspaper serialisation. At that stage, the column for the *Sunday Times* had still not been written and the *Sunday Independent* had no idea that Keane was, in essence, about to switch sides. Earlier that week Keane had phoned her editor at the *Sunday Independent*, Anne Harris, to say that she had made her decision and was going to stay at the *Sunday Independent*. Anne Harris did not even know there was a decision to be made and only found out on the Friday afternoon that Keane was going on the *Late Late Show* just a few hours later.[101] After the dramatic lunch on the Thursday, Keane and Haughey went their separate ways and never met again, although they spoke on the phone at least twice during the following week. Keane met with the editor of the Irish edition of the *Sunday Times*, Rory Godson, and the journalists John Ryan and Michael Ross to draft the column.[102] Keane's *Late Late Show* revelation was followed the next month by a four-part serialisation in the *Sunday Times* of what was expected to be Keane's memoirs. It never appeared.

In an RTÉ television documentary, *Terry*, broadcast in April 2000, Keane told her interviewer, Cathal O'Shannon, that the affair was in effect a perfect situation for Haughey: 'He had wife and his family and he had his girlfriend.' She described Haughey as an ostrich with his head in the sand. He was aware that everyone knew about the affair and yet did not want it to be official or for there to be any proof – this is why he told her at their Le Coq Hardi meeting that he wanted to return all his photographs and mementoes of the affair. She declared that she was staggered and profoundly upset by his actions: 'If he feels after all this time that he wants to deny me even when he's dead, it sort of put everything into perspective and maybe I sort of, I think I probably did question the whole relationship in a way I never had ever before.'[103] She stated that she wanted reassurances from him which he would not give. This, in essence, forced her to give her side of the story.

On the night Keane told the nation of the affair, Haughey was in Malahide having dinner with Maureen and their friends Arthur and Phyllis Gibney. The following four weeks were perhaps the most painful of Haughey's life. Keane revealed various stories in the *Sunday Times*, some of which were clearly embellished, others not. Her belief that she was influential in Haughey's political thinking was treated with disdain and contempt by many who knew him. She alleged that he was on the verge of resigning after the February 1982 general election. He had thought of leaving for the South of France and was going to ask her to join him there because, supposedly, 'He could not take it any more.'[104] Given the all-consuming nature of politics and power in Haughey's life, this was extremely unlikely.

At the same time as the Keane serialisation, the Moriarty Tribunal was in session. It revealed details of a £300,000 donation to Haughey from the property developer Patrick Gallagher. At seven o'clock on the morning after the *Late Late Show*, Haughey rang his friend James Morrissey seeking advice on how to deal with the fallout. Morrissey told him that there was only one thing he could do and 'that was to spend the rest of his life, dedicated to and looking after the great woman who was in the room next door, his wife'.[105] In her interview on the *Late Late Show* Keane told Gay Byrne that the Haughey family would recognise what she said and her story as the truth and that she did not think it would hurt them. The truth was that it did hurt them, profoundly. Maureen Haughey had suffered greatly in the week of the Keane revelations and had stayed at home in Abbeville. By the following weekend and the second episode in the serialisation of the Keane memoirs in the *Sunday Times* she had returned to her normal routine. She told her husband that they would never speak of it but would just continue to live their lives. She remained steadfastly loyal to him over the remaining seven years of his life.

Keane was deeply hurt by the end of the affair and came to bitterly regret her revelations on the *Late Late Show*. She made another appearance on the *Late Late Show* in March 2006, just three months before Haughey died. She told the host, Pat Kenny, that she regretted having caused so much hurt and pain by taking part in the original interview, and that it had hurt innocent people, including both her own family and Haughey's family. She said that she panicked at the thought of a book coming out that was going to tell the story of her relationship with Haughey, and that if anyone was going to tell her story it should be herself. She told Kenny that she thought she was wrong to appear on the original show, and had made 'a big mistake' because she was under serious pressure. She had just been diagnosed with heart disease and felt that she had been both misguided, and misled by people who had done very well out of her appearance and had something to gain by it. There was much speculation about Keane's motives for doing the original *Late Late Show* interview in 1999, and for serialising her memoirs. These included revenge for Haughey attempting to erase her from his life; the devastating impact of her diagnosis with heart disease; circulation wars between the *Sunday Independent* and the *Sunday Times*; and needing money after a disastrous investment went wrong. Keane was paid £60,000 by the *Sunday Times* for the initial four instalments and a salary of £50,000 a year for what came to be a two-year contract, but as the *Irish Times* obituary of her in 2008 noted: 'In one fell swoop, she broke her pact with her readers, alienated public opinion, burned her bridges with Charles Haughey and the *Sunday Independent* and caused pain to her family and friends.'[106] In June 2006, on the Sunday after Haughey died, the tabloid newspaper *Ireland on Sunday* printed a long interview with Keane that she had insisted should only be published after his death. It included various photographs of her and Haughey together and basically retold the same stories the *Sunday Times* had printed some seven years earlier. Coming just three months after her regret about revealing the original affair in 1999, it was a strange way of paying respect to a man barely cold in the grave.

The ending of the affair was extremely difficult for both Keane and Haughey. As the Keane family friend Sarah Carey pointed out: 'It was a very sad ending to a genuinely meaningful relationship. Terry paid a high price for their relationship yet Haughey continued on in his marriage, which of course she understood. In the end, I think he broke her heart. When she went public, it was done in pain. She regretted it terribly afterwards. I felt very sorry for her. However, part of me thinks she was right. Without that personal testimony, everyone around Haughey would persist in denying her existence in his life.'[107] Keane's part in his life was, however, unknown to Haughey's children, whose eyes were opened by Keane's explosive interview with Byrne. In the documentary *Terry*, Keane told Cathal O'Shannon she was absolutely certain that Maureen Haughey and Haughey's children knew about the affair, just as her own family did. Yet, notwithstanding all the rumours about Haughey and Keane and her continuous references to him in her column 'The Keane Edge', the Haughey children viewed it as simply one of a never-ending series of rumours about their father which was best ignored. In those columns, Haughey was routinely referred to as 'Sweetie' but was also frequently called Charlie and on occasions as the Taoiseach.[108] The revelation of the affair caused deep pain in the Haughey household.

There is little doubt that the affair between Haughey and Keane was long-lasting, genuine and meaningful. It was one of the many lives of Charles Haughey, along with his public persona and his relationships with his wife and children. At heart, Haughey was able to compartmentalise the different strands in his life. The pictures published in the *Sunday Times* and *Ireland on Sunday*, although somewhat tawdry and certainly embarrassing to Haughey, testified to the longevity of the relationship. It is doubtful that Keane had any real influence on Haughey's politics or public policy decisions, but they clearly spent much time together in France and Ireland. Much was made by Keane of Haughey's love of France, and perhaps at its heart Haughey's view of the affair was quintessentially French; straying discreetly was permissible, but family break-ups should certainly be avoided. In 1992 he told Anne Harris that despite demands from some in his inner coterie of Fianna Fáil advisers, including P.J. Mara, that he end his relationship with Keane, he refused, telling the journalist, 'I simply could not do it.'[109] While the affair was known to the journalistic and chattering classes of Dublin's southside, it came as a shock to much of the rest of Ireland, and Haughey certainly did not want it revealed. In May 1999, as Haughey's travails with the tribunal were lengthening, the possibility of him facing the second criminal trial of his life beckoned, and he was suffering from prostate cancer, the existence of the affair and its revelation in the most public of Irish forums was yet another shattering blow to him and his family.

EVIDENCE

By June 2000, the criminal case against Haughey arising from his alleged obstruction of the McCracken Tribunal was suspended indefinitely by Judge Kevin Haugh, on the grounds of potentially prejudicial media coverage, including an interview with then Tánaiste Mary Harney, who said that she thought Haughey should be convicted and go to jail.[110] That same year he made a tax settlement of £6 million with the Revenue Commissioners, financed by selling fifteen acres of the Abbeville estate to the property developers Treasury Holdings. The remainder of the estate was sold to Manor Park Homes five years later for a price reported to be in the region of €45 million. The details of the sale were never made public by either party but a figure of €35 million is more accurate. Haughey was allowed to stay for the remainder of his life in what had been his home since 1969.

The conclusions of the McCracken Tribunal forced the Oireachtas to establish another tribunal, under Justice Michael Moriarty, to examine whether business interests might have secured favourable policy decisions from Lowry or Haughey during their respective ministerial careers, and, in Haughey's case, when he was Taoiseach. The Moriarty Tribunal ran in parallel with the ongoing criminal charges. Between Friday 21 July 2000 and Thursday 15 March 2001, Haughey appeared before the Moriarty Tribunal a total of thirty-three times. He gave evidence for five days in July, and then for another eight days from 22 September (just six days after his seventy-fifth birthday) to 3 October. He testified in two-hour blocks because of his advancing age and various medical issues.

On his first day he told the tribunal that during the 1970s, when his indebtedness was worsening, he was 'borrowing from Peter to pay Paul'.[111] He said that his finances had been managed by the late Des Traynor since 1960, even though extensive documentation from Allied Irish Bank in the 1970s showed that Haughey was heavily involved in his own affairs. By the time Haughey became Taoiseach in December 1979 his overdraft stood at over £1 million before £400,000 was written off by the bank. Furnished with specific documentation about meetings he had with his bankers from 1971 to 1974 – ergo he did not simply leave his finances to Des Traynor – Haughey neither confirmed nor denied that these meetings had taken place. He said that he was overwhelmed by the documentation the tribunal had produced and that he was incapable of grasping it. At one point, he added: 'Quite frankly, I'm lost. It confuses me.'[112]

When the tribunal resumed in January 2001 Haughey gave his evidence in private and for one hour in the mornings. In October 2000, his legal team had requested that he should be recused from giving any more testimony due to the progressive nature of his prostate cancer. His consultant, Peter McLean, had furnished a report to the tribunal that Haughey was suffering from fatigue, stress and disorientation and should not have to give evidence again. The tribunal commissioned two reports, one from a neurologist and one from a urologist, both from Britain, who believed he was able to continue to give evidence, but it should be for just one hour a day and in private. Haughey decided not to contest this and gave evidence on twenty more occasions between 20 January and 15 March 2001. Over the course of his evidence Haughey was questioned about donations made to him between 1979 and 1996, including his control of the Fianna Fáil party leader's account. Donations intended for the treatment of Brian Lenihan in 1987 were among the funds lodged to this account. Haughey gave evidence on 2 February 2001 about the medical treatment of Brian Lenihan, who had died in 1995:

> My efforts on behalf of Brian Lenihan at that time were the most compassionate thing I have ever done in my life and I think it is absolutely preposterous that this whole genuine charitable effort on my part at that time should now, twenty years or so later, be sought to be turned against me in the most cruel fashion, that I would deliberately divert to my own purposes money that was subscribed by well-meaning people for the good and salvation for my friend Brian Lenihan … The fact is that I, to save my friend's life, took an initiative, instituted the raising of funds, all of which funds were spent in his best interest and I did not, could not and would not divert one penny of those funds for any other purpose.[113]

For their part, the Lenihan family were always grateful to Haughey for initiating that fundraising drive.

During his testimony Haughey consistently denied that he had done any favours for any of his donors. He maintained that it was quite acceptable that a statesman should receive financial assistance from admirers. In March 1999, Martin Mansergh had sent him a note, via his son Seán, about how he might approach his testimony, outlining a defence of his travails with the tribunal.[114] This was to be the basis for much of Haughey's testimony. He acknowledged that not many people would agree with the way he organised his personal affairs, that it was far from ideal, that certain dangers were attached to it, and it was not a model for anyone. He stated that he left the management of his personal finances largely to others, who were models of discretion, and he would not be the only well-known and extremely busy person to put management of his finances in the hands of an accountant, which enabled him to concentrate on his political work. The note stated that many people had difficulties with the banks and everyone had to negotiate with them, asking had banks ever been known to bully or intimidate anyone and that of 'all the pathetic victims of bullying, is AIB with its huge profits really a plausible candidate?'[115] It pointed out that Haughey was often critical of the lack of encouragement banks gave to small businesses and that in 1984, he had co-operated with the Garret FitzGerald-led government to pass emergency legislation to save the Insurance Corporation of Ireland, a subsidiary of AIB, but stated he wanted to ensure the cost would not fall, as originally intended, on the taxpayer.

Mansergh pointed to the use of Abbeville as a place where much important government work was done and how Haughey had cancelled the project for an official residence for the Taoiseach in January 1980, saving the taxpayer an estimated £7 million in capital by the time it would have been completed, and running costs of several thousand pounds a year: 'Perhaps that decision to cancel the official residence, which probably by now saved the taxpayers £20m, was the biggest political mistake of a lifetime made in terms of personal cost and cost to reputation.' The note added that the contributions to Haughey were to enable him to do the job of Taoiseach without distraction: 'Contributors did it because they believed in the person, because they thought his service would be of benefit to the country. It was not done for motives of personal gain, nor was there any.'[116] It pointed to precedents where politicians in difficulty accepted financial help from supporters without any quid pro quo being sought or given, albeit in a more structured way. It alluded to the financial difficulties that the famous British prime ministers Benjamin Disraeli and Winston Churchill had gone through and the fact that Margaret Thatcher had a foundation established for her. In the Irish context it pointed to the public collections for both Charles Stewart Parnell and Daniel O'Connell. The note ended by saying that Haughey's taxes were organised in such a way as not to incur liabilities and that the establishment of Celtic Helicopters, run by Haughey's son Ciarán, was an attempt to found a small family business in an area of public demand which complemented, rather than competed against, the work of Irish Helicopters.[117] These were the defences that Haughey used in his evidence to the tribunal. They left many people unconvinced.

END

On Thursday 15 March 2001, Haughey finished his evidence at the tribunal at 12 p.m. and returned to Abbeville. He had been thinking of going to Inishvickillane for the weekend but was not feeling well and decided to stay at home. Over the weekend he felt more tired, and late on Sunday night he collapsed. An ambulance quickly arrived and he was taken to Beaumont Hospital. At the hospital the medical registrar on call, Dr Kevin Moore, was taking a breather after a hectic night. The St Patrick's Day weekend had been a busy one at the hospital. Things had just quietened down when Moore was paged at 1 a.m. and told that a seventy-five-year-old local man with a recent history of bronchial and respiratory problems, who also had prostate cancer, was being brought to the hospital having suffered a serious cardiac incident. He was then told the name of the patient, who, he was informed, was slipping in and out of consciousness and was in an extremely weak state. On receiving the call, Moore paged Dr Emily Ho, the cardiac registrar, who immediately made her way to the hospital. Moore met the ambulance crew at the door of Beaumont. Haughey was unconscious. His blood pressure was very low and his heartbeat abnormally fast. Essentially, he was in cardiogenic shock following a serious arrhythmic episode. Haughey needed fluids for rehydration and to be stabilised as a matter of some urgency. Moore resuscitated Haughey and for the following half an hour, Moore, Ho and their team worked to save Haughey's life.

By this stage a number of journalists, who had received a tip-off that Haughey was in hospital and was seriously ill, started to arrive at Beaumont. Just before 2 a.m., having restored a regular rhythm to Haughey's heartbeat, Moore and Ho had him moved to intensive care, where he was placed on a ventilator. Haughey had been in grave danger of dying.[118] He was helped by the skill of his doctors and nurses, the fact that the ambulance arrived at Abbeville quickly, and because the hospital, the building of which he himself had signed off on as Minister for Health, was just ten miles away. Haughey was then placed under the care of Professor Eoin O'Brien, the consultant cardiologist at Beaumont Hospital, and the anaesthetist Dr Brian Lamont. He stayed in hospital for ten days.

A few weeks later he received an Easter card from Fr Alec Reid: 'May the joy of Easter bless you with new hope and courage for the future.'[119] By that stage it was clear to Haughey and his family that his future would be mainly confined to home. His customary daily early morning horse ride with his friends John Carberry and Standish Collen had had to be curtailed after he fell off his horse on Portmarnock strand in January 1998 and broke his thigh. One of the supportive messages he received after this accident was from President Mary McAleese, who in a handwritten note told him that he showed remarkable courage in the immediate aftermath of his dreadful fall: 'I'm sure that feisty spirit has helped over the long, bedridden days since.'[120] McAleese had run unsuccessfully for Fianna Fáil in the 1987 general election in Dublin South East. Prior to the Anglo-Irish Agreement in 1985 she had written to Haughey expressing scepticism about the then coalition government's efforts to resolve the Northern Ireland conflict: 'I dread to think what the coalition ministers have been up to with the Brits to make the latter think that another go at an internal settlement would find support in Dublin. Even if Garret personally drafted the blessed thing, Northern nationalists won't wear it, whatever about the unionists.'[121] Now, over a decade later, Haughey was grateful to her for her support during this difficult time, wishing her 'not just success but happiness and fulfilment every day of your term in office as President'.[122] His cancer was terminal and his heart trouble meant he could not travel any significant distance. He was to spend the last five years of his life in Abbeville.

Over those last few years, various friends visited Haughey at Abbeville. Vincent Browne was a regular visitor. Others included his lifelong friend, Austin Dunphy, who Haughey had appointed to the National Heritage Council, and his wife, Stella, Gillian Bowler, James Morrissey, Oliver Barry, Des Peelo and members of the farming community around Kinsaley. Garret FitzGerald showed up in September 2005, a fact he inadvertently revealed to the media a few months later, leading him to send a note of apology. Haughey replied: 'my worry was that you might be inclined to think the publicity emanated from my side', and with that the battle that had both encapsulated and enraptured Ireland in the 1980s ended.[123] Many of those with whom Haughey had served made brief appearances, among them Ray MacSharry and Pádraig Ó hUiginn, the two men he considered to have done most, alongside him, to fix the economy and restore Ireland's international reputation in the post-1987 period. Others, such as Bertie Ahern and Charlie McCreevy, also made the odd appearance to check in on him. Haughey's solicitors, Ivor Fitzpatrick and Deirdre Courtney, were regular visitors, and they kept him updated on the Moriarty Tribunal. In February 2002, they considered issuing proceedings against Sebastian Barry and the Abbey Theatre over its staging of Barry's play *Hinterland*, which both the author and theatre admitted was partly based on Haughey's life. The two solicitors believed that it was defamatory, insulting and humiliating to Haughey and his family, but in the end Haughey, following a lifelong tradition, decided not to sue.[124]

Haughey's sister Eithne died in February 2002, and his brother Jock in October 2003. He could see his own death looming ever closer but maintained he was not ready to die – he wanted to spend more time with his grandchildren, who had become his main source of joy in his troubled last years.[125] He had begun to write poetry at this stage and celebrated the lives of his grandchildren in one of his poems. His prostate cancer, which had been manageable since its diagnosis in late 1994, became aggressive in the middle of 2005, and for much of Haughey's last twelve months he was in significant pain. Haughey was not one to complain, however, considering it part of life's cycle that some people got cancer and had to live with it. To queries from his family and friends, he would utter a phrase many an Irish person suffering from a similar ailment might use: 'I'm grand.' At Easter 2005, he took one last trip to Kerry and boated around Sneem with his daughter Eimear, son Conor and some of his grandchildren.[126] Haughey had long held an obsession with water. He was perhaps at his happiest when he was on Inishvickillane and near the sea, which he believed had a therapeutic effect. When he was close to the end he was very anxious that the history of Inishvickillane that Mícheál Ó Dubhshláine was working on would be published. Inishvickillane was the place where he would go to forget his worries, to contemplate life. His Hy Brasil.

Haughey was under the care of his Clontarf-based GP, Dr Paddy Kelly, who regularly attended to him at Abbeville, and had a fortnightly check-up at the Mater Private Hospital for the last year of his life. Haughey was never a religious person, but he did become more spiritual and contemplative in those last months. His friendship with his brother Eoghan, always close, deepened as he reflected on his life. While Fr Eoghan looked after Haughey's spiritual care, his wife, Maureen, provided for everything else. By the first week of June 2006, Haughey was extremely ill and in the last stages of his life. A few close friends called to pay their final respects. Dermot Desmond and two of his sons, Brett and Ross, came to visit for a few hours. On Friday 9 June, the former Canadian Prime Minister Brian Mulroney was in Dublin and went to Abbeville to visit Haughey for the afternoon; they reminisced on their respective times in office in the 1980s and early 1990s.

The following day Maureen Haughey arranged one last gathering of Haughey's friends and neighbours from the locality. The same people had been coming for years. They were the ones who stood with him when he was at his lowest ebb and they returned on that Saturday for one last get-together in the bar at Abbeville. Haughey sipped at a glass of wine, while Pearle and Tess, his Daffodil nurses from St Francis Hospice, Raheny, fought to get him to go back to his sickbed. Eventually they gave up and let his neighbours have their final farewell. On Monday afternoon Haughey slipped into unconsciousness. He died in his bedroom at home in Abbeville at 10 a.m. on Tuesday 13 June 2006. At his bedside were his wife, Maureen, his children, Eimear, Conor, Ciarán and Seán, and his daughters-in-law, Jackie and Orla. Also in his bedroom was Marie Sheahan, his loyal personal secretary since 1969, who had come to be a close friend. Catherine Ward and Haughey's nephew, Niall Haughey, who were employed in his private office at the time, were also there. His brother Fr Eoghan arrived just after his passing to say some final prayers. A family united in grief prepared themselves for the long days and nights ahead as Charles Haughey passed from them into the pages of history.

CHAPTER 23

AFTERDEATH

FUNERAL

As a former Taoiseach, Charles Haughey was accorded a full state funeral. In his last year he had spent a lot of time thinking about the type of service he wanted. He had discussed it with both his brother Fr Eoghan and the undertaker, John Stafford of Stafford's funeral homes. In the end it was a traditional affair; a wake in the house for family and close friends, removal to the church, a public viewing, mass, and graveyard burial with a graveside oration. An hour after Haughey's death, John Stafford arrived at Abbeville to take away and prepare Haughey's body for viewing and burial. Haughey's daughter, Eimear, accompanied Stafford to his premises on the Malahide Road. In the early afternoon they arrived back at Kinsaley, where Maureen, her sons, Conor, Ciarán and Seán, and Haughey's eight grandchildren were there to welcome him back to his beloved Abbeville for the last time. Haughey was laid out in the main reception room off the hall in Abbeville, and over the following day and a half a steady stream of friends and admirers arrived to pay their respects. His family took it in turns to stay by his coffin until, at 10.45 a.m. on Thursday 15 June 2006, Haughey left Abbeville for the last time. Gardaí escorted his coffin on to the hearse and a guard of honour made up of friends and neighbours lined the driveway from Abbeville to the main road. As the hearse slowly made the short journey to the Church of Our Lady of Consolation in Donnycarney, led by four Garda motorbike outriders, the streets were lined with onlookers, including schoolchildren from the nearby St Nicholas of Myra National School on the Malahide Road. The hearse arrived at the church at eleven o'clock and for the next six hours, Haughey's body was on display in the heartland of his constituency.

At 5 p.m., Haughey's coffin, draped in the tricolour, was taken from the mortuary chapel by Defence Forces pallbearers and received at the main entrance to the church by Fr Eoghan Haughey and the Archbishop of Dublin, Diarmuid Martin. After a homily by Fr Eoghan, Anthony Cronin, Haughey's long-time adviser, gave a brief reflection. He began by quoting the song from Shakespeare's play *Cymbeline*: 'Fear no more the heat o' the sun, Nor the furious winter's rages …' He told the packed congregation that he was 'Charlie Haughey's friend for sixty years or thereabouts. In all those years there never was a time when I regretted that friendship, or was in any way regretful about it, or felt I had cause to be other than extremely proud of it.' After bringing the congregation through their friendship, Cronin ended by reciting his own short poem 'Completion':

> All things tend to completion,
> Towards a resultant end.
> The heat of a harvest noon-day
> With an august night will blend.
> The rose burns out in its calyx.
> The leaf yields to the ground.
> Almost every appearance
> Is with disappearance crowned.[1]

Fr Eoghan and Archbishop Diarmuid Martin were joined in celebrating Haughey's funeral mass at noon the following day by a number of other priests, including the parish priest in Donnycarney, Fr Peter Finnerty, and Fr Alec Reid, with whom Haughey had spent so much time in the search for peace. Beyond the immediate Haughey family, President Mary McAleese, who had cut short a state visit to Africa, and her husband, Martin, led the mourners, who included many of Haughey's old political friends and rivals, among them Garret FitzGerald, Patrick Hillery, Mary Harney, John Hume, Gerry Adams and the then Taoiseach, Bertie Ahern. Albert Reynolds, who was ill, was represented by his wife, Kathleen. Representatives of the social partners with whom Haughey had worked to revive the economy were in attendance, as were many of the civil servants he had worked with over his long career.

The mourners were welcomed with a mass booklet that included a drawing of an early Christian oratory at Inishvickillane (Inis Mhicileáin) by Pat Liddy, and Ralph Waldo Emerson's oft quoted words: 'To laugh often and much; to win the respect of intelligent people and the affection of children; to earn the appreciation of honest critics and endure the betrayal of false friends; to appreciate beauty; to find the best in others; to leave the world a bit better … to know that one life has breathed easier because you have lived. This is to have succeeded.' Brian Lenihan, the son of the former Tánaiste Brian Lenihan, with whom Haughey had shared the dramatic highs and crushing lows of political life, gave the first reading, from Jeremiah; the second reading, from the Second Epistle to Timothy, was delivered by Haughey's daughter, Eimear. Fr Eoghan gave a moving homily, which touched on Haughey's public and family life, noting that 'whatever about the greatness or otherwise of his achievements, C.J. certainly attracted the storms'. Prayers of the faithful were read by family, friends and political allies: Ciarán Haughey, P.J. Mara, Brian Dennis, Siobhán O'Connor, Mary Murphy, and former Fianna Fáil politicians Tom Fitzgerald from Kerry and Seamus Cullimore from Wexford.

Haughey's son Seán read a reflection on behalf of the family. It offered a strong defence of his father, and touched on Haughey's role as father, grandfather, statesman, local politician, and friend to many. He ended by recalling his father's words to Dáil Éireann on his retirement in February 1992: 'He served the people, all the people, to the best of his ability.' This was followed by a recitation by Áine Uí Laoithe of Seamus Heaney's poem 'The Given Note', which begins: 'On the most westerly Blasket / In a dry-stone hut / He got this air out of the night.' This was accompanied by the piper Liam O'Flynn playing the piper's lament known as Port na bPúcaí (the tune of the fairies) about the Blasket fiddler who retrieves the mysterious Port na bPúcaí from Inishvickillane, embodying both the real and ethereal worlds. Haughey's long-time friend the poet Brendan Kennelly gave the final tribute. He pointed to Haughey's qualities as a real Dubliner – witty, quick, positive and determined. Kennelly was a regular correspondent of Haughey's over the years, telling him in the dark days after the McCracken Tribunal report and at the beginning of the Moriarty Tribunal that there was a sense of style in Dublin and that 'more than anyone in the second half of this battered old century you created that style. Ya boy ya.'[2]

There was a simplicity of style to the end of Haughey's funeral that encapsulated his life. Before his coffin was taken from the church, another friend, the musician Finbar Furey, played a haunting version of his classic composition 'The Lonesome Boatman'. Haughey's coffin was then shouldered out of the church by pallbearers from the 2nd Military Police Company at Cathal Brugha Barracks. The coffin was placed into the hearse and followed a military company procession drawn from the three arms of the Defence Forces, Army, Naval Service and Air Corps, who led it on its final journey to St Fintan's cemetery in Sutton.

Haughey was buried at 4 p.m. on Friday 16 June 2006. Military Police pallbearers carried the coffin to the graveside, where they removed the tricolour and presented it to Maureen Haughey before the prayer service began. The Taoiseach, Bertie Ahern, delivered a graveside oration in which he said Haughey was blessed with a strong intellect, natural charisma and driving spirit. He had led a career full to the brim of achievements which benefited immensely his constituents and his country. Haughey was a consummate politician, who exhibited grace under pressure, an incisive mind and superb parliamentary skills. He also had a proud identity with all of Ireland and a profound respect in victory and defeat for the democratic institutions of the state: 'If the definition of a patriot is someone who devotes all their energy to the betterment of their country Charles Haughey was a patriot to his fingertips.'[3] The ceremony ended with a Naval Service firing party delivering three volleys over the grave, while the Defence Forces' Band played the Last Post and Reveille.

And with that final act, the man who had dominated Irish political life for much of the latter part of the twentieth century was silenced. He lies under a simple headstone, which reads: 'He served his people and loved his kind.'

TRIBUNAL

Six months after Haughey's burial, on 19 December 2006, the Moriarty Tribunal issued its first report regarding payments made to the former Taoiseach between 1979 and 1996. It stated that Haughey had received just over £9.1 million in payments from various quarters and rejected his evidence that he accepted these personal donations on the basis that they were from disinterested citizens seeking to assist a politician whose views they supported. It also rejected his view that this was in accordance with practices gleaned from the biographies of English political leaders down the years. It noted that apart from the almost invariably secretive nature of payments from senior members of the business community, their very incidence and scale, particularly during difficult economic times nationally, and when governments led by Haughey were championing austerity, 'can only be said to have devalued the quality of a modern democracy'.[4] The report also refused to accept Haughey's testimony that he knew virtually nothing of his financial arrangements, and left such matters to Des Traynor. It reproached him for what it described as his attempts to saddle such individuals as Eileen Foy, Paul Kavanagh and Jack Stakelum with responsibility for particular aspects of his financial affairs.

The report made three specific negative findings in relation to actions Haughey had taken in respect of Ben Dunne, Mahmoud Fustok and the late Brian Lenihan. In relation to Ben Dunne, the tribunal found that in arranging a meeting between Dunne and the chairman of the Revenue Commissioners, Séamus Paircéir, just after he had been elected Taoiseach in 1987, Haughey sought to and did confer a benefit on Dunne. The substantial payments made by Dunne to Haughey had to be regarded as payments primarily motivated by Haughey's resumption of the office of Taoiseach in 1987. The terms of settlement offered by Paircéir to Dunne constituted a real and tangible benefit to Dunne, in that they gave him an option that he did not have before Haughey's intervention.[5]

The tribunal further determined that a payment by Mahmoud Fustok of £50,000 to Haughey in February 1985, through the bank account of Dr John O'Connell, was made in circumstances that influenced the discharge of Haughey's political duties. Fustok was a wealthy Saudi Arabian bloodstock breeder and diplomat who was introduced to Haughey by O'Connell, who himself had a peripatetic career as a Labour, Independent, and finally Fianna Fáil public representative and was Fustok's bloodstock agent in Ireland. O'Connell joined Fianna Fáil in 1985, the same year he facilitated the donation to Haughey by Fustok. Fustok had asked O'Connell to transmit the money to Haughey on his behalf. When O'Connell lost his seat in the 1987 general election, Haughey appointed him to the Seanad. In evidence to the tribunal in July 1999, O'Connell recounted that he had been dining with Fustok in London shortly before February 1985 when Fustok told him that he owed money to Haughey for the purchase of a yearling from Haughey's stud farm, and asked O'Connell to transmit a payment on his behalf. O'Connell agreed to do so, and subsequently received a cheque from Fustok which he lodged to his own account. He later drew a cheque on this account which he delivered to Haughey. The tribunal maintained that Fustok's motive for making the payment was connected with public offices held by Haughey. The payment had the potential to, and did, influence the discharge of those offices in connection with the granting of Irish citizenship to relatives of Fustok and in particular to a woman named Faten Moubarak.[6] In all, fourteen relatives or close associates of Fustok, including his brother, were granted Irish naturalisation between June 1981 and December 1982, when Haughey was Taoiseach, with a further naturalisation taking place in May 1990 when Haughey was again back in the Taoiseach's office.

In relation to Brian Lenihan, the tribunal found that a sizeable proportion of the excess funds collected for Lenihan's treatment in the USA was misappropriated by Haughey for his personal use. The tribunal had established that as much as £265,000 may have been collected for the benefit of Lenihan. Of those funds, no more than just over £70,000 was used to meet the costs and expenses for his medical treatment in the United States.[7] The tribunal maintained that fundraising for the general election campaign of 1989 was run in conjunction with the campaign to raise funds for Lenihan, and was also used by Haughey to bolster his personal finances. It accused him of 'deliberately and skilfully' arranging the manner in which various payments were made to Fianna Fáil to enable him to retain significant amounts of that money for his own use. It reckoned that this amounted to some £85,000 of the £160,000 donated.[8]

When the tribunal's report was published, the Haughey family issued a strongly worded nine-page statement specifically rejecting the charges laid against Charles Haughey by Justice Moriarty. It placed on the public record an extract of the submission the family had made to the tribunal on the proposed findings relating to Ben Dunne, Mahmoud Fustok and Brian Lenihan. The family described the findings as perverse. They said that it was wrong that the report did not make any positive findings relating to the fact that Haughey did not carry out any act or make any decision to benefit persons or companies who made donations to him during the seventeen years between 1979 and 1996, which were the subject of the tribunal's investigations. In fact, the only positive finding in relation to Haughey was one in relation to Glen Ding, near Blessington in Wicklow, where state lands were sold to a part of the Cement Roadstone Holdings group of companies in 1990. The tribunal's inquiries into the disposal and the conduct of the sale of the Glen Ding lands were prompted by the part played by Cement Roadstone Holdings in the operation of the Ansbacher accounts. It found that there was no connection between Haughey and the disposal of the lands; and there was no connection between the operation of the Ansbacher accounts and the disposal of the lands.

In their insistence that the tribunal should have found that Haughey had made no act or decision affecting a number of people or companies in the period the tribunal was investigating, the Haughey family specifically mentioned the following: Michael Smurfit; Dermot Desmond; the late P.V. Doyle; John Byrne; Edmund Farrell; Mark Kavanagh; Celtic Helicopters Ltd; the sale of the B&I Line; the acquisition of Irish Distillers by Pernod Ricard; the controversy surrounding the Carysfort Site; the dealings between AIB and the government in connection with the funding of Beaumont Hospital; the siting of the Whiddy Oil terminal; the late Patrick Gallagher; Guinness Mahon Ireland Ltd; John Magnier; Nicholas Fitzpatrick; Seamus Tully; Oliver Murphy, and Laurence Goodman.[9]

What particularly exercised the Haughey family was that Haughey was never made aware of the proposed findings of the tribunal. In particular, although his dealings with the tribunal ended in 2001, at no stage was there any communication from the tribunal suggesting that adverse opinions were to be made against him. Had Haughey and his solicitors been made aware of such a possibility in 2001, it would have given them the opportunity to deal with each of those allegations and to answer them or produce evidence for the tribunal to consider. This would have been Haughey's legal entitlement, but it was not given by the tribunal. In relation to the three negative findings against Haughey, his family issued strong denials in all cases. In the case of the tribunal's finding that monies for Brian Lenihan's treatment in the US were misappropriated by Haughey for his personal use, the Haughey family cited Haughey's evidence to the tribunal that it was his initiative to raise the funds for Lenihan's trip to the United States and that it was Haughey's belief that more money was expended on Lenihan's medical treatment than was accounted for. They argued that other monies were intermingled with the Brian Lenihan fund monies, including election funds, all of which were placed in the same account and that no precise records were kept at that time.[10]

Regarding the Fustok payment, the Haughey family again quoted Haughey's evidence that he was reasonably certain that Fustok had actually purchased a yearling from Abbeville Stud, took it into his bloodstock empire, and paid for it. They argued that the evidence available to the tribunal supported the evidence that a sale involving a yearling took place between Fustok and Abbeville Stud. Haughey had at the time been trying to persuade Fustok to invest in Ireland by bringing some of his racing business to the country; in his view, it was important for Irish racing and bloodstock breeding to have an owner of Fustok's international standing operating in Ireland. At no time did the tribunal suggest to any of the witnesses, and neither did they allege to Fustok himself in correspondence, that no sale had taken place. Dr John O'Connell gave evidence to the tribunal that he was the main proposer, supporter and lobbyist for all of those granted passports who were known to Fustok and that he did so on humanitarian grounds. In that context, the Haughey family maintained, the finding was perverse; the payment of £50,000 was not received by Mr Haughey by reason of the naturalisation of Ms Faten Moubarak or indeed any of those who had received Irish naturalisation.

The events of the Fustok payment to Haughey in February 1985 had been brought to Haughey's attention by O'Connell in January 1992. At a private meeting in the Sutton home of the businessman Dermot O'Leary, whom Haughey had appointed to the board of CIÉ in 1989, O'Connell told Haughey that he could not guarantee that the details of Fustok's payment to Haughey would remain secret. According to the journalist Sam Smyth, O'Leary led a secret group of influential Fianna Fáil activists who were backing Albert Reynolds for the leadership of the party.[11] As a revelation of any payment to Haughey, particularly from a Saudi businessman, no matter in what context, would have had devastating effects on his political life, Haughey privately agreed to step down in the near future. When Haughey was eventually replaced by Albert Reynolds just a few weeks later, O'Connell was appointed Minister for Health. Reynolds later appointed O'Leary to the board of Aer Rianta and to the position of chairman of CIÉ.

A few years earlier, in December 1989, O'Connell had told Haughey that he was becoming increasingly concerned by cuts to the health service and that the policies being pursued by Haughey's government were leading to a crisis situation across the country. He said he was finding it increasingly difficult to support the Minister for Health and demanded Haughey take remedial action. O'Connell received little succour from Haughey's reply. The Taoiseach told him: 'You will recall the critical situation we faced when we came into office in 1987. It is no exaggeration to say that the country was heading for national bankruptcy … We simply had to take drastic action. We are providing more funds in 1990 but I am still not satisfied that the solution is simply to provide more money.'[12] O'Connell had been disappointed when Haughey failed to appoint him to the cabinet after the 1989 election and their relationship turned sour. Over the next two years O'Connell became increasingly disillusioned by Haughey, although he voted for him in the leadership contest of November 1991. Suggestions that O'Connell was working with Reynolds to overthrow Haughey were denied by both men, but O'Connell was certainly instrumental in persuading Haughey to resign in early 1992.

In relation to the Séamus Paircéir–Ben Dunne meeting, the Haughey family claimed that the tribunal had not identified the alleged benefit sought by or conferred on Dunne by Haughey. Paircéir told the tribunal that, as the head of the Revenue Commissioners, he was going to have a meeting with Ben Dunne about the tax situation of the Dunne Family Trust, whether or not Haughey contacted him. The original Revenue Commissioners' estimate of the liability of the Dunne Family Trust was £38.8 million. They reduced this to £23.6 million, and finally offered Dunnes a settlement of £16 million. Ben Dunne rejected the offer and when the case went before the Tax Appeals Commissioner in November 1988, Dunnes won and paid no tax at all.[13] The tribunal did not say that Haughey had influenced the negotiations between Paircéir and Dunne. Moreover, the McCracken Tribunal had already found that apart from arranging the meeting, 'no representations were made by Mr. Charles Haughey on behalf of Mr. Ben Dunne or the Dunnes Stores group. The Tribunal is satisfied that there was no wrongful use of his position by Mr. Haughey in this regard.'[14] Essentially, the only thing that Haughey did was to effect an introduction between Paircéir and Dunne, which, the Haughey family submitted, he was obliged to do and did as a public representative.

In a famous piece of reportage for the *Irish Times* during the general election of 1989, entitled 'Charles Haughey's Irelands', Nuala O'Faolain wrote of Haughey:

Like most Irish TDs, too, he is asked for, and promises, help and favour. The difference between him and the TDs who complain about this clientelism (in private) is that he believes in it. 'Why should they hear from some faceless bureaucracy that they've got a pension? Why shouldn't they ask someone they know to get it for them? Why shouldn't someone they know personally tell them they've got it?' He was fervent about this. He doesn't see political patronage as keeping the people in subjection. He sees the politician as protecting the individual against indifference. What's more he sees this as the way the Irish people like to do things. And his commitment is to preserving the Irish way.[15]

That is essentially what Haughey was doing when he introduced Ben Dunne to Séamus Paircéir. Justice Brian McCracken was unimpressed with Dunne's donations to Haughey, noting that in accepting them Haughey failed in his obligations to his constituents and to the citizens of the state by making himself dependent on wealthy businessmen.[16] Haughey certainly did not see it that way. He believed that in introducing Dunne to Paircéir he was in effect simply protecting the individual against bureaucratic indifference. This was something he did for all constituents.

In July 2007, the Moriarty Tribunal wrote to Pádraig Ó hUiginn asking for his comments on the standards of proof and evidence that it should apply in its inquiry into Michael Lowry. Ó hUiginn had become a director of Esat Telecom in 1995 and the tribunal was investigating the awarding of the state's second mobile telephone licence to the company later that same year. Ó hUiginn, who had worked with Haughey for so long, replied that he profoundly disagreed with the standards the tribunal had applied in the Haughey module: 'There is no acceptable principle of jurisprudence or equity to justify "opinion" as the basis for findings in matters of such gravity which in the minds of the public involve criminal issues of bribery and corruption. I think such findings are unconstitutional. I also question the right of the tribunal to invent a new principle that "opinion" is sufficient proof in the matters it was set up to investigate.'[17] He had been outraged by the tribunal's treatment of Haughey during the thirty-three days it questioned him. He also considered the report iniquitous and unfair.[18] Many of Haughey's loyalists from his Taoiseach days felt the same. While he was giving his evidence to the tribunal his old press secretary Frank Dunlop told him, 'History will be kinder to you. In the police state in which we now live, truth, honour service to the State and other attributes are swept aside.'[19] Both Dunlop and Ó hUiginn remained loyal to Haughey in death. While the Haughey family, Dunlop, Ó hUiginn and others, including Dermot Desmond, considered Haughey to have been wronged by the Moriarty Tribunal, many more took the view that the tribunal had reached the correct conclusions about him.

MYTHS AND CONTRADICTIONS

In his note for Haughey's unpublished autobiography, Martin Mansergh suggested Haughey use the following paragraph:

> Some years after my retirement my private financial arrangements were accidentally brought to light in a way that has been embarrassing to myself, my family, and the country. They are capable, as I have discovered to my cost, of having a very negative but largely unjustified construction put upon them. All of this together with some other matters have resulted in a tribunal of investigation being established which has required me to explain and justify in more detail than my memory can supply the financial assistance which was collected for me by friends during public life and since. These funds made it possible for me to give generous help where it was most needed, to carry out my duties in a style which I thought appropriate (though others may fundamentally disagree), as well as to enjoy the company of friends. Since these revelations my reputation has been assailed from all quarters. While I accept that there is much in my public and private life that can be legitimately criticised, I have been accused of practically every crime not recognised by law that it is possible for a politician to

commit. Virtually anything can be written about me, without fear or contradiction. Without seeking to downplay my own heavy responsibility for the circumstances in which I now find myself, or to take away from my deep regret for the hurt and disappointment that this has caused others, especially those nearest and dearest to me, I have to reflect that it has been the lot of political leaders throughout history to have careers that end on a melancholy note. To climb the peak is a perilous and challenging journey in which a lot of opposition has to be overcome and on which it is easy to lose one's footing more than once ... Sooner or later, however, descent is inevitable, and often precipitous. Of my fellow European leaders who sat around the table with me in Dublin Castle at the European Council in June 1990 during the Irish presidency, men like Chancellor Helmut Kohl, President Mitterrand of France, and Prime Ministers Andreotti of Italy and Papandreou of Greece all made important and enduring contributions to their country but have suffered serious damage since to their representation arising from other circumstances in which they may or may not have been involved ... But in time more balanced assessments will have a chance to emerge, provided that complete myths are not allowed to prevail through want of contradiction.[20]

The aim of this particular work has been to provide such a balanced assessment of Haughey; to see through the myths, many of which Haughey created himself, and present a portrait of a man who was by far the most complex and divisive figure in modern Ireland. In his graveside oration at Haughey's funeral, Bertie Ahern accurately said of Haughey that he 'did not ride the winds and tides, he sought to change them'. There were times when Haughey succeeded magnificently and others when he failed deeply. Yet Haughey's life was also a mass of contradictions. He was the man of the towering intellect and the deep humanity. He was the statesman who, as the 1991 Notre Dame citation said, worked might and main to achieve historic agreements in which the parties of Northern Ireland pledged and ultimately succeeded in their attempts at reconciliation. The arms trial, however, haunted him throughout his life from his acquittal in 1970. He was the statesman who presided over an enormously successful European presidency, who played a crucial role in a pivotal period of European history and who had the respect and admiration of his peers on the world stage. He was the dominant figure in the revival of the Irish economy in 1987 through his vision of social partnership and his insistence in office of cutting public expenditure to regain international confidence in the Irish state. Yet he contributed to the dismal economic situation in the 1980s by his reluctance in his first two administrations to correct the public finances. His own personal finances were a mess of colossal proportions and left him open to the humiliation he suffered in his last decade. He was the patron of the arts who also understood the needs and wants of ordinary Irish people. Much to the chagrin of many, those same ordinary people kept voting for him in their thousands. He was also the man who took the money of Ireland's monied elite as if it were his due, and who brought ignominy to himself and his family. They remained steadfastly loyal to him in life as well as death. He died having long since made his peace with those who mattered to him – his wife and family – but the legacy that he himself so dearly wanted as the architect of modern Ireland was denied him.

In March 1987, just after taking the position of Taoiseach for the third time, Charles Haughey replied to a letter of encouragement he had received from the Church of Ireland Archbishop of Armagh, Robin Eames. Haughey wrote: 'I am very conscious of the daunting task ahead of me, but like John Bunyan's pilgrim we will be valiant and suffer no discouragement.'[21] Bunyan's great archetypal tale is at its heart a quest, fraught with danger, that takes his pilgrim, Christian, through the Slough of Despond, Vanity Fair and the Delectable Mountains. Haughey's own life was a similar quest. In his case the prize was power. The power he yearned for and used in so many different ways brought with it triumph and despair in differing measures. It saw the child of poverty experience both the bitter lows of the Slough of Despond and the dramatic highs of the Delectable Mountains in a life unparalleled in modern Irish political history.

ACKNOWLEDGEMENTS

My earliest political memory is of coming home from Sullivan's Quay primary school in Cork City on the afternoon of Friday 7 December 1979 to discover that Charles Haughey had won the Fianna Fáil leadership election. My late father, Jack Murphy, a painter in the Cork Harbour Commissioners, was looking at our television set in amazement. I had never heard him utter an expletive before, and never would do again, but on that day he let out an exasperated curse that earned him a stern rebuke from my mother. Like many people across the country, he was shocked that Fianna Fáil's TDs had chosen Haughey over George Colley, the preferred candidate of Jack Lynch, to lead the party. Both my parents were born into homes in Blackpool on Cork's northside, where Lynch hailed from. While ours was a non-political home, Lynch was spoken of in generally reverential terms. That evening I watched RTÉ news wondering who this Haughey character was. The following week I followed every news programme I could and began a new found interest in the politics page of Cork's *Evening Echo*, the paper of choice in our home. I have been obsessed with Irish politics and Haughey ever since.

This book is the culmination of some eight years' work, but in my mind it has been over forty years in the making, ever since I decided as an eleven-year-old that I needed to find out more about Charles

Haughey and how his victory in the Fianna Fáil leadership election led to the stunned reaction in my own home and across the country. I have amassed significant intellectual and personal debts in the course of my research and am glad to be able to repay some of them now.

I owe a major debt of gratitude to the family of Charles Haughey for allowing me access to his archive in Dublin City University, for opening many doors for me, and for speaking so frankly to me about him. I am particularly grateful to his children, Eimear Mulhern, Conor Haughey and Seán Haughey, and their families, for welcoming me into their homes and sharing their memories of their father, and mother, Maureen, with me.

I am very grateful to those who agreed to be interviewed for my research and gave me so much of their time. Some are now sadly deceased. I want to pay a particular thanks to Seán Aylward for his friendship and support. For many years I have been in and out of various libraries and archives tracking down various aspects of the career of Charles Haughey. I thank Seán Dorgan of Fianna Fáil for allowing me access to the Fianna Fáil papers and for offering many avenues of research. I am particularly grateful to the staff of the National Archives of Ireland, the National Library of Ireland, the University College Dublin Archives, and the Hesburgh library at the University of Notre Dame. Much of the work for this book was undertaken in the library of Dublin City University, where the Haughey papers are now held. I spent countless hours in the care of the University's librarians John McDonough and Chris Pressler and their team, particularly, Joe Dooley, Killian Downing, Gordon Kennedy, David Meehan, Felix Meehan and Liam O'Dwyer. I thank them for their professionalism, guidance and good humour. I am also grateful to the former President of DCU, Brian MacCraith, and the current President, Daire Keogh, for their encouragement and support of my work over the years. I thank DCU's Faculty of Humanities and Social Sciences Research Support Scheme for supporting this publication.

DCU is a vibrant and stimulating place to teach, research, and write. I have been very fortunate to work there for over twenty-five years among so many dedicated scholars and students. My work in the University has been aided and facilitated by many friends and colleagues, among them Alex Baturo, Eileen Connolly, Aisling de Paor, John Doyle, Barbara Flood, James Galvin, Jimmy Kelly, Eugene Kennedy, Katie Keogh, Christine Loscher, Ken McDonagh, Iain McMenamin, Ross Munnelly, Donnacha Ó Beacháin, Mark O'Brien, Deiric Ó Broin, Philip O'Connor, Cormac O'Sullivan, Declan Raftery and Mary Shine Thompson. I owe a particular thanks to my colleague Yvonne Daly for help with Irish translations and to Adam McAuley for advice on various legal aspects of Haughey's career.

I have learned much about Charles Haughey and Irish politics from conversations with many people over the years. I thank Nicholas Allen, Frank Barry, Elaine Byrne, Sarah Carey, Ken Carty, Raj Chari, Mick Clifford, John Coakley, Shane Coleman, Stephen Collins, Tommy Conlon, Matt Cooper, Liam Cullen, Deaglán de Bréadún, Eamon Delaney, Anne Dolan, Johnny Fallon, David Farrell, Michael Gallagher, Yvonne Galligan, Brian Girvin, Gerry Gregg, Anne Harris, Eoghan Harris, Mary Jones, Jerry Kelleher, Michael Kennedy, Dermot Keogh, Bill Kissane, Brian Lynch, Martin Mansergh, Michael Marsh, Shane Martin, Patrick Maume, Andrew McCarthy, Justine McCarthy, David McCullagh, Enda McEvoy, Harry McGee, Monica McWilliams, Ciara Meehan, John Mooney, Brian Murphy, Mary Murphy, James Morrissey, Miriam O'Callaghan, Anthony O'Connor, Tim O'Connor, Eoin O'Dell, Mary Ann O'Neil, Tim O'Neil, Mary O'Rourke, Terry Prone, Niamh Puirséil, Theresa Reidy, Paul Rouse, Rob Savage, Stephen Weir and Kevin Whelan. Two people who taught me much about political leadership, and Fianna Fáil, Robert Elgie and Noel Whelan, died within days of each other in July 2019. Both were taken much too soon and are sadly missed.

I spent two separate semesters working on this book as a guest of the Keough Naughton Institute for Irish Studies at the University of Notre Dame. I thank its directors Chris Fox and Patrick Griffin for hosting me so generously and making me a part of their wonderful community. I am very grateful to Seán McGraw for his guidance and friendship at Notre Dame and elsewhere. At Notre Dame I benefited greatly from the support of Beth Bland, Aedín Clements, Eugene Costello, Bob and

Martha Dunn, Mary Hendrickson, John and Chris Kelly, Declan and Beth Kiberd, Sarah McKibben, Tara McLeod, Peter McQuillan, Bríona Nic Dhiarmada, Stephen O'Neill, Bob Schmuhl and Enrico Terrinoni. A special thanks to Brian Ó Conchubhair. I am particularly grateful to Mary O'Callaghan and Diarmuid Ó Giolláin for their friendship, support and encouragement.

This book owes much to the insight, guidance and support of my friends and colleagues John Horgan, Eunan O'Halpin, Eoin O'Malley and Kevin Rafter. They all encouraged me to start it and told me to finish it. In the intervening years they kept me going with encouragement, advice, and dinner. They might not agree with all that is in the book but it is certainly better for their perceptive comments over the years.

Away from my desk, my friends Breda Griffith, Dave Hannigan, Michael Moynihan, Aengus Nolan, Joe O'Hara, and Colm O'Reilly remain pillars of support. Thanks especially to Michael O'Brien for Gillabbey Rock and much else besides, and Colm O'Callaghan for, well, everything.

I thank Nicki Howard, the Director of Gill Books, and her team including Teresa Daly, Ellen Monnelly and Claire O'Flynn for their professionalism and support, and in Nicki's case, considerable patience as she waited for my manuscript. That manuscript has been much improved by the sublime editing skills of Deirdre Nolan, my copyeditor Jane Rogers and the brilliant Aoibheann Molumby, who has dealt patiently and generously with my many queries as she saw this book to completion. I also thank Laura King for her tremendous work in compiling the photographic section. I am very grateful to them all. I owe a debt of gratitude to Michael Gill and Conor Nagle who suggested I publish with Gill in the first place and I am very happy I have.

Finally, although I cannot repay my debts to them this book would not exist without the support and love of my wife, Mandy, and children, Amy, Aoife and Jack. They have lived with the Haughey project for almost as long as I have, and I am eternally grateful to them for persevering with me, enduring my many absences and encouraging me over what at times seemed like a never-ending finishing line. They make my life complete. I also thank the wider Murphy family, especially my mother, Margaret, and siblings, Liam, Gina, Eric and Jacqui for their ongoing love and support. I am grateful for the friendship of Chris Lee. Finally, in the course of the writing of this book, Oliver Lee and Annabel Lee emerged into my world and have changed it so much for the better.

Gary Murphy
Dublin, July 2021

NOTES

INTRODUCTION

1. The area is widely referred to as Kinsealy, but Kinsaley is the spelling Haughey used in his own correspondence.
2. Interview with Maureen Haughey, 14 March 2014. I met Maureen Haughey in the company of her son Seán, and she told me of the sixty-odd years she had spent with Charles Haughey.
3. *Charles Haughey's Ireland* was shown on Channel 4 in the UK on 23 March 1986. It is available at https://www.youtube.com/watch?v=Rhodf3xTc0U&t=5s. In the draft script for the programme Haughey adds in his own handwriting the words 'like most Irish mothers'. The draft script is in the Haughey papers, Dublin City University, C7/106 (1).

1. CATHAL

1. 'The making of a Taoiseach' appeared in *Magill* on 30 January 1980.
2. Interview with Haughey's private secretaries Seán Aylward, 17 August 2016; and Donagh Morgan, 6 September 2017. Aylward was Haughey's private secretary from 1979 to 1981 and again in 1982. Morgan was Haughey's private secretary from 1987 to 1991.
3. Browne to Haughey, 18 January 1979, Haughey papers, C7/80. While Browne's letter is dated January 1979 it is clear that he is writing to Haughey as Taoiseach. It is stamped 21 January 1980 by the Department of the Taoiseach. Browne is mistaken in the spelling of Haughey's youngest brother's name as Owen; the spelling is 'Eoghan'.
4. Both John Haughey's and Sarah Haughey's military pensions files are available from the Military Service Pensions Collection at www.militaryarchives.ie, file number 24SP9208. A copy of parts of both John Haughey's and Sarah Haughey's pension files are in the Haughey papers, C7/123. This box consists of notes about John and Sarah Haughey.
5. Notes on wedding, birth and baptismal certificates (by CJH), Haughey papers, C7/123.
6. Haughey to Daly, 25 October 1989, Haughey papers, C7/55 (2).
7. A useful summation of John Haughey's file was provided by Ronan McGreevy in the *Irish Times* on 11 May 2018 under the headline 'Travails of Charles Haughey's father sheds new light on family trauma', available at https://www.irishtimes.com/news/ireland/irish-news/travails-of-charles-haughey-s-father-sheds-new-light-on-family-trauma-1.3491044.
8. Tim Pat Coogan (1990) *Michael Collins*. London: Macmillan, p. 351. This page is photocopied and in the Haughey papers, C7/123.
9. Louis Walsh to Charles Haughey, undated but by context late 1981, Haughey papers, C7/123.
10. See Johnnie Haughey's pension file. Also McGreevy, 'Travails of Charles Haughey's father'.
11. *An Cosantóir*, the Irish Defence Forces' journal, November 1983, p. 355.
12. See Johnnie Haughey's pension file. Also McGreevy, 'Travails of Charles Haughey's father'.
13. See John Haughey's pension file.
14. Unsigned profile of Charles James Haughey, *Irish Times*, 9 June 1969.
15. Haughey to Broughan, 6 February 1980, Haughey papers, C7/122 (1). Broughan became a Labour Party TD in 1989, contesting and winning elections in the same constituency as Haughey's son Seán. He left the Labour Party in 2014 and ran successfully as an independent in 2016.
16. Thomas Patrick Broughan (1980) *An Leabhar Uí hEochada Ulad (Notes on the Origins and History of the Surname Ó hEachaid, O'Haughey)* (hereafter *Haughey*), p. 370. Copy in possession of the author.
17. Interview with Fr Eoghan Haughey, 25 February 2014.
18. See also Ronan McGreevy, 'Charles Haughey's father blamed ill health on IRA service', *Irish Times*, 11 May 2018, available at

https://www.irishtimes.com/news/ireland/
irish-news/charles-haughey-s-father-blamed-
ill-health-on-ira-service-1.3491033.

19 MacErlean to Haughey, Haughey papers,
C7/123. The date given is just 1957, the year
Haughey was elected to the Dáil.

20 Young to Haughey, 10 May 1983, Haughey
papers, C7/123.

21 Egar to Haughey, 19 July 1991, Haughey
papers, C7/123.

22 *An Cosantóir*, the Irish Defence Forces'
journal, November 1983, p. 353.

23 Tobin to Haughey, 12 March 1984; Haughey
to Tobin 15 March 1984, Haughey papers,
C7/7 (1).

24 Bruce Arnold (1993) *Haughey: His Life and
Unlucky Deeds*. London: Harper Collins.
Tobin to Haughey, 19 May 1993; Haughey to
Tobin, 27 May, Haughey papers, C7/7 (5).

25 Phillips to Haughey, 16 July 1997; Haughey
to Phillips, 6 August 1997, Haughey papers,
C7/152 (2).

26 Notes on wedding, birth and baptismal
certificates (by CJH), Haughey papers, C7/123.

27 'Summary of Sworn Evidence Given Before
The Interviewing Officers By The Applicant
Mrs Sara Haughey – Nee Williams – (F.N.
44123) on the 7th November 1940 And
Agreed To By Her', Haughey papers, C7/123.
Sarah's maiden name was McWilliams, not
Williams; and she spelled her forename Sarah,
not Sara, in correspondence with officialdom.
She was known as Sadie to her family in
Derry. For convenience I have called her
Sarah in this work.

28 Sarah Haughey to secretary, Military Service
Pensions Board, 13 December 1940, Haughey
papers, C7/123.

29 See Sarah Haughey's Military Pension File at
www.militaryarchives.ie. The file number is
24SP9208.

30 Notes on wedding, birth and baptismal
certificates (by CJH), Haughey papers, C7/123.

31 Interview with Seán Haughey, Charles
Haughey's youngest son, 28 November 2020.
I have held a number of interviews with
Seán Haughey over the last few years and am
grateful for his time.

32 'The night Charlie was born', *Sunday World*,
24 September 2000. A copy is in the Haughey
papers, C7/121 (1).

33 Haughey's birth and baptismal certificates are
in the Haughey papers, C7/121 (1).

34 Bobby Molloy to Charles Haughey, 9 May
1978, Haughey papers, C7/121 (1). Molloy,
who would later fall out with Haughey
and leave Fianna Fáil for the Progressive
Democrats, was passing on the good wishes
of Chancellor Corcoran.

35 Interview with Seán Haughey, 27 May 2016.

36 I would like to thank Professor Amanda
Phelan of the School of Nursing and
Midwifery, Trinity College Dublin for this
information. The statistics suggest that one in
80,000 babies are born with a caul.

37 Martin Mansergh (ed.) (1986) *The Spirit
of the Nation: The Speeches and Statements
of Charles J. Haughey (1957–1986)*. Cork:
Mercier Press.

38 Interview with Monica McWilliams,
14 September 2018. McWilliams is a first
cousin of Charles Haughey and the daughter
of Owen McWilliams.

39 Interview with Seamus McWilliams, 20
September 2018. McWilliams is another
first cousin of Charles Haughey and the
son of Patsy McWilliams. He still lives in
Stranagone. I spent the day of 20 September
2018 touring Swatragh and Stranagone with
him, where he showed me the tunnel Johnnie
Haughey stayed in while on the run. I am
very grateful to him for his time and insights
into the history of this area of south Derry.

40 Patrick Maume, 'Haughey, Charles James
(C.J.)', *Dictionary of Irish Biography*, available
at https://www.dib.ie/biography/haughey-
charles-james-c-j-a9531, p.1. See also Justin
O'Brien (2000) *The Arms Trial*. Dublin: Gill
and Macmillan, p. 100; Stephen Kelly (2016)
'A Failed Political Entity', *Charles Haughey
and the Northern Ireland Question*. Dublin:
Merrion Press, p. 24.

41 Monica McWilliams interview.

42 David Burke, 'Charles Haughey did not run
guns to the IRA in 1970 but his father Seán
did decades earlier. And on the orders of
Michael Collins!', *Village* magazine, May
2020.

43 Eoghan Haughey interview.

44 Burke, 'Charles Haughey'.

45 Jean Healy, 'Genetic factor is key to
Haughey's survival', *Cork Examiner*,
26 October 1991. There is a copy in the
Haughey papers, C7/123.

46 See John Haughey's pension file.

47 O'Shiel to McKeon, 20 April 1928, Haughey
papers, C7/123.

48 See John Donohoe, 'Haughey's Meath roots',
Meath Chronicle, 26 July 1997. A copy is in the
Haughey archive, C7/121 (1).

49 *Meath Chronicle*, 27 September 2003,
Haughey papers, C7/121 (1).

50 Two of Haughey's early school copybooks
remain intact and are in his papers, C7/121 (1).
They were located in Abbeville in April 2002
having survived his childhood in Belton Park
and his adult changes of address – Howth
Road, Grangemore in Raheny and finally
Abbeville.

51 See Jean Healy, 'Genetic factor is key to Haughey's survival.'

52 Ibid.

53 This story was related to me by Kate Nugent in an interview on 13 August 2019. Kate Nugent was for many years Charles Haughey's constituency secretary. Her grandparents, the Ormondes, lived in Hazel Road, next to Belton Park Road, and were friendly with the Haugheys. Cathal Haughey was a childhood friend of her uncles.

54 Contribution of Deaglán de Bréadún in the question-and-answer session of a talk given by the author on the life of Charles Haughey, Trinity College, Dublin, 29 March 2017.

55 Anthony Cronin, 'Portrayal of former leader has serious errors of actuality', *Irish Independent*, 10 January 2015.

56 Answers prepared for Eleanor Walsh, Haughey papers, C7/134 (2). Walsh was working on a thesis regarding Haughey's time as Minister for Justice.

2. EDUCATION

1 Campion to Haughey, 14 December 1979, Haughey papers, C7/4 (2).

2 See *Irish Press* and *Irish Independent*, 17 August 1938. The clippings are in the Haughey papers, C7/121 (1). The *Irish Independent* is mistaken when it describes Seán as Cathal's younger brother. He was of course his older brother.

3 Rowe to Haughey: undated, but his reply thanking her is dated 3 January 1980 and she congratulates him on becoming Taoiseach in her first line, Haughey papers, C7/123.

4 Fr Eoghan Haughey told me that this chant was often sung by the Haughey boys when celebrating good news such as exam results and school and club football and hurling victories.

5 Ó Mórdha to Haughey, 17 June 2003, Haughey papers, C7/121 (1). Haughey rang him back to thank him for sending this reminder of his childhood.

6 Annraoi Ó Beolláin (Harry Boland), 'Bóithrín na Smaointe', St Joseph's Past Pupils' Newsletter, February 1993, a reminiscence on the fiftieth anniversary of the Leaving Certificate class of 1943 in which the writer recalled the fondness with which Brother Ó Catháin, 'The Goof', was regarded by the pupils. Copy in the Haughey papers, C7/121 (1).

7 Gerard Brockie (1988) *St Joseph's CBS, Fairview, 1888–1988*. Copy in the Haughey papers, C7/245.

8 Broughan, *Haughey*, p. 371.

9 Broughan, *Haughey*, p. 374.

10 As recalled by his St Joseph's contemporary, Art McGann, in episode one of the four-part RTÉ and Mint Productions documentary *Haughey*. It was screened on 13 June 2005 and can be seen at https://www.youtube.com/watch?v=10kJzyD2bKs&t=787s.

11 Ó Beolláin, 'Bóithrín na Smaointe'.

12 Enda McEvoy (1998) *Fennessy's Field: A Century of Hurling History at St. Kieran's College, Kilkenny*. Kilkenny: Red Lion Press has a brief account of the game (pp. 61–2). I am grateful to Enda McEvoy, one of Ireland's leading hurling journalists, for providing me with this information.

13 I am grateful to Professor Paul Rouse of UCD's School of History and Archives for providing me with this information. There is some debate as to whether Haughey actually started the game. Although he is named in the official programme, Jim Wren notes that he was actually a substitute in the game; see William Nolan (ed.) (2005) *The Gaelic Athletic Association in Dublin 1884–2000*, Vol. 3. Dublin: Geography Publications, p. 1145.

14 Sheila Walsh, in a letter to Haughey dated 12 October 1961, on his appointment as Minister for Justice, reminded him of the story of those black boots with the white laces; Haughey papers, C7/8 (1).

15 Eoghan Haughey interview.

16 Again I am grateful to Paul Rouse for providing me with this information. The allegiances in the Haughey household when it came to GAA were mixed as Charles Haughey's younger brother, Pádraig (known as Jock), played all his life with St Vincent's, winning an All-Ireland senior football medal with Dublin in 1958 when they beat Derry, some of whose players came from the Stranagone area of south Derry.

17 Nolan, *The Gaelic Athletic Association in Dublin*, p. 344.

18 Claffey to Haughey, 28 September 1995; Haughey to Claffey, 3 October 1995, Haughey papers, C7/152 (1).

19 Eoghan Haughey interview.

20 Kate Nugent interview

21 Kiberd is quoted in Episode 1 of the RTÉ documentary *Haughey*. The episode is pertinently called 'The Outsider'. I have learned much about Haughey from various conversations with Professor Kiberd and am grateful to him for his insights.

22 Eoghan Haughey interview.

23 Brockie, *St Joseph's CBS*, p. 53.

24 Broughan, *Haughey*, p. 375.

25 Sam Smyth (1997) *Thanks a Million Big Fella*. Dublin: Blackwater Press, pp. 9–10. Maureen

Haughey confirmed the essence of this story to me.

26 See for instance his CV on being appointed Minister for Agriculture and Fisheries in October 1964, Haughey papers, C7/19; see also Kelly, *Failed Political Entity*, p. 26. The FCÁ was the successor to the Local Defence Forces, which was stood down at the end of the war.

27 Haughey to Artane Company, 12 October 1956, Haughey papers, C7/19.

28 Haughey to BOC [Battalion Officer Commanding], North Co. Dublin Battalion, FCA, 12 February 1957, Haughey papers, C7/19.

29 Haughey to secretary, Clontarf Golf Club, 23 August 1956, Haughey papers, C7/19.

30 Secretary of Clontarf Golf Club to Haughey, 24 August 1956, Haughey papers, C7/19.

31 Eoghan Haughey interview.

32 Haughey's UCD identity cards are in the Haughey papers, C7/121 (1).

33 Maureen Haughey interview.

34 RTÉ and BBC Northern Ireland, *Seven Ages*, produced and directed by Seán Ó Mórdha. FitzGerald is interviewed in Episode 7, 'Haughey and FitzGerald: Great Adversaries of the Eighties', available at https://www.youtube.com/watch?v=xvRji-YFx8A&t=2961s.

35 Garret FitzGerald (1992) *All in a Life: An Autobiography*. Dublin: Gill and Macmillan, p. 31.

36 Maureen Haughey interview.

37 Kelly, *Failed Political Entity*, p. 23.

38 That Haughey led the demonstration is the recollection of his college friend at UCD, Kevin Burke, as told in Episode 1 of the RTÉ documentary *Haughey*.

39 Arnold, *Haughey*, p. 14.

40 *Irish Times*, 8 May 1945. In a piece on the 75th anniversary of the incident the *Irish Times* journalist Ronan McGreevy pieced together the events of that day. See https://www.irishtimes.com/news/ireland/irish-news/ve-day-75-haughey-fitzgerald-and-that-irish-times-front-page-1.4247916. There is also a lively account of the incident in the 'History Hub', 'Hidden History of UCD', at https://ucdhiddenhistory.wordpress.com/2009/04/27/7-charles-haughey/.

41 Burke recollection, *Haughey* documentary.

42 Maureen Haughey interview.

43 McGreevy, 75th anniversary, *Irish Times*.

44 FitzGerald in Episode 1 of the RTÉ documentary *Haughey*.

45 Kelly, *Failed Political Entity*, p. 28.

46 See the review of Kelly's *Failed Political Entity* by Martin Mansergh in *History Ireland*, 25:1, January/February 2017.

47 Mac Liammóir to Haughey, 18 September 1970, Haughey papers, C7/13 (3).

48 Haughey to Mac Liammóir, 20 September 1970, Haughey papers, C7/13 (3).

49 Maureen Haughey interview. When she died in 2017 at the age of 91 her obituary in the *Irish Times* noted that 'she was an astute observer of politics, and interested in history, but kept her views largely for her family circle and friends.' *Irish Times*, 25 March 2017.

50 Kathleen Lemass is quoted in John Horgan (1997) *Seán Lemass: The Enigmatic Patriot*. Dublin: Gill and Macmillan, p. 98.

51 *Irish Press*, 25 May 1945. A cutting of this report of the UCD Commerce Society is in the Haughey papers, C7/121 (1).

52 Treanor to Haughey, 22 December 1992, Haughey papers, C7/7 (5).

53 James Dooley to Haughey, 12 February 1991, Haughey papers, C7/48 (1).

54 Mulvin to Haughey, 12 October 1961; Haughey to Mulvin, 23 October 1961, Haughey papers, C7/8 (1).

55 In 1996 the UCD golden jubilee celebration for graduates of 1946 reported that seventeen students graduated with a BComm that year, including Haughey and Harry Boland. UCD Golden Jubilee Ceremony: Graduates of 1946, 18 September 1996, Haughey papers, C7/121.

56 Eoghan Haughey interview.

57 Interview with Eimear Mulhern, 8 January 2016. Eimear Mulhern is Haughey's eldest child.

58 I am grateful to Seán Aylward, former Under Treasurer at King's Inns, and Renate Ní Uigín, the librarian at King's Inns who provided me with copies of the documentation relating to Haughey's entrance to King's Inns and his acceptance to the Bar.

59 As told in *Seven Ages*, Episode 7.

60 Alex A. McCarthy, Registrar, National University of Ireland, to Haughey, 10 July 1947, Haughey papers, C7/121 (1).

61 This is one of two of Haughey's essays that survive from this period in his papers. The other is from his second year and is entitled 'Political Economy'. He was known to the UCD authorities as James Haughey but submitted his papers as Charles James Haughey.

62 Charles James Haughey 'The Financing of Industry in Ireland'; an essay submitted in pursuance of the prescribed regulations for the Bursary in Commerce, 1947. Haughey sent the finished manuscript to a typist for final submission. Haughey papers, C7/121 (1).

63   Interview with Deirdre Courtney, 29 November 2018.

64   Smyth, *Thanks a Million*, p. 10.

65   Maureen Haughey interview.

66   Edward Haughey to Charles Haughey, 9 December 1979, Haughey papers, C7/4 (2).

67   J. Crawford, secretary and treasurer of the Institute of Chartered Accountants in Ireland, to C.J. Haughey, 21 December 1948, Haughey papers, C7/121 (1).

68   Buchanan to Haughey, Haughey papers, C7/121 (1).

69   Lynch to Haughey, 15 November 1996, Haughey papers, C7/152 (2).

70   See Niamh Puirséil (2005) 'Political and Party Competition in Post War Ireland' in Brian Girvin and Gary Murphy (eds), *The Lemass Era: Politics and Society in the Ireland of Seán Lemass*. Dublin: UCD Press, pp. 14–15.

71   Haughey handwrote an undated document outlining the aims of the committee that produced *Firinne Fáil*. This was the basis of the report sent to the Dublin North East comhairle ceantair seeking permission to go ahead with the project. It is in the Haughey papers, C7/97 (1). A literal translation of An Coisde Craoladh would be 'the Broadcasting Commission', although Coisde would more normally be spelled Coiste.

72   Patrick Colley to Haughey, 13 July 1948, Haughey papers, C7/97 (1).

73   Haughey note on *Firinne Fáil*.

74   Vincent Browne, 'The Charlie Haughey story', *Sunday Independent*, 3 September 1978 –The clipping is in the Haughey papers, C7/18.

75   Haughey to the Secretaries of all Cumainn, Dublin North East, 21 September 1948, Haughey papers, C7/97 (1).

76   The draft letter of invitation is dated 25 February 1949, Haughey papers, C7/97 (1).

77   Traynor to Haughey, 9 March 1949, Haughey papers, C7/97 (1).

78   Maume, *Haughey*, p. 2.

79   'A Member of Fianna Fáil', Haughey papers, C7/97 (1).

80   Haughey to the Department of Industry and Commerce, for the attention of Mr Slattery, 15 June 1951, Haughey papers, C7/19.

81   Colm Keena (2001) *Haughey's Millions: Charlie's Money Trail*. Dublin: Gill and Macmillan, pp. 16–17.

82   Maureen Haughey interview.

83   Kelly, *Failed Political Entity*, p. 29.

84   Burke recollection, Haughey documentary.

85   The *Irish Independent* of 20 September 1951 announced the wedding as being between Cathal Haughey and Máirín Lemass.

86   A declaration of income prepared for Haughey by Annraoi O'Beollain in December 1951 gave his address as 53 Palmerston Road, Rathmines, Dublin. Annraoi O'Beollain was how Harry Boland always signed his name. Haughey papers, C7/243.

87   Maureen Haughey interview.

3. CHARLIE

1   Haughey to de Valera, 5 September 1951, Haughey papers, C7/97 (1).

2   Maureen Haughey interview.

3   Fleming to Haughey, 10 December 2003; Haughey to Fleming, 22 December 2003, Haughey papers, C7/97 (2).

4   The statement of Haughey's income as prepared by O'Beollain is in the Haughey papers, C7/243. There is no evidence of any of these firms ever trading.

5   Interview with P.J. Mara, 17 April 2014.

6   Haughey to S. Richardson, Norwich Union Fire Insurance Society Limited, 30 October 1951, Haughey papers, C7/19.

7   G.M. Goodbody, Friends Provident Building Society to Haughey, 4 September 1951, Haughey papers, C7/243.

8   Maurice Moynihan (1975) *Currency and Central Banking in Ireland, 1922–1960*. Dublin: Gill and Macmillian, p. 390.

9   Maureen Haughey interview.

10   University College Dublin Archives, Fianna Fáil papers, P167. Fianna Fáil Parliamentary Party Minutes 441/A, 14 January 1953.

11   Fianna Fáil Parliamentary Party Minutes 441/A, 22 July 1953.

12   Maureen Haughey interview.

13   These figures are taken from the ElectionsIreland.org website.

14   Fianna Fáil East Wall cumann to Haughey, 18 March 1954, Haughey papers, C7/97 (1).

15   Haughey to Tomás Ó Maoláin, Ard Runai FF, 20 Jan 1954, Haughey papers, C7/97 (1).

16   Lemass to Haughey, 8 August 1954, Haughey papers, C7/100 (1).

17   See Horgan, *Lemass*, p. 160; Maume, *Haughey*, p. 2. Conor Lenihan (2015) *Haughey: Prince of Power*. Dublin: Blackwater Press, p. 26 claims Lemass was in effect grooming his own leadership group with this initiative.

18   Haughey to the Director of Organisations, 28 April 1955, Haughey papers, C7/100 (1).

19   Haughey to the Director of Organisations, 12 February 1956, Haughey papers, C7/100 (1).

20   Report on Borris Comhairle Ceantair Re-Organisation Meeting, 18 May 1962, Haughey papers, C7/92 (1).

21   Lemass to Haughey, 8 October 1954, Haughey papers, C7/100 (2).

22 Lenihan, *Haughey*, p. 29.

23 Haughey to Ms Smith, Irish Countrywomen's Association, 25 November 1955, Haughey papers, C7/100 (1).

24 Haughey to Lemass, 3 March 1956, enclosing report to the Director of Organization from An Chomh Chomhairle Atha Cliath, Haughey papers, C7/100 (1).

25 Kavanagh to Haughey, 31 October 1955, Haughey papers, C7/100 (1).

26 Haughey to Smith, 25 November 1955. The report on the activities of the Chomhairle's first year gives the speakers, discussants and titles of the talks.

27 Lemass to Haughey, 7 September 1955, Haughey papers, C7/100 (1).

28 A detailed account of the Clery's ballroom speech is provided in Horgan, *Lemass*, pp. 164–8. A different view of the speech is provided by Bryce Evans (2011) *Seán Lemass: Democratic Dictator*. Cork: Collins Press.

29 Haughey's Ard Chomhairle agenda is in C7/100 (2) of his papers.

30 Haughey to committee members of An Chomh Chomhairle Atha Cliath, 13 September 1955.

31 Report to the Director of Organization from An Chomh Chomhairle Atha Cliath, 3 March 1956.

32 Andrews to Haughey, 12 November 1958, Haughey papers, C7/100 (1).

33 The Dublin No. 1 Area Corporation results are given in the *Irish Press*, 25 June 1955. Fianna Fáil emerged as the largest party but lost four seats in the city.

34 Maureen Haughey interview.

35 The *Irish Times*, *Irish Independent* and *Irish Press* all carried wide coverage of the flooding on 9 December 1954.

36 Byrne to Haughey, December 1954. There is no day given. Haughey papers, C7/97 (1).

37 The *Evening Herald* and *Evening Press* of 15 March 1956 and the *Irish Times*, *Irish Independent* and *Irish Press* of 16 March 1956 all extensively covered Byrne's funeral.

38 Profiles of the Fianna Fáil candidates in the 1955 local elections are in the Haughey papers, C7/97 (2).

39 David McCullagh (2018) *De Valera: Rule (1932–1975)*. Dublin: Gill, p. 344.

40 Haughey's speaking schedule for the last week of the campaign is in the Haughey papers, C7/97 (2).

41 *Irish Press*, 1 May 1956.

42 Vivion de Valera to Haughey, 1 May 1956, Haughey papers, C7/97 (2).

43 Haughey to de Valera, 8 May 1956, Haughey papers, C7/97 (2).

44 Haughey to Feehan, 8 May 1956; Haughey to Gageby, 8 May 1956. The draft letter to Gageby is dated 8 April but is clearly in May as it thanks Gageby for the 'wonderful help and assistance which you gave me in the recent Bye-Election campaign'. Haughey papers, C7/97 (2).

45 Feehan to Haughey, 16 May 1956, Haughey papers, C7/97 (2).

46 Haughey to Traynor, 14 July 1955, Haughey papers, C7/100 (2).

47 Traynor to Haughey, 19 July 1955, Haughey papers, C7/100 (2).

48 Healy to Haughey, 19 April 1956, Haughey papers, C7/97 (2).

49 Haughey to Healy, 4 May 1956, Haughey papers, C7/97 (2).

50 *Meath Chronicle*, 3 February 2010.

51 Donnacha Ó Beacháin (2011) *Destiny of the Soldiers: Fianna Fáil, Irish Republicanism and the IRA, 1926–1973*. Dublin: Gill and Macmillan, p. 234.

52 Kelly, Failed *Political Entity*, pp. 29–36. He is particularly critical of John Horgan's *Lemass* and Donnacha Ó Beacháin's *Destiny of the Soldiers*, accusing them both of missing its true significance. The original memorandum can be seen in the Fianna Fáil papers, P176/46.

53 Kelly, Failed *Political Entity*, pp. 33–4.

54 Thomas Mullins, Ard Runai, Fianna Fáil to Each Member Anti Partition Committee, 25 January 1955, Haughey papers, C7/100 (2).

55 Niall Haughey wrote to Charles Haughey's son Seán about this memorandum, in October 2007 when he was in the process of collating Charles Haughey's papers. He recalled discussing this memorandum with Haughey two years earlier in 2005. At this stage, Charles Haughey's final illness was quite far progressed and his memory failing, so it is not surprising that he had doubts about his involvement in the document's authorship. I am grateful to Seán Haughey for providing me with this information.

56 Lemass and Groome to Haughey, 21 December 1954, Haughey papers, C7/100 (2).

57 Kelly, Failed *Political Entity*, p. 37.

58 Horgan, *Lemass*, pp. 170–2.

59 Maureen Haughey interview.

60 Puirséil, *Political and Party Competition*, p. 23.

61 McCullagh, *De Valera: Rule*, pp. 346–7.

62 Haughey papers, C7/100 (1).

63 Details of the count are in the *Irish Press*, 7 and 8 March 1957.

4.IN THE DÁIL

1   Vincent Browne, *Sunday Independent*, 3 September 1978.

2   Colley to Haughey, 9 April 1957, Haughey papers, C7/97 (2).

3   Haughey speech at Traynor/Haughey presentation, 22 February 1962, Haughey papers, C7/92 (2).

4   Speech by Seán F. Lemass at dinner making presentation to Oscar Traynor and Harry Colley, Clery's Restaurant, Thursday 22 February 1962, Haughey papers, C7/92 (2).

5   Haughey to Guiney, 1 March 1962, Haughey papers, C7/92 (2).

6   Reffo to Haughey, 10 March 1962, Haughey papers, C7/92 (2).

7   See Emily O'Reilly, 'Thoroughly Modern Charlie', *Irish Press*, 1 October 1992.

8   Interview with Paddy Terry, 18 June 2020. Paddy Terry worked in the Department of Justice from 1946 to 1985 before retiring at the grade of Assistant Secretary. He later worked as legal adviser in the Department of Equality and Law Reform, and then as a parliamentary draftsman in the Office of the Attorney General, until he finally retired from public life at the age of 88 in 2008. I interviewed him in his home in June 2020, in the company of his daughter, Emer, when he was aged 100. He died a few months later on 28 September 2020. I am very grateful to Emer Terry for her kindness in arranging our interview in the midst of the Covid 19 pandemic. Paddy Terry also recounts this story in his unpublished private memoir, *70 Years in the Public Service*, which he prepared for his family. He gave me a copy of this memoir and I quote from it here with his daughter Emer's permission.

9   I am grateful to Seán Aylward for discussing this issue with me.

10   Interview with Brendan O'Donnell, 1 May 2018. O'Donnell served as Haughey's private secretary during his period as Minister for Agriculture and Minister for Finance from 1964 to 1970. He was transferred to the Department of Health and Social Welfare in 1977 at Haughey's request when he became minister and he followed to the Taoiseach's office on his election in 1979.

11   Part of Haughey's maiden Dáil speech is in Mansergh's *Spirit of the Nation*, pp. 1–3. The full speech can be found at https://www. oireachtas.ie/en/debates/debate/dail/1957-05-14/74/#spk_432.

12   Kelly, *Failed Political Entity*, p. 41. The full debate can be accessed at https://www. oireachtas.ie/en/debates/debate/dail/1957-07-04/41/.

13   Haughey to Ó Briain, 25 June 1958, Haughey papers, C7/100 (2). Haughey addresses his letter to Dhonncadha O Briain.

14   Ibid.

15   An outline schedule and draft film script of Channel 4's *Charles Haughey's Ireland* is in the Haughey papers, C7/106 (1).

16   Haughey to Michael Hayes, City Sherriff, 1 November 1957, Haughey papers, C7/19.

17   Dunlevy and Barry to Haughey, 2 December, Haughey papers, C7/19.

18   Haughey to Dunlevy and Barry, 11 December 1957, Haughey papers, C7/19.

19   Haughey papers, C7/100 (1).

20   Kate Nugent interview.

21   Haughey to Aiken, 20 January 1958, Haughey papers, C7/92 (1).

22   Dudley Edwards to Haughey, February 1958; Haughey to Dudley Edwards, 6 February 1958, Haughey papers, C7/92 (1). Dudley Edwards was the secretary of the 1913 club. Other members were David Thornley (chairman) and John Horgan, later an *Irish Times* journalist, TD, MEP, DCU academic, and biographer of Seán Lemass.

23   Haughey to An Rúnaí Príobháideach don Taoisigh, 22 March 1958, Haughey papers, C7/19.

24   Haughey to Terry O'Leary, 2 April 1958, Haughey papers, C7/19.

25   O'Leary to Haughey, 14 April 1958, Haughey papers, C7/19.

26   Kurt Schaefer to Haughey, 16 December 1957, Haughey papers, C7/19.

27   Haughey to Schaefer, 7 February 1958, Haughey papers, C7/19.

28   Gary Murphy (2009) *In Search of the Promised Land: The Politics of Post-war Ireland*. Cork: Mercier Press, p. 130.

29   Richard Aldous and Niamh Puirséil (2008) *We Declare: Landmark Documents in Ireland's History*. London: Trafalgar Square, p. 172.

30   Bryan Fanning (2008) *The Quest for Modern Ireland: The Battle for Ideas 1912–1986*. Dublin: Irish Academic Press, p. 197.

31   Fianna Fáil Parliamentary Party Minutes, FF441/B, 11 December 1958.

32   Fianna Fáil Parliamentary Party Minutes, FF441/B, 28 January 1959.

33   See for example Fianna Fáil Parliamentary Party Minutes, FF441/B, 4 March, 11 March, 29 April 1959.

34   Horgan, *Lemass*, p. 177.

35   Haughey to O'Brien, 4 November 1958, Haughey papers, C7/19

36   See the short-lived Fianna Fáil magazine *Cuisle*, Edition 2, Spring 2012, which has a brief history of Fianna Fáil Ard Fheiseanna and is available at https://

irishelectionliterature.files.wordpress.
com/2012/03/85163547-cuisle-edition-02.pdf.

37 Murphy, *Promised Land*, p. 132.

38 I am grateful to Monica McWilliams for this
information.

39 Haughey to Ó Caoimh, 18 September 1958,
Haughey papers, C7/19.

40 Monica McWilliams interview.

41 *Irish Press*, 29 September 1958.

42 Speech at Gillooly Hall, Sligo, 15 February
1959, Haughey papers, C7/149.

43 Speech at Cork School of Music, 14 March
1959, Haughey papers, C7/149.

44 Horgan, *Lemass*, p. 182.

45 This letter was sent to Fianna Fáil supporters,
and the template is undated and addressed
as A Chara. It was sent from Fianna Fáil
headquarters at 72 Amiens Street. Haughey
was Director of Finance and George Colley
was Agent and Director Publicity. Haughey
papers, C7/149.

46 McCullagh, *De Valera: Rule*, p. 372.

47 The results for the Dublin constituencies are
given in the *Irish Press*, 19 June 1959.

48 De Valera to Haughey, 23 June 1959, Haughey
papers, C7/19. I would like to thank my DCU
colleague Dr Yvonne Daly for her help in
translating this letter.

49 Haughey to de Valera, 2 July 1959, Haughey
papers, C7/19.

50 Haughey to McDonnell, 4 November 1958,
Haughey papers, C7/19. The reference to
Hamlet comes from the play's final scene
where Claudius turns to Gertrude and says
that Hamlet will win his duel against Laertes
and Gertrude replies, 'He's fat and scant of
breath.'

51 Undated note from Dr Maurice B. Berger, but
by context early 1959, Haughey papers, C7/97
(2).

52 I am grateful to Dr Anthony O'Connor,
consultant gastroenterologist at Tallaght
University Hospital for discussing the
intricacies of calories and body mass index
with me and for his incisive insights into
Haughey's health.

53 Haughey's dietary notes for this period are in
his papers, C7/97 (2).

54 Maureen Haughey interview. Haughey's
private secretaries, Seán Aylward and
Donagh Morgan both confirm that as
Taoiseach he ate relatively little during the
day and at working dinners would always
have fish. By contrast he constantly drank
tea throughout the day. In December 1967
Maureen Haughey wrote to the wife of the
Indian Ambassador to Ireland to thank
her for a Christmas gift of a box of Indian

tea that she and her husband had sent to
the Haugheys, and stated that both 'my
husband and myself are great tea drinkers
and look forward very much to sampling
this wonderful beverage.' Maureen Haughey
to Kamla Reni Tandon, 22 December 1967,
Haughey papers, C7/147 (1).

55 Haughey to McDonnell, 4 November 1958.

56 C. Garrett Walker to Haughey, 31 December
1979; Haughey to Walker, 7 January 1980,
Haughey papers, C7/3 (3).

57 Maureen Haughey interview.

58 Smyth, *Thanks a million*, p. 23.

59 Personal statement by Charles J. Haughey,
Minister for Finance, undated but by context,
early June 1959. Haughey papers, C7/91 (2). A
second copy is in C7/148 (1).

60 Statement by the Government Information
Bureau on behalf of the Attorney General,
9 June 1969, Haughey papers, C7/91 (2). A
second copy is in C7/148 (1).

61 Keena, *Haughey's Millions*, p. 26.

62 Gallagher in RTÉ *Haughey* documentary,
Episode 1.

63 Donegan to Haughey, 7 June 1969; Haughey
to Donegan, 10 June 1969, Haughey papers,
C7/91 (2).

64 MacDonagh to Haughey, 20 July 1967;
Haughey to MacDonagh, 24 July 1967,
Haughey papers, C7/147 (2).

65 MacDonagh to Haughey, 25 July 1967,
Haughey papers, C7/147 (2).

66 Haughey to Reverend Patrick Bruen, 17 June
1966, Haughey papers, C7/147 (2).

67 Smith to Haughey, 15 July 1966, Haughey
papers, C7/146 (2).

68 Haughey to Smith, 20 July 1966, Haughey
papers, C7/146 (2).

5. JUSTICE

1 Haughey alluded to Traynor's illness in an
interview he did with Lemass's biographer,
John Horgan, in October 1994. I am grateful
to Professor Horgan for providing me with
the notes of this interview. I have learned
much about Haughey from Professor Horgan
over many conversations.

2 This information comes from an interview
John Horgan did with Traynor's ministerial
colleague, Kevin Boland, in November 1994.
Again, I am grateful to Professor Horgan for
supplying me with his notes of that interview.

3 Arnold, *Haughey*, pp. 30–1. At this stage,
Berry was assistant secretary of the
Department of Justice but was its de facto
head as the secretary, T.J. Coyne, was out on
sick leave.

4   This quotation is taken from *Magill*, June 1980, and cited by Arnold, *Haughey*, p. 30.

5   'Berry Diaries', *Magill*, June 1980.

6   Maureen Haughey interview.

7   The first recorded evidence of this quote is in Mansergh, *Spirit of the Nation*, pp. xxii–xxiii.

8   Terry interview; memoir.

9   I am grateful to both Paddy Terry and Seán Aylward for discussing this issue with me.

10   Downey in the RTÉ *Haughey* documentary, Episode 1.

11   Terry interview; memoir.

12   Terry interview; memoir.

13   This was the reflection of many of the civil servants interviewed for this book who worked with Haughey over the course of his ministerial career.

14   Haughey to Sarah Murphy, 12 July 1983, Haughey papers, C7/62 (1).

15   Correspondence from Professor Eunan O'Halpin, 17 June 2020. O'Halpin, the son of Padraic O'Halpin, was a friend of the Harkins in their later years.

16   *Irish Times*, 17 December 1960.

17   Mansergh, *Spirit of the Nation*, p. 43.

18   See, for instance, the editorial 'Changes in the defamation law', *Irish Times*, 12 July 2003.

19   This speech is from the second stage of the 1961 Defamation Bill, 3 May 1961; https://www.oireachtas.ie/en/debates/debate/dail/1961-05-03/36/.

20   Professor Eoin O'Dell of TCD provides a useful summation of the debate in his online blog. It can be accessed at http://www.cearta.ie/2008/03/infamy-defamation-haughey/. I am grateful to Professor O'Dell for discussing this with me.

21   *Irish Times*, 17 December 1960.

22   Terry interview; memoir.

23   A good example of the style of debate between McGilligan and Haughey can be seen in their joust on Thursday 22 June 1961; https://www.oireachtas.ie/en/debates/debate/dail/1961-06-22/3/.

24   *Sunday Review*, 13 May 1962.

25   *Irish Times*, 11 May 1962.

26   *Irish Press*, 15 May 1962.

27   Terry interview; memoir.

28   Terry interview; memoir.

29   Walsh interviewed Haughey on 19 May 1998. She sent him a number of questions in advance and he had typed up his answers for her; Haughey papers, C7/134 (2). See Eleanor Walsh (1998) *The Minister as legislator: Charles J. Haughey as Minister for Justice, 1961 to 1964*. MA thesis, University College Cork.

30   Maureen Haughey interview.

31   Terry interview. A biographical note on Kellett by the Royal Irish Academy notes that Haughey was one of her pupils. See https://www.ria.ie/news/dictionary-irish-biography/iris-kellett-renowned-equestrian.

32   Haughey to Lemass, 23 July 1960; Lemass to Haughey, 25 July 1960, Haughey papers, C7/93 (2).

33   On 30 August 1995, I interviewed Colm Barnes about his relationship with Lemass. On that occasion he mentioned Haughey as having the right ideas about free trade and European integration in this stage of his career. Barnes fell out with Haughey and joined the Progressive Democrats in 1987 over his dismay at Fianna Fáil's reluctance to repudiate explicitly what he saw as its state-directed capitalism and unreconstructed Irish nationalism. See Terry Clavin's elegant *Dictionary of Irish Biography* entry on Barnes, https://www.dib.ie/biography/barnes-colm-a9338.

34   Barnes to Haughey, 7 July 1960, Haughey papers, C7/92 (1).

35   Haughey to Barnes, 8 July 1960, Haughey papers, C7/92 (1).

36   *Irish Times*, 17 December 1960 featured Haughey in its '*talking to*' series.

37   Haughey to Colley, 21 March 1961, Haughey papers, C7/93 (2).

38   Colley to Haughey, 6 April 1961, Haughey papers, C7/93 (2).

39   'The Reform of the Law', speech to An Chomh Chomhairle, Fianna Fáil, 15 April 1961, Haughey papers, C7/93 (2). Parts of the speech are underlined in red pen.

40   *Irish Times*, 17 December 1960.

41   Report of the Television Joint Committee to the Fianna Fáil National Executive, March 1961, Haughey papers, C7/92 (1). The committee consisted of T.J. O'Reilly (chair), Joseph Groome, Lionel Booth, Anthony Hederman, and Haughey.

42   Horgan, *Lemass*, p. 315.

43   See Robert Savage (2010) *A Loss of Innocence? Television and Irish Society 1960–72*. Manchester: Manchester University Press, pp. 64–6.

44   Interview with Mike Burns, 28 February 2020. Burns joined RTÉ in 1963 and worked there until 1991 in a variety of roles in both radio and television. He interviewed Haughey on numerous occasions. He died in February 2021.

45   Haughey to Blaney 29 August 1962, Haughey papers, C7/91 (1).

46 Interview with Terry Prone, 14 May 2019. Haughey used Carr Communications, the agency led by Tom Savage and Terry Prone, to prepare for numerous television appearances in the 1980s and early 1990s. Terry Prone commented that his professionalism in preparation was meticulous.

47 Raymond Shiel to Haughey, 14 October 1961, Haughey papers, C7/8 (1).

48 P. O'Meachair to Haughey, 15 September 1961; Haughey to O'Meachair, 16 September 1961, Haughey papers, C7/92 (2).

49 O'Sullivan to Haughey, 30 September 1961, Haughey papers, C7/92 (2).

50 Aylward interview. The original Burma Road linked Lashio in eastern Burma (now Myanmar), with Kunming, in Yunnan province, China and was 1,154 km (717 miles) long. The Chinese began construction of the road after the outbreak of the Sino-Japanese War in 1937 and completed it in 1939. It was a vital supply route to China from the outside world. In April 1942 the Japanese overran Burma, seized Lashio, and closed the road.

51 Haughey to Raymond Shiel, 17 October 1961, Haughey papers, C7/8 (1). Shiel had originally suggested to him that he would have to put up with suggestions of nepotism, which 'no doubt, will bother you hugely!', Shiel to Haughey, 14 October 1961, Haughey papers, C7/8 (1).

52 Doyle to Haughey, 9 October 1961, Haughey papers, C7/8 (1). The underlining of 'are' is in the original.

53 Haughey to Doyle, 19 October 1961, Haughey papers, C7/8 (1).

54 Walsh to Haughey, 12 October 1961; Haughey to Walsh, 16 October 1961, Haughey papers, C7/8 (1). Walsh was a long-term journalist at the *Irish Press* who ended up as the paper's women's editor. Her wedding diary was an integral part of the *Irish Press* and a major part of the success of the Saturday editions of the paper. My thanks to John Horgan and Seamus Dooley for this information.

55 Haughey to Gemma Boyd Barrett, 24 October 1961, Haughey papers, C7/93 (1).

56 Castelnau to Haughey, 12 October 1961, Haughey papers, C7/8 (1).

57 Terry interview; memoir.

58 Terry interview; memoir.

59 The Dáil debate on the issue is at https://www.oireachtas.ie/en/debates/debate/dail/1958-11-25/44/.

60 This account of the Macushla affair is drawn from Conor Brady (2014) *The Guarding of Ireland: The Garda Síochána and the Irish State 1960–2014*. Dublin: Gill and Macmillan; Vicky Conway (2014) *Policing Twentieth-Century Ireland: A History of An Garda Síochána*. London: Routledge.

61 This was recalled by Desmond Anderson of M.G. Anderson Insurances in a letter to Haughey on 4 February 1980 thanking him for his support in this matter. Haughey papers, C7/3 (2).

62 Thomas Mark Muldoon, General Secretary, Garda Representative Body for Inspectors, Station-Sergeants and Sergeants to Haughey, 9 June 1971, Haughey papers, C7/102 (2).

63 Mullen to Haughey, 11 November 1991, Haughey papers, C7/2 (1).

64 Haughey to Diarmuid Ó hAlmhain, 3 January 1963, Haughey papers, C7/93 (2).

65 Answers prepared for Eleanor Walsh, Haughey papers, C7/134 (2).

66 Terry interview; memoir.

67 O'Donovan to Haughey, 27 August 1964, Haughey papers, C7/146 (2).

68 Haughey to O'Donovan, 31 August 1964, Haughey papers, C7/146 (2).

69 In a letter dated 14 October, Ó Mórdha wrote to Haughey thanking him for meeting him the day before. The year is not mentioned but is most probably 1998. Ó Mórdha's landmark series, *Seven Ages*, aired in February and March 2000.

70 For a good account of the Succession Act and its importance in Irish life, see Finola Kennedy (2001) *Cottage to Crèche: Family Change in Ireland*. Dublin: Institute of Public Administration, pp. 224–34.

71 Answer prepared for Eleanor Walsh, Haughey papers, C7/134 (2).

72 Mansergh, *Spirit of the Nation*, p. 47.

73 Haughey to Hobson, 16 July 1964, Haughey papers, C7/146 (1).

74 Mansergh, *Spirit of the Nation*, p. 47.

75 Cohn to Haughey, 23 November 1964, Haughey papers, C7/14 (2).

76 Maguire to Haughey, Haughey papers, C7/147 (2). The letter is undated and simply says 'Monday'. The reply, sent on behalf of Haughey by his then private secretary Brendan O'Donnell, is dated 11 October 1967.

77 A copy of this speech is in the Haughey papers, C7/153 (2).

78 Answer prepared for Eleanor Walsh, Haughey papers, C7/134 (2).

79 Haughey to Hinkson, 16 April 1964 Haughey papers, C7/146 (1).

80 Speech by the Minister for Finance, Charles J. Haughey, at a meeting of Comhdhail Atha Cliath in the Shelbourne Hotel, 10 June 1969, Haughey papers, C7/8 (1).

81   Keynote address by the Taoiseach, Charles J. Haughey, at the Conference organised by the Council for the Status of Women, 1 February 1992, Haughey papers, C7/154.

82   Kelly, *Failed Political Entity*, p. 43.

83   Berry to Lynch, 8 June 1970 quoted in John Bowman, 'Letter tells of Haughey role in "breaking" IRA', *Irish Times*, 2 January 2001.

84   Ó Beacháin, *Destiny of the Soldiers*, p. 250.

85   Charles J. Haughey statement on the end of the border campaign, 27 February 1962 in Mansergh, *Spirit of the Nation*, pp. 4–5.

86   Haughey to Sister M. Frances Teresa, 26 March 1965, Haughey papers, C7/146 (1).

87   T. Ryle Dwyer (1987) *Charlie. The Political Biography of Charles Haughey*. Dublin: Gill and Macmillan, p. 37. On the death penalty in Ireland see David M. Doyle and Liam O'Callaghan (2019) *Capital Punishment in Independent Ireland*. Liverpool: Liverpool University Press; Ian O'Donnell (2017) *Justice, Mercy, and Caprice: Clemency and the Death Penalty in Ireland*. Oxford: Oxford University Press. See also Mary Rogan (2011) *Prison Policy in Ireland: Politics, Penal-Welfarism and Political Imprisonment*. Abingdon: Routledge.

88   Terry interview; memoir.

89   Mansergh, *Spirit of the Nation*, p. 22.

90   Doyle and O'Callaghan, *Capital Punishment in Independent Ireland*, p. 202.

91   Michie to Haughey, 12 June 1985; Haughey to Michie, 19 June 1985, Haughey papers, C7/74 (1).

92   Michael Kennedy (2000) *Division and Consensus: The Politics of Cross-Border Relations in Ireland, 1925–1969*. Dublin: Institute of Public Administration, p. 203.

93   Ruadhán Mac Cormaic (2016) *The Supreme Court*. Dublin: Penguin Ireland, p. 93.

94   Mansergh, *Spirit of the Nation*, p. 26.

95   Terry interview; memoir.

96   Answers prepared for Eleanor Walsh, Haughey papers, C7/134 (2).

97   B.H. Hayden, Chairman, Mountjoy Prison Visiting Committee, to Haughey, 27 November 1964, Haughey papers, C7/146 (1).

98   Mac Cormaic's *The Supreme Court* provides very good accounts of the careers of both Ó Dálaigh and Walsh.

99   Ó Dálaigh to Haughey, 12 October 1964, Haughey papers, C7/146 (2).

100   Walsh to Haughey, 9 October 1964, Haughey papers, C7/150.

6. AGRICULTURE

1   Note to the voters of Dublin North East from the Minister for Justice, Charles J. Haughey, undated but by context May 1963 as the by-election was held on 30 May, Haughey papers, C7/91 (1).

2   Haughey to Prince Rainier, 14 August 1963, Haughey papers, C7/19.

3   Haughey to Maloney, 20 November 1963, Haughey papers, C7/19.

4   See David Fitzpatrick (1996) '"Unofficial emissaries": British Army boxers in the Irish Free State, 1926', *Irish Historical Studies*, Vol. 30, No. 118, 206–32, at p. 209.

5   O'Flynn to Haughey, 28 January 1964, Haughey papers, C7/146 (2).

6   Interviews with his private secretaries Brendan O'Donnell, Seán Aylward and Donagh Morgan confirmed Haughey's periodic bouts of stress. His wife and children also confirmed his difficulties with kidney stones.

7   Report to C.J. Haughey, TD, the Minister for Justice, November 1963, Memorandum on the Public Image of the Fianna Fáil Party, Haughey papers, C7/91 (1).

8   A copy of Thornley's lecture is in the Haughey papers, C7/92 (1). Thornley was elected for the Labour Party in Dublin North West in 1969 and 1973. On his life and career see Yseult Thorney (ed.) (2008) *Unquiet Spirit: Essays in Honour of David Thornley*. Dublin: Liberties Press; Edward Thornley (2012) *Lone Crusader: David Thornley and the Intellectuals*. Dublin: Ashfield Press.

9   Tomás Ó Maoláin to Each Member Organisation Committee, 21 August 1964, Haughey papers, C7/92 (1).

10   Thornley to Haughey, 4 June 1970, Haughey papers, C7/13 (3).

11   I am grateful to Leo Powell, editor of the *Irish Field*, for providing me with this information and discussing Haughey's career as a horse owner and stud farmer with me.

12   In a letter to Lady Anne Hemphill on 14 January 1964, Haughey outlined Maureen's increased interest in hunting and mentioned that he himself had had some good recent hunting with Wards; Haughey papers, C7/146 (1).

13   *Irish Press*, 9 October 1964.

14   Smith's resignation letter is reproduced in Brian Farrell (1971) *Chairman or Chief? The Role of Taoiseach in Irish Government*. Dublin: Gill and Macmillan, pp. 66–7. Lemass was keen to have the trade union movement support the government's EEC

application, which had lapsed in January 1963 after Charles de Gaulle vetoed the British application.

15 National Archives and Records Administration of the United States (NARA), RG59, 2343, Pol 2-1 Ire, Dublin Embassy to State Department, 9 October 1964.

16 NARA RG59, 2343, Pol 15-1 Ire, Dublin Embassy to State Department, 16 October 1964.

17 *Irish Times*, 10 October 1964.

18 *Irish Times*, 15 October 1964.

19 Horgan, *Lemass*, p. 356.

20 Mary Daly (2002) *The First Department: A History of the Department of Agriculture.* Dublin: Institute of Public Administration, p. 459.

21 C.S. Andrews (1982) *Man of No Property: An Autobiography.* Dublin: Lilliput Press, p. 242.

22 National Archives of Ireland, Department of the Taoiseach, NAI, DT, S.17543A/63, Lemass to Smith, 5 November 1963. Lemass was telling Smith of a meeting he had had with Deasy at which he expressed these views.

23 Maurice Manning (1986) *The Blueshirts*, 2nd edn. Dublin: Gill and Macmillan, p. 57.

24 Lemass was speaking in the Dáil debate on this issue on 12 December 1963. See https://www.oireachtas.ie/en/debates/debate/dail/1963-12-12/5/.

25 This memorandum is quoted in Murphy, *Promised Land*, p. 232.

26 Childers to Haughey, 12 October 1964, Haughey papers, C7/19.

27 Griffin to Haughey, 10 October 1964, Haughey papers, C7/150.

28 Tinsley to Haughey, 12 October 1964, Haughey papers, C7/150.

29 Harrower to Haughey, 20 October 1964, Haughey papers, C7/146 (1).

30 Doyle to Haughey, 19 October 1964, Haughey papers, C7/150.

31 This description is cited in Daly, *The First Department*, p. 343.

32 Deasy to Haughey, 12 October 1964, Haughey papers, C7/91 (1).

33 Creedon to Haughey, 20 January 1988, Haughey papers, C7/37 (7).

34 On 31 August 1994 I interviewed Jack Nagle at his home in Rathgar, Dublin about his long career in the civil service as part of my PhD research. He recalled that the difference between Haughey and Smith in their approach to agriculture brief was stark. Smith was happy to let his officials take the lead on policy, whereas Haughey made it clear that he was open to all sorts of ideas from within the department but it was he who was firmly in charge of its policy orientation.

35 Haughey to M. Mooney, 8 June 1965, Haughey papers, C7/146 (1).

36 Address at the inaugural meeting of the Dublin Institute of Catholic Sociology, 21 November 1964 in Mansergh, *Spirit of the Nation*, pp. 49–51. The Dublin Institute of Catholic Sociology was headed by a priest named Liam Carey, who was put into that role by Archbishop John Charles McQuaid at a time when he felt that he might have been losing his grip on the Department of Sociology in University College, Dublin, which was, despite his best efforts, being slowly infiltrated by younger lay academics.

37 Elizabeth O'Brien to Haughey, 18 December 1964, Haughey papers, C7/151 (1). Macra na Tuaithe was the youth branch of Macra na Feirme.

38 Haughey to O'Brien, 22 December 1964, Haughey papers, C7/151 (1).

39 The programme for the event can be seen at Alan Kinsella's excellent Irish election literature website at https://irishelectionliterature.com/2016/03/06/1964-programme-for-a-dinner-to-mark-the-40th-anniversary-of-sean-lemass-as-a-t-d/.

40 Haughey to Robert P. Chalker, 1 October 1964, Haughey papers, C7/146 (1).

41 For a breezy account of the Kennedy visit to Ireland see Ryan Tubridy (2010) *JFK in Ireland: Four Days that Changed a President.* London: HarperCollins. See also Brian Murphy and Donnacha Ó Beacháin (eds) (2021) *From Whence I Came: The Kennedy Legacy, Ireland and America.* Dublin: Irish Academic Press.

42 Haughey to O'Higgins, 2 December 1964, Haughey papers, C7/146 (2).

43 Bowen to Haughey, 29 July 1965 which includes the *Financial Times* clipping of 27 July; Haughey to Bowen, 3 August 1965, Haughey papers, C7/146 (1). The debate was actually held on 24 November 1964 and Haughey told the Dáil he made a profit of £874. Haughey was debating with the Labour Party's Michael Pat Murphy who told him that 'Down the country people who have been dealing with hens for years say that at present prices every hen dies in debt.' The debate can be accessed at https://www.oireachtas.ie/en/debates/debate/dail/1964-11-24/28/.

44 Text of proposed interview with Charles Haughey for *Pigs and Poultry* magazine, 23 February 1965, Haughey papers, C7/244.

45 Haughey to Mansholt, 8 February 1965, Haughey papers, C7/146 (1).

46 Haughey to Brandt, 5 February 1965, Haughey papers, C7/146 (1). The Internationale Grüne Woche translates as International Green Week.

47 Address by Charles J. Haughey, TD, Minister for Agriculture, at the Queen's University Literary and Scientific Society Debate on 'The Future of Irish Politics', 9 February 1958, Haughey papers, C7/91 (1).

48 Patrick Maume, 'West, Harry (Henry William)', Dictionary of Irish Biography, available at https://www.dib.ie/biography/west-harry-henry-william-a9368. West would later become leader of the Ulster Unionist Party from 1974 to 1979 and ran against the hunger striker Bobby Sands in the famous Fermanagh–South Tyrone by-election of April 1981.

49 Interview with Bertie Ahern, 21 August 2018. Ahern, who was close to Haughey during the 1980s, maintained that Haughey was very proud of his relationship with West and other contacts which he built up during the 1960s, but which were diluted after the arms trial of 1970.

50 Kennedy, Division and Consensus, p. 246.

51 West to Haughey, 18 February 1965, Haughey papers, C7/146 (2). For the later meetings between Haughey and West, see Anthony Craig (2010) Crisis of Confidence: Anglo-Irish Relations in the Early Troubles. Dublin: Irish Academic Press, p. 33.

52 Kennedy, Division and Consensus, p. 264.

53 Faulkner to Haughey, 28 January 1966, Haughey papers, C7/147 (2).

54 Haughey to Faulkner, 1 February 1966, Haughey papers, C7/147 (2). 'Up there' was a euphemism often used by Haughey to refer to Northern Ireland.

55 Address at the Irish Club, London, St Patrick's Day, 17 March 1965, in Mansergh, Spirit of the Nation, p. 51.

56 A brief clip of the event can be seen on the RTÉ website at https://www.rte.ie/archives/2015/0318/687812-haughey-attends-irish-club-banquet-in-london/.

57 Kennedy, Division and Consensus, p. 245.

58 Horgan, Lemass, p. 206.

59 In April 1991, as a postgraduate student in UCC, I interviewed Flor Crowley about his political career. Haughey was in his third stint as Taoiseach at this stage and Crowley was still in touch with him and remained a staunch defender. He died suddenly at his home in Bandon in May 1997.

60 Stephen Collins and Ciara Meehan (2020) Saving the State: Fine Gael from Collins to Varadkar. Dublin: Gill Books, p. 107.

61 Haughey speech to the Oscar Traynor Cumann, Raheny, 25 March 1965, Haughey papers, C7/90 (1).

62 Haughey speech to the Dublin North East Fianna Fáil Convention, Whitehall, 19 March 1965, Haughey papers, C7/90 (1).

63 Horgan, Lemass, p. 207.

64 Corry to Haughey, 17 April 1965, Haughey papers, C7/90 (1).

65 For Corry's role in the 1920–22 War of Independence and Civil War era, see Gerard Murphy (2010) The Year of Disappearances: Political Killing in Cork 1921–1922. Dublin: Gill and Macmillan. See also the documentary by Eunan O'Halpin In the Name of the Republic shown on TV3 in March 2013, available at https://www.youtube.com/watch?v=rPpZ1u0Ra1M.

66 Haughey to Seán MacCarthy, 19 March 1965, Haughey papers, C7/91 (1).

67 MacCarthy to Haughey, 18 March 1965, Haughey papers, C7/91 (1).

68 Breen to Lemass, 7 April 1965, copy in the Haughey papers, C7/91 (1).

69 Lemass to Haughey, 9 April 1965, Haughey papers, C7/91 (1).

70 Haughey to Breen, 14 April 1965, Haughey papers, C7/91 (1). The book Haughey refers to is Breen's famous account of his role in the War of Independence and Civil War, My Fight for Irish Freedom, first published by Talbot Press in 1924. He was involved in the ambush and killing of two RIC policemen at Soloheadbeg in Tipperary, widely regarded as the act that started the War of Independence.

71 Breen to Haughey, 14 April 1965, Haughey papers, C7/91 (1). This letter is dated the same day as Haughey's to Breen but seems clearly to be a reply to Haughey's original.

72 Thomas Murray to Haughey, 2 April 1965, Haughey papers, C7/90 (1).

73 Haughey to Murray, 5 April 1965, Haughey papers, C7/90 (1).

74 FitzGerald to Haughey, undated May 1965, Haughey papers, C7/90 (1).

75 Haughey to FitzGerald, 5 May 1965, Haughey papers, C7/90 (1).

76 Nagle to Haughey, 25 April 1965, Haughey papers, C7/150.

77 Tim Pat Coogan (1966) Ireland Since the Rising. London: Pall Mall Books, p. 110.

78 Coogan to Haughey, undated but received in the Department of Agriculture 24 November 1964, Haughey papers, C7/146 (1). Haughey replied the same day.

79 Haughey is quoted in Episode 5 of the Seán Ó Mórdha series Seven Ages. The episode

is titled 'The Modernisation of Ireland' and is available at https://www.youtube.com/watch?v=Lu7mCngeGvE.

80   Lenihan, *Haughey*, p. 34.

81   For a history of Jammet's see Alison Maxwell and Shay Harpur (2011) *Jammet's of Dublin 1901 to 1967*. Dublin: Lilliput Press.

82   Peart to Haughey, 13 May 1965, Haughey papers, C7/146 (2). The incident took place the previous week, on 6 May. Wilson was Prime Minister and leader of the Labour Party, and Brown was deputy leader and deputy prime minister.

83   Haughey to Peart, 17 May 1965, Haughey papers, C7/146 (2).

84   Boston to Haughey, 11 May 1965, Haughey papers, C7/146 (1); Tyrell to Haughey, 6 May 1965, Haughey papers, C7/146 (2).

85   Haughey to Tyrell, 10 May 1965, Haughey papers, C7/146 (2).

86   Haughey to Boston, 11 May 1965, Haughey papers, C7/146 (1).

87   MacGabhainn to Haughey, 6 May 1965; Haughey to MacGabhainn, 10 May 1965, Haughey papers, C7/146 (1).

88   Wilson to Haughey, 7 May 1965, Haughey papers, C7/150.

89   Dermot Keogh (2008) *Jack Lynch: A Biography*. Dublin: Gill and Macmillan, p. 94.

90   Mary Daly (2016) *Sixties Ireland: Reshaping the Economy, State and Society, 1957–1973*. Cambridge: Cambridge University Press, p. 56.

91   Keogh, *Lynch*, p. 96.

92   Lynch's Dáil budget speech of 11 May 1965 is available at https://www.oireachtas.ie/en/debates/debate/dail/1965-05-11/57/.

93   Haughey to Lemass, 10 May 1965, Haughey papers, C7/146 (1).

7. OF FARMERS AND ELECTIONS

1   O'Donnell interview.

2   See Purcell's obituary in the *Irish Times*, 29 March 2003, 'Head of family business that was world leader in shipping of live cattle'. It is available at https://www.irishtimes.com/news/head-of-family-business-that-was-world-leader-in-shipping-of-live-cattle-1.353953.

3   Aiken to Haughey, 28 January 1965, Haughey papers, C7/146 (1).

4   Haughey to Aiken, 4 February 1965, Haughey papers, C7/146 (1).

5   Smyth, *Thanks a Million*, p. 13.

6   *The Death of an Irish Town* was originally published by Mercier Press in 1968. It was reissued twenty years later under the title *No One Shouted Stop* in 1988 and published

under Healy's own imprint, The House of Healy.

7   See Conor Brady, 'Healy, John', *Dictionary of Irish Biography*, https://www.dib.ie/biography/healy-john-a3896.

8   See Mark O'Brien (2014) '"Sources say … "': Political Journalism since 1921', in Mark O'Brien and Donnacha Ó Beacháin (eds), *Political Communication in the Republic of Ireland*. Liverpool: Liverpool University Press, p. 84.

9   Information from John Horgan.

10   Healy to Haughey, undated but by context it is before the election of 1965; Haughey papers, C7/91 (1).

11   See Dennehy's obituary in the *Irish Times*, 24 July 1999. It is available at https://www.irishtimes.com/news/innovator-who-was-one-of-the-pioneers-of-public-relations-1.210018.

12   Information from John Horgan.

13   Healy to Haughey.

14   The Dáil debate on the Anglo-Irish Free Trade Agreement on 5 January 1966 can be seen at https://www.oireachtas.ie/en/debates/debate/dail/1966-01-05/3/. Parts of Haughey's speech are reproduced in Mansergh, *Spirit of the Nation*, pp. 54–9.

15   Mansergh, *Spirit of the Nation*, p. 59.

16   Haughey to Peart, 16 November 1966, Haughey papers, C7/147 (1). Haughey had actually taken up the position of Minister for Finance the previous week, on 11 November.

17   See Ray Ryan, 'The historic battle to increase price of milk', *Irish Examiner*, 6 August 2016.

18   Collins and Meehan, *Saving the State*, pp. 114–15. Sweetman tragically died in a car crash in Monasterevin in January 1970. His unexpected death at the age of 61 was a grievous blow to the conservative wing of Fine Gael and the party as a whole.

19   Gary Murphy and Theresa Reidy (2012) 'Presidential elections in Ireland: From partisan predictability to the end of loyalty', *Irish Political Studies* 27:4, 615–34, at pp. 623–4.

20   Ciara Meehan (2012) 'Constructing the Irish presidency: The early incumbents, 1938–1973', *Irish Political Studies* 27:4, 559–75, at p. 571.

21   Earl of Longford and T.P. O'Neill (1970) *Éamon de Valera*. London: Hutchinson, p. 461.

22   Report on the 1966 Presidential Election by Director of Elections, Charles Haughey, Haughey papers, C7/92 (1).

23   Groome, an honorary secretary of Fianna Fáil, and his wife, Patti, owned Groome's Hotel, where Haughey, Lenihan, O'Malley

24 Haughey to the secretary, each Comhairle Dáil Cheantair, undated but by context late March 1966, Haughey papers, C7/92 (1).

25 Ray Ryan, 'How Dev almost lost the 1966 presidential election', *Irish Times*, 20 August 2018, available at https://www.irishtimes.com/news/politics/how-dev-almost-lost-the-1966-presidential-election-1.3601119.

26 Haughey to Padraig O'Fathaigh, 16 May 1966, Haughey papers, C7/92 (1). The proposed poster design is also in this box.

27 Haughey Report on the 1966 Presidential Election.

28 O'Higgins to Haughey, 16 May 1966, Haughey papers, C7/90 (1).

29 Frank Ryan to Haughey, 18 May 1966, Haughey papers, C7/90 (1).

30 Speech at Bray, 27 May 1966, Haughey papers, C7/90 (1).

31 Haughey Report on the 1966 Presidential Election.

32 Haughey Report on the 1966 Presidential Election.

33 Ryan to Haughey, 1 February 1966, Haughey papers, C7/147 (1).

34 Report by Frank Ryan Public Relations 'Presidential Election, 1966 and its Meaning for the Future', undated, Haughey papers, C7/92 (1).

35 NARA, RG59, 2344, Pol 15, Government Ire, 20 July 1966.

36 Haughey to Revelstoke, 23 August 1966, Haughey papers, C7/147 (1).

37 There are good accounts of O'Reilly's role in Bord Bainne and his relationship with Haughey in Ivor Fallon (1994) *The Player: The Life of Tony O'Reilly*. London: Hodder and Stoughton; and Matt Cooper (2015) *The Maximalist: The Rise and Fall of Tony O'Reilly*. Dublin: Gill and Macmillan.

38 Haughey to Moran, 16 August 1966, Haughey papers, C7/147 (1).

39 Savage, *A Loss of Innocence?*, pp. 78–80, provides an excellent account of this incident.

40 The nine men were Deasy, Jim Bergin, Tom Cahill, Joe Dunphy, Michael Gibbons, Sean Holland, Hugh Leddy, TJ Maher and Bob Stack. Stack was hospitalised towards the end of the sit-down protest.

41 Savage, *A Loss of Innocence?*, p. 81.

42 On Lemass's speech, see John Horgan and Roddy Flynn (2017) *Irish Media: A Critical History*. Dublin: Four Courts Press, p. 99.

43 Horgan, *Lemass*, p. 331.

44 *Irish Independent*, 1 November 1966.

45 McQuaid to Haughey, 26 October 1966, Haughey papers, C7/1 (1).

46 The *Irish Press* of 22 October 1966 has a vivid front-page description of the incident alongside a poignant story of the Aberfan mine disaster in Wales, which had killed 144 people, mostly children, the previous day.

47 As reported in the *Irish Press*, 22 October 1966.

48 Keon to Haughey, 24 October 1966, Haughey papers, C7/150.

49 Maguire to Haughey, 11 November 1966, Haughey papers, C7/150.

50 O'Donnell interview.

51 Lemass is quoted in *Irish Press*, 27 October 1966.

52 Roe to Haughey, 12 October 1966, Haughey papers, C7/147 (1).

53 Haughey to Roe, 14 October 1966, Haughey papers, C7/147 (1).

54 Roe sent a copy of his letter to the NFA, dated 22 October 1966, to Haughey on the same day. It was enclosed with a letter of his own to Haughey. Both are in the Haughey papers, C7/150.

55 Roe to Haughey, 22 October 1966, Haughey papers, C7/150.

56 Haughey to Roe, 28 October 1966, Haughey papers, C7/150.

57 Seán Doyle to Haughey, 11 October 1966, Haughey papers, C7/151 (1).

58 Bernard Canning to Haughey, 26 October 1966, Haughey papers, C7/150.

59 Charley Lydon to Haughey, 1 November 1966, Haughey papers, C7/151 (1).

60 Jim McGuire to Haughey, 3 November 1966, C7/147 (1).

61 Ryan to Haughey, 8 November 1966, Haughey papers, C7/150.

62 Love to Haughey, 1 November 1966, Haughey papers, C7/150.

63 *Irish Press*, 1 November 1966.

64 *Irish Press*, 2 November 1966.

65 John O'Connor to Haughey, 1 December 1966, Haughey papers, C7/151 (1).

66 Michael O'Connor to Haughey, 2 November 1966, Haughey papers, C7/151 (1).

67 Haughey to O'Connor, 7 November 1966, Haughey papers, C7/151 (1).

68 See Jack Lynch 'My life and times', *Magill*, November 1979.

69 Keogh, *Lynch*, p.116; Bruce Arnold (2001) *Jack Lynch: Hero in Crisis*. Dublin: Merlin, pp. 67–8.

70 Horgan, *Lemass*, pp. 330–1.

71 Lenihan, *Haughey*, pp. 46–7.

72 Horgan, *Lemass*, p. 334

73 *Irish Times*, 2 November 1966.

74 Maureen Haughey interview.

75 Lenihan, *Haughey*, p. 48.

76 Kevin Rafter (1993) *Neil Blaney: A Soldier of Destiny*. Dublin: Blackwater Press, p. 37.

77 Keogh, *Lynch*, pp. 118–19.

78 Horgan, *Lemass*, pp. 336–7.

79 Kelly to Haughey, 7 December 1966, Haughey papers, C7/147 (2). Kelly was a former IRA member who was arrested and interned in the Curragh during the Second World War. He was released in 1946 and became a journalist, working in RTÉ from 1961 to 1966. He died in 1974 at the relatively young age of 57.

80 Kelly to Haughey, 14 April 1967, Haughey papers, C7/147 (2). 'Paddy O'Hanrahan' is a reference to Pádraig Ó hAnnracháin, who was head of the Government Information Bureau. After Lynch took office, he moved Ó hAnnracháin out of the GIB to the Department of Education. He would later become one of Haughey's most trusted advisers.

81 McCourt is not mentioned by name in either of Kelly's letters to Haughey; he is referred to as the Director General. For a full treatment of his life see Eugene McCague (2009) *My Dear Mr McCourt*. Dublin: Gill Books.

82 Haughey to Kelly, 17 April 1967, Haughey papers, C7/147 (2).

83 This letter is in the Haughey papers, C7/243. It is a two-page undated letter, which is printed, with the handwritten signature 'Jack'. It is addressed 'Dear Charlie' and begins, 'Hereunder is a conversation I had with Seán F Lemass in Dáil Éireann on the night he handed over to Lynch.' It then recounts the conversation. That conversation ends with Lemass saying 'Go home to Peggy. Good night Jack.' Peggy is a reference to Lemass's daughter, Peggy Lemass, who was Jack O'Brien's wife. Both Seán Haughey and Eimear Haughey confirmed to me that their father, Charles Haughey, said the letter was from Jack O'Brien and was given to him at some stage during the arms crisis.

84 O'Brien letter.

85 See Peggy Lemass's obituary, *Irish Times*, 24 July 2004, available at https://www.irishtimes.com/news/interest-in-public-affairs-persisted-1.1150638.

86 This trait of Lemass's was mentioned by Hillery in an interview with Lemass's biographer John Horgan in December 1994. I am grateful to Professor Horgan for providing me with his notes of this interview.

87 Information from John Horgan.

88 Clemens to Haughey, 24 October 1966, Haughey papers, C7/150. The salutation in the letter was Charles Haulghey. Mark Twain was the pen name of Samuel Clemens.

89 Haughey to Clemens, 7 November 1966, Haughey papers, C7/150.

90 Deasy is quoted in a comprehensive report of the meeting in the *Irish Independent*, 9 November 1966.

91 Owen Patten to Haughey, 10 November 1966, Haughey papers, C7/150.

92 Haughey to McKenzie, 23 November 1966, Haughey papers, C7/147 (1). McKenzie was Kenyan Minister for Agriculture from 1959 to 1961 and again from 1963 to 1970. The only white man to serve in the government of Jomo Kenyatta, he was widely believed to have been a spy for Britain and for Israel. He was assassinated in 1978 on the orders of the Ugandan dictator Idi Amin when the plane in which he was flying from Uganda to Kenya blew up after a bomb on board exploded.

93 Moran to Haughey, 17 May 1968, Haughey papers, C7/148 (1).

94 The *Irish Press*, *Irish Independent* and *Irish Times* of 14 November 1966 all carried front page accounts of the fire.

8. THE MINISTER FOR FINANCE

1 Callaghan to Haughey, 27 November 1966, Haughey papers, C7/191 (2).

2 Beddy to Haughey, 10 November 1966, Haughey papers, C7/150. For Beddy's career, see his entry in the *Dictionary of Irish Biography* by Pauric J. Dempsey and Shaun Boylan, available at https://www.dib.ie/biography/beddy-james-patrick-a0536.

3 Griffin to Haughey, 11 November 1966, Haughey papers, C7/150.

4 Haughey to Griffin, 11 November 1966, Haughey papers, C7/150.

5 Noel Whelan (2011) *Fianna Fáil: A Biography of the Party*. Dublin: Gill and Macmillan, p. 133.

6 There are good accounts of the free education scheme in P.J. Browne (2008) *Unfulfilled Promise: Memories of Donogh O'Malley*. Dublin: Currach Press; and John Walsh (2009) *The Politics of Expansion: The Transformation of Educational Policy in the Republic of Ireland, 1957–72*. Manchester: Manchester University Press. Horgan's *Lemass* and Keogh's *Lynch* offer equally good accounts of the schemes from the perspectives of their subjects.

7 See John Walsh, 'The Politics of Educational Expansion' in Girvin and Murphy, *The Lemass Era*, p. 146.

8   John Bowman's weekly radio archive programme *Bowman: Sunday: 8.30* ran a feature on the free secondary scheme in its episode of 17 January 2021 celebrating the centenary of O'Malley's birth on 17 January 1921. It features clips of O'Malley, Haughey and Lynch and can be accessed at https://www.rte.ie/radio/radioplayer/html5/#/radio1/11272316.

9   Whelan, *Fianna Fáil*, p. 135.

10   Horgan, *Lemass*, p. 301.

11   O'Malley is quoted in Walsh, *Politics of Educational Expansion*, p. 161.

12   *Limerick Leader*, 11 March 1968.

13   Haughey to Mother Bernard, 31 March 1999, Haughey papers, C7/152 (2).

14   Haughey to Mother Bernard, 15 May 1971, Haughey papers, C7/114 (1).

15   Eoghan O'Catháin to Haughey, 4 January 1967, Haughey papers, C7/150.

16   O'Donnell interview.

17   Whitaker to Haughey, 10 January 1967, Haughey papers, C7/147 (1).

18   Fallon, *The Player*, p. 148; Cooper, *The Maximalist*, pp. 71–2

19   The Dáil debate is entitled 'Heinz-Erin Ltd. – Statement by Minister for Finance' and can be accessed at https://www.oireachtas.ie/en/debates/debate/dail/1967-04-05/24/.

20   MacHale to Haughey, 13 January 1967, Haughey papers, C7/147 (2).

21   Haughey to MacHale, Haughey papers, C7/147 (2).

22   See Terry Clavin's entry for Gallagher in the *Dictionary of Irish Biography* at https://www.dib.ie/biography/gallagher-matt-a9609.

23   Keena, *Haughey's Millions*, p. 30.

24   All quotations in this paragraph are taken from the Dáil debate on the Committee on Finance, 27 April 1967, available at https://www.oireachtas.ie/en/debates/debate/dail/1967-04-27/30/.

25   Haughey to O'Halpin, 26 October 1964, Haughey papers, C7/151 (1).

26   Part of reply to Budget Debate, FF file, 1967, Haughey papers, C7/151 (2).

27   Joseph Groome and Kevin Boland, Runaithe Oinigh Fianna Fáil, to the Officers and Members of each Cumann: Dublin Area, Haughey papers, C7/151 (1). The national collection was cancelled in 1965 to allow each constituency to concentrate on raising funds for that year's general election.

28   Elaine Byrne (2012) *Political Corruption in Ireland 1922–2010: A Crooked Harp.* Manchester: Manchester University Press, p. 89.

29   T. Ryle Dwyer (1992) *Haughey's Thirty Years of Controversy.* Cork: Mercier Press, p. 33.

30   MacEntee to Haughey, 12 April 1967, Haughey papers, C7/243.

31   Haughey to MacEntee, 12 April 1967, Haughey papers, C7/150.

32   Maureen Haughey interview.

33   Whitaker is quoted in the RTÉ documentary *Haughey*, Episode 1.

34   Interview with Rory O'Hanlon, 21 April 2016. O'Hanlon was a TD for Cavan Monaghan from 1997 to 2011. He served as Minister for Health in two of Haughey's three governments from March 1987 to November 1991. He served as Minister for the Environment between November 1991 and February 1992, when he was sacked by Albert Reynolds.

35   Seán Haughey interview.

36   Haughey's budget speech is at https://www.oireachtas.ie/en/debates/debate/dail/1967-04-11/35/.

37   Haughey to J.D. Milburn, 18 April 1967; Milburn to Haughey 13 April 1967, Haughey papers, C7/150.

38   O'Donnell interview.

39   Haughey 1967 budget speech.

40   McGuire to Haughey, 13 April 1967, Haughey papers, C7/150.

41   Roth to Haughey, 19 May 1967; Haughey to Roth, 26 May 1967, Haughey papers, C7/147 (1).

42   See Savage, *A Loss of Innocence?*, pp. 44–7 for the end of Roth's career in RTÉ.

43   Cohane to Haughey, 27 June 1967, Haughey papers, C7/147 (2).

44   Haughey to Cohane, 3 July 1967, Haughey papers, C7/147 (2).

45   *Irish Times*, 11 August 1967.

46   Cohane to Haughey, 12 June 1967, Haughey papers, C7/147 (1).

47   Cohane to Haughey, 27 June 1967.

48   This quote is taken from Ed Walsh (2011) *Upstart: Friends, Foes and Founding a University.* Cork: Collins Press. Walsh, the founding president of the University of Limerick, socialised with Cohane on occasions.

49   Cohane to Haughey, 27 June 1967.

50   Patrick O'Doherty to Haughey, undated but by context early 1967, Haughey papers, C7/147 (1).

51   O'Donnell's note is attached to the original letter.

52   Haughey to Patrick O'Doherty, 13 February 1967, Haughey papers, C7/147 (1).

53   O'Donnell interview.

54   P.A. Howard to Rúnaí Príobháideach, Cathaoirleach na gCoimsinéirí Ioncaim, 7 April 1967, Haughey papers, C7/151 (2).

55   Tony Ó Dáilaigh to Haughey, 9 August 1967, Haughey papers, C7/151 (2). Attached to the Ó

Dáilaigh letter is that from the Department of Education to the chairman of the Laois Vocational Education Committee, 3 August, 1967.

56 Wikipedia https://en.wikipedia.org/wiki/Charles_W._Engelhard_Jr.

57 O'Brien to Haughey, 11 December 1968, Haughey papers, C7/148 (2).

58 Haughey to O'Brien, 13 December 1968, Haughey papers, C7/148 (2).

59 Haughey speech to Cork City Comhairle Dáil Ceanntair, 21 October 1967, Haughey papers, C7/151 (2).

60 Lynch, quoted in the *Irish Press*, 4 November 1967.

61 For a detailed discussion of the complex machinations of EEC entry in the 1960s see Michael J. Geary (2010) *An Inconvenient Wait: Ireland's Quest for Membership of the EEC, 1957–73*. Dublin: Institute of Public Administration.

62 Lynch to Haughey, 27 October 1967, Haughey papers, C7/151 (2).

63 Haughey to Mother Mary Gemma, Missionary Sisters of St Columban, 19 October 1967, Haughey papers, C7/147 (2).

64 Interview with Gerry Collins, 11 April 2019.

65 Report to the Sub Committee on Organisation: Visit to Democratic Party Election Rooms at Mineola, Nassau County, Long Island, October 1966, Haughey papers, C7/91 (1).

66 Des O'Malley (2014) *Conduct Unbecoming: A Memoir*. Dublin: Gill and Macmillan, p. 30.

67 Hilda O'Malley to Lynch, 8 May 1968, Haughey papers, C7/148 (2). Lynch forwarded a copy of this letter to Haughey on 10 May, and all his other ministers, as O'Malley had asked him to do so.

68 Hilda O'Malley received 3,361 first preference votes, just over 9.3 per cent of the vote, placing her fifth on the first count in the four-seat constituency. Des O'Malley, by contrast, received 5,960 votes, 16.6 per cent of the vote, and was comfortably elected.

69 O'Malley, *Conduct Unbecoming*, p. 41.

70 Hilda O'Malley to Haughey, Haughey papers, C7/13 (1). The letter is simply dated Friday, but by context is May 1970 after Haughey had been sacked by Lynch. It is most likely Friday 8 May, two days after Haughey's sacking.

71 O'Malley, *Conduct Unbecoming*, p. 39. This was a point Des O'Malley reiterated to me in an interview in his home on 21 September 2017.

9. HORSEMAN, PASS BY

1 *Irish Times*, 10 January 1998; Keena, *Haughey's Millions*, p. 27. See also 'Charlie Haughey's finances: The Kaiser and the Boss', *Magill*, January 1998, available at https://magill.ie/archive/charlie-haugheys-finances-kaiser-and-boss.

2 Haughey to Freddie Tinsley, 30 January 1976, Haughey papers, C7/115 (2).

3 Evidence from the Moriarty Tribunal of Inquiry, 25 July 2000, available at https://moriarty-tribunal.ie/wp-content/uploads/2016/09/transcript_129.pdf.

4 Smyth, *Thanks a Million*, p. 20.

5 PA to Charles Haughey to Margaret Heffernan, 1 February 1984, Haughey papers, C7/116 (2). There is no record of Heffernan's query in Haughey's papers, but it could, of course, have been made in a different way or lost.

6 Brian P. Kennedy (1990) *Dreams and Responsibilities: The State and the Arts in Independent Ireland*. Dublin: Arts Council, p. 154.

7 Terence Brown (1985) *Ireland: A Social and Cultural History 1922–1985*. London: Fontana Press, p. 315.

8 Tim Pat Coogan (2003) *Ireland in the Twentieth Century*. London, Arrow Books, p. 511.

9 Mansergh, *Spirit of the Nation*, p. 85.

10 Aylward interview.

11 FitzGibbon to Haughey, Haughey papers, C7/148 (1). FitzGerald makes no mention at all of FitzGibbon or of the scheme in his memoirs.

12 Coogan to Haughey, 2 February 1968, Haughey papers, C7/148 (1).

13 Haughey to Coogan, 7 March 1968, Haughey papers, C7/148 (1).

14 Michael Mills (2006) *Hurler on the Ditch: Memoir of a Journalist Who Became Ireland's First Ombudsman*. Dublin: Currach Press. See also Mills's obituary in the *Irish Times*, 19 April 2008, available at https://www.irishtimes.com/news/state-s-first-ombudsman-who-shone-as-political-journalist-1.915115; and Terry Clavin's entry on him in the *Dictionary of Irish Biography* at https://www.dib.ie/biography/mills-michael-a9638.

15 This is the only reference to the artists in the entire speech delivered on 7 May 1969, which can be read at https://www.oireachtas.ie/ga/debates/debate/dail/1969-05-07/47/.

16 Eamon Delaney (2009) *Breaking the Mould: A Story of Art and Ireland*. Dublin: New Island Press, p. 234.

17   Interview with Eamon Delaney, 17 February 2017. Delaney is the son of Edward Delaney and worked for a period in the Department of Foreign Affairs when Haughey was Taoiseach from 1987 to 1992. See Eamon Delaney (2001) *The Accidental Diplomat: My Years in the Irish Foreign Service, 1987–1995*. Dublin: New Island Press.

18   Sheikh Ali Ahmed to Haughey, 22 April 1968, Haughey papers, C7/1 (1).

19   Paddy Harte (2005) *Young Tigers and Mongrel Foxes. A Life in Politics*. O'Brien Press: Dublin, p. 101.

20   Collins and Meehan *Saving the State*, p. 119.

21   'For Ireland: For Democracy.' Fianna Fáil pamphlet for the 1968 referendum, Haughey papers, C7/90 (2).

22   'Why are we having this referendum now?' Fianna Fáil advertisement in the Sunday papers, 4 August 1968, Haughey papers, C7/90 (2).

23   Niamh Puirséil (2007) *The Irish Labour Party 1922–73*. Dublin: University College Dublin Press, p. 254.

24   'Give Irish Politics the Kiss of Life', Fianna Fáil pamphlet for the 1968 referendum, Haughey papers, C7/90 (2).

25   Haughey notes on the 1968 referendum campaign, Haughey papers, C7/90 (2).

26   Keery to Haughey, 8 August 1968, Haughey papers, C7/90 (2). Interview with Neville Keery, 5 September 2017. Keery joined Fianna Fáil in the mid-1960s and was an active member in the Dún Laoghaire–Rathdown constituency. He stood unsuccessfully as a candidate for the Dáil in the 1969 and 1973 general elections. He was a senator from 1969 to 1973 and later worked for Fianna Fáil and the European Commission.

27   'Edenmore Can Have Its Own TD', Fianna Fáil leaflet for the 1968 referendum, Haughey papers, C7/90 (2).

28   Mara to Haughey, undated but by context during the referendum campaign, Haughey papers, C7/90 (2).

29   *Irish Press*, 13 September 1968.

30   Haughey's handwritten notes on the 1968 referendum campaign, Haughey papers, C7/90 (2).

31   Haughey to Walter Doody, 21 November 1968, Haughey papers, C7/148 (1).

32   Hermens to Haughey, 16 August 1968, Haughey papers, C7/90 (2).

33   Haughey to Hermens, 22 August 1968, Haughey papers, C7/90 (2).

34   *Irish Press*, 2 September 1968.

35   Results are given in the broadsheet newspapers on 18 October 1968.

36   Reports of the accident appeared on the front pages of the four broadsheet newspapers on 21 September 1968.

37   O'Donnell interview.

38   Lenihan to Haughey, 29 March 1966, Haughey papers, C7/147 (1).

39   Maureen Haughey interview.

40   Haughey to Lenihan, 25 March 1966, Haughey papers, C7/19.

41   *Cork Examiner*, 30 March 1966.

42   Haughey to Garda Commissioner William Quinn, 26 February 1965, Haughey papers, C7/146 (2).

43   Haughey to Garda Commissioner Eugene Crowley, 18 December 1990, Haughey papers, C7/56 (5).

44   Aylward interview.

45   O'Donnell interview.

46   O'Malley to Haughey, 23 October 1968, Haughey papers, C7/16 (1)

47   Ryan to Haughey, 25 October 1968; Haughey to Ryan, 29 October, Haughey papers, C7/16 (3).

48   Niamh O'Sullivan to Haughey, 29 October 1968; Haughey to O'Sullivan, 31 October 1968, Haughey papers, C7/16 (1). See the appreciation for Niamh O'Sullivan which references her culinary skills in the *Irish Times*, 8 September 1997, written by 'P.J.'. This is most likely P.J. Mara and is available at https://www.irishtimes.com/opinion/niamh-o-sullivan-1.104208.

49   O'Halpin to Haughey, undated but by context in the aftermath of the crash, Haughey papers, C7/16 (2).

50   Moore to Haughey, 25 September 1968, Haughey papers, C7/16 (2).

51   Corboy to Haughey, 3 December 1968, Haughey papers, C7/16 (1).

52   Mills to Haughey, 21 October 1968, Haughey papers, C7/16 (2).

53   McRedmond to Haughey, 18 October 1968, Haughey papers, C7/16 (2).

54   Coogan to Haughey, Haughey papers, C7/16 (1).

55   Haughey to Coogan, Haughey papers, C7/16 (1).

56   Haughey to Guest, Haughey papers, C7/16 (1).

57   Legge to Haughey, 16 December 1968; Haughey to Legge, 19 December 1968, Haughey papers, C7/148 (1). For Legge's career at the *Sunday Independent*, see Kevin Rafter (2012) 'A Tale of "Womanly Intuition": Hector Legge at the *Sunday Independent*, 1940–70' in Mark O'Brien and Kevin Rafter (eds) *Independent Newspapers: A History*. Dublin: Four Courts Press.

58   *Irish Times*, 11 June 1969.

59   Viney to Haughey, 9 June 1969, Haughey papers, C7/91 (2).

60   Haughey to Earl of Harrington, 2 January 1969, Haughey papers, C7/148 (1).

61   Ryan to Haughey, 6 November 1968, Haughey papers, C7/151 (3).

62   Childers to Haughey, 7 January 1969, Haughey papers, C7/89 (2).

63   O'Kennedy to Haughey, 31 March 1970, Haughey papers, C7/151 (3).

64   *Irish Press*, 8 May 1969.

65   Coogan, *Ireland in the Twentieth Century*, p. 512.

66   *Irish Press*, 8 May 1969.

67   Haughey, budget speech, 7 May 1969.

68   *Irish Independent*, 8 May 1969.

69   *Cork Examiner*, 8 May 1969.

70   *Irish Independent*, 8 May 1969.

71   *Irish Times*, 8 May 1969.

72   Griffin to Haughey, 13 May 1969, Haughey papers, C7/150.

73   Haughey to Griffin, 14 May 1969, Haughey papers, C7/150.

74   Terry to Haughey, 9 May 1969, Haughey papers, C7/150.

75   David Andrews to Haughey, Haughey papers, C7/150. The letter is simply dated Wednesday, which was the day of the budget, and Haughey replied two days later.

76   Terry de Valera to Haughey, 8 May 1969, Haughey papers, C7/150.

77   MacGonigal is quoted in the *Irish Press*, 8 May 1969. The Royal Hibernian Academy was an artist-led organisation whose core remit was to support contemporary art and artists in Ireland through exhibition, education and advocacy.

78   MacGonigal is quoted in Delaney, *Breaking the Mould*, p. 234.

79   Todd Andrews to Haughey, 8 May 1969, Haughey papers, C7/150.

80   Walsh to Haughey, 7 May 1969; Haughey to Walsh, 9 May 1969, Haughey papers, C7/150.

81   De Vere White to Haughey, Haughey papers, C7/150. The date in this letter is Wednesday night, the night of the budget.

82   *Irish Times*, 8 May 1970.

83   Eamonn Andrews to Haughey, 22 May 1969, Haughey papers, C7/150.

84   Leonard to Haughey, 24 November 1969, Haughey papers, C7/151 (3).

85   Leonard is quoted in the *Irish Independent*, 18 June 2006. See https://www.independent.ie/opinion/analysis/he-was-a-fantasist-a-noble-statesman-who-dreamed-of-being-a-gentleman-26413055.html.

86   Leonard to Haughey, 18 March 1970, Haughey papers, C7/243.

87   See Patrick Maume's eloquent entry for Leonard in the *Dictionary of Irish Biography* at https://www.dib.ie/biography/leonard-hugh-a9703.

88   James Cummins to Haughey, 25 November 1969. In congratulating Haughey on the initiative Cummins sent him a copy of the *Saturday Review*; Haughey papers, C7/148 (1).

89   *New York Times*, 29 December 1969. A clipping of the article, entitled 'Dublin: A new tax haven beckoning', was sent to Haughey by Joe Malone of the Irish Tourist Board in New York; Haughey papers, C7/148 (1).

90   McClory to Haughey, 13 April 1970, Haughey papers, C7/148 (1).

91   Latimer to Haughey, 6 November 1972, Haughey papers, C7/141 (3).

92   Haughey to Latimer, 14 November 1972, Haughey papers, C7/141 (3).

93   Arnold talks at length about Haughey in dismissive tones in a documentary called *Charles Haughey: Patronising the Arts* which was shown on RTÉ 1 on 12 February 2007. It was produced by Clíona Ní Bhuachalla and directed by Charlie McCarthy.

94   Ballagh also talks at length about Haughey in *Patronising the Arts* (ibid.). See also his autobiographical memoir (2018), *A Reluctant Memoir*. London: Head of Zeus.

95   Flanagan to Haughey, 29 September 1990, Haughey papers, C7/1 (2).

96   The report, 'Voting Study for Fianna Fáil', May 1960, was prepared by Conrad Jameson Associates, London, marked 'strictly confidential' and addressed to Fianna Fáil, care of Minister of Finance. Haughey papers, C7/89 (2).

97   Puirséil, *Irish Labour Party*, p. 264.

98   Collins and Meehan, *Saving the State*, pp. 119–20.

99   Conrad Jameson, 'Voting Study for Fianna Fáil'.

100   Jameson to Haughey, 29 May 1969, Haughey papers, C7/89 (2). Rather intriguingly, the letter is addressed to Haughey care of Sam Stephenson, of Stephenson, Gibney and Associates. Stephenson, Gibney was one of Ireland's leading architectural firms. Stephenson was an active member of Fianna Fáil in the 1960s, was a member of Taca, and friendly with Haughey. See his obituary in the *Irish Times*, 11 November 2006, available at https://www.irishtimes.com/news/a-bold-and-controversial-architect-who-left-his-mark-on-dublin-1.1028028.

101   Jameson to Haughey, 29 May 1969.

102   Jameson to Haughey, 29 May 1969.

103 Speech by Minister for Finance, Charles Haughey at Raheny, 3 June 1969, Haughey papers, C7/151 (3).

104 Note from Haughey marked 'Urgent and Confidential' to Every Director and Candidate in Dublin City and County, Haughey papers, C7/91 (2).

105 Mac Conghail to Haughey, 12 June 1969, Haughey papers, C7/91 (2).

106 Niall Andrews to Haughey, 10 June 1969, Haughey papers, C7/91 (2).

107 Television programme report on *Seven Days* produced by Muiris Mac Conghail, 10 June 1969. Copy in the Haughey papers, C7/92 (1).

108 Roe to Haughey, 24 April 1968; Haughey to Roe, 25 April 1968, Haughey papers, C7/149.

109 Haughey to Seamus Puirséil, 12 June 1969, Haughey papers, C7/91 (2).

110 Haughey to Paddy Smith, 4 June 1969, Haughey papers, C7/91 (2).

111 On the purchase of Abbeville, see Mary Rose Doorly (1996) *Abbeville: The family home of Charles J. Haughey*. Dublin: Town House and Country House, pp. 9–10. Keena, *Haughey's Millions*, p. 37 states that the price paid was £146,977.

112 Haughey to John Franklyn, 3 December 1968, Haughey papers, C7/148 (1).

113 *Evening Herald*, 29 May 1969.

114 Personal statement by Charles J. Haughey, Minister for Finance, June 1969.

115 O'Connor to Director General, RTÉ, 25 June 1969, Haughey papers, C7/92 (1).

116 Irvine to O'Connor, 26 June 1969, Haughey papers, C7/92 (1).

117 O'Kennedy to Haughey, 23 June 1969, Haughey papers, C7/8 (1).

118 Ryan to Haughey, 2 July 1969, Haughey papers, C7/89 (1).

119 O'Reilly to Haughey, 3 July 1969, Haughey papers, C7/89 (1).

120 Máirín Lynch to Haughey, 30 June 1969, Haughey papers, C7/1 (1). For an assessment of Máirín Lynch, see Dermot Keogh, *Jack Lynch*, pp. 459–69. I am grateful to Professor Keogh for many discussions over the years about Jack Lynch.

121 Jack Lynch to Haughey, 23 June 1969, Haughey papers, C7/89 (1).

10. MR HAUGHEY'S ATTITUDE

1 Undated notes of interview preparation, Haughey papers, C7/101 (2). The context here is clearly the aftermath of Haughey's acquittal in the arms trial of October 1970.

2 Moylan to Haughey, 13 August 1969, Haughey papers, C7/120 (1).

3 O'Brien, *The Arms Trial*, p. 42.

4 A copy of Lynch's statement can be found in the National Archives of Ireland, NAI 2000/5/12, Lynch TV address, 13 August 1969. There is also a copy in the Haughey papers, C7/120 (1).

5 David Burke (2020) *Deception and Lies: The Hidden History of the Arms Crisis 1970*. Cork: Mercier Press, p. 45; Barry White (1984) *John Hume: Statesman of the Troubles*. Belfast: Blackstaff Press, p. 88; Paddy Doherty (2001) *Paddy Bogside*. Cork: Mercier Press, p. 194.

6 Eunan O'Halpin (2008) '"A Greek authoritarian phase"? The Irish army and the Irish crisis, 1969–70', *Irish Political Studies*, 23:4, 487.

7 Burke, *Deception and Lies*, p. 43.

8 Blaney is quoted in Michael Heney (2020) *The Arms Crisis of 1970: The Plot That Never Was*. London: Head of Zeus, p. 24.

9 See Pádraig Faulkner (2005) *As I Saw It: Reviewing Over 30 Years of Fianna Fáil and Irish Politics*. Dublin: Wolfhound Press, p. 90; John Walsh (2008) *Patrick Hillery: The Official Biography*. Dublin: New Island, p. 210; O'Malley, *Conduct Unbecoming*, p. 54. Boland is quoted in Burke, *Deception and Lies*, p. 44, and in Heney, *Plot that Never Was*, p. 21 as saying there was no suggestion of any crossing of the border 'unless the situation was so bad no action of ours could make it worse'.

10 Kevin Boland (1976) *Up Dev!* Dublin: K. Boland, p. 42.

11 See Angela Clifford (2006) *Military Aspects of Ireland's Arms Crisis of 1969–70*. Belfast: Belfast Magazine, p. 22; Heney, *Plot that Never Was*, pp. 22–5; Kennedy, *Division and Consensus*, p. 342; Ó Beacháin, *Destiny of the Soldiers*, p. 289–90.

12 Kennedy, *Division and Consensus*, p. 342.

13 See Donnacha Ó Beacháin (2019) *From Partition to Brexit: The Irish Government and Northern Ireland*. Manchester: Manchester University Press, p. 107.

14 Faulkner, *As I Saw It*, pp. 93-4.

15 O'Halpin, 'Greek authoritarian phase', p. 484.

16 Ó Beacháin, *Destiny of the Soldiers*, p. 290.

17 Kennedy, *Division and Consensus*, p. 342.

18 NAI 2000/9/1, Government Cabinet Minutes, 16 August 1969. See also Mansergh, *Spirit of the Nation*, p. xxxvi.

19 Dwyer, *Thirty Years of Controversy*, pp. 37–8.

20 Note by Leslie Bean de Barra entitled 'Six County Relief Operation'. The note is undated but refers to the total contributions received by the organisation to 22 September 1969 as being £45,130 5s 9d. Haughey papers, C7/243.

De Barra also refers to a statement she gave at the 21st International Conference of the Red Cross, Istanbul, September 1969.

21 McQuaid to Lynch, 16 August 1969; McQuaid to Haughey, 19 August 1969; Haughey to McQuaid, 20 August 1969, Haughey papers, C7/120 (1).

22 Daley to Haughey, 17 October 1969, Haughey papers, C7/120 (1).

23 Undated notes of interview preparation, Haughey papers, C7/101 (2).

24 Keogh, *Lynch*; Arnold, *Jack Lynch*; T. Ryle Dwyer (2001) *Nice Fellow: A Biography of Jack Lynch*. Cork: Mercier Press; T.P. O'Mahony (1991) *Jack Lynch: A Biography*. Cork: Blackwater Press.

25 Lenihan, *Haughey*, p. 78.

26 Burke, *Deception and Lies*, p. 241.

27 Heney, *Plot that Never Was*, p. 3.

28 See Des O'Malley's comment piece in the *Sunday Independent*, 'I know what happened because I was there', 27 September 2020, where he dismisses Heney and Burke as having written books which 'might compete for prizes in fiction rather than serious historical analysis'.

29 Arms Trial Notes: 'Other Defendants', undated, Haughey papers C7/120 (1).

30 Arms Trial Notes: 'Other Defendants', undated, Haughey papers C7/120 (1).

31 Kelly, *Failed Political Entity*, p. 67.

32 Burke, *Deception and Lies*, pp. 114–17.

33 Heney, *Plot that Never Was*, pp. 76–7.

34 Arms Trial Notes: 'The Attorney General – v – Luykx and Others', Haughey papers, C7/120 (1).

35 Accounts of the Haughey–Gilchrist meeting are to be found in Burke, *Deception and Lies*, pp. 116–17; Clifford, *Ireland's Arms Crisis*, p. 663; Craig, *Crisis of Confidence*, p. 68; Heney, *Plot that Never Was*, p. 77; Kelly, *Failed Political Entity*, p. 67; O'Brien, *Arms Trial*, p. 75.

36 Gilchrist to Haughey, 19 March, Haughey papers, C7/148 (1). The year is not given but it was clearly 1970.

37 Haughey to Gilchrist, 20 March 1970, Haughey papers, C7/148 (1).

38 Heney, *Plot that Never Was*, pp. 75–6.

39 Heney, *Plot that Never Was*, p. 82.

40 FitzGibbon to Haughey, 17 January 1980, Haughey papers, C7/116 (1). Hastings's letter to FitzGibbon dated 14 January 1980 is enclosed with the original letter.

41 *Evening Standard*, 18 December 1979, Haughey papers, C7/116 (1).

42 See Stephen Kelly (2020) 'Charles J. Haughey and the arms crisis', *History Ireland*, 28:5, 47.

43 Arms Trial Notes, Haughey papers, C7/120 (1). The notes on Peter Berry are untitled. In later notes I use the name 'Peter Berry' for convenience.

44 See 'Arms Crisis 1970: The inside story', *Magill*, 31 May 1980.

45 Arms Trial Notes, 'Peter Berry'.

46 'Arms Crisis 1970: The inside story', *Magill*, 31 May 1980.

47 Arms Trial Notes, 'Peter Berry'.

48 'Arms Crisis 1970: The Inside Story', *Magill*, 31 May 1980.

49 Arms Trial Notes, 'Peter Berry'.

50 Arms Trial Notes: 'The Attorney General – v – Luykx and Others', Haughey papers, C7/120 (1).

51 Heney, *Plot that Never Was*, p. 189.

52 Arms Trial Notes: 'The Attorney General – v – Albert A. Luykx and Others, Haughey papers, C7/120 (1).

53 Ibid., Haughey papers, C7/120 (1).

54 Fagan's handwritten statement of 13 May 1970, and his witness statement to Gardaí of 14 May 1970 are available at NAI, 2001/61/1.

55 Arms Trial Notes: 'Other Defendants', undated, Haughey papers C7/120 (1).

56 Arms Trial Notes: 'The Attorney General – v – Luykx and Others', Haughey papers, C7/120 (1).

57 Ibid., Haughey papers, C7/120 (1).

58 Statement of Evidence of Peter Berry, Secretary. Department of Justice, witness no. 25, Haughey papers, C7/120 (1).

59 Arms Trial Notes: 'Other Defendants', undated, Haughey papers C7/120 (1).

60 Clifford, *Arms Conspiracy Trial*, p. 47; Heney, *Plot that Never Was*, p. 186.

61 Arms Trial Notes: 'The Attorney General – v – Luykx and Others', Haughey papers, C7/120 (1).

62 Tom McIntyre (1971) *Through the Bridewell Gate. A Diary of the Dublin Arms Trial*. London: Faber and Faber, p. 169.

63 Arms Trial Notes: 'The Attorney General – v – Luykx and Others', Haughey papers, C7/120 (1).

64 Heney, *Plot that Never Was*, p. 193.

65 Statement of Evidence of James Gibbons, Minister for Agriculture and Fisheries, witness no. 26, Haughey papers, C7/120 (1).

66 Arms Trial Notes: 'Mr. Fagan's statement', Haughey papers, C7/120 (1).

67 Ibid.

68 Haughey to Stan O'Brien, 2 March 1964, Haughey papers, C7/146 (2).

69 Arms Trial Notes: 'Mr. Fagan's statement', Haughey papers, C7/120 (1).

70 Ibid.

71 Ó Beacháin, *Destiny of the Soldiers*, pp. 293–4.
72 See Paul Bew (2007) *Ireland: The Politics of Enmity 1789–2006*. Oxford: Oxford University Press, pp. 500–1.
73 Diarmaid Ferriter (2012) *Ambiguous Republic: Ireland in the 1970s*. London: Profile Books, p. 146.
74 Kelly's self-published books *Orders for the Captain* (Dublin 1971) and The *Thimble Riggers* (Dublin 1999) outline his own position.
75 Ó Beacháin, *Destiny of the Soldiers*, pp. 294–5.

11. THIS TIRESOME BUSINESS OF THE TRIAL

1 On 11 May 1970 Haughey's solicitor, Pat O'Connor, read a statement to the media outlining Haughey's injuries. It can be seen at https://www.rte.ie/archives/category/politics/2015/0422/695843-taoiseach-delivers-budget-after-minister-has-horse-fall/.
2 Ruth Young, under her married name, Ruth Henderson, later sued a number of newspapers and publishing houses who claimed that Haughey was beaten up in a public house in either north Dublin, west Dublin, or Meath the night before the accident.
3 Maureen Haughey interview; Eimear Mulhern interview.
4 Maureen Haughey interview.
5 Arms Trial Notes: 'The Attorney General – v – Luykx and Others', Haughey papers, C7/120 (1).
6 Arms Crisis Timeline with comments by Charles Haughey's legal team, undated, Haughey papers, C7/120 (1).
7 Lynch was speaking in the Dáil on 25 November 1980 in a debate entitled 'Magill Magazine Allegations'. It can be read at https://www.oireachtas.ie/en/debates/debate/dail/1980-11-25/22/. Lynch gave a forceful defence of his own position at the time of the Arms Crisis. See Keogh, *Jack Lynch*, p. 259.
8 Maureen Haughey interview.
9 Maureen Haughey interview. Brian Dennis would later give one of the Prayers of the Faithful at Charles Haughey's funeral mass.
10 Connolly to Haughey, 7 May 1970, Haughey papers, C7/13 (1).
11 Mara to Haughey, 6 May 1970, Haughey papers, C7/13 (1).
12 Arnold to Haughey, 11 May 1970, Haughey papers, C7/13 (1).
13 Haughey to Arnold, 8 June 1970, Haughey papers, C7/13 (1).
14 Leonard to Haughey, 10 June 1970, Haughey papers, C7/13 (2).

15 Edwards and Mac Liammóir to Haughey, 12 May 1970, Haughey papers, C7/13 (1).
16 Feeney to Haughey, 10 May 1970, Haughey papers, C7/13 (1). Feeney was tragically killed in a light air crash off the south-east coast of England in November 1984, which claimed the lives of nine people including four Irish journalists.
17 Morrissey to Haughey, 7 May 1970, Haughey papers, C7/13 (2).
18 Kennedy to Haughey, 19 May 1970, Haughey papers, C7/13 (2).
19 Whitaker to Haughey, 20 May 1970, Haughey papers, C7/13 (1).
20 Statement from Charles J. Haughey Esq. T.D., 8 May 1970, Haughey papers, C7/120 (1).
21 Report On Meeting dated 25 May 1970 at Abbeville, Kinsealy, Co. Dublin at 11 a.m. Haughey papers, C7/120 (1). The names of Patrick Doocey and Bryan Alton are misspelled in the report.
22 Statement of Evidence by Detective Chief Superintendent John Fleming, *Attorney General v Albert A. Luykx and Others*, District Court, pp. 58–60, Haughey papers, C7/120 (1).
23 Heney, *Plot that Never Was*, p. 271.
24 Maureen Haughey interview. Pat O'Connor's daughter Niamh O'Connor told me in an interview that her father considered the arrest of Charles Haughey to be completely bogus and clearly political. He had been assured by Superintendent Fleming that nothing would happen until he had a chance to ask Haughey the questions he wanted. Interview with Niamh O'Connor, 16 June 2017.
25 *Irish Press*, 28 May 1970.
26 Maureen Haughey interview.
27 All the main Irish broadsheets carried extensive reports of the arrests and charges in their editions of Friday 29 May 1970. The main headlines, however, related to the demand of another ex-minister, Kevin Boland, that Lynch call a special Ard Fheis accusing the Taoiseach of the greatest act of treachery of which an Irishman could be guilty.
28 Máirín Lynch is quoted in the *Cork Examiner* and the *Irish Independent*, 29 May 1970.
29 Haughey to Gibbons, 16 July 1970, Haughey papers, C7/14 (1).
30 Flanagan to Haughey, 27 July 1970, Haughey papers, C7/14 (1). Flanagan was one of only two government ministers not to attend Jack Lynch's homecoming from a UN General Assembly meeting in New York three days after the defendants were acquitted in the second arms trial. He was in London at a

conference for World Conservation Year but from this letter it is clear where his sympathies lay in relation to Haughey's charge.

31 O'Halpin to Haughey, 12 August 1970, Haughey papers, C7/14 (1).

32 McIntyre, *Bridewell Gate*, p. 18.

33 Doherty to Haughey, 1 September 1970, Haughey papers, C7/120 (1).

34 Mac Liammóir to Haughey, Haughey papers, C7/13 (3).

35 Haughey to Mac Liammóir, 22 September 1970, C7/13 (3).

36 Healy to Haughey, 20 September 1970, Haughey papers, C7/13 (2).

37 Maureen Haughey interview; Niamh O'Connor interview.

38 Eimear Mulhern interview.

39 McIntyre, *Bridewell Gate*, p. 75.

40 *Irish Independent*, 23 September 1970.

41 McIntyre, Bridewell Gate, p. 164.

42 *Irish Independent*, 24 October 1970.

43 All the newspapers on the day after the verdict carried extensive coverage of Haughey's press conference.

44 *Irish Independent*, 24 October 1970.

45 Interview with Séamus Puirséil, 28 July 2016. Puirséil was a Fianna Fáil activist for a number of decades from the mid-1960s and acted as Haughey's director of elections in 1989. He attended the arms trial on several days and was present when Haughey came into the bar after his press conference. He later became president of the Irish National Teachers' Organisation and chief executive of the Higher Education and Training Awards Council.

46 See Dáil debate of 9 November 1971 at https://www.oireachtas.ie/en/debates/debate/dail/1971-11-09/42/.

47 The statement is reproduced in full in the *Irish Press*, 9 November 1971.

48 Boland is quoted in Episode 2 of the RTÉ *Haughey* documentary, entitled 'Arise and Follow'.

49 John Coakley (2010) 'The rise and fall of minor parties in Ireland', *Irish Political Studies* 25:4, 526.

50 *Irish Press*, 20 September 1971.

51 See Patrick Maume, 'Boland, Kevin', *Dictionary of Irish Biography*, https://www.dib.ie/biography/boland-kevin-a0768.

52 Boland to Haughey, 23 August 1971, Haughey papers, C7/1 (1). Boland always signed his letters and official documents in Irish, Caoimhghín Ó Beoláin.

53 Haughey to Honan, 22 September 1970, Haughey papers, C7/13 (2).

54 Colleary to Haughey, 15 February 1971, Haughey papers, C7/140 (1).

55 Haughey to Colleary, 25 February 1971, Haughey papers, C7/140 (1).

56 O'Connor to Haughey, 16 August 1971, Haughey papers, C7/140 (2).

57 Haughey to O'Connor, 17 August 1971, Haughey papers, C7/140 (2).

58 Wilson to Haughey, 7 November 1971, Haughey papers, C7/17 (2).

59 Brendan Mulligan to Haughey, 7 December 1971, Haughey papers, C7/93 (1).

60 Barry to Haughey, 11 November 1971, Haughey papers, C7/17 (2).

61 Maureen Haughey interview.

62 Mulhern interview.

63 Interview with Kevin Healy, 28 February 2020. Healy began his career in journalism at the *Cork Examiner* before moving to RTÉ, where he had a long and distinguished career, presenting, among other programmes, the *News at 1.30* and *This Week* and later becoming Head of Radio.

64 Healy interview. This interview took place on 12 January 1981. Kevin Healy kindly gave me a copy of his contemporaneous notes of the interview, for which I am very grateful.

65 O'Brien wrote to Haughey on 21 November 2000. The date on his note is just '21 November', but it is clear that the year is 2000; Haughey papers, C7/134 (1). O'Brien was seeking an interview for a thesis he was writing on Fianna Fáil at Queen's University, Belfast. He later published *The Modern Prince: Charles J. Haughey and the Quest for Power* (2002). Dublin: Merlin Press, which was quite critical of Haughey.

66 Browne to Haughey, 12 May 1971, Haughey papers, C7/114 (1).

67 Haughey to Browne, 15 May 1971, Haughey papers, C7/114 (1).

68 Colleary to Haughey, 17 August 1971, Haughey papers, C7/101 (1).

69 Haughey to Paul O'Dwyer, 11 January 1973; Haughey to Joe Malone, 11 January 1973, Haughey papers, C7/141 (3).

70 Handwritten note by Charles J. Haughey on Department of Health notepaper, 15 September 1978. This letter was in Haughey's private safe in Kinsaley and found after his death by his children. I am grateful to Seán Haughey for providing me with a copy.

71 See 'The Peter Berry papers', *Magill*, June 1980, p. 54. The Berry Diaries, as they have become known, were edited by Vincent Browne and created huge interest when published in *Magill* in 1980.

72 See 'Arms crisis 1970: The inside story', *Magill*, 31 May 1980. See also Patrick Maume's biography of Berry in the *Dictionary of Irish Biography* at https://www.dib.ie/biography/berry-peter-a0629.

73 Heney, *Plot that Never Was*, pp. 126-32 offers the most detailed critique of the meeting where he sides with Berry's account arguing that Lynch and his Minister for Defence not only failed to act at the time but later pretended that they had never got the warning.

74 Browne to Haughey, dated Mon. Dec. 11. There is no year given but it is certainly 1978. Haughey papers, C7/145 (2).

75 Maureen Haughey interview.

76 Maureen Haughey interview. This story was repeated by Seán Haughey on a special *Liveline* programme on RTÉ Radio 1 on the fiftieth anniversary of the arms crisis on 22 September 2020. It can be accessed at https://www.rte.ie/radio1/liveline/programmes/2020/0922/1166843-liveline-tuesday-22-september-2020/.

77 Aide-memoire by Charles Haughey dated 16 July 1979. The written copy and a transcript are in the Haughey papers, C7/120 (1). Haughey spells MacEoin as McEoin and Hefferon as Heffron.

78 Memo by General Seán MacEoin on Directive of 6th Feb 1970, 21 July 1979, Haughey papers, C7/120 (1).

79 MacEoin memorandum, 21 July 1979.

80 The document is dated 5 June and is reproduced in Heney, *Plot that Never Was*, pp. 350–6.

81 MacEoin memorandum, 21 July 1979.

82 Heney, *Plot that Never Was*, p. 103.

83 Des O'Malley, 'I know what happened because I was there', dismisses Heney's theory as a misreading of the evidence of the 6 February authorisation.

84 See Eoin O'Malley's review of Heney's *Plot that Never Was* in the *Sunday Times*, 12 April 2020.

85 Lyons to Haughey, 10 December 1979, Haughey papers, C7/3 (2).

86 Haughey to Lyons, 17 December 1979, Haughey papers, C7/3 (2).

87 Kelly to Haughey, 13 August 1980, Haughey papers, C7/1 (1).

88 Haughey to Kelly, August 1980, nd, Haughey papers, C7/1 (1).

89 Kelly to Haughey, 23 September 1980, Haughey papers, C7/1 (1).

90 Hederman to Haughey, 8 January 1981, Haughey papers, C7/1 (1).

91 Haughey to Kelly, 13 January 1981, Haughey papers, C7/1 (1).

92 Interview with Suzanne Kelly, 17 November 2017. Suzanne Kelly is the daughter of Captain James Kelly and a successful tax lawyer. She has long campaigned for a full state vindication of her father.

93 Sheila Kelly to Haughey, 1 February 1984; Haughey to Sheila Kelly, 8 February 1984, Haughey papers, C7/116 (2).

94 For a thorough synopsis of Kelly's career, see his entry in the *Dictionary of Irish Biography* by Patrick Maume at https://www.dib.ie/biography/kelly-james-a9336.

95 Sheridan to Haughey, 30 January 1992, Haughey papers, C7/120 (3). Sheridan was appointed as a judge of the Circuit Court in 1978 and appointed as President of the Circuit Court in 1998 where he served for less than a year.

12. ISOLATION

1 Croke to Haughey, 27 October 1970, Haughey papers, C7/13 (1).

2 See the *Sunday Independent*, 6 May 2001, which headlined a piece by Brendan O'Connor as 'The idiot's guide to the arms trial'.

3 Alton to Haughey, 26 October 1970, Haughey papers, C7/14 (1).

4 Haughey to T.H. Whitty, 28 June 1972, Haughey papers, C7/141 (2).

5 Sr Mary Leontia to Haughey, 13 January 1971; Haughey to Sr Mary Leontia, 14 January 1971, Haughey papers, C7/114 (1).

6 As recalled by Eamonn Blaney, the son of Neil Blaney, on *Liveline*, 22 September 2020; Suzanne Kelly interview.

7 Haughey to Mac Anna, 12 July 1977, Haughey papers, C7/8 (2).

8 Haughey to Mullen, 25 June 1977, Haughey papers, C7/8 (2).

9 Ó Beacháin, *Destiny of the Soldiers* has a comprehensive account of the Ard Fheis, pp. 311–16.

10 See *Irish Times*, 22 February 1971 for a dramatic description of these remarkable scenes. John Walsh, *Hillery*, pp. 245–9, provides an account of the Ard Fheis from Hillery's perspective.

11 John Walsh, *Hillery*, pp. 247–8.

12 Footage of the Ard Fheis can be seen in the RTÉ *Haughey* documentary, Episode 2, 'Arise and Follow Charlie'.

13 Peck is quoted in Ó Beacháin, *Destiny of the Soldiers*, p. 311.

14 Mara interview.

15 The walk was known as the Jimmy Savile walk. See the obituary of Lady Goulding in the *Irish Times*, 2 August 2003, available at

https://www.irishtimes.com/news/aristocrat-who-did-something-with-her-life-1.368360.

16   Lady Goulding to Haughey, 21 October 1971, Haughey papers, C7/102 (1).

17   This is the recollection of Cora Keogh, who was Lady Goulding's personal assistant. Cora Keogh is the mother of DCU's president, Daire Keogh, and I am grateful to him for this information.

18   J.W. Good to Manager, Bank of Ireland, 20 October 1971, Haughey papers, C7/102 (1).

19   Minutes of the meeting of the fundraising committee of the Central Remedial Clinic, 13 June 1972, Haughey papers, C7/102 (1).

20   Fitzgerald to Haughey, 2 March 1973, Haughey papers, C7/92 (1).

21   Keena, *Haughey's Millions*, p. 48.

22   A number of lists of firms to be approached for support, both typed and in Haughey's handwriting, can be seen in C7/102 (1) of Haughey's papers.

23   Minutes of the meeting of the fundraising committee of the Central Remedial Clinic, 13 June 1972.

24   C.V.D. Wardell, Chairman of the Board of Governors of St Patrick's Hospital to Haughey, 15 October 1974, Haughey papers, C7/102 (1).

25   See for instance Shane Ross's column in the *Sunday Independent*, 'Noble vision hijacked by FF cronies', 1 December 2013.

26   Haughey to Robert McGonigal, 25 January 1972, Haughey papers, C7/114 (1).

27   Haughey to Thomas Collins, 16 April 1973, Haughey papers, C7/142 (1).

28   Minutes of meeting between Charles Haughey, Thomas Collins and Angela Kelly, Malahide, 13 October 1972; Haughey to Collins, 29 January 1973, Haughey papers, C7/114 (2).

29   Goulding to Haughey, 26 May 1980, NAI, 2013/100/768.

30   Aylward interview.

31   Haughey to Raymond Shiel, 9 March 1973, Haughey papers, C7/141 (3).

32   Haughey to Lady Goulding, 12 May 1982, Haughey papers, C7/163 (3).

33   As cited in Lady Goulding's obituary in the *Irish Times*, 2 August 2003.

34   De Valera to Haughey, 4 November 1971, Haughey papers, C7/140 (2). On 3 March 2021 an RTÉ Investigations documentary, *Who Am I: Ireland's Illegal Adoptions* revealed that Prof. de Valera facilitated the illegal adoption of Irish babies long after the introduction of the 1952 Adoption Act, which made the practice a criminal offence.

35   Norma D. Roth to Haughey 27 January 1977; Haughey to Roth, 31 January 1977, Haughey papers, C7/136 (1).

36   Betty Moran to Haughey, 6 March 1971, Haughey papers, C7/140 (1).

37   Eva Keogh to Haughey, undated; Haughey to Keogh, 9 August 1971, Haughey papers, C7/140 (2).

38   Mullen to Haughey, 17 November 1972; Haughey to Mullen, 5 December 1972, Haughey papers, C7/141 (3).

39   Muldoon to Haughey, 9 June 1971, Haughey papers, C7/102 (2).

40   Haughey to Muldoon, 14 June 1971, Haughey papers, C7/102 (2).

41   Charles Haughey Memorandum for Representative Body for Inspectors, Station-Sergeants and Sergeants File, 24 June 1971, Haughey papers, C7/102 (2).

42   Wymes to Muldoon, 16 September 1971, re: Application for Authorisation to employ consultant to R.B.I.S.S., Haughey papers, C7/102 (2).

43   The relevant statutory instrument is S.I. No. 64/1962 – Garda Síochána (Representative Bodies) Regulations, 1962. It can be seen at http://www.irishstatutebook.ie/eli/1962/si/64/.

44   Muldoon to Wymes, 4 October 1971, Haughey papers, C7/102 (2).

45   Wymes to Muldoon, 22 December 1971, Haughey papers, C7/102 (2).

46   Thomas A. O'Grady, General Secretary of the Representative Body for Inspectors, Station-Sergeants and Sergeants to Haughey, 2 April 1974 and 11 April 1974, Haughey papers, C7/102 (2).

47   Haughey to Tom Kelly, 8 December 1972, Haughey papers, C7/141 (3).

48   Mara interview.

49   Haughey to Mara, 1 July 1965, Haughey papers, C7/151 (1).

50   Interview with Ray MacSharry, 4 January 2017. MacSharry was first elected in 1969 and became a hugely important figure in Fianna Fáil over the next two decades. He was a close observer of the class differences between Fianna Fáil and Fine Gael in rural Ireland. P.J. Mara made a similar point about urban Ireland.

51   O'Hanlon interview.

52   Haughey to Butt, 4 July 1973, Haughey papers, C7/114 (2).

53   See Michael Kennedy (2010). '"Where's the Taj Mahal?": Indian restaurants in Dublin since 1908", *History Ireland*, 4:18, p. 52.

54   Albert Reynolds (2009) *My Autobiography*. London: Transworld Ireland, pp. 67–8. See also Lenihan, *Haughey*, p. 82.

55   Mara interview.

56   Haughey to B.H. Jellett, 27 September 1973, Haughey papers, C7/114 (2).

57   Charles Crowley to Haughey, 1971, Haughey papers, C7/114 (1).

58   Cabot to Haughey, 9 September 1971, Haughey papers, C7/114 (1).

59   Interview with David Cabot, 26 April 2016.

60   Adams to Haughey, 29 January 1972, Haughey papers, C7/141 (1).

61   Adams to Haughey, 30 March 1972, Haughey papers, C7/14 (2).

62   Cronin to Haughey, 12 June 1972, Haughey papers, C7/14 (2).

63   Haughey to Cronin, 19 June 1972, Haughey papers, C7/14 (2).

64   A copy of the speech, entitled 'Arts and the Majority', with various annotations, is in the Haughey papers, C7/14 (2).

65   Haughey to Mary Purcell, 9 August 1972, Haughey papers, C7/141 (2).

66   J.C. Duignan to Haughey, 20 June 1972, Haughey papers, C7/14 (2).

67   'Irish MP Urges Tax Exemption For Artists', Haughey papers, C7/14 (2).

68   Haughey to Mother Bernard, 21 July 1972, Haughey papers, C7/114 (2).

69   Mary Purcell to Haughey, 7 August 1972, Haughey papers, C7/141 (2).

70   Correspondence with Agnes Aylward, 22 March 2020. Agnes Aylward, formerly Breathnach, went on to have a distinguished career in the civil service where she worked in a variety of roles in the Department of Industry, Trade and Tourism and the Department of the Taoiseach. She is currently the project director of the Lafcadio Hearn Japanese Gardens in Tramore.

71   Interview with Paul Kavanagh, 15 July 2015. Kavanagh was appointed chief fundraiser for Fianna Fáil in 1982 and held that position until Haughey retired in 1992. He was one of Haughey's appointees to the Seanad in 1989.

72   Sr M. Margaret, Manor House School to Mr and Mrs Haughey 29 April 1971; Haughey to Sr M. Margaret, 10 May 1971, Haughey papers, C7/114 (1).

73   M. Payne to Haughey, 14 April 1971, Haughey papers, C7/114 (1).

74   Chairman, Goffs Bloodstocks Sales to Haughey, 2 October 1972, Haughey papers, C7/114 (2).

75   See the Seanad National Stud Bill, 1969: Second and Subsequent Stages, 24 July 1969, at https://www.oireachtas.ie/en/debates/debate/seanad/1969-07-24/6/.

76   Leo Powell interview. Leo Powell has penned an important piece on Haughey and equestrianism on the Haughey family website available at https://www.charlesjhaughey.ie/articles/equestrian.

77   'Accounting for Charles Haughey: Finances and frozen assets', Magill, March 1998. See https://magill.ie/archive/accounting-charles-haughey-finances-and-frozen-assets.

78   In his 2020 memoir, Burning Heresies: A Memoir of a Life in Conflict, 1979–2020, p. 108, the journalist Kevin Myers, quoting Michael Osborne of the Irish National Stud in Kildare, wrote that every racing stables in Ireland bought a Haughey yearling for making the industry wholly tax free but would not buy another as Haughey did not have an eye for bloodstock, although he thought he had. This probably says more about Myers's antipathy to Haughey than it does about Haughey's tax exemption scheme and his abilities as a breeder. It is clear that the Ballsbridge International Bloodstock Sales company had much faith in him. Some correspondence and minutes of meetings of the company are in the Haughey papers, C7/101 (1).

79   Again I am grateful to Leo Powell for his help in taking me through Haughey's career as a horse owner.

80   Haughey to O'Brien, 8 April 1970, Haughey papers, C7/148 (2). In his note to Haughey expressing pleasure on having him and Maureen visit Ballydoyle, O'Brien told Haughey it was most kind of him to see the stretch on the river and that he knew Haughey would do what he could about it.

81   O'Brien to Haughey, 30 September 1978, Haughey papers, C7/244.

82   O'Brien to Haughey, 9 October 1978, Haughey papers, C7/1 (2).

83   Lemass to Haughey, 13 July 1971; Haughey to Lemass, 19 July 1971, Haughey papers, C7/114 (1).

84   Keane recalled her first meeting with Haughey in the Sunday Times, 16 July 1999, having appeared on the Late Late Show two nights earlier, when she revealed the affair. After Haughey's death the newspaper Ireland on Sunday carried an interview with Keane on 18 June 2006 which repeated this story.

85   A self-published book, Sweetie, by the journalist Kevin O'Connor appeared later in 1999; it mentioned the affair but not in any particularly extensive detail.

86   Interview with Ivor Fitzpatrick, 29 November 2018. Fitzpatrick served as Haughey's solicitor for many years and represented him at the McCracken and Moriarty tribunals.

87   Mara interview.

88   Interview with Anne Harris, 24 April 2019.

89   Interview with Sarah Carey, 19 March 2017.

90   Simonds-Gooding to Haughey, undated,
      September 1971, and 7 November 1971,
      Haughey papers, C7/114 (1).

91   See Rosita Boland, 'Settled into an Irish
      cottage, Peig style', *Irish Times*, 9 November
      2019.

92   Simonds-Gooding to Haughey, 4 June 1970,
      Haughey papers, C7/14 (1).

93   See Donal Hickey, 'Inis, natural wonderland,
      lost paradise', *Irish Examiner*, 5 October 2009.

94   Haughey to Tom Walsh, 17 December 1974,
      Haughey papers, C7/114 (2).

95   Haughey to W.E. Curran, 11 June 1974,
      Haughey papers, C7/143 (1).

96   Diarmaid Ferriter (2018) *On The Edge:
      Ireland's Offshore Islands: A Modern History*.
      London: Profile Books, p. 133.

97   Kiberd uses the wall metaphor in the RTÉ
      documentary *Haughey*, Episode 2: 'Arise and
      Follow Charlie'.

98   Interview with Conor Haughey, 7 December
      2017.

99   Terry Prone interview.

100   J.P. Kane to Haughey, 20 April 1974, Haughey
      papers, C7/115 (1).

101   Clive Hutchinson to Haughey, 4 May 74;
      Haughey to Hutchinson, 11 June 1974,
      Haughey papers, C7/114 (3).

102   Haughey to Gerry Collins, 30 August 1974,
      Haughey papers, C7/144 (3).

103   Mulhern interview.

104   Interview with Gerry Wrixon, 4 April 2019.
      Wrixon is a former president of University
      College, Cork. He advised Haughey on
      various aspects of the state's energy policy
      during the 1980s when he was Professor of
      Microelectronics at UCC.

105   Cabot interview. See also Mícheál Ó
      Dubhshláine (2009) *Inisvickillane: A Unique
      Portrait of the Blasket Island*. Dingle: Brandon
      Books.

106   Cabot interview.

107   Haughey to Robert McCabe, 30 October 1987,
      Haughey papers, C7/33 (1).

108   Vincent Sheridan to Haughey, 23 November
      1981, Haughey papers, C7/157 (2).

109   Cabot interview.

110   C.J. Falconer to Haughey, 23 July 1975;
      Haughey to Falconer, 24 July 1975, Haughey
      papers, C7/144 (1).

111   On Hy Brasil, see https://www.ria.ie/news/
      library-library-blog/mythical-island-hy-
      brasil-and-book-olees.

13. A CORINTHIAN, A LAD OF METTLE, A GOOD BOY

1   Seamus Puirséil interview.

2   Séamus Puirséil interview.

3   See Jock Haughey's obituary in the *Irish
      Times*, 18 October 2003, 'Controversial figure
      in political drama', available at https://www.
      irishtimes.com/news/controversial-figure-in-
      political-drama-1.385037.

4   Haughey to Malone, 8 March 1973, Haughey
      papers, C7/114 (2).

5   Maguire to Haughey, 2 March 1973, Haughey
      papers, C7/8 (2).

6   Yeats to Haughey, 3 March 1973, Haughey
      papers, C7/8 (2).

7   Donough O'Connor to Haughey, 3 March
      1973, Haughey papers, C7/92 (1).

8   Hart to Haughey, 2 March 1973, Haughey
      papers, C7/142 (1). The underlining of know
      is in the original letter.

9   See Bryce Evans and Stephen Kelly (2014)
      'Conclusion' in Bryce Evans and Stephen
      Kelly (eds) *Frank Aiken: Nationalist and
      Internationalist*. Dublin: Irish Academic
      Press, p. 313.

10   Carty to Haughey, 23 April 1973, Haughey
      papers, C7/142 (1). Professor Carty
      interviewed a number of leading political
      figures in this period. He wrote to George
      Colley seeking an interview but was told
      that Colley was too busy. These interviews
      formed part of his doctoral thesis and his
      extraordinarily influential book, *Party and
      Parish Pump: Electoral Politics in Ireland*
      (1981). Ontario: Wilfrid Laurier University
      Press.

11   Interview with Professor Ken Carty,
      20 October 2019. I am grateful to Professor
      Carty for providing me with a copy of the
      notes from his interview with Haughey on
      1 May 1973.

12   Carty interview.

13   Matt Ryan to Haughey, 11 February 1974,
      Haughey papers, C7/142 (3).

14   Haughey to Willie Ryan, 2 October 1974,
      Haughey papers, C7/143 (1).

15   Haughey is quoted in the *Kerryman*,
      1 November 1974.

16   'The impudence of Charles Haughey',
      Kerryman, 8 November 1974.

17   Haughey to Stephenson, 14 November 1974,
      Haughey papers, C7/143 (2).

18   Rosita Sweetman (1972) *On Our Knees:
      Ireland 1972*. London: Pan Books, pp. 132–4.

19   Gallagher to Haughey, 3 July 1972, Haughey
      papers, C7/141 (2).

20   Haughey to Gallagher, 5 July 1972, Haughey
      papers, C7/141 (2).

21   Mulcahy to Haughey, 18 August 1972, Haughey papers, C7/141 (3).

22   Conor Cruise O'Brien (1972) *States of Ireland*. London: Hutchinson, p. 189.

23   Haughey to Mulcahy, 22 August 1972, Haughey papers, C7/141 (3).

24   Vincent Browne, 'The making of a Taoiseach', *Magill*, 30 January 1980, available at https://magill.ie/archive/making-taoiseach.

25   *Irish Press*, 31 January 1975.

26   Undated notes of interview preparation; Haughey papers, C7/101 (2).

27   Notes on interview preparation, DO'D, 14 May 1975, Haughey papers, C7/101 (2).

28   Question and answer interview preparation, undated, Haughey papers, C7/102 (2).

29   *People and Power* was first broadcast by RTÉ on 8 July 1975. Haughey appeared on 22 July. The format was a simple question and answer session with Haughey and Farrell facing each other.

30   Brendan Flanagan to Haughey, 26 July 1975, Haughey papers, C7/144 (2).

31   Carty interview.

32   Haughey to Lawlor, 1 August 1975, Haughey papers, C7/144 (2).

33   Haughey to Mother Bernard, 11 June 1975, Haughey papers, C7/115 (1).

34   A report of the case appeared on the front pages of the *Irish Times* and *Irish Press*, 23 September 1975.

35   Gallagher to Haughey, 23 September 1975; Haughey to Gallagher, 29 September 1975, Haughey papers, C7/115 (2).

36   Seán Haughey interview.

37   Reports of the accident were carried on the front pages of the Irish broadsheet newspapers on 7 July 1976. On the same evening as Haughey's crash, the Fine Gael TD for Roscommon Leitrim, Joan Burke, was also involved in a motor accident on the Dublin–Galway road at Kilcock. Her daughter and a friend were in the car with her.

38   Loughnane to Haughey, 7 September 1976; Haughey to Loughnane, 9 September 1976, Haughey papers, C7/115 (2).

39   Speech by Charles J. Haughey in reply to the debate on the Honorary Secretary's Report, Fianna Fáil Ard Fheis, 17 February 1978, Haughey papers, C7/93 (2).

40   Martin O'Donoghue in an interview with Cormac O'Sullivan, 24 June 2010, quoted in Cormac O'Sullivan, '"The Greatest Comeback Since Lazarus": The Fianna Fáil General Election Campaign of 1977, a Milestone in Irish Political Communication', MA in Political Communication, Dublin City University, 2010, p. 43.

41   Gary Murphy (2015) '"The Irish People Should Feel Ashamed of Themselves for What They had Done": Party Politics and the Fianna Fáil Manifesto of 1977' in Kevin Rafter and Mark O'Brien (eds) *The State in Transition: Essays in Honour of John Horgan*. Dublin: New Island Press, p. 142.

42   Fianna Fáil, *Manifesto: An Action Plan for National Reconstruction*, 1977, p. 1. The manifesto is available at the National Library of Ireland and at the Fianna Fáil archives in UCD. There is also a copy in the Haughey papers, C7/82.

43   O'Donoghue, cited in O'Sullivan, 'Lazarus', p. 43.

44   Frank Dunlop (2004) *Yes, Taoiseach: Irish Politics from Behind Closed Doors*. Dublin, Penguin, pp. 80–1.

45   Ciara Meehan (2013) *A Just Society for Ireland? 1964–1987.* London: Palgrave, p. 91.

46   Stephen Collins (2001) *The Power Game: Ireland under Fianna Fáil*. Dublin: O'Brien Press, p. 106.

47   Whelan, *Fianna Fáil*, p. 186.

48   Keogh, *Jack Lynch*, p. 403.

49   J.J. Lee (1989) *Ireland, 1912–1985: Politics and Society.* Cambridge: Cambridge University Press, p. 490.

50   O'Sullivan, 'Lazarus', pp. 19–20; 49–50.

51   Keogh, *Jack Lynch*, p. 407.

52   Dunlop, *Yes, Taoiseach*, p. 68.

53   Eoin O'Malley and Gary Murphy (2018) 'The Leadership Difference? Context and Choice in Fianna Fáil's Party Leadership' in Eoin O'Malley and Seán McGraw (eds) *One-Party Dominance: Fianna Fáil and Irish Politics 1926–2016*. Abingdon: Routledge, p. 125.

54   Bertie Ahern (2010) *Bertie Ahern: The Autobiography*. London: Hutchinson, p. 43. Bertie Ahern interview.

55   Interview with Michael Woods, 21 February 2017.

56   *Irish Press*, 1 June 1977.

57   Mara interview.

58   Haughey's full statement is reprinted in Mansergh, *Spirit of the Nation*, p. 241.

59   The *Irish Independent* reported O'Brien's comments under the large headline 'Haughey security under fire', 2 June 1977.

60   Collins and Meehan, *Saving the State*, p. 166.

61   Stephen O'Byrnes (1986) *Hiding Behind a Face: Fine Gael under FitzGerald*. Dublin: Gill and Macmillan, p. 2.

62   For a contemporary assessment of the campaign see Brian Farrell and Maurice Manning (1978) 'The Election' in Howard R. Penniman (ed.), *Ireland at the Polls: The Dáil Election of 1977*. Washington DC: American Enterprise Institute. For later assessments

see Stephen Collins (1996) *The Cosgrave Legacy*. Dublin: Blackwater Press, pp. 148–52; Michael Gallagher and Michael Marsh (2002) *Days of Blue Loyalty: The Politics of Membership of the Fine Gael Party*. Dublin: PSAI Press, pp. 28–9; Collins and Meehan, *Saving the State*, pp. 162–7.

63   Neville Keery interview; Fianna Fáil General Election 1977 Manifesto, pp. 22–3.

64   Note of visit to Abbeville, 14 June 1977, Haughey papers, C7/136 (2).

65   Haughey to Robinson, 10 March 1977, Haughey papers, C7/136 (2).

66   Brendan O'Donnell interview.

67   Albert and Kathleen Reynolds to Haughey, 5 March 1978, Haughey papers, C7/145 (2).

68   Edwards to Haughey, 13 March 1978, Haughey papers, C7/145 (2).

69   Haughey to Edward McGuire, 22 March 1978; to Albert and Kathleen Reynolds, 23 March 1978; to Hilton Edwards 23 March 1978, Haughey papers, C7/145 (2).

70   Maev-Ann Wren (2003) *Unhealthy State: Anatomy of a Sick Society*. Dublin: New Island, p. 58.

71   Haughey to Muireann Egan, February 1978, Haughey papers, C7/93 (1).

72   Weldon to Haughey, 14 December 1993, Haughey papers, C7/7 (5).

73   Browne to Haughey, 6 November 1997, Haughey papers, C7/244.

74   Whelan, *Fianna Fáil*, pp. 196–7.

75   Fianna Fáil General Election 1977 Manifesto, p. 25.

76   Mac Cormaic, *The Supreme Court*, pp. 156–77 has an excellent account of the McGee case.

77   Brendan O'Donnell interview.

78   Brian Girvin (2018) 'An Irish solution to an Irish problem: Catholicism, contraception and change, 1922–1979', *Contemporary European History* 27:4, 16. Girvin provides an extremely comprehensive and nuanced account of the difficulties of enacting contraception legislation.

79   Haughey to Cohan, 2 April 1969, Haughey papers, C7/151 (3). A copy of the questionnaire with Haughey's short answers is also included in this box.

80   Horan to Haughey, 28 May 1975; Haughey to Horan, 3 June 1975, Haughey papers, C7/144 (1).

81   Diarmaid Ferriter (2009) *Occasions of Sin: Sex and Society in Modern Ireland*. London: Profile Books, p. 423.

82   Girvin, 'Irish solution', p. 20.

83   Interview with Jimmy Guerin, 25 June 2021. Jimmy Guerin was a family friend of the Haugheys for many years. He was in Abbeville the night before Haughey introduced the Bill, where Haughey told him that he had just come back from the Archbishop's palace and had received the final seal of approval from Ryan for the proposal.

84   Brendan O'Donnell interview.

85   The debate held on 23 February 1979 can be accessed at https://www.oireachtas.ie/en/debates/debate/dail/1979-02-28/3/.

86   Brendan O'Donnell interview.

87   As told to *Seven Ages*, Episode 6, 'The Seventies: A Decade of Terror, Tension and Transformation'.

88   Aneurin Bevan was a particular political hero of Haughey's. He had been brought up in dire poverty in the South Wales valleys and in 1945 was appointed Minister of Health, and given responsibility for establishing the National Health Service.

89   Seanad debate on Health (Family Planning) Bill, 1978: Report and Final Stages, Tuesday 17 July 1979.

90   Haughey to F. Kelleher, secretary, University College, Cork, 5 October 1979, Haughey papers, C7/116 (2).

14. I HAVE THE VOTES

1   Browne to Haughey, 11 December 1979, Haughey papers, C7/80 (2).

2   Browne, 'The making of a Taoiseach'.

3   This one-page petition is in the Haughey papers, C7/231 (2).

4   Dunlop, *Yes, Taoiseach*, p. 106.

5   *Irish Press*, 3 September 1979.

6   Keogh, *Jack Lynch*, p. 422.

7   Correspondence to the author from David Neligan, 2 April 2021. David Neligan was the Head of the Anglo-Irish section of the Department of Foreign Affairs and was in attendance at this meeting. I am very grateful to him for his insights into this matter.

8   *Irish Press*, 5 and 6 October 1979.

9   See *Irish Times*, 17 September 1979; also Keogh, *Jack Lynch*, p. 423.

10   See Michael Mills, 'How Lynch era came to an end', *Irish Times*, 28 April 1998.

11   *Irish Independent*, 12 November 1979.

12   *Irish Independent*, 12 November 1979.

13   Browne, 'The making of a Taoiseach'.

14   Mills, *Hurler on the Ditch*, p. 124.

15   Kevin Healy interview.

16   *Irish Press*, 16 November 1979.

17   In interviews with P.J. Mara, Brendan O'Donnell and Seamus Puirséil, all confirmed that Lynch's declaration that he was stepping down caught Haughey by surprise.

18 *Irish Independent*, 3 December 1979.

19 See Padraig O'Morain (2003) *Access to Justice for All: The History of the Free Legal Advice Centres 1969–2003*, p. 28. Available at https://www.flac.ie/assets/files/pdf/access_to_justice_for_all.pdf.

20 Coolock Community Law Centre – Discussions with Minister, December 1979, Haughey papers, C7/107.

21 Note by P.J. Wylie, 19 January 1979, Haughey papers, C7/107.

22 *Irish Times*, 5 December 1979.

23 Interview with Geraldine Kennedy, 29 January 2019.

24 Keogh, *Jack Lynch*, p. 425.

25 FitzGerald, *All in a Life*, p. 339.

26 O'Malley, *Conduct Unbecoming*, p. 126.

27 Aylward interview.

28 Ray MacSharry interview.

29 Browne, 'The making of a Taoiseach'.

30 MacSharry interview.

31 *Irish Press*, 8 December 1979.

32 O'Donnell interview.

33 Dunlop, *Yes, Taoiseach*, p. 134.

34 Browne, 'The making of a Taoiseach'.

35 Haughey's comments were reported in all the Irish broadsheets of 8 December 1979.

36 Mills, 'How Lynch era came to an end'.

37 Interview with Charlie McCreevy, 26 October 2019. McCreevy soon turned against Haughey and was involved in a number of heaves against him. He later held a number of ministerial posts under Albert Reynolds and Bertie Ahern.

38 P.J. Mara interview; Brendan O'Donnell interview.

39 Reports of Haughey's press conference appeared in all the newspapers of Saturday 8 December 1979.

40 Speech by George Colley at the Camelot Hotel, Baldoyle, 20 December 1979, Haughey papers, C7/94 (2).

41 O'Malley, *Conduct Unbecoming*, pp. 129–30.

42 Haughey's handwritten notes of who might be in his cabinet are in C7/98 of his papers.

43 Interview with Máire Geoghegan-Quinn, 25 October 2019. Geoghegan-Quinn only served as a full minister in the first of Haughey's four governments. She was a minister for state in the other two and later served as a full minister under Albert Reynolds. She was Ireland's European Commissioner between 2010 and 2014.

44 Haughey to Geoghegan-Quinn, 23 July 1979, Haughey papers, C7/116 (1).

45 Geoghegan-Quinn to Haughey, 13 July 1979, Haughey papers, C7/116 (1).

46 Eoghan Haughey interview.

47 The full debate, held on Tuesday 11 December 1979, can be seen at https://www.oireachtas.ie/en/debates/debate/dail/1979-12-11/4/.

48 FitzGerald, *All in a Life*, p. 340.

49 Eoghan Haughey interview.

50 Mansergh in Episode 2 of the RTÉ documentary *Haughey*.

51 Brendan O'Donnell interview.

52 Dáil debate on nomination of Taoiseach, 11 September 1979.

53 Interview with Noel Whelan, 30 March 2017. Whelan was appointed secretary to the Department of Economic Planning and Development in July 1977. He later became secretary to the Department of the Taoiseach in 1980, before being appointed Vice-President to the European Investment Bank in 1982.

54 Paddy Moriarty to Haughey, 11 December 1979, Haughey papers, C7/4 (3). Moriarty, the chairman of the RTÉ Authority, was in Bahrain on the day Haughey was elected leader of Fianna Fáil and recounted this story to him.

55 Gallagher in Episode 2 of the RTÉ documentary *Haughey*.

56 Eimear Mulhern interview.

57 Aylward interview.

58 Dunlop, *Yes, Taoiseach*, p. 195.

59 Kiberd in Episode 2 of the RTÉ documentary *Haughey*.

60 Browne to Haughey, 11 December 1979.

61 Fergal Foley to Haughey, 13 December 1979, Haughey papers, C7/3 (1).

62 Susan McWeeney Forsythe to Haughey, 12 December 1979, Haughey papers, C7/3 (2).

63 Lehane to Haughey, 12 December 1979, Haughey papers, C7/4 (3).

64 Telegram from Vidal to Haughey, December 1979, Haughey papers, C7/4 (3).

65 Telegram from Browne to Haughey, December 1979, Haughey papers, C7/4 (1). The reference is to Miss Amelia Havisham, the wealthy spinster in Dickens's novel *Great Expectations*.

66 Ryan to Haughey, 9 December 1979, Haughey papers, C7/4 (4).

67 John Crowley to Haughey, 7 December 1979, Haughey papers, C7/4 (3).

68 Lynch to Haughey, 30 December 1979, Haughey papers, C7/1 (1).

69 John Horgan diary, 24 March 1980. I am grateful to Professor Horgan for providing me with a copy of his diary from his archive.

70 Aylward interview.

15. TAOISEACH

1   Aylward interview.
2   Aylward interview; Morgan interview.
3   Graham Pointon, Pronunciation Advisor, BBC, to Haughey, 10 December 1979; S.C. O'Riordan to Pointon, 21 December 1979 Haughey papers, C7/121 (2).
4   Noel Whelan interview.
5   Dunlop, *Yes, Taoiseach*, pp. 192–3.
6   Neligan to the author, 2 April 2021.
7   John Horgan interview.
8   Geraldine Kennedy interview.
9   A clip of this famous broadcast can be seen at https://www.rte.ie/archives/2015/0109/671262-haughey-warns-we-are-living-beyond-our-means/. The text is in Mansergh, *Spirit of the Nation*, pp. 323–6.
10 Geraldine Kennedy interview.
11 Slogans for Ard Fheis, Haughey papers, C7/95 (2)
12 Philip O'Connor (2019) 'A Very Political Project: Charles Haughey, Social Partnership and the Engineering of an "Irish Economic Miracle", 1969–92'. PhD thesis, School of Law and Government, Dublin City University, p. 87.
13 John Horgan interview.
14 Haughey's speech is in his papers, C7/95 (2). It is also in Mansergh, *Spirit of the Nation*, pp. 327–38.
15 Des O'Malley interview.
16 Haughey Ard Fheis speech, 16 February 1980.
17 O'Connor, 'A Very Political Project', pp. 85–6.
18 O'Malley, *Conduct Unbecoming*, p. 123.
19 Stephen Collins, 'Haughey settled bill for 1979 postal strikers' food and drink', *Irish Times*, 8 November 2014.
20 O'Connor, 'A Very Political Project', p. 87.
21 Minister from M.F. Doyle, 1 July 1980, Haughey papers, C7/81.
22 Minister from M.F. Doyle, 1 July 1980, Haughey papers, C7/81.
23 Barnes to Haughey, 1 March 1981, Haughey papers, C7/139 (2).
24 Haughey to Barnes, 30 March 1981, Haughey papers, C7/139 (2).
25 *Irish Times*, 17 July 1980.
26 *Kilkenny People*, 18 April 1980. While Gibbons's remarks did not make the front page of his local paper, they were the lead story in the *Irish Independent* of the same date.
27 Both Haughey's and Gibbons's statements are in the Haughey papers, C7/94 (2).
28 *Kilkenny People*, 25 April 1980.
29 O'Connor, 'A Very Political Project', p. 88.
30 Healy to Haughey, 10 September 1980, Haughey papers, C7/1 (1).
31 'Haughey tries for a comeback', cable from US Embassy Dublin to State Department, 16 November 1974, available at https://www.wikileaks.org/plusd/cables/1974DUBLIN01609_b.html.
32 In March of 1980 Fionbarr Ó Catháin of Drew University reminded Haughey that they had met in Hume's house on the morning of the funerals. Haughey later replied that he recalled the meeting and was glad of Ó Catháin's advice on the current situation in Northern Ireland. Haughey papers, C7/3 (2).
33 Haughey to Mother Bernard, 6 February 1973, Haughey papers, C7/114 (2).
34 Haughey to Robert Haughey, 7 January 1976, Haughey papers, C7/115 (2).
35 Legge to Haughey, 17 February 1980, Haughey papers, C7/8 (3).
36 Browne to Haughey, 11 December 1979.
37 Confidential Report of British Embassy on Charles Haughey, 9 April 1980, quoted in Ó Beacháin, *From Partition to Brexit*, pp. 170–2.
38 P.J. Mara interview.
39 Interview with Noel Dorr, 23 May 2017.
40 Interview with Wally Kirwan, 16 April 2019. In June of 1983, four days after her landslide re-election triumph, Ticher wrote to Thatcher telling her that the teapot Haughey gave her came from his collection and offering her a sugar bowl and cream jug to go with it. Ticher to Thatcher, 13 June 1983, Haughey papers, C7/116 (2).
41 Aylward interview.
42 Confidential Report of British Embassy on Charles Haughey, 9 April 1980, quoted in Ó Beacháin, *From Partition to Brexit*, p. 172.
43 Eunan O'Halpin interview with Dermot Nally, 13 January 2009. I am grateful to Professor O'Halpin for providing me with a copy of his notes of his talk with Nally.
44 Blaney is cited in Seán Donlon, 'NI policy with Haughey in power', *Irish Times*, 27 July 2009.
45 On Noraid, see Brian Hanley (2004) 'The politics of Noraid', *Irish Political Studies*, 19:1.
46 Donlon, 'NI policy with Haughey in power'.
47 Haughey to Flaherty, 30 January 1980, Haughey papers, C7/158 (1).
48 Seán Donlon, 'Haughey bid to tighten grip on Northern policy derailed', *Irish Times*, 28 July 2009.
49 Aylward interview.
50 Michael Mills, 'Top envoys in reshuffle', *Irish Press*, 5 July 1980.
51 Donlon, 'Haughey bid to tighten grip'.
52 Nally interview with Eunan O'Halpin.

53   Chris Glennon, 'Govt. backs down on
      ambassador', *Irish Independent*, 10 July 1980.
54   *Irish Independent*, 28 July 1980.
55   Brendan O'Donnell interview.
56   Noel Dorr interview.
57   Interview with Daithí Ó Ceallaigh,
      6 December 2017.
58   Donlon, 'Haughey bid to tighten grip'.
59   Carey to Haughey, 25 December 1989,
      Haughey papers, C7/7 (3).
60   Brendan O'Donnell interview; Ray
      MacSharry interview.
61   Speech by An Taoiseach, Letterkenny,
      1 November 1980, Haughey papers, C7/83 (1).
62   *Irish Press*, 3 November 1980.
63   Brendan O'Donnell interview.
64   Ó Beacháin, *From Partition to Brexit*,
      pp. 181–2.
65   *Irish Independent*, 6 November 1980;
      MacSharry interview.
66   *Irish Independent*, 8 November 1980.
67   McGowan to Haughey, 14 November 1980;
      Haughey to Ciarán Haughey, 17 November
      1980, Haughey papers, C7/83 (1).
68   Arnold to Haughey, 12 November 1980,
      Haughey papers, C7/243. A copy is in C7/1
      (1).
69   *Irish Press*, 8 December 1980.
70   NAI, DFA, 2010/53/930, Meeting between the
      Taoiseach and the British Prime Minister,
      8 December 1980.
71   A copy of the joint communiqué is in the
      Haughey papers, C7/231 (1).
72   Neligan to the author, 2 April 2021. This
      account was given to me by the Irish official
      David Neligan, who was at the meeting.
73   Margaret Thatcher (1993) *The Downing Street
      Years*. London: HarperCollins, p. 390.
74   *Irish Times*, 9 May 1980.
75   Ó Beacháin, *From Partition to Brexit*,
      pp. 183–4.
76   Nally interview with Eunan O'Halpin.
77   Wally Kirwan interview.
78   FCO letter to No.10 ('Anglo/Irish
      Summit') [addressing Taoiseach Haughey's
      'presentational issues' regarding communiqué
      on Anglo-Irish cooperation], available from
      the Margaret Thatcher archive, at https://
      www.margaretthatcher.org/document/125319.
      I am grateful to my DCU colleague, Professor
      Eoin O'Malley for bringing this document to
      my attention.
79   Thatcher to Haughey, 11 December 1980;
      Haughey to Thatcher, dated December 1980,
      Haughey papers, C7/191 (2).
80   Wally Kirwan interview.

16. RISE AND FOLLOW

1   Haughey to Michael MacGinty of Donegal
      Linens, 5 January 1981, Haughey papers,
      C7/157 (3).
2   P.J. Mara interview.
3   Interview with Frank Wall, 10 September
      2015. Wall was appointed general secretary
      of Fianna Fáil in 1981 and served throughout
      Haughey's period as leader.
4   Geraldine Kennedy interview.
5   Frank Wall interview.
6   Mara is quoted in John Horgan (2001)
      '"Government Sources Said Last Night …":
      The Development of the Parliamentary Press
      Lobby in Modern Ireland' in Hiram Morgan
      (ed.), *Information, Media and Power Through
      the Ages*. Dublin: UCD Press, p. 267.
7   Interview with Pádraig Ó hUiginn, 25 March
      2014.
8   Irish Congress of Trade Unions, *Annual
      Report 1980*, p. 22.
9   See Gary Murphy and John Hogan (2008)
      'Fianna Fáil, the trade union movement,
      and the politics of macroeconomic crises,
      1970–82', *Irish Political Studies* 23:4, 591.
10   Paul Tansey, 'A good deal – at a price', *Irish
      Times*, 6 January 1981.
11   O'Connor, 'A Very Political Project', p. 92.
12   O'Malley is quoted in Niamh Hardiman
      (1988) *Pay and Economic Performance in
      Ireland 1970–1987*. Oxford: Clarendon, p. 212.
13   Paul Tansey, 'Understanding unemployment',
      Irish Times, 5 January 1981.
14   Des O'Malley interview.
15   Mullen to Haughey, 5 August 1981, 14 August
      1981, Haughey papers, C7/116 (1).
16   Haughey to Mullen, 7 September 1981,
      Haughey papers, C7/116 (1).
17   Alton to Haughey, 9 February 1981, Haughey
      papers, C7/116 (1).
18   Owens to Gibney, 21 January 1981, Haughey
      papers, C7/94 (1).
19   Frank Wall interview.
20   Neil Fetherstonhaugh and Tony McCullagh
      (2006) *They Never Came Home: The Stardust
      Story*. Dublin: Merlin provides a poignant
      account of the tragedy.
21   P.J. Mara interview.
22   Bertie Ahern interview.
23   Fetherstonhaugh and McCullagh, *They Never
      Came Home*, p. 96.
24   Interview with Martin Mansergh, 30 March
      2016.
25   Frank Wall interview.
26   Seán Aylward interview.
27   There is a large literature on the hunger
      strikes of 1980 and 1981. For a riveting early
      account see David Breresford (1987) *Ten Men*

Dead: The Story of the 1981 Irish Hunger Strike. London: HarperCollins. See also Thomas Hennessy (2013) *Hunger Strike: Margaret Thatcher's Battle with the IRA 1980–1981.* Dublin: Irish Academic Press.

28 Ray MacSharry interview.

29 Anthony Cronin, 'How Aosdána began', Aosdána pamphlet on the tenth anniversary of its inception. Copy in possession of the author.

30 Brian P. Kennedy (1990) *Dreams and Responsibilities: The State and the Arts in Independent Ireland.* Dublin: Arts Council, p. 199.

31 Ballagh to Haughey, undated, but by context early 1981, Haughey papers, C7/1 (2).

32 Cronin discussed the founding of Aosdána in the RTÉ programme *Arts Express*, broadcast on 12 April 1991, to honour the tenth anniversary of its founding.

33 Kennedy, *Dreams and Responsibilities*, pp. 199–200.

34 Cronin to Chairman, The Arts Council, 4 October 1990, private collections. Copy in possession of the author.

35 Anthony Cronin, 'Facts, figures, and the state of the arts', *Irish Times*, 1 September 1990.

36 Cronin, 'How Aosdána began'.

37 See for instance Fintan O'Toole, 'How Charlie came to be painted as a man of the arts', *Irish Times*, 10 February 2007.

38 See Michael O'Loughlin, 'Why we should stand up for Aosdána this Bloomsday', *Irish Times*, 16 June 2017.

39 Haughey to Louis and Ann le Brocquy, 27 October 1987, Haughey papers, C7/51 (6).

40 Haughey's address is in Mansergh, *Spirit of the Nation*, pp. 462–81.

41 Reports of the speech and reaction to it were published in all the national newspapers on 13 April 1981.

42 *Irish Press*, 13 April 1981.

43 O'Brien to Haughey, 21 April 1981; Haughey to O'Brien, 22 April 1981, Haughey papers, C7/139 (2).

44 Ray MacSharry interview.

45 Bertie Ahern interview.

46 Ó Beacháin, *From Partition to Brexit*, p. 186.

47 Seán Aylward interview.

48 All the major papers reported on the Sands' family visit to Abbeville, and the summonsing of the British ambassador.

49 Kelly, *Failed Political Entity*, p. 223.

50 Interview with Declan O'Donovan, 15 May 2017. O'Donovan was a senior official in the Department of Foreign Affairs at this time. He was later promoted to the position of assistant secretary and sent by Haughey to Northern Ireland in 1989 as Head of Mission, at essentially the ambassadorial grade.

51 Haughey to Figg, 14 September 1981, Haughey papers, C7/116 (1).

52 Collins and Meehan, *Saving the State*, pp. 185–8.

53 St John Blake to Haughey, 24 February 1981, Haughey papers, C7/96 (1).

54 1981 General Election File, 'Press Advertising', Haughey papers, C7/94 (1).

55 1981 General Election File, 'General Election Information Centre', Haughey papers, C7/94 (1).

56 1981 General Election File, 'The Labour Election Programme and Comparisons with the Fine Gael Programme', Haughey papers, C7/94 (1).

57 1981 General Election File, 'How does your team compare', Haughey papers, C7/94 (1).

58 1981 General Election File, 'Notes for Press Conference, 3 pm, Wednesday 3 June', Haughey papers, C7/94 (1).

59 In interviews with the journalists Mike Burns, Kevin Healy and Geraldine Kennedy, they all confirmed their surprise at the success of the H-Block candidates.

60 Des Byrne, IMS, to Frank Wall, 10 August 1981, Haughey papers, C7/98.

61 Frank Wall interview.

62 Ray MacSharry interview.

63 Coogan to Haughey, 10 July 1981, Haughey papers, C7/81.

64 Daly to Haughey, 3 July 1981, Haughey papers, C7/81.

65 Haughey to Daly, 14 July 1981, Haughey papers, C7/81.

66 Whelan, *Fianna Fáil*, p. 208.

67 Frank Wall interview.

68 Michael Woods interview.

69 Liam Weeks (2017) *Independents in Irish Party Democracy.* Manchester: Manchester University Press, pp. 220–1.

70 Collins and Meehan, *Saving the State*, p. 201.

71 Maurice O'Connell (2020) *No Complaints: A Memoir of Life in Rural Ireland and in the Irish Public Service.* Kerry: Kingdom Books, pp. 86–7. O'Connell died in 2019 and his memoir, published the following year, was edited by J. Anthony Gaughan.

72 Stephen O'Byrnes (1986) *Hiding Behind a Face: Fine Gael under FitzGerald.* Dublin: Gill and Macmillan, p. 134; Stephen Collins (1992). *The Haughey File: The Unprecedented Career and Last Years of the Boss.* Dublin: O'Brien Press, p. 52.

73 John Walsh *(2008) Patrick Hillery: The Official Biography.* Dublin: New Island, p. 476.

74 Loftus delivered his view of the events of that day and night in an interview with Liam Weeks in 2008. See Liam Weeks *Independents in Irish Party Democracy*, p. 108.

75 Walsh, *Hillery*, pp. 475–6.

76 Whelan, *Fianna Fáil*, p. 209.

77 Ned O'Neill to Haughey, 22 February 1982, Haughey papers, C7/170 (2).

78 Dáil debate of 26 January 1982, available at https://www.oireachtas.ie/en/debates/debate/dail/1982-01-26/2/.

79 On the politics of abortion and the 1983 referendum see Brian Girvin (1986) 'Social change and moral politics: the Irish constitutional referendum 1983', *Political Studies* 34:1, 61–81; Tom Hesketh (1990) *The Second Partitioning of Ireland: The Abortion Referendum of 1983*. Dublin: Brandsma Books.

80 O'Dwyer to Haughey, 28 April 1981, Haughey papers, C7/139 (2).

81 Haughey to O'Dwyer, 1 May 1981, Haughey papers, C7/139 (2).

82 FitzGerald, *All in a Life*, p. 416.

83 Seán Aylward interview.

84 Haughey to Vaughan, 14 May 1981, Haughey papers, C7/162 (1).

85 FitzGerald, *All in a Life*, p. 416.

86 Haughey is quoted in Emily O'Reilly (1992) *Masterminds of the Right*. Dublin: Attic Press, p. 75.

87 Haughey to Attorney General, 31 March 1982, Haughey papers, C7/163 (1).

88 Frank Wall interview.

89 Neeson to Haughey, 11 February 1982, Haughey papers, C7/94 (3).

90 Terry Prone interview.

91 *Irish Independent*, 17 February 1982.

92 FitzGerald, *All in a Life*, p. 401.

93 Doyle to Haughey, 17 November 1982. The note Doyle gave to Haughey with his letter is headed 'Proposed Borrowing from the Central Bank in 1981'. Haughey papers, C7/81.

94 *Irish Press*, 17 February 1982.

95 *Irish Independent*, 17 February 1982.

96 *Irish Press*, 17 February 1982.

97 O'Donovan to Haughey, 23 February 1982, Haughey papers, C7/157.

98 *Evening Herald*, 18 February 1982.

99 Kate Nugent interview.

100 *Irish Times*, 21 April 1982.

17. 1982

1 Mara used this expression in Episode 2 of the RTÉ documentary *Haughey*.

2 Joe Joyce and Peter Murtagh (1983) *The Boss: Charles J. Haughey in Government*. Dublin: Poolbeg, pp. 32–3.

3 O'Malley, *Conduct Unbecoming*, p. 131.

4 *Irish Times*, 24 February 1982; *Cork Examiner*, 22 February 1982.

5 *Irish Independent*, 24 February 1982.

6 *Irish Independent*, 26 February 1982.

7 *Irish Times*, 26 February 1982.

8 Dunsany to Haughey, 24 February 1982; Haughey to Dunsany, 25 March 1982, Haughey papers, C7/10 (2).

9 Fennell to Haughey, 27 February 1982, Haughey papers, C7/10 (3).

10 Flinn to Haughey, 24 February 1982, Haughey papers, C7/116 (2).

11 Haughey to Flinn, 1 March 1982, Haughey papers, C7/116 (2).

12 See Robbie Gilligan (2011) *Tony Gregory: The Biography of a True Irish Political Legend*. Dublin: O'Brien Press.

13 Kevin Rafter, *Neil Blaney*, p. 99.

14 Noel McGinley, Fianna Fáil Donegal NE Dáilcheantair to Haughey, 21 May 1982, Haughey papers, C7/94 (3).

15 'Tony Gregory – Priority Issues', undated but by context March 1982, Haughey papers, C7/80 (1).

16 'Tony Gregory – Priority Issues'. The profile was written by 'KR', most likely Ken Ryan, who was a Fianna Fáil press officer in this period.

17 Shannon to Gregory, 8 March 1982, Haughey papers, C7/157.

18 *Irish Independent*, *Irish Press*, *Irish Times*, 10 March 1982.

19 Gillígan, *Tony Gregory*, p. 109.

20 *Irish Independent*, 10 March 1982.

21 Bertie Ahern interview.

22 Colley's statement was referred to in all the broadsheet papers of 10 March 1982.

23 Des O'Malley interview.

24 Máire Geoghegan-Quinn interview.

25 McCafferty to Haughey, 30 March 1982, Haughey papers, C7/116 (2).

26 Haughey to McCafferty, 22 April 1982, Haughey papers, C7/116 (2).

27 NSC Minutes of the meeting of 30 April 1982, available at https://www.margaretthatcher.org/document/114329.

28 See Reagan's diary entry of 30 April 1982, available at https://www.reaganfoundation.org/ronald-reagan/white-house-diaries/diary-entry-04301982/.

29 Mates to Haughey, 14 May 1982, Haughey papers, C7/10 (2).

30 For a detailed account of the hectic diplomatic relations at the UN over the Falklands conflict see Noel Dorr (2011) *A Small State at the Top Table: Memories of Ireland on the UN Security Council, 1981–82*. Dublin: Institute of Public Administration.

31 Ó Beacháin, *Partition to Brexit*, p. 193.
32 Dáithí Ó Ceallaigh interview. At this stage Ó Ceallaigh was press officer at the embassy.
33 Wally Kirwan interview.
34 Dunlop, *Yes, Taoiseach*, pp. 267–8; J.J. Power, letter to the *Irish Times*, 'Sinking of the "Belgrano"', 31 January 2012.
35 *Irish Independent*, 6 May 1982.
36 The text of Irish statement is reproduced in Dorr, *A Small State at the Top Table*, pp. 182–3.
37 *Irish Independent*, 6 May 1982.
38 Noel Dorr interview.
39 Gerry Collins interview.
40 Brendan O'Donnell interview.
41 Lawrence Freedman (2005) *The Official History of the Falklands Campaign*, Vol. 2: *War and Diplomacy*. Abingdon: Routledge, p. 425.
42 See Lillis's review of Dorr's book: 'Mr Haughey's dud Exocet', *Dublin Review of Books* Issue 21, available at https://drb.ie/articles/mr-haugheys-dud-exocet/. Lillis reiterated this point to me in an interview in his home in Dublin on 11 October 2018.
43 Noel Dorr interview.
44 Dáil debate, Tuesday 11 May 1982, available at https://www.oireachtas.ie/en/debates/debate/dail/1982-05-11/10/.
45 Eamonn O'Kane (2012) *Britain, Ireland and Northern Ireland since 1980: The Totality of Relationships*. Abingdon: Routledge, p. 32.
46 See Charles Moore (2013) *Margaret Thatcher: The Authorized Biography*, Vol. 1: *Not For Turning*. London: Penguin, pp. 621–2.
47 Noel Dorr interview.
48 See NAI, DT, 2012/90/982.
49 Haughey to McKimm, 25 June 1982, Haughey papers, C7/164 (1).
50 Moore, *Not For Turning*, p. 621.
51 Deaglán de Bréadún, 'Falklands a ridiculous war, said Haughey', *Irish Times*, 28 December 2017.
52 Lillis interview.
53 Dáithí Ó Ceallaigh interview.
54 Wally Kirwan interview.
55 Mansergh interview. See also his review of Kelly's *Failed Political Entity*.
56 Declan O'Donovan interview.
57 'Haughey is right on the Malvinas', *Magill*, 31 May 1982.
58 Andrews to Haughey, 21 April 1983, Haughey papers, C7/243.
59 Andrews to Haughey, 24 June 1982, Haughey papers, C7/94 (3).
60 Burke to Haughey, 14 March 1982, Haughey papers, C7/1 (1).
61 FitzGerald, *All in a Life*, p. 406.
62 *Irish Independent*, 31 March 1981.
63 Dublin West Candidates Canvas Notes, Haughey papers, C7/82.
64 Ray MacSharry interview.
65 *Irish Press*, 7 June 1982.
66 *Irish Independent*, 17 June 1982.
67 See Dáil debate, 16 June 1982, available at https://www.oireachtas.ie/en/debates/debate/dail/1982-06-16/6/.
68 See for instance his letter to Anna May Miley, 4 July 1982, Haughey papers, C7/164 (2).
69 See Thomas Murray (2016) *Contesting Economic and Social Rights in Ireland: Constitution, State and Society, 1848–2016*. Cambridge: Cambridge University Press, p. 317; Emmet O'Connor (2011) *A Labour History of Ireland, 1824–2000*. Dublin: University College Dublin Press, p. 236.
70 *Irish Press*, 19 July 1982.
71 Pádraig Ó hUiginn interview.
72 Haughey's recollections are told in the Haughey family website at https://www.charlesjhaughey.ie/articles/social-partnership.
73 Pádraig Ó hUiginn interview.
74 *Irish Press*, 28 July 1982.
75 Seán Aylward interview.
76 Joyce and Murtagh, *The Boss*, p. 227.
77 A timeline of the events from Friday 13 August to Sunday 15 August 1982 is in Haughey's papers, C7/81.
78 Joyce and Murtagh, *The Boss*, p. 229.
79 Seán Aylward interview.
80 Timeline of events, Haughey papers.
81 Dunlop, *Yes, Taoiseach*, p. 272.
82 A copy of Connolly's statement is in Haughey's papers, C7/81.
83 Dunlop, *Yes, Taoiseach*, pp. 274–5.
84 Joyce and Murtagh, *The Boss*, p. 234.
85 Statement issued by the Taoiseach, Haughey papers, C7/81.
86 Connolly to Haughey, 17 March 1984, Haughey papers, C7/116 (2).
87 Haughey to Connolly, 15 June 1984, Haughey papers, C7/116 (2).
88 McCreevy to Haughey, 1 October 1982, Haughey papers, C7/1 (1).
89 McCreevy to Ahern, 1 October 1982, Haughey papers, C7/1 (1).
90 Bertie Ahern interview.
91 Charlie McCreevy interview.
92 Ahern, *The Autobiography*, p. 67.
93 *Irish Press*, 5 October 1982.
94 *Irish Press*, 6 October 1982.
95 Ahern, *Autobiography*, p. 68.
96 Tom McGrath and Michael Murphy to Haughey, 4 October 1982, Haughey papers, C7/10 (2).
97 Dunlop, *Yes, Taoiseach*, pp. 296-7.
98 Ray MacSharry interview.
99 Bertie Ahern interview.

18. PHONE TAPPING

1   Constituency Report, 11 November 1982, Haughey papers, C7/82.

2   Conroy to Haughey, 7 October 1982, Haughey papers, C7/10 (1).

3   Dorothy Ravenswood to Edward Brazil, 27 November 1982, Haughey papers, C7/10 (2). Brazil forwarded a copy of the letter to Haughey.

4   Dervla Murphy, letter to the editor, *Irish Times*, 30 November 1982. The letter was entitled: 'The Duke Who Came In From The Cold'.

5   Wall, letter to the editor, *Irish Times*, 30 November 1982, Haughey papers, C7/165 (2).

6   Tim Pat Coogan, interviewed by Dermot Moran (1984). *The Crane Bag Book of Irish Studies*, 8:2, 'The Media and Popular Culture', p. 25.

7   Haughey to Eoghan Haughey, 29 November 1982, Haughey papers, C7/165 (2).

8   The most detailed account of the Dowra affair is in Joyce and Murtagh, *The Boss*, pp. 240–50.

9   Dunlop, *Yes, Taoiseach*, p. 276.

10 Peter Dolan, Killinagh Cumann Fianna Fáil to Haughey, 2 October 1982, Haughey papers, C7/82.

11 Joyce and Murtagh, *The Boss*, pp. 237–8.

12 This story was recounted by Pat Rabbitte in the *Sunday Business Post*, 18 April 2021.

13 Hugh Munroe to Haughey, 8 February 1983, Haughey papers, C7/54 (4).

14 P.J. Mara interview.

15 Martin Mansergh, 'C.J. Haughey and the phone tapping saga', *Irish Independent*, 24 January 1992.

16 *Irish Times*, 18 December 1982.

17 Joyce and Murtagh, *The Boss*, pp. 304–6.

18 Haughey made this claim in his statement rejecting Doherty's allegations in 1992 that he – Haughey – knew about the telephone taps on the phones of Arnold and Kennedy. Haughey's press conference statement is in his papers, C7/49.

19 Haughey to Castro, 9 December 1982, Haughey papers, C7/165 (2).

20 Haughey to Deighton, 10 January 1983, Haughey papers, C7/7 (1).

21 *Irish Press*, 25 January 1983.

22 Ray MacSharry interview.

23 *Irish Independent*, 24 January 1983.

24 Ahern, *The Autobiography*, p. 72.

25 P.J. Mara interview.

26 The obituary was entitled 'CJ Haughey – man of controversy', *Irish Press*, 27 January

1983. Later the editor Tim Pat Coogan said its inclusion was the fault of a production error. See Tim Pat Coogan (2008) *A Memoir*. London: Weidenfeld and Nicolson, p. 259.

27 *Irish Independent*, 28 January 1983.

28 Mara made this comment in Episode 3 of the RTÉ *Haughey* documentary. The episode was entitled 'The Survivor'.

29 Bertie Ahern, *The Autobiography*, p. 73.

30 Grattan Bannister to Haughey, 3 February 1983, Haughey papers, C7/54 (4).

31 Message to all members of the Fianna Fáil Organisation throughout the country from the leader, Charles J. Haughey, 3 February 1983, Haughey papers, C7/60 (2).

32 *Irish Press*, 5 February 1983.

33 Briscoe in *Haughey*, 'The Survivor'.

34 Whelan, *Fianna Fáil*, p. 217.

35 *Irish Press*, 8 February 1983.

36 *Irish Press*, 9 February 1983.

37 Bertie Ahern, *The Autobiography*, pp. 68-9.

38 Paul Kavanagh interview.

39 Doherty to Haughey, 8 February 1983, Haughey papers, C7/243.

40 O'Donoghue to Haughey, 9 February 1983, Haughey papers, C7/243.

41 See obituary of Shea Healy, *Irish Times*, 17 April 2021.

42 *Irish Times*, 22 January 1992.

43 Terry Prone interview.

44 Haughey press conference statement 22 January 1992, C7/49. The statement was reproduced in all the following day's newspapers.

45 *Irish Times*, 22 January 1992, with handwritten emendations by Haughey, Haughey papers, C7/49.

46 *Irish Press*, 23 January 1992.

47 Ainsworth to Haughey, 19 February 1987, Haughey papers, C7/6 (3).

48 Feehan to Haughey, 15 January 1984, Haughey papers, C7/1 (1).

49 See Maume, *Haughey*, p. 18.

50 Feehan to Haughey, 23 November 1987, Haughey papers, C7/7 (2).

51 Haughey to Feehan, 16 July 1987, Haughey papers, C7/51 (4).

52 MacBride to Haughey, 9 March 1985, Haughey papers, C7/62 (3).

53 Eogan to Haughey, 23 February 1987, Haughey papers, C7/62 (3).

54 Eogan to Fianna Fáil, 30 January 1983, Haughey papers, C7/10 (5).

55 Ainsworth to Haughey, 18 January 1992, copy in possession of the author.

56 Ainsworth Note, 'Confidential', 18 January 1992, copy in possession of the author.

57 Joe Ainsworth, 'My memory of events in 1982 gives a very different picture', *Irish Times*, 10 October 2012.

58 Maureen Haughey interview.

59 P.J. Mara interview.

60 Tim Ryan (1992) *Mara PJ*. Dublin: Blackwater Press, p. 144.

61 Martin Mansergh, 'C.J. Haughey and the phone tapping saga.' The reference to January is to 1982, when Michael Noonan confirmed the existence of the tapping.

62 *Irish Independent*, 6 December 1984.

63 See Doherty's obituary: 'A 25-year political career dogged by controversy', *Irish Times*, 8 June 2005.

64 Haughey to Des Bruen, 1 April 1987, Haughey papers, C7/51 (1).

65 T. Ryle Dwyer, *Haughey's Thirty Years of Controversy*. Cork: Mercier Press, p. 176.

66 Des O'Malley interview.

67 *Irish Times*, 17 April 2021.

68 O'Malley, *Conduct Unbecoming*, p. 189.

69 John O'Leary (2015) *On the Doorsteps: Memoirs of a Long-serving TD*. Killarney: Irish Political Memoirs, p. 261.

70 Reynolds, *My Autobiography*, p. 146.

71 Terry Prone interview.

19. HAUGHEY'S IRELAND

1 New Ireland Forum Report, p. 1. A copy of the report is in Haughey's papers, C7/61 (3).

2 Paddy McCarthy to Haughey, 28 May 1983, Haughey papers, C7/63 (3).

3 Statement by Charles J. Haughey at the conclusion of the public session of the forum 21 September 1983, Haughey papers, C7/61 (3).

4 'The Case for a Unitary State', Haughey papers, C7/63 (3).

5 *Irish Independent*, 14 May 1984.

6 *Irish Times*, 11 May 1984.

7 *Irish Press*, 14 May 1984.

8 *Irish Press*, 19 May 1984.

9 O'Malley, *Conduct Unbecoming*, p. 146.

10 P.J. Mara interview.

11 *Irish Independent*, 27 February 1985.

12 O'Malley, *Conduct Unbecoming*, p. 152.

13 Eamonn Ryan to Haughey, 27 February 1985, Haughey papers, C7/61 (4).

14 Ó Beacháin, *From Partition to Brexit*, p. 206.

15 Dáithí Ó Ceallaigh interview.

16 Niamh O'Connor interview. O'Connor worked for Fianna Fáil in Leinster House at this stage.

17 Máire Geoghegan-Quinn interview.

18 Dáil debate, 19 November 1985, available at https://www.oireachtas.ie/en/debates/debate/dail/1985-11-19/21/.

19 Ibid.

20 James Downey (1998) *Brian Lenihan: His Life and Times*. Dublin: New Island, p. 140.

21 Lenihan, *Haughey*, p. 147.

22 O'Hanlon interview.

23 Dáil debate, 19 November 1985.

24 Dáil debate, 19 November 1985.

25 Whelan, *Fianna Fáil*, p. 221.

26 O'Hanlon interview.

27 Dáil debate, 19 November 1985.

28 *Irish Independent*, 15 November 1985.

29 Haughey used this phrase in a January 1982 pamphlet replying to the Unionist politician Robert McCartney, who presented the 'Unionist Case' to both the then Taoiseach, Garret FitzGerald, and Haughey in October 1981. Haughey's reply is in the Haughey papers, C7/117.

30 Seamus Mallon with Andy Pollak (2019) *A Shared Home Place*. Dublin: The Lilliput Press, p. 69.

31 Mallon to Haughey, 10 February 1992, Haughey papers, C7/2 (1).

32 Daly to Haughey, 17 November 1995, Haughey papers, C7/156.

33 Ken Cotter, Riverstown–Glounthane Comhairle Ceantar, to Haughey, 24 January 1985, Haughey papers, C7/170 (1). The date here is mistaken. It should be January 1986. Getting the year wrong in January letters was quite common among Haughey's correspondents.

34 Haughey to Brian Hunt, Thomas Clarke Cumann, Waterford, 12 February 1986, Haughey papers, C7/138 (1).

35 On the formation of the Progressive Democrats, see Stephen Collins (2005) *Breaking the Mould: How the PDs Changed Irish Politics*. Dublin: Gill and Macmillan.

36 Máire Geoghegan-Quinn interview.

37 Interview with Mary O'Rourke, 12 April 2018. O'Rourke was frontbench spokesperson on education, and would later serve as Minister in Haughey's final two governments.

38 Bertie Ahern interview.

39 Terry Prone interview.

40 Haughey is quoted in Brian Girvin (1987) 'The Campaign' in Michael Laver, Peter Mair and Richard Sinnott (eds), *How Ireland Voted: The Irish General Election 1987*. Dublin: Poolbeg Press, p. 13.

41 See John Walsh (2019) *The Globalist: Peter Sutherland – His Life and Legacy*. London: William Collins.

42 'Some Points About The New Amendment', undated, Haughey papers, C7/98.

43 Haughey to Dermot O'Sullivan, 19 April 83, Haughey papers, C7/62 (5).

44   James Joyce to Haughey, 24 August 1983, Haughey papers, C7/98.

45   Haughey to Reverend Stephen Redmond, 30 August 1983, Haughey papers, C7/62 (5).

46   B.M. Carroll to Haughey, 4 August 1983, Haughey papers, C7/62 (5).

47   Haughey to Brenda Weir, 2 September 1983, Haughey papers, C7/62 (5).

48   Yvonne Galligan (1998) *Women and Politics in Contemporary Ireland: From the Margins to the Mainstream*. London: Pinter, p. 102.

49   Fergus Finlay (1998) *Snakes and Ladders*. Dublin: New Island Press, p. 33.

50   Collins and Meehan, *Saving the State*, p. 218.

51   FitzGerald, *All in a Life*, pp. 630–1.

52   Haughey to Arthur McRory, 5 June 1986, Haughey papers, C7/62 (4).

53   Mansergh, *Spirit of the Nation*, p. 1122.

54   See for instance Fintan O'Toole, 'Brass neck allowed Haughey to get away with the big lie', *Irish Times*, 18 May 1999.

55   1986 Ard Fheis Working Paper, Haughey papers, C7/106 (2).

56   W. Salters Sterling to Haughey, 5 December 1986, Haughey papers, C7/62 (4).

57   Haughey to Sterling, 7 January 1987, Haughey papers, C7/62 (4).

58   Maureen Haughey interview.

59   Conor Haughey interview.

60   All the daily newspapers carried reports of the accident and rescue on Monday 30 September 1985. This account also draws on the report in the *Sunday Tribune*, 6 October 1985, entitled: 'The Man They Cannot Sink.' In my interview with Conor Haughey on 7 December 2017 he played down his own part in the rescue, beyond saying simply, 'It was a tense time but sure I did what needed to be done.' I am grateful to him for sharing with me his recollections of that dramatic night.

61   Cummins to Haughey, 13 September 1989; Haughey to Cummins, 4 October 1989, Haughey papers, C7/31 (2).

62   Haughey to Coveney, 9 October 1985, Haughey papers, C7/121 (2). Coveney's postcard is undated.

63   Haughey to Avner, 9 October 1985, Haughey papers, C7/121 (2).

64   Channel 4 to Haughey, 4 April 1986, Haughey papers, C7/121 (2).

65   The programme can be seen at https://www.youtube.com/watch?v=Rhodf3xTc0U.

66   Kurland was quoted in the *Sunday Independent*, 25 June 2006.

67   Channel 4, *Charles Haughey's Ireland*, draft Film Script, Haughey papers, C7/106 (1).

20. NATIONAL RECOVERY

1   Gary Murphy (2016) *Electoral Competition in Ireland Since 1987: The Politics of Triumph and Despair*. Manchester: Manchester University Press, p. 30.

2   MacSharry interview.

3   Bertie Ahern, *The Autobiography*, p. 92.

4   Interview with Peter Cassells, 29 July 2016. Cassells was a senior ICTU official in this period. He became General Secretary in 1989, overseeing ICTU's membership of the social partnership process.

5   Bertie Ahern interview.

6   See Conor Brady (2005) *Up with the Times*. Dublin: Gill and Macmillan, pp. 6–7; Terence Brown (2015) *The Irish Times: 150 Years of Influence*. London: Bloomsbury, pp. 339–40.

7   See *Irish Times* editorial, 'The Gregory option', 2 March 1987.

8   Paul Kavanagh interview.

9   Desmond to Haughey, 27 February 1986, Haughey papers, C7/60 (1).

10   Desmond to Haughey, 9 May 1986, Haughey papers, C7/64 (1).

11   Interview with Dermot Desmond, 14 March 2019.

12   Desmond to Haughey, 26 January 1987, Haughey papers, C7/60 (2).

13   Buckley to Haughey, 28 January 1987, Haughey papers, C7/60 (2).

14   Haughey to James Dorney, General Secretary, Teachers' Union of Ireland, 14 January 1987, Haughey papers, C7/65 (1).

15   Haughey to Mulvey, 5 February 1987, Haughey papers, C7/65 (1).

16   Interview with Alan Dukes, 25 February 2020.

17   MacSharry interview.

18   Ray MacSharry and Padraic White (2000) *The Making of the Celtic Tiger: The Inside Story of Ireland's Boom Economy*. Cork: Mercier Press, p. 75.

19   *Irish Times*, 10 October 1987.

20   O'Connor, 'A Very Political Project', pp. 160–2. Philip O'Connor provides a wealth of detail on the painstaking negotiations involved in finalising the Programme for National Recovery. I am grateful to him for allowing me to draw on his work for this section.

21   MacSharry and White, *The Making of the Celtic Tiger*, p. 126.

22   Charles J. Haughey, 'Social Partnership: Its Origins and Achievements', https://www.charlesjhaughey.ie/articles/social-partnership.

23   Pádraig Ó hUiginn interview.

24   Charlie McCreevy attributed this comment to Haughey and it is quoted in Tim Hastings, Brian Sheehan and Padraig Yeates (2007)

Saving the Future: How Social Partnership Shaped Ireland's Economic Success. Dublin: Blackhall, p. 178. McCreevy repeated it to me in our interview.

25 Address by the Taoiseach, Charles J. Haughey to the first meeting of the International Financial Services Committee in Government Buildings, 9 April 1987, Haughey papers, C7/224.

26 Interview with Michael Somers, 28 November 2018.

27 Pádraig Ó hUiginn interview; Somers interview.

28 See Sweeney's obituary, 'Key figure in the State's first marine policy', *Irish Times*, 19 August 2017.

29 De Courcy Ireland to Haughey, 23 November 1989, Haughey papers, C7/31 (2).

30 Paul Durcan, 'Charlie Haughey and Knock International Airport', available at https://www.charlesjhaughey.ie/articles/charlie-haughey-and-knock-international-airport.

31 Durcan to Haughey, 6 June 1986, Haughey papers, C7/64 (3).

32 Somers interview.

33 Carol Coulter, 'Nothing allowed to disturb the sound of harmony', *Irish Times*, 10 October 1987.

34 Opening Remarks by An Taoiseach Charles J. Haughey at a press conference to launch the Programme for National Recovery, 9 October 1987, Haughey papers, C7/224.

35 Brendan Keenan, 'Haughey … giving away a lot less than it seems', *Irish Independent*, 10 October 1987.

36 O'Connor, 'A Very Political Project', p. 164.

37 Haughey to Fionnuala Prendergast, 1 April 1998, Haughey papers, C7/129 (1).

38 Haughey, 'Social Partnership: Its Origins and Achievements'.

39 Coveney to Haughey, dated 'Saturday', but by context mid to late June 1987, Haughey papers, C7/31 (2).

40 Crowley to Haughey, 16 September 1988, Haughey papers, C7/31 (2).

41 Haughey to All Ministers, 31 March 1988, Haughey papers, C7/40 (3).

42 Haughey to All Ministers, 19 April 1989, Haughey papers, C7/40 (3).

43 O'Hanlon to Haughey, 12 May 1989, Haughey papers, C7/40 (4).

44 O'Hanlon interview.

45 Damian Corless (2007) *Party Nation: Ireland's General Elections, the Strokes, Jokes, Spinners and Winners*. Dublin: Merlin Press, p. 233.

46 Interview with Noel Dempsey, 10 April 2019.

47 Interview with Paddy Teahon, 9 May 2019.

48 Pádraig Ó hUiginn interview.

49 Bertie Ahern interview.

50 O'Rourke interview.

51 Dukes to Haughey, 20 March 1989, Haughey papers, C7/38 (1).

52 Wren, *Unhealthy State*, p. 61.

53 Robb to Haughey, 22 October 1988, Haughey papers, C7/1 (1).

54 *Cork Examiner*, 20 October 1988.

55 *Cork Examiner*, 21 October 1988.

56 *Irish Press*, 29 October 1988.

57 *Cork Examiner*, 5 December 1988.

58 Taoiseach's meeting with Mr. Gorbachev – 2 April 1989. Summary Speaking Note (Revised), Haughey papers, C7/153 (2).

59 Haughey to Takeshita, 28 April 1989, Haughey papers, C7/54 (3).

60 John Horgan diary, 5 February 1999.

61 O'Rourke interview.

62 Dempsey interview.

63 Ahern, *The Autobiography*, p. 105.

64 Brian Girvin (1990) 'The Campaign' in Michael Gallagher, Michael Laver and Richard Sinnott (eds), *How Ireland Voted 1989*. Galway: PSAI Press, p. 21.

65 Mulvey to Haughey, 21 June 1989, Haughey papers, C7/7 (3).

66 Dukes interview.

67 Haughey to Dukes, 22 June 1989, Haughey papers, C7/38 (3).

68 Interview with Charlie McCreevy, 26 October 2019.

69 McCreevy to Haughey, 14 September 1987, Haughey papers, C7/38 (6).

70 McCreevy to Haughey, 3 March 1988, Haughey papers, C7/7 (2).

71 O'Malley, *Conduct Unbecoming*, p. 183. See also T. Ryle Dwyer (1999) *Short Fellow: A Biography of Charles J Haughey*. Dublin: Marino Books, p. 358.

72 Haughey to Dukes, 29 June 1989, Haughey papers, C7/38 (3).

73 Brian Farrell (1990) 'Forming the Government', in Gallagher et al., *How Ireland Voted 1989*, p. 185.

74 Whelan, *Fianna Fáil*, p. 234.

75 Collins, *The Power Game*, p. 199.

76 Collins, *The Haughey File*, p. 163.

77 Dáil debate, 6 July 1989, available at https://www.oireachtas.ie/en/debates/debate/dail/1989-07-06/2/.

78 Reynolds, *My Autobiography*, p. 132.

79 Collins, *The Power Game*, p. 200.

21. WE WILL BE RELYING ON YOU

1 The citation is available at http://archives.nd.edu/ndr/NDR-20/NDR-1991-06-14.pdf.

2 Haughey to Malloy, 18 January 1991, Haughey papers, C7/56 (5).

3 Haughey to Keough, 25 July 1991, Haughey papers, C7/57 (1).

4 See Eamonn Mallie and David McKittrick (1996) *The Fight for Peace: The Secret Story Behind the Irish Peace Process*. London: Heinemann, pp. 115–17.

5 Haughey to Major, 19 March 1991, Haughey papers, C7/56 (6).

6 See Kevin Rafter (2002) *Martin Mansergh: A Biography*. Dublin: New Island, p. 180.

7 Adams to Haughey, 15 January 1986, Haughey papers, C7/191 (1).

8 Adams to Haughey. The letter is dated 17 Meitheamh. By context it is clearly 1986 as it was written after the Anglo-Irish Agreement and before Haughey returned to power. Haughey papers, C7/191 (1).

9 Martin Mansergh interview.

10 Ed Moloney (2003) *A Secret History of the IRA*. London: Penguin, p. 261.

11 Coogan, *A Memoir*, p. 304.

12 Moloney, *Secret History*, p. 269.

13 Rafter, *Mansergh*, p. 182.

14 Reid to Haughey, 11 May 1987, Haughey papers, C7/191 (2). The letter was published in the second edition of Moloney's *Secret History* (2007). The week after Haughey's death in 2006, Moloney published a piece in the *Irish Times* in which he revealed the existence of the letter. It was entitled 'Haughey risked his career in daring search for peace', 19 June 2006. Moloney's piece is reprinted on the Haughey family website at https://www.charlesjhaughey.ie/articles/daring-search-for-peace.

15 Mansergh interview.

16 Interview with Seán Ó hUiginn, 27 November 2018.

17 Dukes interview.

18 Ó Beacháin, *From Partition to Brexit*, p. 208.

19 Catherine O'Donnell (2007) *Fianna Fáil, Irish Republicanism and the Northern Irish Troubles, 1968–2005*. Dublin: Irish Academic Press, p. 73.

20 Mansergh interview.

21 Interview with Dermot Ahern, 9 March 2019.

22 Reid to Haughey, 21 December 1988, Haughey papers, C7/191 (1).

23 NAI, DT, 2017/10/34. Ed Moloney reproduced a picture of the letter in his blog: https://thebrokenelbow.com/2018/01/04/that-uvf-letter-to-haughey-here-it-is/.

24 Gerry Collins interview.

25 The undated letter from the UDA is in the Haughey papers, C7/119 (1).

26 Army Council, Irish Republican Army to Charlie Haughey, undated but by context the late 1980s, speaking as it does of the past

twenty years of conflict, Haughey papers, C7/231 (2).

27 Correspondence with Martin Mansergh, 8 May 2021.

28 Mansergh to Taoiseach, 6 December 1989. Gallagher's memo on his meeting with Hume is dated 5 December 1989 and is titled 'Secret'. Haughey papers, C7/191 (1).

29 Secret and Personal. Meeting between the Taoiseach and Prime Minister Major, London, 21 June 1991, Haughey papers, C7/191 (1).

30 Ibid.

31 Drafts of *A Strategy for Peace and Justice in Ireland* are in the Haughey papers, C7/191 (1).

32 Mallie and McKittrick, *Fight for Peace*, pp. 118–21.

33 *Irish Times*, 5 December 1991.

34 Haughey to Sutherland, 16 November 1988, Haughey papers, C7/53 (4).

35 Meeting between the Taoiseach and Prime Minister Thatcher in Downing Street, 13 June 1990, Haughey papers, C7/191 (1).

36 Fahey to Haughey, 19 March 1987, Haughey papers, C7/42 (3).

37 Haughey to All Ministers, 31 July 1989, Haughey papers, C7/54 (5).

38 Haughey to Cassells, 25 July 1989, Haughey papers, C7/54 (5).

39 Haughey to All Ministers, 6 June 1990, Haughey papers, C7/56 (1).

40 McGowan to Haughey, 28 June 1990, Haughey papers, C7/40 (4).

41 Haughey to Delors, 29 January 1991, Haughey papers, C7/56 (6).

42 Haughey to Delors, 15 February 1990, Haughey papers, C7/41 (2).

43 Haughey to Delors, 1 August 1989, Haughey papers, C7/54 (5).

44 Haughey to Delors, 17 May 1989, Haughey papers, C7/54 (4).

45 Cabot interview.

46 Bertie Ahern interview.

47 Interview with Ted Barrington, 1 February 2021. Barrington was assistant secretary in the Department of Foreign Affairs at this time and played a central role during the EU presidency.

48 Kirwan interview.

49 Brittan to Haughey, 8 January 1989, Haughey papers, C7/40 (4). The handwritten note from Brittan is dated 1989, but he obviously meant 1990, and the letter is marked as received by the Department of the Taoiseach on 9 January 1990.

50 Haughey to Thatcher, 16 February 1990, Haughey papers, C7/55 (5).

51 Haughey to Kohl, 13 February 1990, Haughey papers, C7/41 (2).

52 Haughey to Thatcher, 25 April 1990, Haughey papers, C7/41 (2).

53 Haughey to Giscard d'Estaing, 14 June 1990, Haughey papers, C7/56 (1).

54 Correspondence to the author from Paul Gillespie, 4 November 2020. Gillespie to Mara, 4 May 1990, Haughey papers, C7/35 (2).

55 *Irish Times*, 27 June 1990.

56 Thatcher to Haughey, 27 June 1990, Haughey papers, C7/119 (2).

57 Meeting between the Taoiseach and Prime Minister Thatcher in Downing Street, 13 June 1990, Haughey papers, C7/191 (1).

58 Kohl to Haughey, 9 November 1990, Haughey papers, C7/1 (2).

59 Haughey to Kohl, 10 February 1992, Haughey papers, C7/1 (2).

60 Walsh, *Hillery*, p. 485.

61 Prone to Mara, 21 March 1990, Haughey papers, C7/154.

62 Haughey to Moore, 6 June 1990, Haughey papers, C7/56 (1).

63 Frank Wall interview.

64 *Irish Times*, 27 October 1990.

65 Pauline Doran – Appointments secretary to Jim Duffy, 22 March 1990, Haughey papers, C7/55 (6).

66 Duffy to Lenihan, 4 October 1990, copy in the Haughey papers, C7/42 (1).

67 This note is simply headed 'Jim Duffy' and is unsigned and undated. Haughey papers, C7/42 (1).

68 Whelan, *Fianna Fáil*, p. 242.

69 O'Malley, *Conduct Unbecoming*, p. 188.

70 Bertie Ahern, *The Autobiography*, p. 117.

71 Eimear Mulhern interview.

72 Brian Lenihan (1991) *For the Record*. Dublin: Blackwater Press, p. 176.

73 Presidential Election Campaign, Haughey papers, C7/42 (1).

74 Reynolds, *My Autobiography*, p. 140.

75 Peter Owens, 'Fianna Fail – A Failure to Communicate', 14 December 1990, Haughey papers, C7/42 (1).

76 Interview with Seán MacCarthaigh, 31 January 2020. MacCarthaigh worked for UPI press agency at the time.

77 Dwyer, *Short Fellow*, p. 400.

78 Haughey to Goodman, 31 March 1987, C7/51 (1).

79 Haughey to His Excellency, Jose Eduardo Dos Santos, President, Popular Republic of Angola, Haughey papers, C7/54 (1).

80 Dempsey to Haughey, 27 September 1991, Haughey papers, C7/38 (2).

81 Dempsey interview.

82 *Irish Independent*, 28 September 1991.

83 Geoghegan-Quinn interview.

84 Interview with Micheál Martin, 3 October 2017.

85 O'Connor interview.

86 *Irish Press*, 11 November 1991.

87 Collins interview.

88 Jim McDaid (1992) 'On the Campaign Trail', in Gallagher and Laver, *How Ireland Voted*, p. 41.

89 John Waters, 'Attempting to depose Fianna Fáil', *Irish Times*, 5 November 1991.

90 McCreevy interview.

91 Waters, 'Attempting to depose Fianna Fáil'.

22. THE PULSE OF THE NATION

1 Robinson to Haughey, 7 December 1990, Haughey papers, C7/1 (1).

2 Corboy to Haughey, 18 November 1980, Haughey papers, C7/99.

3 Robinson to Haughey, 4 August 1976, Haughey papers, C7/137 (2).

4 Haughey to Robinson, 9 September 1976, Haughey papers, C7/137 (2).

5 *Irish Times*, 30 December 1998.

6 Olivia O'Leary and Helen Lucy Burke (1998) *Mary Robinson: The Authorised Biography*. London: Hodder & Stoughton, p. 153.

7 Robinson to Haughey, 18 June 1991, Haughey papers, C7/39 (7).

8 Haughey to Robinson, 18 June 1991, Haughey papers, C7/39 (7).

9 Dermot Ahern interview.

10 Bertie Ahern, *The Autobiography*, p. 132.

11 Charles Haughey's handwritten note, '23 Oct 91', Haughey papers, C7/49.

12 Charles Haughey's handwritten note, 'Thursday 30/1/92', Haughey papers, C7/49.

13 Address by the Taoiseach Mr. Charles J. Haughey, TD, at a meeting of the Fianna Fáil Parliamentary Party, Thursday, 30 January, 1992, Haughey papers, C7/49.

14 Reynolds, *My Autobiography*, p. 150.

15 Haughey to Major, 7 February 1992, Haughey papers, C7/57 (5).

16 Nally to Taoiseach, Secret and Personal. Northern Ireland. 10 February 1992, Haughey papers, C7/191 (1).

17 Byrne to Haughey, 1 February 1992, Haughey papers, C7/1 (1).

18 McGuinness to Haughey, 31 January 1992, Haughey papers, C7/1 (2).

19 Keaveney to Haughey, 4 February 1992, Haughey papers, C7/1 (1).

20 Wallace to Haughey, 17 February 1992, Haughey papers, C7/2 (1).

21 Heaney to Haughey, 19 April 1988, Haughey papers, C7/41 (1).

22 Martin to Haughey, 5 February 1992, Haughey papers, C7/1 (1).

23   Kenny to Haughey, 6 February 1992, Haughey papers, C7/1 (1).

24   Connell to Haughey, 10 February 1992, Haughey papers, C7/2 (1).

25   McDonald to Haughey, 4 February 1992, Haughey papers, C7/2 (1).

26   Magahy to Haughey, 10 February 1992, Haughey papers, C7/2 (1).

27   Bono to Haughey, undated, but by context late 1988, Haughey papers, C7/7 (3).

28   Haughey to Bono, 7 February 1989, Haughey papers, C7/7 (3).

29   Sutherland to Haughey, 6 February 1992, Haughey papers, C7/1 (1).

30   See the Department of the Taoiseach, 'History of Government Buildings', available at https://www.gov.ie/en/organisation-information/eff3cc-history-of-government-buildings/.

31   Major to Haughey, 13 December 1991, Haughey papers, C7/41 (3).

32   Interview with Austin and Stella Dunphy, 13 August 2019. Austin Dunphy was an architect and lifelong friend of Haughey.

33   The resignation statement is in the Haughey papers, C7/49.

34   Kiberd made this comment in Episode 4 of the RTÉ documentary Haughey. The episode was entitled 'Disclosure'.

35   As recalled by Catherine Butler in Haughey, 'Disclosure'.

36   Andrews to Haughey, 23 February 1992, Haughey papers, C7/2 (1).

37   Dorr to Haughey, 25 February 1992, Haughey papers, C7/2 (1).

38   Haughey to Christy Twomey, 20 November 1995, Haughey papers, C7/152 (1).

39   Haughey to O'Reilly, 13 February 1989, Haughey papers, C7/33 (2).

40   'Flashback 1987 ... CJ heads to the Champs-Élysées', available at https://www.independent.ie/life/flashback-1987-cj-heads-to-the-champs-elysees-31396129.html.

41   Irish Independent, 27 July 1987.

42   O'Brien to Haughey, 10 March 1994, Haughey papers, C7/152 (1).

43   Haughey to Fergus McCann, 5 July 1995, Haughey papers, C7/152 (1).

44   Haughey to Donal Uasal O'Murchu, 5 December 1992, Haughey papers, C7/12 (2).

45   Haughey to Brenda Cleary, 29 January 1993, Haughey papers, C7/12 (2).

46   Haughey to Healy-Rae, 11 January 1993, Haughey papers, C7/7 (5).

47   Haughey to Michael Denieffe, 18 January 1993, Haughey papers, C7/7 (5).

48   Daly to Haughey, 12 September 1994, Haughey papers, C7/152 (1).

49   Haughey to Daly, 5 October 1994, Haughey papers, C7/152 (1).

50   Hume to Haughey, 18 September 1995, Haughey papers, C7/152 (1).

51   Haughey to Hume, 16 October 1998, Haughey papers, C7/152 (2).

52   Ware to Haughey, 29 November 1994, Haughey papers, C7/152 (1). In Haughey's handwriting he notes: 'talked to Mr Ware on overall picture without details or attribution'.

53   Speech at the launch of Seán Lemass: A Biography by Michael O'Sullivan, at 85 St Stephen's Green, 24 November 1994, Haughey papers, C7/154.

54   O'Reilly to Haughey, 4 January 1994; Haughey to O'Reilly, 18 January 1994, Haughey papers, C7/152 (1).

55   Power to Haughey, 11 May 1994; Haughey to Power, 18 May 1994, Haughey papers, C7/152 (1).

56   O'Shannon to Haughey, 25 June 1998, Haughey papers, C7/231 (2).

57   Sheehy to Haughey, 12 July 1999, Haughey papers, C7/231 (2). Haughey's handwritten note is dated 23 July 99.

58   Pearson to Haughey, 1 March 2000, Haughey papers, C7/134 (1).

59   Interview with Miriam O'Callaghan, 10 May 2021.

60   O'Connor interview.

61   See, for instance, Muiris Mac Conghail, 'Dice loaded in favour of Haughey', Irish Times, 6 July 2005.

62   Ó hUiginn to Haughey, 3 November 1998, Haughey papers, C7/131 (1).

63   Lee, Ireland 1912-1985, p. 509.

64   Handwritten notes by Haughey on Seven Ages outline by Seán Ó Mórdha, Haughey papers, C7/131 (1).

65   Ó Mórdha to Haughey, 5 February 2000, Haughey papers, C7/131 (1).

66   Seven Ages, 'Haughey and FitzGerald Great Adversaries of the Eighties', available at https://www.youtube.com/watch?v=xvRji-YFx8A&t=517s.

67   Mansergh to Haughey, 7 March 2001, Haughey papers, C7/231 (2).

68   Kevin Rafter (2015) "'Never Justify. Never Explain': Some Thoughts on Irish Political Memoirs' in Rafter and O'Brien, The State in Transition, p. 284.

69   'Foreword' attached to Martin Mansergh letter, 7 March 2001, Haughey papers, C7/231 (2).

70   Correspondence to the author from Martin Mansergh, 6 May 2021.

71   Travers to Haughey, 3 December 2001, Haughey papers, C7/134 (2).

72   Correspondence to the author from John Travers, 2 March 2021.

73   Rafter, '"Never Justify. Never Explain"', p. 284.

74   See Vincent Browne, 'Haughey: The final years', *Village* magazine, June 2006, available at https://magill.ie/archive/haughey-final-years.

75   *Irish Times*, 22 April 1997.

76   Haughey to McCourt, 7 May 1997, Haughey papers, C7/129 (1).

77   Dorgan to Haughey, 19 May 1997, Haughey papers, C7/129 (1). There is also a copy of this letter in C7/1 (2).

78   Binchy to Haughey, 14 July 1997, Haughey papers, C7/129 (1).

79   Keena, *Haughey's Millions*, p. 249.

80   Smyth, *Thanks a Million*, pp. 142-9.

81   *Irish Independent*, 10 July 1997.

82   Eimear Mulhern interview.

83   Keena, *Haughey's Millions*, pp. 235–44.

84   Mr Justice Brian McCracken (1997) *Report of the Tribunal of Inquiry (Dunnes Payments)*. Dublin: Stationery Office.

85   Charlie McCreevy interview.

86   *Sunday Independent*, 4 February 2018.

87   Desmond interview.

88   Haughey to Inspector A. Glennon, Bridewell Garda Station, 18 October 1999, Haughey papers, C7/152 (2).

89   See for instance, Michael Moynihan (2018) *Crisis and Comeback: Cork in the Eighties*. Cork: Collins Press.

90   Haughey to Tomás Ó Murchu, Runaí, Glen Rovers Hurling Club, 6 October 1980 Haughey papers, C7/159 (3).

91   Mary O'Shea to Haughey, undated, but by context February 1983. Haughey papers, C7/11 (2).

92   McCarthy to Haughey, 7 November 1986, Haughey papers, C7/62 (3).

93   Haughey to Brosnan, 11 February 1988, Haughey papers, C7/52 (3).

94   Conor Haughey interview.

95   *Irish Independent*, 24 October 1999.

96   Liam Nolan to Haughey, 29 October 1999, Haughey papers, C7/129 (1).

97   Cardinal Cahal Daly to Reverend Eoghan Haughey, 15 June 2006. Eoghan Haughey gave me this letter before he died in October 2016. I quote it here with his permission and that of the Haughey family.

98   Interview with James Morrissey, 31 August 2018.

99   Haughey to Joe Briscoe, 3 November 1999, Haughey papers, C7/129 (1).

100   *Ireland on Sunday*, 18 June 2006.

101   Harris interview.

102   Interview with Rory Godson, 10 January 2020. Godson was the editor of the Irish edition of the *Sunday Times* at this time.

103   *Terry* aired on RTÉ on 25 April 2000. It was a Tyrone Production for RTÉ, directed by Joanne McGrath with Cathal O'Shannon as interviewer, although he does not appear on screen. The last words Terry Keane utters are that she was looking forward to a new future without Haughey, ending with 'What more can I say?' as Charles Aznavour's 'She' is played in the background. She then gulps quite noticeably as the credits begin to play.

104   *Sunday Times*, 16 May 1999.

105   James Morrissey interview.

106   'Diarist who later regretted her TV revelation of affair', *Irish Times*, 7 June 2008.

107   Sarah Carey interview.

108   See Donal Lynch, 'Deconstructing Sweetie: not so veiled a secret', *Sunday Independent*, 25 January 2015.

109   Harris interview.

110   Irish Independent, 27 May 2000.

111   *Irish Times*, 22 July 2000.

112   *Irish Independent*, 22 July 2000.

113   The transcript of Haughey's evidence is available at https://moriarty-tribunal.ie/wp-content/uploads/2016/09/transcript_159.pdf.

114   Mansergh to Seán Haughey, 10 March 1999, Haughey papers, C7/231 (2).

115   'Notes', attached to Martin Mansergh letter to Seán Haughey, 10 March 1999.

116   Ibid.

117   Ibid.

118   This section is based on the author's interview with Dr Kevin Moore, 27 November 2020. I am very grateful to Dr Moore for his recollection of that night.

119   Reid to Haughey, Easter 2001, Haughey papers, C7/134 (1).

120   McAleese to Haughey, 20 February 1998, Haughey papers, C7/129 (1).

121   McAleese to Haughey, 17 June 1985, Haughey papers, C7/62 (5).

122   Haughey to McAleese, 11 March 1998, Haughey papers, C7/129 (1).

123   FitzGerald to Haughey, 6 February 2006; Haughey to FitzGerald, 7 February 2006, Haughey papers, C7/243.

124   Draft of letter from Ivor Fitzpatrick Solicitors to The Director, The Abbey Theatre, 11 February 2002, Haughey papers, C7/244.

125   Conor Haughey interview.

126   Eimear Mulhern interview.

23. AFTERDEATH

1   Anthony Cronin's reflection was reprinted
     in the *Sunday Independent*, 18 June 2006. It
     was published in Anthony Cronin's *Collected
     Poems* (2004) and is reproduced here with
     permission of New Island Books.

2   Kennelly to Haughey, 6 October 1998,
     Haughey papers, C7/130.

3   Ahern's words were quoted in the *Irish Times*
     and *Irish Independent*, 17 June 2006.

4   First report of the Moriarty Tribunal, p. 544.

5   Ibid., p. 395.

6   Ibid., p. 106.

7   Ibid., p. 167.

8   Ibid., p. 167.

9   The Haughey family issued a press release
     through their solicitors, Ivor Fitzpatrick and
     Company, on the night of 19 December 2006.
     It can be seen on the Haughey family website
     at https://www.charlesjhaughey.ie/articles/
     press-statement-moriarty-tribunal.

10   Ibid.

11   See Sam Smyth, 'Charlie, the Saudi "gift" and
     truth about his overthrow', Irish *Mail on
     Sunday*, 22 October 2017.

12   O'Connell to Haughey, 29 December 1989;
     Haughey to O'Connell, 11 January 1990,
     Haughey papers, C7/38 (6).

13   *Irish Times*, 5 February 1999.

14   McCracken Tribunal report, p. 51.

15   Nuala O'Faolain, 'Charles Haughey's Irelands',
     Irish Times, 10 June 1989. The piece was
     reprinted in O'Faolain's memoir, *Are You
     Somebody?* Dublin: New Island, 1996,
     pp. 245–52.

16   McCracken Tribunal report, p. 51.

17   Ó hUiginn to Stuart Brady, Solicitor, Tribunal
     of Enquiry, 20 September 2007. Pádraig Ó
     hUiginn gave me a copy of this letter during
     one of my many interviews with him. I quote
     from it here with the express permission he
     gave me before his death in April 2019.

18   Ó hUiginn interview.

19   Frank and Sheila Dunlop to Haughey,
     16 October 2000, Haughey papers, C7/1 (3).

20   Martin Mansergh, 'Foreword', 7 March 2001.

21   Eames to Haughey, 23 March 1987; Haughey
     to Eames, 6 April 1987, Haughey papers,
     C7/6 (3).

SOURCES

INTERVIEWS AND CORRESPONDENCE

Bertie Ahern, Fianna Fáil politician. He was chief whip and later a minister in a number of Haughey's governments (21 August 2018)

Dermot Ahern, Fianna Fáil politician and chief whip in Haughey's last government (9 March 2019)

Agnes Aylward, formerly Breathneach, senior civil servant in the Department of Industry, Trade and Tourism and the Department of the Taoiseach, and currently the project director of the Lafcadio Hearn Japanese Gardens in Tramore (22 March 2020)

Sean Aylward, Haughey's private secretary 1979–1981 and 1982 (17 August 2016, 21 October 2016, 6 February 2018)

Colm Barnes, leading industrialist (Glen Abbey textiles), who approved of Haughey's early views on free trade and European integration, but later fell out with him; he joined the Progressive Democrats in 1987 (30 August 1995)

Ted Barrington, assistant secretary in the Department of Foreign Affairs. He played a central role during Ireland's EU presidency (1 February 2021)

Mike Burns joined RTÉ in 1963 and worked there until 1991 in a variety of roles in both radio and television. He interviewed Haughey on numerous occasions (28 February 2020)

David Cabot, Haughey's adviser on the environment (26 April 2016)

Sarah Carey, journalist and friend of Terry Keane's children (19 March 2017)

Ken Carty, Canadian academic who wrote the influential book *Party and Parish Pump* (20 October 2019)

Peter Cassells became general secretary of ICTU in 1989 and oversaw ICTU's membership of the social partnership process (29 July 2016)

Gerry Collins was appointed Fianna Fáil's assistant general secretary in 1965 and was later a minister in all of Haughey's governments (11 April 2019)

Deirdre Courtney, Haughey's solicitor (29 November 2018)

Eamon Delaney, civil servant in the Department of Foreign Affairs 1987–1992 (17 February 2017)

Noel Dempsey, Fianna Fáil politician and an internal critic of Haughey in his last government (10 April 2019)

Dermot Desmond, financier, entrepreneur and friend of Haughey (14 March 2019)

Noel Dorr, former general secretary of the Department of Foreign Affairs who also served as Irish ambassador to the United Kingdom and the United Nations (23 May 2017)

Austin and Stella Dunphy, lifelong friends of Haughey (13 August 2019)

Alan Dukes, Fine Gael politician and leader of the party from 1987 to 1990 (25 February 2020)

Ivor Fitzpatrick, Haughey's solicitor (29 November 2018)

Tony Foley, economist at Dublin City University who advised Haughey in the 1980s (21 August 2018)

Máire Geoghegan-Quinn, Minister for the Gaeltacht in the first of Haughey's four governments. She was a minister for state in the other two and later served as a full minister under Albert Reynolds. She was Ireland's European Commissioner between 2010 and 2014 (25 October 2019)

Paul Gillespie, *Irish Times* journalist specialising in European affairs (4 November 2020)

Rory Godson, editor of the *Sunday Times* during the Terry Keane revelations (10 January 2020)

Jimmy Guerin, lifelong friend of the Haughey family (25 June 2021)

Anne Harris, former editor of the *Sunday Independent*. She also edited the column 'The Keane Edge' (24 April 2019)

Conor Haughey, Charles Haughey's eldest son (7 December 2017)

Fr Eoghan Haughey, Haughey's youngest brother (25 February 2014)

Maureen Haughey, née Lemass, Haughey's wife. When she died in 2017 at the age of ninety-one, her obituary in the *Irish Times* noted that 'she was an astute observer of politics, and interested in history, but kept her views largely for her family circle and friends' (14 March 2014)

Seán Haughey, Charles Haughey's youngest son (27 May 2016, 5 January 2018, 28 November 2020)

Kevin Healy began his career in journalism at the *Cork Examiner* before moving to RTÉ, where he presented, among other programmes, the *News at 1.30* and *This Week* (28 February 2020)

John Horgan, former Labour Party TD, senator and MEP. He also had a distinguished career as a journalist and academic (22 October 2018)

Paul Kavanagh, chief fundraiser for Fianna Fáil during Haughey's leadership (15 July 2015)

Neville Keery, Fianna Fáil activist who was a senator from 1969 to 1973 and later worked for the party and for the European Commission (5 September 2017)

Suzanne Kelly, the daughter of Captain James Kelly and a successful tax lawyer. She has long campaigned for a full state vindication of her father (17 November 2017)

Geraldine Kennedy, a journalist and later politician who was the first female editor of the *Irish Times*. She was a close observer of Haughey's career as Taoiseach (29 January 2019)

Wally Kirwan, senior civil servant in the Department of the Taoiseach (16 April 2019)

Michael Lillis, senior civil servant in the Department of Foreign Affairs (11 October 2018)

Seán MacCarthaigh worked for UPI press agency (31 January 2020)

Charlie McCreevy, Fianna Fáil politician who supported Haughey in his leadership election and who was later involved in a number of heaves against him. He held a number of ministerial posts under Albert Reynolds and Bertie Ahern (26 October 2019)

Ray MacSharry, first elected in 1969, became a hugely important figure in Fianna Fáil over the next two decades serving as Tánaiste and Minister for Finance under Haughey (4 January 2017)

Monica McWilliams, a first cousin of Charles Haughey and the daughter of Owen McWilliams (14 September 2018)

Seamus McWilliams, a first cousin of Charles Haughey and the son of Patsy McWilliams (20 September 2018)

Martin Mansergh, senior adviser to Haughey throughout his period as leader of Fianna Fáil (30 March 2016, 6 May 2021)

P.J. Mara, Haughey's long-standing press secretary (17 April 2014)

Micheál Martin, first-time TD in Haughey's last government. He became leader of Fianna Fáil in 2011 (3 October 2017)

Kevin Moore, formerly registrar at Beaumont Hospital and now consultant endocrinologist at Tallaght hospital (27 November 2020)

Donagh Morgan, Haughey's private secretary 1987–1991 (6 September 2017)

James Morrissey public relations executive, author, and friend of Haughey (31 August 2018)

Eimear Mulhern, Haughey's eldest child (8 January 2016)

Jack Nagle, secretary of the Department of Agriculture (31 October 1994)

David Neligan, senior official in the Department of Foreign Affairs (2 April 2021)

Kate and Bob Nugent, Kate Nugent was for many years Haughey's constituency secretary. She and her husband, Bob Nugent, were also friends of the Haugheys (13 August 2019)

Miriam O'Callaghan, broadcaster and journalist, who co-produced the 2005 RTÉ documentary, *Haughey* (10 May 2021)

Dáithí Ó Ceallaigh, senior official in the Department of Foreign Affairs (6 December 2017)

Niamh O'Connor, daughter of Pat O'Connor, Haughey's solicitor. For a time she worked for Fianna Fáil at Leinster House (16 June 2017)

Brendan O'Donnell, Haughey's private secretary during his period as Minister for Agriculture and Minister for Finance from 1964 to 1970. He was transferred to the Department of Health and Social Welfare in 1977 at Haughey's request when he became minister and he followed him to the Taoiseach's office on his election in 1979 (1 May 2018)

Declan O'Donovan, senior official in the Department of Foreign Affairs (15 May 2017)

Rory O'Hanlon, Fianna Fáil politician. He was Minister for Health from 1987 to 1991

SOURCES

and then Minister for the Environment
from November 1991 to February 1992 in
Haughey's last two governments
Pádraig Ó hUiginn, Haughey's closest civil
service adviser. He served as secretary of
the Department of the Taoiseach from
1982 to 1993 (25 March 2014, 12 May 2016,
16 April 2018)
Seán Ó hUiginn (27 November 2018), senior
official in the Department of Foreign
Affairs
Des O'Malley (21 September 2017), Fianna Fáil
and Progressive Democrat politician. He
was an implacable opponent of Haughey
throughout his career
Mary O'Rourke, Fianna Fáil politician who
served as a minister in Haughey's final
two governments (12 April 2018)
Leo Powell, editor of the *Irish Field*
(30 November 2018)
Terry Prone, managing director of Carr
Communications, the agency Haughey
used to prepare for numerous television
appearances in the 1980s and early 1990s
(14 May 2019)
Séamus Puirséil, a Fianna Fáil activist who acted
as Haughey's director of elections in 1989
and later became president of the Irish
National Teachers' Organisation and chief
executive of the Higher Education and
Training Awards Council (28 July 2016)
Michael Somers, secretary of national debt
management at the Department of
Finance, later the first director of the
NTMA (28 November 2018)
Paddy Teahon, senior official in the Department
of the Taoiseach. He was secretary of the
department from 1993 to 2000 (9 May
2019)
Paddy Terry worked in the Department of
Justice from 1946 to 1985 before retiring
at the grade of assistant secretary. He later
worked as legal adviser in the Department
of Equality and Law Reform, and then as
a parliamentary draftsman in the Office of
the Attorney General, finally retiring from
public life at the age of 88 in 2008
(18 June 2020)
John Travers, senior civil servant in the
Department of the Taoiseach and the
Department of Industry and Commerce
(2 March 2021)
Frank Wall was appointed general secretary of
Fianna Fáil in 1981 and served throughout
Haughey's period as leader (10 September
2015)
Noel Whelan was appointed secretary of the
Department of Economic Planning

and Development in July 1977. He later
became secretary to the Department
of the Taoiseach in 1980, before being
appointed Vice-President to the European
Investment Bank in 1982 (30 March 2017)
T.K. Whitaker, secretary of the Department of
Finance from 1956 to 1969 and Governor
of the Central Bank from 1969 to 1976
(18 May 1994)
Michael Woods, Fianna Fáil politician and
minister in all of Haughey's four
governments (21 February 2017)
Gerry Wrixon, microelectronics expert, energy
adviser and former president of UCC
(4 April 2019)
John Horgan's interviews with Kevin Boland
(24 November 1994), Charles Haughey
(24 October 1994), Patrick Hillery
(14 December 1994)
Eunan O'Halpin's interview with Dermot Nally
(13 January 2009)

MANUSCRIPT AND ARCHIVAL SOURCES
Broughan, Thomas Patrick (1980) *An Leabhar
Uí hEochada Ulad (Notes on the origins
and history of the surname Ó hEachaid,
O'Haughey).* Copy in possession of the
author
Cabinet Minutes, National Archives, Dublin
Charles J. Haughey Papers, Dublin City
University, IE DCUA C7
Department of the Taoiseach Files, National
Archives, Dublin
Fianna Fáil Papers, University College, Dublin
Margaret Thatcher archive at www.
margaretthatcher.org
Military Service Pensions Collection, Military
Archives, Dublin
Paddy Terry memoir. *70 Years in the Public
Service.* Copy in possession of the author.
Ronald Reagan diary at https://www.
reaganfoundation.org/ronald-reagan/
white-house-diaries
State Department Files, National Archives and
Records Administration of the United
States
John Horgan diary. Copy in possession of the
author
Wikileaks

TELEVISION AND RADIO PROGRAMMES
7 Ages, RTÉ 2000
Arts Express, RTÉ 1991
Bowman: Sunday: 8.30, RTÉ Radio 1
Charles Haughey: Patronising the Arts, RTÉ 2007
Gunplot, RTÉ, 2020
Haughey, RTÉ 2005
Haughey's Ireland, Channel 4 1986

685

In the Name of the Republic, TV3 2013
Kenny Live, RTÉ 1994
Liveline, RTÉ Radio One, 21 January 2015,
    22 September 2020
People and Power, RTÉ 1975
Prime Time, RTÉ, 2006
Terry, RTÉ 2006
The Late Late Show, RTÉ

NEWSPAPERS AND PERIODICALS

An Cosantóir, the Irish Defence Journal
An Phoblacht
Cork Examiner
Crane Bag
Dublin Review of Books
Evening Herald
Evening Press
Financial Times
Irish Examiner
Irish Independent
Ireland on Sunday
Irish Press
Irish Times
Kerryman
Kilkenny People
Limerick Leader
Magill
Mail on Sunday
Meath Chronicle
Sunday Business Post
Sunday Independent
Sunday Review
Sunday Times
Sunday Tribune
Sunday World
Village Magazine
Western People

PARLIAMENTARY DEBATES

Dáil Éireann Debates
Seanad Éireann Debates

SELECT BIBLIOGRAPHY

Adams, Gerry (2003) *Hope and History: Making Peace in Ireland*. London: Brandon Books.

Ahern, Bertie (2010) *Bertie Ahern: The Autobiography*. London: Hutchinson.

Aldous, Richard and Niamh Puirséil (2008) *We Declare: Landmark Documents in Ireland's History*. London: Trafalgar Square.

Andrews, C.S. (1982) *Man of No Property: An Autobiography*. Dublin: Lilliput Press.

Arnold, Bruce (1993) *Haughey: His Life and Unlucky Deeds*. London: Harper Collins.

Arnold, Bruce (2001) *Jack Lynch: Hero in Crisis*. Dublin: Merlin.

Ballagh, Robert (2018) *A Reluctant Memoir*. London: Head of Zeus.

Barrington, Ruth (1987) *Health, Medicine and Politics in Ireland 1900–1970*. Dublin: Institute for Public Administration.

Bew, Paul (2007) *Ireland: The Politics of Enmity, 1789–2006*. Oxford: Oxford University Press.

Boland, Kevin (1976) *Up Dev!* Dublin: K. Boland.

Boland, Kevin (1982) *The Rise and Decline of Fianna Fáil* Cork. Mercier Press.

Bowman, John (1982) *De Valera and the Ulster Question*. Oxford: Clarendon Press.

Brady, Conor (2005) *Up with the Times*. Dublin: Gill and Macmillan.

Brady, Conor (2014) *The Guarding of Ireland: The Garda Síochána and the Irish State 1960–2014*. Dublin: Gill and Macmillan.

Breresford, David (1987) *Ten Men Dead: The Story of the 1981 Irish Hunger Strike*. London: HarperCollins.

Brockie, Gerard (1988) *St. Joseph's CBS, Fairview, 1888–1988*. Dublin: St. Joseph's.

Brown, Terence (1985) *Ireland: A Social and Cultural History 1922–1985*. London: Fontana Press.

Brown, Terence (2015) *The Irish Times: 150 Years of Influence*. London: Bloomsbury.

Browne, P.J. (2008) *Unfulfilled Promise: Memories of Donogh O'Malley*. Dublin: Currach Press.

Burke, David (2020) *Deception and Lies: The Hidden History of the Arms Crisis 1970*. Cork: Mercier Press.

Byrne, Elaine (2012) *Political Corruption in Ireland 1922–2010: A Crooked Harp?* Manchester: Manchester University Press.

Carty, R.K. (1981) *Party and Parish Pump: Electoral Politics in Ireland*. Ontario: Wilfrid Laurier University Press.

Chambers, Anne (2014) *T.K. Whitaker: Portrait of a Patriot*. Dublin: Doubleday Ireland.

Clifford, Angela (2006) *Military Aspects of Ireland's Arms Crisis of 1969–70*. Belfast: Belfast Magazine.

Clifford, Angela (2009) *The Arms Conspiracy Trial: Ireland 1970: The Prosecution of Charles Haughey, Captain Kelly, John Kelly, and Albert Luykx*. Belfast: Athol Books.

Coakley, John (2010) 'The rise and fall of minor parties in Ireland', *Irish Political Studies* 25:4.

Coakley, John and Kevin Rafter (eds) (2013) *The Irish Presidency: Power, Ceremony and Politics*. Dublin: Irish Academic Press.

Coakley, John and Jennifer Todd (2020) *Negotiating a Settlement in Northern Ireland, 1969–2019*. Oxford: Oxford University Press.

Cohan, Al (1972) *The Irish Political Elite*. Dublin: Gill and Macmillan.

Collins, Neil and Mary O'Shea (2000) *Understanding Political Corruption in Ireland*. Cork: Cork University Press.

Collins, Stephen (1992) *The Haughey File: The Unprecedented Career and Last Years of The Boss*. Dublin: O'Brien Press.

Collins, Stephen (1996) *The Cosgrave Legacy*. Dublin: Blackwater Press.

Collins, Stephen (2001) *The Power Game: Ireland under Fianna Fáil*. Dublin: O'Brien Press.

Collins, Stephen (2005) *Breaking the Mould: How the PDs Changed Irish Politics*. Dublin: Gill and Macmillan.

Collins, Stephen and Ciara Meehan (2020) *Saving the State: Fine Gael from Collins to Varadkar*. Dublin: Gill Books.

Conway, Vicky (2014) *Policing Twentieth-Century Ireland: A History of An Garda Síochána*. London: Routledge.

Coogan, Tim Pat (1966) *Ireland Since the Rising*. London: Pall Mall Books.

Coogan, Tim Pat (1990) *Michael Collins*. London: Macmillan.

Coogan, Tim Pat (2003) *Ireland in the Twentieth Century*. London: Arrow Books.

Coogan, Tim Pat (2008) *A Memoir*. London: Weidenfeld and Nicolson.

Cooper, Matt (2015) *The Maximalist: The Rise and Fall of Tony O'Reilly*. Dublin: Gill and Macmillan.

Corless, Damian (2007) *Party Nation: Ireland's General Elections, the Strokes, Jokes, Spinners and Winners*. Dublin: Merlin Press.

Craig, Anthony (2010) *Crisis of Confidence: Anglo-Irish Relations in the Early Troubles*. Dublin: Irish Academic Press.

Cruise O'Brien, Conor (1972) *States of Ireland*. London: Hutchinson.

Cruise O'Brien, Conor (1998) *Memoir: My Life and Themes*. Dublin: Poolbeg.

Daly, Mary (2002) *The First Department: A History of the Department of Agriculture*. Dublin: Institute of Public Administration.

Daly, Mary (2016) *Sixties Ireland: Reshaping the Economy, State and Society, 1957–1973*. Cambridge: Cambridge University Press.

Delaney, Eamon (2001) *The Accidental Diplomat: My Years in the Irish Foreign Service, 1987–1995*. Dublin: New Island.

Delaney, Eamon (2009) *Breaking the Mould. A Story of Art and Ireland*. Dublin: New Island.

Desmond, Barry (2000) *Finally and in Conclusion: A Political Memoir*. Dublin: New Island.

Dictionary of Irish Biography, Cambridge University Press, https://www.dib.ie/

Doherty, Paddy (2001) *Paddy Bogside*. Cork: Mercier Press.

Doorly, Mary Rose (1996) *Abbeville: The Family Home of Charles J. Haughey*. Dublin: Town House and Country House.

Dorr, Noel (2011) *A Small State at the Top Table: Memories of Ireland on the UN Security Council, 1981–82*. Dublin: Institute of Public Administration.

Downey, James (1998) *Brian Lenihan: His Life and Times*. Dublin: New Island.

Downey, James (2009) *In My Own Time: Inside Irish Politics and Society*. Dublin: Gill and Macmillan.

Doyle, David M. and Liam O'Callaghan (2019) *Capital Punishment in Independent Ireland*. Liverpool: Liverpool University Press.

Dunlop, Frank (2004) *Yes, Taoiseach: Irish Politics from Behind Closed Doors*. Dublin: Penguin Ireland.

Dwyer, T. Ryle (1987) *Charlie: The Political Biography of Charles Haughey*. Dublin: Gill and Macmillan.

Dwyer, T. Ryle (1992) *Haughey's Thirty Years of Controversy*. Cork: Mercier Press.

Dwyer, T. Ryle (1999) *Short Fellow: A Biography of Charles J. Haughey*. Dublin: Marino Books.

Dwyer, T. Ryle (2001) *Nice Fellow: A Biography of Jack Lynch*. Cork: Mercier Press.

Evans, Bryce (2011) *Seán Lemass: Democratic Dictator*. Cork: Collins Press.

Evans, Bryce and Stephen Kelly (eds) (2014) *Frank Aiken: Nationalist and Internationalist*. Dublin: Irish Academic Press.

Fallon, Ivor (1994) *The Player: The Life of Tony O'Reilly*. London: Hodder and Stoughton.

Fallon, Johnny (2011) *Dynasties: Irish Political Families*. Dublin: New Island.

Fanning, Bryan (2008) *The Quest for Modern Ireland: The Battle for Ideas, 1912–1986*. Dublin: Irish Academic Press.

Fanning, Ronan (1978) *The Irish Department of Finance 1922–58*. Dublin: Institute of Public Administration.

Farrell, Brian (1971) *Chairman or Chief? The Role of Taoiseach in Irish Government*. Dublin: Gill and Macmillan.

Farrell, Brian (1990) 'Forming the Government' in Michael Gallagher and Richard Sinnott (eds), *How Ireland Voted 1989*. Galway: PSAI Press.

Farrell, Brian and Maurice Manning (1978) 'The Election' in Howard R. Penniman (ed.), *Ireland at the Polls: The Dáil Election of 1977*. Washington DC: American Enterprise Institute.

Faulkner, Pádraig (2005) *As I Saw It: Reviewing over 30 years of Fianna Fáil and Irish Politics*. Dublin: Wolfhound Press.

Feehan, John (1984) *Operation Brogue: A Study of the Vilification of Charles Haughey*. Cork: Mercier Press.

Feehan, John (1985) *The Statesman: A Study of the Role of Charles Haughey in the Ireland of the Future*. Cork: Mercier Press.

Feehan, John (1988) *An Apology to the Irish People*. Cork: Mercier Press.

Ferriter, Diarmaid (2005) *The Transformation of Ireland*. London: Profile Books.

Ferriter, Diarmaid (2009) *Occasions of Sin: Sex and Society in Modern Ireland*. London: Profile Books.

Ferriter, Diarmaid (2012) *Ambiguous Republic: Ireland in the 1970s*. London: Profile Books.

Ferriter, Diarmaid (2018) *On The Edge: Ireland's Offshore Islands A Modern History*. London: Profile Books.

Fetherstonhaugh, Neil and Tony McCullagh (2006) *They Never Came Home: The Stardust Story*. Dublin: Merlin Press.

Finlay, Fergus (1998) *Snakes and Ladders*. Dublin: New Island.

FitzGerald, Garret (1991) *All in a Life: An Autobiography*. Dublin: Gill and Macmillan.

FitzGerald, Garret (2005) *Reflections on the Irish State*. Dublin: Irish Academic Press.

FitzGerald, Garret (2010) *Just Garret: Tales from the Political Frontline*. Dublin: Liberties Press.

Fitzpatrick, David (1996) '"Unofficial emissaries": British Army boxers in the Irish Free State, 1926', *Irish Historical Studies* 30:118.

Foster, Roy (1988) *Modern Ireland: 1600–1972*. London: Penguin.

Foster, Roy (2007) *Luck and the Irish: A Brief History of Change, 1970–2000*. London: Allen Lane.

Freedman, Lawrence (2005) *The Official History of the Falklands Campaign*, Vol. 2: *War and Diplomacy*. Abingdon: Routledge.

Gallagher, Michael and Michael Marsh (2002) *Days of Blue Loyalty: The Politics of Membership of the Fine Gael Party*. Dublin: PSAI Press.

Galligan, Yvonne (1998) *Women and Politics in Contemporary Ireland: From the Margins to the Mainstream*. London: Pinter.

Garvin, Tom (2004) *Preventing the Future: Why was Ireland so Poor for so Long?* Dublin: Gill and Macmillan.

Geary, Michael J. (2010) *An Inconvenient Wait: Ireland's Quest for Membership of the EEC, 1957–73*. Dublin: Institute of Public Administration.

Gilligan, Robbie (2011) *Tony Gregory: The Biography of a True Irish Political Legend*. Dublin: O'Brien Press.

Girvin, Brian (1986) 'Social change and moral politics: the Irish constitutional referendum 1983', *Political Studies* 34:1.

Girvin, Brian (1987a) 'The Campaign' in Laver, Michael, Peter Mair, Richard Sinnott (eds), *How Ireland Voted: The Irish General Election 1987*. Dublin: Poolbeg.

Girvin, Brian (1987b) 'The Divorce Referendum in the Republic, June 1986', *Irish Political Studies* 2.

Girvin, Brian (1990) 'The Campaign' in Michael Gallagher and Richard Sinnott (eds), *How Ireland Voted 1989*. Galway: PSAI Press.

Girvin, Brian (1993) 'The Road to the Election' in Michael Gallagher and Michael Laver (eds), *How Ireland Voted 1992*. Dublin: Folens.

Girvin, Brian (2002) *From Union to Union: Nationalism, Religion and Democracy from the Act of Union to the European Union*. Dublin: Gill and Macmillan.

Girvin, Brian (2018) 'An Irish solution to an Irish problem: Catholicism, contraception and change, 1922–1979', *Contemporary European History* 27:4.

Hanley, Brian (2004) 'The politics of Noraid', *Irish Political Studies* 19:1.

Hanley, Brian and Scott Millar (2010) *The Lost Revolution: The Story of the Official IRA and the Workers' Party*. Dublin: Penguin Ireland.

Hardiman, Niamh (1988) *Pay, Politics and Economic Performance in Ireland, 1970–1987*. Oxford: Clarendon.

Harte, Paddy (2005) *Young Tigers and Mongrel Foxes: A Life in Politics*. Dublin: O'Brien Press.

Hastings, Tim, Brian Sheehan and Padraig Yeates (2007) *Saving the Future: How Social Partnership Shaped Ireland's Economic Success*. Dublin: Blackhall.

Healy, John (1968) *Death of an Irish Town*. Cork: Mercier Press.

Healy, John (1988) *No One Shouted Stop*. Mayo: House of Healy.

Heney, Michael (2020) *The Arms Crisis of 1970: The Plot That Never Was*. London: Head of Zeus.

Hennessy, Thomas (2013) *Hunger Strike: Margaret Thatcher's Battle with the IRA 1980–1981*. Dublin: Irish Academic Press.

Hesketh, Tom (1990) *The Second Partitioning of Ireland: The Abortion Referendum of 1983*. Dublin: Brandsma Books.

Horgan, John (1997) *Seán Lemass: The Enigmatic Patriot*. Dublin: Gill and Macmillan.

Horgan, John (2000) *Noel Browne: Passionate Outsider*. Dublin: Gill and Macmillan.

Horgan, John (2001) '"Government sources said last night …": The development of the parliamentary press lobby in modern Ireland' in Hiram Morgan (ed.), *Information, Media and Power Through the Ages*. Dublin: UCD Press.

Horgan, John and Roddy Flynn (2017) *Irish Media: A Critical History*. Dublin: Four Courts Press.

Hussey, Gemma (1990) *At the Cutting Edge: Cabinet Diaries*. Dublin: Gill and Macmillan.

Ivory, Gareth (1997), 'Fianna Fáil, constitutional republicanism and the issue of consent: 1980–1996', *Éire Ireland* 32:2.

Ivory, Gareth (2014) 'Fianna Fáil, Northern Ireland and the limits on conciliation, 1969–1973', *Irish Political Studies* 29:4.

Jones, Jack (2001) *In Your Opinion: Political and Social Trends in Ireland through the Eyes of the Electorate*. Dublin: Townhouse and Countryhouse.

Joyce, Joe and Peter Murtagh (1983) *The Boss: Charles J Haughey in Government*. Dublin: Poolbeg.

Keena, Colm (2001) *Haughey's Millions: Charlie's Money Trail*. Dublin: Gill and Macmillan.

Keena, Colm (2003) *The Ansbacher Conspiracy*. Dublin: Gill and Macmillan.

Kelly, James (1971) *Orders for the Captain*. Dublin: James Kelly.

Kelly, James (1999) *The Thimbleriggers: The Dublin Arms Trials of 1970*. Dublin: James Kelly.

Kelly, Stephen (2012) 'Fresh evidence from the archives: the genesis of Charles J. Haughey's attitude to Northern Ireland', *Irish Studies in International Affairs* vol. 23.

Kelly, Stephen (2013) *Fianna Fáil, Partition and Northern Ireland, 1926–1971*. Dublin: Irish Academic Press.

Kelly, Stephen (2016) '*A Failed Political Entity*': *Charles Haughey and the Northern Ireland Question*. Dublin: Merrion Press.

Kelly, Stephen (2020) 'Charles J. Haughey and the arms crisis', *History Ireland* 28:5.

Kennedy, Brian P. (1990) *Dreams and Responsibilities: The State and the Arts in Independent Ireland*. Dublin: Arts Council.

Kennedy, Finola (2001) *From Cottage to Crèche: Family Change in Ireland*. Dublin: Institute of Public Administration.

Kennedy, Michael (2000) *Division and Consensus: The Politics of Cross-Border Relations in Ireland, 1925–1969*. Dublin: Institute of Public Administration.

Kennedy, Michael (2010) '"Where's the Taj Mahal?": Indian restaurants in Dublin since 1908', *History Ireland* 4:18.

Kennedy, Michael and Deirdre McMahon (2005) *Obligations and Responsibilities: Ireland and the United Nations, 1955–2005*. Dublin: Institute of Public Administration.

Keogh, Dermot (2008) *Jack Lynch: A Biography*. Dublin: Gill and Macmillan.

Keogh, Dermot with Andrew McCarthy (2005) *Twentieth Century Ireland: Revolution and State Building*. Dublin: Gill and Macmillan.

Kiberd, Declan (1995) *Inventing Ireland: The Literature of a Modern Nation*. London: Jonathan Cape.

Kiberd, Declan (2018) *After Ireland: Writing the Nation from Beckett to the Present*. London. Head of Zeus.

Kissane, Bill (2002) *Explaining Irish Democracy*. Dublin: University College Dublin Press.

Laver, Michael and Audrey Arkins (1990) 'Coalition and Fianna Fáil', in Michael Gallagher and Richard Sinnott (eds), *How Ireland Voted 1989*. Galway: PSAI Press

Lee, J.J. (1989) *Ireland, 1912–1985: Politics and Society*. Cambridge: Cambridge University Press.

Lenihan, Brian (1991) *For the Record*. Dublin: Blackwater Press.

Lenihan, Conor (2015) *Haughey: Prince of Power*. Dublin: Blackwater Press.

Longford, Earl of and T.P. O'Neill (1970) *Eamon de Valera*. London: Hutchinson & Co.

McCague, Eugene (2009) *My Dear Mr McCourt*. Dublin: Gill and Macmillan.

MacCarthaigh, Muiris (2005) *Accountability in Irish Parliamentary Politics*. Dublin: Institute of Public Administration.

Mac Cormaic, Ruadhán (2016) *The Supreme Court*. Dublin: Penguin Ireland.

McCracken, Mr Justice Brian (1997) *Report of the Tribunal of Inquiry (Dunnes Payments)*. Dublin: Stationery Office.

McCullagh, David (2018) *De Valera: Rule (1932–1975)*. Dublin: Gill Books.

McDaid, Jim (1992) 'On the Campaign Trail' in Michael Gallagher and Michael Laver (eds), *How Ireland Voted 1992*. Dublin: Folens.

McDonald, Frank (1985) *The Destruction of Dublin*. Dublin: Gill and Macmillan.

McDonald, Frank (2018) *Truly Frank: A Dublin Memoir*. Dublin: Penguin Ireland.

McEvoy, Enda (1998) *Fennessy's Field: A Century of Hurling History at St. Kieran's College, Kilkenny*. Kilkenny: Red Lion Press.

McGraw, Sean D. (2015) *How Parties Win: Shaping the Irish Political Arena*. Ann Arbor: University of Michigan Press.

McIntyre, Tom (1971) *Through the Bridewell Gate: A Diary of the Dublin Arms Trial*. London: Faber and Faber.

MacSharry, Ray and Padraic White (2000) *The Making of the Celtic Tiger: The Inside Story of Ireland's Boom Economy*. Cork: Mercier Press.

Mair, Peter (1987) *The Changing Irish Party System: Organisation, Ideology and Electoral Competition*. London: Pinter.

Mallie, Eamonn and David McKittrick (1996) *The Fight for Peace: The Secret Story Behind the Irish Peace Process*. London: Heinemann.

Mallon, Seamus with Andy Pollak (2019) *A Shared Home Place*. Dublin: Lilliput Press.

Manning, Maurice (1986) *The Blueshirts*, 2nd ed. Dublin: Gill and Macmillan.

Mansergh, Martin (ed.) (1986) *The Spirit of the Nation: The Speeches and Statements of Charles J. Haughey (1957–1986)*. Cork: Mercier Press.

Mansergh, Martin (1995) 'The background to the peace process', *Irish Studies in International Affairs* vol. 6.

Marsh, Michael, Richard Sinnott, John Garry and Fiachra Kennedy (2008) *The Irish Voter: The Nature of Electoral Competition in the Republic of Ireland*. Manchester: Manchester University Press.

Maxwell, Alison and Shay Harpur (2011) *Jammet's of Dublin 1901 to 1967*. Dublin: Lilliput Press.

Meehan, Ciara (2012) 'Constructing the Irish presidency: The early incumbents, 1938–1973', *Irish Political Studies* 27:4.

Meehan, Ciara (2013) *A Just Society for Ireland? 1964–1987*. London: Palgrave.

Mills, Michael (2006) *Hurler on the Ditch: Memoir of a Journalist Who became Ireland's First Ombudsman*. Dublin: Currach Press.

Moloney, Ed (2003, 2nd edn 2007) *A Secret History of the IRA*. London: Penguin.

Moore, Charles (2013) *Margaret Thatcher: The Authorized Biography*, Vol. 1: *Not For Turning*. London: Penguin.

Moriarty, Mr Justice Michael (2006) *The Moriarty Tribunal Report. Report of the Tribunal of Inquiry into Payments to Politicians and Related Matters, Part 1*. Dublin: Stationery Office.

Moynihan, Maurice (1975) *Currency and Central Banking in Ireland, 1922–1960*. Dublin: Gill and Macmillan.

Moynihan, Michael (2018) *Crisis and Comeback: Cork in the Eighties*. Cork: Collins Press.

Mulroe, Patrick (2017) *Bombs, Bullets and the Border Policing Ireland's Frontier: Irish Security Policy, 1969–1978*. Dublin: Irish Academic Press.

Murphy, Brian and Donnacha Ó Beacháin (eds) (2021) *From Whence I Came: The Kennedy Legacy, Ireland and America*. Dublin: Irish Academic Press.

Murphy, Gary (2006) 'Payments for No Political Response? Political Corruption and Tribunals of Inquiry in Ireland, 1991–2003', in John Garrard and James L. Newell (eds), *Scandals in Past and Contemporary Politics*. Manchester: Manchester University Press.

Murphy, Gary (2009) *In Search of the Promised Land: The Politics of Post-war Ireland*. Cork: Mercier Press.

Murphy, Gary (2015) '"The Irish people should feel ashamed of themselves for what they had done": Party Politics and the Fianna Fáil Manifesto of 1977' in Kevin Rafter and Mark O'Brien (eds), *The State in Transition: Essays in Honour of John Horgan*. Dublin: New Island.

Murphy, Gary (2016) *Electoral Competition in Ireland since 1987: The Politics of Triumph and Despair*. Manchester: Manchester University Press.

Murphy, Gary and John Hogan (2008) 'Fianna Fáil, the trade union movement and the politics of macroeconomic crises, 1970–1982', *Irish Political Studies* 23:4.

Murphy, Gary and Niamh Puirséil (2008) '"Is it a New Allowance?": Irish entry to the EEC and popular opinion', *Irish Political Studies* 23:4.

Murphy, Gary and Theresa Reidy (2012) 'Presidential elections in Ireland: From partisan predictability to the end of loyalty', *Irish Political Studies* 27:4.

Murphy, Gary and Theresa Reidy (2013) 'Presidential Elections: The Collapse of Partisanship?' in John Coakley and Kevin Rafter (eds), *The Irish Presidency: Power, Ceremony and Politics*. Dublin: Irish Academic Press.

Murphy, Gerard (2010) *The Year of Disappearances: Political Killing in Cork 1921–1922*. Dublin: Gill and Macmillan.

Murray, Gerard (1998) *John Hume and the SDLP: Impact and Survival in Northern Ireland*. Dublin: Irish Academic Press.

Murray, Thomas (2016) *Contesting Economic and Social Rights in Ireland: Constitution, State and Society, 1848–2016*. Cambridge: Cambridge University Press.

Myers, Kevin (2020) *Burning Heresies: A Memoir of a Life in Conflict, 1979–2020*. Dublin: Irish Academic Press.

Nolan, William (ed.) (2005) *The Gaelic Athletic Association in Dublin 1884–2000*, Vol. 3. Dublin: Geography Publications.

Ó Beacháin, Donnacha (2011) *Destiny of the Soldiers: Fianna Fáil, Irish Republicanism and the IRA, 1926–1973*. Dublin: Gill and Macmillan.

Ó Beacháin, Donnacha (2019) *From Partition to Brexit: The Irish Government and Northern Ireland*. Manchester: Manchester University Press.

O'Brien, Justin (2000) *The Arms Trial*. Dublin: Gill and Macmillan.

O'Brien, Justin (2002) *The Modern Prince: Charles J. Haughey and the Quest for Power*. Dublin: Merlin.

O'Brien, Mark (2001) *De Valera, Fianna Fail and the Irish Press: The Truth in the News*. Dublin: Irish Academic Press.

O'Brien, Mark (2008) *The Irish Times: A History*. Dublin: Four Courts Press.

O'Brien, Mark (2014) '"Sources Say …": Political Journalism Since 1921' in Mark O'Brien and Donnacha Ó Beacháin (eds), *Political Communication in the Republic of Ireland*. Liverpool: Liverpool University Press.

O'Byrnes, Stephen (1986) *Hiding Behind a Face: Fine Gael under FitzGerald*. Dublin: Gill and Macmillan.

O'Connell, John (1989) *Dr John: Crusading Doctor and Politician*. Dublin: Poolbeg.

O'Connell, Maurice (ed. J. Anthony Gaughan) (2020) *No Complaints: A Memoir of Life in Rural Ireland and in the Irish Public Service*. Kerry: Kingdom Books.

O'Connor, Emmet (2011) *A Labour History of Ireland, 1824-2000*. Dublin: University College Dublin Press.

O'Connor, Kevin (1999) *Sweetie*. Dublin: Kevin O'Connor.

O'Connor, Philip (2019) 'A Very Political Project: Charles Haughey, Social Partnership and the Engineering of an "Irish economic miracle", 1969–92. PhD thesis, School of Law and Government, Dublin City University.

O'Donnell, Catherine (2007) *Fianna Fáil, Irish Republicanism and the Northern Irish Troubles, 1968–2005*. Dublin: Irish Academic Press.

O'Donnell, Ian (2017) *Justice, Mercy, and Caprice: Clemency and the Death Penalty in Ireland*. Oxford: Oxford University Press.

O'Donoghue, Martin (1990) 'Irish economic policy, 1977–79', *Studies* 79.

Ó Dubhshláine, Mícheál (2009) *Inishvickillane: A Unique Portrait of the Blasket Island*. Dingle: Brandon Books.

O'Faolain, Nuala (1996) *Are You Somebody?* Dublin: New Island.

O'Gráda, Cormac (1997) *A Rocky Road: The Irish Economy since the 1920s*. Manchester: Manchester University Press.

O'Halpin, Eunan (1999) *Defending Ireland: The Irish State and its Enemies since 1922*. Oxford: Oxford University Press.

O'Halpin, Eunan (2000) '"Ah they've given us a good bit of stuff …": Tribunals and Irish political life at the turn of the century', *Irish Political Studies* 15.

O'Halpin, Eunan (2008) '"A Greek authoritarian phase"? The Irish army and the Irish crisis, 1969–70', *Irish Political Studies* 23:4.

O'Kane, Eamonn (2012) *Britain, Ireland and Northern Ireland Since 1980: The Totality of Relationships*. Abingdon: Routledge.

O'Leary, Brendan (2019) *A Treatise on Northern Ireland*, Vol. 3, *Consociation and Confederation: From Antagonism to Accommodation?* Oxford: Oxford University Press.

O'Leary, John (2015) *On the Doorsteps: Memoirs of a Long-serving TD*. Killarney: Irish Political Memoirs.

O'Leary, Olivia and Helen Lucy Burke (1998) *Mary Robinson: The Authorised Biography*. London: Hodder & Stoughton.

O'Mahony, T.P. (1991) *Jack Lynch: A Biography*. Cork: Blackwater Press.

O'Malley, Desmond (2014) *Conduct Unbecoming: A Memoir*. Dublin: Gill and Macmillan.

O'Malley, Eoin (2006) 'Ministerial selection in Ireland: Limited choice in a political village', *Irish Political Studies* 21:3.

O'Malley, Eoin (2011) *Contemporary Ireland*. Basingstoke: London.

O'Malley, Eoin and Gary Murphy (2018) 'The Leadership Difference? Context and Choice in Fianna Fáil's Party Leadership' in Eoin O'Malley and Seán McGraw (eds), *One Party Dominance: Fianna Fáil and Irish Politics 1926–2016*. Abingdon: Routledge.

O'Reilly, Emily (1991) *Candidate: The Truth Behind the Presidential Campaign*. Dublin: Attic Press.

O'Reilly, Emily (1992) *Masterminds of the Right*. Dublin: Attic Press.

O'Rourke, Mary (2012) *Just Mary: A Memoir*. Dublin: Gill and Macmillan.

O'Sullivan, Cormac (2010) '"The Greatest Comeback Since Lazarus": The Fianna Fáil General Election Campaign of 1977, a Milestone in Irish Political

Communication', MA in Political Communication, Dublin City University.

O'Sullivan, Eoin (1991) 'The 1990 presidential election in the Republic of Ireland', *Irish Political Studies* vol. 6.

O'Toole, Fintan (1995) *Meanwhile Back at the Ranch: The Politics of Irish Beef*. London: Vintage.

Patterson, Henry (2002) *Ireland Since 1939*. Oxford: Oxford University Press.

Puirséil, Niamh (2005) 'Political and Party Competition in Post War Ireland', in Brian Girvin and Gary Murphy (eds), *The Lemass Era: Politics and Society in the Ireland of Seán Lemass*. Dublin: UCD Press.

Puirséil, Niamh (2007) *The Irish Labour Party 1922–73*. Dublin: University College Dublin Press.

Quinn, Ruairi (2005) *Straight Left: A Journey in Politics*. Dublin: Hachette.

Rafter, Kevin (1993) *Neil Blaney: A Soldier of Destiny*. Dublin: Blackwater Press.

Rafter, Kevin (2002) *Martin Mansergh: A Biography*. Dublin: New Island.

Rafter, Kevin (2009) *Fine Gael: Party at the Crossroads*. Dublin: New Island.

Rafter, Kevin (2012) 'A Tale of "Womanly Intuition": Hector Legge at the *Sunday Independent*, 1940–70' in Mark O'Brien and Kevin Rafter (eds), *Independent Newspapers: A History*. Dublin: Four Courts Press.

Rafter, Kevin (2015) '"Never Justify. Never Explain": Some Thoughts on Irish Political Memoirs' in Kevin Rafter and Mark O'Brien, *The State in Transition: Essays in Honour of John Horgan*. Dublin: New Island.

Reddan, Fiona (2008) *Ireland's IFSC: A Story of Global Financial Success*. Cork: Mercier Press.

Reynolds, Albert (2009) *My Autobiography*. London: Transworld.

Rogan, Mary (2011) *Prison Policy in Ireland: Politics, Penal-Welfarism and Political Imprisonment*. Abingdon: Routledge.

Ryan, Tim (1992) *Mara PJ*. Dublin: Blackwater Press.

Savage, Robert (2010) *A Loss of Innocence? Television and Irish Society 1960–72*. Manchester: Manchester University Press.

Sinnott, Richard (1995) *Irish Voters Decide: Voting Behaviour in Elections and Referendums Since 1918*. Manchester: Manchester University Press.

Smyth, Sam (1997) *Thanks a Million Big Fella*. Dublin: Blackwater Press.

Sweeney, Eamon (2010) *Down Down Deeper and Down: Ireland in the 70s & 80s*. Dublin: Gill and Macmillan.

Sweetman, Rosita (1972) *On Our Knees: Ireland 1972*. London: Pan Books.

Thatcher, Margaret (1993) *The Downing Street Years*. London: HarperCollins.

Thornley, Edward (2012) *Lone Crusader: David Thornley and the Intellectuals*. Dublin: Ashfield Press.

Thorney, Yseult (ed.) (2008) *Unquiet Spirit: Essays in Honour of David Thornley*. Dublin: Liberties Press.

Tobin, Fergal (1996) *The Best of Decades: Ireland in the 1960s*. Dublin: Gill and Macmillan.

Tubridy, Ryan (2010) *JFK in Ireland: Four Days that Changed a President*. London: HarperCollins.

Walsh, Dick (1986) *The Party: Inside Fianna Fáil*. Dublin: Gill and Macmillan.

Walsh, Ed (2011) *Upstart: Friends, Foes and Founding a University*. Cork: Collins Press.

Walsh, Eleanor (1998) 'The Minister as Legislator: Charles J. Haughey as Minister for Justice, 1961 to 1964', MA thesis, University College Cork.

Walsh, John (2005) 'The Politics of Educational Expansion', in Brian Girvin and Gary Murphy (eds), *The Lemass Era: Politics and Society in the Ireland of Seán Lemass*. Dublin: UCD Press.

Walsh, John (2008) *Patrick Hillery: The Official Biography*. Dublin: New Island.

Walsh, John (2009) *The Politics of Expansion: The Transformation of Educational Policy in the Republic of Ireland, 1957–72*. Manchester: Manchester University Press.

Walsh, John (2019) *The Globalist: Peter Sutherland – His Life and Legacy*. London: William Collins.

Waters, John (1991) *Jiving at the Crossroads*. Belfast: Blackstaff Press.

Weeks, Liam (2017) *Independents in Irish Party Democracy*. Manchester: Manchester University Press.

Whelan, Noel (2011) *Fianna Fáil: A Biography of the Party*. Dublin: Gill and Macmillan.

Whitaker, T.K. (1983) *Interests*. Dublin: Institute of Public Administration.

White, Barry (1984) *John Hume: Statesman of the Troubles*. Belfast: Blackstaff Press.

Wren, Maev-Ann (2003) *Unhealthy State: Anatomy of a Sick Society*. Dublin: New Island.

INDEX